HIGH TREASON
2

HARRISON EDWARD LIVINGSTONE

HIGH TREASON 2

THE GREAT COVER-UP:
THE ASSASSINATION OF
PRESIDENT JOHN F. KENNEDY

Carroll & Graf Publishers, Inc.
New York

Copyright © 1992 by Harrison Edward Livingstone

Drawings copyrighted 1992 by Neil O. Hardy, except where otherwise noted.

First Carroll & Graf edition 1992

Carroll & Graf Publishers, Inc.
260 Fifth Avenue
New York, NY 10001

Library of Congress Cataloging-in-Publication Data

Livingstone, Harrison Edward.
    High treason 2 : the great cover-up : the assassination of President John
  F. Kennedy / by Harrison Edward Livingstone. — 1st Carroll & Graf ed.
      p.   cm.
    Continues: High treason / Robert J. Groden.
    Includes bibliographical references and index.
    ISBN 0-88184-809-3 : $25.95
    1. Kennedy, John F. (John Fitzgerald), 1917–1963—Assassination.
  I. Groden, Robert J. High treason. II. title.
  E842.9.L58 1992
  364.1'524—dc20   92-6903
                                                                       CIP

First printing 1992
Fourth printing 1992

Manufactured in the United States of America

Permission was kindly granted by Mr. Steve Mills to reprint his letter in the
Appendix.

This book is dedicated to the people in it, who for the most part hold the truth of the tragedy of John Kennedy's murder within them.

It is their patience with me and the time they took that made the book possible.

Thank you.

History and posterity must decide. Customarily they reserve the mantle of greatness for those who win great wars, not those who prevent them. But in my unobjective view I think it will be difficult to measure John Kennedy by any ordinary historical yardstick. For he was an extraordinary man, an extraordinary politician and an extraordinary President. Just as no chart on the history of weapons could accurately reflect the advent of the atom, so it is my belief that no scale of good and bad presidents can rate John Fitzgerald Kennedy. A mind so free of fear and myth and prejudice, so opposed to cant and clichés, so unwilling to feign or be fooled, to accept or reflect mediocrity, is rare in our world—and even rarer in American politics. Without demeaning any of the great men who have helped the presidency in this century, I do not see how John Kennedy could be ranked below any one of them. . . . He was a big man—much bigger than anyone thought—and all of us are better for having lived in the days of Kennedy.

—Theodore Sorensen, *Kennedy*

CONTENTS

Acknowledgments

As with every book, many people often help out and sometimes go unsung or accidentally forgotten. If I forgot somebody, it was not intentional.

This is particularly to thank Mark Crouch for the great amount of time we have spent together and his insightful thinking on many aspects of the case. He has had a unique opportunity to study the autopsy photographs over the years, and so, had some ideas of his own, particularly about other researchers most closely connected to the investigation we have been conducting. Mark also held my hand throughout a most difficult time in my life, before I got going well on this book, and throughout the whole project. For that I thank him greatly.

I also thank Richard Waybright, Jr., who came knocking on my door one day in 1989, and pushed me back into this investigation. This book flows out of his early prodding which he kept up, until the book began to have a life of its own, and then he had the good sense to leave me alone for long periods of time so that I could work without letup.

Kathlee Fitzgerald rendered invaluable research assistance to me at a time when I began to fold from too many months of work almost with hardly a day off. Her great ability to find things or people, and to sense what I need and get it done, was a tribute to a "can-do" attitude that is hard to come by. She had a lot else to do at the time with her family and job and a bad back, but she came through for me.

I'm also indebted to Martin Shackelford, a longtime assassination researcher, for his steady help and faith. Pat Dumais, Vince Palamara, Ray Carroll, Paul Hoch, Semi Heninger, John Long, Rick Matthews, Steve Mills, Chip Hardgrave, Gary Rowell, Gary Shaw, Larry Howard, Ken Degazio, Andy at the Last Hurrah Book Shop in Williamsport, Pennsylvania, and Jennifer Nelson and Jim Lesar at the Assassination Archives and Research Center in Washington also provided help at key moments. Professor Jerry Rose has been quite patient. Many others sent in useful materials and otherwise helped me.

Then there is Harold Weisberg, who, having endured a painful triple bypass operation and many serious infirmities of age, puts up with me

11

and the many questions I should know better than to ask. But we must always go to the father to test our sometimes incredibly wild or dumb ideas, and Harold is the man to kick them in the ass. I am grateful for his time and great help and friendship, though I am sure he wishes I were dead.

Others provided priceless moral support when I was reaching out to write a better and more important book than the first one, a rather unique achievement for an author, if I have so succeeded.

I am really thankful for the support of the huge companies that helped me prove that someone could basically self-publish a book and get it out there in America, as I did with *High Treason*. The American Dream is not dead, and where there is a will, there is a way, as my father always used to say. I found a way around the roadblocks, thanks to a lot of help from many wholesalers and book chains, who went out of their way to license me as a vendor to them, and work with me— just a one-man small press—and finally, to get this book published.

I am grateful to my neighbors, who put up with me, and were trained, in the end, to leave the parking space in front of my house vacant, because it was mine.

Lastly, I would like to thank my editor, Kent Carroll, for the great care and time he took with this book, doing one of the best editing jobs I have ever seen or imagined. Not many publishers edit books anymore, and among those that do, none would have taken the care that Mr. Carroll has taken. And thanks to you too, Herman Graf, a great book-man.

Introduction

I was one of those people who lost their innocence, idealism, and confidence. I am now sixty-three years old and can still remember that awful day. I still hurt. I followed John F. Kennedy from the time he ran for Congress for the first time until the assassination. Then I continued until the day Robert died. I saw President Kennedy two days before he became President when he came to Waterbury, Connecticut, at three o'clock in the morning and 3,000 people were waiting for him. I was in the front row between the National Guard. He walked to the end of the balcony and spotted me and waved and gave me that wonderful smile. I could but stand in awe.

I was only five feet tall, and so I looked like a child. I received many letters from the White House when he was there, as I wrote him about everything and always received a reply—a letter every week. Also, many papers about what he was doing. When he was killed, I sent Robert Kennedy a picture that had been taken that morning of the President with a blind girl with a Kennedy hat. The President had laid his head against hers. Robert Kennedy wrote back and told me how much that meant to the family.

Robert and Ted Kennedy both came back to Waterbury. They never forgot what Waterbury did for the President. I used to walk to work in the morning and say to myself that we are in good hands.

I spent my vacations at the Cape and saw the Kennedy family many times at church. I saw Mrs. Kennedy in church after Robert was killed, and told her of my sorrow. She was very gracious and kind.

I felt in my heart that big money was paid to kill the President. I also believe that Robert Kennedy knew it, too, but would not reveal it because he felt it would destroy the country and so he, too, was killed.

Thank you for the good book and for telling the world the truth.

This letter was sent to me by Dorothy M. Gauvin, of Worcester, Massachusetts. Of the many wonderful letters I received after publishing my book *High Treason*, this letter touched me the most. It captures what many of us felt for John Kennedy, what none of us who have researched this case can get out of his head, and what so many readers cannot forget when they seek anything written on the case, anything that might lead to the awful truth that everyone suspected: that John Kennedy was overthrown, murdered in a foul conspiracy based in the United States, part of it reaching into the highest areas of our government and the Establishment that has the power in this nation.

How else could it have been covered up? There had to be great power at work to manipulate the Chief Justice of the Supreme Court, the succeeding president, and the law enforcement agencies normally charged with investigating such crimes. They have never remotely done that job.

Only we, the people, have taken that job and go on with it. And that is what this book is about. I have gone on with this investigation, which has cost me considerable money and time, although there are other things I would much rather do. The writing of the first book debilitated me to the point where I thought I would not survive it. But like a lot of others, I am obsessed with the case, and it has become a part of my life. And some folks close to me have pushed me back into this investigation in the hope that the job can be finished, or at least that we can learn more. This book uncovers more new evidence, some of it quite explosive, and it compares the crime of the murder of President Kennedy to other such crimes.

Let us look at what this country was like in 1960, the year when the young John Kennedy ran against Richard Nixon. I'll never forget that election day in November, when I frantically booked a flight back to Baltimore to vote. I had just crept off a sailboat after a rough voyage through tremendous storms to Miami, and was still walking into telephone poles, still gripping the boat's wheel in my mind so hard, someone had to help uncurl my fingers from its spokes when the hurricane finally abated. My face was badly bruised from one such encounter with a lamppost, and as I remember it, shortly after deplaning I crashed into a table in the converted church in Bolton Hill, where the voting booths were, and fell down.

So there was a sacrifice I could be proud of for the rest of my days. I weathered a terrible storm in a small boat, gave up a chance to vacation (perhaps forever?) on a tropical isle surrounded by bathing beauties, and with only one day in Florida returned as fast as I could to the salubrious warmth of quaint old Baltimore. That was before they renovated it.

How were we as a country then? What would motivate me and so many others to go home to vote for young John Kennedy?

We were a nation dishonest with ourselves, living double standards in every part of our lives, a smoky industrial nation still fighting its way out from beneath the ignorance of its rural past, still not adjusted to its role as the most powerful nation on earth, a nation living lies and telling itself lies, still flexing its muscles as though it alone won World War II and the deaths of vast millions in the agony of China and of the Soviet Union in their struggle with the Axis had nothing to do with it.

A nation that raised its smallest children in fear of atomic attack and nuclear war, a nation still traumatized from World War II like so many other countries on the earth, a nation putrid with environmental pollution and virulent racism, a nation that considered women still more or less possessions of men, and which refused to admit its darkest secrets of child abuse. A nation whose college students made a way of life of drunken fraternity parties and date rape, a nation that bashed its homosexuals and rejected their humanity and creativity, a country that threw stones at people with beards, brought its children up to think of blacks or Jews and in some areas even Catholics as beyond the pale.

When John Kennedy came to power, it was because he struck a deep wellspring of the untapped best that was in this country; he recognized in his opponent, Richard Nixon, something venal, cruel, and illegal in his very appearance, and in Kennedy there was grace and charm, wit and a great articulate brilliance.

That brilliance came through in the three debates with Nixon, and Kennedy—who had won the primaries—was still an unknown quantity, whereas Nixon had been vice president under Dwight David Eisenhower, the hero of World War II. Kennedy would not have won the election except for those three debates in which he looked better and talked better than Nixon. That, and Mayor Daley of Chicago, won it for Kennedy—as old Joe Kennedy had won the West Virginia primary for John Kennedy some months before.

John Kennedy planted a hope in the breast of many of the young and intelligent in this nation, a hope that we might finally move toward our fulfillment, that the American Dream would become a reality if we helped him. *Ask not what your country can do for you, but what you can do for your country.* Soon a lot of us went off in the Peace Corps, as I did, little knowing that Kennedy's evocation was so radical that it helped roll the forces forward that would finally kill him.

We had hope for the first time in a way that had not been here before. There was a younger spark at work, not the fatherly or grandfatherly image of Eisenhower and the good men who went before him. For we had been blessed with an age of titans and heroes, of great presidents and prime ministers and generals in the world who had gotten us through the most terrible war in all of human history and somehow had put the world back together again. What was next? Those were a lot of tough acts to follow, even for the greatest of charismatic leaders in need of issues and causes.

The Eisenhower years were somnolent. Problems piled up and little was done. Most of these problems weren't even talked about. Powerful people didn't know about those problems, or didn't want to know. There were a lot of things we didn't talk about in public in those days. We've come a long way, haven't we, for those who remember.

The masses of people grew restless. Strikes and factionalism threatened the country, and the nation's social structure was terribly rent from the huge lies we lived in our own land. Our Statue of Liberty was a beacon to the world, but what were our lives like amid such diseases as McCarthyism and racism?

Kennedy was hope. He gave us hope. He was filled with optimism and was willing to dare, willing to move away from the status quo to New Frontiers. And we wanted to go with him. Those one thousand days of his presidency was one of the most exciting times in our history. How we thrilled to watch him on television. His press conferences were an event. He was a star, and people crowded into the corner taverns to watch him. The jukeboxes were turned off. Nobody talked, and everyone got ready to laugh, because we all knew that no matter what the problems coming at us, he would get a laugh out of us somehow. And we passed through a number of great crises in those thousand days, including the threat of nuclear holocaust. Few presidents had so much serious trouble befall them in three years' time.

And this nation began slowly, somehow, to respond to the challenges, to move forward into a new age that no one could see quite clearly then, from a time when black folks could not sit down to eat with us in some cities in a public place, or live where they wanted to, or travel in the seats of their choosing, or use the same bathrooms or drinking fountains as white people.

This book presents new evidence in the assassination of President Kennedy. This book is also a sort of oral history, as I was fortunate in obtaining many personal remembrances of that tragic day in 1963, and, along with them, evidence that goes a long way to clearing up many of the as-yet-unsolved puzzles.

When Kennedy died, his successor, President Johnson, set up the Warren Commission to examine the murder, ostensibly to investigate it. Chief Justice Warren and his Commission relied primarily upon the materials provided by the FBI, the CIA, and the Dallas police, but they also held hearings and questioned very many witnesses. It is unfortunate that some of what the witnesses had to say that indicated things the Commission did not want to hear was distorted.

The Commission and the government had a secret agenda all along, and that was to substantiate the previous findings of the police and FBI that one crazed, lone gunman—a Communist sympathizer—killed the President. That gunman was Lee Harvey Oswald.

From the start there were public suspicions that something else had happened. Within months our policy concerning the Vietnam War changed, and reports of witnesses in Dallas meeting early deaths slipped out. Soon books and articles began to appear that proposed that there had been a conspiracy. The known evidence and reports from Dallas certainly seemed conflicting, so the Warren Commission published a section dealing with "rumors."

We know now, and I know from talking to most—in fact nearly all—of the medical witnesses, that something was indeed hidden from the nation and the world. The autopsy report was fudged, and as I demonstrate in my last book and this one, the photographs and X-rays were forged. Evidence of more shots, and shots from different directions—indicating more than one gunman—was covered up.

But why? Did the Government know all along that there was a conspiracy but did not know who was behind it—and had to put out a cover story for the time being? Or did persons within the Government overthrow the administration and plant the fake evidence themselves?

This book endeavors to answer those questions. First, we will review the history of Kennedy's presidency and his medical history, and his intent to withdraw from Vietnam. Then we will delve deeply into the medical evidence in the case, but it will also discuss the murder of his brother Robert, and the murders of numerous others during the tough ten years from November 22, 1963, through Watergate.

The first time I saw John Kennedy was in a hearing room of the United States Senate in 1956 or so. If I recall correctly, the Capitol was being renovated, and space was short. Kennedy was a member of the Foreign

Relations Committee, and on that day John Foster Dulles, the Secretary of State, was asked about his work. Old Senator Greene of Rhode Island was asleep down at one end of the table in the very small but crowded room, and there was space for only a handful of spectators— perhaps ten at the most. This was not the kind of hearing room that we normally see on television in the great public, staged hearings.

I was in college nearby and wanted to see what I could learn by attending hearings. I found myself sitting just behind Kennedy, and I came back several times because I was so impressed by him, and I knew I was in a special presence.

It was a long time before Kennedy got to talk. The speakers seemed to go by seniority, when I look back on it now, nobody asked anything that might be considered a probing question in that special club within the citadel of American government. The hearing went something like this, to paraphrase it: "How are things goin' in the world, Mister Secretary?" old, gruff Senator Claghorn would ask.

"Fine, fine. Everything is running along smoothly, Senator."

"And Russia?"

"No problem there," the patrician, perfectly groomed Wasp establishmentarian in the blue pinstripe suit would reply.

"And how is your department goin'? Everythin' all right down yonder at Foggy Bottom?" He was thinking of the bean soup, corn bread, and Virginia ham waiting in the dining room down below.

"Fine, fine."

And so on. Then it was the turn of another senator. They had a couple of hours to kill, according to the schedule that was published in the *Washington Post*. But then it was John Kennedy's turn. There was a noticeable stir in the room. Those people knew something I didn't know. People sat straight in their chairs, and Senator Greene woke up. Since Kennedy was young and new, he was last to speak. Thirty minutes later I knew I had seen something that was not only out of the ordinary but I had seen an extraordinary man. Everybody felt it, Kennedy had a strong presence, and people sat up and took notice.

"Mr. Secretary, my understanding is that three electrical generators in the foreign assistance program under bill number 3612 were sent to Marseilles as part of a transshipment to North Africa. Investigators have traced these same generators, made by General Electric, with serial numbers 36251214, 36251215, and 36251216 to a dock in Santiago, Chile, where they are waiting transportation to a private buyer in Bolivia. Mr. Secretary, these generators have actually been traced clear around the world before they reached Santiago. What information do you have on their misappropriation?"

After harrumphing and scowling, Dulles would mumble something and try to slide by it, but Kennedy was relentless, and pursued his point as far as he could.

Or, Kennedy would have a list of facts and figures in front of him and never need to consult it. He had an almost photographic recall of the statistics and figures that staggered his targets and made them feel small.

And sometimes I would smile at Kennedy with all the idiocy of an idolizing student. And he would smile back, or I would give him a bit of a wave, and he would wave back as he left, and one day I spoke to him, having for an hour tried to figure out a gambit that I could offer that might get some word from him, some response.

"I think that you are the best man in here," I blurted out. That wasn't the thing that I had planned to hit him with, but it was what I felt.

"Well, I wouldn't say that, but thank you anyway. Are you a student?" His Boston accent came through loud and clear, with his long A's. He called Cuba "Cuber."

"Yes."

"Well, study hard, ["haaad"] and maybe someday you can be here, too, and do better than we do!" And he smiled with a twinkle in his eye and a bit of a patronizing air, and went on. He could patronize me any day.

Of course, five years later John Foster Dulles's brother Allen, the head of the CIA whom Kennedy had fired not long after he became President, was sitting on the Warren Commission making a show of looking into the assassination of President Kennedy, and he displayed about as much incisiveness and probity as his brother. In other words, the evidence of conspiracy was in front of them, but they wouldn't see it, for they long ago had lost the facility to see their noses clearly, and it wasn't because of age.

One day after attending one of his hearings, I was having a beer in a bar on Pennsylvania Avenue near Capitol Hill which often is frequented by workers from the House and Senate Office Buildings, the high and low, senator and secretary, congressman and file clerk, and who should sidle up to me but John Kennedy. Why, I've had Woody Allen, Clint Eastwood, Ernest Hemingway, John Steinbeck, James Jones, and Kim Novak standing beside me at Elaine's, the Hog's Breath, and other famous saloons, but this was a star of the first water, a star that was going to last in a way that nobody but Hemingway in that time could equal.

"I think I saw you at the hearing again today, that right?"

"Yes, that was me."

"Well, what is your opinion of the foreign situation—as a student?"

"I think we have got to work something out with the Soviet Union."

"I agree." Well, he knew that even then, before he began to hammer out a détente with Russia which has finally borne fruit a generation later. The important thing was, I was talking to a United States senator. Little did I know that he would run for president not long afterward. But one thing was sure, this gentleman was one of the top people I would ever know. You never get over their passing, so we can all imagine how his close friends, his family, his widow, felt when he died so brutally. And they are still too wounded to respond, to deal with it. To pursue it.

It is significant to my way of thinking that America's greatest writer, when Kennedy was elected, was Ernest Hemingway, and the John F. Kennedy Library in Boston is devoted not just to Kennedy, but also has the entire Hemingway collection, everything he every wrote, published in many languages and many editions, his manuscripts, his letters, his memorabilia and snapshots. It seems to me more than fitting that in death those two men would be brought together in that large and ethereal, soaring, otherworldly building. One might wonder that the life of a president could generate such a tremendous load of material that it takes a large building to deal with it, but that is the case. I am grateful for the symbolism of Hemingway and Kennedy being together under one roof there, for it was Kennedy who promoted the arts in a way that had never before happened in the United States. He made the arts legitimate. We no longer taught and worshipped only dead artists and writers, but took an interest in what was in our time.

In my student days in the Washington area I had stuffed envelopes in the campaigns of the liberal Wayne Morse of Oregon and the even more liberal Adlai Stevenson for president, hoping against hope that some liberal could change things. What that meant wasn't so clear. We were not thinking of spending our way out of problems, but hoped more for a change in attitude, in spirit. When John Kennedy came along and began his run, I was out there stuffing envelopes and putting them under thousands of doors. Kennedy came to Baltimore on his campaign, and I stood in the reception line at the Emerson Hotel and shook his hand, and I'll never forget it. Never forget seeing him that one last time close-up. I'm sure the thousand other people there felt the same way.

After that he was President, and I was going off to sea, living my nightmares, bumming through Europe, going to law school, and trying to write books. I felt like none of us ever got to really know him because he didn't live long enough. Like one of Kennedy's advance men, Gary Underwood, said, "He wasn't a great President. He didn't have the chance."

Gary said this with bitterness. There will never be anyone again like John Kennedy. He was a great president and a great leader who got us through crisis after crisis, and laid the groundwork for the tremendous civil rights legislation that followed his death when he made it clear with federal troops that the law would be obeyed. Kennedy improved this nation in a way it desperately needed. He energized America and prepared us for vast changes in our society so that we could all start to relate to one another in a better way, in relationships that were based on honesty and not power.

That may be his ultimate legacy. Kennedy gave us a great deal, but he broke the shackles of the past and freed the vast tolerant and liberal force within the large majority of Americans that set loose a new burst of creativity and hope in our young—in fact, in the whole country.

Sadly, it was soon to be slowly ground down by the years of disorder and war that followed his death and that flowed from his death—in fact happened only because he was out of the way. He would have stopped it—not let it happen.

All that disorder in our Time of Troubles occurred only when certain people could get him out of the way, and much of it was because of the despair everybody felt when he was struck down.

But the spirit has not died, and he left us with much. We did get moving again, and soared into the space age. Most of all, some of the worst things in this country were changed because of his life, and perhaps because of his death. We have him to thank for that.

Someday the rage that so many of us still feel twenty-eight years after the murder of the President we loved will get through to all those people who have done nothing or who through apathy or indifference have helped to bury this case and this tragedy. The rage that burns within us will someday force Congress to admit that it is even more of a crime to allow the lie that this nation has been living all of these years to go on.

*   *   *

We can only hope that the fight to preserve and expand the progress that was made will throw back the forces of darkness, working to engulf us once again. Eternal vigilance is the price of freedom, and why this book was written.

Steven Mills, a fellow researcher, wrote me that "it wasn't just the man they killed. It was the ideal that the people are the government."

HIGH TREASON
2

"If we cannot end now our differences, at least we can help make the world safe for diversity. For, in the final analysis, our most basic common link is that we all inhabit this planet. We all breathe the same air. We all cherish our children's future. And we are all mortal. This generation of Americans has already had enough—more than enough—of war and hate and oppression. . . . We shall do our part to build a world of peace where the weak are safe and the strong are just. We are not helpless before that task or hopeless of its success. Confident and unafraid, we labor on—not toward a strategy of annihilation but toward a strategy of peace."

—John F. Kennedy at
American University
June 1963

CHAPTER 1

THE KENNEDY PRESIDENCY

"The Kennedy message—self-criticism, wit, ideas, the vision of a civilized society—opened up a new era in the American political consciousness. The President stood, in John P. Roche's valuable phrase, for the politics of modernity. 'Liberalism and conservatism,' Kennedy remarked one night, 'are categories of the thirties, and they don't apply anymore. . . . The trouble with conservatives today is that most of their thinking is so naive. As for the liberals, their thinking is more sophisticated; but their function ought to be to provide new ideas, and they don't come up with any.' His effort was to dissolve the myths which had masked the merging realities in both domestic and foreign affairs. His hope was to lead the nation beyond the obsessive issues of the past and to call forth the new perceptions required for the contemporary world." So wrote Arthur Schlesinger.[1]

In other words, Kennedy was tampering with the fundamental idea

25

structure of the United States, trying to educate and reshape a country that was not in the least prepared for the rapidly changing world preparing for the Twenty-first Century. Some might say it still isn't.

We all know that to tamper with someone's idée fixe can be very dangerous.

But first we must remember John Kennedy with the love and affection that so many of us had for him. He made mistakes as all men make mistakes. But when one is the king, the leader, or the president, mistakes can have very far-reaching consequences and sometimes be catastrophic.

Operation Zapata, an invasion by Cuban exiles trained and equipped by the United States, was planned and intended to enter Cuba toward the end of President Eisenhower's term of office, but there were delays, and when Kennedy entered office, the operation was presented to him. The invasion was all set to go, and certain misrepresentations were made to Kennedy about it, and he went along with the plan. The Bay of Pigs was a catastrophe for the men who were captured or killed, though there was mercifully little bloodshed. The fact is that the way Kennedy ultimately handled it probably saved this nation from a much larger war with the socialist states.

But those men came back to the United States, when they got out of prison in Cuba with our help, and they felt betrayed. We believe that some of them helped kill Kennedy when the time came to eliminate him.

The Cuban Missile Crisis followed along in the next year of John Kennedy's presidency, and there were those in the military and the intelligence agencies and in the power centers and among the radical rightists of the cold warrior sect who began to hate him because in their opinion this crisis flowed out of the failure not to conquer Cuba in the first place.

It is unfortunate that the real issue behind the Missile Crisis was never revealed to the general public because it put us in the position of not playing fair, if we can call it that.

That issue had to do with our placement of intercontinental ballistic missiles in Turkey, aimed at the Soviet Union. Russia responded to this great provocation on its border, and to the threat to its security by our doctrine of Containment by putting its missiles into Cuba pointed at us. In my view, all that the Soviets wanted to do was make a trade.

I am sure that were it not for Kennedy, we would have bombed Cuba and there would have been a war. Our generals pushed him to do that during the crisis, and Cuba had its defenders. They pushed him to invade with our Army and Marines. There would have been a terrible bloodbath in Cuba which would haunt us as a nation forever, and probably cost us the world. We would have been sucked into a guerrilla war that perhaps never would have ended, with all of South America helping Cuba, for they all hated us.

Instead, Kennedy created the Alliance for Progress and the Peace Corps, and when he went to Latin America, very many millions of people turned out. It was like the visit of the Pope, only bigger.

It is my opinion that we might have saved ourselves the *entire* Cold War and the near bankruptcy it has cost us if we had better understood Russia's problems and worked with the Soviets rather than against them. Admittedly, this was not easy after World War II ended and Stalin, the great dictator, was still alive, but we had certainly worked with them before (as we did during the war), and with dictators throughout the world for a long time. I have no doubt but that Russia would have liberalized a lot sooner, and in better conditions for it than the present.

We built a "defense" based on accumulating an arsenal of atomic weapons after World War II, never dreaming that there would be a response. It never occurred to us that the more we escalated, the more somebody in the world would feel bound to constrain us, to keep up with us or outproduce us. Every arms race in history was like that. When one side builds a new battleship, the other must.

In fact, the "Empire Americanus" that existed for years after World War II was not so benign, but threatened much of the world. Even NATO, according to British and Canadian historians, was created to control *us* more than it was to contain the Soviet Union. Europe understood Russia, but we did not, and we were determined to fight a Cold War against communism even though it was apparent to any student of history that it would fall of its own weight. Had we not kept up such a tremendous military pressure on Russia, it would not have had to keep up with us in arms production at such high levels that it required a dictatorship of the Party to produce the weapons.

Russia has followed regular cycles in its history for the past one thousand years. The 1917 Communist revolution did not really change the patterns of repression and liberalization Russia had followed for centuries.

Kennedy inherited the Cold War from Eisenhower and the CIA, and he was uncomfortable with it. But Kennedy, like most, had no doubt of the need for a strong defense—with such major nations in the world as unstable, aggressive, repressive, and authoritarian as the U.S.S.R.

Kennedy was a capitalist, but a liberal who accepted a few socialist ideas. So did the majority of the American people, who repeatedly elected Democrats. A lot of those basic programs such as social security, unemployment compensation, government investment in some sectors of the economy, regulation for everybody's protection, remain good ideas, and in fact have saved us from great trouble.

Then there was organized crime. The Mob was a deadly disease so pervasive that it threatened the country. Organized crime had grown in power through a secret alliance with government, working hand in glove with the CIA, local police, and other officials.

Robert Kennedy had been part of that racket busting. He was not only in trouble with the Army for his role in investigating it during the McCarthy years, but he was in hot pursuit of Jimmy Hoffa, the head of the Teamsters union and numerous others of the criminal elite. They hated him, and he hated them. John Kennedy's election insured the greatest prosecution of mobsters in our history, and that, as we know, declined by eighty percent when John Kennedy died. RFK had lost his power, and his backing.

Atomic Testing

There was a time in American history after World War II when the U.S. military took upon itself to expose its own troops and some of those from the rest of the Free World to atomic weapons. Ultimately, over a half million men were marched through ground zero moments after an atomic weapon was set off in Nevada, or otherwise exposed to radiation at close range both in Nevada and in the Pacific island test sites.

This was one of the greatest crimes in our history. How any nation—knowing full well the effects of radiation from our use of the fission bombs on Hiroshima and Nagasaki—could expose human beings to this deliberately, I'll never know. It is an example, perhaps a symbol, of what we really were as a nation in the years preceding Kennedy's election to the presidency. We might point out how a vestige of this remains today—the enormous violence we find on our television sets every night. Hardly a moment goes by, flicking the dial, when we don't find a gun pointed at us, or see people killed. Then we wonder why we have so much violence in our country. As we saw in the film *A Clockwork Orange*, people are conditioned to violence—made insensitive to it.

Towns and cities were downwind of the atomic testing in the late forties and throughout the fifties. Significant and perhaps dangerous fallout was recorded as far away as Buffalo, New York. Shortly after the bombs were set off in Nevada, entire herds of sheep were found dead in Utah, and today many people in the towns of Utah and other surrounding areas have died or are dying from leukemia and other forms of cancer and radiation poisoning.

Today, among us still, are the dead and dying, derelict veterans in large numbers, many of whom have helped destroy themselves, drowning their physical and emotional pain with drink and drugs, some of whom have no idea why they are suffering so. The Veterans Administration refused for very many years to take responsibility for these men, and they got nothing, not even medical care. After all, to care for that many men would bankrupt us. But the tests went on.

The military was trying to find out what would happen, as for example what happened at the Battle of Petersburg in the American Civil War when Union miners tunneled under the Confederate lines, painfully, slowly, and secretly, and placed a boxcar full of gunpowder under the Southern trenches and battlements and set it off. The intent was to blow a hole in the lines and thus having breached them, to march through and win the day.

But when the blast went off, everyone was so in awe and so shocked, nobody did anything. By the time the Yankees moved forward, the Rebels woke up and filled the breech with fresh troops, and stopped the Yankee charge. Though the engineers succeeded, the whole long and expensive effort failed.

So, a hundred years later, the generals were still befuddled by this, and needed to know that if a huge army was marching down from the Bering Strait, and if an atomic bomb was set off and blew a hole in the advancing Chinese and Russian formations—would our own men be brave enough to go right through there and cut them up. So, could they march through ground zero five or ten minutes after the blast went off? At least this is how the tests were rationalized.

Well, they could. But the generals had to see if Indian troops could do it. And Canadian troops, and troops from all over the world. They had to keep trying it on American soldiers—hundreds of thousands of them for years.[2]

As a teenager in Arizona I used to see those bombs going off in the predawn dimness to the northwest. Little did I know that some boys who were watching them from their ranches closer to the blasts would soon die.

Well, John Kennedy was almost alone in seeing what was going on, and he stopped the tests. He then worked with the Russians to try to get some sort of a treaty. The Russians continued testing, so under great pressure from the military, JFK let them go on, but *underground.*

He was then able to get a treaty with the Soviet Union banning any further aboveground tests. This was one of his greatest achievements, but it came in the face of bitter opposition from the military and the radical right wing that was moving into a position to take over and control the United States, and wanted weapons of terror.

I believe Kennedy paid the ultimate price for this treaty and some of the other things mentioned in this section. The treaty earned him a great hatred from his enemies, and they got him back.

Make Love, Not War

President Kennedy was the "first American president to give art, literature, and music a place of dignity and honor in our national life," Lewis Mumford said. And only Washington and Jefferson had much feel for architecture. After all, when John Kennedy became president, we were to a certain extent an artistically barbaric country. This was not a gentle country, but a country whose rural pastimes, at a period when the majority of our population was still outside the principal urban population centers, were cruising on the main drags, young men making target practice of road signs, gay bashing, racial slander, lynching, and American Joe drinking beer on the couch and watching television.

"A wave of intellectual interest and excitement rippled out from the White House. Learning and culture were in style. 'The quality of American life,' said the President, 'must keep pace with the quantity of American goods. This country cannot afford to be materially rich and spiritually poor.' "[3]

Do you get the idea from this—those of you who were not alive or don't recall—that there was a deep spiritual malaise in America before Kennedy? Those of us who were young and naive then will never forget the powerful wind of fresh spring air that came in with John Kennedy, for the idea of Camelot was no joke. Everything started to change. And

John Kennedy's leadership was also a leadership of the young by the youthful.

And his First Lady was stunning and wonderful in our perception. Most everyone loved her. We had a government that was somehow so different from any government anywhere that the vast majority were thrilled every day with the glamour and excitement of it all. The modernity, actually. And once again these very things would breed hatred. Resentment would grow like a disease and finally consume the beauty we had then for one brief moment in history.

"He cared deeply and personally about education, human rights, better health, cleaner cities, and greater dignity for the aged. Believing that 'a nation reveals itself not only by the men it produces but also by the men it honors,' he initiated the new Medal of Freedom Awards. . . .

"The White House became both a showplace and a dwelling place for the distinctive, the creative, and the cultivated. It was also, cracked the President to one gathering of intellectuals, 'becoming a sort of eating place for artists. But *they* never ask *us* out!' "[4]

Kennedy stayed close to Robert Frost throughout his presidency, and André Malraux, the novelist and Minister of Cultural Affairs of France, as well. Sorensen tells us that he gave Malraux as much attention as he gave the foreign ministers of many nations.

Perhaps this was another crime that might have been added to the "Wanted for Treason" poster published in the newspaper in Dallas the day he died.

He also had to dinner the Americans who had won the Nobel Prize; it was the first official U. S. recognition of their achievements.

There were only a couple of significant ballet companies, and only a few opera companies, including two or three great ones. Petipa and the Kirov were names known only to a few Americans, and George Balanchine had a most difficult time keeping his fledgling New York City Ballet going. It turned out to be the greatest ballet company in the world. Our symphony orchestras, though often very good, were almost always led by great European conductors, and the musical taste of the audiences ran only to the war-horses of classical music, the compositions of Bach, Beethoven, Brahms, and Tchaikovsky. Little did anyone know of the other great composers. Leonard Bernstein, the flashy showman leading the New York Philharmonic, became the darling of the liberal crowd in those years as he began to introduce the new art forms of jazz and Broadway to more "serious" music, and perform composers that few here had heard before. We were until Kennedy a country without taste.

It was almost impossible to get a cup of tea in a public place in the South, or find a sidewalk café in all of the United States except for North Beach in San Francisco's Italian section. Practically the only coffeehouses America had were in North Beach or Greenwich Village, and such meeting places were essential to many creative people trying to gestate a book, a play, a painting, a poem, or a musical composition. Maine was the end of the world in North America, America knew little about Canada or Mexico.

But those lovely evenings at the White House when Pablo Casals and so many other great artists and musicians came to a command performance for the President! In my judgment, it was this single act of the President and his wife that gave American artistic creativity the shot in the arm it so desperately needed. Kennedy gave everyone hope, and the wondrous excitement was so infectious that it spread like wildfire through the artistic community in America. A nation's art and culture, its writing and music, is the core of a nation's soul, and ours had lain dormant and suppressed for so long beneath a cloak of militarism and intolerance.

Politics

"At the time it seemed that Kennedy suffered from the illusion so common to new presidents (even Roosevelt had it till 1935), that he, unlike any of his predecessors, could really be president of all the people and achieve his purposes without pain or trauma. Some of us, however, thought argument the best way to break national apathy and communicate the reality of problems. We believed that the educational value of fights in drawing the line between the administration and its opponents would guarantee that even if we did not have a law, we would have an issue," Schlesinger wrote.[5]

Listen to some more of this, for this is as deep as any philosopher ever got in discussing the leadership of a nation. Schlesinger and other presidential advisors thought Kennedy was mistaken in avoiding a particular fight. "We thought him mistaken in 1962 in making the entirely respectable, safe, and overrated trade expansion bill his top legislative priority instead of staging a knockdown–drag-out fight over federal aid to education or Medicare. To the President I would cite the Roosevelts, Wilson, Jackson, and so on in arguing the inevitability and superiority of the politics of combat as against the politics of consensus. But while he did not dispute the historical points, he plainly saw no reason for rushing prematurely into battle.

"I think now he had deeper reasons for this than I understood at the time—that his cast of mind had a profounder source than a pragmatist's preference for a law over an issue, than a rationalist's distaste for give-'em-hell partisanship, or even than a statesman's need to hoard national confidence against the possibility that foreign crises might require swift and unpopular presidential decisions. I believe today that its basic source may have been an acute and anguished sense of the fragility of the membranes of civilization, stretched so thin over a nation so disparate in its composition, so tense in its interior relationships, so cunningly enmeshed in underground fears and antagonisms, so entrapped by history in the ethos of violence. In 1963 Kennedy spoke to Robert Stein of *Redbook* about the destructive instincts 'that have been implanted in us growing out of the dust' and added, 'We have done reasonably well—but only reasonably well' in controlling them. His hope was that it might be possible to keep the country and the world moving fast enough to prevent unreason from rending the skin of civility. But he had peered into the abyss and knew the potentiality of chaos."[6]

"Kennedy communicated, first of all, a deeply critical attitude toward the ideas and institutions which American society had come in the fifties to regard with such enormous self-satisfaction. Social criticism had fallen into disrepute during the Eisenhower decade. In some influential quarters, it was almost deemed treasonous to raise doubts about the perfection of the American way of life. But the message of Kennedy's 1960s campaign had been that the American way of life was in terrible shape, that our economy was slowing down, that we were neglectful of our young and our old, callous toward our poor and our minorities, that our cities and schools and landscapes were a mess, that our motives were materialistic and ignoble, and that we were fast becoming a country without purpose and without ideas. As president, he proceeded to document the indictment. In so doing, he released the nation's critical energy. Self-criticism became not only legitimate but patriotic. The McCarthy anxieties were forgotten. Critics began to question the verities again, and defenders of the status quo no longer had the heart, or nerve, to call them Communists. The President, in effect, created his own muckraking movement."[7]

But you see, as in the Soviet Union, to do this would antagonize the ultimate holders of power in this country: those with guns and those who controlled the military. The radical right thought of Kennedy as a Communist for the very attitudes stated above. They hated him for these things. These men were effected by Kennedy's forcing the steel companies to roll back their price hikes in violation of the antitrust laws, and they were threatened to the core of their lives by Kennedy's proposal to reduce the oil-depletion allowances which had made the Rockefellers and the H. L. Hunts and the Syd Richardsons and the Clint Murchisons of this country rich.

Economics

Kennedy was a patrician, an aristocrat who cared deeply for the people. He was not a demagogue and not a traitor to his class as the radical-right Republicans thought of him and Roosevelt. A primary reason why they didn't like his father was that Roosevelt had appointed Joe Kennedy as the first head of the Securities and Exchange Commission, and coming out of the Great Depression, Joseph Kennedy's regulations reigned in very many flagrant abuses of fiduciary responsibility over the investing public. That was a great achievement, considering the degree to which fraud was practiced in those days. We can see the catastrophic results of deregulation of financial institutions by President Reagan. Draconian measures are almost a necessity in that area of our economic life.

But Kennedy was about as economically conservative as could be, though he subscribed to the "new" ideas of John Maynard Keynes. Keynes believed that in times of recession, the government should spend, borrowing money if necessary, to pump up the economy, and save when the economy was doing well. The idea was to rearrange the tax base so that more tax money proportionately flowed in when times were good, without hindering the economy.

Since then the Federal Reserve and the leading economists of the country have further learned to tinker with the economy so that it never seems to fall too far. The Great Depression was in part a product of overproduction, when mass production was still relatively new, and when we could not keep computerized inventories. It was easy to overproduce and then have to close down assembly lines. Supply and demand always has to be relatively close together.

The stock market crash also reflected both the rampant speculation that existed in those days, with far too large a line of credit margin allowed speculators, and the realization by investors that factories had overproduced.

Kennedy As a Man

Kennedy had a social conscience. He had what was always called a sense of stewardship. One looked after those who were with us, whether our retainers or the public. This was in fact the philosophy of the Democratic party, which for a long time was run by such intellectuals and patricians as Wilson, Kennedy, and Roosevelt, who had a sense of responsibility to the general public, to the middle class and workingman. They did not—in their alliance with the unions—believe in the "trickle down" theory that the Republicans subscribe to, and which represented some of the worst abuses of capitalism.

Now that the power of the unions is being broken, and the power of the Democratic party largely evaporated since the extermination of its liberal centrist leadership, we may wonder what protection we have now that the great counterbalance of Soviet communism is no longer there to scare the devil out of those robber barons who will go right back to taking everything away from us, and reducing us to minimum wages and penury.

Then there was civil rights. Kennedy's detractors try to downplay the role he took in that, or say that he utilized it merely for political ends. Some political ends when sympathizing with the plight of blacks or agitating for civil rights could and did bring a lot of people a swift death.

"We're taking names," some radical right-wing types and cops have told me from time to time when I spoke too freely. Some of us might well expect to die of an accident or a gunshot.

Kennedy cared. He assessed the situation and acted. He sent troops to Mississippi and enforced the law. And that is the way it went throughout his presidency. His brother, the Attorney General, took it as a primary task to insure that United States attorneys looked into voting rights violations, and that people were prosecuted for violating anyone's civil rights. A race killing was considered a violation of their rights and the issue became a federal matter when whites were let go by southern courts for killing blacks. To interfere with peaceful marchers was considered a violation of civil rights. As long as they had a permit.

School segregation, lunch-counter and bus segregation, were all considered in violation of the law. The Supreme Court made those findings, and Attorney General Robert Kennedy—the Kennedy White House—enforced the will of the courts.

And Kennedy introduced his Omnibus Civil Rights legislation, which, when finally passed, forever changed the social and political landscape of America. Martin Luther King, Jr., had for his most important human ally (this is an allusion to God being his other ally) President John F. Kennedy.

Kennedy had a sense of stewardship.

He had something else. When he went to Mexico City, two million people came to see and hear him. A million or more people in Berlin. It was often like that. Every tiny *tienda,* hut, and hovel around the world had his picture. He spoke to all of the people everywhere. Americans may not really know how great this man was, and what he meant everywhere in the world. Perhaps seeing again the films of his funeral cortege might hint at it, when presidents, premiers, kings, and queens walked on the street like commoners for miles behind his caisson, behind his riderless white horse with its saddle turned backward. Even General Charles de Gaulle, the President of France, walked there among all of those mourners.

And we mourned. Even many of his detractors knew what they had lost and that things would get a lot worse without him.

Because Kennedy had so much style, so much class, publicly. He and his wife. And his children. I mean, we don't often have small children running around the White House, crawling under the presidential desk during interviews and meetings, as happened in those days.

Maybe those children so close helped remind him just how precious life was, and he refrained from acts that would have led to far larger conflagrations in the world. They made him and kept him the more human.

The Wall

We know of the major crises that erupted one after the other during his presidency. They were almost stopped dead with the first one, the Bay of Pigs. He had to admit, as Eisenhower admitted that he had lied about our U-2 spy plane being shot down over Russia, that he had sent the men into Cuba, and that we had failed miserably. In a parliamentary system there would have been a call for a vote of confidence, and the government might have fallen.

The East Germans built a wall across Berlin, imprisoning their own people, unable to compete with the glitter, decadence, glamour, and prosperity of West Berlin. Our generals counseled war over that. Kennedy sent a token force of 1,500 men or so, and that was all that was needed. No one doubted the legal right of East Germany to do what it did, but nobody felt that it was right to do it.

I can tell you that were it not for Kennedy, we would have gone to war right there. Now the Wall is down. Many people over the years were shot trying to get over it or under it, and the division lasted for years. But the truth was, those who fought against Germany in World War II were not too eager to have Germany reunited again, not for a long time, until Germany could again be trusted. The Cold War kept Germany divided.

General Taylor

General Maxwell Taylor was a man President Kennedy appeared to trust. He had been in retirement when Kennedy brought him back to government service, and it was Taylor who played a principal role at the beginning of Kennedy's presidency when Robert Kennedy headed up an informal but intense investigation of what really happened at the Bay of Pigs debacle.

The invasion of Cuba by a group of Cuban exiles had been planned by the CIA and the Pentagon during the last year of Eisenhower's presidency. Due to delays, the invasion did not come off before Eisenhower left office. John Kennedy had to be told what was in the works, and he was lied to extensively about the situation and the facts. After the invasion failed, he had RFK and Maxwell Taylor investigate it. Allen Dulles was greatly angered by what they found.

Robert Kennedy attended all the meetings as many witnesses were interviewed, and Taylor used those meetings to press his counterinsurgency ideas in between the lines of what the meetings were about— the failure of the Bay of Pigs invasion. He had quite a different concept of warfare to sell than traditional frontal assault, as we saw with the invasion itself, or in wars of maneuver that meant nothing in guerrilla insurrections and jungle terrain such as Vietnam.

These ideas appealed to Kennedy, and he was drawn in because his tendency was to avoid anything that might lead to large-scale conflict and war, if possible. The fact that Taylor was in reality a militant cold warrior and a hawk all down the line on many issues went right by Kennedy. Taylor was a wolf in sheep's clothing. A lot of people when tapped by a president for a job in an administration, especially for the first time, will carefully conceal whatever part of their character might be in conflict with that president, either for the egotism of having a job close to the chief of state, or for the purposes of manipulating him.

In addition, it is not possible for a president to investigate fully the thoughts, beliefs, and background of everyone he asks to work for him. Presidents are all too frequently embarrassed by the men they have hired or appointed to top posts.

It is worth noting that nearly every person whom Kennedy had tapped for his staff or for the government when he was inaugurated was in his job when Kennedy died. Ordinarily, there is a very high attrition rate among White House staff due to the terrible pressure and stress of any job there, working at all hours, seven days a week often enough, and for only about $20,000 a year at the time. Any of those men could have made far more money anywhere else.

As the three brief years of the Kennedy presidency passed, certain events transpired that drew out of Taylor some of his real feelings. Seeing things in a strictly linear fashion, he felt that the Kennedy administration did not know its own mind.

Death of the Ngo Brothers

An example dealt with the problems raised by an impending coup by a group of generals developing in Vietnam in late August 1963. The following may teach several lessons. Ambassador (to South Vietnam)

Henry Cabot Lodge had wired the State Department that the outlook for the coup was good, and the "chances for success would be diminished by delay."[8] But a cable to the contrary saying that the rebels did not command sufficient forces to overcome the Ngos was sent by General Paul D. Harkins and read by Kennedy. Suspicious, Kennedy investigated.

Kennedy requested a copy of General Taylor's wire to Harkins asking him for his advice. Dean Rusk writes; "The last paragraph, however, seemed to suggest how General Harkins should answer the inquiry: 'FYI State to Saigon 243 was prepared without DOD or JCS participation. Authorities are now having second thoughts.'

"Taylor's telegram angered the President. The cable not only tainted Harkins's assessment but also implied Kennedy was running a government incapable of making up its mind. The dissension within the Kennedy administration grew sharper at the noon August 28 NSC meeting. The State Department officials promoting the coup argued that the U.S. 'must decide now to go through to a successful overthrow.' Ambassador Frederick Nolting disagreed. By abandoning Diem and Nhu, said Nolting, the U.S. would be reneging on past commitments. At that, Averell Harriman, known as 'the crocodile,' sharply denounced Nolting's political judgment and advice, charging that he had not adequately represented U.S. interests during his term as ambassador. Deputy Secretary of Defense Roswell Gilpatric could not recall when anyone in the presence of the President 'took the tongue-lashing that Nolting did from Harriman.'

" 'The President was appalled at the emotions this problem had stirred up and the basic lack of information about Vietnam,' remembered Michael Forrestal. 'He just couldn't understand how so many Americans could divide almost down the middle in their opinions of what was going on in the country and what should be done about it.'

"The growing rift among the President's advisors and General Taylor's 'second thoughts' cable prompted Kennedy to seek new and independent advice from Ambassador Henry Cabot Lodge and General Harkins. In his instructions of the twenty-eighth to Lodge, the President reaffirmed his pro-coup policy, 'But this judgment in turn is heavily dependent on your on-the-spot advice, and I trust you will not hesitate to recommend delay or change in plans if at any time you think it is wise.' "[9]

It is clear from all the other evidence of his presidency that Kennedy stayed very close to problems, and the above is an example of his personally investigating each problem he perceived. Most other presidents would not have even seen a conflict or problem, but Kennedy could bring conflict out into the open. He wasn't afraid of that, but it set some of his men against each other, and against him in some cases.

There is a benefit in having staff sort out their differences, with an overseer to determine whose ideas are the soundest, and that was what Kennedy was doing. And sometimes we also uncover tricks, as might be said of Taylor's attempt to manipulate General Harkins's answer.

We also see Kennedy's attitude in his talk with Lodge, who unconditionally supported the coup by saying, "I know from experience [the Bay of Pigs] that failure is more destructive than an appearance of indecision. . . . When we go, we must go to win, but it will be better to change our minds than fail."[10]

Following the above closely was the dispute between the Kennedy advisors and State Department officials, Paul Kattenburg and Roger Hilsman and the Pentagon. Kennedy's men insisted that Ngos and Nhu had no support in South Vietnam, but General Taylor and Secretary Robert McNamara resisted this to the end.

Kattenburg was a specialist on Indochina and very disturbed over the failure in this country to understand what was going on there. Ambassador Lodge had said that if we continued to support Ngos and Nhu, "this repressive regime, with its bayonets at every street corner and its transparent negotiations with puppet bonzes, we are going to be thrown out of the country in six months."[11] William Rust writes: "Believing that Kennedy's advisors 'were leading themselves down a garden path to tragedy,' Kattenburg then blurted out the unthinkable: 'At this juncture, it would be better for us to make the decision to get out honorably.' "[12]

Dean Rusk, the Secretary of State, said,[13] "We will not pull out of Vietnam until the war is won, and . . . we will not run a coup."[14] He was for sticking with the status quo—with the Ngos.

Vice President Lyndon Johnson was also at the State Department meeting that day, and Rusk asked him what he thought, "a man whose views on Vietnam were seldom sought by Kennedy. . . . Appalled by the previous week's plot to overthrow Diem, Johnson believed there was no real alternative leadership to the South Vietnamese president. When asked by Rusk if he had any contribution to make, the Vice President replied, 'we should stop playing cops and robbers' and 'get back to talking straight' with Diem. The U.S., said Johnson, 'should once again go about winning the war.' "[15]

Vietnam

We have the right to change our mind. Kennedy did not heavily commit the United States in Vietnam itself at any time in his presidency. He sent military advisors over there, but from Tom Wicker's view,[16] Kennedy's statements were confusing with reference to his position on Vietnam in the last days of his life.

Clearly, Kennedy was under conflicting pressures with regard to Vietnam, as any president or leader would be when faced with the decision of war or peace.

The pressure that Kennedy was under can better be understood when we recall that it appears that both his Secretary of Defense (McNamara) and his Chairman of the Joint Chiefs of Staff (Taylor), seemed to be recommending withdrawal to Kennedy, and these *same* men, in fact much of his Cabinet—after his death—led us into that war in a big way two years later. The implication is that Kennedy was being double dealt. Kennedy was in fact under pressure from these same men to escalate. So, almost alone in his administration he had come to the conclusion to get out. Kenneth O'Donnell, his close friend, said that he did not think Kennedy had told Dean Rusk, the Secretary of State, that he was going to get out. O'Donnell[17] said that he thought that Kennedy had never presented his plan clearly to the National Security Council, but that McNamara knew of it.

Both Generals de Gaulle and MacArthur talked long and hard at Kennedy in 1961 about not getting heavily involved in Vietnam. The meeting with General MacArthur lasted three hours. Among other reasons, from their point of view any land war in Asia was an overextension of the sea and airlift capacity of any major western state on the other side of the world. We would also be fighting Chinese soldiers dressed up like Vietnamese, and it was easy to underestimate the capacity of the enemy in that place to fight to the death.

O'Donnell tells us in his book that MacArthur told Kennedy that in the modern age the Domino Theory was ridiculous. The General said that the nation's domestic problems were more important than Vietnam and had to be dealt with (as we soon learned to our horror). "Kennedy came out of the meeting stunned. That a man like MacArthur should give him such unmilitary advice impressed him enormously."

But this was in the time of a national passion against the hold of the Communists on much of the world and the threat of their already bankrupt political system. Americans as a whole were not well disposed to ignoring Communist aggression.

After returning from a trip to Vietnam in 1962, Senator Mike Mansfield also reasoned with Kennedy and told him to withdraw. Kennedy told O'Donnell after the meeting: "I got angry with Mike for disagreeing with our policy so completely, and I got angry with myself because I found myself agreeing with him."

There was also a political equation. Kennedy had to wait until the next election. He told Senator Mike Mansfield in the Oval Office in Kenneth O'Donnell's presence that he agreed with Mansfield that we had to withdraw all of the military from Vietnam but he said, "I can't do it until 1965—after I'm reelected." When Mansfield left the office, Kennedy said to O'Donnell: "In 1965, I'll be damned everywhere as a Communist appeaser. But I don't care. If I tried to pull out completely now, we would have another Joe McCarthy Red scare on our hands, but I can do it after I'm reelected. So we had better make damn sure that I *am* reelected."[18]

Kennedy was not chicken. That is not why he began to sidestep out of Vietnam. He had proved his manhood in World War II and in the 1962 Cuban Missile Crisis. The fact is, he had learned from the Bay of Pigs that military solutions are not always the best.

But as Mansfield, a close friend of Kennedy's, had said, "It was not unusual for him to shift position. There is no doubt that he had shifted definitely and unequivocally on Vietnam, but he never had the chance to put the plan into effect." (Speaking of the intent to withdraw from Vietnam)[19] Mansfield also said in that interview with the *Post* that Kennedy "had definitely and unequivocally made that decision." This was at a congressional breakfast with Kennedy. "President Kennedy didn't waste words. He was pretty sparse with his language."

The issue here is one of statecraft. There is the Machiavellian view of doing whatever you have to do, ruthlessly if necessary, to achieve your goal. That means lying, murder, whatever. *The Prince* was Machiavelli's crucial work on the subject, and his philosophy was adhered to for centuries by rulers.

The expectations of the Cubans at the Bay of Pigs may have been unrealistic, and of course colored with the false promises or implied promises of American military backing for their invasion.

Since some of these same Cubans may have later helped kill Kennedy, we need to think long and hard about what we say as well as what we do. If the government is going to support rebellions, as we have so often, but then repeatedly hang these people out to dry when it is convenient for us so to do, then sometimes this can blow back in our face.

It is not clear to me that Kennedy in any way betrayed these people. He himself was being tricked and lied to by his military intelligence advisors. He was told that the men would be landed near mountains which they could easily reach and sustain themselves therein for a long-term rebellion. But they were landed two hundred miles from the Escambray Mountains in a swamp with basically no exit.

No president is in a position to review an entire plan for each of many operations. He is the Commander in Chief and cannot micromanage every detail. He could not have known that the military and CIA would be so stupid as to put all the ammunition on one ship which was easily blown up with a few bullets from one small trainer jet plane.

Kennedy got the whole Bay of Pigs operation dumped on him at the very start of his presidency. He was put into the position of lying about what happened, but he had the decency to admit the lie a few days later, as Eisenhower admitted his lie about the U-2 incident. After Kennedy's death, presidents stopped admitting their lies, and from that moment on, the United States government has not had any credibility. There has been one enormous lie after another, and the *double-speak* of National Security Action Memorandum (NSAM) 273 is a good example of where it started. The Gulf of Tonkin incident is a case in point of a great fraud perpetrated on the public. Like the Germans dressing up mental patients in Polish uniforms and shooting them down in an abortive raid on a German border post in order to justify the invasion of Poland.

The French have noted a sort of creeping disease that tended to bog down and ultimately paralyze a government agency or a corporate office, called "the bureaucratic phenomenon."* The British have said for some time that it seemed to make no difference which party was voted into power. A prime minister and his cabinet ultimately could not seem to change policy according to their mandate because of the tough resis-

---

* Michel Crozier, *The Bureaucratic Phenomenon* (Chicago: University of Chicago Press, 1964).

tance of government bureaucrats they depended upon to effect such change. The lead article in the *Baltimore Sunday Sun* for March 31, 1991, dealt with the same phenomenon: "Enforcement of New Laws Often Delayed; Stalling in Agencies, Congress's Directives Blamed for Problem."[20]

The result is that the status quo is more likely to carry on from generation to generation once bureaucratic monsters are created than for constructive, progressive change to occur as needed. Government or business can become unresponsive, and ultimately so much friction will be created that the whole apparatus breaks down.

The publicly unstated counterargument of those who favor such a situation is that an entrenched official constitutes a check and balance to the arbitrary acts of an autocrat or a demagogic legislative body. The particular keepers of the keys in the U.S., of course, are agents of the plutocracy, of the oligarchy that is the real government. Very many of the men surrounding Kennedy represented the main northeastern power controllers among the wealthy Establishment that usually called the shots in those years, and they resented both the upstart Celtic Kennedy and the power of his father. Since the Kennedy money was slightly newer and therefore tainted, the bottom line was one of resentment when it became clear that Kennedy was his own man and not wholly their creature.

The great fear of the secret shadow government in the U.S. is the simple fact that an elected president has a certain mandate for constructive change. John Kennedy was therefore a grave threat because he made way for the many changes necessary for our society to initiate at the time or explode. The problem with these unelected checks and balance characters is that they run counter to our whole theory of government, and these secret controllers and obstructers sit as judge and jury without benefit of public debate or election. These guards become our keepers.

What we were doing in South Vietnam with our 16,000 advisors in the early sixties has to be seen within the context of Indochina as a whole, and how that balanced out what was happening in Cuba, where there were 16,000 Soviet advisors. Playing these chess games seems to keep us endlessly going, and perhaps finally gets us far less than simple straightforward dealing. If that is possible. That is what we need the debate for.

Americans have got to understand the fundamental mechanism of how all this works: We *create* rebellions that we then have to go and fight. We engage in extensive covert activities in violation of some other country's sovereignty, and then having created a big problem have to go in with the military to straighten out the situation. Problem with that is, we don't always intend to win these affairs, don't intend to do anything but feed the jaws of war, eating up material and money which enslaves us all. That was what Vietnam was all about, and that is what this chapter is about. NSAM 273 made it clear without President Kennedy knowing it that a program of extensive covert activities was to be undertaken against *North Vietnam,* and this led directly to the Gulf of Tonkin incident, which created public justification for large-scale American military forces to go to that theater of war.

Another example is the fact that the CIA sent operatives into Cuba to help Castro overthrow Batista. Frank Sturgis of Watergate fame was one of them. There are a whole lot of incidents of this where some might say, well, we didn't know the guy was a Communist. Many times we have backed people who later turned on us, but more likely than not we always knew it very well (the alternative of an intelligence agency not knowing the political background and proclivities of the person they were supporting is too frightening to contemplate) and either believed we could control them or *wanted* Communists in power so we could fight them, make money, keep the Cold War going—which was very valuable to that segment of our country leeching off the rest of us. Even the Russians have recognized that they were entrapped by the militant Cold Warrior Sect there who fed off everyone else's fears and who obstructed any attempt at détente. Kennedy's big mistake which helped lead him to his doom was trying to work out a peaceful accommodation with the Soviets.

In the Gulf of Tonkin incident, Americans were led to believe that our ships were attacked on the high seas, not that we weren't already seriously interfering with North Vietnam. Kennedy recognized that the people of South Vietnam were rebelling against a repressive regime, and unless that regime changed its internal policies, we had no hope or reason to save it.

The Last Year

In the summer of 1963 the President's wife gave birth to a baby boy prematurely, and he died just two days later.

Arthur Schlesinger tells us about what it was like in the autumn of

1963. He writes in *A Thousand Days* that "in public policy the Presidency of John F. Kennedy was coming into its own. He was doing at last in the summer of 1963 what he had been reluctant to do before: Put the office of the Presidency on the line at the risk of defeat. He was staking his authority and his reelection on behalf of equal rights, the test ban, planned deficits in economic policy, doing so not without political apprehension but with absolute moral and intellectual resolve. As he had anticipated, the civil rights fight in particular was biting into his popularity. In November Gallup would report that national approval of his administration was down to fifty-nine percent. Most of this decline was in the South: There, if the Republicans, as he came to believe they would, nominated Barry Goldwater, Kennedy expected to carry only two or three states. Moreover, this had been the hardest of his congressional sessions. At the end of July, according to the *Congressional Quarterly,* thirty-eight percent of the administration's proposals had not yet been acted on by either house. Civil rights and tax reduction were making very slow progress. Knives were sharpening for foreign aid. Even routine appropriation bills were held up."

But then the Senate ratified his nuclear test ban treaty. Schlesinger tells us that it had been a rough, sad summer, but that the ratification of the test ban renewed his strength. Kennedy said, "There is a rhythm to personal and national and international life, and it flows and ebbs."[21]

Kennedy was getting renewed strength and energy and the plotters close to him must have sensed it. They knew that it was time to act.

The great liberal influence Kennedy represented and fostered must never be allowed to die. Without it, this nation is truly a nation without a soul.

It is worth it to end this chapter with what some of those who were closest to John Kennedy thought of him. We don't get from them some phony moralistic judgment or slanderous accusation, but instead, we have their view of just what he really was and meant. A politician's private life should remain private unless it is so grossly illegal or criminal that it has to be brought out.

"His untimely and violent death will affect the judgment of historians, and the danger is that it will relegate his greatness to legend. Even though he was himself almost a legendary figure in life, Kennedy was a constant critic of the myth. It would be an ironic twist of fate if his martyrdom should now make a myth of the mortal man."[22]

Martyrdom. Sorensen goes on to end his book with this: "In my view, the man was greater than the legend. His life, not his death, created his greatness. In November, 1963, some saw it for the first time. Others realized that they had too casually accepted it. Others mourned that they had not previously admitted it to themselves. But the greatness was there, and it may well loom even larger as the passage of years lends perspective.

"One of the doctors at the Parkland Hospital in Dallas, observing John Kennedy's six-foot frame on the operating table, was later heard to remark: 'I had never seen the President before. He was a big man, bigger than I thought.'

"He was a big man—much bigger than anyone thought—and all of us are better for having lived in the days of Kennedy."

"It was all gone now—the life-affirming, life-enhancing zest, the brilliance, the wit, the cool commitment, the steady purpose. . . . He had so little time. . . . Yet he had accomplished so much: the new hope for peace on earth, the elimination of nuclear testing in the atmosphere and the abolition of nuclear diplomacy, the new policies toward Latin America and the third world, the reordering of American defense, the emancipation of the American Negro, the revolution in national economic policy, the concern for poverty, the stimulus to the arts, the fight for reason against extremism and mythology. Lifting us beyond our capacities, he gave his country back to its best self, wiping away the world's impression of an old nation of old men, weary, played out, fearful of ideas, change, and the future; he taught mankind that the process of rediscovering America was not over. He reestablished the republic as the first generation of our leaders saw it—young, brave, civilized, rational, gay, tough, questing, exultant in the excitement and potentiality of history. He transformed the American spirit—and the response of his people to his murder, the absence of intolerance and hatred, was a monument to his memory. The energies he released, the standards he set, the purposes he inspired, the goals he established would guide the land he loved for years to come. Above all he gave the world for an imperishable moment the vision of a leader who greatly understood the terror and the hope, the diversity and the possibility, of life on this planet, and who made people look beyond nation and race to the future of humanity. So the people of the world grieved as if they had terribly lost their own leader, friend, brother.'"*

* Arthur M. Schlesinger, Jr.: *A Thousand Days,* closing pages.

That surged in the depth of his too proud heart
And spiked the punch of New England so tart
Men would call him thoughtful, sincere,
They would not see through to the Last Cavalier.

Jacqueline Kennedy's poem to her husband, 1953

CHAPTER 2

PRESIDENT KENNEDY'S MEDICAL HISTORY

There was seldom a day in John Kennedy's life when he was not in pain or in physical trouble. "At least one half of the days that he spent on this earth were days of intense physical pain. He had scarlet fever when he was very young and serious back trouble when he was older.[1] In between, he had almost every other conceivable ailment. When we were growing up together, we used to laugh about the great risk a mosquito took in biting Jack Kennedy—with some of his blood the mosquito was almost sure to die," his brother Robert wrote.[2]

Jack was often sick as a youngster, with numerous stays, sometimes for months, in hospitals.[3] His real story is one of triumph over great illness, only to be shot down in a street. His mother wrote: "He went along for many years thinking to himself—or at least trying to make others think—that he was a strong, robust, quite healthy person who just happened to be sick a good deal of the time."[4]

Like President Theodore Roosevelt, Kennedy had asthma,[5] a disease that destroys self-confidence in the young, and causes them to overcompensate, ultimately often to try to be a hero. There were various barbaric forms of treatment available, including radium treatments, which it has recently been found caused a high incidence of thyroid cancer in later years. Mostly, sufferers wheezed, strangled, and gasped for each breath of air, and were always subject to dangerous attacks, sometimes proving fatal—precipitated by cigarette, cigar, and pipe smoke, cats, dogs, allergies of all kinds, and the fumes given off by modern building materials.[6]

49

The next major and terrible medical problem Jack had was a very bad back, or as his Boston doctor, Elmer Bartels, called it, an "unstable back." This came from his early youth, and it was not caused by his war experiences or playing football at Harvard. He twice nearly lost his life during dangerous operations attempting to deal with his severe back problems.[7] Bartels told Joan and Clay Blair that Kennedy was "born with an unstable back."[8] The Blairs write: "An unstable back lasts a lifetime. It is a back that can be normal for long periods of time and then go out of whack for no apparent reason. When it goes out of whack, the pain can be excruciating, lasting days or weeks." They asked Dr. Bartels again: "You say Jack Kennedy was *born* with an unstable back?"

"Yes."

A friend at Harvard said that Kennedy was often sick when he was at school there. And "he had a bad back when he was at Harvard. He wore a corset all the time to brace it. It was real bad. If I'd been anywhere near the shape he was in, I wouldn't have gone out for football or anything else." And there was the story of his being in the Harvard infirmary (Stillman) and crawling out to go to the swimming tryouts.[9] "Jack couldn't possibly have won. He just wanted to be there. It showed a determination." Courage.[10]

The corset Jack wore kept him upright, like a doll, like a perfect target, while the bullets found him on the terrible day he died. The corset was six inches wide with metal stays and a plastic pad over the sacrum. The whole thing was laced up tight. He then tied the corset more tightly to his body with a six-inch Ace bandage which he tied between his legs and around his midsection in a figure eight. He did this every day of his adult life. It is speculated that the long-standing cortisone therapy had become counterproductive and was loosening his joints. He packaged himself like this to hold himself together, as his joints had loosened in the sacroiliac.

In his youth Kennedy had everything from German measles,[11] scarlet fever, a serious gastrointestinal disorder—perhaps even ulcers— whooping cough, chicken pox, bronchitis,[12] appendicitis,[13] "severe illness" (which the doctors suspect was hepatitis or jaundice)[14] in his fifth form at Choate in 1933–34 which followed the removal of his tonsils and adenoids. He had trouble climbing stairs at college.[15] Rip Horton told the story—"After he had climbed two flights of stairs he was so fatigued that he stood out on the fire escape, took off his coat, and threw it down. . . . He was overheated and overexerted on that trip up to our room!"[16]

Young Kennedy traveled to the London School of Economics in October 1935 to study under the famous Harold Laski, but fell so ill he was in the hospital for some time before being taken back to the United States.[17] Kennedy started at Princeton, then had to leave due to illness and spent two months at Peter Bent Brigham Hospital in Boston, cause unknown. He went out west to try to recover his health on a ranch in Arizona, where asthmatics (and this author) were traditionally sent. After transfer to Harvard and withdrawals for work/study in Europe, Jack finally graduated in 1940 and spent some time at Stanford in Palo Alto, where a friend said "he was in frail health out there. He had come to Stanford because of the mild climate, I think. He wasn't excited by Stanford academically. He had the Harvard view, of course."[18]

Kennedy made it through one quarter at Stanford in 1940 before starting back early in the following year to see doctors in New York and Boston. He was put into the Lahey Clinic and the New England Baptist Hospital. What was wrong with him this time? Along the way he had been seen at the Mayo Clinic after Christmas of 1945,[19] but we don't know why. I followed a lot of the same route, being an asthmatic, and was sent to the Mayo Brothers because they were important in respiratory problems. Maybe that is why he was there. Looking back on medicine in the mid-twentieth century, it reminds one of the eighteenth century, when they used to bleed people.

World War II

Then there was the war. How Kennedy got into the Navy with his physical disabilities was a story of extraordinary pull. And how he then managed to get combat status, in his zeal to risk his life and serve his country, was another incredible maneuver. He repeatedly was ill and landed in hospitals, where he met a nurse—Ann McGillicuddy—who helped him greatly. Lennie Thom, a shipmate, wrote his wife that he "was worried about Jack's health. He wrote me that Jack was ill—he didn't say what was the matter—but that a team of horses couldn't get him to report to sick bay. Lennie said Jack feigned being *well*, but that he knew he was always working under duress. I think Lennie actually admired Jack's courage for that, for not reporting sick. He and Lennie worked together very well."[20] But Jack concealed it from his commanding officer, Alvin Peyton Cluster, who told the Blairs: "As far as I can remember, his health was good. I don't remember any illnesses at that point. If there had been any serious problems, I would certainly have relieved him of command of the (PT) 109."[21]

Jack's PT boat was run over in the dark by a Japanese destroyer, which is about as close as anybody in the Navy could get to their opponent—who is often out of sight or at a great distance. He spent the night in the water swimming, saving the lives of the men, and ultimately keeping them together long enough to be rescued from an island swarming with the enemy. Kennedy swallowed a lot of gasoline while he was in the water, which led to serious stomach problems, badly hurt his bad back again, and "other illnesses arose from the disaster."[22]

Kennedy had long absences from active duty while he was in the hospital, including six months for an operation in spring 1942.[23] In 1944 Torby Macdonald, a friend, wrote in *Coronet* that he had come to see Kennedy, who "was lying in bed all strapped up as part of the treatment to mend his back. He was suffering from a recurrence of malaria, and his skin had turned yellow. His weight had dropped from 160 to 125 pounds.[24] When I came into his room, he raised a bony wrist and gave me a shaky wave. I asked him how he felt. He tried to lift his head. I had to lean over to hear him.

" 'I feel great,' he said. 'Great?' I echoed. 'Well,' he smiled, 'great considering the shape I'm in.' "[25]

You see, there is an unseen saga behind this man, and it is difficult for the average person to grasp just how hard life was for Jack, who was born with a silver spoon in his mouth. This man ultimately cared so much for all of us that his every decision weighed the fate of humanity. He knew the finiteness and fragility of life with every breath he took.

Addison's Disease

As many know, there was always suspicion and rumor about the possibility that Kennedy had Addison's disease, an insufficiency of the adrenal glands. Addison's is an atrophying of the adrenal cortex, and without the adrenals the body does not have the hormones necessary to regulate sodium and potassium. The modern treatment in the early sixties was cortisone.

Addison's was nearly always fatal until the late 1940s, when hormones and other treatments became available. It became possible for most sufferers to lead relatively normal lives. That is, if the diagnosis was correct.

Addison's is caused by either tuberculosis or an as-yet-unknown cause which atrophies the adrenals. About half of Addison's patients have had tuberculosis. Tuberculosis often lies dormant in the body and can be benign for years, not causing any problem. But it can have damaged the adrenals, which might cause shock and other life-threatening problems when the body is subjected to trauma or stress. The adrenals lie against the back on both sides of the spine, and that is the specific area where Kennedy had so much trouble, pain, and very dangerous operations at the time. He was given last rites several times in his life.

"The diagnosis of Addison's disease could have been firmly established at autopsy and perhaps the etiology determined. However, the autopsy protocol is curiously silent on this point as well as on details of the pituitary, of his vertebral column, and sacroiliac joints. The silence on these points may be due to (a) accidental or intentional failure to search and observe, or (b) suppression of autopsy findings and existing clinical records by relatives or federal officials or both," writes Dr. John Nichols in *Journal of the American Medical Association.*[26]

Nichols goes on to note that *because* there was a failure to report on the adrenals at the autopsy, there is a *presumption* of Addison's disease, taking into account Kennedy's medical history. Then he says that "the most unfortunate aspect is concealment of the diagnosis. Addison's disease, formerly fatal, is an honorable disease and is not a disease to be concealed. It had no stigmata to be avoided."

Then Nichols proposes that "the fact that President Kennedy was continuously engaged in strenuous mental and physical activity, tolerated extensive mental and physical activity, tolerated extensive surgical trauma, and became the father of four children, all without decrease in life expectancy, is noteworthy."

Or Pott's Disease?

The final statement could really mean something else: Kennedy did not have nor could he have had Addison's and done all that he did. Therefore, there is a presumption that he had another disease, and the prime candidate is Pott's disease, which is tuberculosis of the spine. Dr. Joseph Theodore Brierre, a U.S. Navy pathologist who was at Bethesda, diagnosed Pott's disease in the President, and Dr. Doyle Rogers, a prominent pathologist who was also in the Navy and who knew all the doctors concerned, concurs.

Dr. Rogers, as it happens, was an intern and was present at Parkland Hospital when President Kennedy was brought there. He then entered the Navy to do his residency, and came to know some of the autopsy doctors. Rogers knew Jack Ruby, the nightclub owner who shot Lee Harvey Oswald to death, rather well.

They had something else to cover up at the autopsy, a number of doctors have said. "He would not have lived through a second term," the Navy doctors told me.[27] If true, this is a major revelation. It could certainly account for the terrible back problems Kennedy suffered from, and is an example of symptoms being treated rather than the cause.

In those days tuberculosis was something that was not mentioned in a family. Every effort was made to cover it up, just as asthmatics did everything possible to conceal their disease. Tuberculosis was thought of in about the same light as leprosy, and was considered greatly contagious and unclean.

Covering up that he had TB contributed to a spiral of misdiagnosis and mismedication.

Dr. Janet Travell told me with regard to the possibility that Kennedy had had TB of the spine in his lifetime, that there was "no indication. Tests were done. No evidence."[28] She was quite alert and steady, old as she is, during my short talk with her. Dr. Travell is the doctor who gave extensive steroid medication to President Kennedy for many years. If he had had Pott's disease, steroids were the worst thing he could receive.[29]

The Autopsy and the Adrenals

Michael Baden, the New York City former Medical Examiner who was allegedly fired for revealing that Nelson Rockefeller died making love to a young lady—not his wife—was on the panel of experts for the House Assassinations Committee. He has been very strong in his defense of the Warren Commission's findings, and he is prone to making inaccurate statements on the medical evidence. For instance, in his book *Unnatural Death,* he states the following: "One of the things that had haunted the President was his Addison's disease. Over the years, rumors that he was debilitated by it had surfaced and been denied. It was a well-kept secret, and the family wanted it to remain one."[30]

The problem with this statement is the very first phrase: *"his* Addison's disease." It was never proved or admitted that Kennedy had it. In fact, as Baden should know, the contrary was proved by the autopsy X-rays. Here we have an attitude of assumption, of stating as fact a supposition. The evidence was that Kennedy had instead Pott's disease, as some of the doctors at Bethesda Naval Hospital believed.

Another example of Baden's tendency to overstate or misstate the facts follows on the same page a little farther down, when he describes the visit of Commander James J. Humes to Baden's panel of experts and the first question he was asked which was about the adrenals (why, when there were other issues of such vast importance?). Baden writes: "Even then, fifteen years later, when it no longer mattered, his feelings of respect were so strong that he refused to comment for the record about Addison's disease. The family didn't want any mention of any diseases that might be present, he said."

It's this sort of outright rationalization that throws into question the credibility of a medical examiner. Perhaps we are not astute enough to weigh each word that we ourselves or others utter, to analyze the implications of things and how they can mean something else. Dr. Humes *never mentioned* anything about the family or Addison's disease in his interview, which follows.[31]

The autopsy report omitted any mention of the adrenal glands, a violation of the protocol of the Armed Forces Institute of Pathology. Rumors about the issue were rife among the medical community in the Baltimore-Washington area in view of the assumption that Kennedy had Addison's disease. In spite of this belief, there is a lack of documentation of it, and the supposed original diagnoses in London and Boston have not been proven.

Dr. Humes absolutely refused to talk about the adrenals to the panel of doctors assembled by the House Assassinations Committee on September 16, 1977.

"First of all, let me start with the question that is on the lips of everyone here, and that is, did you or didn't you look at the adrenals?"

"I would ask, you—did that bear, or does that bear, on your investigation of the event that took place that night?"

"No, all we were wondering was—we noticed that that was noticeably absent from the autopsy report."

"Since I don't think it bore directly on the death of the president, I'd prefer not to discuss it with you, Doctor."

"All right. Fine. If you prefer not to, that's fine with me. We were just curious because normally we examine adrenals in the general course of the autopsy as we undertake it. Okay, so—"

"I'd only comment for you that I have strong personal reasons and certain other obligations that suggest to me that it might not be preferable."[32]

Tell me, dear reader, don't you suspect that there is something strange going on here? Not only was the meeting getting off to a bad start, but the very first question tied everyone up in a knot. Why?

And what did Humes mean when he spoke of "personal reasons and certain other obligations" for not discussing President Kennedy's adrenals? What difference could it possibly make? After his death, there would have been no reason for covering up the fact that Kennedy had Addison's disease.

Kennedy was well known to be suffering from a severe adrenal insufficiency, and was accused by John Connally during his 1960 campaign for the presidency of having Addison's disease, and some thought this made him physically unfit for the office of president of the United States. But it was never documented publicly or proven that he had Addison's disease, though one of the surgeons who operated on him in 1954, Dr. James Nicholas, told me flatly that Kennedy had Addison's disease at that time, which seems a severe contraindication to their decision to operate, and their expressed doubts before the operation that Kennedy had Addison's and therefore it was safe to operate.[33]

Pott's disease can cause a severe adrenal insufficiency. If this is what he had, and not Addison's, then he was wrongly treated. Disastrously so. Kennedy was being treated with steroids for his medical problems, and the facts are that that particular regimen of steroids will incapacitate and eventually kill the victim if he has Pott's disease. Steroids destroy the liver and activate the dormant tuberculosis.

Steroid treatment also can raise the libido, driving up virility.

In other words, John Kennedy was being killed by the medical treatment he was receiving.

Along with William Greer at the autopsy—the driver of the fatal car —was the President's personal physician, Dr. George Burkley, of the United States Navy, who had been with him in Dallas. In fact, at Parkland Hospital, Kennedy was immediately given a shot of procortisone by his doctor, Admiral Burkley, before he died.

The suspicion arises concerning the deliberateness of what was going on: Was this a method of control, to create such enormous physical pain in the man every day and every hour that he could find almost no relief from it other than sexual release? Admiral Burkley, the President's personal physician, described in an oral history how he stopped Janet Travell from giving JFK procaine, a painkiller.[34] Why? He doesn't say, but implies she was wrong for giving it to the president. The steroid treatment continued. Was she an unwitting instrument of the plotters?

I am told by doctors that Pott's disease is relatively simple to diagnose, and was so in 1963. As Dr. James Nicholas told me, JFK had in fact contracted TB as a child, a common childhood medical hazard in those days—which had lain dormant.[35] What Nicholas didn't say was that the TB would be activated by steroid treatment, which he knew was being continued. In fact, Nicholas says he arranged for Dr. Travell to become Kennedy's personal doctor. We all have heard stories that military doctors may leave something to be desired in terms of their level of competence, but there are a lot of questions to be answered here if the above report is true. But Janet Travell, a civilian, was his doctor, too, in spite of Admiral Burkley's attempt to drive her out. She maintained an office in the White House until May 31, 1965, long after Kennedy was dead.

Burkley controlled the dispensary of drugs for Kennedy right up to the end, and went on to be President Johnson's doctor until he quit the Presidency.

I don't honestly feel that Dr. Humes has had a fair shake in all of this. His whole life was changed by the accident of having to do the President's autopsy. His report, although fudged and mistaken on some crucial counts—if he in fact wrote it—is essentially correct in his placement of the large head wound, and coincides with what the majority of the Dallas doctors and nurses say today. What he later had to say publicly before the House Committee's television cameras and before the Warren Commission in session conflicts somewhat with what he wrote, but it is my belief that Dr. Humes left us clues all along the way, or tried to, and people simply misread him, as they have so much else in this case.

In addition, the question of the adrenals could just as easily have been interpreted as an attempt to protect Kennedy's doctors, in particular his Navy doctors, who perhaps had misdiagnosed him and were mistreating him. Perhaps killing him.

Dr. Brierre, at Bethesda Naval Hospital at the time, believes that this was in fact the case, that Kennedy would have died in his second term, and that his doctor, Admiral Burkley, was "no doctor at all." There are a lot of others that said that Burkley drank too much to know what he was doing.

Crisis

In September 1947 John Kennedy was a freshman congressman from Massachusetts, and had taken a trip to Europe to do some fact-finding for the problems that Europe had in rebuilding and in labor relations after World War II. He became desperately ill in London and was taken to the London Clinic.[36] It was there that the first story that he had Addison's disease surfaced, told by Sir Daniel Davis, his doctor, who said that Kennedy did not have a year to live.[37]

Mary Davis told the Blairs: "He really wasn't a strong person. He'd had all those illnesses and London, cold and dreary, isn't the best place, so I wasn't surprised."[38] They dispatched a nurse, Ann McGillicuddy, a young lady who had been close to Jack during other serious illnesses when he was in the Navy in World War II, to take care of him, and she flew from Boston to London on the night of October 9, 1947. Shortly after she arrived the next day, they sailed on the Cunard Line's *Queen Mary,* and Ann got him safely back to the United States.[39]

The Boston papers said that Jack had been a "a patient in the ship's hospital."[40] An ambulance met the ship in New York and took him to the airport, where he was flown by chartered plane to Boston, and taken on a stretcher to the New England Baptist Hospital and cared for at the Lahey Clinic. He was described by a reporter as "thin and wan."

His friend, Frank Waldrop, said that "I guess the truth was that it was the onset of the Addison's. I know he was given extreme unction and brought off the ship on a stretcher and it was touch and go."[41]

Jack's color was very yellow at the time, and since he had contracted malaria in the war,[42] it was easy to cover up another ailment by saying that he had a recurrence of malaria, which may have in fact been the problem rather than Addison's. At the time there were often great differences of opinion between British and American doctors. His unusual skin color, which was not normal for him but which showed up again in the pictures of him swimming in California in 1963 with a horde of people around him—not just bronzed, but very strange-looking—certainly looked like he had malaria, "or a side effect from Atabrine used to treat malaria."[43]

The Boston *Herald* wrote on October 7, 1947, when he was still in the London Clinic, that "Congressman John F. Kennedy announced today that he was 'much better' after a month's bout with malaria and planned to sail for home this week. Kennedy, who has suffered malaria since 1943, said the attack began while he was visiting Ireland, forcing him to abandon plans for a tour of France and Italy." The possibility that he had in fact had an attack of malaria has been expressed as a "cover story," by the Blairs[44] and others. "The 'malaria' cover story would come back to haunt them, but at first it succeeded splendidly. In the coming years it was trotted out as necessary to explain other hospital confinements—for example, in Okinawa in November 1951, and in Washington in July 1953."[45]

In Boston, Jack was under the care of Dr. Elmer Bartels, who had previously been dealing with Kennedy's bad back. Bartels was a gland specialist "with a great deal of expertise in endocrinology."[46] The Blairs say that if Jack's London problem was the onset of Addison's disease, Bartels was the logical person to treat him.

"Dr. Bartels was willing to talk to us about it. He said that he thought that the truth should now be made known. He told us flatly and unequivocally that Jack had been diagnosed in England as having Addison's disease and had been sent to Boston to continue treatment. It was not a 'partial adrenal insufficiency,' but truly Addison's disease."[47]

At the time the standard treatment was the implantation in the patient's thighs of DOCA pellets. In 1949 cortisone came along and soon became the standard treatment for Addison's, allowing patients to lead nearly normal lives.

In 1954 Jack Kennedy was receiving the standard treatment for Addison's disease. "He had implanted DOCA pellets of 150 mg. which were replaced every three or four months. In addition he daily took 25 mgs of cortisone orally."[48]

Thorn[49] writes that the almost magical effect of cortisone treatment were "those of markedly increased sense of well-being approaching a state of euphoria accompanied by a real increase in energy, concentrating power, muscular strength, and endurance. There was a marked improvement in appetite and an increased feeling of warmth in the skin," and, as most male patients discovered, cortisone markedly increased sexual desire.

It is well to consider this last statement when judging John Kennedy's character by his alleged sexual exploits. His severe back problems did not permit him to have normal intercourse, according to some famous authorities. But if it is ever proven that Kennedy had a great need for tactile reassurance and release, he was as much a victim of his own medicines and constant brushes with death as with normal male desire.

The Back Operation

Dr. Bartels said, "Jack's unstable back continued to plague him during the late 1940s and into the 1950s. By 1954, seven years after Bartels began treating Jack for Addison's disease, the back pain was so intense Jack could barely walk, and then only with crutches. He was told by some medical authorities that a 'double-fusion' operation on his back might stabilize it and enable him to function without pain. But because Jack had Addison's disease,[50] the doctors at the Lahey Clinic firmly opposed the idea of the operation." Bartels recalled: "We didn't want him to be operated on. That's one of the problems of Addison's disease: the increased risk in an operation, even with hormones. The patient doesn't tolerate surgery well. We simply wouldn't do the operation in Boston. Ned Haggart recommended conservative treatment. Physiotherapy, exercise, et cetera. We didn't want him to have any stress other than what was positively necessary. We were not sold on the *need* for the operation.

"It was questioned whether it was absolutely certain that Jack had Addison's disease. I went down to the hospital in New York to see him before he was operated on. I stressed the increased risk of doing surgery on a patient with Addison's disease."[51] Jack had gone to doctors in New York to see if they could help him, and they evidently were not too sure that he had Addison's. They operated on him in October of 1954, and he was released on December 20th. He reentered the New York hospital on the 15th of February for another operation and was released on February 26, 1955.[52]

The operation was written up in the *Journal of the American Medical Association Archive of Surgery,* November 1955, without naming Jack Kennedy as the subject. The doctors were eager to report that it was possible to perform major surgery on a patient with Addison's disease.

The article flatly stated that the patient had Addison's disease for the previous seven years, but nobody linked the report to Kennedy until his first year in the White House.

The surgeons reported no Addisonian crisis during the two separate operations they performed. Jack had a lumbosacral fusing and a sacroiliac fusion. Four months later he had another operation to remove a plate that had been implanted. Still no crisis.[53]

There was no Addisonian crisis, but Kennedy almost died from a postoperative infection. Rose Kennedy wrote: "He nearly died: He received the last rites of the Church."[54] His father went to see Arthur Krock at the *New York Times* and broke down crying, saying that his son was dying. "He told me he thought Jack was dying and he wept sitting in the chair opposite me in the office."[55]

Interview with Dr. James A. Nicholas

Dr. James Nicholas operated on John Kennedy in 1954 and 1955, when Kennedy was no longer able to go on with his life due to the severity of his back pain. He had been advised that the chances of surviving the operation were very slender, but he took the chance. Indeed, he almost died more than once, as the interview below reveals.[56]

"Dr. Nicholas?"

"Yes."

"This has to do with the operation on President Kennedy about 1954."

"Right."

"We have a report that Kennedy actually had Pott's disease."

"Pott's disease?"

"Did you see that when you operated on him?"

"We were aware that he—as a young man—had acquired tuberculosis. But there is no evidence in his spine."

"But wouldn't the steroid treatments which he had been receiving before he came under your treatment—wouldn't that activate the tuberculosis?"

"He had adrenal insufficiency. He had Addison's disease. You know that, don't you?"

"Well, there was always a question of whether or not he had it—"

"He did have it. I managed it, together with Ephram Shorr. He had hypoadrenalism even to the day he died, when they gave him steroids at the time he was in Texas (when he was dying). That was the first thing they got into his vein."

"Did you write the article that was published which didn't mention Kennedy's name?" (The article about the success of a major operation on an Addisonian.)

"I wrote the article. Correct. We used a case report with his initials. I think you know that. Then John Nichols wrote a pathological report from Kansas. I think you know that."

"What I am trying to get at is that my understanding is that it has been stated that Kennedy was being treated in Boston."

"At the Lahey Clinic."

"Yes. He did not trust the diagnosis. They did not want him operated on. And he went to see you folks, and you found that it was safe—even though he was an Addisonian—to operate on him. But the statement that I saw was that there was a question by the doctors—and I assumed it was you, or your colleagues—questioned whether or not he in fact had Addison's. Therefore you decided to go ahead."

"We worked him up at special surgery before we operated on him and confirmed the fact that he had hypoadrenalism. Meaning, decreased adrenal function. When Addison described that disease fifty years ago, he was looking at people who were terminal. In those days they didn't have any way of describing it except when they came into autopsy, or at the end of their life. Dark skin. Collapse. He was not that bad. It was a matter of degree. So we call that hypoadrenalism. That was what the diagnosis was. *Hypo*adrenalism. Decreased adrenal function."

"But you did not feel that he had complete or straight Addison's disease. That is why you operated on him?"

"We operated on him because he insisted on getting relief from a terrible back problem which was curtailing his activity and his future. He was operated on with the full knowledge that he was a high risk. Indeed, we had a long consultation with a seventy-nine-page record, which I haven't released, on him. And he consented to the operation knowing that he might face a terrible problem—because in those days, managing Addison's disease or hypoadrenalism, was a very, very lethal experience. That article I wrote was a sample of that, and of course the drugs we used were not the drugs we use today. And, indeed, after the operation I slept with him for five nights and five days, because we had to manage crises which were not as devastating as you have in the paper where he almost lost his life. He never did that."

"Did he get a staph infection there?"

"He got a staph infection, yes. He always had boils. That was part of the Addison's problem. There was a risk of a staph infection.

"He had it after the operation?"

"He had it after the operation, and that created a problem for us because we used a plate, and that had to be taken out later."

"And you say he had boils?"

"He had boils in his skin, previous to the operation, periodically. But he was disabled at the time. He couldn't function. He was on crutches, and he would have to resign from his activities and not go to the Senate. And he got well enough to play golf, subsequently. And I did secure myself—I got Janet Travell for him. And she managed the tight muscles and the rehabilitation period and Burkley, the White House physician. And I saw him up to the time of his death, periodically. And that's it!"

"When you looked, if he'd had tuberculosis of the spine, would you have been able to see it?"

"Yes, when you take the tissue out. We did a sacra fusion on both sacra joints which looked abnormal. We did not find infection."

"There was no infection?"

"There was no tuberculosis. The basis of tuberculosis I think probably was suspected as a cause of his hypoadrenalism at the Lahey Clinic when he acquired this over in England before that."

"I'm wondering, was there any documentation—you started the conversation by mentioning that he had TB as a child. Is there proof?"

"Well, you know in those days everybody got exposed to TB. It was called 'childhood TB.' If you took a tuberculum test, and I have, and I'm positive. That was the term used in those days, and he was positive for that."

"Did you take tissue samples when you operated on him?"

"There was nothing there."

"Did you do that as a matter of course when you perform an operation?"

"Yeah. Right."

"In the autopsy photographs of his back, there is a circular hole about seven inches down on his back to the right of the spine. We are questioning whether or not it is a bullet hole or a scar of some kind."

"He had a large hole in his spine. It was healed. It was a scar. It was scar tissue. In the midline. And over both sides of the pelvis."

"I'm talking about a circular hole that looks like a bullet hole—"

"It's probably a bullet hole. It's not from a scar."

"It couldn't have been from the operation?"

"No. Not from the operation, no."

"You did take tissue samples, then? Is that documented anywhere?"

"Yes, it's in his hospital records."

"If there was anything there—"

"If there was anything there, he would have been treated for it. That was done to see why he had this condition. When he was operated on we took tissue out and sent it to the laboratory."

"So you would have done it as a matter of course?"

"As a matter of course. Nothing was bad except a bad disc, and inflammation of his joints, which was part of the pain problem."

"But you feel that it is pretty solid that he had tuberculosis as a youngster?"

"Well, this is what the Lahey Clinic had diagnosed. And I had a positive tuberculoma test. I don't know if the autopsy showed about his adrenal glands—whether he had tuberculosis of the adrenals. That was always possibly suspect. But nobody proved it, so I can't tell you that."

"When they autopsied him—do you have a report on his adrenal glands?"

"No, I don't know what happened at autopsy. One would like to know about his adrenal glands. After all, he had a deficiency of the adrenal glands."

"Do you have any reason to suspect that the TB had seated itself in the glands?"

"That's all hindsight. Retrospectively, one might argue, well, maybe that caused the hypoadrenalism. Why did he get hypoadrenalism? I don't have any answers to that."

"The reason why this has come up is that some of the Navy doctors said that he did not have Addison's disease, but that he had Pott's disease."

"He did not have Pott's disease. There was no evidence of it. If there was any evidence, there must have been some tissue to make the diagnosis."

"That was retrospectively."

"Well, when you get an infection in the spine—a staph infection—if you look at autopsy materials, I'm sure you will get signs of infection.

He did not have TB. There was no evidence of it whatsoever. I can state that categorically."

"If he had Pott's disease, and he had been receiving steroids—"

"Absolutely, it would have been wrong."

"It would have been the wrong treatment?"

"No, he had adrenal insufficiency. We had an excellent man named Dr. Ephram Shorr, one of the nation's outstanding endocrinologists, go over this. He died subsequently. That's in the record. He was also seen by Dr. Frank Glenn. There was no evidence of anything like that whatsoever. He did have Addison's disease. He had all the criteria. He had twenty-four urinary tests. He was thoroughly worked up. He had decreased adrenal function and indeed he went into shock several times. We had to give him steroids to pull him out of shock. And over the years, he had to take cortisone. For many years. You would never do that—if he had TB, the TB would have been worse."

"When he was in your hospital he was in shock several times?"

"Yeah, after the operation, which is why we slept with him for five days and five nights. Adrenal insufficiency is characterized by shock and death. And in that article[57] I wrote—I think there are several other cases—we had to give huge doses of steroids, to people who had arthritis, and so on, whom we had to give steroids to because their own bodies stop making steroids."

Improvement

Jack became a relatively healthy man after this operation, which was opposed and nearly stopped by his doctors in Boston. When he died he was in the pink of physical fitness except for the chronic problems he could ignore. He still needed a board to sleep on, a back brace to wear, and medication. But he was basically healthy, and his heroism in the face of such deadly illness throughout his life gave him a strength and life perspective healthy people lack. In my opinion, surviving such great and long-term physical adversity would also give the victim a political maturity and historical understanding far beyond the average person who had never suffered. These were attributes Kennedy came to possess in later life in great measure.

When Jack was in the Senate in the 1950s, there were stories all over Washington and Baltimore that he had some serious illness such as tuberculosis, according to James MacGregor Burns. In Baltimore the medical community was aware of these stories when Jack was president. But the real story is of a man who had sometimes been down to 125 pounds in weight, and who had found the strength and stamina to achieve the presidency.

Of course, the Kennedy family and campaign people had to do a certain amount of covering up, and as much as possible of his grave medical past was pushed off on his war injuries. A first-class cover-up allowed Kennedy to seek higher office. Addison's did not have a good ring to the average layman, and it had been at one time a fatal disease. Nobody wanted him to die in office.

Dr. Janet Travell became Jack's medical spokesperson as he began his drive to the White House. She had prescribed for him a regime of physical therapy and the use of what was to become his famous rocking chair. In her statements and those she authorized, she never denied the charge that he had Addison's disease.

But Jack clearly denied it when he told his friend Arthur Schlesinger in 1959. "He said that after the war, fevers associated with malaria had produced a malfunctioning of the adrenal glands, but that this had been brought under control. He pointed out that he had none of the symptoms of Addison's disease—yellowed skin, black spots in the mouth, unusual vulnerability to infection. 'No one who has the real Addison's disease should run for the presidency, but I do not have it.' "[58]

James MacGregor Burns wrote in 1959: "While Kennedy's adrenal insufficiency might well be diagnosed by some doctors as a mild case of Addison's disease, it was not diagnosed as the classic type of Addison's disease, which is due to tuberculosis. Other conditions, often not known, can cause inadequate functioning of the adrenal glands. As in Kennedy's case, this can be fully controlled by medication taken by mouth and requires a routine endocrinologic checkup as part of a regular physical examination once or twice a year."[59]

The main thing in this statement is that he is implying that there is a kind of Addison's disease, but not the one that is caused by tuberculosis, which in this case would be Pott's disease.

During the primaries in the presidential campaign of 1960, some tried hard to bring out the issue of Kennedy's health, and some of the established Democratic Party leaders, including former president Harry S Truman, John Connally, and Senator Lyndon Johnson—who had had a heart attack—came out against Kennedy's candidacy. An aide to Johnson, India Edwards, said at a press conference on July 4, 1960, that several doctors told her that Kennedy had Addison's disease. "Doctors have told me he would not be alive if it were not for cortisone." At the time, Jack obviously looked great, and the other candidates were rapidly becoming afraid of him. Mrs. Edwards, a Johnson aide, said that she objected to "his muscle-flexing in boasting about his youth."[60]

As Pierre Salinger reports in *With Kennedy,* the press generally felt that the attacks on Kennedy over his health were totally unfair.

The fact was that the once-sickly youth and young man was rapidly overwhelming his opposition, and coming out of nowhere to challenge the establishment within the Democratic Party. He and his beautiful wife represented youth, glamour, wealth, excitement, and vibrant health, and there are always those among us who will hate and kill out of jealousy.

"I have never had Addison's disease. In regard to my health, it was fully explained in a press statement in the middle of July, and my health is excellent. I have been through a long and difficult campaign and my health is very good today."[61]

Assessment

We are indebted to Dr. Lattimer, a urologist, who was the first outsider allowed to examine the autopsy X-rays and photographs of the late President, for demonstrating that the X-rays of the President's lower torso are also fake. He wrote in the May 1972 issue of *Resident and Staff Physician Magazine:* "The adrenal gland areas were well visualized on the X-rays of the mid-portion of the body and no abnormal calcification could be seen in those areas to suggest tuberculosis or haemorrhage of the adrenals. It is the author's firm belief that the President suffered from bilateral adrenal atrophy." There is no sign of Addison's disease.

Unless the X-rays Dr. John Lattimer speaks of showing the adrenals are fake, as it would appear the skull X-rays are, then Kennedy did not have Addison's disease. I can see no reason why they would cover that up after death with a forged X-ray.

Bilateral adrenal atrophy can arise from Pott's disease.

"The adrenals are invisible to X-rays, and do not show up on films unless especially treated with dye," my advisor tells me, a chief radiologist, Dr. Donald Siple of Baltimore. Obviously, the X-rays of the President in the National Archives were antemortem, but passed off as being from the autopsy.

Of course, Dr. Lattimer, previous to expressing his expert opinion on radiographic materials and showing for the first time that an X-ray can show the normally invisible, had demonstrated the exception to Newton's Law of Motion with his invention of the "jet effect." He made himself an expert in the use of the Mannlicher-Carcano rifle, noted the movement of melons on a post when shot, and accepted that President Kennedy's face was blown away—after viewing the X-rays of same, without questioning the fact that Kennedy's face remained in the photographs he allegedly saw.

Both Dr. Lattimer and Dr. John Nichols felt that the truth should come out—if he did have Addison's—because of the encouragement it offers other victims who might similarly overcome that particular severe handicap, and go on to high achievement.

Joan and Clay Blair wrote: "It must be said in any event that Jack's progress through life bearing this burden bespeaks, among other things, a truly awesome indomitability. He had unlimited alternatives to the pursuit of an active and demanding career. A life of drink and indolence would not have been an astonishing choice for a healthy young man of his inherited wealth and power. For one of Jack's frailty (and pain—Bobby's statement, it is clear, cannot have been much of an exaggeration and may have been an understatement), it would have been not merely forgivable but almost natural. His refusal to surrender is surely a choice of positive heroism."[62]

His brother Robert wrote this about John Kennedy: "I never heard him complain. I never heard him say anything that would indicate that he felt God had dealt with him unjustly. Those who knew him well would know he was suffering only because his face was a little whiter, the lines around his eyes were a little deeper, his words a little sharper. Those who did not know him well detected nothing."

"When I was young in Texas, I used to know a cross-eyed boy. His eyes were crossed, and so was his character. . . . That was God's retribution for people who were bad, and so you should be careful of cross-eyed people because God put his mark on them. . . . Sometimes I think that, when you remember the assassination of Trujillo and the assassination of Diem, what happened to Kennedy may have been divine retribution."

—President Lyndon Baines Johnson to Pierre Salinger

CHAPTER 3

A NEW LOOK AT THE CASE

We are just second-class citizens, you and I. We are not worthy of being told the truth or even part of it. Nations just lie to their public, and when a government is overthrown from within, the easiest way to handle it is to pretend it did not happen. That is what happened to us in 1963, when President John F. Kennedy was assassinated.

"I think the Warren Commission has, in fact, collapsed like a house of cards. And I believe the Warren Commission was set up at the time to feed pabulum to the American people for reasons not yet known, and that one of the biggest cover-ups in the history of our country occurred at that time," Senator Richard Schweiker of Pennsylvania told Anthony Summers in 1978.[1]

Pabulum. And this man was a member of the United States Senate.

Schweiker was replaced in the Senate by Arlen Specter. Specter perpetrated a great deal of the cover-up as a counsel for the Warren Commission when he and Representative Gerald Ford invented the Magic Bullet Theory and ignored the testimony that told the real story.

Specter is a Republican and was a lowly assistant counsel on the Warren Commission. How come it was left to him to do the crucial interviewing of most or all of the principal medical witnesses, and of the

Secret Service agents and other close witnesses to the murder in the motorcade?

The Warren Commission was composed of five Republicans, one of whom was the former Director of the Central Intelligence Agency whom Kennedy had fired, and two conservative southern Democrats— all of them the political enemies of John Kennedy. Chief Justice War- ren was a primary supporter of Richard Nixon, whom Kennedy had defeated three years before in the 1960 presidential campaign. On the face of it, doesn't this smell? Warren thought highly of the Teamsters as well. Their leader, Jimmy Hoffa, was imprisoned by Robert Kennedy, and has been accused of participating in John Kennedy's death. Hoffa disappeared in 1975 without a trace.

Were there no independents or liberal Democrats in this country who could have been placed on the Commission?

It was certainly inappropriate for there to have been a presidential commission investigating and preparing a report on the assassination of the previous president, when it was already suspected that President Johnson had something to do with the death of his predecessor. This was like the FBI or the CIA investigating itself. We needed an indepen- dent judicial body to look into the murder.

Specter was replaced as the chief architect of the "great cover-up" by his legal colleague and office mate in the Philadelphia district attor- ney's office—Richard Sprague—a man around whom scandal swirled, hired as the first chief counsel of the House Assassinations Committee in 1976, and fired only when it was made clear to him that he was bringing down not only the Committee, but some good congressmen, and maybe the House itself.

How come the congressman Thomas Downing, who hired Sprague— nominally a Democrat—was rated one hundred percent by a right-wing conservative southern think tank? Let this book speak out as a ringing document against injustice and what John Kennedy was against, be- cause the so-called investigations of his death were co-opted by the Republican party, which acquiesced in the murder, covered it up, and seized power.

The Author's Investigation

I have talked to most of the medical witnesses in the assassination. Their statements right now are the best evidence in the case—when they repeat what they were originally known to have said, and fits with what everyone else said independently.

I have collected so much data that I believe that certain findings are conclusive, and that some major problems of the case are solved. I am overwhelmed by the force and unanimity of what the witnesses have to say on certain points. When you—as I have—have listened again and again to the tapes of the operating nurses, doctors, and others at Dallas, insisting that the back of the head is missing, and then hear the same thing in 1991 from some of the autopsy doctors and morticians present, all to the exclusion of a wound in any other part of the head, to the exclusion of any semantic confusion as to where that large defect in the head and scalp was, then it is conclusive and overwhelming.

It is crystal-clear that there was no back of the head. There was more bone missing back there than scalp, and the photographs and X-rays showing the back of the head are false and cannot possibly be correct.

My investigation has established some indisputable facts: The autopsy evidence was faked. The photographs and X-rays are forgeries.

The official bodies ignored many facts that indicated or proved more shots, more gunmen, planted and forged evidence. The Warren Commission's Arlen Specter, when he interviewed witnesses, repeatedly ignored, twisted, or distorted statements when they tended to conflict with the conclusion he wanted. He tortured out of witnesses the answers he wanted, which would show no conspiracy. The "flurry" of shots, for instance, which the Secret Service men heard at the time of the fatal head shot, became one shot.[2]

Roy Kellerman even tells Arlen Specter: "First, Mr. Congressman, I wanted to look this car over for—let me go back a little bit. When this car was checked over that night for its return to Washington, I was informed the following day of the pieces of these missiles that were found in the front seat, and I believe aside from the skull, that was in the rear seat, I couldn't conceive even from elevation how this shot hit President Kennedy like it did. . . ."[3] This man was an experienced police officer. Do you get the idea that he is trying to tell us that there was something very peculiar about the shots, and that it could not have come from above?

"In the rear seat."

Speaking of the body shot that hit Kennedy, Dr. Humes, for instance, admits that the same bullet might very well have gone through both Kennedy's neck and Connally's torso, but *not* his wrist, ending up in his thigh.[4] This conclusion is totally backed up by simple laws of nature. There was more lead in Connally's wrist and thigh than was lost by the bullet that supposedly went through his chest. If some of the contortions of the Warren Commission are correct—that one bullet did in fact strike both men but could not have inflicted the rest of the wounds on Connally—then there had to be *two* gunmen firing from behind, as Senator Christopher Dodd has written,[5] in addition to shots from in front, from a third location.

Dodd's conclusions were from the acoustical evidence, which said that a fourth shot was fired from the Grassy Knoll, and there are clear indications of two more shooters. Two of the shots provable acoustically to have been from behind were too close together to have been fired from the alleged Oswald's alleged gun.

The real evidence that proves conspiracy and high-level government involvement in this case has always been overlooked. It was overlooked because it is secret. The real pieces of evidence are the autopsy photographs and X-rays—which are prima facie forged.

The Autopsy

The FBI men who were at the autopsy were careful to note exactly what everyone else noted: A bullet that hit Kennedy from behind did not penetrate the chest, and certainly did not come out the throat. "Further probing determined that the distance traveled by this missile was a short distance inasmuch as the end of the opening could be felt with the finger."[6]

The autopsy doctors—whose job it was to conduct an autopsy and nothing more, and not to solve the case—according to the same FBI report, along with the FBI men present, concluded that after external cardiac message, "it was entirely possible that through such movement the bullet had worked its way back out of the point of entry (in the back) and had fallen on the stretcher."[7] The doctors implied that the FBI was lying when it concluded that the same bullet did not pass through John Kennedy and strike John Connally, as the Warren Commission later reported. The FBI has never retreated from this. They may have their own special findings and evidence which they may ignore or lie about, but not this.

The FBI believes to this day that two separate bullets struck Kennedy and Connally. The fact that they so believe does not negate the official speculation of a lone gunman in their view because they do not accept the acoustical evidence of a gunman in front of the car, nor do they accept that a whole bullet missed both men and caused fragments of pavement to strike a spectator, James Tague, in the face.

As the years passed, officials tried to tie up some of the loose ends left by the Warren Commission in 1964, and more and more questions began to be asked. A newspaper account, for example, in 1966, said, "The *autopsy report* [author's emphasis] concluded that a single bullet hit both Kennedy and Connally, and Dr. Boswell said, 'There is absolutely no doubt in our minds, now.' "[8] This was not his area of scientific study, but the doctor is being used as the tool of the official line.

The trouble with the above is that the autopsy report did not make any such finding. That was what the Warren Commission and its "Magic" Bullet Theory was all about.

A second spot on Dr. J. Thornton Boswell's drawing was even more interesting. That showed where a bullet had entered the back of the head, presumably. The spot is down near the hairline, near the center of the head, and he said nothing about that. Could *both places*—precisely noted by his assistant, James Curtis Jenkins—on the same drawing with measurements as to their placement have been wrong?

No. In 1977 both doctors strongly persisted in noting that the rear head entry wound was more than four inches below where we find it in the alleged autopsy photographs.[9] The doctors resisted recanting what they had written in their autopsy report about the placement of the entrance wound on the back of the head until 1978[10] during public hearings before the House of Representatives, when Dr. Humes appeared to bow to the superior and relentless power clearly at work in the case and imply that they had been wrong about that too. But not really. There wasn't any entrance wound there in the first place. There couldn't have been because there wasn't any head there, unless he was hit twice from front and back in the head, and they reconstructed the skull.

What was forcing these changes?

The autopsy photographs and X-rays. And why? They showed wounds quite different from what was seen at Parkland Hospital in Dallas and at the autopsy in Maryland.

One of the keys to this case is the "spherical" bullet fragment on the outer table of the skull seen near the cowlick, in the occipital area, about a half inch from the most recently alleged rear entrance hole in the back of the head.[11] That fragment could not have been left there by any bullet entering the back of the head a half inch away. It could get there only after penetrating the skull from within, from a shot that came from the right front or side and was exiting there, and one part of the bullet did not make it all the way out. It had to have come from a shot in front.

That is, if there was bone there.

The autopsy photographs and X-rays are forged, and I will present considerable new evidence backing up those forgeries, as well as a complete picture of what actually happened with regard to the medical evidence.

In addition, I have made a most startling discovery.

It was always believed among the critics that there were major differences in what was known to be the medical facts at Parkland Hospital in Dallas and what was reported from the autopsy by the Warren Commission. The Warren Commission published drawings of the wounded body that wholly misled the public.

My investigation delved into what exactly was seen and reported at the autopsy. After some time I began to suspect that the wounds that were seen at both hospitals—the incision in the throat for the tracheotomy tube and the large hole in the back of the head—*were the same* in both hospitals. That is, they did not change. Nobody altered the body. Two wounds—the bullet holes in the back and the throat—each were seen in one but not the other hospital. The small wound of entry in the throat seen in Dallas was not seen at Bethesda, and the back wound was not seen at Parkland.

It took me years to locate and interview anyone who participated in the autopsy and would talk about what they had seen. Finally, I found nearly all. The body had not been altered in order to fool the camera, but was it tampered with and bullets removed?

The Smear Campaign

One way in which the murder of the Kennedy brothers has been covered up is to besmirch their memories with scandal, and revel in the missteps of their survivors in the family. It is said that they were not worthy of commitment, or their murders were not worthy of serious investigation, and so why bother?

There is a question of character with regard to reporters and sensationalists such as Thomas Reeves, who pin arguments on their own judgmental notions of what is right or wrong, and slander a man long dead as though his very memory and ghost haunts them with fear. They are afraid of the memory of John Kennedy. As Ben Bradlee, managing editor of the *Washington Post,* and so many others said who knew him, he was unique. The rules did not apply. His wife had lost two children and he had a country to run. His own personal life was filled with often excruciating pain and much tragedy. Whatever this man's personal life was, it should remain private.

Those perilous times at the beginning of the terrible sixties were days when the fate of this world hung by a hair. The whole world could have been blown up at any moment, and Kennedy was the man. He was the one who prevented it, and many people knew it.

Whatever Kennedy needed, he got. He did not abuse it, and in my judgment and the judgment of history, he was the better for it, and made this world a better place.

The original injustice here was done to the Kennedy family and his widow, who to this day remain strangely reluctant to discuss the case with anyone. It wasn't just Kenny O'Donnell and Dave Powers* and many other witnesses who were told to shut up, or that the autopsy found something different from what they thought, or that they only imagined that they saw a gunman on the Grassy Knoll, but it is quite evident to me that the Kennedys themselves were silenced by J. Edgar Hoover. Hoover's close friend was Lyndon Baines Johnson, who took over as President, who had himself sworn in on Kennedy's plane bearing the President's body back to Washington, insensitively forcing everyone else on the plane, and making the widow, covered with her husband's blood, stand there and observe the swearing in as a witness. This act alone, not to speak of some of those that soon followed, was enough to shock the dead President's loyalists into silence, afraid to say anything at all in the face of such brutal power.

It is possible but highly unlikely that the body was stolen during that staged swearing in or at some other time, but this isn't required to

---

* Kenneth O'Donnell and David Powers were assistants to the president, though Dave doubled as "court jester." They were as close to Kennedy as anyone outside the family ever was.

prove that the autopsy pictures were forged. It is not necessary to have the body stolen to cover up the facts of the murder. It is necessary only to be in a position to forge and plant the evidence, and frame a patsy. The logical time to steal the body was during the swearing in, when only General Godfrey McHugh was guarding the body, and not before.

The original injustice to that family was done by the United States in giving the President a dishonest autopsy and a totally dishonest investigation of that murder. And the injustice continued with the murder of the President's brother, Senator Robert F. Kennedy, and by allowing the terrorizing of the entire family by the systematic murder of witnesses.*

Whatever aberrations that have flowed from Senator Edward Kennedy or other members of his family are aberrations that flow from psychic murder, from that original terror. People get unhinged from such an onslaught, and only a few can get through it without taking too much to drink, or finding other ways to forget, making some mistake or serious misstep along the way.

In the course of my investigation, I found only a few people who would not talk to me. There was a pattern among them. They seemed to recite a litany, a line with regard to the assassination, then swallowed wholly the line of the Warren Commission. They were not believable. When you have two people using the same words, the same language, you feel as though they have been ordered to recite their piece. So they do it.

Yet other witnesses talk freely. But the Dallas witnesses were advised not to discuss the case. Sometimes they would say something so improbable to me that one might think they are unwittingly being used to plant considerable and powerful misinformation.

Many of the witnesses did not actually see everything that they speak of, but got it through surmise, imagination, or from someone else. There are now—as in other famous events in the past—professional witnesses.

Conspiracy Claimants

There are those who feel they live in obscurity, so they wish to be a part of the action—some action, any action—and come forth with any story

* See Chapter 7 on "Strange Deaths" in *High Treason.*

at all that will bring them some limelight, notoriety, travel, or money. It's perfectly understandable. The trouble is, they may be telling the truth, and it is often too easy to dismiss what these people say out of hand.

Or they may simply be mistaken.

In the past, some have come forward to claim involvement in the conspiracy: "Saul," in Hugh McDonald's *Appointment in Dallas,* Robert Easterling in Henry Hurt's *Reasonable Doubt,* Ricky and Geneva White claiming that Ricky's late father, Geneva's late husband, Roscoe White, was the shooter on the Grassy Knoll (see Chapter 23), and reports that Charles Harrelson, the convicted assassin of Judge John H. Wood in Texas, had claimed to have been involved, or was the man in one of the photos of tramps arrested that day, along with Howard Hunt of Watergate fame.

One can have a gut feeling that Harrelson was indeed involved, though he later denied it, and that the other stories are not credible. The Roscoe White story may be corroborated someday, and so might the other stories, but it hasn't been as of early 1992. Texans who have seen or know Harrelson say that he is the tall tramp in the photograph of the men arrested shortly after the assassination in the railroad yards behind the Plaza.

There have been others who have said that they know something about the murder, and were frightened. Some appeared to have foreknowledge, such as Rose Cherami, the girl thrown from a car by two of Ruby's thugs in Louisiana just before the assassination. She told the doctors who treated her that the President was about to die in Dallas, and when things happened the way she said they would, the story came out—and still no one believed her. She was soon thereafter killed in a hit-and-run accident.

There was Madeleine Duncan Brown, President Johnson's mistress, who said that he told her what was going to happen to Kennedy before it happened. She said that Lyndon Johnson told her that "those goddamned Kennedys won't embarrass me again after today. That's not a threat, that's a promise!" She claimed that after the public began to suspect that LBJ had something to do with the murder, Johnson slammed his fist into his hand and said, "It was ordered by oilmen and the CIA!"[12]

There was Richard Case Nagell, the man who shot off his gun in a bank to get himself arrested just before the assassination so that he would be in jail and have an alibi when the murder took place.[13] There was Abraham Bolden, the first black Secret Service man, who said that he knew something about what really happened. He was imprisoned after seemingly having been framed. He was no longer credible, and this was the fate of so many in this case who claimed to have real knowledge.

Theories

We have all heard the theory that the Russians killed Kennedy, or that Castro did it, or the Mob did it.

But what was in it for the Russians? They had just signed a major treaty with the United States as a result of Kennedy's efforts, and many more benefits would have come to them. It was not reasonable for the Soviets to have killed Kennedy—they stood to lose too much. In spite of the fact that Lee Harvey Oswald had lived in Russia, and the questions that have been raised about whether it was really he who came back, there is no strong evidence that either Oswald shot Kennedy or that the Soviet Union was behind it.

The same is true for Castro. The theory has been put forth by Jack Anderson and others that the assassins the CIA sent to kill Castro were captured and turned around and pointed at Kennedy, but there is no evidence for this whatsoever. At least none that would be admissible in court. This theory is based only on what one mobster supposedly said. Meanwhile, Jack Anderson claimed that the photo studies he had made indicated certain CIA operatives were, in fact, present in Dealey Plaza shortly after the fatal shots.[14] This would seem to preclude his own previous implications of Castro having killed Kennedy.

Another major theory that was voiced in the past by a lot of people is that the Mob killed Kennedy.[15] The trouble with that is the Mafia was not equipped to forge the autopsy evidence, plant sophisticated forged evidence that would implicate Oswald, or pull off a sophisticated military-style ambush alone. John L. Davis, the author of *Mafia Kingfish,* said as much at a conference of researchers at the State University of New York at Fredonia in June 1991, hosted by Professor Jerry Rose, when he gave a lecture that implicated the CIA in the murder, something he gave no hint of in his book. Of course, the CIA didn't do it either, although some believe this.

It is possible if not probable that the Mob was used in the assassination in a peripheral way, as Jack Ruby, a known thug, was used to eliminate Oswald. But they were at a very low level, as was John Wilkes Booth, in the murder of Lincoln.

Then there is Milton William Cooper, who claims that William Greer, the driver of the fatal limousine, turned around and shot President Kennedy in the head. He says he sees this in the Zapruder film,* which shows no such thing. Cooper gets thirty-five dollars per seat for his presentation on UFOs and the assassination.

Then there was Howard Donahue of Baltimore, who claimed that a Secret Service man stood up in the Queen Mary, the following car, and accidentally shot Kennedy.[16] Trouble with that is, he didn't shoot Kennedy *several times* accidentally. He didn't shoot him from in the front. He didn't fake a lot of evidence implicating Oswald months in advance.* And at least one frame of one of the many films, or some photograph, would have captured an image of the accidental shooting. But the thousands of photographic images taken show no gun which could have performed the deed in any of the men's hands before Kennedy was struck even the last time.

Another theory belongs to the Warren Commission, which says that one person alone (Lee Harvey Oswald) shot President Kennedy from behind with a cheap rifle, hitting both Connally and Kennedy with one of two shots. The other struck Kennedy in the head and killed him. This is impossible. There is too much evidence that proves a conspiracy, and what follows reviews that evidence and presents new evidence that leads to the only possible conclusion.

Parkland

The most trouble occurs in the case when we try to interpret what is known about the wounds or see the autopsy photographs. Things don't add up. (See Chapter 4.) All sorts of explanations arise, and here is an example: Jane Carolyn Wester, a nurse in the operating room upstairs at Parkland Hospital reported in her interview with the Warren Commission that she received a call from the emergency room "asking us to set up for a craniotomy."[17] Mary Ferrell, a principal researcher in the

---

* Abraham Zapruder was a Dallas dress manufacturer who took a home movie of the assassination and sold it for a large sum to *Life.* It is considered very important evidence that a shot was fired in front of the President.
* See Chapter 9 in *High Treason.*

case, and many others reading this began to get the idea that something such as an autopsy happened in Dallas.[18] Audrey Bell, as she told me,[19] was the supervising nurse that telephoned Jane Wester in the operating room suites upstairs and told her to get ready to operate on the President's head to repair the damage. But Kennedy died first. A craniotomy is standard language referring to brain operations, and not just the removal of the skull cap at autopsies.

Some information surfaced—very slender—that there was a short "autopsy" at Parkland Hospital before the body left. The body did not leave for an hour and a quarter after the President died, during which time the last rites were given, the tubes were removed, and the body was partly washed, wrapped in sheets and a mattress cover, and placed in the coffin. It took about twenty minutes just to wrap the body.[20]

Concerning body tampering, possible alteration, or clandestine extraction of bullets, John Long, a retired New York State Police officer, now a member of the country legislature, wrote me that, "the opportunity might have been provided when the Secret Service ordered the emergency room cleared after JFK had been pronounced dead. At that moment they would have had two primary objectives: 1) Using the available X-ray equipment to identify bullet fragments within the skull which may contradict later false ballistic information provided, they would want to remove the projectile material. 2) I believe that this and the head alteration surgical work could be done quick and dirty at this time. Since Aubrey Rike (the ambulance driver who helped put JFK in his coffin) had no personal information on what would have been the correct condition of the President's skull, he may not have been able to detect anything out of the ordinary when JFK was placed in the casket. To me the emergency room offered the best opportunity for what needed to be done from the conspirator's point of view."[21]

But Dr. Charles Crenshaw has insisted to me, along with Dr. Robert McClelland, Nursing Supervisor Audrey Bell, and some of the other witnesses present, that there was no opportunity for anyone to get at the body after the President was officially pronounced dead at one P.M. About one and a quarter hours passed before the body was taken away, and one or another of the well-known Parkland doctors and nurses was probably present at all times. Jacqueline Kennedy was either in the room or close by. Part of the time was taken up with a partial washing of the body, removal of the tubes, and wrapping the body in sheets, during which time Mrs. Kennedy was just outside the door. When they were finished, she came in and remained with the body until it left the hospital.

I have talked to and questioned nearly all of the witnesses about it, and there was no time when the body was left alone. It would seem highly unlikely that either someone posing as a pathologist, let alone the four or five who supposedly signed the preliminary autopsy report there, could have come in without it being known to us, or any stranger posing as a doctor. It also would be unlikely that one of the Secret Service detail or anyone else could have gotten away with either digging into the neck or the brain for bullets, without anyone seeing him and the story coming out.

That leaves one last possibility in Dallas, if the ambulance was not diverted on the way to Love Field for loading on the plane. I have established a chain of evidence from Parkland, with Aubrey Rike keeping the ambulance in his sight all the way to Love Field[22] as he drove after it, and the ambulance did not stop. Of course the more macabre among us might argue that someone opened the coffin on the short trip to the airport, and with the widow and others present, removed bullets. Admiral Burkley, a doctor, was there. But his odd behavior throughout the day would indicate a total inability to have the coolness needed to perform such an operation in the minutes available to him, even if he was carrying a James Bond thriller in his medical kit, as we are told.

The body could not have been stolen during the first fourteen minutes it was on the plane—before Johnson was sworn in—as explained elsewhere (the body was not unattended by Kennedy's close friends, widow, or entourage at any time), but it might possibly have been stolen *during* the swearing in, when only General Godfrey McHugh of Fort Worth was supposed to be guarding it. The body had either to have been concealed on the plane or taken off before the plane departed. Either scenario seems all but impossible.

That leaves some sort of unscheduled stop after the casket was put into the Navy ambulance at Andrews Air Force Base. I believe Francis X. O'Neill when he told me that he kept the ambulance in sight all the way to Bethesda and that there were no stops.[23] There were plenty of other people in the motorcade, and certainly no word has ever leaked out about any stop. I checked out another story of a stop at Andrews, but it was false.

The only people who can answer the questions posed here as to whether anyone got at the body during these times, or who might have had the opportunity, are Dave Powers and Jacqueline Kennedy.

If the body had been stolen with the knowledge of Mrs. Kennedy and some of the others, it might explain why she has remained silent all these years.

At about two P.M. at Parkland Hospital there was a tremendous commotion in the hall outside the emergency room. As the President's party attempted to leave with the coffin. Dr. Earl Rose, the Medical Examiner of Dallas County, tried to stop the body from leaving.[24] Researchers speculate that either before or while this was going on and the body was in the charge of only the funeral director and his men, some doctors or somebody disguised as a doctor came in and "examined" the body and removed a bullet or bullets. Ken Raley told me that there "definitely was a post," and that Justice of the Peace Theran Ward authorized the examination.[25] I think this is a simple confusion. Theran Ward did come in and take a look at the body, and the emergency room doctors have described to me what cursory examinations they conducted during the short time that was available.[26]

Raley was a reserve policeman and a medical technologist. He says that he had a copy of the report, signed by four or five "pathologists." He told me that he tried to obtain this paper again—which he at one time possessed and has now lost. Larry Howard, the director of the JFK Information Center in Dallas, said he saw it many years earlier, and now says he didn't see it.[27] Raley says that they tried to trace the bullet tracks and examined the brain. If this examination happened, it would have been done in half an hour. The so-called pre-autopsy or pre-exam may have been an elaborate cover for someone to get at the body and remove bullets.

Almost nobody else has ever heard this story, kept out of the rumor mill, which makes it impossible to investigate. But it is an alternate explanation of the very extensive testimony that one of the autopsy personnel offers that there had been a pre-exam and that the brain had been previously severed with a scalpel from its stem.

Dr. Charles Wilber told me that the very fact that all of the President's clothes were removed at Parkland Hospital indicated that an autopsy had begun on the spot. Normally, during an emergency, only essentials are cut away, and clothes are otherwise not removed. But Audrey Bell told me the same day[28] that it was their practice to remove all the clothes and partially clean up the body for removal to a morgue for autopsy, taking care not to interfere with any evidence that might be present.

* * *

I spoke to Theran Ward, who has been retired for ten years. He convinced me that there was no pre-autopsy autopsy at Parkland, and that he neither authorized such a thing nor knew of it.[29] To the contrary, Ward made it clear that his reading of the law was that the federal government had the right to intervene and take the body from Dallas to a military hospital, since the President was Commander in Chief of the military. Ward in fact authorized the removal of the body from the jurisdiction of Dallas County on that day in November 1963.

He expressed fear even today over the fact that some thirteen people died in Dallas not long after the assassination and that it was not wise for him to talk much about the case. "It's not safe," he told me.

Many folks establish franchises in murder cases on some bit of supposed or real evidence. They keep something secret, hoping to sell it. Often when they go public it blows up in their face, which is a major reason for being reticent.

In Dallas I have been offered all sorts of stories, many of them requiring hundreds or thousands of dollars up front to hear or for a look-see at a mysterious locked trunk containing little more than magazines and books about the assassination left by someone connected to the case. One such story was from the daughter of a man she claimed was called at the time of the shooting and asked to go to Parkland. The story we were told by a third party was that he was to remove bullets. At first I was told he was a doctor, and I was asked to pay before meeting the daughter. Then I was told he was dead and not a doctor, but trained enough to be able to remove bullets. A lot of these people are hoping to sell their life story. I never got to meet the girl.

Sometime later, Larry Howard explained that the man was not in fact a doctor, but had been trained in the military to prepare bodies for burial. "I never said he got in there and removed bullets," Larry told me. Larry has done his best to dig up and present new information, whatever it is, in this case, and tries however he can to keep the case alive. For his trouble, Howard has been called an impresario, or the P. T. Barnum of the assassination. He created a small museum presenting alternate theories of the murder, which in other respects is no different from that run by the city at the Texas School Book Depository. And there certainly hasn't been any money in it, as it depends on donations for the most part, to pay the rent and expenses.

A healthy democracy needs a loyal opposition, which Howard represents. His presentations at the JFK Information Center in Dallas have brought about major changes at the "official" museum down the street. I support the Center's efforts and have given a lot of money and free books for them to sell. Their other big backers were Bernard Fensterwald, Robert Cutler, and Oliver Stone.*

Little Lynn

Then there is the story that "Little Lynn" (Karen Bennett Carlin [married name], aka Karen Lynn Bennett, Teresa Norton) is alive and not dead, as Penn Jones, Jr., had reported.[30] Little Lynn was one of Jack Ruby's strippers, very young and pretty, and was a principal defense witness for Ruby.

Gary Shaw came to believe that she was alive, as does my investigator, Richard Waybright. Robert Sam Anson, a writer noted for using secondary sources and "cooking" his work, says that she was found shot to death in August 1964 under the name of Teresa Norton. His source was Sylvia Meagher. Carlin testified a second time to the Warren Commission on August 24, 1964, so if she died, it had to be after that date. Some reports (Penn Jones) say that she died in Houston in 1965, and others in Dallas. In any event, there is no verifiable death record. Waybright suggests that she is in a witness protection program, and Gary Shaw has been getting calls from Carlin's girlfriend, who says that she is alive and well. Waybright searched death records in Houston and Dallas and found nothing.

Norton had a baby boy on April 23, 1964, in Fort Worth.[31] This baby still does not have a name. We would like to find him. A record of the birth is still unattainable. Karen, of course, might be able to tell us a lot about what really happened in this case.

There are some other hot items that walked in off the street at the Dallas Center, both daughters of important figures in the case, but I am not at liberty to divulge this information at this time. I'd like to, but I

---

* Bernard Fensterwald was the lawyer for James McCord in the Watergate affair, and at one point also represented James Earl Ray, the convicted killer of Martin Luther King, Jr. Oliver Stone is the director of *JFK,* a film about the murder of President Kennedy and Jim Garrison's prosecution of Clay Shaw in the conspiracy.

have to develop it first. One of them may involve the greatest treasure trove of the century.

I don't find any credible evidence at this point that the body was tampered with at Parkland. Theran Ward held an inquest two weeks later, at which time testimony was taken from Dr. Perry and others, and a death certificate was signed.[32] In his death certificate the delineation of the shots that killed Kennedy was colored by the official autopsy report from Bethesda Naval Hospital. "The record of inquest details that the formal inquest on John Fitzgerald Kennedy was held on November 22, 1963, at 1 p.m. at Parkland Memorial Hospital in Dallas, TEX., and that the date of death was November 22, 1963, at Parkland Hospital. The 'Nature of Information given J.P.' was 'Death as a result of two gunshot wounds of head and neck.' The document states that the information was provided by Dr. Malcolm Perry, M.D., Parkland Memorial Hospital, Dallas, Tex. It also contains the official 'findings by the Justice:'

"I, Theran Ward, justice of the peace, Precinct No. 2, Dallas County, Tex., after viewing the dead body of John Fitzgerald Kennedy and hearing the evidence, find that he came to his death as a result of multiple gunshot wounds of the head and neck. With this, my hand, officially, this the 10th [sic] day of November A.D. 1963, Theran Ward, justice of the peace, precinct No. 2, Dallas County, Tex."

The House committee goes on to state that "other than the official record of inquest, which states specifically that Ward did, in fact, view the remains of President Kennedy, there is no record of a formal inquest or other procedure to gather evidence from the body within the territorial jurisdiction of death."[33]

Dr. Earl Rose told me that he had no assistants and he was the only person working at the morgue at Parkland, where they normally saw a lot of gunshot wounds. Rose denied the story that there was any sort of examination or an autopsy performed or started at Parkland. "I would have known about it. In fact, I was the only person who could legally do that."[34]

One of the major theories in the case is that the body had been stolen. The question is, was it really possible for the body to have been stolen from the possession of Mrs. Kennedy and the presidential party without their knowing about it, or saying a word?

It is slightly possible that the body was secreted out of Parkland

Hospital, for whatever reason, and brought to Bethesda. At this point, no one can prove that this was not done, nor can we prove that it was done. Professor Jerry Rose has given us a possible scenario for this,[35] and we know that the Secret Service asked to see other exits, including the tunnel exit from Parkland.[36]

Medical personnel at Parkland tell me that it would have been difficult to get a body out that way.[37] There is no direct evidence at all that the body was stolen. In my opinion, it was impossible to steal the body at Parkland without others seeing or knowing it.

Tampering and Alteration

There is no clear-cut evidence that the body had in fact been tampered with and that the wounds were enlarged, altered, or faked. The testimony I have collected indicates that for the most part, the wounds seen in both Parkland Hospital Bethesda were precisely the same. There are only shreds of indications of body tampering, and not at all what we would expect if such tampering had in fact occurred. I don't believe that there is any room for judgment in this, since I filmed the witnesses, and they described the appearance of the wounds, their size, and their placement quite clearly. Others who have seen the wounds feel the same way. The body was not altered.

The fact that the throat wound appears to be altered photographically (retouched) does not demonstrate that anyone had been digging there for a bullet. The retouching appears to create an "exit" wound. The wound was not enlarged.

I have shown that it was probably impossible for a theft from the coffin on the plane to have occurred.[38] Since it cannot be demonstrated one way or the other, we have to assume it never happened.

The idea that the body had been altered, forged, and wounds faked is a deduction or speculation based on false premises and assumptions, distorted facts, and uncorroborated statements.

The way I operate in this research is that I try to corroborate each piece of evidence with several other witnesses. I need to see how testimony matches the hard evidence.

The important point here is that all of those witnesses established in 1988 that there was a large hole in the back of the head in the exact spot where all of the witnesses had seen it in Dallas in 1963. With *no scalp* other than a few shreds over it. Therefore, the body *could not be* a "perfect medical forgery" before they received it, as is fantastically claimed.

The Casket

Kathlee Fitzgerald, my research assistant, and I met with the president of Gawler's, the Washington funeral home that buried Presidents Eisenhower, Wilson, Taft, Roosevelt, and Kennedy. This gentleman, Joseph Hagen, told me quite some stories about Vernon Oneal—the funeral director from Dallas—coming to see Hagen and trying to shake him down for the money for the casket he provided to transport the body to Washington, and which was not used to bury the President. Oneal, apparently, was not willing to make a donation of the casket and his services that tragic day, but wanted his money.

A *Washington Post* article[39] describes a meeting between Oneal and the former mayor of Dallas, Earle Cabell, when JFK was killed, by then the congressman from Dallas, in Washington, wherein it was agreed that the government would pay Oneal $3,495 for his casket and services. Oneal had wanted $500 more. Yet, the document allegedly from the "National Funeral Registry" provided by Larry Howard in Dallas stated that Oneal actually got a check for $13,495. If true, was this a payoff?

Joe Hagen investigated the National Funeral Registry story for me, and could find no such organization.[40] Larry Howard must have the name wrong.

Vernon Oneal got his casket, and was paid for it. According to an affidavit made by Pete Rupay of Denton, Texas, a few months before he died, "Mr. Vernon Oneal explained to me that he indeed received back from the government, after lengthy delays, the bronze casket that was used to transport President Kennedy's body from Parkland Hospital to Love Field following the assassination. He also told me that it was *undamaged* (Mr. Rupay underlined this himself) and that he later used it again, presumably to bury someone else."[41]

Well, there might be something wrong here, because we all had been told that that casket was damaged getting it in and out of *Air Force 1,* and it had to be replaced.

But, since the government paid for the casket, you would think it was stored in a government warehouse in Virginia, as some have said. Oneal must have gotten a different casket, if he got one at all.

I tried to trace the casket, and the General Services Administration told me that they do not have it. The Smithsonian and the JFK Library in Boston do not have it either.

Ardeen Vaughn told Larry Howard in Dallas that he was at a convention with Vernon Oneal and "during their conversation, the Kennedy assassination was brought up. Mr. Oneal said it took him over two years before he received any money for the casket. He also stated that he got the casket back and it was in pretty good shape. Oneal said he had offers from many people wanting to buy the casket from him. Mr. Vaughn said he was sure that Mr. Oneal did have the bronze casket. Mr. Vaughn now owns the Oneal hearse that took Kennedy's body to Love Field."

There are persistent rumors and witnesses in Dallas who say there was either an unscheduled stop at Oneal's on the way to Love Field with the body, or another vehicle went there with a bunch of Secret Service men or their look-alikes, who picked up two large green oxygen tanks and a body bag.

The tanks were put in the President's casket when his body was removed from it during LBJ's swearing in, according to this story, and his body was taken out of the plane in the body bag and flown to Washington from the Dallas Naval Air Station in Irving. They claimed that when the bronze casket came back to Dallas, it had green chips of paint in it from two oxygen tanks that were put into the casket to simulate the weight of the President, and no blood. The body was either operated on in flight to remove the bullets, or at Walter Reed.

The only people who would know if the body was secreted out of its casket at Parkland or if there was such a pre-exam at Parkland in Dallas would be Vernon Oneal, now deceased, and his men, one of whom is deceased. The other is Police Officer Aubrey Rike. After the President died and Jackie left the emergency room—having put her ring on the President's finger—only these men were present as far as we know. More than an hour passed from the time Kennedy died to the time his body was taken away.

Larry Howard flew twice to Minneapolis to interview a former federal agent about the alleged body switch. The source told Howard that as part of the investigation "he interviewed a number of people at Oneal's funeral home and was told that a stop was made by government officials at the funeral home prior to *Air Force 1* leaving Dallas. Items were discovered missing at Oneal's that consisted of oxygen bottles and a body bag. He stated he did not know what these were for, but they were taken. He stated that he knew more about the case, including things that went on at Parkland Hospital, but would not tell me at this time, but would do so at a later date."[42]

The Dallas casket was perceived in different ways by both those at Parkland and by those at Bethesda. There is more trouble with the time of arrival of the casket at Bethesda.

More troubling still is the perception of Jim Metzler, one of the men who helped carry in the casket and who saw the head wounds, who said that the casket came in while it was still light, but this simply cannot be so. The casket and body would have had to come from Dallas in a rocket to get there before dark at five-thirty or so. Since Metzler is certain that it was the Dallas casket, his perceptions contradict all possibility. He says he saw it opened and saw Kennedy inside.

It is possible that what Metzler saw was the reflection of the city lights off the low cloud cover that night. It had been raining off and on that evening.

It is probable that the men unloaded another body shortly before the President's body arrived. Jim Jenkins is insistent that the body of an Air Force major arrived in a viewing casket not long before. The men could have confused this casket with the other. Paul O'Connor never meant that the casket he saw was a "shipping casket" per se, which he was widely quoted as saying. (See Chapter 12.) It is unfortunate that several statements made by O'Connor are difficult to properly understand—for the same reason that he did not express himself clearly.

Jim Metzler is important because he is part of a vital chain of evidence from the arrival of the body outside at the loading dock to the opening of the coffin and unwrapping of the body inside. He has no memory of the specific type or color of vehicle the coffin came in, but he does recall the pick-up truck and the honor guard from all of the services who helped carry the casket in. He remembers an old admiral trying to help carry it in.[43] "The guys that were in the pick-up truck offloaded the coffin. They all had different uniforms on—from all of the services."

The coffin was put down in the morgue and immediately the body was taken out and unwrapped. Metzler got a look at the wound in the back of the head. "There was no body bag, I can tell you that."[44]

Speculation

In addition, there may have been the body of a Secret Service agent brought to Bethesda. There seems never to have been a retraction or investigation by the press or anyone else of the AP report the afternoon of November 22 that a Secret Service man had been killed. It either didn't happen, or the man did not matter enough for anyone to care. Or, obviously, somebody is covering up a lot more. We had also a report in Dallas of a large pool of blood in an alley near the Depository at the time of the assassination,[45] and rumor that a Secret Service man had been killed there.[46]

In his interviews with James Fox, Mark Crouch reports that even some members of the Secret Service believed an agent was lost. Crouch's forthcoming book, *An Absence of Responsibility,* further details his relationship with Fox and the enormous wealth of information Fox possessed, as well as his own set of autopsy photographs.

And in addition to that, some of the men have talked about a coffin being rushed into the emergency ward at another end of the hospital.[47] With this many coffins and bodies, there easily could have been a deliberate shell game either to avoid the press and the public, or as part of the plot itself. The men believe that decoys were used, but that is only their speculation and rumor.

Paul O'Connor told the House Committee investigators that the body arrived in a body bag.[48] I don't feel that he was ever consistent as to whether JFK was merely *wrapped* in it, or was actually in it. He has told me that Kennedy was wrapped in it. Since the zippered gurney mattress covers used at Parkland to line the coffin were similar, and the same color, I think this is another mistake by O'Connor, but I may be wrong. Such a mattress cover was used to line the coffin and Kennedy's body was put in it.

The whole body-alteration thesis depended upon the statement that there had been surgery to the head area, that the body arrived in a body bag and a shipping casket, that the large defect in the head and the throat wound were larger than they were in Dallas, and that there was no brain in the head.

If the body were stolen at Parkland—concealed behind a screen, then slipped out later—there would have been plenty of time to get to Washington on a military jet from one of the nearby bases. Trouble is, it would have been impossible to get away with this at Parkland and no one see it.

If the body was taken from *Air Force 1* while LBJ was being sworn in, there would have been less time to get it back to Washington, and it would have been extremely difficult to get the body off the plane without anyone seeing what was going on. It certainly was not concealed on the plane as "luggage."

Another smoke screen might be the implication that the body was taken to some other location such as Walter Reed for the removal of bullets. It is possible the body was never in the bronze casket when it left Dallas. If it was stolen, it is more likely that it went to Washington on another plane and was operated on during the flight. That's how we can get "surgery to the head area" in the FBI report of the autopsy, unless, as we have discussed, it was operated on right at Parkland, or even at Bethesda. After all, an hour passed before the official on-the-record examination of the body began.

None of this is credible.

The next day pieces of lead were taped to some bone fragments and X-rayed and passed off as President Kennedy's head. (See Chapter 10.) Since the bullets used were not all of the same type, they had to be switched. If somebody actually shot John Kennedy in the head from the sewer alongside the car, it was from where Sam Pate of KBOX in Dallas said it came. Pate saw what appeared to him to be gun smoke, and the shooter would have used a pistol because of the close range. The bullet would be different from Oswald's alleged rifle.

The Evidence

I find that some of the men from the autopsy are not credible insofar as their more fantastic statements are concerned. They make too many mistakes in the evidence for us to believe everything they say. But they are all agreed on what the wounds looked like and their size and placement, which coincides completely with what the Dallas doctors described to me most recently, and I believe made clear in their reports in the past.

And they agree with the autopsy report's description and placement of the wounds. I have reconciled the conflicts about the wounds.

The misinformation in this case had to do with the size of the hole seen in Dallas. Some researchers did not differentiate between the size of the missing scalp and the size of the missing bone. The two missing areas were considerably different. Some of the Dallas doctors did not closely examine the wound and so could not know that the underlying loss of bone was larger than the "egg-shaped" loss of scalp about three inches across in the back of the head. Some of the Dallas doctors, of course, *did* see the full extent of the head wound, and they reported it and drew that bony defect on our heads and on the head of a mannequin.

In 1979 each of the Dallas doctors (except Dr. Clark) laid their hands on my head and that of Ben Bradlee Jr.,* and otherwise outlined on our heads the large defect. It was as big as one's hand and about five inches long. They repeated this to myself and Al Fisher in 1991, and we filmed it. The autopsy report had the same size and essentially the same area.

Therefore, the head wound, like the throat wound, did not grow between Dallas and Bethesda. There was no body alteration. Tampering to remove bullets remains a possibility, but it would not have resulted in the type of massive changes to the body that others suppose, and it is not necessary to explain this conspiracy, which has a simple answer. Harold Weisberg has always tried to teach us to look for the simple answer, and here it is: All that was necessary to cover up this case was to forge the photographs and X-rays.

Even that may not be so simple, but it is a lot easier than stealing and altering or "forging" a body and then putting it back into a coffin for removal a few minutes later.

We know that the autopsy pictures have been tampered with because the evidence of retouching is intrinsic in the pictures themselves. In addition, they contradict each other, and the X-rays, and the medical witnesses, and the autopsy report.

Perhaps what may turn out to be vital evidence are the statements of James Curtis Jenkins that the brain showed signs that it had been previously removed from the head before it ever got to the autopsy. He described a clean scalpel cut through the brain stem. This had seemed to be backed up by the statement in the FBI report that there had been surgery to the head area, noted at the beginning of the autopsy. Wilber says it would have been impossible for a gunshot wound to the brain to

* Ben Bradlee, Jr., a reporter for the *Boston Globe,* worked under my direction for a time in this investigation, and interviewed the Parkland doctors and nurses, showing them the picture of the back of the head.

rip the brain stem apart. It certainly would not look as though it were cleanly severed. The bullet did not pass through the brain stem itself. The statement about surgery was repudiated by Jim Sibert, an FBI man who said he had made a mistake. The mistake was prompted by a discussion at the autopsy table as to whether or not there had been surgery at Dallas. That referred to the tracheostomy and did not refer to anything done to the skull or to the top of the skull. We have to take this on faith.

They would have had to cut twelve cranial nerves, and in addition the blood vessels, to remove the brain. If the brain in fact fell out into Dr. Humes's hands, as the witness says, it would seem that it could not have done so without having been previously removed from the skull.

It is my belief that when the large defect was made slightly bigger at the autopsy in order to remove the brain, the brain did tumble from the head into Dr. Humes's hands. A quick cut was made to free it, which Jenkins did not see. I am sure that the large hole was simply not large enough for the brain to have been previously in and out of the head, in spite of Audrey Bell's postulation that it might have been done by a very skillful person. Just barely, she said.

This is also implied from Jenkins himself, who describes the cuts made by the doctors to enlarge the hole to get it out of there.

In the end, we do not have to have the body tampered with at all prior to the autopsy at Bethesda. If bullets had been found, they could have disappeared just as quickly and the doctors forced to lie about it. All that was necessary was to fake the photographs and X-rays and show those at a later date. Some doctors and nurses at Parkland and some of the autopsy personnel at Bethesda have tried to tell us the truth on some matters, but they are ignored or ridiculed.

Dr. Burkley placed the back wound at the level of the third thoracic vertebra, which is, according to Dr. Charles Wilber, in fact five inches down on the back, and therefore the autopsy photograph has to be a fake. In fact, there are clearly *two* bullet holes in the back in that picture.

I believe that the autopsy report and the autopsy crew did the best they could under terrible circumstances, and that report and those of the Dallas witnesses constitute the best evidence in the case, not the photographs, films, and X-rays. As previously stated by the House Committee on Assassinations, none of the later material from that night that was in the possession of the Secret Service has been authenticated, and would not be admissible in court. Therefore, it should not

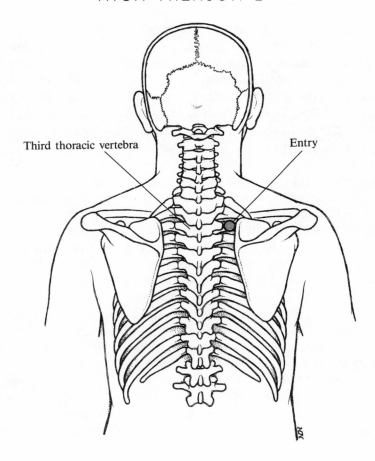

Third thoracic vertebra   Entry

have been relied upon for any of the conclusions that were finally made by the Committee.

They could not go that far because it would publicly cast doubt on this phony material—and open up a snake pit: that the assassination of President Kennedy in fact was not solved in 1963–64, and that there was a conspiracy reaching into the highest levels of government. They could not say or imply this. Nobody had the courage.

For the most part, the autopsy report backs up the crucial medical testimony from Dallas on the head wounds, but some of it, it seems to me, is clearly fudged, if not fabricated. That does not mean the doctors are responsible for that. It is quite clear that the autopsy photographs and X-rays were faked in order to cover up the murder.

The Researchers and the Show-Biz Element

There has been a vast misinformation campaign among the critics in this case. It has become a game, a growth industry, and sometimes a ripoff. If the government had done its job, we could all go home. But they let it happen. If the government had planned this, they couldn't have done it better.

It appears to me that some of the leaders of the "critical community" —meaning those who criticised the Warren Report—are there to mislead us. They give us a lot of criticism, a bit of the truth, and then lead us down the wrong road.

And let us not forget all the books that come out with fantastical stories trying to explain the murder of John Kennedy. We have had everything but UFO's, though maybe I missed that one.

I have encountered people with some of the worst character I have ever known among this bunch of duplicitous opportunists, as I wade through the morass of intrigue.

Long-term involvement in this case teaches many things about life. To quote my chief investigator, Officer Richard Waybright of the Baltimore City Police, "I certainly learned a lot about people and relationships."

My cop friends say to me when I ask them "what do you think about the case?" "The pictures aren't right. I know that." They've always said it to me, and I believe they truly believe it. Besides, it's obvious.

Maybe I am being watched. So what? We have to learn to live with a lot of things. I don't blame the watchers. I'd want to watch a guy like me too. After all, besides God, what gives me the right to do what I'm doing? All writers are policed in this country, even Ernest Hemingway.*

Sound familiar? Do you find this in your line of work? I trusted and believed in the critics in hope of finding out the truth in the murder of John Kennedy. I feel that I have made several major breakthroughs and know something of what really happened, but I did it on my own. Along the way I was initiated into the deeper mysteries of life, so to speak. I am not interested in being a part of the scavenger crowd. This is my

* *The New Yorker,* October 5, 1987. Herbert Mitgang, "Policing America's Writers."

historical statement and one last spurt of research on my part, and that's it for me. I have to go back to *life,* much as I care about the cause.

Some try to keep this case alive however they can in an "operation of forced disclosure" for altruistic reasons, and some who have made a career out of this case do it for the money.

Yet rising above this swamp is a certain amount of real truth, of facts that are unassailable. My job has been to chart a course through for us, and lately I have come into new and unknown waters in this investigation, where I feel close to discovering the real and simple truth, hidden beneath so much complexity. It lies at the bottom of a mountain of manure.

The Medical Evidence

I always felt that the medical evidence held the key to the mystery. I was right. In fact, I think it's a good thing they got the body out of Dallas, because I doubt that that autopsy would have been straight, or at least the findings of it. Some of the murder plot was hatched and operated in Dallas. The Bethesda autopsy report tells a great deal, but the Washington allies of the Texas plotters covered it up and frightened the doctors into statements they otherwise might not have made.

So much of what the witnesses had to say was astonishing. Certainly a lot more than what others reported. Some of the researchers were vastly wrong on their principal theories.

The key piece in the puzzle was that the head wound seen in Bethesda was exactly the same as the one seen in Dallas. Witnesses from both hospitals, independently and together on camera, drew lines on their own heads or that of models which depicted the wounds, and the large defect in the head was *exactly* the same.[49]

As for the tracheotomy incision, the wound shown in the photographs of the body is the *same* as the wound left after the incision was made in Dallas. It was not enlarged.[50]

A certain element of judgment might enter into these equations, but I feel that my findings are conclusive, *exact,* and unassailable. We filmed the witnesses, and I have done an exhaustive survey of their recollections, which are, of course, so fresh even today. Other researchers relied on selectively inaccurate reports from Dallas, saying that "in sworn testimony from the doctors in Dallas, the wound of exit in the back of the head was only 23/4 of an inch." In fact, they described a huge defect of scalp and bone in the back of the head, in the same place and of the same size as that seen at Bethesda. The 2³/₄ inches referred to the area of *scalp* that could not be replaced over a much larger hole in the skull, for which they did not have the bone.

Others implied or said that the incision in the throat that shows in the autopsy photographs is a false exit wound made by the conspirators. They insisted that it was enlarged to remove a bullet. I found that it is merely a normal trach incision (in those special circumstances), made to fit the large flange that had to be slipped inside the skin and the muscles of the neck to prevent it from closing over the breathing tube. They never knew about that flange and how it was shaped because they either didn't ask or want to listen to what they were being told. In addition, the wound looks distended and enlarged in the photographs because the head is hanging back as far as it can go on the brace over the edge of the table, pulling the wound wide open.

I am certain that if others had kept an open mind and been better scholars, they would have found the same things I did. But I know from interviewing the witnesses that often what they said was not reported—which conflicted with the theories of major competitors for public attention in this case. For instance, Dr. Ronald Jones, Chairman of the Surgery Department at Baylor, whom we filmed, said that the throat incision in the pictures was exactly like the one he and Dr. Malcolm Perry made.

In later chapters we will present the proofs of the forgeries of the autopsy photographs and X-rays. It was through these means that Chief Justice Warren and the Commission were tricked. On October 10, 1968, Arlen Specter was quoted in *U.S. News & World Report* as saying "the complete set of pictures taken at the autopsy was not made available to me or to the Commission." Why not? Who controlled that? Who showed Warren the pictures? Specter said, "I was shown one picture of the back of a body which was represented to be the back of the President, although it was not authenticated. It showed a hole in the position identified in the autopsy report. To the best of my knowledge, the Commission did not see any photographs or X-rays. . . . The photographs and X-rays would, in the thinking of the Commission, not have been crucial, because they would have served only to corroborate what the autopsy surgeons had testified to under oath as opposed to adding any new facts for the Commission." Of course, the pictures and X-rays *contradict* the autopsy report on all the key points.

There are *two* apparent bullet holes in that picture of the back. Specter could not have been very awake to ignore the fact that there may be two holes in the picture. The one that is now being claimed as an entry wound may not be a hole at all, but a blood spot, and it appears to be only about three inches from the edge of the shoulder.

Some witnesses have insisted that a deep indentation showing in the photograph of the back which looks like a bullet penetration about six inches down on the back to the right of the spinal column is the wound. Some outsiders will say it could be a surgical scar. Unfortunately, Kennedy's private medical records have never been released, and I am unable to resolve this last conflict. Doctors tell me they know of no operation that would heal like that, leaving a deep hole, and Dr. James A. Nicholas, who performed Kennedy's back operation in 1954, tells me that the hole cannot be a surgical scar. He said that his incisions healed over cleanly.[51]

The pictures were flashed at some of the men of the Warren Commission, including the Chief Justice,[52] on an unofficial basis. This proved to them that there was photographic evidence for history's sake, and that was all they needed to know. They did not investigate it. They assumed like everyone else that pictures don't lie and it wasn't necessary to know too much of what was in them. Besides, the photographs were very gory, and why subject oneself to such disgusting experiences? They didn't really look at or study them.

We assume—in the kindest scenario—it did not occur to the Commission that the photos might be fake. It did not occur that there was a long tradition in some more primitive jurisdictions in our country of police faking of evidence, of phony medical examinations and coroners' reports to cover up official brutality and criminality. It did not occur that anything coming from the National Medical Center of the United States Navy could be fake. Some doctors don't get to be a medical examiner unless they are willing to cover up official crime and police murders. There are some jurisdictions in the United States where police death squads and excessive police brutality resulting in death are never or were not beyond the realm of possibility. In such a jurisdiction, secret societies and organizations of right wing extremists stack the deck in their favor. To repeat what a prominent medical examiner told me in my last book, "If the government wanted to commit a murder, Maryland is the place to do it."

Not only was the autopsy report faked in certain respects, but so were the photographs and X-rays.

Mark Crouch had proposed what I feel is an original concept in this case—the "buffet of evidence." Evidence was established throughout every aspect of the case, and some of it was not representative of the necessary facts. The plotters simply picked and chose what would be used as the situation developed.

Nevertheless, I believe that someone from the conspiracy was in the autopsy room and saw to it that certain things were done.

For instance, before the autopsy began, X-rays were taken of the skull which showed the back of the head missing. Much later, after the autopsy was over (if the X-rays are in fact of Kennedy), the frontal bone on the right side, including the right eye socket, may have been removed for some reason. Dr. Boswell and the other witnesses have insisted to me that the right front forehead, or frontal bone, was never touched or removed either in a search to extract the fragment behind the right eye in the bone,[53] or for any other reason, and that it was intact. The morticians also insisted to me that it was intact.

After the autopsy was over at eleven-thirty or so, alleged bones from the back of the head arrived from Dallas and a reconstruction of the back of the head began to be done.[54] Commander John H. Ebersole came in and made new X-rays, after midnight, as he has described.[55] We now have an X-ray that shows the back of the head intact, and the right front of the face missing, as though it had been blown out by a shot from behind—the exact opposite of what the head had looked like when it came in. What I just described is what we see in the X-rays (A-P and lateral views) that survived after the Secret Service burned most of the evidence a few days later. (As per many interviews with Mark Crouch, from his longtime friendship with James K. Fox.)

The frontal bone is then carefully fitted back into place, and the head filled with plaster by Paul O'Connor. The morticians are brought in to do their work. "The frontal bone was absolutely intact," Tom Robinson, the mortician, told me. In fact, all of them told me the same thing.[56]

The autopsy report as well as the photographs and X-rays which normally would be called the best evidence, were not really studied by the Commission. Here was the most important part of the whole investigation, and it went right by the Commission.

In addition, Arlen Specter personally managed to discredit any medical testimony that contradicted the findings he wanted.

I do not believe that any frontal bone was removed to make these false X-rays. They are composites.

* * *

Of course, a tough lawyer can say, anyone can get a witness to change his recollections or poke holes in his story. I will try to present the testimony and the way it came about so that the reader can judge for himself. In addition, I will try to present enough corroboration to make it stick. I am trying to avoid theory as much as possible, just present the facts and whatever conclusions seem to logically flow from those facts. A lot depends on the credibility of the facts as we have found them. A lot depends on the credibility of the witnesses, and on my credibility.

Above all else, because of these phony pictures, the Warren Commission ignored other evidence pointing to more than three shots, and more than one gunman, as well as evidence which indicated that Oswald was set up to be the patsy, and evidence of a wider conspiracy.

And the proof of it is that slug on the outer table of the skull on the back of the head. *It had to have come from in front* to get to where it is in the X-ray. The fragment almost penetrated the skull, but not quite enough to get away. It certainly didn't come from behind, unless this was some sort of MIRV bullet, with one of the warheads being a dud.

Unless, of course, it was taped there, as Custer's statements indicate. How come nobody noticed that before?

"The key thing for the country is a new foreign policy that will break out of the confines of the cold war. Then we can build a decent relationship with developing nations and begin to respond to their needs. We can stop the vicious circle of the arms race and promote diversity and peaceful change within the Soviet bloc. We can get this country moving again on its domestic problems."

—Senator John F. Kennedy to Harris Wofford

CHAPTER 4

PARKLAND MEMORIAL HOSPITAL

The terrible events of November 22, 1963, descended upon Parkland Hospital with a sudden fury. Emotions all but overwhelmed the competent professionals who were ready to deal with any medical emergency but never expected to have the President of the United States and the Governor of their state brought there mortally wounded. Within a half hour all that changed.

And they never expected to be so misunderstood, maligned, ignored, abused, frightened, and harassed afterward.

This is the way Doris Nelson, a chief nurse, described it in her report. She had just had her lunch, and at "12:33 P.M. I answered the phone which was ringing in the Major-Surgery Nurses' station. Mrs. Bartlett, the telephone operator, informed me that the President had been shot, and was being brought to the hospital. I told her to 'stop kidding me.' She said, 'I am not. I have the police dispatcher on the line.' I thanked her, and immediately hung up the phone.

"I asked Dr. Dulaney, the Surgery Resident, to come into Trauma Room No. 1. I wished to talk with him alone because I did not wish to alert everyone, which might have caused general pandemonium in the Emergency Room. I informed Mrs. Standridge, and she told me that Room No. 1 was set up, so I proceeded into Room No. 2 and opened one bottle of Ringer's Lactate when I heard someone call for carriages.

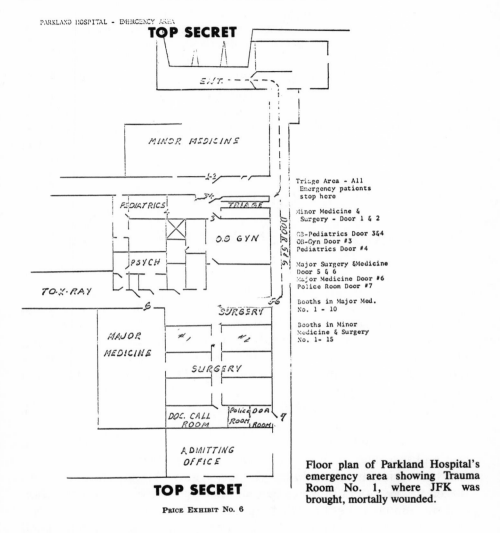

Floor plan of Parkland Hospital's emergency area showing Trauma Room No. 1, where JFK was brought, mortally wounded.

PRICE EXHIBIT No. 6

"Seconds later Governor Connally was brought into Room No. 2. I opened his shirt, and saw that he had received a gunshot wound of the chest. Mrs. Standridge was in the room assisting the doctor, so as I walked out of the room to check on the President, he was wheeled into Trauma Room No. 1. I checked in the room to determine what type of injury he had sustained, and was asked by the Secret Service to screen all personnel at the doorway leading to the trauma rooms. In the meantime, I answered the phone in the Surgery Nurses' station, and Dr. Baxter was on the line. He asked what we wanted. I told him that the

President had been shot, and he said, 'Yes—what else is new?' I said: 'Get down here,' and he said: 'I'm on my way.'

"I stood at the doorway with a city policeman and Secret Service agent, and screened each doctor that went in the area. I offered to get Mrs. Kennedy, who was sitting outside Trauma Room No. 1, a towel, and asked her if she would like to remove her gloves which were saturated with blood. She said: 'No, thank you, I'm all right.' On one occasion she got up and went into the room the President was in. I went in and asked her if she had rather wait outside, and she said 'no.' One of the Secret Service men said to let her stay in the room. She came out shortly thereafter.

"Several White House aides and secretaries came in, and embraced Mrs. Kennedy, and I believe Mrs. Lyndon Johnson was among them. Dr. Kemp Clark arrived. The cardio-verter was carried into the room, and Dr. Jenkins from Anesthesia came with an anesthesia cart. Shortly after Dr. Clark arrived, two priests arrived and gave the President last rites. Dr. Clark came out of the room and talked briefly with Mrs. Kennedy. Then the priest came out, and I talked with the First Lady also. I was informed by Dr. Clark of the President's expiration. . . .

"The President's doctor informed me that arrangements had been made to obtain a casket for the body. Shortly afterwards, Mr. Oneal of the Oneal Ambulance Company arrived with a bronze casket. Miss Hinchliffe came out, and asked for some plastic to put inside the casket. I sent Mrs. Hutton to the second floor to obtain a plastic mattress cover. . . . I asked David Sanders to assist the nurses in preparing the President's body before placing it in the casket. I instructed the nurses and attendants to clean up the room and mop the floor.

"After Mr. Oneal and some of the boys who work with him . . . placed the President in the casket and closed it, Mrs. Kennedy went in, and sat in a chair beside it, leaning her head on the casket."[1]

I asked Doris Nelson if she had seen a bullet entry wound in the back of the head or in the back. "No, not at all," she said.

"Nothing in the President's back?"

"No."

"Did you see this entry wound in the cowlick, here?"

"All I saw was missing skull and brains on the back of his head right there."

"Could you see the edges of the wound in the skull?"

"Yes. There wasn't any bone there where that entry hole shows in the picture."

I showed her the picture in *Six Seconds in Dallas,* which shows a large hole through the skull in the right back of the head. "No. It looked like that, but it's too low. It was where the cowlick is in this picture. There was nothing there." She said the same thing about that drawing which Dr. McClelland had told me. "The hole in the drawing was too low. It was right *there,* in the right rear. In the *right rear!"*

This demonstrates how an ordinary citizen stands up to powerful people, and has the courage to dispute without hesitation the official photographs of the body of the late President. When I showed Mrs. Nelson—who had ripped the President's shirt open and who had a "fairly" good look at his head injury—copies of the photographs of the back of the President's head, she told me, *"It's not true!* The back of his head was blown away and his brains had fallen out on the stretcher."

She said it was on the right-hand side. She saw it when they put Kennedy in his coffin, before it was wrapped. "Does the picture show the wounds that you saw?"

"No. Not at all."

"Why not?"

"There wasn't any hair. It was blown away. There wasn't even hair back there."

"Where was it missing? How far back?"

"The whole scalp in the right rear was blown out."

"Wasn't there a loose flap of scalp there?"

"No. Most of it was exposed brain. There wasn't any hair."

I now think there was something of a badly damaged and holed flap there, as was described by Audrey Bell and Jim Metzler, but that it was pushed aside at times and not noticed.

"You sure that it wasn't on the side?"

"Yes. It was in the back."

"Farther back than that flap?"

"Of course!"

I showed her Dr. John Lattimer's drawing, which he made in part from the X-rays he had seen, but moved the large blow-out up on the head a bit, still leaving it in the front of the head. "Was it like that?"

"There was no bullet that came out of the front of his head. There was no wound in the front of his head at all. He was shot from the side and it blew the back of his head off." She repeated it word for word, but with more emphasis.

"This drawing—actually it's a tracing like the other picture of the back of the head—does this show the trachea wound that you saw? Was it this big, or was it smaller? I am told that Dr. Perry would not have made such a large gash. That must be almost three inches across."

"That's distended. It was about that big because they had to get the cuff in. Maybe after he died it got a bit larger. That happens, and I think Perry has said that."

"It was that big?"

"Well, it wasn't much smaller, because there was a bullet hole there and they had to see what they were doing, what kind of damage was done in there, as he was going in."

"So the picture doesn't look like what you saw?"

"It's about right."

"His head is hanging back off the table in the picture that that tracing of the neck was made from."

"That would pull the neck incision open more."[2]

Margaret Hinchliffe wrote: "It wasn't but a few minutes later that the doctors pronounced the President dead. For a few moments everyone just stood, not really believing the President was really dead. Then Mrs. Kennedy and the priest entered the room, at which time the last rites were said.

"After Mrs. Kennedy and the priests left the room, Miss Bowron and myself, with the assistance of David Sanders, the orderly, prepared the body. All of his clothing and belongings were put into a paper bag and given to the Secret Service men. We remained with the body until he was placed in the casket. Then Mrs. Kennedy entered the room and everyone left the room and waited outside until the President's body was taken from the hospital."[3]

Nurse Diana Bowron wrote: "Miss Hinchliffe and myself prepared the body by removing the remaining clothes . . . we then washed the blood from the President's face and body and covered him with a sheet. During this time, we were assisted by David Sanders, the orderly. . . ."[4]

In early 1991 I once again journeyed to Dallas, this time to film some of the witnesses along with some of the Bethesda autopsy personnel for the first time. I had a pretty good idea that certain false information was being planted in the case. Evidence was being distorted or fabricated in recent years, and this was what I was investigating. (See Chapter 14.)

I was able to solve some of the big questions that had been created for us by determining that both the head wound and the throat wound seen in both hospitals after the tracheostomy were the same, but that entirely new false information seemed to be coming forward. Once again I was in quicksand, wading through a swamp of muck and manure that often seemed to have no bottom.

Some of the Dallas doctors were going out of town for the weekend we had the filming of the Bethesda witnesses scheduled, but saw us during the week, and we filmed them or I interviewed them over the phone. One of my main concerns was the throat wound.

We went to see Dr. Ronald Coy Jones, the chairman of the Department of Surgery at Baylor University, in his office. He was very gracious while we set up our camera. Dr. Jones, who was senior resident in 1963, told me: "That's accurate [the picture]. The cuff was a good two inches wide."[5] He got a good look at it because he was standing alongside the body and made one of the incisions for the chest drainage tubes. Dr. Paul Peters made the other, with Dr. Charles Baxter assisting him. All three doctors insist today that Dr. Humes was wrong and that the incisions entered the chest after the pump was started. "I saw it sucking air," Dr. Baxter told me.[6] Their observations after the pump started was that they could not tell if the chest had been violated by a bullet. "There was a high risk that it had been."[7]

At 12:30 that fatal day in 1963, Dr. Jones was eating lunch with Dr. Malcolm Perry, who a few moments later made the trach incision. Dr. James Carrico was already in the ER, and inserted a trach tube down the throat. Jones heard them paging Dr. George Shires and Dr. Kemp Clark. Dr. Marion Jenkins, the anesthesiologist, and Audrey Bell, the chief nursing supervisor, were at the table with Jones. "You all aren't going to believe this, but the President has been shot." They went into action, running to the ER. He said that Drs. Clark, Giesecke, and Jenkins had the best look at the head wound.

"There was no damage to the face," Jones told me. He said that it had relaxed somewhat, from the lack of scalp in the back not pulling it taut. He thought that the X-rays showing all of the frontal bone from the right eye and forehead missing very peculiar. He couldn't tell "how it got out," speaking of the frontal bone. He said that the picture of the intact face was accurate. He saw no fracture or wounds on the right side, where we see a flap sticking out in front of the ear.

He got a good look at the bullet wound in the throat before it was obliterated with the trach incision. "It was not very large. It had smooth edges. Between one quarter and three eighths of an inch across. It looked like an entrance wound. My initial statement was that I saw it as an entrance wound. I made the assumption. That was what my interpretation was. I thought someone had come up and shot him in the neck with a handgun at close range."

Jones had seen at least one hundred gunshot wounds in the preceding five years, and knew what he was talking about, like all the other doctors and nurses down there in what was then the as yet wild, rough, and violent West.[8] Dallas responded to the national criticism and hate. It changed and became a more tolerant, sophisticated, and cultured city after the murder.

See Chapter 2 of *High Treason* for an extensive presentation of some of the many interviews I either conducted or had conducted more than a decade ago, which established for the first time beyond any doubt that the head wound is not depicted in the official autopsy photographs. I was the first person to ever show those pictures to the Dallas witnesses, and the first person to bring witnesses from both hospitals together to meet.

Dr. David Stewart, formerly of Parkland, wrote me that "there was never any controversy concerning the wounds between the doctors in attendance. I was with them either separately or in groups on many occasions over a long period of time." Before I quote the next statement in his letter, I must ask if it is reasonable to expect that so many doctors who have never disputed among themselves the wounds that they all saw together could have seen something different from what was seen at Bethesda. The answer is, they did not see anything very different. Confusion arose only because of the inability of some critics to understand what was being described.

"Concerning Exhibit F-48 [the photograph of the back of the President's head], there is no way the wound described to me by Dr. Perry and others could be the wound shown in this picture. The massive destructive wound could not remotely be pulled together well enough to give a normal contour to the head that is present in this picture."[9]

Dr. Richard Dulaney and his wife also gave us a lot of time, and over the years, like so many of the other Dallas witnesses, have gone out of their way to tell what they know. Everyone in Dallas wants the truth to be known. And after twenty-nine years, they are all still talking fearlessly.

"The head looked relatively intact. I really could not see the wound until Buddy [Giesecke] picked up the scalp and hair on top of the head to show the wound. I could see into the wound quite well."[10] (Someone shined a flashlight inside.) "It included the occipital region, but was also parietal."

Dulaney said, "I remember noting to myself just how intact the face and head was. I didn't see any damage to the face." Also, he did not see any wound to the right or left temple.

I produced the pictures showing the throat wound and asked him what he thought. "It looks pretty much like what I saw."

He remembered the tubes being in the chest. He said that the pictures that we were showing him were the ones that he saw in the National Archives. He noted that the X-rays made the bone loss look "more anterior."

He said that the gurney mattress covers were "rubberized dark black material. They could have been dark greenish." They were closed with a zipper. In my opinion, these mattress covers certainly could have been mixed up with a body bag in certain people's mind in the great stress that was to follow at Bethesda.

Dulaney placed the large defect more toward the top of the head, and disputed the present photograph which shows an intact back of the head. He said that the pictures he saw at the National Archives were compatible (not necessarily perfectly accurate) with what he saw in Dallas, "after the body had been wetted down and washed and prepared for an autopsy." He said that the pictures in the Archives were basically the same as the tracings published by the House Committee.

The hair on the back of the head in the color pictures does looked washed—though there is still blood on the scalp in one of the color pictures, if not all of them—and if that is a flap (though hinged on the wrong side), then it might be fairly accurate, except for the holes that nearly everyone agrees were through the scalp. It was more shredded and macerated than what we see in the picture.

The Throat Wound

On the throat wound, which Dulaney saw after the trach tube was taken out, he said that what is in the picture is what he saw.[11]

Dr. Peters told me that the incisions shown in the photographs were accurate. He said that Dr. Perry had to cut at least two and a half inches across to get the cuff in.[12] "I wouldn't argue between two and three fourths of an inch and three inches. It was around that range. You can't really measure what is in the photograph, but it's no bigger than what we saw in Dallas. The cut *had* to be at least two inches. If someone says it was three inches, I wouldn't argue with that."

Perry looked down into the chest once he had the throat open. He had to separate the strap muscles and see what damage was done to the trachea. Dr. Perry had to have total control over the area where he was cutting, and this is not achieved by simply puncturing a small hole in the throat. He had to explore the wound itself before he put in a tube and cuff. He told the Warren Commission: "I made a transverse incision right through this wound [the bullet hole in the neck] and carried it down to the superficial fascia, to expose the strap muscles overlying the thyroid and the trachea. There was an injury to the right lateral aspect of the trachea at the level of the external wound. The trachea was deviated slightly to the left and it was necessary to drive the strap muscles on the left side in order to gain access to the trachea. At this point, I recall, Dr. Jones, just on my left, was placing a catheter into a vein in the left arm, because he handed me a necessary instrument which I needed in the performance of the procedure.

"The wound in the trachea was then enlarged to admit a cuffed tracheotomy tube to support respiration. I noted that there was free air and blood in the superior right mediastinum.

"Although I saw no injury to the lung or to the plural space, the presence of this free blood and air in this area could be indicative of a wound of the right hemothorax, and I asked that someone put a right chest tube in for seal drainage."[13] It's quite clear that in those few moments Perry had another job to do besides get a breathing tube in. He needed to make a large incision in the throat in order to look at the lungs and the blood vessels of the neck, along with the trachea, since a bullet had entered in the area.

A little more than one hour passed from the time the President died until the time the body was taken away.

"Jackie was in the emergency room the whole time, just about. She didn't leave until the last rites," Dr. Peters told me, speaking of the period starting from the time the President was brought into the hospital.[14]

"I was making the incision and was startled to find her standing beside me at the table," Dr. Peters told me.

After the last rites, she went just outside the door to sit in a chair that had been provided for her, and Congressman Henry Gonzalez brought her some water and lit a cigarette for her.[15] She smoked it and then reentered the room. "I don't think she left it again until the casket left," Dr. Peters said.

Dr. Crenshaw

Dr. Charles Crenshaw was a junior resident at the time, and so was not very experienced compared to the staff available and working to save the President. But he noted much of what was going on, and his recollections are extensive. I asked him if there could have been some sort of pre-exam or pre-autopsy just after John Kennedy died at Parkland. He told me that he "went back in with the ambulance fellows. After all the furor, Kennedy was pronounced dead at one o'clock. After that there was the wrangle over having the autopsy done there." He said some of the doctors went back in to look at the body from time to time. (Dr. Adolph "Bud" Giesecke had described in 1979 how they had shined a flashlight into the large defect in the back of the head after lifting it up.) Crenshaw does not remember the time. "There was a small amount of time—it could have been two o'clock.

"I don't know how anyone could have gotten at the body," he told me.

"I don't think that the autopsy doctor was competent. It was a bad autopsy. That would have not happened if our Dr. Rose could have done it here."

I told him that Boswell stated that the large defect was primarily located in the back of the head. "Yeah, it was in the parietal-occipital area," he said. This repeats what everyone else told me, which is detailed in *High Treason.*[16]

"Do you know anything about the cerebellum?"

"Yes, it was hanging by a thread. You could barely see it. . . . You could see it there, portions of it on a thread of tissue. Blood was seeping through it. The cerebellum hanging outside of the wound."

Crenshaw imparted to me his opinion, which was commonly held by the medical staff at Parkland who saw the body and knew something about the case: "I still believe he was shot from the front."

I brought up the subject of the treatment Kennedy was receiving before he died. "The big question was: Who was prescribing the steroids?"

"Now, they were in the admiral's [Burkley] kit bag. He gave the cortisone to Jim Carrico to give to him in the emergency ward. Likewise that was the first time I saw the James Bond books in his kit bag. I don't know if he was reading them or if they were for Kennedy! But he carried the steroids with him."

"So you looked in his bag?!"

"Yep. It was rather interesting to see what he was carrying in there."

I brought up the question of the forgeries of photographs and X-rays. "Did you see any fracture in . . . do you see that flap sticking out on the right side of the head in the photograph?"

"There was no fracture there. No flap like that."

"That fracture changes orientation as the camera moves around for different views."

"That's exactly right. It doesn't look like the same head, you know."

"But do you remember any flap—"

"No."

"If Jackie had closed it, could you have seen it?"

"No. The way they are pulling up the scalp in the picture, I didn't even know what that fracture was hanging on to. But it was *not* present in Dallas."

"Do you remember a laceration extending into the forehead over the right eye?"

"No. That was a clot."

"In the photograph there is a laceration extending a half inch into the forehead—"

"They would have had to have done that either before Bethesda, or at Bethesda. That wasn't present in Dallas. The autopsy people make a cut and pull the scalp down over the face."

"So you think that is what that laceration is?"

"That is the *only* thing it could have been. Because when the scalp was pulled back, his face was not marred. The eyes were divergent. It was thought that there was a wound on the left [temple] but that was not true. It was a huge clot in the hair."

He again repeated the evidence for a gunshot wound from in front in the head. "I think the bullet came in from the front, because what I observed was that the scalp was torn by the hole in his head, and the brain was scooped out and the cerebellum was hanging there in the parietal-occipital."

"How lacerated was the scalp in the back of the head? Was there enough to cover that hole—the big defect in the bone?"

"It was just parted where the defect had come out. I think the bullet came in from the front and came out the parietal-occipital."

He described to me the preparation of the body for the trip back to Washington. He says that he was in and out of the room quite a bit as it was going on. "Sheets were put around him and he was put on a mattress cover."

"I remember the nurses got a covering, and it was my recollection that it was a plastic mattress cover, and blood was still seeping out."

"But you didn't see the cover?"

"Well, yes, it was a clear plastic cover."

"It was clear plastic? You could see through it?"

"Yes."

"Did you see them wrap the head up in sheets and towels? Did you see the body wrapped up and put into the coffin?"

"Yes."

"Were towels used?'

"No. I remember the sheets."

"Aubrey Rike held the head as they put it into the coffin. . . ."

"Right. I watched him."

"He said that he could feel the edges of the bone in the back of the head, so he knew where the large hole was. He says because of that, he doesn't remember any towels around the head."

"I don't remember any towels at all."

"How close were you standing?"

"I was standing right in back of him. The girls were there."

"You were very close when they were preparing the body?"

"Right. I cannot say there weren't towels, but I do not remember them."

"You watched them put the sheet around the head, right?"

"Yes."

"On the frontal bone, forward of the coronal suture—do you feel there was any damage? From all the witnesses I have talked to, there was no damage to the face whatsoever, but the right eye was askew."

"Well, it was divergent."

"You know that the forensic dentist who authenticated the skull X-rays as Kennedy's said he did it partly on the basis of a right frontal sinus. The problem with that is that there is no bone on the right side of the face there."

"Right."

"Would you agree with that, from what you saw of the X-rays?"

"Sure."

"We have found indications of forgery and retouching in most of the pictures."

"Oh, yeah, it has got to have been." Crenshaw laughed here.

"The throat wound, though, it looks rather large. Would you say the throat wound is or is not pretty much the way it was after—"

"It was enlarged, but not with a knife. It looks like it was extended and probed with the fingers for a bullet, because that was a frontal wound too." (He didn't know that the picture appears to have been retouched to make the wound look more jagged, like an exit wound, and he did not take into account the fact that the neck is flexed, the head hanging back, pulling the wound open.)

"Malcolm Perry was the best operator we had. He made the smallest incision and the prettiest work. He would not do that. And for him to do any slash like that was impossible. It looks like a butcher did it. I know he said that. Somebody enlarged that, and put their finger in there—I'm sure they were probing for a bullet," he said.

"You don't think that Perry could have done this, then, do you?"

"No way," he said.

"Kennedy expired at one—" I said.

"He was dead before that, but we waited for the priest to come in. There was one Catholic there—a cardiologist—technically, so that he could receive the last rites, it was arbitrarily put at one [o'clock]."

"There was a time frame of an hour and a quarter from the time he died to the time he was removed at a few minutes after two."

"Of course, Jacqueline came in, the priest came in."

"Was there any X-ray machine anywhere around that emergency room?"

"No. I have heard this theory, but I never did see one. An X-ray machine is the easiest way, but you can put your finger in and feel around. It's a bit inadequate because the bullets can go anyplace."

"During the time frame after he died and the priest came, how much of the time were you there?"

"I was there twenty or thirty minutes. Jackie was in there. . . ."

"Between what time and what time?"

"We put the sheet up to him. Then the priest walked in, then Jacqueline walked in, kissed his great toe, and put her ring on his finger."

"Yes."

"There wasn't a dry face in the whole place. Then she put her wedding ring on his finger."

"You think that was about one o'clock, right?"

"It was before we announced his death so that the priest could be there to give him the last rites. Then Kemp Clark went ahead and signed the death certificate."

"That was actually one o'clock. All this was going on. It did not take long."

"All of this happened about one o'clock?"

"Right, so then Baxter and I got Mrs. Kennedy out and she stood there, and I tried to give her a phenobarbital, and she said no. And she stood there in the door and then started to talk to people in the entourage. . . ."

"She was between Trauma Room one and two in that little hall, standing there outside the door holding her pillbox hat."

"Did you have any reason to suspect any of the Secret Service men, anybody who was there, who was not part of the medical team?"

"They didn't even know each other. The Secret Service men were there while we started to work on Mr. Kennedy. Clint Hill had a gun out and cocked and we were afraid he was going to shoot one of us. And Doris Nelson went around saying he's okay, he's okay, he's okay, and got him finally out of the room. It was sheer bedlam. I don't think anyone moved for a while. They had Thompson submachine guns."

"In this time frame of the one hour before the body was removed—it is possible that someone had plenty of time to tamper with the body," I said.

"I was back and forth. I walked in and I walked out. The door was open part of that time."

"Is there any chance that the body could have then been removed from the casket and put behind a curtain?"

"No. I saw the body go into the casket."

"I mean after that, when the fight started over the autopsy."

"No. I saw Aubrey Rike close the casket."

"But there was a fifteen-minute or more battle over the body leaving Texas."

"I believe it was about that time. But the body was coming out of the room by then, with us standing there, and Mrs. Kennedy was there. I don't think there was any possibility of the body being taken out of the casket. Then she walked out into that gaggle of people."

"Were the guns drawn?"

"The guy with the submachine gun had his, and the others had their coats pulled back, showing their holsters. There was no question in anybody's mind that they would have used them."

"Yes."

"And I think they probably would have if they'd had to." Crenshaw laughed again.

"I'm trying to explain that Back-of-the-Head picture, and the X-rays. It's not logical that—during that hour and quarter . . ."

"The time was taken up with cleaning him up, wrapping him, and so on."

"But is it possible that some people posing as pathologists or doctors got in there and got at the body?"

"I don't believe it."

"I know they covered it up," he said. Dr. Crenshaw told me the story of the cover-up, and how LBJ told the police what to do in Dallas. "The President called Fritz up and told him not to say a thing, and they had Hosty burn that note. That was LBJ."

"With regard to the X-ray, double-checking—the frontal bone from the forehead back as far as the coronal suture and into the right temple area which is missing in the X-ray—from your standpoint—that was not like that in Dallas?

"No. I never saw that wound with the bone sticking out there on the right side. It was in the parietal-occipital."

"The face was all right?"

"Not marred at all. It would have fallen in if all that bone were missing."

"Could they have gotten it at that one hour at Parkland?"

"I would say there is no way at Parkland. It had to have happened after the plane or at Bethesda, and I have always thought that it was done at Bethesda."

"You are not alone in that feeling."[17]

Aubrey Rike

Aubrey Rike, a young ambulance driver, worked at Oneal's funeral home. He and Dennis McGuire had picked up a man with an epileptic seizure just minutes before the assassination, at Dealey Plaza on 100 N. Houston Street, and proceeded to Parkland Hospital. The man did not appear in bad shape, but he was slightly injured. He walked off during the ensuing confusion.[18]

Within moments of their arriving, President Kennedy and John Connally were rushed into the trauma rooms. The Secret Service asked Rike to remain in case they needed his ambulance. "Rike stated he cleared the hospital at three P.M. and returned to Oneal Incorporated, Funeral Directors," according to the FBI report.[19]

Aubrey (Al) Rike, currently a police officer in the posh Dallas suburb of Highland Park, by a chance coincidence was a witness to that tragic scene. In 1991 he was hired by the film director Oliver Stone as a technical advisor on the events of that terrible November day in 1963. He was one of the men who put the body in the coffin, after the nurses were through cleaning it up and wrapping it in sheets.

He described the Elgin Britannia coffin which Vernon Oneal brought in another ambulance as a "sealer." He told me on June 10, 1991, that it had a screw on the back of it. "You drain all the air out and tighten it up and its sealed. Otherwise it could pop open somewhere. This way there is no chance of it popping open or anything like that."

I had asked him about a Ziegler case. "Never seen one," he said. I described for him how this is a coffin that fits inside a casket to protect it against seepage, and keep the odors in when the body has been dead for some time and is decomposing. "That casket we put him in—you couldn't put another casket inside of it either."

"It was bronze, right?"

"Yeah."

"You're saying there was a screw on the back of it? You mean like an air lock?"

"Yeah. An air-lock sealing screw."

"Was the lid screwed down?"

"Yeah, that tightens the lid—once you put the lid down and it's closed and locked. Once you tighten that seal up—the only way you can open that lid up is to unscrew the lock and let the air back in and that'll repressurize it."

"How do you draw the air out when you screw it down?"

"It'll come out all right. It'll have some air in it. It'll not be completely airtight. Around the seals it'll be airtight but it'll have some air in it."

"When Jackie came in, did you see her put her ring on him?"

"Yeah, I helped her."

"You waited about thirty minutes for the priest to come in?"

"Yeah. Probably thirty to forty-five minutes."

"When did she put the ring on—after that?"

"No. She came in after we brought the casket in."

"So she saw you put the body in the casket?"

"Yes."

"Then she came over and put her ring on?"

"No, that was when he was still on the table. We left him on the cot until after he was blessed and given his last rites."

"He was on the gurney or whatever it was?"

"Yeah."

"Then he was blessed and he was on the table and then she put the ring on. . . ."

"She did that before he was given the last rites—that was the first thing she did when she came in. She stood there and looked at him for a few minutes. Then she pulled the sheet back and got his hand and took her ring off and tried to put it on him, but of course it wouldn't go on. We got some K-Y jelly and put it on him and slid the ring up."

"Then you put him in the casket?"

"Well, the priest came and gave him the last rites. Then we put him in the casket. . . ."

"And then it was closed. You closed it?"

"Yes."

"Then, did it go right out into the middle of that battle?"

"Probably five to ten minutes after that." This means that the casket remained in the room, and perhaps it was not always attended. Mrs. Kennedy may have gone to the bathroom. Everyone's attention was distracted by the struggle between the President's party, who were trying to take the body to Washington, and the medical examiner of Dallas and those supporting his demand that the body stay in compliance with the law and be autopsied there.

It is conceivable that someone might have slipped the body out of its coffin and hid it behind a curtain, then removed it from the hospital via the OB-GYN delivery room, and out through the tunnel to the staff residency, just as has been shown to one of the Secret Service men when he asked directions for an alternative route out that would not be seen by reporters and everyone else.

"After the lid went on?"

"Yes."

"Did it stay in the room while the battle was going on?"

"Yes."

"Then you left?"

"Yes."

"Did you follow it all the way out of the hospital?"

"I pulled it all the way out."

"Pulled it out?"

"I was at the head and Peanuts [McGuire] was at the foot."

"At any time was the casket alone in the room while the fight was going on?"

"No. No."

"People have said that battle lasted fifteen or twenty minutes."

"No. About ten minutes. It seemed like it was longer. . . ."

"Are you sure there could not have been a Ziegler case inside the Britannia?"

"No. No way. There wasn't a casket inside that casket. No shipping casket inside that casket either. In fact, I had to adjust the pillow and everything in it and I felt the springs all over the bottom. You couldn't fit a casket inside. There was no casket inside."

Dr. Kemp Clark described it as a "bronze-colored plastic casket."[20] Another hospital administrator described it as a "plain bronze casket."[21]

"I know the back of the head was gone," he told me. On April 6, 1991, he described having felt the edges of the large hole on the back of the head through the sheet, when he lifted the head end of the body to put it in the coffin.

"From the time you closed the lid, was it ever out of your sight?"

"We wheeled it out. . . . I was with it. . . . I never really lost sight of it all the way to the airport, except when it was inside the hearse and we took it to the airport. The hearse never stopped. We had eyesight on the hearse all the way in the motorcade."

"Was Jackie in the hearse?"

"Yes. She was back in the back, catercorner to the casket."

Al Rike says that it was unlikely that there were towels beneath the sheet wrapped around the head because he could feel the edges of the large defect, which he said was on the back of the head.[22]

James Curtis Jenkins said that there were towels wrapped around the head at the autopsy, beneath the sheet.[23]

So far there is no mention of towels in the depositions of the nurses, and no other mention of towels by any other witness.

Time of Casket Departure

Parkland security officer Charles Gerloff said the casket left at 1:30 P.M.[24]

Dr. Kemp Clark said 2 P.M. (Author of statement not perfectly clear.)[25]

Nurse Doris Nelson said the body left at 2:10 P.M.[26]

Aubrey Rike told the FBI he cleared the hospital at 3 P.M.[27] He wrote me about this in 1991, saying that he had guessed at the time. The Dallas Police Radio Log[28] has a conversation between Rike's ambulance (606) already at Love Field and the police dispatcher at 2:13 P.M. as follows:

"606."

"606."

"Do you have any idea where this casket coach is that we're supposed to get."

"606."

"Was it supposed to be at Love Field?"

"606."

"10-4. We're approaching Air Cargo now. An officer out at Parkland told us to contact you and have 39 [Butcher and Comer] meet us."

"10-4. Stand by."

On August 15, 1991, Al Rike wrote me to say: "I was driving ambulance No. 606 and the Secret Service drove the hearse to Love Field. We [Mr. Oneal and myself] were to meet the Secret Service at *Air Force 1*. The Dallas police department had the street blocked so we could not get to the plane. I asked the DPD dispatcher the question so she could ask the Command Officer. The Command Supervisor was on another channel, one which we did not have in 606. The hearse belonged to Oneal's funeral home and we wanted it back after they were through with it.

"I was driving 606 and I don't think anybody knocked on the window because the window was rolled down at the time. Mr. Oneal believed that he was going to drive the hearse to the funeral home and embalm the body. He didn't believe the body was leaving Dallas without being embalmed. But he found out differently only when the body was loaded in the hearse and the Secret Service took off with his hearse."

He also wrote that Oneal owned the ambulance and not the city. Oneal contracted with the city of Dallas to run emergencies.

"I talked to the FBI almost a year after the shooting. I was still afraid of the FBI, and don't know what I said to them. I was guessing at the time I cleared from the hospital, and I don't remember what all we talked about. I do know we talked for over an hour."

He also wrote that "I was with the casket at all times after we closed the lid."

Rike's ambulance went to Love Field about the time that Doris Nelson said they had in fact left with the body. There is no other mention by the Secret Service in their testimony and papers before the Warren Commission of a trip to Love Field with that ambulance.

Numerous researchers have contacted Al Rike over the years, and he has been unstinting with his help and time. The universal judgment of all who have met him is that he is thoroughly honest and intelligent.

Roy Kellerman testified that the body left Parkland at 2:04 P.M. for Love Field.[29] He said it took about ten minutes to get there.

The Laceration

The Superior Right Profile autopsy photograph shows a long laceration or incision extending a half inch into the forehead above the right eyebrow and going straight back toward the back of the head. *Nobody* in Dallas saw this. "It did not exist," Dr. Peters told me.[30]

Dr. Crenshaw said that he thought it was the sort of cut made at an autopsy when the scalp is reflected back in order to do a craniotomy. Dr. Boswell and Dr. Karnei told me that it was a laceration and not an incision, and that it was made by a fracture pushing the bones upward and breaking the scalp. They volunteered this information.

I think that it might have happened during transport of the body when the Secret Service agents almost dropped the heavy casket—struggling first to get it disconnected from the floor of the ambulance at Love Field and then up the stairs and into the plane.

I am trying to give everyone the benefit of the doubt, avoiding sinister explanations as much as possible, because every one of these witnesses, though perhaps wrong on one thing, brings important evidence that is corroborated by others. The above laceration/incision is an issue because some think that perhaps it is evidence of a pre-autopsy or of some tampering with the body at some point. It is not rational to me that any cut would have been made that would extend into the face that was not seen in Dallas.

Mark Crouch has discovered that in the black and white Stare-of-Death photographs, the part of the laceration/incision that extends into the forehead has been blacked out with a small black reference triangle. Somebody did not want that cut into the face to show.[31]

The Calls and the Throat Wound

"Dr. Perry was up all night. He came into my office the next day and sat down and looked terrible, having not slept. I never saw anybody look so dejected! They called him from Bethesda two or three times in the middle of the night to try to get him to change the entrance wound in the throat to an exit wound," Audrey Bell told me.[32]

"My whole credibility as a trauma surgeon was at stake," Perry told me. "I *couldn't* have made a mistake like that. It destroys my integrity if I don't know an entrance wound from an exit wound!" he said.[33]

"They really grilled Perry about it," Bell said. "They hounded him for a long time." Arlen Specter in fact went to great lengths to change what Perry had originally been quoted as saying.[34] Specter's problem was that the entire staff at Parkland who had seen the wound insist today that it was an entrance wound.

Half of the entry wound is clearly visible in the photographs of the throat incision as a neat, perfect semicircle the diameter of a bullet at the bottom of the cut, in the center. An exit wound would appear quite jagged and torn, and would be quite a bit larger.

"He was senior man. He'd been doing trauma for years. He was really hounded about a lot of things," Bell told me.[35] "They hounded all of the senior residents about that, and Oswald's death: 'Could they have saved him?'"

Perry denied, in a letter to me, saying to anyone that the cut in the photograph was larger than he had made it. "I've neither verified nor challenged the accuracy of any photos."[36]

The autopsy doctors put the Dallas team in a bad light on a number of points. The Bethesda team made them look incompetent because of the question of whether the chest tubes had actually gone into the President's chest, which Humes said they did not. And the Bethesda doctors impugned their competence with regard to a unanimous opinion in Dallas that the throat wound was an entry wound.

The Warren Commission itself dealt the final blow by publicly disgracing the Dallas doctors, who unanimously felt that the large defect in the posterior skull was an exit wound and that the President had been shot from the front. The Warren Commission simply hid the fact and pretended the exit wound was in the front of the head, based on the false X-ray which a urologist, a Dr. Lattimer, was the first person allowed to see and publicize at an early stage.

Many of those who actually saw the bullet hole in the throat insist to this day that it was an entry wound. It is unreasonable for medical men and women who have seen countless such wounds in their life to continue to insist that it was an entry wound if they could be mistaken. In addition, the throat would have been much more damaged and the skin punched out, ragged, and torn, as would the trachea, if the bullet had been coming out rather than going in. Instead, the wound was small and neat, so many thought it was an entrance.

By casting doubt on the credibility of the Dallas medical team at one of the world's great teaching hospitals, a place seeing many gunshot wounds, the actual medical evidence of an entirely different assassination scenario was discredited at the outset.

Not that the Bethesda doctors had not themselves fudged their report, since they did not at any time during the autopsy know that the President had a bullet wound in the throat. Upon that fact hung the entire fantasy of the single-bullet theory and the government's only possible explanation of the event which would eliminate a conspiracy.

The evidence is unassailable that the bullet hole in the back did not penetrate the chest. What is glossed over is that there are *two* bullet holes in the back. As for the lower hole in the back, "that bullet could have hit his back brace," Audrey Bell told me.[37] "And the bullet that hit him in the throat could have coursed downward and entered his chest." The evidence indicates that *something* may have entered his chest, but not from behind.

A conspiracy which they could not explain, they could not have.

Home

The body arrived at the plane about 2:14 P.M.,[38] and Lyndon Johnson was sworn in at 2:38 P.M.[39] *Air Force 1* took off at 2:47 P.M. CST, or 3:47 EST.[40] In Greenwich Mean Time (Zulu) the plane left at 2047 hours; 2047 Zulu is 8:47 P.M. in England. In winter there is a five-hour time difference between Eastern Standard Time and Greenwich Mean Time, so six hours from 8:47 P.M. is 2:47 CST.

Colonel Swindall "estimated block time Andrews at 2305Z." That is, the plane would land at 6:05 P.M. EST. It was a two hour and fifteen minute flight. The air speed was 520 miles per hour, and the plane had an 80 knot tail wind, which combined for a 600 miles per hour ground speed. It landed in Washington at 5:58 P.M.

The terrible events of the day passed into night. The body was taken off the plane at Andrews Air Force Base and was driven through Washington to Bethesda National Naval Medical Center for the autopsy.

CHAPTER 5

BETHESDA NAVAL HOSPITAL

As noted elsewhere, there is a clear conflict about when the body arrived at Bethesda National Naval Medical Center; when the autopsy started—what is meant by the "start of the autopsy"—and whether that meant the making of the Y incision or the examination of the head after photographs and X-rays were made.

Such questions, which still are not properly answered or documented three decades later, have thrown fuel on the fire of many crazy theories about body theft, alteration, or tampering. Quite frankly, there is a lot of fraud in this case from all sides—not just possible lies in Dallas and the confusion wrought by researchers, but lies about the evidence and the autopsy itself—which fudged certain key matters.

An indication that President Kennedy's body might have been stolen somewhere along the line is found in the statements of one man— James Curtis Jenkins—who says that the brain stem seemed neatly severed with a knife before the brain came out of the head at the autopsy. Additional statements were made by some naval personnel that they thought the body arrived at the hospital before Jackie Kennedy did, and that it was in a different casket (see Chapter 12) and wrapped in a body bag.[1]

One of the men who took the X-rays, Jerrol Custer (see Chapter 10), had previously said that as he was going upstairs to develop films taken of the body of President Kennedy, he saw Jacqueline Kennedy surrounded by people near the entranceway, and that he thought she was just arriving. The enlisted men believe that Jacqueline Kennedy was supposed to have gone immediately to the seventeenth floor when she arrived to await the finish of the autopsy. But she did not in fact do that, and others describe her as being in the hallway after the body came in.

Custer thought she was coming in for the first time, but of course this was only a surmise, and he did not *know*—just as Dennis David did not know *who* was in the coffin he helped take out of a vehicle. Being *told* that Kennedy was in the coffin, and *seeing* him in it are two different things, and guessing that he was seeing Jackie's first arrival is not the same as knowing.

There was a sitting room beside the foyer at Bethesda. Like nearly all hospitals, Bethesda had a waiting room, and that was it. "Beyond the room where the late President's body was taken was a large sitting room where several relatives and close friends had already gathered."[2] Mrs. Kennedy was waiting for the arrival of Ethel Kennedy and others before being taken upstairs.

"When we arrived at Bethesda, we went to some room, some reception room, where the family was."[3]

Custer made it clear to me that he took no X-rays for at least forty-five minutes *after* the body arrived, having been asked to leave the morgue.[4] Therefore, the story that Jackie arrived from Andrews *after* the body arrived and he had taken X-rays is totally false, since she had to be there when he finally got around to taking X-rays sometime after eight P.M. She was there at seven.

Kathlee Fitzgerald offers the explanation of what is known as "memory merge." During periods of great stress, in a crisis or emergency when events are unfolding with great rapidity—such as the events of November 22, 1963—the mind plays tricks and does not register each detail. Some events are imprinted in the brain and merge with others, missing connecting links. Having been involved in shootouts and other warlike experiences, I know this to be true. We think we saw something that we did not.

It is my belief that until proven otherwise, some of the until now nearly unexplainable details of the assassination have to do with the faulty memories of witnesses. How do we know when they are accurate? For Jan Rudnicki (see Chapter 9) and others to have seen Jackie coming down the hallway outside his lab on the first floor before they had the body and began working on it shows that she was there before the body came. The vast weight of the evidence supports this; it does not support the idea that Jackie arrived *after* the body came. This conclusion is not a deduction based upon the official story, but because the likelihood is one of mistake, since Custer could not *know* that she was just arriving, or that she had not stepped outside the door for a moment to greet another person. In any event, as reported at the end of Chapter 10, Jerrol Custer has made it clear that he could not have seen Jacqueline for about one hour after she had to have been there.

I need Custer's testimony and what I know to be his great honesty and intelligence for the purpose of this book. I am faced with the same problem with almost every witness in the case, nearly all of whom are guilty of some mistake in their recollection, but who offer evidence in other respects that checks out. From my investigations I have been able to put together a much better picture which I think will stand the test of time. It requires some patience from the reader though.

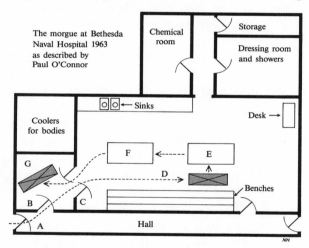

"This is the morgue as it was in 1963. It's gone now and I'm sad about that. (A) The shipping casket came in through this back door. (B) It came in through the cooler room door. (C) Came in through the double doors into the main morgue. (D) Was set down and opened. Inside was the body bag (crash bag)—a greenish gray. (E) We lifted the body out of the body bag and placed it on the table where the autopsy was done. (F) The body was then put onto the second table where Gawler's Funeral Home embalmed the body, and then (G) we took the body and placed it in the casket."—Paul O'Connor

I have no doubt that some Navy rating said—when they received the body of the "Air Force officer" that afternoon—that the body was that of President Kennedy. The officer's body came in a shipping casket in a black hearse and was ready for burial, as James Jenkins has said. The body obviously had to be unloaded by a crew of Navy men from the hospital. Except for Jenkins and Rudnicki, they simply did not know *who* was in that coffin, which stayed in the morgue throughout the autopsy of President Kennedy. And some man probably said, "Well, they had him over at Walter Reed first, but sent him over to us because we're better, and JFK was a Navy man!"

Some of the men believe that the body was at Walter Reed first, which is where the officer's body probably came from, and once again we have an example of memory merge. One of the two casket teams *did* come over from Walter Reed, and it did arrive in a helicopter.[5] The men got into a pickup truck, just as Metzler remembers, and met them at the loading dock when the casket and Navy ambulance arrived.

O'Connor said he heard two helicopters, which had to be the two honor guard teams arriving. Two helicopters *did* land. "The morgue was full of people. We were all in there. There were two helicopters and one landed out in the rear someplace, and I think it was in the Officers' Club parking lot. Yeah, and as soon as that happened, it was about, oh, three or four minutes later that the door burst open and in came the casket and we started."

There were several helicopter arrivals and departures at Andrews, and the Honor Guard from Walter Reed was flown to Bethesda by helicopter.[6] They got into a pickup truck and went to look for the casket.

"Captain Canada had been advised that Kennedy would arrive by helicopter. He had placed an honor guard at the helipad; two helicopters arrived, but they carried the Andrews Air Force Base honor guard, which wanted to be on hand at Bethesda when the body arrived. Both honor guards were standing at attention at the pads."[7]

Jim Bishop writes that "the body was driven to a rear entrance. It was taken out of the ambulance and placed in an empty and well-lighted corridor. There it reposed. McHugh stood by it and wondered what had happened. Kellerman and Greer stood looking around. No one spoke. No one appeared. They waited."[8] If this is true, then we can account for some of the missing time, since the casket was left in the ambulance in front of the hospital for some minutes before it was driven around back and unloaded as well.[9]

Air Force 1 landed at Andrews Air Force Base at 5:58 P.M.[10] The casket and Mrs. Kennedy and Robert Kennedy were in the ambulance and left by a quarter after six. The trip took forty-five minutes and no more.[11] There was a short delay before the body was taken to the back. Now we come to a problem with regard to the period that followed.

Roy Kellerman, the chief of the Secret Service detail with President Kennedy, testified to the Warren Commission: "By the time it took us to take the body from the plane into the ambulance, and a couple of carloads of staff people who followed us, we may have spent fifteen minutes there. And in driving from Andrews to the U.S. Naval Hospital, I would judge, a good forty-five minutes. So there is seven o'clock. We went immediately over, without too much delay on the outside of the hospital, into the morgue. The Navy people had their staff in readiness right then. There wasn't anybody to call. They were all there. So at the latest, 7:30, they began to work on the autopsy."[12]

Some might think there is a half hour after the arrival missing, and that half hour is crucial because of what might have happened off the record at Bethesda. The House Committee[13] and Humes[14] has it come into the morgue at 7:35.

I wonder why the arrival time is not mentioned in the FBI report? That report says that the first incision was made at 8:15, and the House Committee found that that was the start of the autopsy, again agreeing with Humes's Warren Commission testimony.[15] The House Committee defined "incision" as the Y incision, and not an examination of the head. If this is accurate, then Jerrol Custer's statement that the Y incision had been made when he was called back to the room to make his first X-rays after about thirty to forty-five minutes—*before* he made any X-rays at all—would be correct, based on a 7:35 arrival time.[16]

The first half to three quarters of an hour was always understood to have been taken up with unwrapping the body and taking photographs and one set of X-rays by Dr. John Ebersole, the acting Chief of Radiology.

The start of an autopsy is always assumed to be when the visual examination begins, *not* when any cut or Y incision is made.

We are told that there was a wait for Dr. Finck to arrive. We also know that X-rays and photographs were made before a more thorough visual examination began. The X-rays began early and the room had to be cleared when the X-ray machine was in operation, to avoid radiation.

Another serious conflict exists as to who took the X-rays. Jerrol Custer says he took the X-rays, and Edward Reed claims to have done it.[17] Paul O'Connor says they helped each other,[18] sometimes one operating the machine, sometimes the other. Later on, Dr. Ebersole was brought in when they could find no bullets, and his statements make it sound like he operated the machine himself, alone—before as well as after the autopsy.

Jerrol Custer told me that normally he always put his initials on each X-ray he took but that he was told by the FBI men not to do so that night.[19]

Custer has repeatedly said that the X-rays now in evidence are not the ones that he took and are not of President Kennedy.[20] In addition, the evidence tends to indicate that there may be two conflicting sets of X-rays in the National Archives: the officially released[21] set [copies] showing all of the right frontal bone missing[22] and the posterior head intact, and a set of skull X-rays showing the face intact with the posterior skull missing.

A grossly conflicting story is told by the men at the autopsy—one of whom says that Kennedy "was taken out of the casket in the atrium before we went into the morgue. As you came into the morgue there was a little room that had the cold boxes. He was in that and logged and tagged with a toe tag there. But he was taken out of that and brought in on a gurney all wrapped in sheets. The body bag was already open. We put him on the table and we were told not to take the towels off his head. We did unwrap him and we did the body work."[23]

So far, all that I have learned at Parkland is that towels were not put around the head, but only a sheet. Dr. Crenshaw saw the body wrapped up and he told me that there were no towels used.[24] None of the nurses described towels being used when they told how they wrapped the head in sheets, and Aubrey Rike picked up the head, wrapped in a sheet, and felt the edges of the large defect in the back of the head when he helped put the body in the casket, which he couldn't have done if there had been towels around the head.

If towels were indeed around the head when Jenkins saw it unwrapped, then it is an indication that someone had access to the body beforehand.

But another great conflict here is whether the body was taken out of the casket in the anteroom (the cold room) or the morgue itself. I believe Paul O'Connor when he says that he helped unload the body from the casket, but he insists that it was in the morgue and not in the cold room. "Paul was in the anteroom," Jenkins said. Jenkins did not get a good look at the casket because he was in the morgue. Paul told me that he was so busy after the body arrived that he did not have time until about eight P.M. to log in the body, that it came in earlier, but he wrote down eight P.M. because that was when he logged it in—not when it arrived.[25]

The body bag spoken of above by Jenkins was also described by O'Connor, who told the House Committee about it. He has often said that the body was inside it and that it was unzipped to remove the body, but he told me several times that the body was *wrapped* in it, not inside it. I was not questioning him about it at the time—he simply mentioned that it was *wrapped* in the body bag.

The body bag might simply be a zippered gurney mattress cover which was the same color, used to line the coffin in Dallas. I note that apparently several people went to get various kinds of plastic covers that could be used to line the coffin when something was requested to protect the coffin before the body went in, and it is not clear which of them was used. Each witness thinks that it was his particular mattress cover which *he* brought that was used. Unfortunately, it is difficult to determine since five of the witnesses who best would know are either dead or can't be found. We should therefore go with the description provided by Aubrey Rike—who lined the coffin—in Chapter 14. The coffin was lined with a creamish-white-colored rubberized or plasticized sheet that covered the upper half of the body only. Rike denied that the body was put into a mattress cover. He got the half sheet from the cabinet and put it around the pillow and protected the sides of the coffin.

The men from the autopsy present at the meeting with Rike and the Parkland witnesses (See Chapter 14.) did not remember any such rubberized sheet, which they would have seen in the coffin. Jenkins said that the head was wrapped in towels under the sheet around it.

Dr. Philip Williams, a young intern at the time, was asked to bring something to wrap the body in and brought a "plastic mattress cover—whitish-gray." Audrey Bell said it was "opaque," and it had a zipper around it. Dr. Williams said he "thought it had elastic around it. Form-fitting." He gave it to Pat Hutton, and didn't know for sure if it was used. Dr. Charles Crenshaw told me that the mattress cover was clear plastic.[26] Naturally, they threw all of this evidence away at Bethesda.

O'Connor has often said that the body bag was made of a rubberized material. William Manchester writes: "Motioning to Orderly David Sanders, Oneal directed him to line the inside of the coffin with a sheet of plastic. Doris Nelson and Diana Bowron swooped around, wrapping the body in a second plastic sheet. Then the undertaker asked Doris to bring him a huge rubber sheath and a batch of rubber bags. Placing the sheath over Sanders's plastic lining, he carefully cut the bags to size, enveloping the President's head in them one by one until he had made certain that there would be seven protective layers of rubber and two of plastic between the damaged scalp and the green satin. All this took twenty minutes."[27] "There was no body bag. Definitely not in a body bag."[28]

A body bag or crash bag is quite different from the above wrappings. But, once again, "body bag" is a euphanism—another example of memory merge.

Now we come to the possibility of a shell game of some kind with the body, if there was tampering with it at Bethesda.

James Jenkins told me: "I remember a nice casket coming in. We were told that we had an Army or Air Force major for burial the next day, which is kind of unusual. We were told not to worry about logging him in, and that was extremely unusual."[29]

Jenkins believed that the major came in a shipping casket. "In a body bag wrapped in sheets and towels. The coffin was there at the same time as Kennedy. They had apparently put him with Kennedy in that coffin. But all of that was done in the atrium there."[30]

I asked him about the other body that was received that afternoon, November 22, 1963. He had previously said that he was told it was the body of an Air Force major. "It came in earlier in the evening, after I arrived from classes. It came in about the time we first went to the morgue. I'm sure it was at least an hour before JFK came in. Maybe quite a bit more."

Jenkins was not allowed to leave the room, except once when Captain John H. Stover told him to eat his lunch. He was gone only a few moments.[31]

"Was the body [of the Air Force major] in the casket?"

"Yes. It wasn't taken out of the casket and put in a cold box. It sat on a pop-up cart in the cold room, not in a cold box, and that's where it remained."

He said it had to be after 3:30 P.M. "when the other kid went off duty. I remember it coming in. It was Paul's and my job to log it in, but they wouldn't let us log it in." *Why not?*

Jim said that he did not actually see the body in the casket, as it was not opened.[32]

Jim said that along with them was a first class (E6) hospital corpsman as the duty corpsman that night. "He was first class and he was one of the few first class in that position. He was an instructor in the School of Lab Sciences, and worked in special chemistry. He was in there the early part of that night. He was there when the major came in. He told me not to log the body in. Said he had been told not to log it in."

He said that the casket the Air Force major was in was a "nice casket," rosewood or red mahogany. "It was not a *cheap casket.* It had brass fixtures." During another interview he said it was mahogany with ornate brass fixtures. "It was a beaut."[33]

"He came in at least an hour before. Maybe more." But the casket of the alleged officer came in after they had started to prepare for the President's autopsy. "It was not there when we came on."

"It was not there when you came on?"

"No. When a body came into the morgue, we had to log it in, Paul and me."

"As soon as they told us classes were cancelled, I was never allowed to leave."

"And you think that was at 3:30?"

"I think so."[34]

From my assessment of the veracity of these witnesses, I believe that there was a shipping casket there. But I believe that the men were falsely told that Kennedy was in it, perhaps as a joke, or as part of the decoy setup, if it in fact existed. Kathlee Fitzgerald has suggested an explanation for this. Jenkins, Metzler, and O'Connor were busy working, preparing the room and materials needed for the autopsy. First Jenkins and O'Connor were alone in the room from mid-afternoon preparing things, and then Metzler arrived and was alone with O'Connor. A shipping casket was brought in from a black hearse with the body of the officer in a body bag, and put down in the cold room, where Jenkins saw it from the morgue itself. The six petty officers detailed to wait on the loading platform spent far too much time there, if they were there until seven P.M. They would have had to go to dinner somewhere along the way. It seems clear to me that they were not, in fact, there all those hours from mid or late afternoon, but had brought in the shipping casket with the body of an officer.

In addition, an honor guard was sent to help take in Kennedy's body, and the six petty officers were no longer present, since some of them do not remember being on the same team as the others.

Some time elapsed and the expensive coffin arrived for the officer and was also put down in the cold room. The body of the officer (in a body bag) through error may have been brought into the morgue and put on one of the two tables there, as some have described, and this may have confused the men. The body may have even been taken out of the bag, and, who knows, it may have looked like Kennedy to boot. The fact is, there is almost nobody who claims to have seen the body come out of a body bag and onto the table. Jenkins may be a bit confused in his nearly thirty-year-old memory of the event, but he saw both caskets in the cold room.

In addition, at times Jenkins was either in the chemical room in the morgue or the changing room, and people and bodies came and went which he could not see. Both rooms were separate from the morgue, but a part of it. The scene changed.

I have spent a couple of years trying to shake Paul O'Connor from some of his ideas. He and the rest of the men may have made some mistakes, and Paul may have exaggerated a thing or two, but he did tell the House Committee investigators that the body was there in a body bag.[35] He told the investigators that the body was *wrapped* in a body bag, and he has told me this too, so he either made the same mistake twice, or it was simply wrapped around JFK. At other times, he says he helped *unzip* it, remove the body from inside, and put it on the table. He has also said that they did not take the sheets off right away but were told to wait. He was sent on a number of errands that night, and it seems to me that if that was the officer's body, it then went back into the cold room when he was out of the room, and the President's casket came in. The body was removed from the casket and O'Connor saw that it was similarly wrapped in a sheet. The men have described how the body remained unwrapped for some time, and the men were taking secret peeks beneath the sheet.

If the officer's body did come into the morgue by mistake or actual intent to do an autopsy, it was sent back to the cold room due to the imminent arrival of the President's body.

In each one of the conflicts in what these men have said—which led to some fantastical theories in the past—we find that some other researcher talked to these men and apparently led them into changing things and saying what ultimatly may be unreasonable.

Speaking again about being stopped from logging the body of the Air Force officer in, Jenkins said, "It was highly irregular. The military was real emphatic about that. Everybody had to be logged in. I mean, you got a body, it had to be tagged immediately. It had to be logged. They didn't ever. They said don't worry about logging him in."

"Did you see the body in that casket?"

"No, I did not."

"I can definitely tell you that there was an ornate type casket already in the laboratory when the President came in."

"How about the bronze casket?"

"That type, whatever it was. It was already there." He was in the morgue and "the doors were open and I could see them come into the cold room." He saw the ornate casket and asked about it. He was told it was the Air Force major. "Do we need to log him into the morgue log?"

"No," he was told. "They said it was too late to take him to Arlington that afternoon. They'd take him over in the morning."[36]

Jan Gail Rudnicki, one of the other enlisted men present, told me that he had a vague recollection of a pick-up of the remains of someone else just before Kennedy's body arrived.[37]

Jerrol Custer, the X-ray tech, said that there was a shipping casket in the morgue but he had no knowledge of the President's body being in it. He said that there was a body of an officer there, in a body bag and in a shipping casket.[38]

The pages of the log were torn out and have never been found. There may have been some opportunity for a shell game of some kind between the two bodies, and it might explain some of the confusion between the caskets, the fact that there were two or more caskets present, that a body was in a body bag, and that a body had come in prior to Kennedy's official arrival.

There is one final, though almost fantastic proposition. The face in some of the autopsy photographs does not look altogether like Kennedy, or like that in some of the other pictures. In addition, because of some of the retouching in some of the pictures, it looks as though the face has been added onto the head in a composite. The X-ray of the skull certainly is not that of Kennedy. My mind is very resistant to the idea, but both Mark Crouch and I wonder that there may be a body double in some way involved. We know that the conspiracy that overthrew Kennedy was greatly sophisticated, and it would seem that the use of a substitute body might not be totally ridiculous. Nothing is too fantastic in this case.

For example, study closely the conflicts in the medical evidence alone, presented in the next chapter. And take a long look at the Right Superior Profile photograph of the body. The face is very white and looks like a much younger Kennedy. It is my opinion that the face has been added to another picture. I got a clue of that when a state police

homicide investigator told me that the entire hairline along the forehead looked painted in.

There is one final scenario, and that is that if the body was not at first
taken over to Walter Reed or somewhere else and operated on, then it
might have happened in some other part of the Bethesda hospital.
Certainly the story that Donald Rebentisch (one of the Navy enlisted
men at Bethesda) tells indicates that the body did not come in the
front, but that an empty casket did, and that Kennedy's casket came in
the back door. "I'm talking about the loading ramps where they used to
bring in supplies. . . . We took the casket out and pushed it down a
long, illuminated hall. Now, this is a service area, not the main part of
the hospital."[39]

Rebentisch describes the scuttlebutt that led to the kind of massive
problem in misinformation that we are now dealing with: "The chief
said we got all the . . . ghouls and reporters and the TV and everybody at the front of the hospital. He said there would be an empty
casket in the ambulance. He said the President's body would really
come in the back."[40] Grizzled old Navy chiefs have told stories like this
from time immemorial to young and foolish enlisted seamen. They
usually don't know more than anyone else. What Rebentisch helped
unload was the gray shipping casket from a black hearse a half hour
before Kennedy came in with the major's body.[41]

The men got some of these ideas because Captain Canada was distressed by the large crowds of people and multitude of reporters in and
around the hospital. "Frantic, he deliberately misled the press, announcing that the President's body would be taken to the emergency
entrance. Then he mobilized all off-duty corpsmen at the heliport. He
expected the worst. As it turned out, he couldn't have been wider of the
mark. The huge mob was to grow huger [sic], but it was docile. Like the
three thousand at Andrews, those here simply gazed."[42]

These people were *not* ghouls, as some have said. They were citizens
who were in shock, and, in a way, who were doing their duty. They were
watching as best they could. They were on guard. They were the ultimate Honor Guard for John Kennedy.

Rebentisch also said that he and five other Navy petty officers took
the coffin in. The *Herald* said that two other Navy men—Richard
Muma and Paul Neigler—had corroborated the story.

Again, like Dennis David, they did not see who was in the casket, and
it was likely the casket of the Air Force officer.

Paul O'Connor has made it clear that his use of the term "shipping casket" was not literal. He meant that it was an inexpensive viewing casket. Even Dr. Clark in Dallas thought it was a "plain plastic casket," as did another witness there. In the stress and pressure of events during those terrible hours, people made all sorts of mistakes, and their memories are not always perfect. In addition, there was a big difference in those days in Texas glitz, or what passed for class, and the real thing, a fact that confused and fooled those researchers who supposed the casket to be very ornate and ceremonial.

Since it is firmly claimed by all that the alleged picture of an intact back of the head was taken before the autopsy began, the picture cannot be true. As for the reconstruction of the skull and filling of it with plaster after the autopsy and before burial, see my comments below. No hairpiece was used.[43]

The alleged autopsy photo of the back of the head shows blood on it, and an entry wound, so it would not be possible that this was a *hairpiece* used in the reconstruction of the head after the autopsy. In addition, the morticians have denied using any hairpiece at all.[44] The coffin was then closed and taken to the White House. There is evidence that pictures continued to be taken right up to the closing of the coffin, but of course these are not in evidence or mentioned anywhere. We have been told that "hundreds" of photographs continued to be taken, but we cannot verify this. Joseph Hagen told me that there were a lot of pictures taken from the gallery (perhaps without a flash), and it is possible that some of the very grainy pictures that are now in evidence was taken from that distance and substituted for the autopsy photographs.

None of the autopsy photographs in evidence was taken after the autopsy or while the body was being prepared for the coffin. The body and head were perfectly clean when the morticians got it. There is no Y incision, and the photograph of the President's back as well as the back of the head shows the body has not been cleaned up. The scalp is bloody in the color pictures, showing that it is not a hairpiece, as some have suggested.

The *Nova* television show on the assassination unintentionally raised questions as to whether there was a set of photographs in the National Archives that showed things other than those in the three sets of photographs owned by former Secret Service agent James K. Fox (in the possession of Mark Crouch) and Robert Groden (which originated from the National Archives via the House Committee) and those seen, traced, and published by the House Committee in the late Seventies, which were claimed to be from the Archives. We all saw on screen doctors entering a room at the Archives where the cameras were not allowed and viewing something alleged to be the autopsy photographs. In addition, the black and white and color photos are not all identical to one another, but some appear to be, except that they may be colorized versions. If true, in addition to the forgeries, there is a major new fraud being perpetrated.

To digress, the National Archives and the Kennedy family lawyer see fit to deny access to this evidence to researchers, policemen (policemen working with me have been denied access), and to the press, but it was granted to phony and misleading shows such as *Nova* (which misrepresented much of the evidence) and the forensically unqualified Dr. Lattimer.

The doctors emerged from the room and said yes, the pictures represented what they saw in 1963. We wondered just what they *did* see. I reinterviewed most of the people who were on *Nova* and feel confident that what they were shown was no different from what we have published in *High Treason,* and not different in any way from any of the known photographs. I say this in spite of the fact that it does not help and perhaps hinders our thesis.

In other words, they were shown a picture of an intact back of the head. Dr. McClelland was led into something he later regretted, when he tried to explain it by saying that the hand seen in the picture was pulling up a flap of scalp to cover the missing bone. He was tricked into saying this in trying to explain how it *might* have happened. He also knows that the scalp was loose and in the form of a flap, but faced in the exact opposite direction. The hinge was on the left of the head, adjoining where we see a hand holding a supposed loose edge of a flap at the right top of the head. He didn't mean to say that it in fact happened that way, and promptly said to me, "Why do they cover it up?" He went on to agree that the X-rays totally contradicted the photographs, and specifically indicated that the forged X-rays were part of the cover-up.[45]

Dr. McClelland then strongly denounced the whole show as misleading and a lie. "We all know the fatal shot came from the Grassy Knoll." The denunciations of the witnesses were very strong. I had the clear impression that leading questions and clever editing were used to get the story they wanted, a common occurrence in this case, just as the

The scalp defect   Skull defect

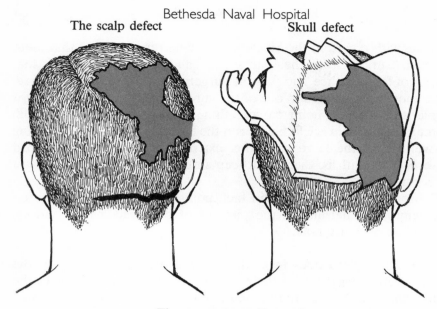

From author's sketch

The can opener effect

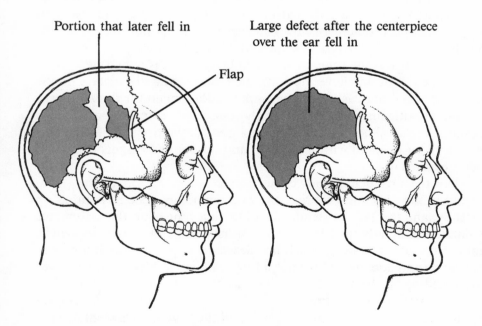

Portion that later fell in

Large defect after the centerpiece over the ear fell in

Flap

From author's sketch

Side view of skull

show did with regard to the Sibert and O'Neill report stating that there had been "surgery to the head area . . ." and then not telling you that the rest of the sentence said that the surgery was to the *top* of the head. The camera then panned to one of the autopsy photographs of the right temple and tried to point to something (a very faint bruise) which Walter Cronkite said might have been the "surgery" they were referring to, overlooking the large laceration extending into the forehead just above it. The truth is, there had been surgery there—to the *bone*—in the X-ray.

We wondered if they were, in fact, pointing to the retouching that exists along the hairline in the pictures of the head, which may be covering up an entry hole.

A crew of Navy enlistees in medical and dental tech schools at the hospital were roused out of their barracks to wait for and unload the coffin, with nobody else around. Some of them carried the coffin inside the morgue and removed the body from the casket and put it on the table. Could it be confused with another body, at least in their minds? Jim Metzler is very certain that it *was* the Dallas casket and that JFK was in it. The problem is, how can the body be gotten back into the Dallas casket if it arrived in some other casket?

Whether it was the same casket as in Dallas, that is not so clear, but I have little doubt. I believe the Navy men unloaded and carried into the cold room another casket, either empty and intended for the Air Force major, or with him inside. This is the one they are calling a shipping casket. A funeral home then brought a good casket for the officer. This was a major hospital with a morgue, and bodies and caskets came and went every day.

Then the President's body came.

According to some theories, the body may have been operated on already, and the bullets removed. All of that hinges on the statements of one man. In addition, bullets do not have to be in a body, especially military jacketed bullets, which are designed to pass through a body.

The motorcade arrived from Andrews Air Force Base with what was supposed to be the President in his casket. They came with a flock of Secret Service men, the President's widow and his brother, who got out of the hearse in front of the hospital, and then the hearse went around to the back, where there were two different unloading areas: the emergency room in one wing of the hospital on the first floor, and the autopsy room in another wing on a sub floor. William Greer, the driver of the fatal car in Dallas drove the ambulance with the bronze casket to the rear, and there Roy Kellerman, the Secret Service man from Dallas, and the FBI men helped unload it. It was taken into the morgue and set down.

X-rays were taken, and the autopsy room had to be cleared each time. Jerrol Custer, the X-ray tech taking the pictures, hand-carried—with an escort—the films upstairs to be developed.

There is only one person to say that the brain was loose in the skull when it arrived at Bethesda. I don't think that he saw Dr. Humes sever the brain stem. His statements to another author became that author's fact, as though the author discovered it, without mentioning that this witness at the autopsy was the source of it.[46]

Dr. Boswell, Dr. Karnei, and others at the autopsy have convinced me that the brain was not completely loose in the head and that it could not have come through the existing large hole in the back of the head without the enlargements they made, and without compressing it, which could have been done as Audrey Bell said, but why go to that trouble?

Paul O'Connor himself has said this, even though he has typified the brain as being partly or entirely blown away. The point is, the hole in the head was not large enough for *any* brain to go through, even one missing as much as Kennedy's was. Jenkins described to me one to three cuts that he thought were in the scalp or skull upon arrival of the body. These were so small, each no more than a half inch or so, if that, and one of them less than an inch, that it seems irrational that anyone would have done that, since it took more cuts to remove the existing brain. In addition, what other evidence is there that these were indeed pre-existing cuts? The fact is, Jenkins did not actually *see* the alleged cuts in the scalp and along the fracture and suture lines he posits were there, which would have allowed the brain to be removed beforehand. They could have been lacerations, normal tears as a result of the exploding skull.

It is a shame that upon such slender opinions an entire two-casket, body-theft-and-alteration theory was erected. It misled countless believers, and directed them away from possible tampering at Bethesda and certain forgery.

"Nobody got to it at Parkland, I can tell you that. The opening in the scalp was not big enough to go ahead and take the brain out," Dr. Robert Karnei told me.[47]

There was a laceration of the scalp extending into the forehead a half inch over the right eye, Dr. Karnei told me in the same interview, but there was no corresponding defect in the frontal bone. The frontal bone was almost completely intact, according to every witness. I have gotten this from the morticians as well as from Dr. Boswell.

Since the autopsy doctors have told me that the large hole was in fact more to the back of the head, where the autopsy report places it as starting, and that the scalp was not intact or whole back there, this and their other testimony puts the lie to the autopsy pictures. So I don't think they have any reason to lie about the one point concerning the brain having been previously cut loose with a knife.

Surgeons at Parkland made a large incision in the President's throat and placed a large tracheal cuff there with a flange. There might have been an opportunity to remove a bullet at that time. But there wasn't any significant damage to his trachea, and it is just plain irrational that a bullet hit him anywhere in the back and came out by the larynx. *Something* hit him in the throat, but what was it? It would seem that it could be a frozen bullet, very small, which the FBI suspected at the autopsy,[48] and which immobilized Kennedy.

The problem with that is, why bother, instead of hitting him in the head first? If they had missed with the first shot, Kennedy would have gotten down out of the way, so he was hit in the neck first by a crack sniper, frozen into place, and then the fusillade began. Rifles would be stupid and unnecessary at some of the close ranges in Dealey Plaza— even against a moving target. Handguns were much more practical, though I have no doubt that one or two rifles were used from much more of a distance than we suppose.

We know that people used false identification that day. We even have people showing up at the autopsy in Maryland who gave names to the FBI men present whom we can find no trace of, such as Dr. George Bakeman, whose name they took.[49] It did not take a doctor to dig in the brain to find a bullet.

The hole in the skull was larger than that in Dallas and in precisely the same spot that the autopsy witnesses place it. The hole through the scalp was about three inches across, true, but the defect in the bone was larger, and that was noted in Dallas. In addition, a large piece of bone above the right ear fell in during the examination at Bethesda, making the large defect in the back communicate and extend to the flap above and just in front of the right ear—beneath some intact scalp. The flap then also fell off. That meant the whole right side of the head all the way to the back and to the top of the head was gone.

What we had in a popularly marketed video and its book were serious distortions of fact and semantic confusions. Important distinctions were not made, for instance, between the exit hole in the scalp and the exit hole in the bone, which was larger. Laceration becomes incision in the mind of the reader or listener, and body tampering becomes body alteration.

Since most of the people writing about this case are trained primarily in a visual or mathematical profession such as engineering, architecture, or accounting, there has long been a serious language problem. Architects and draftsmen are pretty sure they can solve the case with a lot of lines and trajectory analysis. Their lines actually tied a lot of people up in knots for years. Engineers dealing with physics or structure are often incompetent when it comes to medicolegal forensic medicine and oral or written testimony.

O'Connor simply was not in the room when the brain was removed.[50] He has given numerous widely differing descriptions of the amount of brain missing, and therefore he was only guessing. When his own close relative, Jim Jenkins, describes the whole procedure of removing the brain and infusing it, then one or the other is wrong. We have to go with the weight of the evidence.

It often seems as though we are talking about two different bodies and two different sets of wounds. I am inclined to think that the conflicts in the evidence stem more from semantics and normal misperceptions under great stress, rather than actual differences in fact.

> "Let us, if we can, step back from the shadows of war
> and seek out the way of peace. And if that journey is
> one thousand miles, or even more, let history record
> that we, in this land, at this time, took the first step."
>
> —John F. Kennedy, when he concluded
> the Nuclear Test Ban Treaty

CHAPTER 6

THE AUTOPSY:
SOME CONFLICTS IN THE EVIDENCE

Sometimes I think when I study the alleged evidence presented from the alleged autopsy of the alleged body of President Kennedy, that it wasn't really his body. They used a look-alike.

Carefully investigating this so that no one knew what was troubling me, I would ask—when showing witnesses the autopsy pictures depicting the President's face—is that him? Is that the way the face looked?

"That's the way he looked."

"That's him all right."

But sometimes someone would ask me, "Is that him? It doesn't look like him."

One person at the autopsy, Paul O'Connor, said that Kennedy looked emaciated. Everybody else said he was fit and in the pink of good health. Some think that the Groden Superior Right Profile picture is of a wax head and not real, and police have told me that at least part of that picture—the tissue hanging over the hair on the top of the head —is painted in, and the hairline along the forehead is painted in.

One says he thinks the body came in just as the last light left the sky— which was about 5:30—long before Jackie Kennedy and the Dallas casket was supposed to have arrived, and Paul O'Connor says Kennedy came in at eight P.M., but he means that the autopsy started then. Officially, the body is supposed to have gotten to Bethesda at seven P.M., but others say it had to be at 7:35 P.M. It could not take that long to get from Andrews Air Force Base, leaving at 6:15 or so, after a forty-five-minute trip. Dr. Humes told the Warren Commission that it came in at twenty-five minutes to eight.[1]

What happened during the long hour before the autopsy official started at eight P.M., or at 8:15, as the House Committee found, along with the FBI report? Kenny O'Donnell told the Warren Commission that it took forty-five minutes to get from Andrews Air Force Base to Bethesda.[2] In fact, it could not have taken them any longer. The plane landed at six o'clock, and the body was removed and the ambulance left at a quarter after six. The body had to have arrived by seven P.M.

Some of the men from the autopsy insist that Kennedy was not in the bronze casket, but another cheaper one, and a leading doctor at Parkland said it was nothing but a plain plastic casket, leading us to wonder if the funeral director in Dallas cheated the government. According to one document, the funeral director in Dallas, Vernon Oneal, eventually collected an extra ten thousand dollars in addition to the already exorbitant fee he had billed the government. And did he then get the casket back or didn't he?

So one might wonder just whose body was autopsied. I am only half serious when I ask this. I imagine it to be Kennedy. But there are so many questions and so many things that don't add up.

For instance, James Curtis Jenkins, who was there, and as far as I am concerned, a major witness at this late stage in the living history of that tragic event, asks how could Humes say so much and write so much about the brain without having dissected and examined it? It would not be possible, he thinks. But Jenkins is not a neurosurgeon, and Dr. Cyril Wecht, coroner of Allegheny County, Pennsylvania, tells me Humes could have seen what he wrote about. After all, the right hemisphere of the brain was torn apart, split along its whole length down to the corpus callosum.

The Chest Tubes

Dr. Charles Wilber asks similar questions: How could the autopsy doctors not discover that the cuts made in Dallas for the chest tubes penetrated the chest? Everyone at the autopsy says that the pleural cavity was not violated. Not by anything, even a bullet. They said the cuts where the chest tubes would have gone were superficial. This certainly contradicts some of the Dallas medical evidence.

"The inability of the pathologists to find evidence of perforation of the inner chest wall by drainage tubes inserted before death by skilled surgeons raises questions about the surgeons or the pathologists. Either the emergency room surgeons botched a routine life-saving procedure or the autopsy pathologists were less than thorough."[3]

Dr. Humes told the Warren Commission: "We examined these wounds very carefully, and found that they, however, did not enter the chest cavity. They only went through the skin. I presume that as they were performing that procedure, it was obvious that the President had died, and they didn't pursue this."[4]

I have interviewed the Dallas doctors and nurses with respect to the chest tubes, and, according to numerous doctors, they were put inside the chest. But there was an indication that they did not finish the job when it was apparent that Kennedy was actually dead. They pretended that he was alive until they could get a priest. So, they too may have fudged some things. In the end there was some fudging here and there by a lot of people, some of whom meant well and had no sinister intent, and that fudging has helped cloud our perception and prevent much possibility of fully discovering or understanding the truth.

The report of Parkland's Dr. Kemp Clark published by the Warren Commission says that "anterior chest tubes were placed in both pleural spaces. These were connected to sealed underwater drainage."[5] Dr. James Carrico told the House Committee investigators the following: "When the chest tubes were inserted, there was a small amount of blood, and a small amount of air, which could have resulted from the actual surgical manipulations or could conceivably be commensurate or compatible with some very small pneumothorax or hemothorax. But basically the chest tubes did not show any signs of massive injury and did not in their insertion improve the situation."

"Did you have sufficient facts from which you could conclude that the pleural cavity was violated?"

"No, we did not."

"Did you believe it was likely that the pleural cavity was violated?"

"We felt there was a high risk that it had been. . . ."[6] Dr. Charles Baxter inserted the chest tube on the right side, and Dr. Ronald Jones put the tube in on the left side.

If one is to choose between the credibility of the doctors from either hospital, the Dallas physicians are the more credible. Unfortunately, the Navy doctors have little credibility, after fudging their report and changing their story too often. In fact, the Navy doctors have given us much of the real story as they dared. It is just very difficult to interpret. I believe that although they may have actually or figuratively had a gun at their head, they have tried in certain coded ways to let us know at least some of the truth, if often between the lines.

It is possible that one group of doctors might be wrong on some points, and right on others, of course.

The Brain

Again, the question has to be asked: "Was that John Kennedy's brain they wrote about in the Supplemental Autopsy Report?"

I ask it because they listed the weight of the brain as 1500 grams. That is the size of a normal brain.

Second, the men at the autopsy reported that at least a quarter of it was missing. So did the witnesses at Parkland Hospital. Granted the possibility that John Kennedy may have possessed a larger brain than usual, it would still seem abnormally large after a quarter of it was blown away. His head was of normal size.

But other questions remain about the brain when the men say that the brain and lacerations described looked nothing like what they saw.

It would seem possible or probable if we believe that there was an examination made before Bethesda and there appeared to be surgery to the head area, as well as a neatly severed brain stem (in James Curtis Jenkins's speculation), that this was not John Kennedy's brain. After all, "it looked rather small," Jenkins told me. "It looked like the brain of a female." That happens. A brain dehydrates and shrinks over the hours. This one lost a lot of fluid from its wound.

In my opinion, due to the angle of the President's head when he received a shot from the front, fired from just above him but almost horizontally, that shot would have cut into the corpus callosum, which was lacerated.

Charles Wilber wrote me that "a rather interesting paragraph is found in the Supplemental Autopsy Report. The right hemisphere of the brain was obviously demolished. The left hemisphere is claimed to be 'intact.' It is further reported that there is *MARKED* over-stuffing or super-filling of the blood vessels of the brain covering (meningeal vessels) on the left hemisphere. This *engorgement* extends from the left temporal region to the frontal region accompanied by 'considerable *associated* subarachnoid haemorrhage.' Subarachnoid space is that area over the brain that lies between the tough outer protective covering of the brain (dura mater) and the delicate inner covering (pia mater). The arachnoid layer of the brain covering is in this space; sometimes it is called the middle serious membrane of the meninges. A subarachnoid haemorrhage is a bleeding into the space between the pia mater and the arachnoid membrane. But then we are told that the gyre and sulci of the left hemisphere are essentially normal. Later we are told that tissue samples are taken from the 'contused left frontoparietal *cortex.*' Under the microscope, sections from this left brain sample were essentially similar to all sections taken from other parts of the brain which show *'EXTENSIVE DISRUPTION OF BRAIN TISSUE WITH ASSO-CIATED HAEMORRHAGE.'* These observations rekindle my interest in the observations made in Dallas on the ER table (by several medical personnel) to the effect that there was an entry hole in the left temporal region, in front of the left ear and at the hair line."[7]

The Supplemental Autopsy Report tells us about the brain—that "in the interest of preserving the specimen, coronal sections are not made."[8] Wilber points out that the doctors are here admitting that they did not dissect the brain as must be done in the case of a gunshot wound, and according to the Armed Forces Institute of Pathology autopsy protocol.

What is of the gravest importance here to the official history are the questions James Curtis Jenkins asked. "How in the world could Dr. Humes write what he wrote without dissecting the brain? How could he say all of this?" Jenkins asked that "if they did not section the brain, how did they find the internal radiating lacerations described by Humes?"

Jenkins, noting that the corpus callosum is buried in the brain, asks how Humes without sectioning the brain could have known that the corpus was lacerated? Humes described the ventricles and the mid-brain, yet could not see any of this without dissecting the brain. He does not mention the blood vessels, doesn't mention the internal carotids, circle of Willis (where the carotids enter the brain), does not really describe the brain stem or peduncle being severed. Richard Waybright, a Baltimore City police officer working for me, comments that it was

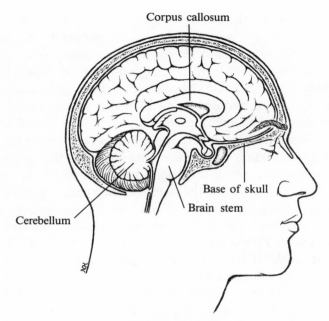

Corpus callosum

Base of skull

Brain stem

Cerebellum

Sagittal section of brain

easy for Humes to see this since "the right hemisphere was largely destroyed by the bullet to the head, thus exposing the corpus."[9]

If a bullet severed the brain stem, where did it go? It did not go through the floor of the skull and up.

If the terrific pressure of the high-powered rifle bullet that presumably entered the skull had torn the brain loose from its stem, the stem would look like taffy that is pulled apart, lacerated and mangled. Stringy. But it did not. The men who saw it say that it was smoothly cut. "I have seen torn brain stems," Jenkins told me, "and they did not look like that."[10] Perhaps what he saw was the cut Humes made before the brain fell out in his hands.

But Charles Wilber says there is a bit to support the idea. He wrote me that "with respect to Jenkins's observations, it is interesting that a sample of tissue, for microscopic examination, was taken from the 'line of transection of the spinal cord.' *No* report was given on the microscopic reading of that tissue. There was a 'superficial' laceration of the basilar aspect of the left temporal lobe; sample for micro was taken. Reported as same as all the brain micro-sections."[11]

Drs. Wecht and Wilber and other pathologists tell me that a bullet cannot severe a brain stem, and it would be *below* the floor of the skull, in any event.

The brain shows through the opening in the very top of the skull in the autopsy photographs, which is the only significant defect that might correspond to what everyone described, though not in that area. The brain *cannot* show there, if that is the large defect described by everyone, because it is intact, and there was a large gouge of brain missing corresponding to the large skull defect, according to Humes in his testimony before the Warren Commission.

Mark Crouch writes: "There is as much confusion surrounding whether the brain is visible in the autopsy photographs as there is surrounding the brain itself at the actual autopsy. One point which helps cloud this issue in the photographs [which is discussed in more depth in Chapter 15] deals with a possible 'colorization' of the photos leaked by the HSCA. The importance of colorization can be appreciated only if one understands that by camouflaging what is clearly brain tissue by painting it red, you greatly confuse what is scalp and what is brain, and therefore confuse how much scalp was missing and where."[12]

The Cerebellum

James Curtis Jenkins said, "I don't remember major damage to the cerebellum. There was major damage to the brain, however."[13] The opinion that the cerebellum was not significantly damaged is backed up by the doctors at the autopsy, and their report. I have a major problem with that because we cannot once again ignore the testimony of the Dallas witnesses.

"The cerebellum was swinging in the breeze."[14] As detailed in *High Treason* and the Warren Report, many of the Dallas witnesses saw the cerebellum out of the head.

"The brain that I saw basically had the cerebellum intact," Jenkins told a meeting of medical witnesses from the hospitals in Dallas and Bethesda which I arranged on April 6, 1991, in Dallas.

Either the autopsy report was fabricated in this regard, due to the necessity of moving the large defect from the back of the head and around to the side or front and top, or we are again dealing with a different body or a different brain.

Spinal Cord

Jenkins describes removing the spinal cord with a Stryker saw, but Dr. Karnei does not remember it having been removed. When I tried to ask Dr. Humes if it had been removed, he hung up on me.[15] Dr. Boswell told me that the cord was not removed.[16]

The question of removal and examination of the spinal cord is important because this would tell us if the tuberculosis Kennedy had been exposed to as a child had been reactivated by the steroids he was being given, and only examination of the tissues of the spinal cord would tell this.

Normally during an autopsy the spinal cord is removed and its condition is reported.

Paul O'Connor reported to me that his spine did not look very well.[17]

The Large Defect

The autopsy report placed the damage as follows: "There is a large irregular defect of the scalp and skull on the right involving chiefly the parietal bone, but extending somewhat into the temporal and occipital regions. In this region there is an actual absence of scalp and bone producing a defect which measures approximately 13 cm. in greatest diameter." *There is no mention of frontal bone* here, which is vastly important, since most or all of the right frontal bone is missing in the X-rays.

In Dallas, of course, the rear of the head was missing, with no damage to the front of the head. After seeing the X-rays at the House of Representatives in 1978, the autopsy radiologist, Dr. John Ebersole, and one of his X-ray technicians, Edward F. Reed (in 1988), said the hole was in the right front of the head. They were totally alone in this perception. The autopsy radiologist described it as being over the right ear, mid portion of the head, measuring around two by three inches. "He emphatically states that 'no rear portion of the head was missing.' "[18] His X-ray assistant, Edward Reed, placed it exactly there also.[19] They are the only witnesses in the entire case who find that the only exit or large defect for the fatal head shot is on that part of the head, in the right temple and forehead, and not in the back of the head.

But Ebersole had said the exact opposite *before* he was shown the new —phony—X-rays he supposedly took himself. He had proclaimed that the back of the head was missing, and that the face was intact.

Interestingly, that is the only large defect on the X-rays, which show that the eye would have been blown away, along with all that part of the face.

There is more trouble with what Ebersole had to say. He told Gil Delaney: "When the body was removed from the casket, there was a very obvious horrible gaping wound to the back of the head."[20] "The front of the body, except for a very slight bruise above the right eye on the forehead, was absolutely intact. It was the back of the head that was blown off."[21]

He said this before he looked at the X-rays in Washington at the House Committee in 1978. When he returned, the X-rays had changed his recollection totally. This cannot be. Ebersole had seen the skull X-rays a month after the assassination and did not change his opinion then. He saw different X-rays in 1978.

Dr. Humes told the Warren Commission: "The third obvious wound at the time of the examination was a huge defect over the *right side of the skull*. This defect involved both the scalp and the underlying skull, and from the brain substance was protruding. This wound measured approximately 13 centimeters in greatest diameter."[22] Humes further defines it as being in the "right lateral vertex of the skull. . . . There was a defect in the scalp and some scalp tissue was not available. . . . We concluded that the large defect to the upper right side of the skull, in fact, would represent a wound of exit."[23] "This area was devoid of any scalp or skull at this present time. We did not have the bone."[24] The autopsy photographs show all the scalp present in that area.

But Arlen Specter did not want the large defect on the right side. He wanted it on top. Of course, others wanted it in *front*, where it appears in the X-rays of the skull. It had started off *behind*, in the rear of the head, and the autopsy report had a good part of it there to begin with, before *each and every wound* began to move somewhere else on the body as time went by and the cover-up continued.

What we have is a fog drawn over the evidence.

As everyone knows by now, every medical witness—in fact every witness to the events in Dallas—said that the back of the President's head was blown off. At the autopsy this wound stayed in the same place. It encompassed part of the top of the head (parietal), extending down to the very back of the head, not far from the hairline. There was no scalp

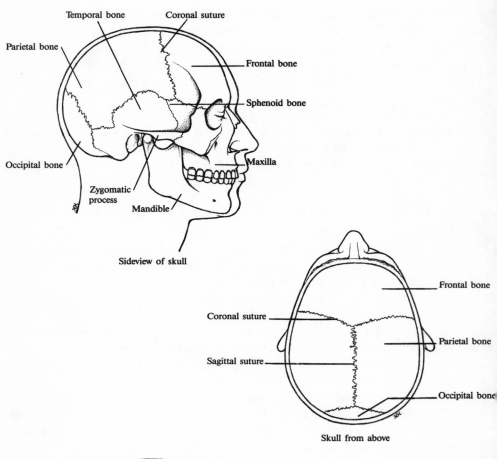

Sideview of skull

Skull from above

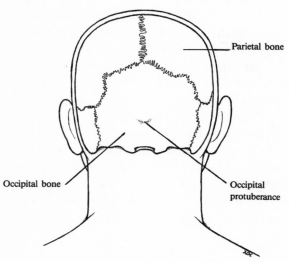

Rear view of skull

or bone in the center of this area covering part of the occiput and part of the parietal area.

There was no bone at all for the largest part of this area, extending some thirteen centimeters, but some shredded scalp remained over part of it. A partial flap existed in Dallas as was later described by witnesses from the autopsy. There was little scalp and bone in the back, but there was a flap of shredded scalp hanging down over the back of the head. Nevertheless, it could not have been drawn over the hole to look as neat and perfect as it does in the present photographs.

By the time Dr. Humes testified to the Warren Commission, the wound seemed to have moved around to the right side of the head and no longer was primarily in the back of the head at all. Yet, Specter asks Humes, "Would you state for the record the size and approximate dimension of the major wound on the top of the head which you have marked wound B?" *Top.*

"This was so large, that localization of it in a descriptive way is somewhat difficult. However, we have mentioned that its major—its greatest dimension was approximately 13 cm."[25] Here we find the wound on *top* of the head, where it is in the photographs, showing all of the brain intact just beneath where the skull is missing.

And we see the large defect on top in the photographs but nowhere else. Not even on the side, other than a small flap of scalp and bone.

The Zapruder film shows us an enormous effusion of apparent brain matter from the right front of the face and temple, but the rest of the front of the head is missing in a few frames. We see only the crescent of the President's hair from the right ear straight up and then back and down the silhouette of the right rear of his hair. All the rest of the head and face are missing. One gets the distinct impression that the effusion from the head is painted on those frames of the film, and that in one of the frames the entire image was superimposed on the background but omitting the face and top of the head forward of the ears.

In a preceding frame there is a black spot—reference *black*—over the place where the witnesses said the skull was blown away. Two of the frames appear to show the hole in the posterior part of the head, about where the photographs show what is alleged to be an entry hole today.

If this is true, the film is quite a forgery. What we have been getting during presentations of the film is a subliminal message that the President had a big exit wound in the face. It is so gory that no one has ever questioned it. The Zapruder film was clandestinely obtained from

Moses Weitzmann whose photo lab processed and then stored the film for *Life* magazine.

Paul O'Connor, Dr. Robert Karnei, and others have said that the hole was not large enough for the brain to be removed without more cuts being made, and yet there is a theory that it had been taken out before it ever got to Bethesda.

As for the top of the head being the locus of the large defect, the autopsy personnel say no, that that wasn't where it was. Nobody in Dallas saw it there, that is for sure.

I think that the answer to all this is that Dr. Humes was essentially correct in his description to Specter. Both Paul O'Connor[26] and Jerrol Custer[27] have made it clear to me that the large defect that they saw did in fact extend from the occiput all the way around the right side of the head as far as just in to the front of the right ear, and that the open flap of bone hanging from a shred of scalp which we see in the photographs was the farthest extent of the wound, but that there was only skin or scalp holding the head together above the right ear until it and the bone attached to it fell in during the examination. Custer made the comment to Ebersole that night that "the only thing that is holding this man's head together is the skin around his face. There was nothing intact."[28] This may explain what appears to me in the last frames of the Zapruder film. There, we can see the head as it sinks to the seat after the fatal shot, the apparent collapse of much of the head.

Custer said that the hole in the temple was continuous to the very back of the head but the frontal bone was not damaged. And of course he denounces the X-rays as forgeries and as being nothing that he or anyone else could have taken at the autopsy. What we essentially have, then, are two major holes through the scalp: One in the back, and one in front of the right ear when the flap is open. As explained in *High Treason,* Jacqueline must have closed it, because no one except Dr. Robert Grossman at Parkland noticed the hole or flap on the side of the head. Grossman saw the fracture line, he says.

"Do you feel that the large defect was enlarged to work there?" I asked O'Connor. "No. It was big enough to do anything you wanted to do."[29] But apparently they did not try to remove the brain without two or three cuts in the scalp and bone to get it though, even though Audrey Bell thought that with some effort it could have been squeezed out. And Paul O'Connor at other times said that the hole was not quite big enough for what remained of the brain to come out.

I think that there is no doubt that the entire back of the head was missing beneath what scalp remained, but that later on during the rough trip to Washington or at the beginning stages of the autopsy a bit more bone fell in along the right side, and that is what was described by Humes, Custer, and O'Connor.

The Forehead-Frontal Bone

Since no witness at Bethesda or Parkland described any damage to the right side of the face, the large hole on the skull including most or all of the right eye, the orbit bottom to top, and the right temple area and forehead cannot be Kennedy's skull. No one has suggested that any part of the bone from the face fell in either before the body arrived or while it was at Bethesda. We know that it was intact during the autopsy and at the end.

In addition, if pieces of bone had fallen in, they would show somewhere in the X-rays and were put back by the doctors later. They were certainly not the pieces of bone that arrived after the autopsy and that were associated only with the large hole in the head toward the rear.

Paul O'Connor is adamant that there was no tampering with the head at the autopsy. He helped fill the cranium with plaster and prepared the body for the morticians. When they got it, it was clean. Speaking of whether or not the frontal bone had been removed, he told me that "there was nothing enlarged that night at the autopsy. Whatever enlargements were made were made before we got the body. . . . Everything in the forehead was intact up to his hairline. Those X-rays are phony. Everything past the hairline—frontal, parietal, temporal, occipital, was gone."[30] But he means a little farther back on the top of the head.

Paul O'Connor, though, was several times out of the room, going to central supply for one thing or another, and these trips took some time. We know that there are matters that he missed that night.

Rear-Head Entry

Then there is the movement of the alleged entry hole in the back of the head some four to five inches from where the autopsy report placed it. None of the enlisted men at the autopsy says he ever saw this, and even the radiologist told Art Smith that "no entrance wound can be seen on the rear of the skull."[31] But Humes and Boswell and the other doctors say that it was there, but low down, near the hairline, just to the right of the occipital protuberance. Their autopsy report placed it just *above* and to the right of the occipital protuberance. Both doctors insisted to the panel of doctors interviewing them years later for the House Committee that it was just *below* it.[32] Humes later was forced by Gary Cornwall, deputy chief counsel of the Assassinations Committee, to retract this during his staged public hearing before the committee, and it moved *five inches* higher.[33]

The Clark Panel of doctors found when examining the alleged autopsy photographs and X-rays that it had moved some *four inches above* where Humes had placed it in his report. This is where the official story and the official controllers of our written history wanted it to end up, so as to give an upward trajectory to that shot coming from the sixth-floor window of the Depository.

They had to have an upward trajectory leading to that window, and the autopsy report didn't give it to them. The unseen hand was at work all these years changing the evidence.

Perhaps some of the answer is in Humes's cryptic statement to the full Warren Commission: "Scientifically, sir, it is impossible for it to have been fired from other than behind. Or to have exited from other than behind."[34] What did he mean by that? Today the enlisted men from the autopsy want to ask him: "Do you think that President Kennedy was struck twice in the head, once from behind, and once from in front?" Note the drawings reproduced in this book and made by James Jenkins, one of the autopsy personnel, which show the evidence he saw for two shots to the head.

The photograph of the large defect in the back of the head shows a semicircle on the edge of the *parietal* bone roughly in the midline and above the occiput. This is referred to as the *exit* due to the beveling on the outer table. A good picture of this is diagramed by the House,[35] and the key point is that it is clearly in the back of the head, where Humes told the Warren Commission it was. Of course, this in itself tends to blow the whole theory that the shot came from behind out of the water.

Scalp Laceration

The Right Superior Profile photograph shows a long laceration starting about a half inch into the forehead above the right eye (the "V" notch) and extending straight back to the occiput—according to both Dr. Boswell and Dr. Karnei in their interviews with me. Paul O'Connor told me that the laceration corresponded to a fracture line on the skull.[36]

Nobody saw any such fracture or laceration of the scalp in Dallas, to my knowledge. During transit to Bethesda, movement of the head in the coffin might conceivably have caused the broken bone, if it existed there, to break the scalp. Dr. Crenshaw suggests that it is in fact an incision, as Joanne Braun, a researcher, suggests. Crenshaw thinks it is the type of cut made at an autopsy to reflect the scalp back, and it certainly would have had to have been cut there in order to remove the frontal bone to make the fake X-ray.

In light of the descriptions and lack of photographic evidence, it is unlikely that the laceration extended all the way to the back of the head, since it seems more rational that the scalp above the ear was intact, as both O'Connor and Custer have told me, and that is what held the head together, since both they and the doctors say that the bone had fallen in or was missing underneath.

In addition, the head was bowed at the time of the fatal shot, and this laceration would have pointed pretty much straight up and down, toward the sky and ground, and it is also unlikely that it represents the crease of a bullet. But that is just my opinion.

Throat Wound

This wound started out as an entrance wound in Dallas and it became an exit wound in Washington.

But all that the autopsy doctors saw was an incision, two inches across, and they never examined the margins of that wound and saw the round cut made by a bullet going in or even coming out. Therefore the doctors lied when they said that they had seen a pathway from the wound in the back wherever it went out through this hole. They did not even know about it. "Attempts to probe in the vicinity of this wound were unsuccessful without fear of making a false passage," Dr. Humes told the Warren Commission.[37]

The whole report was fudged on this point, but it laid the groundwork for the crazy theory the two Republicans, Gerald Ford and Arlen Specter, would invent to say that one bullet hit Kennedy and Connally.

Dr. Crenshaw told me that the cut that Dr. Malcolm Perry made was much smaller and that he never would have made such a cut. The original report I had in 1979 from an interview I arranged but was not present for with Dr. Perry indicated that the cut was not the one he made. Dr. Perry will not dispute the photograph showing a two-inch cut, which Audrey Bell[38] and all other Parkland witnesses—some of whom were filmed[39]—now have told me is accurate. Perry himself indicated to me that the photograph is accurate, though I admit the manner in which he did so was greatly convoluted and mysterious.

Dr. John Ebersole did in fact claim that the wound had arrived from Dallas neatly sutured, when there was no evidence for this whatsoever.[40]

The government of the United States was not only taken away from its chief elected representative, John Kennedy, with bullets—but the crime was covered up by his political enemies.

Back Wound

This wound started out six inches down the President's back and it was gradually moved up to the shoulder, about three inches below the shoulder, and then to the neck. First it was a wound of "the upper right posterior thorax," according to Humes in his autopsy report, but by the time he talked to the Warren Commission, it became a neck wound. There is something of a difference.

Since the back wound was not proven at the autopsy to have come out the throat[41] it had to penetrate something in order to satisfy an ambitious young prosecutor on his eventual way to the United States Senate. Arlen Specter managed to get each witness before him to reverse something in order to conform with the cover-up he was perpetrating, though perhaps unwittingly.

Specter made a career ignoring truth, accusing its messengers of perjury, and accepting what was politically expedient. His hatred for at least one Kennedy was clearly apparent during the Senate confirmation

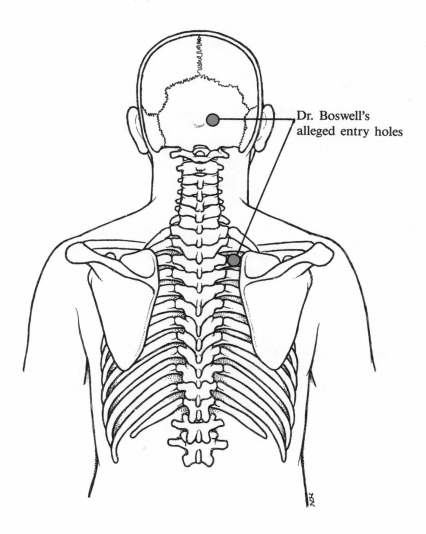

Dr. Boswell's
alleged entry holes

hearings of Clarence Thomas in October 1991, and during which he
accused Professor Anita Hill, an unblemished woman with no reason or
motive to lie, of "flat-out perjury."

Roy Kellerman, the Secret Service man in the front seat of the President's limousine, tried to explain that the bullet that hit Kennedy in the
back did not go anywhere, let alone through the body. He testified that
"a Colonel Finck—during the examination of the President, from the
hole that was in his shoulder, and with a probe, and we were standing
right alongside of him, he is probing inside the shoulder with his instru-

ment and I said 'Colonel, where did it go?' He said, 'There are no lanes for an outlet of this entry in this man's shoulder.' "[42]

If Kennedy was in fact hit in the shoulder or the back, where did the bullet go? They at first thought the bullet had fallen out at Parkland. Was the hole in the back manufactured somewhere along the line, as some of the more crackpot critics suggest?

And did Kellerman really say it was in the "shoulder," or did someone change his testimony? I ask this because some of the other men said they saw the bullet hole six inches down on Kennedy's back. "I saw an opening in the back, about 6 inches below the neckline to the right-hand side of the spinal column."[43] There is no possible way that six inches down on the back, which coincides with the holes in his shirt and coat, could be confused with the apparently painted-in wound two or three inches from the shoulder line in the photograph. Maybe it's just a clot.

Because of the position of the obvious hole (a deep depression in the back) perhaps even lower than six inches in the same photograph, it seems to me that the bullet struck his back brace and therefore was stopped and apparently fell out somewhere, as some have described, without penetrating inside the body.

Francis X. O'Neill told me that the back wound did not penetrate the chest, describing the probing exactly as had Jenkins and Finck.[44] "They used a surgical probe and it just went in so far. In fact, there was a question as to how could it go in and not come out. And Jim Sibert went out and called the FBI laboratories and asked if there was such a thing as an ice bullet. When he came back in we just learned that they had found a bullet on a stretcher in Dallas. That explained it." Or, rather, headed it off at the pass. "As far as you could see, it did not penetrate into the chest?"

"As far as I could see, it did not penetrate."

Floyd Riebe, the Navy photographer at the autopsy, claimed that the lower hole was the wound.

Study carefully the language of the FBI report: "During the later stages of this autopsy, Dr. Humes located an opening which *appeared* [emphasis added] to be a bullet hole which was below the shoulders and two inches to the right of the middle line of the spinal column. This opening was probed by Dr. Humes with the finger, at which time it was determined that the trajectory of the missile entering at this point had entered at a downward position of 45 to 60 degrees. Further probing determined that the distance traveled by this missile was a short distance inasmuch as the end of the opening could be felt with the finger.

"Inasmuch as no complete bullet of any size could be located in the brain area and likewise no bullet could be located in the back or any other area of the body as determined by total body X-rays and *inspection revealing there was no point of exit* [emphasis added], the individuals performing the autopsy were at a loss to explain why they could find no bullets."[45]

Dr. Humes, testifying to the Warren Commission, talked about the back and throat wound. He said, "We examined carefully the bony structures in this vicinity as well as the X-rays, to see if there was any evidence of fracture or of deposition of metallic fragments in the depths of this wound, and we saw no such evidence, that is, no fracture of the bones of the shoulder girdle, or of the vertical column, and no metallic fragments were detectable by X-ray examination."[46]

Compare this with *neck region:* "Several small metallic fragments are present in this region." This was when the Clark Panel examined the films and X-rays in 1968.

Humes has the courage to tell us and the Warren Commission that the bullet that he says may have passed through Kennedy could not be the one they say went through Connally. "I think that extremely unlikely. The reports, again Exhibit 392 from Parkland, tell of an entrance wound on the lower mid-thigh of the Governor, and X-rays taken there are described as showing metallic fragments in the bone, which apparently by this report were not removed and are still present in Governor Connally's thigh. I can't conceive of where they came from this missile."[47]

For once we have every single medical witness in the case agreed in both Dallas and Bethesda. But do you know what this means? If two different bullets hit both men during the space of one and a half seconds, there were *two* men firing at them from *behind,* plus a gunman firing from in front of the car.

The fact is, the photographs of the back have it both ways: There are *two* bullet holes in the back. I'm the only person who ever noticed that. Why?

What Senator Arlen Specter and the Warren Commission then did was perpetrate upon the people of the United States the most colossal lie in history. Specter claimed that a bullet struck President Kennedy in the back of the neck and came out his chest, striking John Connally. This is the famous "Magic" Bullet Theory. It truly is magic!

Tissues

Dr. Charles Wilber, the eminent forensic pathologist, writes: "A listing of tissues that were sampled for microscopic examination was given in this supplement. Brief descriptions of the microscopic sections of the following organs were given: brain at torn edges, heart, lungs, liver, spleen, kidneys, and skin wounds. No mention was made of endocrine organs such as thyroid or adrenals. No reference was made to sections from the anterior throat wound (skin or tracheal cartilages). Apparently no bone was taken from the edges of the bullet entry hole in the back of the head.[48]

"The skin wounds mentioned were confusing. 'Sections through wounds in the occipital and upper right posterior thoracic regions are essentially similar.' Note the admission that the wound in the back of the President's body was in the thoracic (chest) region, not the cervical (neck) region. How could a section through the scalp at the back of the head be 'essentially similar' to a section through the hairless skin of the posterior thorax? A beginning histology student knows differently.

"No mention was made of signs of putrefaction or autolysis in the various tissue sections at the cellular level. The President was pronounced legally dead about one P.M. Dallas time. The President's remains were logged into Bethesda Naval Hospital at about 7:35 P.M. November 22, 1963.[49] 'X-rays and photographs were taken preliminarily and the pathological examination began at about eight P.M., EST.'[50]

"At one P.M. in the heat of Dallas, the remains had been put into a casket; no mention of embalming or refrigeration was made. The dead body was transported from Texas to Maryland. Tissue samples were not fixed any earlier than the time the autopsy began, i.e., about eight P.M. It is strange that all the sections were 'normal' and that none showed cellular signs of decomposition. Liver and lung are prone to break down relatively quickly after death; spleen also does not resist decomposition. In the supplemental report the liver sections showed well-preserved normal cell structure. Lung and kidney sections showed nothing remarkable."[51]

Is this Kennedy's body a good ten hours before they took specimens?

Casket and Body Bag

There is considerable dispute over what casket the President arrived in and when. A few of the men believe the body arrived before Jacqueline Kennedy and the party from Dallas, and that it came in a different casket and was either wrapped in a body bag, or zipped in one. This evidence is very slender at best, and the memories of the men saying one or another of the above is faulty in regard to some other details. Paul O'Connor told the investigator for the House Committee that the body came wrapped in a body bag.[52] He has repeated this many times.

Jerrol Custer has also stated to me that the body came in a body bag.[53]

Custer had been called to the morgue right away in the early part of the evening. "Seven?" "Yeah, it would have to be around there, because it was after dinner—it'd have to be at least a couple of hours after dinner." He was in the morgue when the body came in, and saw it come out of the casket. "I was off to the side, and they took the body out of the casket, and that's when I saw the body bag."

"Not a mattress cover?"

"No. It was a body bag."

"He was inside of it?"

"Right."

"Zipped in?"

"Right."

"Zipped inside of it?"

"Right."

"Did they unwrap it right away and take the body out?"

"Well, this is when Ebersole turned around and looked at us and said, we don't need you right now. So we left the morgue for about a half hour."

"You are absolutely certain?"

"Yes."

"When you came back, was the body on the table?"

"When I came back, the body was on the table. We came back down and that's when we took X-rays."

"Was Reed with you?" [Reed was an X-ray student.]

"Absolutely."

He said that when he came back in, they had already opened up the body. "When I was told they didn't need me right then, that's when they made the Y cut."

Custer strongly disputed the recorded start of the autopsy, "because I was back in there and they were already sautéing the liver, cutting up the lungs, weighing things." When I told him that it was supposed to have started at 8:15, he said, "No! I don't believe it." But if the body came in at twenty-five minutes to eight, as Humes said, then Custer would not have come back in the room before the Y incision was made at 8:15, according to his own statement to me that he was out for forty-five minutes. (See the end of Chapter 10.) He was asked to leave the autopsy room along with some or all of the other men as soon as they removed the body from the casket.

Condition of the Body

Paul O'Connor says that the President was a "thin, small man" or emaciated. Others say that he looked large on the table in the emergency room at Dallas. Most say that he looked very healthy.

The Start of the Autopsy

This is one of the most confusing issues. Officially, it began at eight or eight-fifteen. Yet it is hard to believe that the body, which had to have come in at about seven P.M., just waited for an hour or more with nothing being done. We are told by some that the examination began immediately, and by others that they waited for Finck. Maybe those people were waiting, but some people did get to work right away.

Jerry Custer, the X-ray tech, and a very responsible professional, says that he saw the body taken out of the coffin after seven P.M. and he and Edward F. Reed were then asked to leave until they were ready for him to take X-rays, which was supposed to be the first thing that was done. He was brought back in after a half hour or more, and he says that the Y incision had already been made.[54]

Yet Custer told journalist Warren Patton that "I think we started shooting about 6:45."[55] A faded memory or misunderstanding about the exact time of an event is understandable up to a point, but there is more than a serious conflict in the above recollections.

Dr. Humes said that he made his first incision. He told the Warren

Commission that it was a "Y-shaped incision from the shoulders over the lower portion of the breastbone and over to the opposite shoulder and reflected the skin and tissues from the interior portion of the chest."[56] This was at 8:15 EST.

It is clear to me that a false record has been made, that certain things were done before they went officially on the record. Mark Crouch speaks of the "buffet of evidence." In this case we are given many different and conflicting facts for each issue, and told to take our pick. To hell with what really happened.

It seems to me that there were two teams of people at the autopsy. Jerry Custer insists that he took the X-rays, and Edward Reed insists that he took them. And "Dr. Ebersole, the acting chief of the radiology department that evening, stated in a deposition to the committee that prior to commencing the autopsy he took several X-rays of the skull, chest, and trunk of the body. Dr. Ebersole further told the Committee that he hand-carried these films in their cassettes to the fourth floor of the hospital, where a darkroom technician developed them and then returned them to him. Ebersole then hand-carried them back to the autopsy room."[57]

But why has the Committee not published and instead made secret Ebersole's deposition until the next century? What did he say—alone among the doctors—that is so secret? We can get a good idea when we consider that the X-rays in the record can't be his.

It is highly unlikely that Ebersole hand-carried anything when he had students and numerous underlings to do so. But more important, throughout the record we had been told that Ebersole was not even present until much later, when Jerry Custer's and Edward Reed's X-rays failed to show any bullets.

There are also apparently two teams, when we consider O'Connor being there and seeing certain things that Jenkins did not see, and vice versa.

Same is true of the two photographers, John Thomas Stringer, Jr., and Floyd Riebe. Each claim, to an extent, the other's work.

Roy Kellerman

Let us apply the lost art of common sense to this case for the next little while and listen to what the three Secret Service agents that rode in the car with the dying President had to say. First, hear Roy Kellerman, who was in the front seat, speaking to the Warren Commission.

"But, Mr. Specter, if President Kennedy had from all reports four wounds, Governor Connally three, there have got to be more than three shots, gentlemen."

SENATOR COOPER: What is that answer? What did he say?

MR. SPECTER: Will you repeat that, Mr. Kellerman?

MR. KELLERMAN: President Kennedy had four wounds, two in the head and shoulder and the neck. Governor Connally, from our reports, had three. There have got to be more than three shots.

REPRESENTATIVE FORD: Is that why you have described—

MR. KELLERMAN: The flurry.

REPRESENTATIVE FORD: The noise as a flurry?

MR. KELLERMAN: That is right, sir.[58]

Here we have a major witness not only anticipating the conclusions of the Commission that was only just then beginning, but he is obviously coached to accept the scenario of just three shots, one of which missed. He *must* have been told what they were going to find, so that, like the others, he would know what to say.

Kellerman is saying two things: That there had to be more than three shots, and that there was a "flurry" of shots. Immediately after this, Arlen Specter goes to work on this testimony to be sure it does not say what was just said, and gets something else. The trouble that Specter has is just about every other witness implies one way or another the things that Kellerman has implied: That there were more shots.

MR. SPECTER: The topic we are on now, Mr. Kellerman, is your own way of relating the description of the wounds, starting with four wounds on President Kennedy. . . .

"I can eclipse an awful lot here and get into the morgue here in Bethesda, because that is where I looked him over. . . . This all transpired in the morgue of the Naval Hospital in Bethesda, sir. He had a large wound this size." *(Demonstrates.)*

MR. SPECTER: *(Indicating a circle with your finger of the diameter of five inches.)* Would that be approximately correct?

"Yes, circular; yes, on this part of the head."

MR. SPECTER: Indicating the rear portion of the head.

"Yes."

"More to the right side of the head?"

"Right. This was removed," Kellerman replied.

MR. SPECTER: When you say, "This was removed," what do you mean by this?

MR. KELLERMAN: The skull part was removed.

"All right."

REPRESENTATIVE FORD: Above the ear and back?

KELLERMAN: To the left of the ear, sir, and a little high; yes. About right in here.

MR. SPECTER: When you say "removed," by that do you mean that it was absent when you saw him, or taken off by the doctor?

"It was absent when I saw him."

"Proceed."

"Entry into this man's head was right below that wound, right here."

"Indicating the bottom of the hairline immediately to the right of the ear about the lower third of the ear?"

(Did Kellerman say *left* and not right? We suspect that some of these transcripts were rewritten. Mrs. Kennedy's and Roger Craig's are examples.)

"Right. But it was in the hairline, sir."

"In his hairline?"

"Yes, sir."

"What was the size of the aperture?"

"The little finger, sir."

"Now, what was the position of that opening with respect to the portion of the skull which you have described as being removed or absent?"

"Well, I am going to have to describe it similar to this. Let's say part of your skull is removed here; this is *below.*"

"You have described a distance of approximately *an inch and a half, two inches, below.*"[59]

Here, the opinion of the autopsy doctors is backed up: The entry hole— or at least one of them—is just below the large exit wound. But it isn't in the same place.

The point of this is that Kellerman tells us the entry hole in the head is at "the bottom of the hairline immediately to the right of the ear about the lower third of the ear." What we have here is a completely different placement of an entry wound, if "to the right of the ear" means what we might think, that there was a hole in the right temple area, where there was some discussion at the autopsy of gray metal on the bone there. It is where a bullet would have hit if it had been fired from the Grassy Knoll.

Kellerman is not mistaken. What he is describing is the *second* head entry hole. Two bullets struck the President in the head.

We also learn from this testimony that the rear portion of the head is missing, more to the right side, which is exactly what all of the Dallas doctors and nurses described, and that it is in the same place as described in the autopsy report, extending into the occiput.

Common sense tells that all of these people can't be wrong, but that there is something wrong with the autopsy pictures, since there is no large exit wound showing anywhere on the head.

"You are now referring to the hole which you describe being below the missing part of the skull?"

"Yes, sir. It was confirmed that the entry of the shell here went right through the top and removed that piece of the skull."

"So you are saying it confirmed that the hole that was below the piece of skull that was removed, was the point of entry of the one bullet which then passed up through the head and took off the skull?"

"Right, sir. That is correct."[60]

It is my contention that throughout this testimony the witnesses are trying to say things that are sometimes unrelated or isolated and therefore confusing. I believe that the transcripts were altered and portions deleted. It is clear to me that Kellerman is describing a shot that took off the rear top of his head with a tangential shot from the front. They could print this much because they could simply say that all of these witnesses were mistaken, and the public would believe it.

The final report, or conclusions of the Commission, could simply *state as fact* their conclusions—which are nothing more than speculation—and ignore so much of the testimony they took.

But when Kellerman is asked if the shot came from the front, he says no. It seems clear to me that the witnesses were coached or threatened on certain points, but they were able to get into the evidence much of their actual descriptions of the damage, and that is the real story.

William Greer

The driver of the fatal limousine was next on the witness stand after Roy Kellerman. He sat next to Kellerman on November 22, 1963. Arlen Specter asked William Greer: "What did you observe about the President with respect to his wounds?"

MR. GREER: His head was all shot, this whole part was all a matter of blood like he had been hit.

"Indicating the top and right rear side of the head."

"Yes, sir. It looked like that was all blown off."[61]

This was what he saw when he got out of the car after driving it to Parkland with its grisly contents, and looked at the President's wounds. A little later Specter asks him about it again.

"Would you describe in very general terms what injury you observed as to the President's head during the course of the autopsy?"

"I would—to the best of my recollection it was in this part of the head right here."

"Upper right?"

"Upper right side," Greer said.

"Upper right side, going toward the rear," Specter said. "And what was the condition of the skull at that point?"

"The skull was completely—this part was completely gone."

"Now, aside from that opening which you have described, and you have indicated a circle with a diameter of approximately five inches, would you say that is about what you have indicated there?"

"Approximately I would say five inches; yes."

"Did you have occasion to look in the back of the head immediately below where the skull was missing?"

Greer replies that he did not. Do you, the reader, get the idea that Specter knows the *back* of the head is missing? One might say that he is merely agreeing with the witness for the sake of advancing the conversation, but it hardly seems likely that this little slip of the tongue is that, but, instead, is something else: An admission that he knows that the back of the head is missing and not the front.

Unless, of course, Senator Arlen Specter is an incredibly stupid man (thus substantiating the Peter Principle) who through inductive reasoning states a conclusion after he rearranges the facts to fit it. That is, he has to have a lone gunman firing from behind, so he reasons that the bullet had to have come from behind and therefore the exit wound has to be in the front of the head. Therefore, all of these people are mistaken, but he isn't going to tell them that.

He will just somehow twist and distort their statements that the wound in the neck was from the front until he has it linked up with the wound in the back, something that was never found at the autopsy.

Clint Hill

Secret Service agent Clint Hill is next on the stand before the Warren
Commission. He described hearing a shot and seeing the President
appear to be hit. "I jumped from the car, realizing that something was
wrong, ran to the Presidential limousine. Just about as I reached it,
there was another sound, which was different than the first sound. I
think I described it (a later shot) in my statement as though someone
was shooting a revolver into a hard object—it seemed to have some
type of echo. I put my right foot, I believe it was, on the left rear step of
the automobile, and I had a hold of the handgrip with my hand, when
the car lurched forward. I lost my footing and I had to run about three
or four more steps before I could get back up in the car."[62]

It sounded like a revolver. There are those who always have believed
that a man was standing inside the sewer alongside the car and shot
Kennedy in the head at short range with a handgun.

"The second noise that I heard had removed a portion of the President's head, and he had slumped noticeably to his left. Mrs. Kennedy
had jumped up from the seat and was, it appeared to me, reaching for
something coming off the right rear bumper of the car, the right rear
tail, when she noticed that I was trying to climb on the car. She turned
toward me and I grabbed her and put her back in the backseat, crawled
up on top of the back seat, and lay there."[63]

"Was there anything back there that you observed, that she might
have been reaching for?"

"I thought I saw something come off the back, too, but I cannot say
that there was. I do know that the next day we found the portion of the
President's head."

"Where did you find that portion of the President's head?"

"It was found in the street. It was turned in, I believe, by a medical
student or somebody in Dallas."[64] (This is the "Harper" fragment,
which a medical student named Billy Harper found on the street. He
took it to his professors, who identified it as occipital bone.)

Hill described the car taking off: "The initial surge was quite violent
because it almost jerked me off the left rear step board."[65]

"Did Mrs. Kennedy say anything as you were proceeding from the
time of the shooting to Parkland Hospital?"

"At the time of the shooting, when I got into the rear of the car, she said, 'My God, they have shot his head off.' Between there and the hospital she just said, 'Jack, Jack, what have they done to you,' and sobbed."[66]

"What did you observe as to President Kennedy's condition on arrival at the hospital?"

"The right rear portion of his head was missing. It was lying in the rear seat of the car. His brain was exposed. There was blood and bits of brain all over the entire rear portion of the car. Mrs. Kennedy was completely covered with blood. There was so much blood you could not tell if there had been any other wound or not, except for the one large gaping wound in the right rear portion of the head."[67]

Can there be any doubt where that wound was? How could it, along with the other wounds, move to somewhere else? Clint Hill was in the best position of anyone, along with the widow, to see what had happened before anyone else saw it. Jacqueline said, "I was trying to hold his hair on. But from the front there was nothing. I suppose there must have been. But from the back you could see, you know, you were trying to hold his hair on, and his skull on."[68]

High Treason detailed the extensive testimony of all the medical witnesses in Dallas saying the same thing, that the back of the head was missing, which is not what we see in the X-ray.

"Did you see any other wound other than the head wound?"

"Yes, sir; I saw an opening in the back, about six inches below the neckline to the right-hand side of the spinal column."[69]

I felt that Humes' interview on national television before the House Select Committee on Assassinations was not just staged. Humes was made to reverse his previous insistence that the alleged autopsy photographs and X-rays did not show the entry hole in the back of the head anywhere near where he had placed it in his autopsy report. Humes spoke with what I felt was a deep-seated bitterness and irony in his statements.

Arlen Specter had pushed him around as he had done with all those Parkland doctors who had previously described an entry wound in the throat from a frontal shot, and he had made Humes link a bullet from there to John Connally, no matter what the FBI and the Zapruder films said or showed.

He could get one bullet through Kennedy and Connally's chest, but not his wrist. All the hocus-pocus about the trajectories and the possibility of one bullet hitting both men ignored the fact that CE 399 (the

"Magic" Bullet) did *not* go through Connally's wrist. Some other bullet did. All of this was a distraction, a distortion, a lie to cover up that single fact.

The actual bullet that had gone through Connally was found in pieces in the backseat of the limousine. There was no bullet in Connally's thigh. The fragments found in his body were much more than what was missing from the planted bullet found on a stretcher at Parkland Hospital.

The Bullet

Now you see it, now you don't. I have started off this chapter showing the juxtapositions of one piece of evidence against another related piece of evidence. Another example exists in that there were no significant bullet fragments described at the autopsy of President Kennedy or seen in the X-rays of the posterior half of the head or the brain. But when Dr. Humes testified to the Warren Commission, there magically appeared (probably taped to a piece of bone the next day and X-rayed at Bethesda as described by Jerrol Custer to me) a large bullet fragment lodged in the skull just behind the right eye. It wasn't mentioned in the X-rays seen by the Clark Panel in 1968.

But the Clark Panel also found another big hunk of lead on the outer table of the skull on the back of the head that had not been there before either.

Kind of like the bullet that Dr. David Osborne said (before retracting his statement) he saw roll from the President's wrappings and the missile that the FBI man at the autopsy had Dennis David write a receipt for, which then disappeared or was converted into fragments.

Three years later there magically appeared to the Clark Panel another large fragment, the full diameter of a bullet, stuck in the outer table of the skull, a half inch from the alleged new entry wound in the cowlick area of the head. "There is embedded in the outer table of the skull close to the lower edge of the hole, a large metallic fragment which on the anterior-posterior film (#1) lies 25mm. to the right of the midline. This fragment as seen in the latter film is round and measures 6.5 mm. in diameter."[70] *Outer table of the skull.*

Is this reasonable? No.

But it just happens to be 6.5mm. across, same as the rifle that was alleged to have been used. Round too. Neat, eh? How come it wasn't there in 1963? The whole point of the autopsy and the many X-rays taken and the presence of a radiologist was to locate any part of a bullet that might be present. It is not reasonable that that large piece of metal was there on November 22, 1963. It certainly wasn't there when the morticians washed and combed the hair, as they told me. It is another proof of the forgeries.

Dr. Humes said, "Actually, from all the X-rays that were taken, and we viewed them all together; when I say 'we,' I am saying the medical people who were in the morgue at the time, the two Bureau agents, myself, and also Mr. Greer, who was in there with me, naturally, they were looking for pieces of fragmentation of this bullet. There was none; only one piece to my knowledge. That was removed inside above the eye, the right eye."[71]

Would not the bullet stuck on the outside of the back of the head have been readily seen by everyone at the autopsy? All autopsists comb the hair carefully, looking for any evidence. They did not see this fragment at the autopsy because it wasn't there.

And how in hell could it be stuck in the head a half inch from the hole the rest of it supposedly went through? Granted, strange things happen to bullets, and even stranger interpretations of Newton's laws of physics have been applied to this case, but we cannot have a major part of a bullet stuck in the outer table of the skull a half inch from the hole the rest of it went through.

Then there is the matter of the lateral skull X-ray which shows that the entire right front of the bone of the face is missing. It contradicts the photographs and every witness who says the President's face was undamaged.

In addition, no metal dust fragments or any other metal were seen in the neck during the examination of many X-rays. Again, a trail of metal dust fragments magically appeared when the Clark Panel saw the new X-rays several years later.

We have described a significant fragment of a bullet that was supposed to have been removed by Dr. Humes during the autopsy from behind the right eye. Yet it does not show in the X-rays. We do see in the X-ray, as the Clark Panel noted, the round diameter of a bullet, conveniently 6.5mm (the size of Oswald's alleged bullets) stuck on the outside of the back of the head. Custer told me "there was *no* metal fragment with a round circumference," in the X-rays.[72]

* * *

Then there is the FBI receipt for a "missile" found at the autopsy. FBI men don't confuse fragments with missiles. The receipt reads "missile removed by J. J. Humes." This promptly disappeared from the evidence. Ebersole told Art Smith: "I have no knowledge of that." He told Smith that X-rays prior and after the incisions showed no bullet. Humes told Smith that "it must have been a very small fragment from the body. It wasn't a whole bullet."[73]

There are, of course, countless such contradictions in every area of the nonmedical evidence. Are these stupid mistakes of the plotters or the footprints of intelligence? It is as though we are being told something. I think that Dr. Humes is *trying* to tell us something by amplifying the contradictions. His honor was put on the line, so he spoke in code to us.

I have to ask whether that is John Kennedy's body in that grave at Arlington National Cemetery.

There have been several exhumations lately, but the one exhumation that should have been made long ago—the most important in American history—remains undone.

Let's face it. There is the official story—the story they fed the rest of us. And there is the real story.

What is that real story? This is what we are trying to determine in this inquiry.

The X-Ray and Photograph Conflict

The key to the case is the fact that the X-rays and photographs are completely incompatible with each other. This proves that they are forgeries. Alone among the researchers, I made the startling discovery of the mismatch in 1978.[74]

In addition, if the X-rays and photos do not show the wounds as Custer and the other Bethesda and Dallas witnesses saw them, then the body was not altered, but the pictures were—so as not to show a shot from the front.

Another major discrepancy is the fact that the photographs of the top of the head show a large hole extending clear across from right to left (corresponding to the hole that was marked "missing" on the autopsy face sheet drawing), equally on both sides of the head. This is completely incompatible with the X-rays which show the large defect on the top right front face extending only as far as the midline, and only as far back as the coronal suture. In addition, there are *no photos* showing the brain inside the head, or at least photos that we have some evidence of.

The head wound that Custer and the other men from the Bethesda autopsy who spoke out in 1988 describe is precisely the same wound seen in Dallas, and which is in fact described in the autopsy report. Like the autopsy doctors themselves in their interview with a panel for the House Committee, they state that there was no entry wound in the cowlick area where it appears on the photographs of the back of the head.

Since I have always maintained that anyone could see that that part of the face was missing in the X-rays and not in the photographs, this assumption assumed two things: That the viewer had access to the autopsy photographs, which were not published until 1988, and which were previously seen by only a few people in the United States.

In addition, it would have to be assumed that the viewer might know something about reading an X-ray. I don't think any of us—not being trained radiologists—could claim that we were absolutely sure of what we were seeing. I certainly wasn't when, in 1979, I showed copies of the X-rays to my closest friend, the chief radiologist at Maryland General Hospital, Dr. Donald Siple, and he interpreted them for me, saying that the face on the right was missing, and I shortly published in a small newspaper that the X-rays were fake.

At the same time, I made available to Steve Parks at the *Baltimore Sun* a viewing of the photographs, which were still secret, and he published a front-page story based on our claim that the pictures of the back of the head were fake.

Compartmentalization, as Mark Crouch says, is the only way to explain the sort of conflicts we have in the medical evidence. One hand did not know what the other was doing. It is glaringly apparent at the autopsy.

Take a look at the conflicts in the case in areas other than the medical evidence, and we are looking at an intelligence or military operation. Such operations are intended to foil investigation or espionage, but in this case it prevents anyone from seeing the whole picture.

One might call it Psy Ops, or psychological operations—psy war. Some say only three shots were fired in Dallas, but extensive evidence indicates that six or more were fired. There was no Alek Hidell identification on Oswald when he was arrested, but it turned up shortly thereafter, and the alias was attributed to him after his arrest. There were no fingerprints or palmprints on the weapons attributed to him at the time of the arrest. There was no evidence that the weapons had been fired. There was no remote proof that Oswald was in the alleged assassin's window. There was evidence that Oswald was in fact a government agent, perhaps working for two or more agencies.

Witnesses saw other gunmen, smoke from other guns, heard other guns, felt bullets go by, placed gunmen in other locations around the Plaza. False Secret Service credentials were shown at the Plaza. There may have been men posing as doctors at Parkland. A doctor listed at the autopsy cannot be documented to have existed. Other important persons were there who are not listed.

There was a big pool of blood near the Depository on the sidewalk. There were wire service front-page stories that a Secret Service man had been killed at the time of the assassination.

Films and cameras were seized from witnesses and disappeared from the evidence. Transcripts of testimony was altered. Witnesses were coached, intimidated, ignored, or bullied. Much evidence disappeared from the National Archives. Other evidence appears to have been planted. Oswald clearly had someone posing as him in the weeks before the assassination. J. Edgar Hoover believed that the Oswald in Russia years before might have been an impostor. There are conflicts about the height and description of the Oswald who returned to the United States.

Much evidence in the case appears to be forged, and gives conflicting information. False information was planted in the media immediately after the assassination and ever since. Investigations were clearly co-opted and rigged.

There is a fog over the evidence, something only a military or civilian intelligence operation can do.

And, like the photographs, not only are some photos incompatible with each other *and* the X-rays, but the lateral skull X-ray is incompatible with the anterior/posterior view. The lateral or right profile shows the *entire face* on the right side missing.

"I think of John Kennedy as a sailor, with a seaman's sins and a skipper's skill. His odyssey was an American one, and it continues."

—Senator Harris Wofford, *Of Kennedys and Kings*

CHAPTER 7

DR. ROBERT FREDERICK KARNEI

I interviewed on August 27, 1991, Dr. Robert Karnei, who retired July 1, 1991, as director of the Armed Forces Institute of Pathology. Dr. Karnei was present throughout nearly all of the autopsy of President John F. Kennedy, and was a U.S. Navy pathologist.

I was conducting an inquiry as to whether President Kennedy had Pott's disease, or TB of the spine, as some doctors had told me. "There was no report, as you know, on the adrenals," I said.

"Mainly because they couldn't find them," Karnei said.

"They couldn't find his adrenals?"

"Right. There was nothing there."

"You mean . . . if they atrophied, that is what will happen—there is nothing left?"

"Right. Jim [Humes] and Jay [Boswell] worked long and hard in that fatty tissue in the adrenal-renal area looking for them, and didn't find anything that looked anything like adrenals."

"Oh, boy."

"And he had been on steroids, of course, for many years, and he was Cushionoid.* He had the hump back—the whole nine yards, as far as

* Cushing's syndrome results from a hypersecretion of the adrenal cortex, and in this case is caused by a prolonged administration of large doses of adreno-cortical hormones. The symptoms are protein loss, adiposity, fatigue and weakness, osteoporosis, amenorrhea, impotence, capillary fragility, edema, excess hair growth, diabetes mellitus, skin discoloration and turgidity, and purplish striae of skin. (Taber's Cyclopedic Medical Dictionary, Philadelphia: F. A. Davis Company, 1970.)

being on exogenous steroids. A combination of the two—atrophy of the adrenals and then, of course, the exogenous steroids contributed to that. There was total atrophy as far as we can see at the autopsy. I mean they cut that fat to a fare-thee-well trying to find anything that looked like adrenals, and there just wasn't."

"Yeah."

On Humes's statement on the adrenals to the House Select Committee's doctors:[1]

"Basically they looked for them and they couldn't find them."

He doubted that Kennedy had Pott's disease: "They did not specifically go ahead and look for anything like that that night."

"He did have injuries to the spinal column there. That's documented. He had back injury."

"Do you mean the fused discs from the operation in 1954?"

"That's right."

"All I can say is that they did not find the adrenals, so Addison's would have been a good example of that, for the adrenals to disappear like that."

"You're sure of this?"

"Absolutely!"

"Nobody got a look at the spine area?"

"Not that I remember. I don't remember anybody going into the spinal area to take a look there."

He confirmed "that is probably true," that JFK would have died from the steroid treatments. "You are trying to replace the steroids that the adrenals normally produce."

"All I can say is that Jim and Jay were really handicapped that night with regards to performing the autopsy."

"Was that Burkley?"

"No. Robert [Kennedy] was really limiting the autopsy."

"In the end, don't you think they performed a complete and good autopsy?"

"I think it was as complete as they were allowed to do. I mean, normally they would have gone into the spinal column and taken the spinal cord and all that sort of thing. And they were not allowed to do that. And there was no way they could have looked at the spinal column there to see if there was any disease in the spinal column."

"They didn't remove the spinal column?"

"No. No. Not that I can remember. I am almost sure they did not touch the spinal column. At first we were not even allowed to extend the incisions to examine the brain. I mean, it was really—it was sort of hairy there during the night!"

"You were in the room, right?"

"Yes. I was in and out."

"Did you know a Dr. George Bakeman?"

"Bakeman?"

"The FBI report lists a Dr. George Bakeman as being present, and nobody knows who this person is."

"I have no idea who Bakeman is. Unless he got in there early in the evening and came in with the body. But, no, I don't know anybody by that name that I allowed in the room."

"You were at the door?"

"Yes. I was in charge of the Marine guard to make certain that nobody got in or out of the room."

"Were you inside the room?"

"Yes. I was inside. I was in and out all night long."

"Do you remember the enlisted men that were there, like Paul O'Connor, or Jim Jenkins?"

"Yeah. I'm trying to think of what their names were, now."

"Paul O'Connor was about twenty-two or twenty-four. Jenkins was nineteen. He was very close to Boswell, I think—helping him."

"There were actually three enlisted people in the room, if I remember right now . . . and a civilian, Mr. Stringer, the photographer."

"There was Floyd Riebe, the Navy enlisted photographer. And Jerrol Custer, the X-ray tech."

"Yeah, I forgot about him."

"So the spinal cord was not removed, so there was no opportunity to take tissue samples from it or study whether or not he might have actually had TB of the spine?"

"No, I don't remember the spinal column ever being touched."

"Have you performed a number of autopsies?"

"Oh, yeah, I've done a couple hundred."

"You are not a forensic pathologist, are you?"

"No, no. I'm a hospital pathologist, but I have done a lot of forensic cases."

"If a brain is hit by a bullet, what are the chances—I guess there are about twelve or fourteen nerve and vessel endings attaching it to the skull—of a bullet just completely loosening it from the brain stem and these other nerve endings and so on?"

"It depends on where the bullet has hit. The injury that he [Kennedy] had caused a lot of damage throughout the brain. He basically was brain dead. There is no way that that brain would have ever functioned from what I could see at the autopsy table. A lot of it was missing, and the part that was there was all ragged."

"The large defect was in the very back of the head?"

"Right, yeah."

"You wouldn't say it was in the front of the head, or the right side of the head, or the top of the head?"

"No. Most of the brain that was missing was in the back part of the head."

"The brain? And how about the bone? Same place?"

"Yeah. Most of the bone that was missing was destroyed in the back of the head."

"The official report says that they started at eight or eight-fifteen. Does that mean when the Y incision was made or when they began examining the head after the photographs were taken?"

"Whenever they begin examining the body, that is when the autopsy starts. It doesn't necessarily start with the Y incision. The Y incision occurred a *long* time later."

"A couple of hours, maybe?"

"Yeah. We had to get permission all of the time from Mrs. Kennedy to proceed with the autopsy."

"My understanding is that they just had to extend the sagittal suture and maybe one or two fracture lines just by even less than an inch of a cut in order to obtain the brain, and then—one description I had is that it just fell out into Humes's hands."

"It was pretty fragmented. I was not in the room exactly at the time they took the brain out. They called me out for something. I was not in the room when they actually took the brain out."

"But Humes would have mentioned to you . . ."

"Yeah."

"Did he mention to you whether or not it fell out without his having to cut the brain stem?"

"Uh, I don't remember his having said that. Normally, the cut is made through the medulla oblongata in order to get the brain stem and that part out of it."

"Is that beneath the floor of the skull?"

"Yeah."

"Is the medulla what we would normally call the brain stem?"

"Yeah."

"So, they had to cut that, or necessarily, or could the bullet have torn it loose?"

"Ah, the bullet would not have torn that loose. That was down deep in the brain. At the base of the brain. Now, how much of the temporal, parietal, and occipital lobes could have fallen out superior to the membrane that is there—between the top part of the brain and the cerebellum, I'm not sure whether that could have fallen out when they opened the scalp and take out the brain or not. The brain that I saw was markedly haemorrhagic. I did see it when it was out of there."

"The enlisted man who took the brain and turned it over and put it into the gauze sling and infused it, examined it quite closely. He felt that the brain stem was neatly severed. The problem that I have is that he did not see—maybe Humes severed it, but there has been a question raging whether or not somebody had access to the brain at Parkland or somewhere?"

"Nobody got to it at Parkland, I can tell you that. The opening in the scalp was not big enough to go ahead and take the brain out."

"Do you think that the brain—in your experience with a gunshot wound—that it could have just fallen out of the head into his hands. The description we have is that when he made these very small cuts, maybe two or three cuts to remove the brain, that it just fell into his hands. Could this happen?"

"It's possible. Especially with a lot of ricochet and a lot of fragmentation, it could go ahead and be markedly fragmented. But I don't remember it being that fragmented to where it would fall out like that."

"The man who infused it, who put it into the gauze sling and put the needles into the veins—he says that the brain stem was neatly cut across, and that it had fallen out into Humes's hands. It raises the question as to whether someone had gotten access to it. So far, I don't see when it could have happened."

"As I said, the hole in the skull was not big enough for someone to have gotten in there and taken the brain out at the time."

"When it came in?"

"Right."

"I have met with the funeral people from Gawler's and they described very, very specifically what was left when they put the head back together, and the man there stated that there was not enough scalp on the back of the head to cover the hole. He said that the area of missing scalp was as big as the palm of your hand, but they could not cover that area, and that is exactly where the large defect was, which was larger than the missing area of scalp entirely on the back of the head. They didn't have to worry about it because the head was on the pillow and it did not show. Does that square with what you recall?"

"Pretty much."

"I don't want to ask leading questions."

"They did a real good job. There was a sort of a laceration that extended beyond the hairline in front. They did a tremendous job of fixing that up."

"You mean on the forehead?"

"Yeah. They did a great job that night. You could hardly tell where that laceration was."

"Was it a sort of V-shaped triangle pointing at the right eye, about half an inch into the forehead?"

"Yeah, something like that. Boy, you are really trying to drag up something."

"If I send you some of the pictures, maybe you could tell me if they're accurate or not?"

"You know, it just extended beyond the hairline. It wasn't very far. A half inch sounds about right. It was just beyond the hairline. They sutured it and covered it with a wax, I guess, is what they use. It was great, I mean, you couldn't tell where it was unless you knew what was there."

"One of the funeral men said there was a small hole in the temple that he put wax in. He said that he didn't have to do anything more with it. He didn't have to use cosmetics. The wax took care of it. It was in the sideburn. He felt that it was from a fragment that came out. But he couldn't remember which side of the head it was on. Do you remember that?"

"Yeah, at the end there, when they were starting to close things up— the only hole that I remember them doing anything with was that laceration, but I don't remember any other hole being there."

"In the forehead?"

"In the forehead, yeah."

"Was all that bone in front of the coronal suture, was that all intact other than a fracture?"

"I'm trying to remember—"

"The right side of the face?"

"Quite a bit of it was there. Normally you would have to cut part of that out in order to get the brain out."

"In the frontal bone?"

"Yeah. What I am trying to say is that normally when you make your incision to take the skull cap off, the incision would have been forward of where the fracture was, where it disappeared again."

"The problem that we have is that the X-rays of the skull that were released have no—the whole right top front of the face is missing. There is no large defect in the back of the head. In fact, there is no large defect anywhere else on the head."

I said, "I've studies this for a long time and my feeling is that Humes did a very good job, but that *something* happened along the way to distort this evidence very drastically. In other words, pictures were released of the back of the head, for instance, which show an entirely intact back of the head. Every single medical witness, including Jackie Kennedy, every doctor, every nurse in Dallas who saw these pictures say that they are fake. The X-rays don't show the wounds. There are serious problems with all this stuff that has been fielded. And, of course, I've badly wanted to talk to someone who knows something about this."

"Have you talked to Jim or Jay?"

"I have tried to, but when I brought up the possibility that this material is forged, they terminated the discussion. I think the reason is that they were forced—and you would know better than I—but they were forced to agree. . . . Let me put it this way, in 1978 there was a meeting of a panel of doctors set up by the House, and they met with Humes and Jay and they were presented with these photos and X-rays, and Humes and Jay insisted that the entry hole in the back of the head was four to five inches away from where it was in the autopsy report and from where they had seen it. Did you know this?"

"No, no."

"They repeatedly stated that—in fact they both answered in unison, 'No, that's not the entrance wound.' So the Committee commented on this in their report, on the 'persistent disparity between its findings and those of the autopsy pathologists.' The end result is that all these years those poor doctors have been accused of having made mistakes, doing something stupid in their work. Same thing for the Dallas doctors. The Dallas doctors repeated to me this year, insisting that the hole in the throat was an entry wound."

"That definitely was an exit wound."

"Did you examine that wound?"

"No, I did not. But I read where the Dallas doctors retracted that."

"No, I am sorry, but they never retracted it. Perry is the only one that sounds like he is waffling. He sounds like he reversed himself, but he really did not."

"Wasn't that in the Warren Report?"

"I think the Report says it, but it was only an assumption. They did not even know there was a bullet hole in the throat."

"At first, yeah, but there was a bullet hole in the neck. They couldn't find the exit wound," he said.

"They didn't know there was a bullet hole in the throat. All they saw was the trach incision."

"Right. Once they talked to the doctors in Dallas, this is around midnight, I think."

"No, it was the next day when he called Perry."[2]*

"Next day?"

"Yes. The body was already gone."

"I was convinced they talked to somebody that night, and finally decided that had to be the exit wound. Pierre Finck, I think, talked to somebody."

"No, the only person that called was Humes. While you were there, there were people in the gallery that were trying to force the issue and say 'did the bullet come out the throat?' But at the time there was no knowledge that there was a bullet hole of any kind in the throat."

"For some reason I thought they had discovered that around midnight. Maybe it was the next day."

"Yes, it was the next day when Humes was sitting at home and called Perry."

"When Dr. Humes came out of that meeting of the panel of doctors for the House Committee, he said to a reporter, 'They didn't ask the right questions.' We have always wondered, what is the right question? Do you think that Kennedy was hit twice in the head, which the film seems to indicate? Do you have any indication that was a possibility?"

---

* Humes stated that he called Perry Saturday morning, the day after the autopsy, after taking his children to church. "I returned and made some phone calls and got hold of the people in Dallas unavailable to us during the course of the examination . . . and spoke with Dr. Perry and learned of the wound in the front of the neck, and things became a lot more obvious to us as to what had occurred. . . ." (I HSCA 330)

"There were two bullets that hit him, if I remember right now. There was one in the neck, and one in the skull. That was the only two bullets that there was any evidence of."

"You know that the photograph of the back appears to show two bullet holes. One is six or seven inches down on the back to the right of the spine, and the other is up on the soft muscles of the shoulder. This seems to be a little bit suspicious. The question is, what is going on here?"

"Yes."

Where the Casket Came In

"Were you there when the casket came in? When the body came in?"

"No. I had my altercation with the press there at the time the body was brought in."

"Was that around the back of the hospital?"

"No, that was in the front. It would be in the passageway leading back to the morgue area."

"Which was downstairs?"

"Yes, it was on the same level—it was right outside the elevators that led back to the autopsy room."

"Could they have had any kind of a decoy thing going on to try to avoid the crowds? Did they have two caskets or two ambulances? Did they go to the old morgue which I think still had the cold room?"

"The old morgue was no longer used, and there were no refrigerators there anymore. That had been closed down for a long time, and they had moved into the new morgue."

"Where the cafeteria is now."

"Right."

"The new morgue is the only place where the casket could have been delivered?"

"As far as I know."

"Could the Navy ambulance have come to the emergency room in the other wing? One of the Navy men described in the newspapers the body being delivered there and being trundled down the corridors to the morgue at the other end of the hospital."

"No! It definitely came in the loading dock, because the only passageway to get back there would have been through me and the Marine guard. Nobody came through that way."

"Do you feel that there was no opportunity for somebody in that room to somehow distort the autopsy itself? I know there were some fragments found, and Dr. Osborne at one time stated that a whole bullet rolled out of the wrappings, or fell out when the back was lifted from the table."

"I had heard that, but I never saw any whole bullet. All I ever saw were fragments that night."

"You would have heard about that, right?"

"Yeah."

I told him about the Clark Panel finding a bullet stuck on the outer table of the skull, and an entry wound in the cowlick.

"No, but bullets can do odd things once they get inside the skull. They can ricochet back and forth depending on the velocity of the bullet. Dr. Perry is much better at that, as he is a real firearms expert."

I asked him about Captain or Dr. Brown. He first thought he might have been chief of surgery. "There was a Captain Brown who subsequently became the Surgeon General, if that is the one you are talking about. I can't recall the first name. Might be Roy."

I asked him if he knows anything about the Custer story of taping fragments to bone the next day.

"I never heard that one."

"I'm going to send you the Clark Panel report with that statement that on the outer table of the skull there is a large fragment in the area I have described to you."

"That's hard to believe."

"Does it raise your curiosity?"

He laughs heartily. "Yeah, it makes you wonder. It's kind of hard to believe that maybe some of the X-rays and photos, maybe they played around with them the next day and they got mixed in with the ones that were taken. The Secret Service people confiscated *everything* that night."

"Had you heard that they had been playing around with X-rays the next day?"

"No. That is the first I've heard of that."

"Do you have any reason to suspect, or did Humes, Boswell, or Finck have any reason to suspect that the Secret Service was doing something strange in this case?"

"No. All I know is that they confiscated everything that night. And then they set a Secret Service man beside the tissue processor all night long. The next day, when they put the tissues in to be processed for the histologic sections, they had a Secret Service man beside the tissue processor, and when they took the sections, when they put the trimmings on the block, they confiscated all those trimmings. They didn't let anything go."

"Have you ever heard of Dr. Lattimer? The urologist? He states in an article that the adrenals were clearly visible and unremarkable in the autopsy X-rays."

"Bullshit."

"Now you're talking!"

"My understanding is that you can't see them, not without a lot of dye, if there are adrenals."

"It's kind of hard to see them on a flat plate, number one."

"There were obviously a lot of problems in doing the autopsy that evening. I have to really take my hat off to Jim and Jay for keeping as cool as they were," he said.

Probing the Back Wound

"Dr. Finck was very clear that that wound in the back did not go anywhere," I said.

"He couldn't get it to go anywhere—the one in the back of the neck —he couldn't get it to go anywhere because his probe would not go anywhere."

"Did you watch this probing?"

"I didn't watch all of it. I know that he was having a hard time."

"Why didn't they turn the body over?"

"Well, they did. They tried every which way to go ahead, and try to move it around, but the rigor mortis was getting to be a problem."

"But this was after the Y incision?"

"Yes."

"The men described being able to see the end of the finger and the probe poking the muscle from inside the empty chest." (But not the finger or the probe itself.)

"They were working all night long with probes trying to make out where that bullet was going on the back there."

"They spent some hours on it?"

"It was a long time. I don't know how long it was."

"Just on that?"

"Just on that, trying to figure out where in the dickens that went."

"Wasn't it about six inches down on the back? Where would the third thoracic vertebra be?"

"The third thoracic vertebra would be about . . ."

"Wouldn't that be about six inches down?"

"Something like that. It's not six inches down from the shoulders. It would be from the base of the skull."

"The third thoracic?"

"I'm trying to think now—if it was that low or not."

"Well, you know, the holes in his coat and shirt were six inches down?"

"They were?"

"Yes. When I send you a copy of the photograph of the back, you will notice two apparent bullet holes, and one of them is down about six or seven inches. The other is up in the soft shoulder, which we think may be painted in."

"Well, I think they did the very best job under the circumstances, and everything after that is a lie," I said.

"Well, I agree with that."[3]

CHAPTER 8

J. THORNTON BOSWELL

On October 2, 1990, my chief investigator, Richard Waybright, a Baltimore City police officer, went to see one of the physicians who helped conduct the autopsy on President Kennedy's body. He came away with startling information.

Until Rick Waybright went to see him, Dr. Thornton Boswell had talked to almost no other independent investigator except myself. And I had been able to obtain precious little information from him. I figured a policeman might have better luck than a mere author or governmental investigating committee.

Boswell was very gracious to my investigator, and answered all of Mr. Waybright's questions to the best of his ability. He promised to locate his notes and at a further meeting explain what some of the markings on his blood-stained drawings made at the autopsy meant. In particular, we wanted to know what the sketch of an apparent wound in the left eye area marked "three centimeters" meant, and what the dot over the left eye was in the full body drawing.[1]

We also wanted to know what the markings for "inshoot" and "outshoot" meant on his drawings, and what exactly was the "missing" area written over the top of the head. Some assumed this referred to surgery. He said that related to the actual dimensions of the missing bone, but that it was not necessarily at the top of the head.

* * *

A key point which Officer Waybright brought out during his interview with Dr. Boswell was the fact that the floor of the orbit of the right eye was cracked, which Dr. Boswell had noted from the X-rays. He pointed out to Waybright that the present X-rays not only do not show that the orbit is cracked, but that there is no orbit at all.

Richard Waybright wrote after seeing this that "in the drawing that he completed at the autopsy [which has bloodstains on it], he indicated that the orbit was cracked through the floor, and in our copies, the floor of the orbit is missing."

Waybright went on to say Dr. Boswell "appeared to be troubled by the X-rays and continued to look at them. He stated that they did not look right, but that he would have to see the originals before he could make a valid judgment."

We note that Dr. Boswell presumably saw the alleged original X-rays in 1977 when they were shown to him by the House Select Committee's panel of doctors. At that time, he and Dr. Humes both took issue with them, finding the rear head entry wound greatly moved from where it had been when they saw it.

We admit that the copies we showed Dr. Boswell, which were out of a book, were not the best, but certain data in the X-rays are reproduced beyond question in the copies, and cannot be mistaken for what they show. That is, the whole top right front of the face is missing. The jaw is also missing or cropped out in the versions that were made public.

Dr. Boswell had drawn a small crescent shape down at the bottom of the overall cover sheet, with a slanted line drawn through it from ten o'clock to four o'clock. Others had assumed that it referred to the top of the skull from the hairline back across the top of the head down to the neck in the back, but Dr. Boswell explained that it was a drawing of a crescent-shaped piece of skull that was brought into the autopsy room later.

Dr. Boswell solidly backed the previous public statements by Paul O'Connor, Jerrol F. Custer, the X-ray tech, and other of the men that the X-rays alleged by the government to be that of President Kennedy are not of Kennedy. Dr. Boswell was not aware that autopsy personnel had denounced both the photographs and X-rays, but he made most of the same observations they had indicating forgery and substitution of the materials.

He reiterated what he had said to the panel of doctors interviewing both him and Dr. Humes for the House Select Committee on Assassinations, that the entry wound in the back of the skull was nowhere near where it appears in the phony X-rays.[2]

Officer Waybright repeatedly went over this ground with Dr. Boswell, who "with rigid tenacity maintained that the entry wound was at or near the occipital protuberance."[3]

Waybright wrote me that "Dr. Boswell indicated that the entrance wound [on the head] was located at the rear of the head where a small piece of brain tissue is visible in the autopsy photographs. He stated that the 'bullet hole' that Ida Dox has highlighted in her drawings of the President's head is not the entrance wound but possibly may be blood or a mixture of blood and water."

This means that the present X-rays, which according to the Clark Panel and independent interpretations show an entry wound near the cowlick area—are substitutions. We know that the dentist who was asked by the Select Committee on Assassinations to authenticate the X-rays, Dr. Lowell Levine, was not allowed to see the whole X-ray of the head because it would reveal the wound area to him,[4] and was therefore asked to authenticate a skull X-ray that could not in fact be proven to be that of President Kennedy in death.

When Drs. Humes and Boswell were shown the X-rays by the above panel of doctors on September 16, 1977, Dr. Angel, one of the interviewing doctors, said, "It's really hard to be sure, square this with the X-ray which shows so much bone lost in this right frontal area."[5] This statement provides the necessary documentation to show that the doctors were presented basically the same X-rays that were published by the House Committee in the same volume on the medical evidence on pages 109–113.

Dr. Charles S. Petty, medical examiner of Dallas County, chimed in. "Well, I think there may be more bone apparently lost than is actually lost in the X-rays." Already a quarter of the face is missing in the X-rays. Dr. Petty then immediately changes the subject. "We don't know when these X-rays were taken. Dr. Humes, do you by chance know at what phase of the autopsy the X-rays were taken? Were these taken before the brain was removed or after?"

Dr. Humes replies, "Yes. All of the X-rays were taken before any manipulations were performed."[6]

First of all, the key observation here is that they find a great hole in the right front of the face, which is what the X-rays show. As we know, the photographs reveal no damage to the face, which would have fallen completely in, or would have been blown away, had any of that frontal bone been missing.

Not only that, but Dr. Petty suggests that "I think there may be *more* bone apparently lost than is actually lost in the X-rays."

And to top it off, Dr. Angel then observes a few lines after that: "So, in that case this exit wound is really in the frontal—it's in front of that notch there—it's in the frontal, see what I mean, it would have to be about here." According to the X-rays, the exit wound has moved from the back of the head to the front of the face.

Yet these doctors, some of whom had great familiarity with the case and the disputes over the medical evidence which have raged for years, never really got down to asking the right questions of Humes and Boswell. They never pursued after this point the issue of all that frontal bone being missing, which is not described in the autopsy report at all.

And what a shame that all of the medical witnesses, both from Bethesda and Dallas, have not been brought together in one room with this phony photographic and X-ray evidence.

As Jerrol Custer pointed out to Sylvia Chase of KRON-TV in San Francisco, the photographs of the face are incompatible with the X-rays. This went right by the few others over the years who might have seen the evidence. It certainly went by the staff of the House Committee.

I don't believe that was an accident. One can put it down to bad staff work or incompetence, but I don't think so. Anyone can see that the photos and X-rays are grossly incompatible, and with so many doctors' observations calling into question numerous things wrong with the films, we would have to say that the mistakes were not accidental, even though the most gracious thing one could say for Andrew Purdy, Mark Flannigan, and Robert Blakey of the House Committee was that it was safer to cover themselves by not dealing with the gross incompatibilities in the films than to say that they were covering up for the conspirators themselves.

Richard Waybright's report to me said, "Dr. Boswell could not explain the markings on the skull diagram that indicate '3.4 cm,' nor could he explain the markings on the body chart [face area] which are located in the area of both eyes. This inability to recall these markings is plausible because it has been twenty-seven years. What this tells me is that there were no entry wounds in the face or left temple area.

"Dr. Boswell was adamant that there were no wounds in the face or left temple area.

"Dr. Boswell stated that when you use his diagrams to locate the wounds you should use only the measurements next to the diagram and not the marks, because they will indicate the true position of the wounds. He stated that the drawings are just to indicate the general area and are not to be considered exact by any means. The marks were to orient the area of the wound and the measurements were to pinpoint it exactly." In addition, Boswell did not make all of the notations on his drawings. Jim Jenkins made some of them.

Waybright also pointed out that Boswell indicated that they were not permitted to track the wounds, but that they probed the back wound briefly and it led toward the throat. He admitted that they were unaware of the throat bullet wound until the next day when Humes spoke to Dr. Malcolm Perry in Dallas on the telephone.

The repeated indications throughout this case that the autopsy doctors were prevented from properly tracking the wounds may be an indication of conspiracy.

On September 1, 1991, I interviewed Dr. Boswell again. My first interview with him had been many years before. This is what he had to say, though we did not have much time. Talking to one of the autopsy doctors is always difficult, at best.

I asked Dr. Boswell about the brain being loose in the head: "Some of the witnesses implied that Jackie Kennedy actually had some or all of the brain in her hand when she came into Parkland."

"No, that's ridiculous!"

"She told Nellie Connally that 'I have his brains in my hand.' "

"Well, that was just a matter of speech. Of course, there was a gunshot wound in the brain that sort of splattered. His brain *was in his skull.*"

I tell him about Jenkins, told him that [his assistant and others] "they describe the brain stem as being neatly severed. There were two or three small cuts in the scalp and along the sagittal suture and along a fracture line."

"None of that is true."

"When the body arrived?"

"When the body arrived, the brain was in the skull, in the head."

"And the brain stem was intact? It was attached to the brain stem?"

"Right."

"It occurred to me that Jenkins just didn't see Dr. Humes sever the brain stem. That's why it looked neatly severed to him."

"Right."

"Was it true that they just needed to make the smallest enlargement of the large defect in order to get it out? It was not necessary to do a craniotomy?"

"Well, there was a pretty good amount of the skull that was—first of all there was a piece of the skull on the pavement down in Dallas."

"Was that known as the Harper fragment? A medical student picked it up."

"It may very well be. I've never heard it called that."

"He had taken it to Methodist Hospital. . . ."

"It was not very large, if you look at the diagrams and X-rays. That was not really very large."

"Was that the trapezoidal shape?"

"Yeah. On a separate diagram. But the scalp was lacerated, and a pretty good size piece of the frontal and right occipital portion of the skull had separated and were stuck to the undersurface of the scalp. So when that was reflected, then it was true, there was a big bony defect in the right side of the skull. And with the fragments—I think the brain was largely removed through that defect. But the scalp was somewhat intact overlying that, so that, that just superficially, externally, you couldn't tell that there was a big hole in the skull."

"The men—I was at Joseph Gawlers's funeral home the other day and Joe Hagen, the president, and his cosmetologist and so on described to me reassembling his head at the end and they stated that when they had finished there was still an area in the back of the head, just in the occipital-parietal area probably three inches across, that there was not enough scalp to cover that. But nobody could see it because the head was on the pillow—"

"Right."

"And that is the way you remember it?"

"Right."

"That there was no scalp there?"

"Right."

"And that was basically the area where the large defect was."

"Well, that defect was a lot larger—do you mean in the skull?"

"Yes. That area of missing scalp was in the center of a larger defect?"

"Well, no, it was more posterior than the defect in the scalp. Most of the scalp could be reattached. It was a laceration. It wasn't an avulsion of scalp, really. I don't even remember a defect once the morticians repaired the skull and everything."

"Did you stay right to the end?"

"Sure did."

"But there was still a little bone missing, that had not come back from Dallas?"

"There wasn't too much missing. And the scalp was closed over the bone. The bone fragments were replaced. Most of them were replaced in the skull. A couple of them may have very well been retained as autopsy material. But the scalp was almost completely restored. Because at that point we didn't know whether anybody would view the body or anything, and the mortician did a magnificent job of restoring the head and skull."

"That is what I was told. There was apparently a laceration that extended about a half inch into the forehead just above the right eye."

"That wasn't apparent after they got through restoring the body."

"Did that laceration sort of go straight back—in other words—front to back across the side of the head there, above the right eye going back?"

"You mean to the posterior of the skull?"

"Yeah, it was only three inches long or so, wasn't it?"

"That laceration extended from around the eyebrow all the way back to the posterior of the skull."

"It was over the top of the large defect of originally missing bone?"

"Yeah, sure. The bullet exploded inside his skull, and just sort of blew the top of his head off, but it separated the scalp with the laceration. And didn't tear it away or anything. That was destroyed."

"So the laceration extending from the right eye—the scalp was basically intact? It was just torn through there?"

"Right."

"I know that there was a fracture in the right orbit, through the floor of the orbit, is that right?"

"Right."

"And maybe one fracture in the frontal bone above that somewhere?"

"Right."

"Basically, the frontal bone forward of the coronal suture, was that intact?"

"Well, without notes or records or anything, I would hesitate to say anything too specific about that for something to be published."

"There is just one more question. The main defect—the circular bone that you drew on your diagram, that was separate from the trapezoidal piece. I think that came in later, flown in from Dallas. But your impression of that main area of the missing bone originally—it seemed to be described as from the occipital bone forward—somewhat on the right side of the head. I just wonder how much it was on the top of the head, in the back there, and how far forward it went."

"I can't tell you that. I vaguely remember the two pieces of bone. The small piece three or four centimeters across, and when we reconstructed that, that was part of the wound of entry. There was one circular area on one side that we determined to be a wound of entry. Or a portion of the bone was a wound of entry."

"On one side of the head?"

"On one side of the piece of bone, yes. It was semicircular piece of bone, and on one side of that piece of bone there was another hole right in the edge, and there was beveling on one side which showed us which was on the inner surface. So the wound of entry was on the outside, with fragments of bone on the inside."

"I was talking to Francis X. O'Neill, who was at the autopsy, and we were talking about the statement in his report that 'there was surgery to the head area.' "

"See, we didn't—that whole question is related to 1) had he had a tracheostomy, and 2) they had started to put tubes in his chest to evacuate blood from his chest. The only thing that we, the autopsy surgeons, were talking about was the tracheostomy. That was related to the wound in the body. He hadn't had any surgery to his head. He had had the wound on his neck which was the wound of exit from the back wound that came out through his larynx, and that had been extended in efforts to do a tracheostomy, which they never did."

"I know that those FBI men misspelled some names and—"

"Well, they also misinterpreted a lot of things that they heard. They didn't know what they were listening to or talking about."

"They wrote that there was 'surgery to the head area, mainly to the top of the head.' That is the quote from their report."

"That was never discussed. There was never any question about that."

"They just made it up? They thought they heard that? It says 'mainly to the top of the head,' and nobody could sort through what that meant."

"That was never a question."

"And the entry hole—I know that you and Dr. Humes insisted that it was near the hairline, where that little tissue is. This is what everybody has described. So it is questionable how it got up into the cowlick area, where you can't really see it in the black and white pictures. It seems to have moved four inches, when Dr. Fisher and Dr. Morgan looked at those X-rays in 1968."

"They weren't there, so there is no way they could tell anything."

"Yes. I think that you stand by your original report that the entry wound was at or near the occipital protuberance?"

"Well, I've got exact measurements where that was in my report."

During another interview later in the year[7] Dr. Boswell told me that they had not removed the spinal cord, which verified what Dr. Karnei[8] had previously told me.

As Tom Robinson, the mortician who prepared the face and head for burial, told me, the head and brain suffered normally during the forensic examination because it was necessary, but he made a point of telling me that the autopsy doctors treated the President's organs and torso "kindly," and did as little damage as possible. They worked with "great care."[9]

Dr. Boswell also patiently answered my questions with regard to the right frontal bone. He made emphatically clear that at no time was that bone removed or put back. "It was intact."

"Did you have to remove the bone to get at the fragment that was lodged behind the right eye?"

"No."

"So the frontal bone as far as the right orbit, was that intact?"

"Yes."

"At no time during the autopsy was any of that forehead removed?"

"Right."

With regard to the brain, I asked, "Did you take the brain out, or was it Dr. Humes?"

"We were both right there."

"Did you have to sever the brain stem?"

"I'm sure we did, but at this point, after thirty years—"

"It's possible that it might have been blown loose?"

"No!"

"Some medical opinion says no, it couldn't have been."

"No, it wasn't."

"Jim Jenkins, one of the enlisted men present, felt that the brain tumbled out of the head and that it had been previously severed."

"That's not true."

"The brain was not loose in the head, then?"

"That's right."[10]

It must be repeated that the photographs and X-rays of the back of the head do not show the large exit wound as it was, and all the medical descriptions of the scalp at the very back of the head state that it was mostly missing and the rest badly shredded. Numerous eyewitnesses have emphatically stated that the scalp was not intact enough to pull over the large hole in the bone in the very back of the head to make the present photograph.

There were quite a few incompatibilities the staff and the Committee clearly overlooked, whatever their intent in so doing.

On the same day that I again spoke with Dr. Boswell, Dr. Lowell Levine, the forensic dentist who authenticated the skull X-rays for the House Committee, told John Long that all of the damage was "occipital-parietal" [in the back of the head]. There seemed no way to explain the massive amount of missing forehead and orbit on the right side. It was also quite clear that there had been no dismantling or reconstruction of the bones of the face or the front of the head, according to the morticians and the doctors.

I would like to close this chapter with a comment Officer Richard Waybright wrote me: "Prior to interviewing Dr. Boswell, my impression was that the autopsy had been conducted by a team of doctors who were either inexperienced or incompetent.

"However, after talking to Dr. Boswell, I left with the strong feeling that, at least in Dr. Boswell's case, he was qualified and capable. I feel that he was honest in his interview with me and that he has been wrongly criticized for his performance at the autopsy. While I do concede that the autopsy was far from perfect, I think that given the situation that they were in, they should not be faulted. I think the autopsy room was in utter chaos with all the witnesses jammed inside.

"I think that a lot of the blame for the irregularities at the autopsy should be laid upon the military commanders who were present and giving the orders."

Rick Waybright said that the autopsy X-rays he showed Boswell deeply troubled the doctor. "I believe that he declined to make a judgment because they were not the right X-rays. However, he had not seen the X-rays in twenty-seven years (if ever) and they may have confused him." He may have declined to further comment because we did not have the originals to show him, as Waybright says.

Waybright closed his report to me by saying, "It is my opinion that these are not the X-rays that Dr. Boswell saw on the night of November 22, 1963.

"His statement that they did not look right and his obvious bewilderment at viewing them tend to indicate that either they are not what he saw, or they are obvious fakes, and he did not want to commit himself at this time."

> "There are three things which are real: God, human folly, and laughter. The first two are beyond our comprehension, so we must do what we can with the third."

> —John Kennedy to Dave Powers

CHAPTER 9

JAN GAIL RUDNICKI

"Nick" Rudnicki was a lab assistant to Dr. Thornton Boswell and was called out by Boswell to help him the night the President's body came in for autopsy at Bethesda Naval Hospital. Nick, as he is known, was not on duty, but ended up working many hours that night. Many of his recollections are quite clear twenty-seven years later, and at no time during my interview did he express confusion or inconsistency with regard to the facts as he remembers them. Rudnicki is presently a sales representative, with two children and a normal life.

Rudnicki was following the case all these years and was intensely aware that there were various controversies raging over what the back of the head had looked like, as well as whether the body had in fact arrived in a body bag and a shipping casket.

I told Nick that Dr. Boswell had told my chief investigator, Richard Waybright, a couple of weeks before that there was no entry wound in the cowlick area as the present photos and X-rays seem to show, and where all the outside doctors who have reviewed those materials have insisted there was a large exit wound. Boswell, of course, had himself insisted that the entry wound in the back of the head was just where they had placed it in the autopsy report, near the hairline at the back of the head, four to five inches lower than where it is now claimed to be in the photographs and X-rays.

He did not recall any entry wound in the back of the head.

In addition, Dr. Boswell had stated most emphatically to my investigator that the floor of the orbit was merely cracked, not entirely missing, as is the case in the official X-ray—which shows the top right side of the face missing.

In other words, Boswell was not retreating from what he and Dr. Humes had insisted upon before the panel of doctors the House Select Committee on Assassinations provided. Even though the autopsy doctors were adamant on that point—a clear red flag that there was something seriously wrong with the autopsy photos and X-rays—they refused to accept the testimony of the autopsy doctors themselves, and said, "They made a mistake," in the autopsy report.

Doctors don't make mistakes like that. This was the price Humes and Boswell were paying for their report which told of a bullet transiting the neck, when they never knew during any part of the autopsy that there was a bullet wound in the front of the neck. All that, of course, was invented later.

To digress a bit more, Dr. Ebersole, the radiologist, stated that he had taken another set of X-rays at one A.M. trying to find a bullet in the body, after he says he was told by the Dallas doctors that there had been a bullet entry wound in the front of the neck.[1] This is another example of confusion, since no such call was made to Dallas until the next day, when Dr. Humes, in the privacy of his own home, after sleeping, called Dallas and talked with Dr. Malcolm Perry.[2]

In addition, Dr. Humes and Dr. Boswell told the panel of doctors interviewing them for the House Assassinations Committee that *"all* of the X-rays were taken before any manipulations were performed."[3]

I told Mr. Rudnicki that Paul O'Connor, Jerry Custer, and the other witnesses insist that "there was no back of the head back there," and he immediately said, "That's correct."

"I was there through the whole autopsy, but most of my time was spent in the back room—the tissue room which adjoined the autopsy room itself." He prepared the slides and put the organs and other tissues in jars of formaldehyde.

"I remember the casket being wheeled in and I helped put the body on the table," he told me.

"I don't ever remember seeing a shipping casket. The only casket I have in my mind's eye is the ornamental one." He said that they were all scooted out while the X-rays and photographs were taken.

There has been some confusion due to the fact that the Kennedy entourage bought another casket to replace the one from Dallas, which had a broken handle.

He thought that the autopsy began at seven or eight o'clock, but could not recall for sure. He said that he was there until about 11:30 P.M., "twelve o'clock maybe," when the mortician was brought in. "I was out of there before the remains were out of there."

I asked him if he personally had a chance to examine the wounds. He said yes, because he was working with Boswell. "I remember the wounds to the throat, the wound to the rear right quadrant of the head."

He said that he did not remember suturing to the throat wound which Ebersole had described as being present when the body arrived from Dallas. (Ebersole was the only witness to ever describe suturing to the throat wound, and he did this unofficially in some interviews in 1978.)[4] Ebersole had made other totally conflicting statements, contradicting both himself and the evidence.

I asked him about the wound to the back of the head: "It was a big hole." He did not see Custer put his hands inside the head.

"Was the scalp missing on the back of the head?"

"Yes."

"Not just shredded, but gone?"

"As far as I could tell, it was *gone* [his emphasis]. I couldn't see any gray matter in there, you know. There was some hair hanging over it. There wasn't a big hole type thing, but there wasn't any scalp there either. It was a lasting impression, as I recall."

I asked Rudnicki if he knew anything about composite photos or X-rays being made right in the Naval Hospital the next day, and he said no. "Is that when they made the new pictures?" he asked. I considered the fact that he used the word "new" when referring to the photos and X-rays, which he had seen, most significant.

"There was some controversy about whether they took the brain out or not," he said. He said he seemed to remember the brain being removed, but wasn't too clear. James Curtis Jenkins recalled taking the brain out very clearly.

He said that he thought there were some discrepancies among the comments of Paul O'Connor and some of the others. Specifically, Rudnicki did not feel that there wasn't any brain at all in the head.

In my discussions with Paul O'Connor, I felt that he was inconsistent on this, and that he was simply not being careful enough with his language when he exaggerated and said that there was no brain in the head when it arrived. He at various times in many talks with me clarified this to mean that there was some brain in the head, but a great deal had been blown away.

I asked him if he recalled the body of an Air Force officer being there that night. He said that he did not recall. He had a vague recollection of a pickup of the remains of someone else just before Kennedy's body arrived.

Once again I asked him if he remembered anything about the body bag and the shipping casket, and he said, "I remember him coming in the bronze casket."

"Did you see the back wound at all?"

"Yeah, I remember—at least I think I remember—a small—what appeared to be an entry wound several inches down on the back."

"Did it look like a real wound—not something that someone had artificially made with a knife to look like he had been shot from behind?"

"No, no, it was real. It seemed like a fine hole.

"I remember them making a comment, and there seemed to be some controversy about looking for a shell fragment, and one was missing, and looking through the sheets. It fell out, or something of that nature."

I asked him if he remembered anything about Admiral Osborne's comment that a whole bullet had fallen out of the sheets or from the back area when they moved him. This was also stated to me by James Curtis Jenkins, who remembered very clearly that a bullet had rolled out of the sheets from the back area. Of course the House Committee got Osborne to appear to retract this. I later found that so many of these "retractions" were anything but.

"Yeah, that may very well be. I may not have been in the room during that time, but I remember some conversations concerning that."

I asked him if it was a whole bullet or a fragment, and he said, "I assume it was a bullet."

Then he said, "There seems to be some controversy as to when Jackie actually arrived at the hospital. I remember seeing her—I peeked my head out—the entourage coming down the corridor. I remember looking out and I remember seeing her, and for some reason he seems to think she wasn't even there at the time I supposedly saw her. So I don't understand that one. I don't see these people every day so I'm sure it wasn't something that happened previously."

He said that he thought the body had not been there when he first saw her coming down the corridor. "She preceded it in?"

"That's correct."

I began going over the ground again of what the photos and X-rays of the back of the head seemed to show. I pointed out that all the witnesses had said there was no bone or scalp in the back of the head on the right.

"Yes, from the ear back, the scalp was either gone or definitely destroyed in that area. I don't know whether it was implosion or explosion. I can't recall that. Not being an expert in forensic medicine or anything, it would look more like it was an exit than an entrance."

He recalled a controversy at the time as to whether the throat wound was a bullet wound or a tracheotomy and whether it was an entry wound or an exit. But he is not sure that he really saw the throat wound. "I did not get down close and look at it."

"I remember seeing it," the big gash in the throat. "I don't have a direct memory of it as I do with the type of wound to the head."

"With the recent pictures that were shown on television I recall the frontal area missing in the X-rays rather than the back area."

"How did the face appear to you?"

"Normal. It looked perfectly normal, if you didn't look at the back of the head."

"What did the top of the head look like? Was there a large hole in the top of the head?"

"No, not that I recall." But he said that he did not get a good look at it. Then he clarified something by saying that when he said that the right rear quadrant of the head was missing; "That could extend to the top of the head."

I again asked him if there was any scalp left in the right rear of the head behind the ear, and he said no, "That was gone."

"Boswell and Humes got dumped on pretty heavily," he said. "I can't imagine that somebody would put out photographs like that when there must have been at least five hundred people who saw it otherwise," he said.

"Nobody was supposed to see these pictures," I said.

"So they just switched the photos for Warren to see and nobody else saw them?!" he said.

He said that everybody was asked to leave the room during the X-rays, because of the radiation.

"The next day we were all up in the office there, and what can I say? It was 'forget everything you saw, everything you said, everything that you knew. Wipe it from your mind!' Like a dutiful little soldier, I did so. And consequently, I didn't make notes."[5]

"Approval of assassination was totally inconsistent with everything I knew about the two men."

—Secretary of Defense Robert McNamara, testifying to the Church committee on CIA-Mafia assassination plots

CHAPTER 10

JERROL F. CUSTER

On October 8, 1990, I conducted one of numerous interviews with Jerrol Custer, the X-ray tech who did the work of taking roentgenograms of the President's body. He told me that he took *many* films, and that he could not understand what had happened to them. Only a few survive.

Today Custer runs the technical end of the large X-ray service at the Presbyterian Hospital in Pittsburgh. He is a respected and level-headed family man who has had a burning anger for many years over the distortions of the evidence he and the other men and doctors obtained at the autopsy.

"I took a lot more films. I X-rayed every inch of the body from head to toe. What happened to them? I made up angles and took many shots to look for bullet fragments." He then clarified this to say that he had not taken films of the feet.

"I took at least five films of the skull, including an oblique/tangential view of the hole in the head. Two of the neck. Two of both shoulders. I took a chest X-ray, a thoracic spine, a lumbar spine, a pelvis. I took femurs. In fact, I went all the way down. The only thing I didn't take was the feet. We took laterals—laterals of the chest. Side pictures of the thoracic spine, and side pictures of the lumbar spine."

"A piece of metal fragment fell out of his back when we picked up the body to place a film under his head. An autopsy pathologist picked it up with forceps and placed it in a bottle with formaldehyde in it."

In another interview conducted with Custer,[1] he told me that the missile that fell from the posterior area of the President when they moved him early after the body arrived had the appearance of a whole bullet and not a fragment, and was mutilated as though it had struck bone. The nose of it had a mushroom shape, with the after part of the bullet the stem of the mushroom. He said it was not a whole bullet, and that it came out around C6 or C7 at the base of the back of the neck.[2]

"Ebersole wanted to see if there were any patterns, shell patterns. He stood there and told us what he wanted to see. He specifically wanted to see a lateral skull X-ray right away. Then he wanted to take a picture of the neck. He commented about fragments in the neck. I remember seeing fragments in the neck.

"When we picked the body up and the one fragment [the mutilated bullet] fell from the back, he was the one who got someone to come over right away and pick it up."

Admiral David Osborne [then captain] had previously stated that a whole bullet was found at the autopsy, which had rolled out of the President's wrappings. He later told the Committee that he wasn't sure.[3]

Custer said that the films showed some destruction in the cervical spine, "but I don't recall at what level."

He said that there was a salt and pepper pattern of fragmentation on the film from the back to the front of the head, in a cone shape from the occipital area. "It fragmented more as it passed through the head and exploded in the front." (He was not sure if the pattern was from front to rear or from rear to front.)

"I don't remember actually seeing any metal fragments in the X-ray films of the neck at all."

"In the autopsy report they don't describe seeing any films of the shoulders, of the thoracic—the upper chest—or anything else."

We talked about the statement by Paul O'Connor that the right eye was slightly popped from the orbit. "That was the only damage to the face as far as I could see," Custer told me. "According to the X-rays, the right eyeball shouldn't have been there because the floor and the outer ridge of the orbit is gone.

"The orbit is missing and it does not match with the autopsy photographs of the face," he said. "From the destruction of the skull, the face should have fallen in. There shouldn't have been any eyeball there with that amount of destruction, that orbit, the floor of the orbit was blown completely out. So it should have fallen completely out. Maybe that was why there was a protrusion of the eyeball, which tells me there may have been some tampering before the body got to Bethesda.

"The whole thing makes me wonder: Was the body tampered with before the autopsy? There definitely was no brain."

"But there had to be some brain left?!"

"There definitely was no brain—I was able to put both my hands inside the skull cavity." (Custer has since clarified this to mean he *could* have put his hands inside Kennedy's head, but that he did not. Secondly, unless people there were more insensitive, stupid, and brutal than we can imagine, it is not rational that he did so. But it does show how Custer, like most if not all of the witnesses at one time or another, has misspoke himself.)[4] "I even made the comment, my God, what is the sense of taking films of the head?

"I saw tissue—surrounding tissue on the skull itself."

"But Jenkins has a very clear memory of taking the brain and infusing it and putting it in a jar of formaldehyde."

"Well, I don't know. I can't honestly say I saw much brain. If there was anything in there, it had to be very small. Why didn't they mention the brain weight on the autopsy report? You have to remember that that night it was total mass confusion. There were too many people in that autopsy room working on that body that shouldn't have been there."

There was a supplemental autopsy report, though, dated December 6, 1963, which published a brain weight of 1500 grams, more than the weight of a larger than average brain that could not have lost any of its mass. Everyone had described a great loss of mass at Parkland Hospital in Dallas. Some felt a quarter of its area had been lost.

This is an example of not only the mind playing tricks on a witness, but the setup itself tricked him because he thought he had been taking the first X-rays when he was first called back into the room, and did not realize that X-rays had already been taken and the brain removed.

He thinks that the reports and data from the autopsy weren't done to "make perfect," but were all "pushed together" in a haphazard way "to change people's perceptions of what happened to the President."

Custer had stated flatly in November 1988 that the X-rays were fake. This author was the first person to call them fake in 1978. Ten years passed before anyone else noted it.

I asked Custer about the fact that the Clark Panel had found a large cross section of a bullet on the outer table of the skull near the alleged entry wound at the cowlick on the back of the head. The bone was actually missing on the back of the head there.

"It can't be," Custer said. "I don't understand where that bullet could have been on the skull because we moved the body all over creation. It would have shown."

I asked him if he examined the X-rays of the head right then, and he said yes.

"When we lifted him up, a bullet dropped from the shoulder area down to the trunk area."

"Did you see any sutures on the neck wound when the body arrived?"

"There were no sutures at all."

"The scalp was so loose from the base of the skull in the occipital region to the front, it drooped. His face was deformed. Instead of how the face normally looked—it seemed like his face was squished. It seemed like someone had taken a clay image of his face and pushed it together. The whole skin part—the scalp and the front part of the face seemed like everything had drooped forward."

"This is lying on his back, right?"

"Right. There was no continuity to the face part at all. He did not look like he looks in the photographs taken at the autopsy. The photos look like a normal body lying there."

"That isn't the way it looked to you?"

"No. Absolutely not!"

"Could the face in the picture be false somehow?"

"It's hard to say. Here's another thing too. On his eyes—I never forgot his eyes—the right eye seemed to protrude a lot further than the left eye. It had a dead, cloudy stare."

Custer made it clear in a later interview that what he describes above about the face is after the scalp had been reflected in the back and the brain removed. The face no longer had anything to hold it tight over the skull.[5] This is important because none of the surviving autopsy pictures show the Y incision, the inside of the chest, or any other indication that they were taken after the first examination of the body.

I again brought up the fact that in 1968 the Clark Panel review of the autopsy materials found numerous facts that were not the case at the autopsy. For example, there is "embedded in the outer table of the skull close to the lower edge of the hole, a large metallic fragment which on the anterior-posterior film (#1) lies 25mm. to the right of the midline. This fragment as seen in the later film is round and measures 6.5mm. in diameter." The Clark Panel said that there was no apparent exit for the bullet: "The photographs do not disclose where this bullet emerged from the head."

Custer immediately said, "You know, it's funny about that. The following day Ebersole, and I think it was Captain Brown [his superior officer in charge of radiology], brought skull fragments up to the main department, and they pulled me out of the department and put me off in a room and they had me X-ray parts of the skull. They had numerous amount of fragments, and he had pieces of skull. I always wondered where they got them from. And in fact the next day he was the one that came upstairs to the main department and had me X-ray fragments of the skull. I was doing this in one of the back rooms where the portable X-ray machines were."[6] He told me that he recognized one of the pieces of bone, which looked like the "skull cap" or part of the top of the head.[7]

"Skull fragments and bullet fragments. And they had me X-ray them *next to the skull.* They had me put a piece of bullet fragment down and a piece of skull and had me shoot it, and there were fragments that they did have—numerous sizes.

"Whose head was it from?"

"Nothing was said about whose it was. They told me they were doing this so they could make a bust of Kennedy. But it never did set right with me. I was never told where this material came from.

"It was a Captain Brown—I think, a four-striper, head of the radiology department." (Loy T. Brown)

I believe that Custer has described for us a step in the forgery of the X-rays, where they held fragments up against pieces of skull from somebody's head and took films of them which were later assembled in composite X-rays.

"Here's what he [Ebersole] told me: 'The only reason why I'm doing this is because they want to make a bust of Kennedy.'

"I said to myself, wait! How in the heck are they going to make a bust of Kennedy if I'm shooting pictures of pieces of skull?"

"But you have no idea where the pieces came from?" I asked.

"I have no idea!"

This story is in part corroborated by Dr. John Ebersole's explanation for pencil marks found on the X-rays which he said he placed there a few days after the assassination when asked to measure the skull for a "bust." Perhaps it was in fact a wax head that was to be used for some of the alleged autopsy photographs, as Cindy McNeill, a Houston attorney, suggests, though he might not have known that.

Again I told him about the findings of the Clark Panel, which noted a large half of a bullet, one embedded in the outer table of the skull near the alleged entry wound located some four inches above its placement in the autopsy report, at which point Custer interjected, "Almost as if it was placed there."

"Ebersole had me shooting pieces of skull and bullet fragments together. I asked him why we were doing this, and he came up with that cock-and-bull story about the bust of Kennedy, which is ridiculous."

I said, "There's not a reason in the world why they would have been doing something like that. . . ."

"That's right!" Custer replied.

He said that he in fact had no idea where the fragments or skull pieces came from, as they could have come from anywhere not connected to the assassination. "That's right." He reiterated that the chief of the department, Captain Brown, was there. This was Captain Loy T. Brown, who had driven all the evening of November 22 back from a meeting in Chicago.

I interviewed Dr. Brown[8] and he said that he had heard about the assassination in Chicago almost immediately. At once, he called his department at Bethesda and told them to get ready, and then started driving east as fast as he could go. Brown denied having been present at any taping of bullet fragments to bone fragments the day after the autopsy.

At the autopsy the day before, Custer said, "As soon as I showed Dr. Ebersole different pictures pertaining to the skull and neck, he grabbed them right away, and I never saw them again.

"Him and Humes were pretty much buddy-buddy. He would see something and he'd take it over and show it to Humes. Humes would write something down. Then Ebersole would come over to me and say, well, here, take a different view of that."

I asked Custer to give me a character judgment about the two men within the context of the conspirators having possibly planned all along to bring the body to Bethesda, where they could control the autopsy or the doctors and get the result they needed. He said he didn't know Ebersole very well, but he knew Humes well. "Humes that night—

seemed to be haphazard. He didn't seem to be organized for what he was doing. I had worked with surgeons before [but not Humes]. Surgeons operate in a methodical manner. He didn't seem to do that."

"You have to take into account the shock factor—this was a president brought in there dead," I said.

"I understand that," Jerry said. "There was a lot of commotion that night. I've never seen four-star generals upset like that. Admirals. It was like the whole Joint Chiefs of Staff were there. But still, in that situation he [Humes] is a professional man. He has a job to do. It wasn't a coordinated front on everything. One person was doing one thing, another person was doing an entirely different thing. Nobody was communicating with each other."

"Do you think there was any plan for that to happen that way?"

"I don't know. It just struck me funny though. If you have ever had any dealings with a criminal investigation, everything is done in a methodical manner. Every piece of evidence—you write down, the weight, everything. Humes was basically waiting for Ebersole to say something to him. It was Ebersole to Humes. Never Humes to Ebersole."

"Do you think Ebersole was controlling the autopsy?"

"Yes, I would say so."

He said that he didn't like Ebersole too much. "He didn't impress me as much of a radiologist," Custer said all in the same breath. "And, he didn't want to dirty his hands, if you know what I mean."

He said he couldn't understand why the investigations ignored the technologists, and "not the so-called doctors." His characterization of the physicians was less than kind, but in line with what many feel about military doctors, or those doctors in particular. "They [the techs] see more than the doctors do sometimes."

He said that usually Ebersole gave the X-rays to Custer to put in the medical records. "Once I gave them to him that night, he never let them out of his sight. There were pictures being taken all the time that evening."

I told him that Ebersole had told Art Smith that he had gone back in there at one in the morning and taken another set of X-rays because they were unable to find an exit wound, but that they had called Dallas and found that there had been a wound in the neck. Custer immediately said, "He did what now?"

I repeated it, and Jerry said: "Dr. Ebersole couldn't operate an X-ray machine." I asked him if he took the second set after the autopsy was over. "No!"

He then said "that you have to understand something about the Navy. A lieutenant commander radiologist would not push a portable X-ray machine into a morgue to X-ray a body. This would be done by a technologist. It's just unheard of."

"Do you know for a fact that he couldn't operate that machine?"

"I know for a fact that he couldn't operate that machine. All he was able to do was fluoro, and interpret films." He then said that Ebersole and Captain Brown came up to the room where Custer was sleeping in the middle of the night, woke him up, and congratulated Custer on what a good job he had done at the autopsy, and how well he had served his country.

"It was beneath him to do a menial job like that. That should tell you what type of person he was."

"Arrogant."

Custer repeated that the impression he had was that Ebersole was controlling the autopsy. But this might only be within the context of Ebersole interpreting X-rays and as soon as he found something, fragments or particles, "he would call Humes over and show it to him and they would go back and do something to the body."

Then I asked him again about the events of the twenty-third. "Well, I had a portable unit, and what he was doing was taping the fragments to the pieces of skull. Big pieces."

"Did the pieces or fragments ring a bell with you?"

"Well, the one that I saw was the one that fell off the body the day before. It was misshaped and I recognized it." He said that he did not recognize any of the pieces of skull that were used. "Ebersole came right out and said these were pieces of Kennedy's skull."

"When we lifted the body out to put a plate under it, the fragment fell out." He said it could have come "from any one of those regions," referring to the back of the head or the back itself. "A misshapen bullet." "Not half of a bullet, not a fragment?" "It was like a bullet. It was misshapen as if it had hit bone and flattened partially out."

"It was fairly sized." (Meaning it was not small, like a .22.)

He said he clearly recognized this bullet the next day when Ebersole had him hold that and other fragments up against pieces of skull bone to make X-rays.

He said that Ebersole could not operate a portable machine, and that he could not have made a second set of X-rays to look for an exit wound or bullets as he said in his 1978 interview with Art Smith.[9] Smith writes in the first paragraph of his story that Ebersole "personally took fourteen X-rays of John Kennedy during the autopsy. . . . He took two sets of X-rays; one at approximately 8:30 to 9:00 and another set around one A.M."

The *Philadelphia Inquirer* story[10] stated that Ebersole merely was on hand and interpreted the X-rays, and that two technicians were there with a portable machine.[11] (We note that that interview seems to be filled with misstatements.) Ebersole said in the *Inquirer* interview, "We found no bullet *in the body.*" Did he mean that they did in fact find a bullet, but it had fallen out and was not in the body?

It must be scientifically impossible for a large cross section of a bullet to be embedded on the outside of a skull some distance from where it is supposed to have entered and passed through. This would appear, therefore, to be part of the faked evidence. But why was it there? To imply that the bullet has actually struck there, and not four inches lower, where the autopsy report had placed an entry? Yet the good doctors of the Clark Panel duly reported this without a second thought.

Custer comments that the present X-rays which the Clark Panel reviewed show the right frontal bone and the orbit completely gone. Yet Dr. Boswell very specifically noted at the autopsy that the orbit was only cracked through the floor, and he repeated this to Rick Waybright. Boswell and the other doctors, as well as Custer, examined carefully the X-rays as they were developed before the autopsy began.

Since there were no metal fragments in the neck, it did not occur to them to dissect that region where they had thought only a tracheotomy had been performed.

The Clark Panel also found that another bullet entered "the decedent's back at the right side of the base of the neck between the shoulder and spine and emerged from the front of his neck near the midline." This is clearly not where the hole is in the photographs, some inches far down the back, as it is in the clothing and in the autopsy report and other reports.

"The cutaneous wound in the back was too small to permit the insertion of a finger. The insertion of a metal probe would have carried the risk of creating a false passage."[12] There is extensive testimony from those at the autopsy that they did in fact stick their fingers and probes into the hole in the back. One again feels that we are talking about two different holes in the back.

The Clark Panel also found that postmortem rigidity had set in, whereas the witnesses from the autopsy told me that it had not yet begun. Either this panel of notable doctors was selected for its incompetence, or they were simply stooges who reported only what they appeared to see.

"I'm the only one that I feel was actually moving the skull around. It was almost as if he was scalped, literally," Custer said to me.

"Someone else was taking photos in civvies." Custer was probably referring to John Thomas Stringer, Jr., the medical photographer who was a civilian, but there are indications that some other men were there taking pictures. Custer later corrected the story to me that he had put his hands in the hole and said that he "could" have put his hands in the head, but of course did not.[13]

"There was a flap of scalp in the back of the head, but it was badly shredded. As I have said, it would not make a picture like the one we now have, which shows the scalp so intact.

"Every time you moved the head, the whole scalp moved forward. It was all loose."

Custer was told by the security chief at the Naval Hospital that the President's body was arriving by helicopter from Walter Reed and would land as close as possible to the Naval Hospital, where it would be brought the rest of the way by ambulance.[14]

He said that there was a shipping casket in the morgue, but he had no knowledge of the President's body being in it. He said that there was a body of an officer there, in a body bag and in a shipping casket.[15]

Custer told me that "there were no towels around Kennedy's head. There were sheets."

"Entirely sheets?"

"Yeah."

"No terry-cloth towels inside the sheet?"

"I don't remember seeing any of that."

"There was a sheet around the outside which everyone remembers. . . ."

"Yeah, I remember seeing that."[16]

*   *   *

"There was a king-size hole—that area was torn [back of the head]. . . . Look at the lateral skull film—looks like part of the front of his face was gone—but look at the autopsy photograph—there's nothing gone there. . . . His eye should have been completely gone on that film."[17] Custer repeated this several different times.

"On the KRON show, I brought out the discrepancy between the X-rays and photos. I think that I didn't actually bring them out, but I said something to the fact that these weren't the X-rays that I had taken."[18]

Were a lot more X-rays taken? "Oh, definitely. Absolutely. At least five at the end that I know of."

"Were they all developed?"

"Everything was perfect. In fact, that was the thing that I was mostly worried about that night."

"There is only one anterior/posterior film and the laterals of the skull," I said.

"There was more than that. I know for a fact there was more than that, because Ebersole had made me X-ray that thing every which way, every angle that I could possibly X-ray.

"There were FBI people there."

"Sibert and O'Neill?"

"Yes. They were just about running the whole show. What was going on, who was to be admitted, who wasn't to be admitted. I had one of them with me at all times, every time I left the morgue. I had to go all the way up to the second and third floor for film."[19]

"Ebersole is wrong. He had nothing whatsoever to do with any of this. The article pertaining to the fact that Ebersole took all the X-rays. He went back in a second time and took a second set of X-rays. He never did any of that. He never brought out the fact that they brought pieces of the skull back the next morning. He had me X-raying them *so they* could make a 'bust,' which was a bald-faced lie. Do you remember last time I talked to you, I had pieces of skull, plus I had pieces of fragments of the bullet, and I was putting bullets next to pieces of the skull and X-raying them at the same time?"

"Yes, but was there any other witness to that?"

"No, not that I can think of. It's been such a long time.

"I was the only person in the room at the time when he told me the next day what he wanted me to X-ray, and he stood there and watched me as I took them. I took the film and he just ran them out of there to have processed. He brought them back, looked at them, and said change this, change that, change this."

"It sounds like the strangest thing on earth," I said.

"The next day during the time that I was taking these X-rays, he seemed sort of prerehearsed—coached—like he had been told what to say."[20]

"Dr. Ebersole was running the show as far as when it came to taking what X-rays. He told me exactly what he wanted and how he wanted it done. As far as taking the X-rays the next day, the bone fragments, how he wanted things."

"Was there anyone giving him orders?"

"Well, there was a civilian there that I remember, and the way he introduced me to him was by saying he was an FBI agent."[21]

"I had copies of the X-rays in the main lobby of the X-ray department and stuck them behind the insignia of the U.S. Navy Medical Center. That's exactly where I hid them. I knew nobody would look there."

"Do you remember what they show?"

"Oh, *yeah!*"

"Did they look anything like the ones we have now that has the right side of the face missing?"

"*No.* See, that's the funny thing. There's some that are missing. There's one that's a lateral shot of the skull—side picture." Custer said that they never showed a lateral shot that showed the fragments spread out (the pattern of spread which gives the direction from whence it came). "There's another—a side or tangential shot—it's strictly of the hole—the elongation of the hole. They never showed that one. I took pictures of the neck. They never showed those. I took pictures of the upper thoracic cavity. They never showed those."[22]

"Kennedy never came directly from Dallas to Bethesda," Custer said.

"How do you know it? Prove it!"

"I know it. I can't prove it. The only thing I know is, the officer of the day, a lieutenant, made the statement to me that night that 'Kennedy will be coming in by helicopter from Walter Reed.' And then they said Alexandria, Virginia, and I said, 'Wait a minute, Walter Reed isn't in Alexandria, is it?' 'No, it's coming in from Walter Reed from Alexandria.' I've never forgotten that. He came up and got me personally."[23]

"When we lifted him up and put plates under his lower back and his upper back, a fragment fell out."

"Was the fragment as big as your thumbnail?"

"It was pretty big. This is what I can't understand. That was the only fragment I saw that night. But the next day Ebersole had additional fragments and bigger bullets. How in hell did he get the rest of that bullet when we found only that one piece that night?"

Custer insisted that Jackie arrived after the autopsy began. "I was coming up from the ward with an FBI agent in front of me and an armful of X-rays and here comes Jacqueline Kennedy in the front door with Bobby Kennedy, and that was supposed to be the whole entourage."

"But you don't know for a fact that she was just arriving then—or that she had walked out and was just walking back in?"

"No, no! She was definitely coming in because I heard them saying it."

"Hearsay."

"Yeah. I heard 'em saying it. She still had that outfit on, and why would she go back out and come back in again?"

"To get some air."

"No. You don't realize how tight that security was. I mean, there were Secret Service agents everywhere."

"Yeah, but whenever she is going to take a step, ten men are going to take the same step, so she went out and they went with her and she came back in. The point is, you don't know for sure—I'm not saying at all that you're wrong, but you don't know for sure that she wasn't already there."

"See, I knew she was coming. That's another thing. I knew she was coming and I saw her come in. In fact, at the time the FBI agent made the comment about it too: 'You guys stand back here. I don't want them to know you are here.' So I knew for a fact that was the first time she was there."[24]

It's unfortunate that there are such severely contradictory statements as in the above. Custer's statements on various points—like those of some of the other men who had a good look at the wounds and with whom events that night registered well, are vitally important.

Some of what they say is discredited by the contradictions, and each other. What stands is what they all agree upon.

But once again we wonder if there was another fresh body look-alike that terrible night now beginning to fade into history, and whether the men were hypnoprogrammed, or, actually saw different things—different bodies—a half hour apart.

"The House Committee covered it up. They had to. That investigator [Purdy] was a real jerk. Why would you call anybody at two o'clock in the morning? He woke me out of a deep sleep and started questioning me at two o'clock in the morning. I told him, I said, hey, buddy, I don't know you from Adam. You want to talk to me, you come here to Pittsburgh and show me some proof that the gag order is off, and I hung up on him. Then he never called me back to make the appointment. He *never* even bothered to come to talk to me. He never came to interview me."

Jerry Custer described to me, after many interviews, the fact that he had been asked to leave the morgue as soon as the body was out of the casket. "Did they open it right away and take the body out?" I asked him.

"Well, that is when Ebersole turned around and looked at us and said, 'We don't need you right now.' So we left the morgue for about a half hour or more. Maybe forty-five minutes." (In a later interview, he said that it was at least an hour.[25])

"You are absolutely certain?"

"Yes."

"When you came back, was the body on the table?"

"When I came back, the body was on the table. We came back down and that's when we took the X-rays. The Y incision was already made."[26]

His statement that the Y incision was already made fits with the time that we know about, since Humes told the Assassinations Committee that the body came in at 7:35[27] and that he made that incision at 8:15.[28] If Custer was out of the room for thirty to forty-five minutes as he says, the Y incision would have been made before he came in.

We know that the men were asked to leave, as Metzler, Reed, Rudnicki, and others have said. Some were called back in about forty-five minutes later, and that is when Custer took his first X-rays. Ebersole, according to him, had already taken X-rays when the men were out of the room.

It would have been impossible for Jackie not to have already been there when Custer saw her as he came down the hallway with his first films to develop, since she had been there for more than an hour. The story we have been told is false.

Mrs. Kennedy had been waiting in an anteroom near the front door for others to arrive, and when she and the others went to the elevator to go up to the seventeenth floor, that is when Custer and the others saw her on the way up to develop his films. Or thought they did.

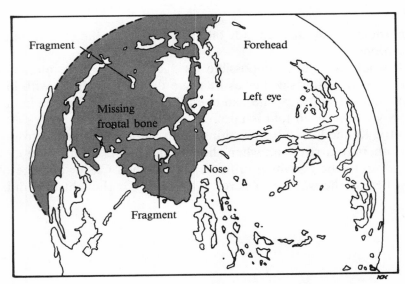

A.P. view

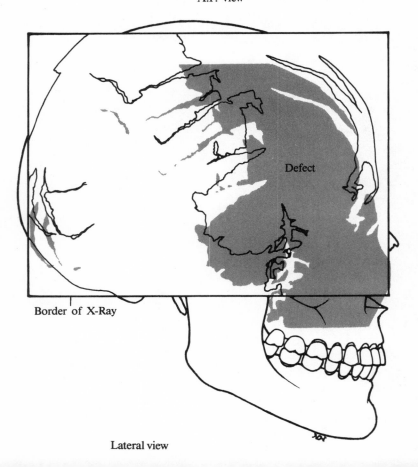

Lateral view

The photographs in this section are from what is known as the Fox set (identified with an F) and the so-called Groden set (identified with a G). The original Fox photos are in black and white. The Groden set is in color. Note that the face is perfectly intact in all of these pictures, but the X-rays show the entire top right front of President Kennedy's face blown away. Compare the X-rays to the Stare-of-Death photograph on the following page.

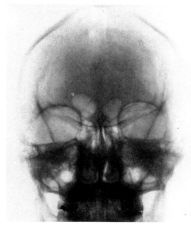

A normal Anterior-Posterior skull X-ray

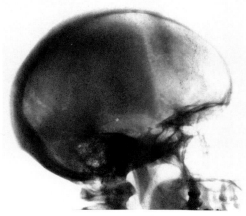

A normal Lateral skull X-ray

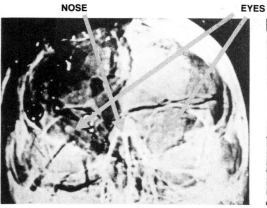

The Kennedy Anterior-Posterior skull X-ray

The Kennedy lateral skull X-ray Note the amount of facial bone that is missing.

These X-rays were allegedly taken of President Kennedy during the autopsy at Bethesda Naval Hospital. Note the large area of missing bone on the right front of the face, including the eye and forehead. According to the testimony and statements of all medical personnel in Dallas and Bethesda, no bone whatsoever was missing, removed, or replaced in any part of the face at any time during or after the autopsy. The skull X-rays are totally incompatible with the photographs of the face.

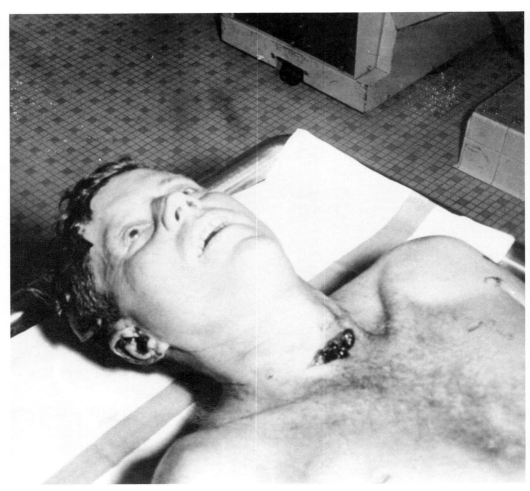

The Stare-of-Death photograph (F1)

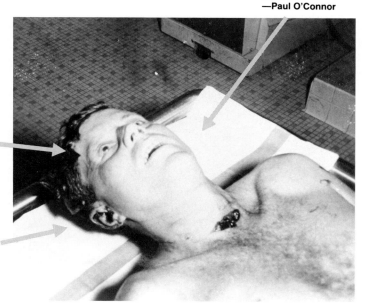

Reference black triangle

This shadow should not be here given the camera angle.

Note how wide the eyes are, yet the eyes are not divergent, nor is the right eye popped from the head as it was described by the medical witnesses. Tom Wilson's computer studies say the right eye has been painted in and is flat black on his gray scale study. It certainly does not look like it is the half-popped-out eye described by all the medical witnesses, and the eyes are not divergent as in the original **Groden Stare-of-Death** photograph I viewed in 1979, which he claims not to have at this time but which has been seen elsewhere by others since then. The eyes were quite askew when I saw Groden's version, and that is the way the eyes were described by the medical witnesses. There seems to be a lack of whiskers and pores in the skin, leading some to speculate that this is a wax head with real hair. Our studies indicate that the hair is in fact entirely fake, the hairline painted in all along the forehead, and the entire right side of the head painted in. Note there is no flap of skull sticking out from the right temple.

The shadow cast by the head on the towel beneath the right ear is in the wrong place for a light source at this camera angle. The camera's flash would leave no shadow in that area. Look carefully at the face. It may actually be a mask, a face from another picture put over this one. The right eye is probably not real.

Study the throat incision (tracheostomy) and compare it to what we see in the Left Profile photograph. There is considerable retouching on one end of the tracheostomy here, and along the edge, to make it look jagged and irregular, larger than it is. This was taken to be an exit wound, not realizing it was made by Dr. Malcolm Perry pretty much like we see it, except for the retouching. You can see the lower half of the bullet entry hole near the center of the bottom lip of the incision. It is almost a perfect semicircle, certainly not what an exiting bullet would leave there, in view of the ragged tear in the trachea which Dr. Perry reported.

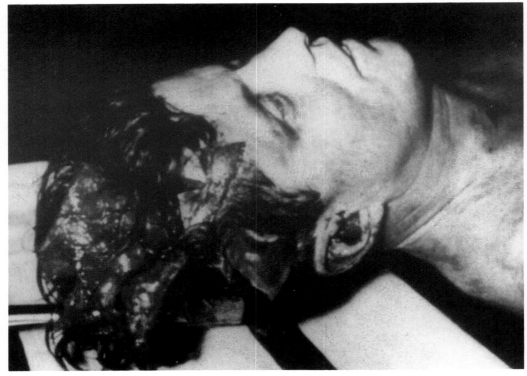

The Groden Superior Right Profile (G1)

This is a black and white print made from a color print in Groden's possession, one of a number of color autopsy pictures he has shown since he was staff consultant to the House Assassinations Committee. Note that the right side of the head is intact except for the apparent wound: what is called the "Devil's Ear" and the "Bat-Wing Configuration," neither of which is in the right place for the small flap of bone we see sticking out from the head in the Back-of-the-Head photographs.

It is impossible for the back of the head to either appear so intact or to have been perched on the steel headrest as we see here, with the large defect described by the autopsists.

The autopsy report makes clear that the large defect extended from the back of the head to just in front of the ear. Except for the flap in the back and on top, the scalp was missing. It would appear, therefore, that the whole right side of the head in this picture has been painted in with a matte overlay, as Paul O'Connor wrote me when he commented on this fake photograph.

Note the laceration extending from a half inch inside the forehead straight back toward the rear. Some have felt that this is an incision made at the autopsy later in the night for reflecting the scalp back, but the autopsy doctors have insisted that the body arrived with this large laceration caused by the fractured bones beneath pushing through. Not only do we not see the laceration in the other pictures, the part that extends into the forehead over the right eye has been masked over with a black triangle in the black and white prints, leading some to think that a bullet entry hole was covered up there. The color picture showing this tear or cut is therefore wholly incompatible with the black and whites showing the right side of the face.

There is no background in this or any of the other Groden pictures. Shadows were airbrushed into them to mask matte lines, and backgrounds were cropped out.

Note that the face appears pasty and white, and yet this was taken before the autopsy began. Although the sharpness of the nose may be due to the camera angle, the nose nevertheless does not appear to be Kennedy's. The moles highly visible on his face in photographs taken in the morning are not seen here, nor are the pores or whiskers. The mouth and eyes are more closed.

Bullet entry into head

"Bat Wing
Configuration"

The Three Stripes:
Scalp or brain?
These were actually
painted on this
photograph.

An anomaly. This is
covered with a black
triangle in the other
black and white
autopsy photos.

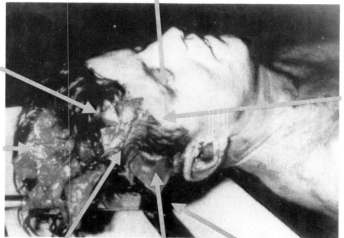

Sutures?

"Devil's Ear"

This area was
painted and
retouched. There
was no bone here
and little scalp.

The three stripes
hanging down on top
of the head are black
here. They were very
red in the color
photo, but they are
white-gray in the
black and white
prints. Note tear into
JFK's forehead over
his right eye. It is
blackened out on
Inferior Right Profile
(See reference black
triangle on Stare-of-
Death photo.).

"Note the scalp is
torn in pieces and
hangs down over the
head wound."
—Paul O'Connor

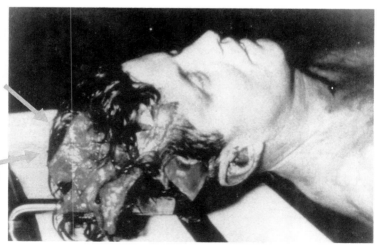

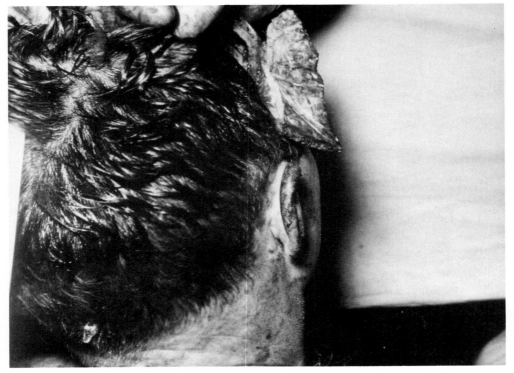

The Back of the Head (F3)

Note the flap sticking out from the head. There are saw marks along the edge of the flap which may correspond to the area in the temple radiologists have told me has been surgically removed from the skull.

Note the area which is out of focus from behind the right ear all along the hairline to the center of the back of the head near the neck. The area that is out of focus is paint covering the edge of the large flap of scalp so that no one could easily see how all the bone escaped the head. There is no bone beneath the scalp. Note also that at the top of the picture by the fingers pulling the flap over the big hole, one can see the edge of the large defect, which is much lower in the other pictures. This picture fooled everyone because it gave the impression there was no real damage to the back of the head.

The apparent wound in the cowlick clearly does not appear (or appears in a slightly different position) in other views showing the back of the head, as Dr. Humes noted. Humes indicated that this and other pictures were printed in black and white from color pictures, and the color pictures are either paintings or in part retouched . One might also suppose that there were additional tracings made from the pictures by Ida Dox, which were then colored and passed to Groden. The alleged wound in the cowlick actually has hairs growing out of it, and is in fact painted onto the photograph on overlays. Humes as much as said this during his HSCA interview.

Groden possesses two similar prints. One may have a slightly different camera angle and the other is probably just a cropped version of the black and white that has been colored. One of these has a series of black crescents a half inch apart and a half inch long all along the hairline. His pictures are clearly colored or painted pieces of art, and not reproductions of this black and white picture.

COMMENTS BY STEVE MILLS

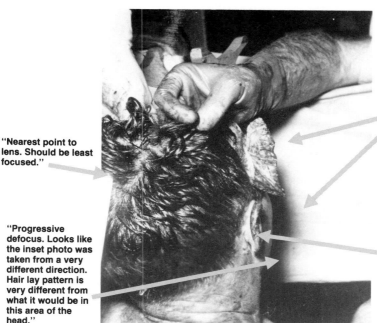

"Nearest point to lens. Should be least focused."

"No shadow cast into this cavity by the hair. All shadows in this one look wrong. They don't relate to what we see, especially the flap. Note the ear's shadow is complete on his cheek."

"Progressive defocus. Looks like the inset photo was taken from a very different direction. Hair lay pattern is very different from what it would be in this area of the head."

"True focal plane of the original photo."

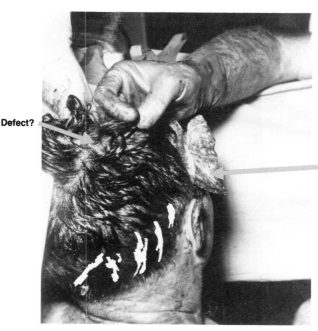

Defect?

Serrated edge from a saw?

Audrey Bell's drawing (white lines on hair) of the edge of the flap of scalp on the back of the head, which rises from the right bottom of the head to the top; an identical description was given by some of the autopsy staff. The flap covers a large loss of bone beneath it.

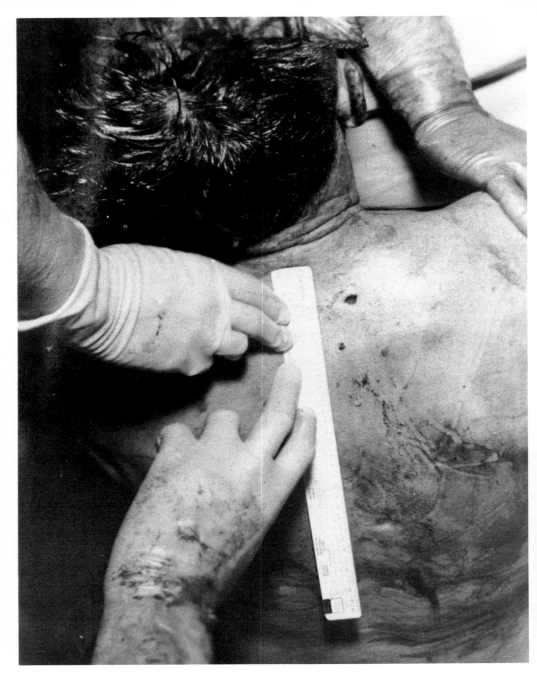

The Back (F5)

Note that there are *two* apparent bullet holes, one near the shoulder, which some witnesses say is only a clot, and a deep indentation some seven inches down on the back near the spine, which the Navy photographer and others say is the real bullet hole. It is not a scar. Note also that there is no bullet hole in the cowlick on the back of the head. This black and white print shows striations on the skin made by the sheets, and other pressure points.

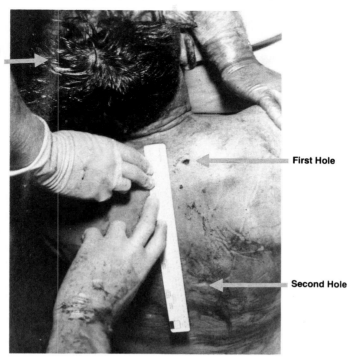

"Note the head. No entry wound."
—Paul O'Connor

First Hole

Second Hole

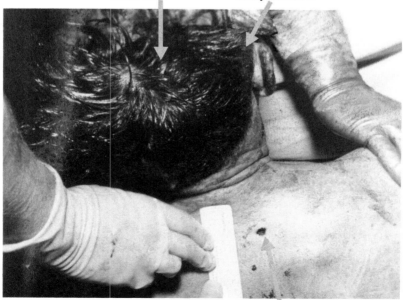

This photo shows no evidence of an entry hole as Dr. James J. Humes said.

Cavity in cranium

Alleged entry in back

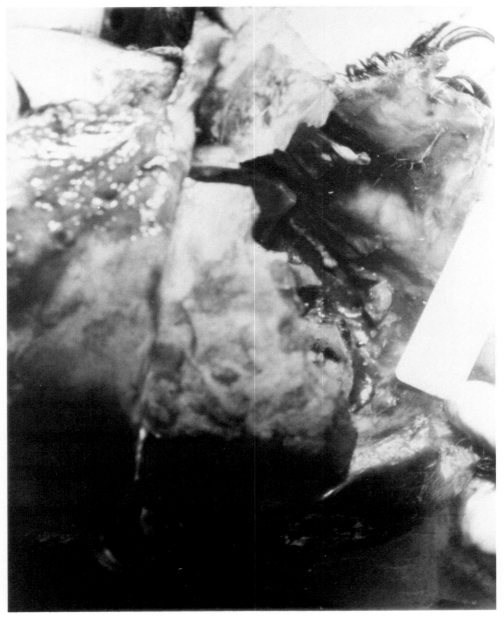

The Large Defect (F8)

Groden possesses a color copy of this photograph, which is identical in all respects. The photograph is difficult to orient, but study the drawing (opposite page) made by Paul O'Connor. On the left side, note the lip of a specimen jar just visible alongside the neck. The right side of the head is by the hand, and the right side of the neck is at the bottom right of the picture, with the left side of the neck on the left margin. The hairline is just barely visible. Note the scalp reflected back to the left. This was "just like a window shade," as Jim Metzler and Audrey Bell described it, and could be peeled aside to reveal the large bony defect beneath, which we see here. No part of this photo appears faked, but the problem is in knowing which part of the head it is in or whose head it is. It proves there was a major hole in the back and right side of the head.

TOP

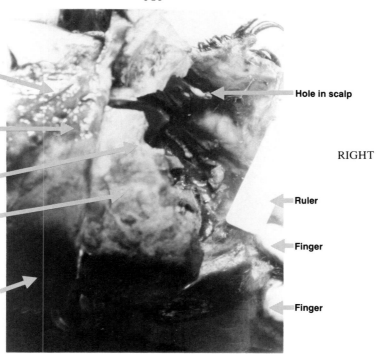

Scalp flap reflected to left.

Hole in scalp

Back-of-head midline

LEFT

RIGHT

Beveled outward exiting fragment

Ruler

Bone

Finger

"You are looking into the wound. The occipital protuberance is above the table over the bottle top."
—Paul O'Connor

Finger

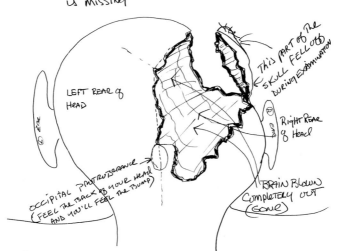

REAR OF HEAD SHOWING APPROXIMATELY HOW MUCH OF THE SKULL is missing

THIS PART OF THE SKULL FELL OFF DURING EXAMINATION

LEFT REAR OF HEAD

RIGHT REAR OF HEAD

OCCIPITAL PROTUBERANCE (FEEL THE BACK OF YOUR HEAD AND YOU'LL FEEL THE BUMP)

BRAIN BLOWN COMPLETELY OUT (GONE)

HARRY: THE WOUND IN THE RIGHT SIDE OF THE SKULL WAS HUGE BUT NOT BIG ENOUGH TO REMOVE THE BRAIN WITHOUT TEARING THE ORGAN APART

P.S. I CAN'T DRAW WELL!

Drawing by Paul O'Connor

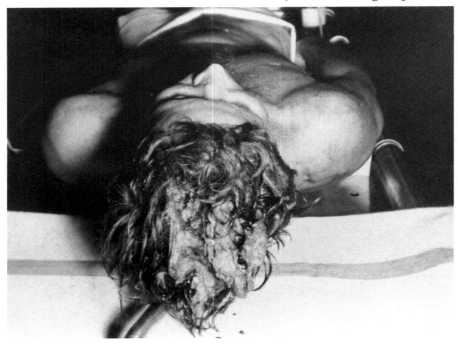

The Top of the Head (F6 and F7)

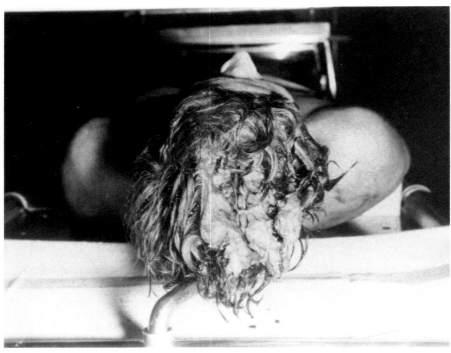

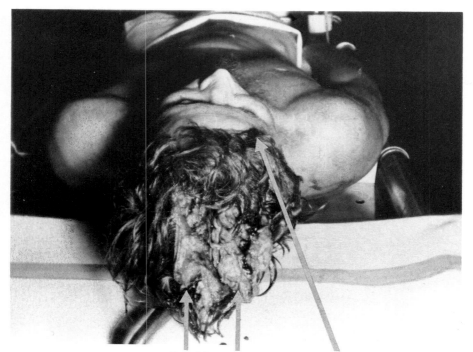

**Brain? Scalp? Matter
is white-gray.**

**The reference black
triangle**

There are two black and white and one color photograph from this angle. Groden's color picture is probably colored from (F6). The second black and white view has the camera a few inches higher. Note that the large defect goes all the way over to the left side of the head, meaning this cannot be Kennedy's body, because the large defect did not cross the midline of his head. In addition, the brain is fully visible to the top of the hole instead of being gouged out and missing as carefully described by Dr. James J. Humes. Further, the hole is nowhere near the main areas described as being missing, in the back and all along the right side, which shows nowhere in any of the other pictures.

Audrey Bell wrote on a copy of this picture: "This does not look like the wound area that I remember seeing."

Note how white or gray the three stripes of matter are hanging down from the top of the head. Turn to the Groden Right Superior Profile picture and note how black they are. They are bright red in the Groden pictures, which goes to black when printed in black and white, and therefore have been painted into his picture.

Note the small black triangle in the hairline over the right eye. This changes orientation in the three pictures it appears in, and covers up the torn or incised skin seen in the Groden Right Superior photograph extending a half inch into the forehead. Mark Crouch, who discovered it, thinks it may cover another bullet hole. No light passes through the triangle on the negatives, and is therefore referred to as "reference black."

Note the small instrument table over the top of the body, which sits on top of the autopsy table. The doctors insist that the little table was not the type they used and did not sit over the body. The Y incision has not been made.

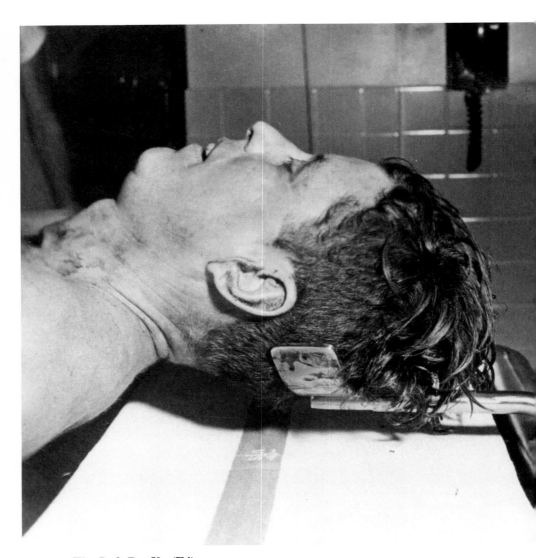

The Left Profile (F4)

The grout line is misaligned.

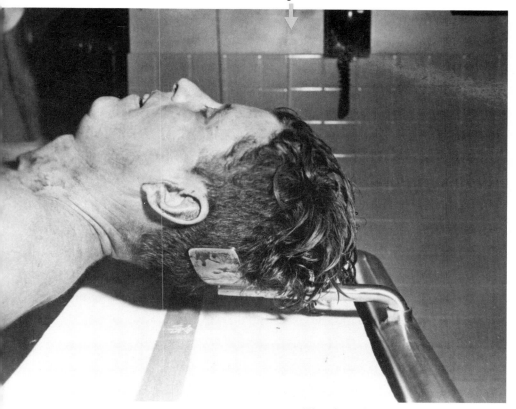

"Note the neck wound. Compare this with [the Stare-of-Death photo]."
—Paul O'Connor

Note the vertical grout line between the tiles where the hair meets the forehead. The tiles to the left side of it are not full-size, as though this were a composite photograph. The autopsy crew say there was no phone at that position on the wall alongside the table. Note the throat incision. No Y incision has been made. The eyes are more closed in this photograph. The throat incision is not particularly large in this view. There is no evidence of a wound or even a small hole anywhere in the left temple area or anywhere else on the left side, and there is none on the X-rays. The Dallas doctors have since said that they made a simple error when they thought there was such a perforation, but had probably seen only a spot of blood. A 6.5 bullet entry hole in the scalp would be very small, partly closed over, and difficult to spot.

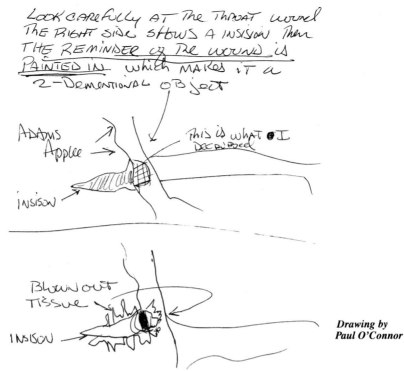

LOOK CAREFULLY AT THE THROAT WOUND
THE RIGHT SIDE SHOWS A INSISON THEN
THE REMINDER OF THE WOUND IS
PAINTED IN WHICH MAKES IT A
2-DEMENTIONAL OBJECT

ADAMS
APPLE →

THIS IS WHAT I
DESCRIBED

INSISON

BLOWN OUT
TISSUE

INSISON

Drawing by
Paul O'Connor

Paul O'Connor insists that the peculiar shape of the throat wound results from photographic retouching.

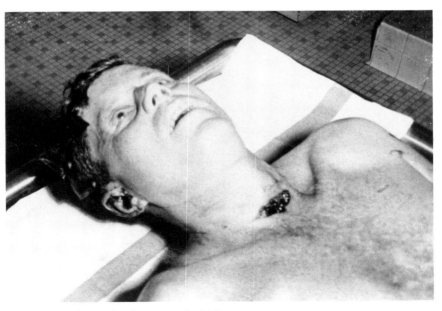

The Stare-of-Death photograph (F1)

"Kennedy . . . still has the possibility of being, in the eyes of history, the greatest president of the United States, the leader who may at last understand that there can be coexistence between capitalists and socialists. . . . He would then be an even greater president than Lincoln."

—Fidel Castro

CHAPTER 11

JAMES CURTIS JENKINS

On October 8, 1990, I interviewed Jim Jenkins at some length. Jenkins was Dr. Thornton Boswell's assistant at the autopsy, and just nineteen years old. He has had a difficult time dealing with the horror of what happened that night in 1963.

"I was talked to by the Assassinations Committee, by Mr. Kelly and Mr. Purdy."

"Did they show you any pictures?"

"They were very intimidating individuals. . . . They lied to me . . . they both told me they were lawyers, and then when you checked their identification, Kelly was an FBI agent, and when I talked to them, they really didn't want to know what I knew. They played games. To be honest with you, I got angry. They took me down to the legal library in Jackson [Mississippi] to show me the pictures of the Warren Commission, which I had already . . . I already knew they were just . . . they were not real."

"They were pictures of the body?"

"Yeah, the ones in the Warren Commission Report." (The drawings, not the photographs. These are highly inaccurate.)

"Paul O'Connor and I were the only two people there on duty that night, and I was in the morgue all night long. There's some things that I remembered, and every time I ever told anybody it's always been implied: 'We don't really care—we want this, this, and this!' "

"They want you to say certain things?" I asked.

"Yes, so I haven't really done much about it. To be quite honest with you, I'm surprised that Paul and Custer talked to you after our first bad experiences [with official investigators and other researchers].

"Then we were not allowed to talk all of those years. They had each one of us under threat of court-martial. Then I received an order that I could talk to Purdy and Kelly, but that was all. No one else.

"I would like to sit down with the other people and verify with them and talk to them about what I remember and what they remember. I have some twenty questions for the people from Parkland, also. And for once I'd just like to get this thing cleared up in my own mind and get it over with."

He does not remember Floyd Riebe. He said that he remembers only the people that he worked with: Humes, Boswell, O'Connor. He said that the handwriting on Boswell's autopsy face sheet drawings giving the organ weights and so forth were his handwriting. He spent almost the whole night at the head of the autopsy table.

"It wasn't necessary to surgically remove the brain from the skull. I remember Humes saying, 'This brain fell out in my hands. The brain stem has been surgically cut.' The brain was there and it was intact, but it was damaged. I remember it was difficult to infuse it because the circle of Willis [an H-shaped circle of vessels underneath the brain] was damaged and it was difficult to get the needles in. The brain would infuse for several hours and then we would drop it into a bucket of formaldehyde.

"I left the next morning and as well as I could remember, the brain was in the bucket. Those are the things I told Purdy and Kelly. They didn't even . . . they were so apathetic about reporting the stuff, they just breezed over it like it wasn't there.

"At that time I was in a Ph.D. program in pathology, and they asked me questions like where is the occipital? I just got to the point where I didn't care to talk to them."[1]

The House Committee people showed him the artist's rendition of the drawings in the Warren Report and talked to him about a hole in the top of the head, and "there was nothing whatsoever like that."

"Nothing like the Warren drawing?"

"No. The only thing that comes close is the flap of scalp and bone a little anterior to the ear, which was similar to what we saw."

"Do you think that the Committee ignored you then?"

"Yes! I know they did."[2]

* * *

"I looked at the back of the head, but all I saw was the massive gaping wound. The head remained wrapped in sheet and towels until the men came in. We were specifically told not to remove the sheet and towels. And all the conversation about no brain—well, *the head wound was not accessible at that point in time.*"

"All that happened in the anteroom where the cold boxes are. When the body came into the morgue proper, it came in on a stretcher wrapped in sheets. There was a casket already in there [in the anteroom or cold room] when Kennedy's body came in."[3]

In response to my questions on October 8, 1990, as to whether or not there was enough intact scalp on the back of the head to completely cover up the large hole described by all witnesses, Jenkins said, *"No.*

"There was a hole in all of it [the scalp and the bone]. There was a hole in the occipital-parietal area. I had seen a wound similar to that before.

"I just never could understand how they came up with the conclusions that they did.

"The other thing that they told me was that there was a wound on the top of the head. I don't remember that. I could almost say that there was none."

"Were you there all of the time?"

"I *was* there all of the time. The only time I was away from the table was probably five or ten minutes when I was told to get a sandwich. But I did not leave the room."

"Were you there when the men from the funeral home came to dress the body?"

"There was only one man who came. And he was striking because I was in the military and he came in with his bowler and his vest and so forth. He did everything. He did the embalming, and he did the cosmetics."

"Were any photographs taken during that period?"

"I'm not sure, to be honest with you. The only photographs that I remember were taken at the beginning of the autopsy." He recalls an older civilian who did the photographic work. In his late forties, or early fifties. Fifty-five." That would be John Stringer.

Jenkins said that when they did the autopsy, the throat wound was listed as a tracheotomy, and "it looked like a trach." At that time no one at the autopsy knew that there had been a bullet wound in the throat, because the tracheostomy performed in Dallas obscured it. "Dr. Boswell did look into the neck cavity. I remember that. If there had been a bullet in there, it would have done considerable damage to the trach and the esophagus and so forth in that area."

He said that when the body was unwrapped and he first saw the throat wound, "it was pretty wide. It looked like a hastily done trach. But two and a half inches is, you know, kind of big." Dr. Perry had insisted to a *Baltimore Sun* reporter in 1979 that he had made the large gash in the throat to insert the cuff for the breathing tube. Perry seems to agree to the picture.

"I would say that it was at least an inch and a half or two inches wide," Jenkins said. "I was real surprised at the fact later on that that was supposed to have been a bullet wound. We found no bullets, no fragments in the *body*. I remember the arguments, the animosities radiating from the gallery because there were no bullet fragments found."

"With regard to the neck wound, I remember the animosities from the gallery [the viewing area overlooking the autopsy table where numerous officers and others observed] because the wound path couldn't be probed into the chest cavity. They tried their damnedest to do that, *almost to the point of making an entrance wound* into the pleural cavity with a metal probe. That was Dr. Humes trying to probe that neck wound. There was nothing found there.

"Stover was down on the floor behind me. Galloway was in the gallery. I didn't know Burkley. Stover was the one who finally told me to go and get something to eat. I walked behind him to the three little rooms just back there, got a sandwich, took a couple of bites, and went back to the table.

"Everything from just above the right ear back was fragmented. It was broken up, but it was being held together by the scalp."

"Was there an area of actual absence of scalp and bone?"

"Yes, there was. There was an area probably along the midline just above the occipital area."

"In the occipital area?"

"Yeah, right at the occipital area. It was higher. One of the things I don't understand is that this would not have been low enough to have gotten into the cerebellum."

Jenkins does not remember the kind of damage to the cerebellum that was described in Dallas, but only to the rest of the brain on the right side.

He does not recall any damage to the face, but says that "they had some problems keeping the right eye closed after they were doing the cosmetics."

When asked about the X-rays showing the top right front of the face missing, he said, "I'm sure that's not the case." This put him in line with Dr. Boswell and all the other witnesses from the autopsy who have talked about it.

I also asked him if he had seen any damage to the left temple area. In Dallas, the death certificate said that the President had died "from a gunshot wound to the left temple." Jenkins said that neither he nor anyone else at the autopsy to the best of his knowledge had seen any such wound.

"I might have gone along with *right* temple," he said. I agree with that because just above the right ear there was some discoloration of the skull cavity with the bone area being gray and there was some speculation that it might be lead.

"There might have been an entry wound there?"

"Yes. And the opening and the way the bone was damaged behind the head would have definitely been a type of exit wound. The reason I have said this is I saw this before in other wounds and it was very striking.

"I have done many autopsies. I would like to talk to the other people because I think that what I remember at Bethesda is true. I'd like to know who wrapped the head at Parkland and what kind of towels they were. I'd like to talk to the individuals who actually cleaned and wrapped the body for shipment."

Jenkins said he never understood why he was never contacted by anyone from the night of the autopsy until the Assassinations Committee investigating the case in 1977 got in touch with him. "I stood right there within three feet of the autopsy all night." But no one was interested, and he feels negatively about the Committee staff who did come to see him. They weren't interested in what he had to say.

He did not know Dennis David, who was not present during the autopsy. He remembers Jan Gail Rudnicki, Jim Metzler.

Jenkins said, "I have a lot of questions. I'd like to get together with Boswell, Humes, and Finck. Humes made the comment that the brain 'fell out in my hand.' I know they didn't do a skull cap because all they did was extend the sagittal suture a little to get the remainder of the brain out. Actually, it was the sagittal suture in the top of the skull. They extended that a little bit. It doesn't make sense to me where they came up with a hole in the top of the head that was that close to the frontal bone.

He said that the autopsy logbook disappeared. "We really never logged the President in that night. Someone told us that he was coming. Someone had penciled in *C & C* up on the right-hand side of the log next to the autopsy number we used.

"I remember a nice casket coming in. We were told that we had an Army or Air Force major for burial the next day, which is kind of unusual. We were told not to worry about logging him in, and that was extremely unusual."

"Did Kennedy come in a shipping casket?"

Jenkins answered, "I don't know," but didn't see that happen. "He [Kennedy] was taken out of the casket in the atrium before we went into the morgue proper. As you came into the morgue there was a little room that had the cold boxes. But he was taken out of that and brought in on a gurney all wrapped in sheets.

"We put him on the table and we were told not to take the towels off his head. We did unwrap him and we did the body work."

Jenkins ended the conversation with saying that "it was a big lie perpetrated in our history. The really bad thing about it was why this was perpetrated. Did they cover it up for the reasons that LBJ gave, that the people couldn't handle it, or was it for more sinister reasons? It has certainly changed my whole perception of the government.

"Sometime before my death I'd like to get to the bottom of it. I'd like to sit down with people who were witnesses. I'd like to read all of the books about it.

"I don't understand the conclusions of the Warren Commission. The things that came out of the autopsy were total fabrications. As naive as I was at that time, it was pretty shocking to me."

He said that the bullet could not have come out the throat and hit Connally because "the angle was wrong and it would have done massive damage in the trach area. There was no such damage. Boswell lifted the Y incision [the major cuts on the torso to remove the organs] or butterfly area of the throat [no dissection of the throat area was done] up and looked in there and felt it with his fingers. If there had been that type of damage there—we're talking about a cartilaginous ring structure—it would have all been shattered."[4]

I have conducted a series of lengthy interviews with Jim Jenkins since

October 1990. On April 6, 1991, he came to the meeting in Dallas with some of the other autopsy witnesses and some of the Parkland witnesses, which we filmed.

On June 16, 1991, he responded to a long series of questions in the following interview.

"When did you hear that the President's body was coming?"

"Three o'clock sticks in my mind because that was about when the classes were canceled and we were told to report to the morgue."

Air Force 1 had not taken off yet. It was airborne at 3:47 EST. But, as many people in the Navy noted, "he was a Navy man. We knew he was coming to Bethesda."

The Air Force Major

I asked him about the other body that was received that afternoon, November 22, 1963. He had previously said that he was told it was the body of an Air Force major. "It came in earlier in the evening, after I arrived from classes. It came in about the time we first went to the morgue. I'm sure it was at least an hour before JFK came in. Maybe quite a bit more."

Jenkins was not allowed to leave the room, except once when Captain Stover told him to eat his lunch. He was gone only a few moments.[5]

"Was the body in the casket?"

"Yes. It wasn't taken out of the casket and put in a cold box. It sat on a pop-up cart in the cold room, not in a cold box, and that's where it remained."

He said it had to be after 3:30 "when the other corpsman went off duty. I remember it coming in. It was Paul's [O'Connor] and my job to log it in, but they wouldn't let us log it in."

Jim said that he did not actually see the body in the casket, as it was not opened.[6]

Jim said that along with them was a first class (E6) hospital corpsman as the duty corpsman that night. "He was first class and he was one of the few first class in that position. He was an instructor in the School of Lab Sciences, and worked in special chemistry. He was in there the early part of that night. He was there when the major came in. He told me not to log the body in. Said he had been told not to log it in."

He said that the casket the Air Force major was in was a "nice casket," rosewood or red mahogany. "It was not a *cheap casket.* It had brass fixtures." During another interview he said it was mahogany, with ornate brass fixtures.[7]

"There was really no one in that room [the cold room] after the autopsy started. The double doors stayed open. A baby was admitted to the morgue that night sometime."

"Was there a clock on the wall?"

"Military rooms don't go without clocks."

"The Air Force major came in at least an hour before. Maybe more." But the casket of the alleged officer came in after they had started to prepare for the President's autopsy. "It was not there when we came on."

"It was not there when you came on?"

"No. When a body came into the morgue, we had to log it in, Paul and me.

"As soon as they told us classes were canceled, the duty people were told to report to the morgue. I was never allowed to leave."

"And you think that was at three-thirty?"

"I think so."[8]

There is a conflict between Metzler's recollection that the casket came directly into the morgue and Jenkins believing that the casket never came in but went to the cold room adjoining the morgue and was unloaded there, the body being wheeled into the morgue.

He told me that four men helped set up the morgue: Paul O'Connor, Jim Metzler, himself, and the first class, who was their boss.

After the body was received and removed from the coffin, they waited twenty minutes before the head was unwrapped.

Jenkins told me that he had originally thought that the casket JFK came in was brown, but he only really remembers the casket JFK was buried in, which was mahogany.

When the President's body came in, Jim did not help take it out of the casket. He saw it come in the morgue on the gurney, wrapped in sheets. "It came out of the casket in the cold room. Paul was in the ante [cold] room." Jenkins says Paul *did* help take it out of the casket. Jenkins was in the morgue.[9] But Jenkins did not get a close look at the casket, as he was in the morgue.

"There were no shipping caskets around there."[10] With regard to this matter, Jenkins feels that Paul O'Connor would know more about the casket the body arrived in.

He doesn't recall logging in the President. There was no name with the autopsy number, but someone wrote *C & C,* which meant Commander in Chief.

"We did a full-scale autopsy on JFK. We removed the testes, the adrenals [which would have been removed with the kidneys], etc. His lungs were very pink. But the question came, does he smoke? It came back that he took an occasional cigar.

"There were sections of the heart and other organs taken."

He remembers a doctor whom he thinks was Grogan. He isn't sure, and that name is not yet known to us. "I remember a resident in pathology. Real thin, curly hair, swarthy, brought something to Humes or Boswell that they had requested."

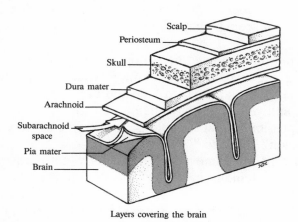

Layers covering the brain

The brain stem was severed very smoothly. The brain was turned upside down and put into a gauze sling and he and Boswell infused it through two vessels—internal carotids, he thinks. "We put a needle in each one of those that was attached to a piece of tubing that went to a five-gallon container of formalin up on top of the cabinets. We would normally let it sit there for three, four hours, then we'd drop it in the bucket which was filled with formalin.

"I remember Dr. Humes questioning whether or not the brain stem had been severed by a bullet, because the brain fell out in his hand. It was a smooth cut that looked like it had been severed with a knife or a scalpel—at the area of the axis [as it enters at the skull] which is at the first vertebra.

"Humes asked someone in the gallery if there had been any surgery at Parkland. From the discussion that I heard, from Humes asking someone in the gallery if there had been surgery to the head area, from the surgical cuts in the area of the wound, from the fact that the brain stem was severed, there had to be an extensive professional exam of the head area before it ever got to Bethesda. I'm sure that minimum incisions were made to get to the brain. They had to be minimum in order to keep it covered. They probably were very calculating in their cuts. It was a mess—blood, brains, skull. But it had to be obvious enough for Dr. Humes to question it. I'm thoroughly convinced.

"Prior to taking the brain out, just looking at the head, I think what prompted the comments in the FBI report was that there were some surgical incisions at the area of the top of the skull near the wound."

He said that the skull was cut with a scalpel along a suture or fracture line. Only one cut, but, "there may have been others." In other words, much of this hinges on seeing what may have been only a one-half to one-inch cut.

"It [surgery] would have to have been done in order to remove the brain. If you were going to remove the brain, it would take a few very small incisions of less than an inch to take the brain out, due to the extensive damage, and you would have had to cut the brain stem also. There is always a possibility that it could be a tear [the surgery to the brain stem], but I don't think so."[11]

Later the spinal cord was removed—a Stryker saw cut both sides of the vertebral column. Jenkins saw Dr. Boswell remove the spinal cord.[12]

Both Dr. Boswell,[13] and Dr. Robert Karnei,[14] who was present in the autopsy room, deny that the spinal cord was removed. Once again it sounds as though we are talking about two different autopsies.

Part of the problem of trying to solve a case with so much conflicting evidence is the way people's minds play tricks on them. A lot of the witnesses did not see certain things because they were momentarily out of the room or otherwise occupied, so they will compensate by making certain assumptions in their mind which then become fact. If they think that Robert Kennedy was limiting the autopsy and they did not see the spinal cord removed, for instance, then they may state that the spinal cord was not removed because Robert did not want it done.

It is very common under stress for people's minds to imagine that they saw something when they did not or to block out memory of certain events. Jackie K. as climbing on the trunk of the car or Nelly Connally going up a flight of stairs.

I am not suggesting that that is what happened here, and that the spinal cord was in fact removed. I don't know at this point. The cord is not properly mentioned in the autopsy report, whereas normally it would be.

"There had to be an examination of the body before it came to Bethesda for the brain stem to be severed. Those were surgical. They had to be done beforehand [the surgery to the skull and brain stem only]."

"Did someone get at the body?" I asked.

"Yes. They would have had to know what they were doing, have the time, and know where the bullets were," he said. The bullets would tell us if different guns were used.

"It would have had to be a concerted effort to accomplish something like this. I know that in my own mind that somewhere between Dallas and Bethesda somebody examined the body," he said.[15]

"Suppose the bullet that hit him in the throat came up that way and came out the back of the head?"

"There would have had to be a hole in the base of the skull."

"And you would have noticed it?"

"Well, yes, sure!"

"Suppose that it came out through the area that was later the large defect?"

"It still would have had to come up through the floor of the skull."

"I think the reason Humes and Boswell never said primarily what they thought was that they never were asked their opinion if there was a possibility of a second bullet from another angle," he said. They were never asked if the President was hit twice in the head.

With reference to the appearance of the body, Jim said, "I wouldn't say that he was emaciated." The consensus, except for Paul O'Connor's caveat, was that Kennedy looked in the pink of health.

"I felt like he was a small man," Jenkins said. Contrast this with the unnamed doctor at Parkland Hospital who is quoted by Theodore Sorensen in *Kennedy* as saying, "I had never seen the President before. He was a big man, bigger than I thought."

On May 9, 1991, I called Jim again. He reported to me that his nephew had examined a set of the autopsy photographs for us. His nephew Charles had two degrees in photography. He reported that Charles had said that "there was definitely not an overlay of two negatives, but it could be an airbrushed negative." What police forensic people I could find could not find a matte line either. Neither could the HSCA.

"The most striking thing is the amount of the pictures which are out of focus. Almost intentionally out of focus."

We talked about the wounds again. "Like we said, there was still an area the size of a silver dollar, a hole left in the back underneath the scalp. In the later stages of the autopsy they were trying to fit the bone fragments together. . . . there may have been some small fragments missing beneath the scalp . . . with the overlapping bone attached to the scalp." This is not clear. Certainly not in the area described.

"Was there any metal found at the autopsy?"

"No, not really. There were some metal fragments that were brought into the autopsy in a small bag. They weren't found in the head or torso at Bethesda."

"That was one of the reasons for the animosities or tensions going on between the gallery and the doctors. That was the reason why the radiologist came in, because there was an insinuation that the guy who was taking the X-rays [Custer] didn't know what he was doing."

"I can't say with authority yes or no if there was a shipping casket. I'm also not sure if it was in a body bag and on a gurney. I don't really know. I can't answer those questions. I do have a memory of the body in sheets.

"I have no doubt but that the body was examined very thoroughly before it got to Bethesda. I don't know where. Probably we could . . ."

And then Jenkins, who has begun to investigate the case himself, asked if photographs of the autopsy room at Walter Reed were available. The men had insisted that some of the features seen in the photographs did not exist in the morgue at Bethesda, but then, they might have been mistaken about that.

"We had basically three wounds, two wounds with no exits—no metal fragments in the back wound [which went nowhere]. The brain that we saw was not that damaged. It was damaged, don't get me wrong, but it wasn't damaged to the point where the cerebellum was totally severed and the midbrain was totally exposed and all of this stuff. The midbrain . . . all of these internal structures . . . the midbrain would have had to be dissected in order to make the statements that were made and to come up with a 1500-gram weight for that brain, it would have been one of two things: Either it was a normal brain [intact] or it had been [undamaged?]. Well, it had been intact."

A bullet can pass through the brain, and what it actually does to brain tissue is traumatize—it jells a little.

"There was a brain. I helped infuse the brain."

He said that the logical place for the pre-examination was on the plane. "There was security. All of the people on the plane had strong emotional or political ties to Kennedy, and it would have been to their advantage not to say anything. That would break everything if one individual who was actually there would speak out.

"Both the Secret Service and the FBI had men who could probe for and remove bullets, and they were both involved. I'm sure a lot of their forensics people who were not physicians could have done it. The type of examination we're talking about, to take out the bullet and so forth —it would take very special people, and they are refusing to talk. But it would take an X-ray, time, and special people to remove the bullet or fragments."

Jenkins felt that if exploding bullets were used, there would be damage and fragments to and in both hemispheres of the brain, but he said that the damage was limited to the right side. There were no fragments on the left side. Prussic acid explodes on contact. If used in exploding bullets, metal fragments would be distributed throughout the brain. "But the brain that I saw was virtually intact, and there were no fragments. The flap in the Zapruder film is much bigger than in the pics and at the autopsy."[16]

The brain was basically intact. "Probably a fourth of it was lost."

"The towels that were on the head were an off green—a lightish greenish." At this time we cannot determine for certain if there were towels on the head when it left Parkland. Aubrey Rike, who could feel the edges of the wound through the sheet when he placed the body in the casket, said no, there were no towels. There is no record of towels having been used to wrap the head at Parkland. Only sheets.

* * *

Jenkins said that he and Paul were told to go to the morgue at three-thirty to four P.M. Jenkins was not allowed to leave the morgue. "Paul was a kind of courier. He always had an escort, and was in and out of the morgue."

"There was a fight in the gallery, or a pushing match. One of the reasons why was that there was someone taking pictures."[17]

He pointed out in one of the photographs of the body the metal block that was used under the neck to raise the head and keep it in place.

Jenkins was reading the Warren Report, which I sent him. "It is almost as though they are talking about two different autopsies," he said.[18]

He said the instrument table would not be over the body until the Y incision was made. "There would have been a scale next to it."[19] The pictures show an instrument table on four short legs sitting astride the body. We used the same type, but it had a hanging scale attached to one corner. "It was a cutting board, really. They put the organs on them and cut them. The one we had at Bethesda had a scale attached."

He recalled taking all the sheets off the body. The phone on the wall was in the wrong place, not as it is in the pictures behind the right side of the head. We see it on the tile wall just above the head, looking at the left side of the face. The color autopsy pictures from the National Archives in the possession of Robert Groden do not show any background at all, and the black and white Fox set seem to have problems with the background, as Jenkins says here.

He said there should have been a portable X-ray machine in the pictures somewhere, and the wooden structure seen in the pictures on the floor did not exist in the autopsy room. He said that the tile step we see on the floor in the pictures would be the beginning of the gallery. But the Bethesda gallery had a rail. The step and beginning of the gallery should be about four feet from the table.

Speaking again about being stopped from logging the body of the Air Force officer in, he said, "It was highly irregular. The military was real emphatic about that. Everybody had to be logged in. I mean, you got a body, it had to be tagged immediately. It had to be logged. They didn't ever. They said don't worry about logging him in."

"Did you see the body in that casket?"

"No, I did not."

"I can definitely tell you that there was an ornate type casket already in the laboratory when the President came in."

On May 29, 1991, Jenkins said, "I am willing to say that when the body had arrived at Bethesda, the brain stem was cut with a knife before it got there. There were enough surgical cuts in the head and scalp area to indicate the brain had been removed and thoroughly examined. There was surgery down in there. They only needed to extend the sagittal sutures a bit to get it out.

"Only Humes, Boswell, and Finck did any dissection of organs from the body."

Jenkins did not recall Floyd Riebe, the medical photographer, coming in until after the autopsy started, which means that Floyd, if this is accurate, did not see the shipping casket.

On July 14, 1991, I had another very long interview with Jim Jenkins. He corrected my misunderstanding of something he had said, and we went on, sometimes breaking new ground. I repeat some of what he said so that it can be compared.

"Humes talks about a deep laceration front to back in the right cerebral hemisphere of the brain. I did not see that. Look at the photograph showing the top of the head—in the center of the head, a little anteriorly, there is a hole there. The thing that I notice about it is that all that tissue seems to be intact. The brain seems to be intact and valid."

This is one of the major contradictions in the evidence—not only do we have four different placements of the large defect in the head (back of the head, right side, right front face in the X-ray, top of the head in the photograph), but instead of a large gouge being missing in the brain corresponding to the large defect in the skull, as Humes described both to the Warren Commission (on the right side of the head), there is no gouge of brain missing according to the photograph: It is intact as seen through the large opening in the top of the skull. Humes described more of a furrow across the brain, front to back, parallel to the midline.

I asked him, "What are the three white stripes hanging down on top of the hair?" The color photographs show these to be a very bloody red, but they come out as white in the black and white photographs. Since a reprint of the color picture of the right side of the face shows them to be black, we have a photographic impossibility. They are bloodred in the color pictures, and red goes to black when black and white prints are made from color pictures. The indication is that the stripes were colorized.

"No, that's scalp. That's the meninges. Right above there you'll see some things inside that are sort of folded—that's brain."

"Does that picture of the top of the head, does that look like what you saw after the body was unwrapped and put on the table?"

"No, not really. That's not brain. That's tissue."

"That's not brain?"

"No, that's not brain. It looks, it seems to me, a little bit too far forward."

"It looks like [the first glossy picture, there, the head in profile] the black stripes, which are really bloodred, are painted in," I said. I have seen the color pictures, and the three stripes of tissue hanging down from the apex of the head are very dark red, and painted in. This visual inspection was backed up by pure science: Red goes to black when a color picture is printed in black and white.

"They show they are right above the ear forward as having the flap opened out—protruding—but there is a difference in where that hole is in the next picture," he said. We were talking about the back-of-the-head picture with the flap sticking out on the right side just above and *in front* of the ear.

"The orientation changes—" I said. This was a key point. In three different back-of-the-head shots, the flap was oriented differently, maybe because the scalp to which a piece of bone on the flap was attached was shifting, but it seemed more likely because the whole thing was faked somehow. On the right front profile picture and the stare-of-death picture showing the neck, the flap does not appear open at all, and if it was closed, is not in the right place, as some witnesses said.

"It seems like in the first two pictures the wound moved forward on the head and on the third one it moves anteriorly back toward the back of the head. But in *none* of these pictures is it actually in the position of where it was."

"Where was it? It was just *anterior* to the ear, right?"

"Well, it started above the ear, about where the flap is and went back —look at the back-of-the-head picture, the one with the hand. Look at the faded area near the hairline [the area that is out of focus]. That would have been about the lower limits of the wound itself. And it would have extended up about the level to the anterior position of the wound on the third photograph. But maybe not that far forward. Maybe about where his fingers are."

"These pictures depict the wound almost in the front of the head—almost in the frontal bone."

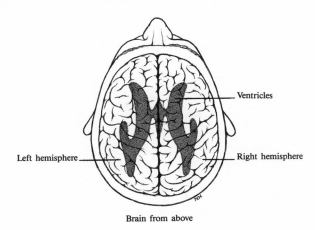

Brain from above

"Who took the brain out of the head?"

"Dr. Humes took the brain out in his hands and handed it to Dr. Boswell."

"Did you assist in some way?"

"I was standing right there. I thought we were going to do a skull cap and they said no. So they just extended the sagittal suture where the wound went into the sagittal suture, which is in the midline of the skull, extending it up, actually, and flipped some of the bone back and the brain—Dr. Humes was ready to cut the stem, and the brain—the brain virtually fell out into his hands."

"Was it still connected just a little?" (Talking about the brain.)

"It wasn't connected."

"And you don't think the weight of it tore it loose?"

"No. You have to understand the relationship of all of these structures to each other. What else would be affected if the brain stem or the peduncle had been severed by a bullet as opposed to being surgically cut," Jenkins proposed.

"You've got a bullet going through there with tremendous force and it's obviously blowing out brain matter and bone as it exits. To what extent in your knowledge would it tear at the brain stem and tear it loose?"

"In my opinion it could not have made such a clean cut. I guess [the] probability is always there of that and there was a discussion of that."

"How long did the discussion continue?"

"Until it was cut off."

"Who cut it off?"

"Basically, the same person who cut all the others off."

"Somebody in the gallery?"

"Yes." (Admiral George Burkley, the President's doctor.)

"Was it fairly lengthy?"

"No. It was basically a proposal that was negated."

"So, Humes asked if there had been surgery at Parkland?"

"Yes. He asked, 'Did they do surgery at *Parkland?*' and he was told that there was no surgery done at *Parkland. . . .*"

"I get the distinct idea that Humes is describing some other brain that wasn't in Jack Kennedy's head!"

"I get that idea, too," Jenkins replied laconically.

"I try to be optimistic, too, but we're talking about 1500 grams of brain, too," Jenkins said, reminding me of that vast anomaly in the evidence. Fifteen hundred grams was the weight of a normal brain.

"You have to remember that the brain had been infiltrated—infiltrated with formaldehyde, which is basically water. I don't really know what volume that will take. You tend to replace all the fluids in the brain with the formaldehyde solution. That way the tissue becomes harder."

"Is a fifteen-hundred-gram brain a normal average weight—is that with the fluids?"

"I don't know—you have to find an expert."

We got back to the wounds of the brain. Jenkins always went back to it. "On the surface of the brain that I saw, I did not see that type of laceration. Humes is saying the laceration was from the frontal area to the tail area—to the corpus callosum. I don't know if he was talking about to the cerebellum, to the ventricles, or what. If he was talking about that type of laceration or tear, then that brain should be virtually falling apart. The right cerebral-temporal area should be laid open like a ripe melon—and the brain was not damaged to that extent. The damaged area of the brain did not seem to correlate to the severity of the damaged area of the skull. The brain tissue is soft—not as firm as the skull area. A good forensics man could tell you if this was possible or not possible. That there could seemingly be a smaller proportion of damage to the brain than to the skull. Seems to me there would probably have been basically a blow-out of the skull itself and some of the brain matter would follow. But, what I saw was that there was not the brain matter missing that was described by Dr. McClelland or by Paul—and sometimes I get the impression not even by Dr. Humes. My rationalization for that is they all saw it at a time of shock and distress.

"I've given my impressions of the brain . . . and the fact that it was small indicated to me that it was female (i.e., that would fit through the hole). I have no anatomical, no scientific fact for that statement at all. It is clearly an impression."

"I don't think the pathological samples would have been turned loose at Bethesda. They would have gone downtown," he said.

"Do we have any report on those samples in any of the published materials?"

"I think, basically, what they are doing—drawing their conclusions from what they *saw* that night." Not from the studies that would have been done later from the samples.

Jenkins noted that the House Committee avoided any discussion of the histology. Humes's refusal to talk about the adrenals cut all the rest of the necessary discussion off. "When he avoided that, they never asked him anything about the lung tissue and so on."

"What else would they have asked him about?"

"I would think that if they were really forensic pathologists, they would have asked about any possible pathology testing that was done. I'm sure there was some done. They should have asked him if there was any disease found in any of the microscopic examination of the organs that they did sections of. One of the things I don't understand is they talk about beveling of the wounds in the skull. I don't remember that the skull was that closely examined. There were certainly no magnifying glasses there. Everything was done on a gross basis. The body was not accessible to them any time after the autopsy. It had already been altered by the cosmetics and the embalming.

"I could hear what they were saying and I remember no discussion about missile wounds beveled in or beveled out. That would be something I would remember."

*   *   *

I asked Jim if "on the long laceration Humes describes from front to back down to the corpus callosum—did you see this that he's talking about?"

"No."

"But you yourself didn't see anything corresponding to that?"

"No. What I describe to you as far as damage to the brain is exactly what I saw."

"So, what basically you saw was a certain amount of brain missing . . ."

"In the area that I pointed out to you."

"In the back of the head where the large defect in the back of the skull would have been?"

"Right!"

I quoted Humes talking about a large defect in the right cerebral hemisphere corresponding to the large defect in the skull. "That would be about five inches or five and a half inches."

"That's a lot. I don't really see how he can describe it. I can take my fist and put my fist in it, and my fist is not five inches. If it had been five inches, then it would have encompassed a fourth, maybe even a third of the total head."

We talked about the "pre-exam." Key issues in the case are whether or not the body was examined and bullets removed, and the statements overheard by the FBI men and noted by them that there had been surgery to the head area when they received the body. Again, I asked Jenkins about this.

"Do you think the scalp and bone had been extended?"

"In the two places Dr. Humes questioned."

"And that was the discussion at the table when he questioned somebody in the gallery about Parkland."

"About surgery at Parkland."

"And he noticed something that looked more like cuts."

"It would have been a surgical incision as opposed to a traumatic laceration."

"These pictures are intentionally vague," he said about the autopsy photographs.

"Did you see where he, Humes, was talking about?"

"I can place where his hand was."

* * *

We tried to figure out the photograph that shows a large hole in the head with some of the scalp reflected back. Of course, almost no one has been able to place this picture as to where it is on a head, whether the large hole it depicts is on the front, side, back, or top of the head. Sometimes we *think* we can orient it, but we are never very sure. The House Committee commented on the poor quality of these pictures and this problem overall, and something is seriously wrong when they leave us a picture like that without any reference photographs taken from a distance that will orient it. Here is where those Secret Service personnel who arbitrarily burned most of this evidence on December 7, 1963, ought to hang. (Mark Crouch tells me that his friend, Secret Service man James Fox, described the burning of most of the autopsy photos and X-rays and other assassination related materials two weeks after the autopsy.) Actually they did not leave it for *us*. They left it for ghosts in the next century—for our posterity who will never have a remote chance of figuring this stuff out.

We studied the photograph of the large defect in the skull, and Jenkins said, "At the base of that photograph there is a darkened area that looked like it may have been penciled out. I'm trying to determine if that's an auditory canal that's coming through. Look at the oblong area there that looks like it may be blacked in. That would be approximately where Dr. Humes described a cut. That should be the occipital area and approximately where Dr. Humes described their entrance wound."

"It looks like a surgical cut there. There's a little white line at the end of it. . . ."

"Well, I think that's just a tear," Jim said.

"If I'm correct, the surgery would have been done at approximately where the end of the V is and also about two thirds up the skull where the piece of bone was."

"Where the black horizontal line is. A slot."

"Right. It would have been in that area."

"Do you think it was someone else's brain or that it was Kennedy's brain?"

"I have a tendency to think that it was Kennedy's brain and that it had been thoroughly examined and bullets removed."

"That it was his brain?"

"I think it probably was. I have no way of knowing."

"But when you say it was smaller—a female brain . . ."

"Again, too, you have to go back to my *impressions*. He was a much smaller man than I thought." Jim later noted on the manuscript of this chapter, which he corrected, that his impressions are colored by the fact that he himself is about six feet six himself, so nearly all men are *small* to him.

"He looks thin on that table. His chest was thin."

"Well, he was fairly well muscled—he looked pretty good. He looked like he might work out."

"Paul said he looked emaciated."

"I didn't see that. When I saw him he had fairly decent muscle tone in the chest and abdominal area. He was thin. He was a small man."

Jim said that he did not see the entrance wound described in the autopsy report and by the doctors in their testimony. He nor the men didn't altogether believe that it was there.

Jim did notice an area in one of the pictures that was blacked in. Reference *black.*

"In the area where Humes is talking about, speaking of the entry wound, right above that was where the large mass of tissue and scalp and so forth was. When we opened it up when they took the sheet off and the towel, there was a large gaping hole there with tissues and bone and so forth hanging from it. I think when he says they reflected the scalp back, they reflected it back to the left side of the head. I think they went to the midline of the skull there and reflected it back to take a look at it."

On the brain, he said, "Sometimes they are saying there is no radiation of bullet fragments to the left side of the brain. All the damage was to the right hemisphere of the brain, primarily to the occipital, parietal area.

"It seems to me that initially everything [the damage] was posterior to this and it would not have touched the frontal bone very much. You have to understand that on most adults the frontal suture runs probably two fingers in front of the ear, and runs all the way across the front of the skull.

"In the temporal area, right in front of the ear, as I told you before, there was a flap of skin there that was hanging on and there was a discussion about some markings on the bone in that area."

"For a possible bullet going in or out?"

"Yes."

"This would be the flap that we see in the photo?"

"Yes."

"We're talking about the Back-of-the-Head picture with the flap sticking straight out of the side of the head by the ear?"

"Yes. The flap was right above and forward of the ear."

"They did not find any bullets in the body." I told Jim about the big fragment on the back of the head seen first by the Clark Panel in 1968. "It wasn't there," Jim said. "If it had been there, they would have been jumping for joy had they found something. They never would have brought the radiologist [Ebersole] in. The radiologist came in to show us how to position the body because, quote, we were 'missing something.' "

"Then the brain was removed and that was when the question came up about the surgery and the suture line was extended. The question about the surgery came up before the brain was removed." Jenkins told me that no one had access to the body in the morgue that night, or in the cold room. "It didn't happen in the morgue there that night. The bottom line is that the head had been very extensively examined."

"Do you think anybody beat on it with a hammer?"

"I don't think so. When you take a hammer and beat a skull, it leaves little semicircle marks. It's actually an impression in the bone. That is not something that someone would miss." But we may have some of those semicircles in the bone. Dr. McClelland thought he saw them.

"You didn't see anything like that?"

"I didn't."

"That's something someone would have commented on."

"I think there would have been a lot of comments on it."

"Now, this long laceration in the brain from front to back—in any way did it look like a slice?"

"It didn't look like anything to me because I didn't see it. I don't know from reading Humes's testimony if it was internal. If when they sectioned the brain, they found it, or if he is implying it was surface. If it came from the external part of the brain and went deep in like if you would take a knife at the top of the brain and slice it from the frontal area back to the back of the brain to open it up down to the depth of the corpus callosum. If that would have been there, I would have seen that.

"I don't know if what Humes is describing was something he found when they examined the brain after the autopsy, and if it was internal.

If it is something they found internally after they sectioned the brain, or if he is saying that it was an incision through the parietal area from the surface to the depth of the corpus callosum."

"An incision?"

"Yeah."

"If it was a surgical incision, it would have been two and a half inches deep and six inches long."

"So what he is describing looked like a trough made by a bullet transiting the brain, but what you actually saw was just a big defect in the right cerebral hemisphere in the after part of it, corresponding to the large hole in the skull?"

"Right."

"The other thing that doesn't make any sense is they simply did not section the brain. How did they find the radiating channels? The corpus callosum is buried between the brain hemispheres—unless it was a laceration that someone had taken a knife and sliced down through it to the corpus callosum. How did they do all of this if they didn't section the brain? The brain was relatively intact on the surface. Only the whole area of the defect—anterior area—the parietal. The whole underside of the brain was relatively intact—"

"That brain would have had to be sectioned in some manner to reach those levels, even to the third ventricle, where they describe damage to the ventricle."

"We have here a statement [in the Supplemental Autopsy Report] that the brain was not sectioned," I said.

"And then all of a sudden we get into all of this description of all those internal structures—" Jim said, meaning that it would not be possible to see them without sectioning the brain. Doctors have since told me that it would be possible in view of the deep laceration down the length of the brain from a bullet passing through.

"Humes does not describe the brain stem to any extent. And you know, that night, it looked like it had been surgically cut. I don't know if it's possible for a bullet fragment to totally sever something like that without damaging a lot more. We're talking about, if a bullet had severed the brain stem, where did it go? Why isn't there extensive damage to the floor of the calvarium? Even if a bullet tore the brain loose, the brain stem would be jagged."

I asked him if he had ever seen a torn brain stem. "I've seen torn brain stems because we tried to bring the brain with the spinal cord out, and ninety percent of the time it tears loose. It's not really shredded, it's stringy, pulled out. It looks like taffy when you pull it apart."

"Looking at the photos in your book, the large defect seems to have slid forward toward the frontal area of the head, too. I can't say that I'm absolutely right, but I feel like if it had been really that far forward in the head, certainly we would have seen it. And I would not have focused on . . ."

"You certainly would have—what?"

"The large defect. That's almost on the top as opposed to the area where we saw it."[20]

"Humes said at the autopsy, 'It fell out in my hand!' referring to the brain, so at first I thought a bullet had severed it.

"When we were having trouble infusing the brain because the blood vessels at the base of the brain were retracted, we were having a hard time getting the needle in."[21]

In a final interview Jenkins insisted to me that he never once left the morgue from about three-thirty or four in the afternoon (two-thirty to three P.M. Dallas time—before or during the plane's takeoff from there) until nine A.M. the following morning.

He repeated what we had first heard in Dallas from him, that he strongly believed that some of the autopsy photographs were not taken in the morgue. Of course, like the Stemmons Freeway sign that was removed the day after the assassination from Dealey Plaza, the morgue was remodeled into a cafeteria, so we can't compare the background in the pictures with the actual facts unless someone has some of those thousands of other autopsy photographs the Navy medical photographic school and the Bethesda hospital autopsy archives had in its files.

He said that the pieces of bone that were brought in from Dallas late that night were small, not much bigger than a quarter, and did not fill up the large area of missing bone in the back of the head, in part contradicting Humes's testimony to the Warren Commission. Humes does say there that the three pieces filled all but one quarter of the large defect.[22] He ridiculed the idea that the X-rays we now have of the skull could have been made from a reconstruction of the head, because such large pieces were not available.

I think that as far as the size of the pieces of bone go, that is a matter of judgment. Jenkins freely admits severe difficulty remembering time frames that night, and the size of things may be an additional category of memory problem, giving Humes the benefit of the doubt in this instance, though I have no real reason to sit in judgment on one or the other of these men with regard to this recollection. I admit failure to reconcile all the conflicts in the evidence in this case. They were too cleverly manufactured.

Jenkins said that no X-rays were developed in the morgue. "We would have had to have tanks and a dark room, and there was no way to set it up like that in the morgue," he told me, contradicting former FBI man O'Neill's statement to me that some or all of the X-rays were developed in the morgue, which seems highly unlikely. To my knowledge, no one else has said what O'Neill told me.

Jenkins strongly insisted again that he believed that the body and brain had been operated on before they ever got it, and that the doctors were lying on major points.

He stated that he was not lying about anything he had said, that no one had influenced him, and that he had an antipathy for some of those who had previously interviewed him who might be accused of getting him to say these things.[23]

Unless what Humes says to the Warren Commission about the condition of the brain can be interpreted as surgery, Jenkins is alone in describing surgery to the head. But he had one powerful ally. One major piece of evidence that corroborated him.

The FBI.

But the FBI agent—James Sibert—who wrote that there had been surgery to the top of the head swore in an affidavit to the HSCA that it was a mistake. Then why did we hear so much about body alteration and prior surgical removal or surgery to the brain for the next ten years?

Somebody made it up, that is why. There was no known evidence, only a deduction based on false premises and no facts. No evidence.

Jim Jenkins did not actually see a cut brain stem before the brain came out of the head. The odds are that what he probably saw was Humes's transection. In addition, he did not see any other cuts on the scalp or bone—but only surmised that they might have been there. He said that they would have only been a half inch or so. Why bother? If a bullet was lodged in the brain, the conspirators would want to get it out, and might have had to remove the brain to do so. But it is highly unlikely that anyone would have made any cut at all if that was all that they were going to cut, risking discovery. The brain might have compressed sufficiently to be removed and then replaced, but it seems to me that a bullet anywhere in the brain could have been extracted through the large hole in the head—without it being necessary to remove the brain at all.

Somehow, I believe Jim Jenkins. I may be wrong, but I think he is too honest, and I believe he saw and heard all that he says.

> "No one who knew Robert and John Kennedy believes that they would conceivably countenance a program of assassination. They were too filled with love of life and so conscious of the ironies of history."

> —Arthur Schlesinger

CHAPTER 12

THE RECOLLECTIONS OF PAUL O'CONNOR

I began interviewing some of the witnesses from among the former enlisted men present at the autopsy of President Kennedy. This followed several talks with the doctors themselves, which in some cases did not yield much or any information, unfortunately. They stonewalled me. The doctors have been in the spotlight too long, and were gunshy and tired.

My first major interview with Paul Kelly O'Connor was on April 20, 1990, followed by an interview on May 9. The following comments are from those two interviews, and then I will relate what he has had to say since then. It's a lot. It was from his statements that other reseachers drew to construct so much of the fantastic theory of body alteration to fool the cameras . . . sidetracking us from the body tampering and photo and X-ray alteration that might have actually happened.

O'Connor worked general crime and homicide as a police officer for three years. He did not have formal training in photo analysis but recognizes retouching when he sees it, and knows what to look for. There are, of course, numerous instances of retouching on the alleged autopsy photographs, and I discuss this in Chapter 15. O'Connor had worked in funeral homes since the age of fourteen, and was twenty-two when he saw the President's body.

O'Connor is adamant that it would have been impossible to remove even half of a brain through the large hole in the skull as it existed when the body was brought into Bethesda Naval Hospital without performing a craniotomy. He said that the brain would have been de-

stroyed if someone had tried to remove it, because the hole was nowhere near large enough.

O'Connor says he was with the body from the moment it arrived until
the coffin was closed. He helped dress the body before it was placed in
the casket, and was the last person to touch the body when he placed a
black rosary in Kennedy's hand. He first told me that he was absent
only once, for about five minutes.

Joseph Hagen, the president of Gawler's Funeral Home, says that
this is untrue, and that he, Joe Hagen, put the rosary in Kennedy's
hand.[1]

O'Connor states that there had been no surgical removal of the brain
from the head, as others claim or imply. It was O'Connor's job to
remove the brain, and in the examination of the head, no such surgery
had been performed. He states that he told other researchers this. The
fact is that Jenkins, had said that he felt the brain had been previously
removed and replaced, but another researcher took this evidence as his
own theory, robbing it of credibility.

He indicates that his previous experience working at the Naval Medical Center put him beyond shock and that he would have accurate
recollections. Nevertheless there are serious problems with what he
remembers, as there are with many of the witnesses.

Nevertheless, all testimony of a given witness should not necessarily
be categorically discredited when just some of it is not corroborated by
other witnesses. The testimony that is corroborated should be considered valid if there is no other explanation for it. In the case of the body-
bag problem, the body had various wrappings which could be called a
body bag but were not strictly a "crash bag" or body bag per se.

There is an equal confusion over the "shipping casket" matter. Paul
makes it clear in these interviews that he did not mean that the body
came in a military shipping casket. It is clear that he was never in a
position to have a good look at the Dallas casket before it got to
Bethesda, and therefore does not really know if the President came in it
or not. There were several coffins present at the morgue and this is a
simple case of memory merge.

Paul's great virtue is his very clear recollection of all matters having
to do with the wounds themselves, which perfectly backs the autopsy
doctors as well as the Parkland doctors. In this respect, he and the
other enlisted men are in agreement, but each of them makes some
statement that is not backed up by any other credible witness, or is
simply not supported by the realm of possibility.

* * *

O'Connor says that rigor mortis had not set in. He says the right eye was slightly popped from the orbit by the force of the explosion in the head, and therefore more wide open than the left eye. He says that he never saw such damage before or since to a body, and he is a veteran of Vietnam, where he saw hundreds of wounds and was badly wounded himself.

He says that he did not think that anyone had touched or tampered with the body before it arrived at Bethesda. He insisted to me that there was no flap of scalp on the back of the head, but only bits of shredded scalp. This is what most of the other witnesses seem to have said, and totally negates the implication of a flap of scalp, which is in fact reported by Metzler, Bell, and McClelland. What both sets of witnesses recall is true. There was a badly shredded flap of scalp that at times was pushed aside and could not be seen.

An important point is that O'Connor (and the other witnesses) insists that the hair was caked with blood and could not be black and shiny—newly washed—as it is in the present photographs of the back of the head.

O'Connor responded to a series of written questions I sent him. He also made extensive notes on his set of autopsy photographs for me, the Fox set, which he possesses. I asked him if anyone could have torn open the throat more than it was—so that it looks something like the large gash we now see in the photograph. In other words, making it look like an exit wound, or trying to find a bullet. He said no, and instead pointed to retouching, which makes the throat wound look larger than it actually was. In other words, they painted in an exit wound. He said that it was actually teardrop shaped.

We note that two members of the staff of the House Select Committee on Assassinations, Andrew Purdy and Mark Flannigan, confronted witnesses with the Ida Dox drawings of the autopsy photographs, though they pretended to me to have actually shown the photographs to the Dallas doctors. These watered-down drawings would conceal the true nature not only of the wounds, but of the retouching. I have no doubt but that the forgeries were deliberately covered up in this fashion during the HSCA. (Ida Dox's drawings are tracings from the photographs themselves, and published by the House.)

Since I independently corroborated that there was airbrushing on the throat wound, I maintain that a finding of forgery with regard to the pictures showing the throat wound is conclusive. Rather than enlarge the incision or make it look like an exit wound, the airbrushing covers up the edges of the entry wound that was there when the surgery was performed for inserting the trach tube and cuff.

The head is lying at a backward angle, stretching the edges of the throat incision open widely so that it could be falsely called a gaping exit wound when shown to Chief Justice Warren and a handful of others who could not know the difference, and who were so shocked at their first view of these gory pictures that they would not ask questions. But the edges of the wound remain clean and neatly incised, and are not the torn, irregular, jagged, or mangled lacerations made by an exiting bullet. Who showed those pictures to Warren, or set it up?

A fog was being drawn over the evidence, which would from that point onward undergo a steady evolution, perhaps including gradual changes in the photos themselves over the years in the Archives. More about this later.

O'Connor said there was no probing of the knife cuts in the chest. He said that there were superficial cuts (above each nipple) that did not penetrate the pleura. He said that he did not see the chest tube incisions, "which does not say they were not there." ("I was at the head of the body during the autopsy and could not see what transpired in the body cavity except to notice blood in the upper right intercostal muscles.")

The fact is that O'Connor, who says that at all times when he was in the room he stood at the head of the table, may not have seen the chest-tube cuts and may have been out of the room before the Y incision was made, which might have prevented him from having a clear view of that part of the chest when he came back in, since the chest was laid open.

O'Connor said that he left the morgue for five minutes to get a small rubber sheet to put over the hole in the head.

He states that there were decoy ambulances and *caskets* (his own emphasis). He said that when they were awaiting the body, they heard a helicopter land behind the hospital and about five minutes later the body came in, at about eight P.M. He said they immediately went to work photographing the body and that every part of the President's body was photographed.

The eight P.M. figure has to be inaccurate, but could have been when O'Connor came back into the room if he was out for a period of time. The body arrived at the hospital at seven P.M. according to the Warren Commission, for which there is sufficient documentation. The House found that the body came into the morgue at 7:35 P.M. O'Connor may mean that as soon as the photography was over, about eight P.M., the head was examined, and as far as he was concerned, the autopsy began then, with the Y incision coming fifteen minutes later.

As for decoys, there is no evidence of this, although it seems not unreasonable that there might have been some.

O'Connor said that no photos were taken after the autopsy began. This is contradicted by statements that photos were taken at several stages of the autopsy.

He says that when they prepared the body for burial, they put the skull together, using the brown rubber sheet which covered an area about three by three inches, and filled it with plaster. Then they washed the hair and combed it back over the large hole so that the body could be viewed. No hairpiece was used. Fragments of bone that had fallen from the head in Dallas were put back over the plaster to fill in all but the above hole.

He states that no photographs were taken of the brain. "There was no brain to photograph." Remember, O'Connor says that his primary job was to remove the brain during an autopsy. Photos of the brain are in evidence and have not disappeared, nor have they been seen outside the House Committee, and are not authenticated easily. A Supplemental Autopsy Report dated December 6, 1963, deals with the brain and gives its weight as 1500 grams, the size of a normal brain having suffered no damage.

With regard to the Sibert and O'Neill FBI report, he says "most of what they say is 'do do'! The information that they gave is incorrect. Much of their report is wrong."

All X-rays were taken on the table with a portable X-ray machine.

O'Connor also points out what some of us have already noticed: That the alleged entry wound in the cowlick in some of the photographs simply isn't there in other photographs. As Dr. Humes all but said, it is apparently painted into the photograph. "I defy you to find it in the black and white photograph."[2]

I might add that Drs. Humes, Finck, and Ebersole continue to refuse to answer questions or discuss the case. Why, all these years after the great tragedy of 1963? Part of the answer has to do with how easily the press twists and distorts things, by asking leading questions or initiating statements, and part is fatigue. And perhaps part is due to fear.

O'Connor said this about the autopsy doctors: "Somebody got to them real bad. Somebody got on their case. They are afraid as death to talk."[3]

He states that Floyd Riebe took pictures under John Stringer's direction. The pictures were then destroyed.

The "best evidence" in this case is the *weight* of the evidence. Certainly not a body which is no longer available, nor the photographs and X-rays which are evidence only of possible forgery or the lack of it. They are not evidence of the definitive nature of the wounds.

"I have a set of photographs with me right now and I know that there are one, two, three good forgeries in there," Paul said.

"Which ones?"

"Yes, okay, the Back-of-the-Head picture," he said. "There was a big hunk of his scalp and hair blown out of the back of the head."[4] He repeated this to me many times, and it meant that the body was not altered before it got to Bethesda to result in such a picture.

He told me: "They could have never showed him [Kennedy's body] to anybody, because there was too much scalp gone up there. It was just all macerated, it was just torn in little shreds."

"The scalp in the back?"

"Yeah, the whole wound area was all to shreds. Uh, pieces of brain kept falling out of the scalp. It was a mess."

"But in the back of the head, was there any scalp at all, or was it all badly shredded?"

"There was scalp, but it was still shredded a lot."

I told him that we thought there was no way the head could be reconstructed that night in the time alloted to make the Back-of-the-Head picture. He did not reply but started talking about the X-rays right away:

"Well, there's an X-ray picture, lateral of the head X-ray. And you see *there's no exit deficit from the rear of the head.* You're darn right that's not his X-ray," he said.

"The lateral?"

"The lateral. It's not right because that's part of the frontal area; now, there was fracture down through there, but it wasn't missing. I can see a fracture into the right orbit. His right eyeball was actually pushed out of the orbit a little bit."

"Wouldn't that show up in the picture?"

"Well, it should, really. I'll turn it around here, the rear of the head, yeah. This is wrong too!"

"Which one?"

"The rear of the head, this is a composite forged photograph masking a large defect in the very back of the head," O'Connor said.

"That's what Mark Crouch and I think," I said.

"They are all forged, just about. . . . There are three good forgeries there. . . . The throat wound is airbrushed in. . . . The whole right side of the head is airbrushed in.

"Top of the head is okay."

"I'll tell you what we had to do that night. His head was so badly fractured all over. Comminuted fractures. Comminution means like you dropped an egg on the floor. You got comminuted fractures of the shell."

"So they're all criss-crossing each other."

"We had to fill his head with plaster of Paris. Just to maintain the form of the skull. Then we put too much in and had to chip some out. There were some nervous and strange moments that night."

"Did you see anything that looked like an entry wound in the left temple area?"

"No."

Another time I asked him if there was an entry wound in the right temple area, and he said no.

"No. You know what it looked like to me?"

"No."

"Looked like somebody planted a small bomb in his head and it blew off. I looked at the whole head, I was at the head all the time. I was at the head of the body the whole time."

"Throughout the autopsy?"

"Yeah."

"And there was no brain in the head when it came in?"

"Well, maybe a handful. Macerated tissue."

"But your impression was that someone had removed the brain?"

"No, I thought he had his brains blown out. If you had seen the size of the hole. That's the reason I know he's been shot twice in the head. It took me a long time to finally realize that, hey, this guy's got hit by somebody else because one bullet just can't do this."

"Yes."

O'Connor told me that Burkley gave the orders in the autopsy room, and that it was him that told them not to probe the neck wound. "Don't do that because the family doesn't want you to do that." He said that the room was half crazy with confusion, pandemonium. The doctors were frightened and were paper pushers with little experience. "Humes was real freaky. They were scared to death anyway when they got down there. And then Admiral Burkley started screaming at them."

They did not turn over the body and discover the back wound until two hours after the autopsy was performed. "And then Humes sticks his finger into it and says, 'It doesn't look like it goes anywhere.' But, you know, he only sticks his finger in there and that was all he did. He didn't probe it. He didn't stick a probe into it or sound into it or anything."

He said that the intercostal muscles in the upper right rear of his back had blood in them.

"It was so strange that night. The important things that they should have looked at they didn't look at. Seems like everyone was focused on the head, and that was it."

He said that he thought they used a fragmentation bullet to the head, and he said that there was in fact no coning effect on the skull bone from bullets entering or leaving, so that there was no way to tell from that which direction a bullet had gone.

He confirmed that the wound in the back was six inches down from the shoulder, and said that the photograph of it was "accurate as the dickens." He meant the lower hole in the picture, not the upper apparent wound.

I again asked him if there was enough scalp over the back of the head to make the present photograph, and he said emphatically no. I brought up the Walter Cronkite appearance on *Nova* and the implication that the doctor's hand was pulling the scalp over the large hole in the skull. "That's a bunch of shit."

"That he wasn't pulling the flap over it?"

"No, there was no flap. And another thing, do you see that one picture? The close-up shows the cowlick? Supposedly there's a hole in there. That's a bunch of shit too."

"There wasn't any hole there?"

"No. That's a touched-up fake job. Well, as a matter of fact, all that scalp is touched up because it was all shredded."

He then pointed out that in the other photograph, which shows the back wound, the back of the head is also visible, and "you look at it real close so you can see the cowlick too. There is no rear head entry wound in that picture." It is true that others noticed that the alleged entry wound in the cowlick is not present in some of the other views of the back of the head. Drs. Humes and Boswell themselves indicated that it wasn't there.

O'Connor also said it was not possible to reconstruct the head to make the forgery.

I said, "I don't know how you could have done the job with all that going on."

"We didn't hardly do the job. It was the worst postmortem I've ever done in my life."

"As we all know."

"If they had just left us alone, gave us a couple of good pathologists, we could have done a real good job."

He said that "Admiral Burkley was a maniac. I'd never seen anybody like that in this life. Scared the hell out of me, I'll tell you. He was yellin' and cussin' and carrying on all night." He said that Burkley "kept saying, 'Don't do this because the Kennedy family won't want that done and don't do this and don't do that.' It's just unbelievable.

"See, that's the reason that such, well, number one, the poor guys that did the autopsy—Boswell and Humes . . ."

"They sounded scared to me."

"Yeah, they are. Particularly—see, these guys had not done an autopsy in probably years. They were the paper pushers. Especially when you get up to be a Commander of the Navy."

"Yes."

"Humes is real freaky," Paul said. "They were scared to death anyway when they got down there. And Admiral Burkley started screaming at them." Paul laughed here.

"Who gave the order not to probe the throat wound?"

"Burkley. Burkley gave all the orders like that. He says, 'Don't do that because the family doesn't want you to do that.' We didn't even know there was a bullet hole in the back, his back."

"You didn't . . ."

"We didn't even know it until about two hours into the autopsy."

"That there was a hole in his back . . ."

"No. We turned him over and 'Oh, look, there's a hole!' That's . . . that's the way that night went. It was just absolutely crazy!"

"Yeah."

"And so Humes sticks his finger into it and says, 'It doesn't look like it goes anywhere.' If they'd done a legal postmortem, especially in the murder, that's what they do in legal postmortems. Well, we wouldn't have all this stuff today."

"Right."

"But you know, Humes only sticks his finger in there and that was all he did. He didn't probe it. He didn't stick a probe into it or sound into it or anything."

"Humes? He didn't probe the back wound?"

"No, just with his finger. You can't go very far with your finger in a bullet hole."

"Right. But didn't Finck testify that he did that, that he put probes in there?"

"Well, I don't know about Finck. . . ."

"Do you think that the back wound went very far into the body?"

"Yeah. That's the wound that comes out his throat. It's the entry wound that comes out his throat."

"You're absolutely certain of that?"

"Yeah, just about."

"How can you be, if it wasn't probed?"

"Well, the wound in his throat that corresponded with the wound in his back was a little to the right of the vertebrae. That bullet did something strange. It actually grazed one of the vertebrae. And a piece of it split off, I think."

"A piece of the bullet split off?"

"I think so, or a fragment of it did. The reason I think this, when we opened him up, eviscerated him . . . the intercostal muscles in the upper right rear of his back had blood in them."

"So you think part of the bullet went down there?"

"Yeah. I think it did. But nobody looked at it, you know. But you know something? It was so strange that night. The important things that they should have looked at, they didn't look at. Seems like everyone was focused on the head, and that was it."

Paul was looking at the photo showing the neck wound. "What puzzles me about this wound as I'm looking at it right now is that it looks like it was painted on the body."

"The throat wound?"

"Yeah. It's just that . . . that it doesn't conform with the anatomy of the throat. If you're gonna do a tracheotomy, you never do it across or laterally, you do it vertically. It's more of a stabbing. I've done it before, I know what I'm talking about. Because if you go across horizontally, you're going to hit the jugular or the carotid artery."

"So the present one we are looking at is horizontal, right?"

"Horizontal, right."

"So, you're saying it should be vertical?"

"Oh, yeah. It should be vertical."

"In other words, from the chin down?"

"Yeah. Now, you can ask Perry which way he did it. That's very important because this is a very dangerous procedure to do if you don't do it right. You can end up with someone dying on you real quick."

O'Connor repeated that part of the gaping throat wound has been painted in, and the implication is that it hides what was a small entry wound at the base of the old tracheostomy.[5]

O'Connor strongly questioned whether on the night of the autopsy when the body arrived from Texas at Andrews Air Force Base, why they would have driven it through the city when they could fly it to Bethesda in a helicopter in a few minutes.[6]

I got back to the Dallas doctors on this. I had good copies of the photographs, and they were able to see the wound quite clearly. They had no doubt but that the wound in the pictures was accurate and what they remember. They made a horizontal incision at Parkland and it was a good two inches across to accommodate the large cuff that had to be inserted to protect the tube. In addition, Dr. Perry needed to make a quick inspection of the area underneath the bullet wound in the skin for significant damage to the trachea or blood vessels present in that area. A fairly large incision was necessary.

I closely questioned Drs. Jones, Carrico, McClelland, and others who had a good look at it or assisted Dr. Perry. They had no question in their mind about what the picture showed, and I concluded that the neck wound had not been altered at all after the doctors at Parkland were finished with it, and the cuff had been removed. It is unfortunate that I have not been able to obtain a cuff of the type used at that time to see for myself exactly how it worked. I also regret the difficulty there is in trying to work with these witnesses and learn anything at all, but all of us understand what they have been through.

* * *

During the long interview of April 20, 1990, Paul and I talked about the head wound. I said, "Now, on the hole in the head, in the pictures there's that flap over the right ear."

"Yeah. That's part of the temple bone. It's parietal temple bone that's popped loose."

"Is that connected to the large hole in the back of the head?" I asked.

"Yeah. The reason you can't see it is because he's got all that scalp and hair."

"In other words, you're saying that there wasn't a piece of bone in between that and the big hole in the head?"

"Well, in the picture I'm looking at in your book here, there's a piece of scalp that's going over the top of that, see, it sort of pops out. You can lift the scalp up. You can see where that bone was back. But it was, actually, it was glued to the scalp area back there. It was actually not attached to the brain. You understand what I'm talking about?"

"That flap that opened up?"

"That bone, that flap of bone is what you're talking about, right?" he asked. "The one that we see in that picture is actually attached to the scalp. Matter of fact, I think it fell off later on."

"The flap?"

"Yeah."

"Okay," I said. "When it's opened up, in other words, it's part of a much bigger hole. . . ."

"Oh, yeah. There's a huge hole. I don't know why they didn't go ahead and open the whole thing up. You know, just peel the scalp back and take a picture of the whole thing. Because what you see there—"

"But you say they didn't do that."

"No. They just took pictures. Went around and took pictures."[7]

Paul said, like the others, that there were no fragments found.

"Was any missile or bullet found?"

"No."

"How about fragments?"

"No."

"No fragments?"

"No fragments, period"

"Well, the FBI men wrote in that report, you know, that everybody quotes and said that, ah, receipt for a missile. What do they mean by that?"

"I don't know. I have no idea. Now, that was another strange thing. Like I said, no definition showing any entry or exit at all. It was like a bomb went off in his head. So it leads me to believe they used a frag bullet."

"You saw wounds in Vietnam, right?"

"Oh, *God,* yes! I treated wounds. I was a hospital corpsman attached to the Marine Corps. In fact, I got wounded myself over there."

"Humes and Boswell were quite obviously scared. They certainly fudged a few things, like they didn't even know he had been shot in the throat, or that there was a wound there," I said.

"Right."

"Because, if you're saying there's no way to see that coning effect to know that's where the entry or exit was . . ."

"Right. There was nothing like that at all."

"No coning?"

"No coning at all."

"Yeah. So then they made it up?"

"Things that go in small come out big. I know that. I've seen it hundreds of times."

He said that the wound that shows near the shoulder is the back wound. This wound is only three inches or so down the back. I think it is another painted-in wound, since it does not correspond to the evidence, nor does it look real.

"Well, the photograph that we have shows an apparent wound in the back. Would you say that that's accurate?"

"Yeah, that's accurate. That's accurate as the dickens, really."

"Yes."

"Was there any damage done to his face at all?"

"No. His right eye was pushed out of the orbit a little bit."

"If there was bone missing in the area that the X-rays show bone to be missing, wouldn't you see that on his face in the photograph?"

"Oh, yeah. The whole face would have been sagged in. The photograph that I've got here is not like that."

"Yes."

"I do remember that. I know exactly how big the wound was. I put my hand in there several times. It was massive. It stretched from temporal, parietal, temporal, just about to the frontal."

"Did you see when the body came in? Did you have any impression that someone might have already been at it? Because it would be hard to know what had happened in Dallas."

"Well, I didn't know," he said. "The reason that I didn't forget like the rest of them is that I started working in a funeral home when I was fourteen years old."

"You were used to it."

"Yeah, I was, but I was scared, don't get me wrong. I was scared to death. It was the President of the United States! . . . I was fortunate enough to work in a funeral home, so I had my wits still in hand. I noticed things there that people never noticed at all. Just like the casket he came in. It wasn't the casket that went on *Air Force 1.*"

"Yeah, well, some called it the big bronze ceremonial casket that went on *Air Force 1,* but you stand by the statement that when you received the body it was in the shipping casket?"

"Yeah. It was in the shipping casket. When I say shipping casket, I use that figuratively because any casket can be a shipping casket. This is a kind of casket that was very cheap, that isn't ornate. The casket that went on *Air Force 1* was, had gothic corners, it was very ornate."

(The photograph of the casket being loaded onto the plane in Dallas showed what seemed a simple enough casket, with rounded corners.)

"Now, on the surgery to the top of the head . . ."

"I don't understand that. These guys that say that kind of stuff—were they doctors that said that at all?" (One was his cousin by marriage who was at the autopsy with him, along with the two FBI men who wrote the report about surgery to the head area.)

"And there was no back of the head all the way down almost to the hairline, right? It was gone?" I asked.

"It was gone. See, the scalp covered it up so you couldn't tell how bad the wound was until he pulled the scalp off."

"All right, but the big question is that the scalp you saw on the very back of the head going down to the hairline would have been whole enough to pull together to make that picture the way it is."

"No," he replied.

"No. It was macerated."

"See, that's the thing. See this one picture where it shows the doctor's hand in there, lifting the scalp?" Paul asked.

"Yeah."

"That's a bunch of shit."

"That he wasn't pulling the flap over it?"

"No. I don't know what!"

"Did you see the Cronkite show, *Nova*?" I asked him.

"Yeah."

"And so you're saying that was bullshit," I asked.

"That's a bunch of bullshit."

"Yes."

Paul said, "You see that one picture? The close-up shows the cowlick?"

"Yes."

"Supposedly there's a hole in there."

"Yeah."

"That's a bunch of shit, too."

"There wasn't any hole there?" I asked.

"No."

"That's painted in," I offered.

"Yeah. That's a touched-up fake job. Well, as a matter of fact, all that scalp is touched up because it was all shredded.

"Look at the scalp there. See the cowlick?"

"We're talking about the back of the head?"

"Yeah. Remember the picture with the bullet wound in the back of the head?" he said.

"Yes."

"You look at it real carefully, real close so you can see the cowlick, too."

"It's undamaged," I said.

"Right."

"But Humes said when he was looking at that picture a few years ago, when he was with the House Committee doctors, he said, 'What's that?' And they were telling him that was the entry wound, and he said, 'What is this that's stuck on here?' "8

"Yeah, that's a bunch of shit."

"So, in your opinion, that picture's a forgery?"

"Yes. Yeah," Paul said.

"And they couldn't have reconstructed the head to make it?"

"No," he said.

I asked him about finding a bullet at the autopsy, in the wrappings. "Remember when Admiral Osborne said that he found a bullet that fell out of the wrapping? Do you remember him?"

"Oh, yeah, Osborne. Yeah, but that wasn't Osborne. That was, there was one captain that said, during the autopsy, that a bullet rolled out of the clothing on top of the table."

"Yes. That was Osborne," I said.

"That guy is absolutely crazy. Number one, when we got the body, Kennedy was completely nude, there was just no way that could happen. Not in that morgue it didn't."

"Did anybody film the autopsy?"

"No."

"Nobody was in there with a movie camera?"

"No. I wasn't aware of anybody, but I do remember that somebody took a couple pictures and they ripped his damn camera apart. And then, the room was so full of people. It was just crazy that night. It's just that unbelievable.

"A lot of strange things happened that night. Number one is I heard two helicopters, all of us heard two helicopters. One landed out in the rear someplace, and I think it was in the Officers' Club parking lot. Had to be."

"That was in the rear?"

"Yeah, and as soon as that happened, it was about, oh, three or four minutes later that the door burst open and in came the casket and we started. We heard that the . . . there were two ambulances, one at the front and one at the back."

"And the door burst open and the casket came in?"

"Yep."

"And which casket was it?"

"It was the big gray cheap casket."

"Okay, now, you were standing there when one door opened?"

"Yeah, I was."

"This was from outside on the loading dock?"

"From the loading dock, no, I was in the morgue."

"Okay."

"They came in from the loading dock and they had to come in through the cool room. And they came in and they brought it right straight down the side. There was an amphitheater, they brought it right alongside the amphitheater and set it down."

"Inside the morgue?"

"Yeah. We opened it up, unzipped the body bag. Which is another thing everybody is going crazy about, too. The body bag. Seems like I'm the only one who remembers that. They brought him in and opened his body bag. He was nude except for a bed sheet wrapped around his head. Which was just totally soaked with blood."

"Okay."

"And I removed the sheet and we got on with it."

"So you couldn't tell from that whether or not there had been any kind of tampering or surgery or anything?"

"No."[9]

"Did anyone ever influence your perceptions of events?"

"No one has *ever* influenced me in any way. What I saw that night were my own observations—no one has ever tried to change my mind on that observation."[10]

He wrote me that "there were decoy ambulances and *caskets* that night before we received the casket with the body. We heard helicopters going overhead—one continued north, then west, the other landed behind the hospital—moments later—about five minutes—the casket containing the President's body was brought in. I believe that the time was eight P.M.—then we, the autopsy team, which included Riebe, Jerry Custer, started doing their jobs. Reibe along with Stringer started photographing the body. Every part of the President's body was photographed."[11]

On May 18, 1990, we talked again. O'Connor said more than once that he did not think that anyone had touched the body beforehand. "No, there wasn't any flap of scalp like that. It was all mostly shredded in the back of the head. Lying on the table, the scalp was all macerated and shredded.

"And another thing too, if you look at the picture of his hair, it's mostly black and shiny. His hair was caked with blood and not black and shiny like it is in the photograph, but bloody and matted. He had brown hair, remember."

Paul flatly stated that he cannot be wrong about the body bag.

O'Connor again said that they couldn't have surgically removed the brain. "The hole wasn't big enough even to remove half a brain. It would have been torn all to pieces."

He said, "There was no brain to fix. Close to one hundred percent of it was gone. All of his brains were blown out of his cranium."

* * *

"Dennis David saw the shipping casket, I was the one who saw the body bag."

"Dennis David didn't see the casket opened up?"

"No."

"So he he didn't know who was in it?"

"No."

"Who else helped you unload it then?"

"There was Humes, Boswell, and maybe Jenkins."

"Did you lift the body bag out?"

"No. We just unzipped the body bag and lifted him right out of the bag."

"Who helped you do that?"

"The whole place was filled up with people. I'm sure that Humes, Boswell, Jenkins, and a whole bunch of other people helped. I was kind of mesmerized by the bloody sheet around his head."

"Is there any possibility that you could be wrong about the body bag?"

"No."

"You had seen a lot of them before?"

"Oh, yes."[12]

"Do you have any reason to think that when you saw the body that anybody had been at it, that they had been digging bullets out of it?"

"Well, yeah, but I didn't think anybody had touched the body before-hand."

"Yes."

"The thing that stunned me was the severity of the head wound. I had never seen anything quite as extensive in my life."

"Was there any kind of huge flap or just the shredded scalp on the back of the head?"

"When they say flap of scalp, no, that one picture of the back of the head showing hands holding up the scalp there, that is a *strange, disturbing picture.*"[13]

A "Dr. Miller" in the Baltimore–D.C. area called O'Connor late one night and said that someone, maybe "X," took a ball peen hammer to the head either at Walter Reed or Bethesda. O'Connor thinks he said it was Bethesda—"to disrupt the wound and the physical characteristics of the wound." Paul thought that "X" had something to do with it. "X" transferred out after the autopsy.[14]

He said that "I was told by this so-called Dr. Michael Miller that 'the body was altered at Walter Reed or at Bethesda, and he thinks it was Bethesda, and put back in the coffin and taken around the corner and down back of the hospital to the morgue.' "

He repeated that he *unzipped* the body bag. Remember, O'Connor told the House Assassinations Committee investigators that the body was wrapped in a body bag.

"The FBI men said the body was put down in the cooler room?"

"No. It didn't happen that way." Said that Jenkins was wrong about that, too. Said that he thought the FBI men did not help take the coffin out of the hearse.

"So there is no possibility that you could have been mistaken?"

"No. Never."

He said that Jenkins brought out things that he didn't know about.[15]

After discussing the matter on April 6, 1991, in Dallas with Jenkins and Al Rike, he said, "The body was altered at Walter Reed or at Bethesda. Miller said he thought it was Bethesda, and put back in the coffin and taken around the corner and down back of the hospital to the morgue."

"What about the shipping casket, Paul?"

"It had to come from someplace in the Washington area [substantiating this is the possible existence of military hospital towels around the head when they unwrapped it]. After the casket went in, the Navy ambulance took off and they couldn't find it for a while. The switch had to be made at Andrews someplace."

"What time?"

"If they were going to do something to his head, I don't think they'd take him to a hospital to do it. I think they'd probably take him someplace and take a ball peen hammer bang bang bang to disrupt the wound and the physical characteristics of the wounds."[16]

"The thing of it is, when I first got the pictures [in 1991] I said, Jesus Christ, they're all phonied up."

He remembered Metzler very well, he said, and thought he could recall Donald Rebentisch.

"I was the one who actually took the sheet off the head." He recalls Jenkins helping him, but not Metzler. He did not see the bronze casket. "It never came in." He doesn't think it was ever there. He thinks Jim Jenkins or somebody said another casket came into the emergency room on the north side of the hospital.

Of the bronze casket he said, "It didn't go in the front door. But they might have brought it around to the ER, where I'm sure there was a bunch of reporters.

"Sibert and O'Neill were right behind me, whispering, and the only reason I remember them is they were taking down names. I turned around and looked at them and they looked at me like I was a spy or something, and they retreated."

"Could they have seen the body come out of the casket?"

"They should have. I'm sure they were in the room.

"The only other casket I remember was the huge monster—a rosewood [it was mahogany] casket they put Kennedy in."

"That was black mahogany."

"Right. That was black mahogany. I was the one who put him in there and a man said, 'Mr. O'Connor, you must be a Catholic. Here, put this rosary in his hand.'

"I don't remember any brain at all." [A few days later Paul admitted that he didn't remember because he probably was not in the room during the period when it was removed and examined.] I asked him about the bucket that the brain was normally put into with formalin. "I don't know what happened to it." He had no memory of the bucket at all. James Metzler remembers labeling it with Kennedy's name before the body came in.

"What time did the casket come in?"

"I remember I looked at the clock and it said eight o'clock."

"The shipping casket?"

"Yeah."

"Could that clock be on Daylight Savings Time?" (The body had to have come in about seven P.M. at the latest.)

"Oh, God, you're asking questions I can't even answer."

I asked him, "In Dallas, they had used gurney covers—like those greenish-gray body bags. It seems to me possible that in Dallas that's what they used to line that coffin to protect it. Could that have simply been wrapped around the body and not necessarily had him zipped in it?"

"You know something, it *could,* because I thought I remember him being in it and having him zipped in it, but sure—to my mind—it was. But it has been so many years and so much has happened, I kind of doubt my own ability to remember fine details."

"But to you, is it possible?"

"Yeah.

"All I remember is heavy rubber, and I don't think the sheets were heavy rubber." O'Connor once again described his experience in Vietnam working with body bags. It is hard to believe that he invented this. "I'm quite sure it was a body bag."

"How about Kennedy being inside of it?"

"Yeah, he was inside of it.

"They brought the casket in and set it down. Jim says it came in on a gurney, but it didn't come in on a gurney. These two guys brought it in and set it down. They set it down beside the table on the floor. I know that emphatically. The casket was opened—I was standing at the head of the casket. It opened up to the left if you were standing at the foot. He had a sheet wrapped around his body and a sheet wrapped around his head. He did not have his back brace on."

"Did they clear the room every time they took X-rays?"

"Back in those days, nobody paid that much attention. Do you know what I'm talking about?"

"You got radiation."

"You got radiation. A bunch of us were moved into the changing room or the cold storage room."

He remembered Reed and Custer taking X-rays, and he remembered leaving the room a time or two. He said that they waited for some time before beginning, for someone to come, probably Finck.

"Hearsay: I heard the body was at Walter Reed." In fact, nearly all of the men had this idea. Their officers had told them that the body was coming over from Walter Reed. The photographs had to be taken somewhere else.

"Was there any long wait? Did everyone just go right to work?"

"Let me think. There's certain things I remember clear as a bell, and certain things that aren't clear."

"Jerry Custer was actually helping everybody."

"I was up at the head of the body. Jenks was down farther."

I described the way the head looked to Metzler when it was unwrapped, that there was a jagged cut all along the hairline, just above it, from behind the right ear down to the back of the neck, in the hairline, with a flap hanging down.[17] Paul agreed that the flap was hanging down, not up, as it appears in the pictures.

"That's exactly how it looked." He explained that Kennedy had a lot of long hair and tissue hanging down. "It was all hanging down in shreds, so you couldn't actually see inside the skull until you pushed all that aside."

"Metzler said there was a real jagged cut all along the hairline, just like a can opener opened it," I said.

"That is the way it looked."

"Do you think Jenkins is mistaken about the brain?"

"No, I don't think he's mistaken. *I just think I was probably out of the room when what was left of the brain was taken out.* I don't remember the brain. I remember pieces of it splattered around."

Paul then recited by memory the autopsy number for the President, which was correct: A 63-272.

"How about the order not to talk?" He said that "that only applied when I was in the military."

"Things might be a lot clearer if the brain had already been removed while you were out of the room."

"*It had to be,*" he said. "You heard Jenkins—the brain stem was already severed. All you had to do was whack whack with scissors along the sagittal suture and scoop it right out. It'd only take about a minute to do that."

"After the FOIA, I had a lot of fruit loops going, calling me," he said with a mixture of resignation and amusement.

Then O'Connor suddenly said, "The body was *wrapped* in a body bag," which again led me to wonder if he had ever meant the body was *inside* it or wrapped in it. I kept getting this both ways—7 HSCA 15 mentions his telling them that the body was *wrapped* in a body bag. I think he was confusing the mattress cover or gurney cover that was used to put around the body in Dallas with a body bag.[18]

"Yes, you have to make your own mind up about what you saw in the physical evidence. And I saw certain physical evidence that night that, ah, that showed me that he was hit twice."

"Now, you don't think that there's any way that you could have made a mistake about the shipping [cheap] casket?"

"Absolutely not. I swear on my mother's grave.[19]

"And I said that just a gray casket—and I went to a funeral director here in town and we talked. He's been in the business for four years. And he says, yes. I remember the same casket you're talking about, if you're talking about the ornate casket that Aubrey Rike put him in, and when we got it. You're talking about a Mercedes and a Chevrolet. Okay?!"

"Yes."

"That's how you grade caskets. That's how they work. I know exactly what it looked like."[20]

We went over some old ground:

"What do you remember about the neck wound when the President was on the table? Did it look like that photograph?"

"No."

"Is that thing painted on somehow?"

"Yeah, it's airbrushed."

"So what did the throat actually look like?"

"Well, it was a mangled-up mess, there was one section where there was an incision and it was on the right-hand side. In this picture I've got, it's very disturbing because of the fact that, ah, they've airbrushed the whole right side of his head in that picture, too. Plus the fact that the picture when it was taken, if you look at it, it was taken from up above. So the whole part of the head should show all the wound and everything, and that was all airbrushed out."[21]

"You're saying the right side of the head has been painted in?"

"Because the shot was straight down into his face. And it was no way it could be dark back in that area. They just colored the whole right side of the head in. His throat wound is airbrushed in too." He continued to have some trouble with the throat wound as it appears in the pictures, but not to the extent of saying that it was not basically the same size in the picture as in reality. It did not look right to him. "No, it's a pretty big gash." What he meant was that normally, in his experience, only a very small hole was made.[22]

"There's two strange things I saw. Also, these are incisions above each breast. I can see the incisions, but I never knew what they were for."

"They put drainage tubes in there."

"No, they didn't. That's a bunch of shit. . . ."

"You think they've been painted in or something?"

"No, no, no, no. I saw them that night. I said, why the hell did they put these things in? It looks like somebody took a scalpel and just gently opened up a little incision just above the breast."

"Right. The thing was, there was a big hunk of his scalp and hair blown out."

"Yes."

"Because we had to go ahead and put plaster of Paris on his skull that night to get uniformity in his skull. So it would come together."

"Yes."

"And there was a great big hunk—I saw a picture in that museum Gary Shaw has got in Dallas and it shows this Goddamn police officer —with a uniformed guy standing there and a plainclothes guy standing there and—"

"Yeah."

"He reaches down, and it looks like a divot in the grass like at a golf club. Like somebody has whacked the grass—and actually it's a big bunch of his scalp, that he picks up and puts in his pocket."[23] Others say they see what they believe is an FBI man putting a .45-caliber slug into his pocket.

Jenkins said that he thought that O'Connor was not there during that time and did not see the brain. O'Connor later admitted to me that he probably was not in the room during the removal of the brain.

"But the bones were in place and not missing altogether?"

"No, like the forehead? The bones were in place there but the rest of the back of the head was all crushy and mushy . . . there were a lot of bones gone. You have to remember that that picture is phonied up. That picture has been spray-brushed . . . I know that's a phony picture. I'm not an expert on photography, but you just look at it and you can see it's all blackened out where it shouldn't be blackened out at all. The background—you study those pictures for a few hours and you'll pick up all sorts of weird things, like the instrument tray that's positioned over the top of the body—we didn't have one like that."

"What did you have?"

"We had an instrument tray that was on a little wheeled cart that came up alongside and the tray swung out over the body. It stood by itself on the floor. What we see in the picture is sitting on the table."[24]

"We were told that you were used as a courier—"

"Yeah, I ran this, that, and the other."

O'Connor considers it "farfetched" that someone, a doctor with a false I.D., could have sliced into the brain to remove bullets if everyone was gotten out of there. "Jenkins was in there full-time." Jenkins is sure that the body had been tampered with before it ever got to the hospital.

"You have to realize something—that night we had a parade of people going in and out, in and out."

"I just wonder if before the formal autopsy began, if someone was able to be alone with the body at Bethesda?"

"No, no. No way.

"You've got to remember that those photographs of the body were not taken at the Bethesda morgue." He said that the phone was on the other wall, "not where it is in the picture."

In another conversation that day he noted that "at four-thirty the chief petty officer came to me, and about five other petty officers, and told us to go to the back of the hospital. They got the men to go out to get a body, then, because he knows the bronze casket—still in the air—is empty. It has to be."

"How did he know that?"

"Well, he had to know that through somebody else who told him to get a crew together to go back there. At three-thirty in the afternoon. Well, at four-thirty in the afternoon *Air Force 1* is still in the air."

"They were broadcasting from the plane," I said.

"Yes, but they already knew the casket that was coming in the front was empty. All right, at four-thirty in the afternoon *Air Force 1* is in the air and is coming back to D.C. All at once at four-thirty the Navy chief gets the order to get this bunch together because he knows the bronze casket is going to be empty. It has to be. So somebody knew it was going to be in another casket before it even landed."

"Who?"

"It probably came from the Officer of the Day, who gave the order to the Chief."

I asked him about the removal of the brain. "It was probably when I was upstairs. I never did see a brain, period. They wanted something right away and I had to go up. It was two stories up."

About the other casket he said, "I heard about that too. Even Dennis David and the other guys heard that another coffin was rushed into the emergency ward. There was a shell game going on."

About JFK he said that "he looked emaciated as hell. He didn't look like a healthy human being."

"They are all fakes and we know they're fakes," he said, speaking again of the autopsy photographs.[25]

Well, it is rather extraordinary, when you think about it, for actual witnesses to such an event to say such things. To call the photographs of the President's body fakes. That takes a lot of courage, and this veteran has plenty of that, even if he hasn't got all of the story perfect.

And he is right.

CHAPTER 13

JOHN THOMAS STRINGER

I had extensive talks with John Stringer, the civilian photographer who took the pictures of the President's body. His camera took both color and black and white. Stringer said that he was there when the body arrived and helped remove it and put it on the table. He said that there was no body bag or shipping casket.

The first interview contrasted sharply with the second, which followed my sending him copies of the autopsy reports and photographs. The first interview seemed quite candid and straightforward, but in the second, Stringer demonstrated great stress. In addition, Stringer greatly contradicted everything he had said in the first interview, when he described a large hole in the very back of the head. After he was shown the picture of the back of the head, he agreed with it and said that was the way it was (intact).

When I told Stringer that the X-rays show the top right front of the face missing, he said, "That's ridiculous!" I then sent him copies of the X-rays and photographs. He later said that he did not recall any wounds to the face.

Stringer said that he had taken pictures of the interior of the chest, but that they were missing.

I brought up the picture of the intact back of the head to Stringer, and after some discussion—he had already seen it—I asked him, "So you're saying that that picture was taken after the autopsy?" and he replied, "Well, I don't know. If it was, then somebody else made it."

"In other words, you didn't make that picture?"

"That's correct." And then a moment later he said he did not see the picture, and in the second interview, sometime later, he said that the picture shows the head as it was.

"Do you remember that there was a large hole in the back of the head?"

"Yes, there was a large hole in the back of the head. . . ."

"And was there any scalp there at all?"

"No, it was macerated."

"But it wasn't whole enough that you could put it back together so it looked perfect."

"I wouldn't think so."

I asked him if the top of the head was missing, and he said, "No, the top of the head looked all right."

My next question was, "You took pictures inside the skull, right?" and he promptly answered, "We took pictures before and during, but we didn't take anything after the autopsy was over."

"The top of the head was *not* gone," he told me. I kept going over this ground with him. "Well, certainly the hair and all [on the top of the head] was intact from what I remember; it was the back of the head that was gone."

Later he said with regard to the missing side of the face in the X-rays: "There's no way that the face was gone, because you knew who it was. Looking at him from the front, you'd never know anything was wrong."

Stringer said that it was discovered at the lab in the hospital that some of the film was missing from the holders that were used in the camera. The inference is that the plotters were obtaining some of the films right then for later forgery, and stealing films such as the missing pictures of the interior of the chest.

In speaking of the throat wound, Stringer said, "Well, at the beginning it was like a tracheotomy thing."

"Just a little teardrop shape?"

"Yeah."

"Very small, in other words?"

"I would say so."

Stringer greatly contradicted himself in the second interview when he said that there was no bone missing from the back of the head but that it was missing from "the side." I then told him that there was a mere flap of bone and scalp there. He responded, "What I am saying is that it was blown open and there was something missing on the side there too.

Now, you can see some bone there, but not all the bone wasn't there as far as I can remember."

He had evidently talked to someone who refreshed his memory in another, contradictory, direction, in the interim.

In the second interview, after I sent him the pictures, I asked him, "What kind of condition was the back of the head in when you photographed it?"

"Well, the back of the head shows in that photograph."

"You say that's accurate?"

"Yes."

That was highly doubtful.

"And there was no bone missing at any part of the back of the head?"

Stringer made his response:

"No." We can see what a lie this is, how this poor man seems to be forced even to this day to cover up the truth—cover up the back of the head—when every single witness including the autopsy report described a lot of bone missing from the back of the head. At the very least, those lying about the appearance of the back of the head would say, well, the bone was missing, but there is obviously a flap of scalp covering it up.[1]

"Our Nation is commissioned by history to be either an observer of freedom's failure or the cause of its success. Our overriding obligation in the months ahead is to fulfill the world's hopes by fulfilling our own faith. It is the fate of this generation to live with a struggle we did not start, in a world we did not make. But the pressures of life are not always distributed by choice. And while no nation has ever faced such a challenge, no nation has ever been so ready to seize the burden and the glory of freedom."

—John F. Kennedy to Congress

CHAPTER 14

NEW EVIDENCE:
THE 1991 DALLAS CONFERENCE

In 1990, reluctantly, I began reinvestigating the case of the assassination of President John F. Kennedy. Part of this effort entailed finding certain of the autopsy witnesses previously interviewed by another author, and, unfortunately, he did not want anyone to know where these men were. It took me several years to find them, and then I was ready to go to work. Locating witnesses can be very difficult, but I felt a little stupid for not being able to locate these particular men easily, and wondered how they were found in the first place. For instance, one seemed to have a rather unique name, but there were four others with the same name in the United States, and the one I wanted did not have a listed phone.

The most important new evidence—which became absolutely clear when I gathered together in the Grand Ballroom of the Stouffer Hotel in Dallas, for the first time, several of the Bethesda autopsy crew, and several of the doctors and nurses from Parkland Hospital in Dallas[1] to film them for the documentary I was making for network television— were clear descriptions of the large exit head wound showing an actual absence of scalp and bone *nearly exactly the same shape and size, and in exactly the same place, as it had been described in Dallas in the back of the head.* The area where the scalp was missing in the back was smaller. Dr. J. Thornton Boswell, one of the autopsy doctors, confirmed this to me on September 1, 1991.

This was of vast importance in understanding this case. I had long ago suspected that what was described in the autopsy report was basically the same in several respects as what was seen in Dallas, but I was probably alone among the critics of the Warren Report in saying this. What controverted this belief was the picture of the President's head made available by the Assassinations Committee which showed the back of the head perfectly intact, and the obscuring of this fact (as well as others) by the Warren Commission.

The fact is, researchers made serious mistakes in interpreting the evidence because it was so difficult to understand. One of the mistakes had to do with the size of the tracheotomy incision, and another was that the large defect was solely in the back of the head. The latter is an example of selective reporting of what some witnesses indeed did say. But several other Parkland witnesses described it more on the *right side of the head,* extending into the back. In addition, statements by some that there was a flap on the back was automatically discounted.

The probability that the flap was pushed aside for a time and not visible did not occur to researchers. Then the question becomes: How badly damaged was that flap? Where was it? I made mistakes myself in interpreting this evidence because there is a powerful force at work in this "critical community" to distort the evidence and direct legitimate inquiry away from the facts, difficult as they may be to determine. In the process, they co-opt the discoveries of others, and stating false facts in the same sentence destroy the credibility of what is important. There are famous operators in this crowd who do almost no real research of their own but who appear to be doing just that, and push aside legitimate research, claiming for themselves the territory.

I had the horrible experience of watching on television numerous critics and writers whom I know and once respected make false statement after false statement. For instance, some of them said that a whole bullet was found in the limousine, that a whole bullet was found in John Connally's leg, that a whole bullet was found in the wrappings at the autopsy. That the CIA killed Kennedy. One writer took as gospel the statement that the doctors thought they saw a bullet hole in the left temple.

There may very well have been a puncture in the left temple, because the mortician told me the head was penetrated in several places by shrapnel,[2] which he filled with wax, but the Dallas doctors later strongly retracted the observation of an entry wound in the temple. One of the critics selectively edits video films of witnesses so that they appear to say something they don't mean. I have one of those films, and I was a victim of this sort of dishonesty. It has been very difficult to get at the truth because of such games being played with the evidence. One film, for instance, took out the last half of a sentence by Andrew Purdy, an investigator for the House Committee, so as to have him saying the opposite of what he in fact said.

"It is important that all of the facts surrounding President Kennedy's assassination be made public in a way which will satisfy people in the United States and abroad that all the facts have been told and that a statement to this effect be made now," Deputy Attorney General Nicholas Katzenbach wrote Bill Moyers—President Johnson's assistant—*on the 25th of November, 1963, three days after President Kennedy died.*

Katzenbach continued: "The public must be satisfied that Oswald was the assassin; that he did not have confederates who are still at large; and that the evidence was such that he would have been convicted at trial. 2. Speculation about Oswald's motivation ought to be cut off, and we should have some basis for rebutting thought that this was a Communist conspiracy or (as the Iron Curtain press is saying) a right-wing conspiracy to blame it on the Communists. Unfortunately, the facts on Oswald seem too pat—too obvious (Marxist, Cuba, Russian wife, etc.)." J. Edgar Hoover told President Johnson's man, Walter Jenkins, on November 24, "The thing I am most concerned about, and so is Mr. Katzenbach, is having something issued so we can convince the public that Oswald was the real assassin."

In other words, the assassination had to be quieted down fast, and all the focus was on Oswald—and none of it was on the medical or other evidence which would have told a far different story had anyone bothered seriously to investigate. Oswald was railroaded postmortem, and whatever might really have happened would be covered up in order to keep the public peace. The easiest way has always been to blame something on a dead person who can't defend himself.

But was the cover-up deliberate? Some think that the case was covered up to prevent a war, and some think it was covered up because the government didn't know what really happened and had to suggest a story quickly to prevent unrest. Both are wrong.

* * *

Dr. Robert McClelland and all the others from Parkland and Bethesda whom we reinterviewed in 1991 made it startlingly clear that underneath the apparent flap of scalp in the alleged autopsy photograph was a large hole in the skull in the back on the right, extending into the occipital area. When I brought the witnesses together from the autopsy and Dallas, they insisted that after the head was assembled and filled with plaster for possible viewing in an open casket after the autopsy, it was impossible to pull all the hair over the hole. This was solidly backed up to me later on by the cosmetitians from Gawler's Funeral Home. The Bethesda and Dallas witnesses drew on a model of a human head —before the television cameras—what it actually looked like, and there remained a fairly large area where there was no scalp at all in the back. *The pictures were fake.*

A theory maintained that the body was made into a "perfect medical forgery"[3] in order to deceive the autopsy doctors and the cameras. Some critics fell for this fantasy, even though Dr. Cyril Wecht and countless other medical people insisted that it was impossible to fake wounds, and most intelligent and thoughtful people did not accept the idea. In addition, it is my opinion that such a fantastic idea would set back solving the case for years, and witnesses who could throw some light on the facts would die or become incapacitated by illness, as has happened with the President's personal physician, Dr. Burkley, Admiral Galloway, and Dr. Bill Voss.

In 1979 I began showing the pictures and X-rays to the Dallas doctors and nurses, and was the first person to do so. We wonder why the official investigating bodies never bothered to do this. Andrew Purdy,[4] told me that he had shown the Parkland doctors the pictures, but they denied that he had done so. If he had, it would be in the reports on his interviews with the doctors. He does mention in his report the meeting with Dr. Malcolm Perry showing him a *drawing* of the wound in the throat, a tracing from the photograph. But why bother showing a drawing? Because he probably did not have access to the photographs, which were kept in the House Committee's safe. Some investigation!

When I began interviewing the autopsy witnesses, what they had to say astonished me. It was as stunning as the insistence of the autopsists, Drs. Humes and Boswell, to a panel of doctors interviewing them for the House Assassinations Committee that the entry wound in the alleged photographs and X-rays of the body had moved some four inches from where they had placed it.

For instance, we were told that no entry wound had been seen at all in the back of the head at the autopsy. Some of the doctors said that the comminuted fractures were simply too great for there to be an entry wound at that site.

It was also clear from the statements of Dr. Kemp Clark and others in Dallas that the casket described by Clark as "a bronze-colored *plastic* casket,"[5] and as "a plain bronze casket," by Charles J. Price, a hospital administrator[6] was not all that it was blown up to be by those calling it a "ceremonial" or "ornamental" casket. In fact, the witnesses repeatedly qualified it, whenever they caught themselves saying "shipping casket," because they never meant that the casket they saw was simply a "shipping casket." By "shipping casket," they meant the casket in which the body was shipped. Some witnesses were color blind, too.

We are therefore concerned about "leading the witness," as they say in the law.

The difference between myself and others was that I put all of these individuals before television cameras with several of the Parkland witnesses, and let the chips fall where they may, even if it were to go against what I suspected was the truth. My attitude has always been that if someone makes a legitimate discovery that needs corroboration and I provide that, then I am glad to give credit where credit is due.

The Large Head Wound

The rest of this chapter presents what was said at the Dallas conference.

"When the head was unwrapped," James Curtis Jenkins said, "there was a large gaping hole in the back with nothing there."

"No scalp?"

"No, nothing. A hole similar to this." He picked up the drawing showing a big hole in the skull.

Dr. Philip Williams asked Jenkins, "There was brain inside the head, wasn't there?"

"Yes."

"And you removed that brain?"

"Yes. Dr. Humes actually removed the brain."

"Did he cut the brain stem?"

"He didn't cut the brain stem. He didn't have to," Jenkins replied.

"In other words, that was a free-floating brain inside the cranium?"

"Yes."

Jenkins describes the fact that the scalp was already reflected back from the large defect, showing bare bone, when they unwrapped the head. But he did not think that someone had done it, but that it was the result of the blast of the bullet exiting the skull there. This would be a flap.

Floyd Riebe, the medical photographer who took photographs of the President's body at the autopsy, stated that some of the photographs—those showing the back of the head—are composites—forgeries—and not what either he or John Stringer took. He stated that the photograph of the back of the head does not show the large wound as it really was. This was confirmed by all other autopsy witnesses I interviewed, as well as at the Dallas filming, and by every single witness from Parkland.

The filming established that the X-rays are incompatible both with the photographs and the memories of the witnesses.

When the head was reassembled after the autopsy by the morticians for possible open-casket viewing, a significantly large area of scalp was missing in the back so that the large defect in the scalp could not be covered. This was drawn on mannequin heads by the autopsy witnesses on camera. In addition, it was demonstrated by Dr. McClelland that the show *Nova* had misrepresented him and that they had gotten him to make a statement that was based on only an "assumption"—a distortion of the facts. (*Nova* also misrepresented onscreen by taking out of context the statement in an FBI report that there was surgery to the head area. I feel that the denial by Dr. Boswell[7] that this is what they were talking about, and that the FBI men misunderstood it [see Chapter 8] is the truth.)

Jim Jenkins said, "I think there is something wrong with that photo [of the back of the head]. . . . There was an area [of scalp] the size of a silver dollar that was missing."

He described a large gaping wound similar to what Dr. McClelland has in his drawing. "It may have been a little higher, but that is irrelevant at this point." He said the scalp could be drawn over "to cover it to a certain extent, but not entirely."

Dr. Robert McClelland said that it "was one of my clear impressions" that one third of the brain had been blasted out [as all the Dallas witnesses who had seen it indicated in 1963–64]. "That there was not only a horrible gaping wound but that it was a cavity that extended down into the head. And as I stood there holding the retractor, I was looking down into it all the time. I was no more than eighteen inches away from the wound all the time, standing just above it, which was ten to fifteen minutes at least. And during that time I had a continuing impression of that gaping cavity. And during that time I had a strong impression that a portion of what appeared to be the cerebellum fell backward through the wound onto the scalp and hair that was hanging back from the head. Whether it fell completely free and loose I don't know—but it fell back out of the wound into my field of vision." McClelland here referred to the flap in the back.

Dr. McClelland had a close enough look at the large head wound to say that it would have been impossible to cover it over completely. "The way the wound was described by Mr. [James Curtis] Jenkins squares very well with what I saw. I think that the reason my wound [in his drawing made many years before] seems lower was because" of the locks of hair hanging down over part of it. "There was a great deal of matted hair and blood around the edges of it and I probably couldn't appreciate the size of it as Mr. Jenkins could at the autopsy table. But it squares with the general location and configuration of the wound.

"I could not tell what percentage of the scalp was missing or still present over the wound. At the National Archives [for the *Nova* show] it was my assumption—and it was just an assumption—that there was enough of the flap left to pull up over the back portion of the wound and to hide the back portion and the front portion of the wound, not because it was covering the front portion of the wound, but simply from the camera angle it didn't permit that portion of the wound to be seen."

McClelland said, "One might be led to believe that this was intact head back here. That's not the case. It wasn't. The skull was missing underneath the scalp [in the back]."

In the opinion of Jim Jenkins, as well as the others at the autopsy, and of Dr. McClelland, the large hole in the back of the head was an exit wound.

The Right Front Head Entry Wound

The witnesses noticed a "graying" area on the right side of the skull above the ear.

"I remember Dr. Finck making a statement: 'Could this possibly be from a bullet?' The hole was examined as such. When the official autopsy report came out, I was stunned," Jim Jenkins said.

Quite clearly, the gray perhaps could only be lead from a bullet entering the skull there. From the front. From the Grassy Knoll.

The autopsy crew found that the flap of skull and scalp on the right side of the head which appears only in the pictures showing a rear view of the head either did not exist when they dealt with the body or was in the wrong place. The flap (on the right side) in the picture of the back of the head was not seen in Dallas. The possibility exists that it was there, but that Jackie had closed it.

Jenkins thought the flap of bone was attached and hinged more to the top of the head. "There was a discussion at the autopsy on graying area on the bone, anterior to the bone on this flap."

"I would have been one hundred percent sure the fatal shot came from the side, from this angle [front right]. I was very surprised, shocked at the conclusions that came out," Jenkins said.

"There was some gray metallic material approximately the size of the end of my finger," Jenkins said, pointing to his head directly in front of the right ear.

"Could it have been the scrapping from a bullet?"

"That was my impression, and that was the discussion between Dr. Finck and Dr. Humes," Jenkins said. "It looked like lead scrapped onto the bone."

Malcolm Kilduff, acting White House press secretary, points to the spot on the autopsy photographs that could be an entry hole, just above the corner of the right eyebrow. Tom Wilson's computer study of that spot, visible on the Groden Right Superior autopsy photograph, indicates that it is in fact a hole through the skull. One of the morticians, Tom Robinson, told the author how he filled a penetrating hole in the same area with wax. "I didn't have to do anything more to it," he said. Robinson thought it was one of a few very small penetrating skull wounds and exits from "shrapnel."

There was some discussion among the witnesses about this. "We did not have at Bethesda the capabilities that I'm aware of to ascertain any basic forensic pathology. Those facilities existed at the Armed Forces Institute of Pathology downtown."

"It would not have been possible to ascertain the entrance wound in the back of the head because of the fragmentation of the bone, maceration of the scalp, et cetera," Jenkins said.

"I agree," McClelland said, "you would not have been able to ascertain that from what I saw of the wound," and he had a good look at the head that day. "You can't typify an entrance wound by beveling in the skull."

JENKINS: I don't think that there was that much bone available in a single piece to make such a judgment.

I interjected, "Certainly not from the pictures and X-rays that we have."

"It's *absurd!*" Dr. McClelland said. In 1968 the Clark Panel of four doctors reviewed the alleged X-rays and photographs of the body and noted no bone loss anywhere in the back of the head, but they did find a small wound of entry on the cowlick area, which later came as quite a surprise to the autopsy doctors. They said that the wound exhibited the cone-shaped beveling characteristically caused by a bullet passing in the direction of the widening cone.

Paul O'Connor noted at this point in the meeting that there appears to be airbrushing in the right temple area along the hairline, precisely where a retired Maryland state police homicide investigator pointed it out to me, and precisely where Jim Jenkins said there was graying as though from metallic or lead scrapping along the bone of the skull.

The Morgue

There was a moment of quiet as the men studied the autopsy photographs, including the photographer who took them. Then the bomb exploded: "This doesn't even look like the morgue!" Paul said.

"What?" I exclaimed.

"That's true," Jenkins said. "It does not look like the morgue [at Bethesda]."

Floyd Riebe said, "No, I just noticed that floor."

"What did the floor look like?"

"Well, it was similar in design, but it was *white!* . . . The floor at Bethesda was stone tile. It was put in there so it would last for years."

"What color was it?"

"It was white and black."

"This area does not exist in that morgue," Jenkins said.

"Does not!" Paul said. "We have *no* wooden structures in the morgue."

"The Bethesda floor had the small dots," Floyd said. We saw them in the picture.

"We didn't have anything wooden in there," Paul said.

"It does not look like the morgue," Jenkins said.

FLOYD: This area here would have been steps going up to a gallery.

JENKINS: That's what it would have been, wooden steps going up to a gallery. And the gallery would have extended to the head of the table.

All insist that the "Death-Stare" picture of the president was not taken in the morgue at Bethesda.

Fractures

Jenkins recalls a fracture at the base of the skull, when Paul asked him if he could remember the fracture in the orbit. "The eye was dilated real bad," Paul said. "In the vomer area."

"Yes," Jenkins said.

When They Received Word That the President's Body Was Coming

"At three o'clock that afternoon we were told the President had been assassinated. They dismissed classes and we were told to report to the morgue," Jenkins said. But both Paul and Jim said they did not have reason to believe the President was coming there "until Admiral Galloway came into the morgue."

"It was in the afternoon. Sometime in the afternoon," Paul said. Jenkins said he did not know who was coming until seven in the evening or so. Paul clearly remembers it early in the afternoon. Did they have or someone have knowledge before even the widow?

Air Force 1 did not take off from Love Field in Dallas until 3:47 P.M. EST, and it was a while before Mrs. Kennedy decided which hospital to go to, after she was given the choice by Admiral Burkley.

Floyd Riebe remembers it clearly: "I got a call from the Washington press. Evidently they knew he was coming to Bethesda. Roughly right at four o'clock because I was getting ready to go to supper."

Normal Procedure

Normally the staff performed autopsies and the resident doctor came in and checked them, or he did the autopsy with the staff. Humes and

Boswell were administrators and did not normally perform autopsies, nor did they have much experience with gunshot wounds.

This autopsy was quite different, and Admiral Burkley, the President's personal physician, "drove us all up the wall," Paul said. "He interfered constantly. 'Don't do this, don't do that,' he said."

There was a small gallery with benches with a view of the table, and it was filled with brass who interfered often enough, getting more and more disturbed as the failure to find a bullet continued.

The Alleged Rear Head Entry Wound

The Bethesda witnesses insisted in our filming that there was no entry wound at all in the back of the head which was earlier described in the autopsy report near the hairline, and which four years later during an examination of the photos and X-rays was found by a panel of doctors to have moved more than four inches.

The Brain

The autopsy staff say that Dr. Humes removed the brain. The comment that Jenkins remembers being made at the autopsy table was "The brain stem is severed. There was speculation at the time as to whether this had been done by a bullet or not."

There was some brain in the head, but it did not appear to be President Kennedy's brain, and the brain weight listed in the Supplemental Autopsy Report was that of a full-sized adult brain, certainly not that of the President, which had a very great loss of matter from the fatal shot.

"It was a small brain," Jenkins commented. Then, astonishingly, he said, "We did not have a weight for the brain." (The Supplemental Autopsy Report indicates that the weight of the brain was obtained later, *after* formalin fixation.)

At every autopsy there are a set of scales over the body or close to it, and each organ is taken out and weighed, and the weight noted down. This was not done for the brain. (For the other organs?)

"The brain was not weighed, which was not an unusual procedure," Jenkins said.

Jenkins and Boswell took the brain to a stainless steel bucket containing formaldehyde and put it in.

He commented that the brain that "I saw basically had the cerebellum intact."

Here we have one of the basic conflicts in the evidence. Some have speculated that the brain was brought to the autopsy after the body arrived "on a gurney" (seems to me that it could be tucked under the arm). Certainly the President's cerebellum was severely damaged and "swinging in the breeze," as it was described by Dr. Philip Williams, one of the Parkland doctors. Certainly, every single doctor at Parkland, all of whom had seen many gunshot wounds and many other head traumas, insisted that the cerebellum was hanging out on the table. Yet the Bethesda witnesses all say that the cerebellum was undamaged, and study of the photographs and X-rays by independent doctors confirm this.

Therefore, it could be deduced by some from the fact that the cerebellum seemed intact (to the autopsy doctors as well) that the brain did not have so much damage to it as was the impression given in Dallas, and that it had not lost much weight, *that this was a different brain.* These statements do not make it a fact.

In checking just what a "normal" brain weight is, Robbins' text quotes average (for men and women) fresh brain weights as being between 1100 and 1400 grams, without formalin fixation.[8] Brains are weighed fresh before fixation or infusion with formalin at an autopsy. It is possible that a brain traps fluid (becomes edematous)[9] when traumatized by a gunshot wound, but in this case, bleeding would have rid the brain of a good part of its weight.

Dr. Jurgen Ludwig reports that the average weight of an adult male brain is 1350 grams.[10] Sunderman reports that male brains range from 1100 to 1700 grams at the highest, and that the average is 1400 grams.[11] Female averages are considerably less. The weight of 1500 grams given in the supplemental autopsy report for President Kennedy's brain includes formalin, which we can assume added a maximum of 50 grams in weight. This leaves Kennedy's brain weighing 1450 grams after being in part destroyed from a gunshot wound, assuming that most of the brain was in fact intact, as the doctors at Bethesda describe it.

Jenkins said that the Parkland description of the cerebellum "was not congruent with what was seen" at Bethesda. "The damage to the brain did not match the damage to the skull or to the wound as we first saw it when we unwrapped the head—the brain was a small brain and it was a female brain. The brain did seem to be small . . . the brain that I saw and helped infuse was not damaged to the extent that you would have expected. There was a small portion of it missing in the appropriate area, but the rest of it seemed to be more traumatized. It seemed to be jelled. Brain tissue—it's traumatized, it gets real soft and mushy."

"How much brain was in the skull?" Dr. McClelland asked the Bethesda autopsy staff.

"I can't reconcile the difference between my recollections and that of Paul, but we both agree on the size of the open gaping wound," Jenkins said. He said that had a third of the brain along with the cerebellum been destroyed, the bottom of the brain and vessels needed would have been impossible to infuse. "We did have difficulties with it, primarily because they had retracted [which is what happens where a vessel is severed]. *I don't feel that the brain weighed 1500 grams!*" (This is the official weight given in the autopsy report.)

"Paul, did it weigh that much?" Dr. McClelland asked.

"No! There was next to *nothing* there when we looked in," Paul said.

"I agree," Dr. McClelland said.

"A large portion was jelled, and there was some of it missing."

"How much was missing?" I asked.

"I'd say the major portion of the brain remained. It was certainly more than two thirds and probably three fourths still there and intact," Jenkins said.

"It was severed from the brain stem?"

"Yes."

"Had it been severed by a bullet?"

"We turned it over to infuse it, and the vessels had been retracted as though they had been cut at some previous time. The brain stem itself had been incised about two thirds. The other third had basically been pulled out."

"Blasted out?"

"No, it really wasn't. It looked like a clean surgical incision. It looked as if it had been cut surgically." Note, we are now talking about two different indications of surgery to the head area prior to the autopsy, and after the body left the trauma room in Dallas.

The Tracheostomy

We established that the large incision in the throat seen in the autopsy photographs is an accurate depiction of the tracheostomy incision made in Dallas, and would not be a bullet exit wound. This finding destroys the theories maintaining that it was either a manufactured false exit wound or that it was a butchered job during a search to find the bullets, or the implied conclusion of the Warren Commission, which maintained that that was an exit wound.

Several doctors, including Drs. McClelland, Jones, Dulaney, Perry, and some of the nurses have described both for my 1991 filming and previously the size of the trach tube's cuff, which is actually fitted inside the incision to prevent it from closing over the breathing tube, and which requires an incision more than two inches or so across. It tended to stretch the incision somewhat.

The autopsy photograph showing this wide incision makes the wound appear to be gaping because the head is hanging downward a bit from the level of the body, not entirely on the table but supported by a metal brace, and this stretches the neck, pulling open the horizontal incision somewhat. Plus, as explained elsewhere, Perry was operating on the throat, examining the bullet track, the blood vessels, the trachea, and looking into the chest as quickly as he safely could. He needed three inches to do all this. There was no point to putting a tube in the trachea if it had been destroyed by the bullet wound that he saw on the outside of the throat.

In spite of questions being asked about this by others, as a lot of trachs are performed vertically on the neck, from top to bottom, and because of the size, I have no doubt but the wound in the picture is exactly as it was, except for retouching. Previously, I had thought it might have been enlarged, but the size of this wound does not preclude the possibility that someone had removed a bullet with forceps beforehand.

McClelland said that the incision "was about right" for the manner in which they were performed at Parkland, perhaps a bit larger than usual, but "performed in haste."

"This is the incision, and it does look like the incision I saw that day. . . . It may be somewhat longer than usual, but I'd say this [in the photograph] is the same length," as what they made November 22, 1963.

Aubrey Rike, who helped place the body in the coffin, said that as Kennedy lay flat on the table, the long throat incision was more closed. He said that the picture was accurate.

When he lifted the body, he could feel through the sheet the head wound in the back with his hands. He could feel the edges of the wound along the broken skull. "It was in the back."

The Face

Dr. McClelland looked at the X-rays of the skull, and noting the large amount of bone missing on the right upper face from the eye to well beyond the hairline, said, "It's inconceivable to me that his face could be intact and not be greatly damaged if he had a wound in this area." The President's face was undamaged, and every single witness who saw him either as he lay dying or after death said that one could not tell that he was wounded, looking at his face. His face was undamaged.

"If he had this sort of injury to the bone, there would have been a great deal of damage to this portion of the face and the forehead. I did not see that at all. He had no damage to his face except for some slight swelling and cyanosis."

"Is there any way that frontal bone could be missing and the face not fall in?"

"No."

Audrey Bell, the chief supervising nurse for the operating rooms, said, "His face was intact." She and everyone else at Parkland and in Dallas who had seen him said this.

All the autopsy crew agreed that there was no damage to the face. Later on, all those present for the meeting of witnesses agreed that the face in the photographs was Kennedy and that it was the way they remembered him.

The Throat Wound

"Somebody in the gallery wanted the bullet in the back to come out the throat," Jenkins said. "We did not know there was a bullet wound in the back."

Jenkins thought that there was no cover-up at the autopsy, but that there was a cover-up afterward, that things were fudged, changed, or invented by both the doctors and the interpretation the Warren Commission put upon their findings. He thought that all procedures of an autopsy were in fact performed. He described the intestines being cut into strips and put back into the body.

"We assumed that there had been a tracheostomy," Jenkins said. "What I saw was a cleaner surgical incision on both sides. One of the questions I have today is how long did the trach tube stay in?" The important point here is that nobody thought for a moment that the big gash in the throat was an exit wound, but it sure fooled a lot of people down the line later on, who never saw the wound itself. *They thought it was an exit wound.*

McClelland said, "Mac [Dr. Malcolm Perry] said it looked like an entrance wound." (McClelland did not see the bullet hole in the neck, as he came into the emergency room just after they had put the tube in.)

It was established both on April 6, 1991, and other days of filming that the surgeons and other witnesses in Dallas saw an entry wound in the throat barely three to five millimeters across. Two chairmen of two surgery departments in two major universities insist to this day that there was an entry wound there and not an exit wound. (The autopsy doctors and their report got around this by *assuming* a bullet had exited there, since they did not know there had been a gunshot wound in the throat until the day after the autopsy, when they were told so by one of the Dallas doctors.)

"Surgery to the Head Area"

We have begun to answer a number of other questions, such as the statement in the FBI report of the autopsy that there was surgery in the top of the head when the body was first seen. Although this appears to refer to something done to the skull or scalp, it is worth mentioning that Jim Jenkins described on April 6, 1991, what appeared to him to be a shot through the head and brain from front to back that might have appeared to others less trained in forensic medicine to be a surgical cut. Jenkins was merely asking if it was possible for Humes to have seen all he described through this laceration without sectioning the brain.

The impression could be drawn from Jenkins's description that the brain had been sliced open, incised from front to back just to the right of the midline, and from behind the right forehead near the temple to well back in the head, though this is not what he was saying. Other authors misunderstood what he was getting at as well, and built an entire theory on it. Jenkins later clarified this to me by saying that he was asking a question about the damage from front to back on the brain just to the right of the midline (parasagittal). The damage he describes is similarly described clearly as a *laceration* by Dr. Humes in the supplemental autopsy report on the brain, and by him in his testimony to the Warren Commission. The drawings made from photographs of the brain, published,[12] clearly show this laceration or disruption of the brain. If it's Kennedy's brain.

Dr. Humes described the laceration in his Supplemental Autopsy Report as being 4.5 centimeters deep into the brain. In addition, he described a laceration of the corpus callosum. It is quite clear that these two separate lacerations were made by bullet fragments plowing through different parts of the brain and that they are *not* connected.[13] Unfortunately, others began to merge the two lacerations in their mind to make it one, and then it began to become a "slice" or *incision* (made with a knife) rather than a tear, or laceration from a bullet. From there it became an easy step to being an operation to remove bullets, though certainly we do not need to connect the two lacerations in order to have a probe go in there to remove a bullet, if one existed. We don't even need an incision to do that. If the laceration, which is clearly not an incision in the published drawings, is but a wildly disrupted brain, then where is the damage done by the bullet if it is an incision?

The plowed trough across the brain front to back on the right also corresponded to or paralleled to some extent a laceration of the scalp shown in the right profile photograph starting a half inch into the forehead over the right eye, straight back to the occipital area. (See Chapter 8, Dr. Boswell's interview with me of September 1, 1991, and with

Dr. Robert Karnei, August 27, 1991.) The frontal bone beneath this laceration was intact.

Clearly, there was enough brain left in the head for the witnesses to see this, and it would appear that this could be misread to mean that the autopsist's recorded statement by the two FBI men said it was also apparent that a tracheotomy had been performed as well as surgery of the head area, namely in the top of the skull, when they may have been referring to the long "laceration" in the scalp starting on the forehead above the right corner of the right eye a half inch into the forehead and going straight to the back of the head. The laceration, if not an incision made at some point to reflect the scalp, was probably made by the bones shifting on the head during transport and breaking the scalp. It was not seen in Dallas, and the doctors insist to me that it was a laceration.

We see it quite clearly in the Right Superior Profile photograph. Importantly, the part of that laceration extending into the forehead is covered up in the Stare-of-Death photograph and others. This indicates that it was evidence of something they did not want seen in the Fox set of pictures, other copies of which were leaked in 1963, though I can't believe Fox was responsible for the leak.

Jim Jenkins corroborated the discussion about surgery, though he did not actually see any incision, and described the discussion about it around the autopsy table.

First Jenkins thought the discussion by autopsists "related to the brain stem." He said it wasn't necessary to do the craniotomy to remove what was left of the brain, but they extended the sagittal suture to get it out. Doctors performing an operation, or anyone stating that a procedure has been completed, may state: "Surgery to the head area has been performed." An inexperienced FBI man having heard this reports it in another context.

Jenkins said that he thought that in the autopsy report there was a statement that "there was an *incision* running in the brain to the level fore and aft of the corpus callosum, and it was a *surgical incision.*" As described by the doctors, the incision would look like the slice an ax would make if it struck the head front to back to the right of the midline, cutting deeply into the head. This is what happens when a witness reads the word *incision* in another book (not the autopsy report), changes it to *laceration,* and becomes confused. Somebody else's extrapolation became a perversion of the known evidence.

We have here an example of words being previously suggested to a witness, because Jenkins several times repeated on film that "yes, they described it as a *surgical incision* (in the autopsy report) to the depth of the corpus." Wrong again. Not only was it never described as an incision, but it was only 4.5 centimeters deep into the brain, and not to the depth of the corpus at the base of the brain. Jenkins knows that something is wrong and said, "That is the reason I asked Dr. Williams, because I couldn't see any purpose for this [the alleged incision] and I was wondering if I was misinterpreting the statement that was made."

I asked, "Could it have been the track of a bullet going through there?"

JENKINS: Again, that would be speculation on my part.

Dr. Philip Williams said, "Well, it could be, possibly, but it certainly wouldn't be a smooth line like an incision, if that's what it was described as."

JENKINS: May I ask a question? Could it possibly have been that a bullet was removed by that technique? That maybe a bullet had been removed actually from the brain to the track that was apparently made [by the bullet]?

DR. WILLIAMS: Yes, that is possible.

Could this mean (since there was no surgery performed at Parkland) that sometime after Parkland but before the body reached the autopsy itself someone had cut into the brain? Jenkins suspected that perhaps a bullet was removed "through the track that was apparently made." Dr. Williams, of Parkland, said, "It's possible."

Dr. Robert McClelland said, "The bullet is certainly an incriminating piece of evidence."

"Relating to that is the fact that we actually found *no metal* in the body at all," Jim Jenkins added.

But it is my opinion that there was no surgery to the head at any time prior to the autopsy start, and that things were being misinterpreted by those with little training or experience. As author and researcher Harold Weisberg asks, When was it possible to perform such surgery?

Jenkins since has told me again that he was asking a question as to whether or not the brain had been sliced open, and did not mean to state as fact that it had been opened up prior to the autopsy. Confusing, eh? For more on this, see Chapter 11.

In addition, conspirators of the sophistication and intelligence that apparently forged and planted evidence in the case would simply use either exploding or fragmenting bullets that would not leave sufficient material to be able to connect to any weapon or person, or military jacketed bullets that pass through the body. It would not be necessary to operate on the body to remove bullets, or to worry that one remained in the body.

X-Rays

I have established beyond question that the X-rays are fake. Dr. Philip Williams, a neurosurgeon, studied the X-rays the government claims are of President Kennedy, and said, "I would not say this is the same skull [as his, or the one in the photographs]. The bone in the back of President Kennedy's head was missing, and none of it is missing in this X-ray. In fact, no bone is missing in these X-rays anywhere behind the ear, except in what they are calling a small entry hole in the cowlick. The large exit wound in these X-rays is *frontal.*"

It was established by Dr. McClelland on April 6, 1991, that the X-rays show a large blow-out of skull in the front of the head on the right, and are therefore totally incompatible with everything that was seen of the face in Dallas as well as in Bethesda, which was totally undamaged.

The fake X-rays of the head and the fake photograph of the back of the head were used to trick Earl Warren into believing that the President was shot only from behind and not ambushed with shots coming from all around him.

The Back Wound

We found that there was an entry hole well down on the back that did not penetrate the chest at all, and that this bullet did not come out of the throat.

Floyd Riebe was absolutely sure that a deep depression showing on the President's back a good six inches down from the shoulder was the rear entry wound. He pointed it out on the picture. It was "pickled in. There is a hole. Colonel Finck and Dr. Boswell had their fingers in. The tissues pulled in, pushed in there. I know for a fact Colonel Finck had his finger in there." (As Finck testified in the trial of Clay Shaw in New Orleans years before.)

Riebe said that the dark spot nearer the shoulder was a birthmark or a spot of blood.

Jenkins disagreed, and said it was almost on the edge of the scapula on the median line. "O'Connor said it was right on the edge of C7."

JENKINS: Right, maybe so.

Jenkins recalls Humes probing it with his finger. "His hands were extremely large to do that. . . . They were trying to force an entry into the pleural cavity, and there was none. You could actually see behind the pleural ridges as they probed into that area, and those ridges were going down, and as Paul says, there were probably down about the middle lobe of the lung. There was never an entrance established into the pleural cavity. It was probed both with his fingers and with a metal probe—I remember the impression of those that I saw from inside the body because the organs had been removed at that point in time."

"Did it penetrate the chest?"

"No, it did not. It also seemed to be in the soft tissue."

"Was it a shallow wound?"

"Yes. It was almost as if it were inside the rib cage."

"Did it look like a bullet hole to you?"

"Yes."

Paul said, "It looked like a punched—bullet hole."

"Could it look like it was cut with a scalpel, falsified to look like a wound?" All the witnesses shook their heads and said no in very certain terms. It was not an artificial wound.

JENKINS: It was a traumatic wound—a traumatized area. It looked as if it was a misfire or something of that nature that actually just did a punch and went down to a certain point [and stopped). . . .

Or hit Kennedy's back brace.

Boswell's Drawings

The autopsy personnel were unable to explain the drawings Dr. Boswell said he made during the autopsy, which he told the *Baltimore Sun* years later were mistaken.[14] "I don't know what that means," Jenkins said, referring to the notation on the drawing "3cm" and an apparent wound at the left eye.

"I can't relate to the drawing because everything is backward."

"I can't understand it either," Paul O'Connor said.

Jenkins could not explain what Boswell meant when he wrote "missing" on the top of the skull, but he did state that the arithmetic figures were his own handwriting on the drawing and that Boswell wrote the descriptions. But Jenkins denied having written "7 × 4mm" on the back of the drawing, which seems to indicate a bullet hole where we all know the President got shot because of the holes in his shirt and coat.

"The wounds seem to be inverted," he said. But he thought that the circle around the right eye referred to "the dilations structure of the eye."

The Fragments

It was established during the filming that more fragments were found in John Connally than could have come from CE 399, the "Magic" Bullet found on the stretcher of a little boy at Parkland. There was no bullet taken from John Connally's leg, but only the smallest of fragments. A very small fragment remains, which is larger than what was missing from CE 399. Statements that a bullet was taken from his leg is another of those misunderstandings based on the misuse of terms, when "bullet" or "missile" is used in place of "fragment."

I asked if anyone had heard any discussion of fragments or bullets being seen on the X-rays during the autopsy. Jenkins said no, but there was controversy over that and that is what brought Dr. Ebersole downstairs to the autopsy room.

"Do you recall any metal in the throat?"

Jenkins said, "No. There was none found in the body [no bullets] and that caused quite a controversy both from the gallery and from the floor. Later, bullet fragments and bone fragments were brought to us in a bag at the autopsy and placed by the head at the autopsy table. Some of the bone fragments were the ones they tried to place into the head."

Audrey Bell said, "Well, we had too much [metal] to go on the 'Magic Bullet!'" She drew a life-size picture for me of the fragments recovered from John Connally that day, which she put into a small vial.

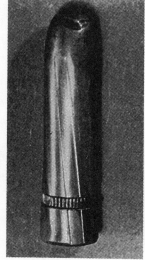

CE 399. The bullet shows no loss such as that which we see in the fragments removed from Governor John Connally.

Life-size drawings of the fragments removed from John Connally and given to nurse Audrey Bell. She put them into a vial the circumference of which we see here, and made this drawing for the author on April 6, 1991. Jerrol Custer, the X-ray tech at Bethesda, identified the fragments in this drawing as looking exactly like those he was asked to tape to pieces of bone he was told were from John Kennedy's skull, the next day, and make X-rays of them.

The Body Theft

It appeared from the testimony filmed in Dallas in April 1991 that the body did not arrive at Bethesda in the same wrappings in which it left Dallas.

The men insist that they had the body and were taking photographs and X-rays before Mrs. Kennedy arrived in the ambulance with the coffin that was supposed to have the body in it. But none of them had personal knowledge of who was in the coffin, and had not in fact taken such pictures and X-rays for at least a half hour after the body arrived.

Floyd Riebe describes the casket as gray.

Dr. McClelland was with the body while they waited for the priest to come to administer last rites. "No one could have tampered with it at any time at Parkland," he said. They waited almost half an hour for the priest. Last rites were administered and then the body was put into the coffin by Rike, Dennis McGuire, and Vernon Oneal, and it was closed. The coffin was rolled out to the hallway, where another fifteen minutes passed during the struggle between the Secret Service men and Dr. Earl Rose. The battle, as William Manchester so well described it, was between the authorities in Dallas who wanted an autopsy there, and the Presidential party that wanted to leave Texas on the spot. Jackie kept her hand on the casket throughout this scene.

The casket was then rolled out of the hospital, put into the hearse, and it went directly to the airport with no stops. Rike followed it the whole way to the airport at breakneck speed: "Code three," he said. Twelve motorcycles accompanied it, and ten to fifteen cars with the Presidential party, the Secret Service, the newsmen.

The Metal Head Brace

Well along in the meeting of the witnesses, they began to question the brace shown in some of the pictures, upon which the back of the head rests.

"As Paul said," Jenkins commented, "we had a chock. It was a block approximately six inches long that had four prongs on it." This was used instead of the metal brace, according to them.

PAUL: It could be turned to different sizes to raise or lower the head.

"And it was matched more or less to the . . . behind the neck as opposed to supporting the back of the head," Jenkins said.

Nobody recalled the metal brace under the head shown in the pictures. They said it was never used. Riebe thought that he had in fact taken the picture (showing the left side of the face), and they felt it was taken in the autopsy room.

The Autopsy Room's Background

They all commented on how much of the poor quality, grainy pictures had much of the background blacked out. Even to the photographer who took some of the pictures this did not make sense.

Jenkins said, "None or very little of the area around the photos shows in the photographs. Almost all of it is blackened out." Riebe said that he was four to five feet from the table, and much of the room would show. He said the pictures are cropped and enlarged.

As they are noting this, O'Connor again emphatically stated—as he looks at these pictures—that he recalls no entry wound in the back of the head. Jenkins agrees and says it would have been impossible anyway.

I ask them if the Back-of-the-Head picture can be accurate. Paul replies, "Look how shiny and clear the hair is," which is not the way it looked that day, what of it there was left. That was covered with blood and gore.

"You don't think any big flap of scalp is being pulled up here to cover the big hole in the back of the head?"

"I don't think so," Jenkins replied.

I ask them what their conclusions would be about the Back-of-the-Head picture.

"I don't think it was taken in the morgue," Jenkins said.

PAUL: They moved the body to the other autopsy table to embalm, dress the body, and so on. I remember helping lift him into the big wood casket.

"You would say there is something wrong with some of these pictures?" I asked.

RIEBE: Definitely, definitely. There's a *lot* wrong with quite a few of them. They are phony. Somebody's dream. . . . I believe that the better part of the pictures we have here today are phony. They're paste-ups.

Riebe said that he took about five rolls of 35mm film, four black and white film packs, twelve in each pack. "Mr. Stringer shot twenty-five to thirty color negatives."

Audrey Bell asked, "Where are all the pictures?"

I asked if someone could have made black and white prints directly from a color negative.

"No," Floyd said, "you had to make what they call an internegative. It could be done. You took your color print, printed it on a piece of film that came out as a positive, then you reversed it."

Scalp

Paul O'Connor described exactly the scene that the others had when the head was being prepared for the coffin. It was filled with plaster and the men pulled the scalp back over as much of the bare plaster as they could, where there was insufficient bone to cover the large defect in the skull.

"There was still an area they couldn't cover a little larger than a silver dollar." This, of course, does not show in the photographs, which depict a perfectly intact scalp over the entire back of the head, except for a very small alleged entry hole at the cowlick, where the big defect was, which we think was painted into the photograph.

The Photographs

Some of the photographs do not appear to have been taken at Bethesda Naval Hospital, but somewhere else. All the men present flatly insisted that some of the background and the floor were not the same at their hospital.

"Somebody's dreamin' about it," Floyd Riebe said. "That's not what I saw," he continued when confronted with the pictures of the back of the head. "I believe it's fake. I believe its a paste-up. A composite-type thing."

Riebe then confirmed that the photograph was out of focus in the middle ground. "That is impossible," he said.

The Wrappings

There was a considerable discussion of the wrappings in which the body left Parkland and arrived at Bethesda. Jim Jenkins had a question in his mind, since the small "barber" towels against the head itself when the body arrived at Bethesda seemed to him to be military towels.

When the body was partially cleaned up at the hospital in Dallas ("You couldn't wash away evidence, so it was just partially cleaned," Audrey Bell had told us), Jenkins said that the head was wrapped in two large towels and then in a sheet. The coffin was lined with a cream-ish-white-colored rubberized or plasticized sheet which covered the up-per half of the body only. Aubrey Rike, the ambulance driver who helped put the body in the coffin, denied that the body was put into a mattress cover. He himself got a half sheet from the cabinet and put it around the pillow and protected the sides of the coffin.

The autopsy personnel present at the meeting with Rike and the Parkland witnesses did not remember any such rubberized sheet, which they would have seen in the coffin.

Dr. Williams, a young intern at the time, was asked to bring some-thing to wrap the body in and brought a "plastic mattress cover—whit-ish-gray." Audrey Bell said it was "opaque," and it had a zipper around it. Dr. Williams said he "thought it had elastic around it. Form-fitting." He gave it to Pat Hutton, and didn't know for sure if it was used.

Aubrey Rike noticed the blue Parkland mark on the sheet.

Jim Jenkins then described the body as he first saw it after it was removed from the coffin. (He did not help take it out, but Paul O'Connor did. O'Connor and Riebe said the body came in a body bag in a shipping casket, not in the ceremonial casket it left Dallas in, and that it was wrapped in sheets.)

Rike described the gurney covers as foam plastic and black, or very dark green with a zipper only on one end, at the top. These could be mistaken for a body bag.

"It was wrapped in sheets," Jenkins said. "I don't know if it was in a body bag. The towels under the head in the autopsy photographs were clean and unstained with blood and were clearly from a military hospital, though they did not normally use towels under a head at an autopsy."

When he said that the bath-size towels were similar to those that were under the head in the autopsy pictures, with a military caduceus on them, perhaps he meant that the bath-size towels they received the body in were from a military hospital. Making this clearer, Jenkins went on to say that "the head was wrapped in a sheet. Underneath that it was wrapped in several bath-size towels, but underneath those [bath towels] in the wound area were towels similar to these [in the pictures]. My impression was that the towels were similar to those in a military hospital." This many towels might seem improbable.

Aubrey Bell asked him if they could have been "laps" (muslin squares). "Did you see those?"

"No. They were definitely towels in this design," he said, pointing to the towels in the photographs. "They were basically a very pale green towel with a dark green center stripe. . . ."

"That was not a Parkland towel!" Audrey Bell said emphatically. "We did not have a green towel with a light stripe in them." She got light and dark mixed up.

Rike said that there were no towels wrapped around the head when he put the body into the coffin. "There was a bloody white sheet wrapped totally around the head." There was extra "padding" around the head.

"The wrappings had a tremendous amount of blood on them," Paul O'Connor said. He made it clear that the towels under the head in the pictures could not be the right ones.

Bell said, "We had green towels in surgery, but I don't think they are the ones you are describing."

"The head was wrapped in two bath-size towels—terry-cloth—and two barber-size towels," Jenkins repeated.

"We had no such towels," Bell said.

McClelland said, "We had no terry-cloth towels."

Aubrey Rike recalls that green towels were given Jackie to wipe away blood, so it would seem that they came from a cabinet that serviced the trauma room. Bell said, "We did not have that kind of linen even down in the emergency room." Al Rike said that the towels they gave Jackie were "greenish color towels. Smooth-type towels." Not terry-cloth. He did not see the mattress cover Dr. Williams had brought.

Jenkins was told not to remove the towels on the head after the sheet was removed. People peeked under the towel. Jenkins asked himself, Why was this type of towel involved in the wrapping of the head?

"When we took the towels off, the wound was gaping. People had looked at the wound before we took the towels off. Then again the injuries were repeated to the people—Paul and I—and to prepare the jars full of the samples and things of that nature. We took the sheets off and we were told not to take the towels off. We had already taken the sheets off the head," Jenkins said.

Drs. Humes and Boswell, the autopsists, removed the towels, throwing them to the wall. Captain Stover, the commanding officer, had them picked up and put in a garbage bag.

"I was never more than three or four feet from the body that night," Jenkins said. "We were all locked in, and only Custer could leave, to develop the X-rays. We stayed until one or two in the morning. There was already present an ornate casket, maybe rosewood, that had been present at the time of the arrival. I was told that it was an Air Force major that was to be buried at Arlington the next day. . . . I was told it was not necessary to log it in, which was extremely unusual.

"Once the body [Kennedy's] was prepared, the casket [wooden] was brought in and the body was placed in that. The coffin was in the cooler room. It was very unusual."

The Hammer

Paul O'Connor received a strange call one night not so long ago—years after the autopsy—from someone who identified himself as Dr. Morgan or as Dr. Miller, in the Washington area. The caller had said that one of the autopsy doctors had taken a hammer to the skull of the president and beat on it before the autopsy began.

Dr. McClelland was staring at a copy of the photographs and a copy of the X-ray of the President's head, and he said the picture showing a large cavity in the skull could be a "picture of somebody else." That "they could be of someone else's head," and "this right here could be the edge of a *ball peen hammer.*"

Dr. Williams asks, "Is that not a picture of the morgue?"

Meanwhile, Jenkins was looking at the photographs, and again says, "That's not a picture of the morgue." Each person was finding something else that was wrong almost at the same moment.

"This was fabricated from . . ." McClelland said, his voice trailing off. Was it the emergency room at Parkland?

Wrap-Up

Floyd Riebe went on to say, "A lot of this evidence was doctored to fit the story that the government wanted to put out. There had to be a conspiracy in order to do all the work that had to be done, to do all that was done to the photographs alone. Somebody had to know about it and not tell."

"And as for faking the wounds," Riebe said, "it's impossible to make a perfect medical forgery out of the body."

"I always thought it was a massive cover-up," O'Connor said. "For this to fall into place like it did, it doesn't happen this way. You just can't in a matter of hours have everything in place to have all of these things happen."

Jenkins said, "After viewing the photographs and relating them to what I remember, I think that the photographs certainly were taken the night of the autopsy, and some of the photographs reflect items that did not exist in the morgue. I have a fairly graphic memory. I think that over the years, certainly, the government has fabricated evidence, manipulated evidence." He said that Dr. McClelland and Nurse Audrey Bell confirmed that what he remembers was very accurate.

He wanted to know where the bullet in the neck went—it would have done considerable damage to the trach area.

Aubrey Rike, the former ambulance driver at Parkland, said the file of his interview with the FBI on November 22, 1963, is missing, and says much else with others is missing. "Everything was covered up, and there's no record of it whatsoever."

AUDREY BELL: Not only did we remove fragments but Governor Connally still had a few fragments left in his thigh. We didn't get all of them. We just got the larger ones.

"So Governor Connally is walking around today with the proof that this was a conspiracy in his leg!" I said.

BELL: What we took off was greater than what is missing from this bullet.

"Much greater?"

"Yes, and I had heard that that's one reason why they disappeared! Because they weighed more!"

Dr. Philip Williams said: "Over all these years it's interesting how such an important event in American history can be recalled with such detail and, certainly, that's the beauty of the human brain. I'm convinced—as I always have been—that this was unexplained, that a lot of the activities of a lot of people in Washington are unexplained. There is a lot yet to be found. It's sad that an investigation like this has not come forth before now and cooperation has not been available.

"I'm saddened that other people who probably have a lot more detailed information which would be helpful in this investigation have not come forward here today, and will realize that and come forward to make their contribution to American history."

"The cost of freedom is always high—but Americans
have always paid it. . . ."

—John F. Kennedy in his message
on the Cuban missile crisis

CHAPTER 15

THE AUTOPSY PHOTOGRAPHS
AND EVIDENCE OF FORGERY

In Chapter 6 I began with a rumination flowing from the great conflicts in each piece of evidence: Is this really President Kennedy's body? I'm not sure if I dare ask this too seriously, but here and there in the works of persons more intimately exposed to the evidence than myself, one comes across statements like the following by Frank Scott—who prepared the report for the House Assassinations Committee on the authenticity of the color photographs of the body: "I conclude that these pictures are authentic photographs. In forming this conclusion, I assume that the object photographed is, indeed, the body of President Kennedy."[1]

People looking at the photographs of the body would sometimes ask me: "Is this really President Kennedy?"

Is that really him in his grave?

There is a certain amount of horror attached to calling what was once a person we loved an object. There is even more horror to what an autopsy does to that person's body. We are fortunate that our culture believes that the spirit never dies and is indestructible. The terrible violation of the body—that which is the cathedral wherein resides the soul—for scientific purposes is viewed without feeling as it is butchered beneath the pathologist's knife.

Scott's report on the authentication of the color photographs is little more than one page long. He relies on stereo pairs and theory. What he does not account for is that stereo viewing is not very good if one does not have prints made from the original negatives. The value of accuracy

313

of a stereoscopic exam is greatly diminished for each generation removed from the original. The House Committee examined prints that
were two generations removed. They did *not* have access to and were
not allowed to study the original color slides in the National Archives.

We can add this to the growing list of dictatorial acts by government
workers and bureaucrats at the Archives who have usurped key artifacts
of our history and who are making it impossible for study and research
of this material, not to speak of all that evidence which by rulings of the
investigative bodies is sequestered in secret at the Archives until the
next century.

"If you had the original color slides, you could tell in a heartbeat if
they are fake or not," Mark Crouch told me on August 17, 1991. The
House Committee had the slides from the Archives taken to a private
firm that made prints from them, which is what was used for the study.
The original film were four by five color positive (slides). There was no
color positive print film in 1963, I am told. Internegatives had to be
made from the slides in order to produce color prints.

The pictures we have are clearly not first generation. The House
Committee commented on the photographs as follows:

1. They are generally of rather poor photographic quality.

2. Some, particularly closeups, were taken in such a manner that it
   is nearly impossible to anatomically orient the direction of view.

3. In many, scaler references are entirely lacking, or when present,
   were positioned in such a manner to make it difficult or impossible to obtain accurate measurements of critical features (such
   as the wound in the upper back) from anatomical landmarks.

4. None of the photographs contains information identifying the
   victim, such as his name, the autopsy case number, the date and
   place of the examination.[2]

There is much more that is wrong with them, but once again—as with
the conspiracy which they admitted to—our representatives in the government did not dare go any further.

In the next paragraph the House Committee comments that a defense would object to introducing "such poorly made and documented
photographs as evidence in a murder trial. . . . Furthermore, even the
prosecution might have second thoughts about using certain of these

photographs since they are more confusing than informative. . . . Some have questioned their very authenticity. These theorists suggest that the body shown in at least some of the photographs is not President Kennedy, but another decedent deliberately mutilated to simulate a pattern of wounds supportive of the Warren Commission's interpretation of their nature and significance . . . the onus of establishing the authenticity of these photographs would have rested with the prosecution."[3]

The House Committee admits here, at the end, that this material would be prima facie inadmissible in evidence and that the prosecution would have to prove authenticity. You, the reader, can safely start out doubting this material. The Committee then went to great trouble to hoke up an authentication. But consider this last quoted paragraph phrase by phrase—since it follows several pages of one of the greatest and most outlandish lies in all of our history, and is then followed by more lying about the authenticity of the photographs and X-rays. First of all, only one critic—Stanley Keeton—ever questioned in writing up to then whether or not that was JFK in the picture, or suggested that the photographs might not be authentic. Almost no critic except Dr. Cyril Wecht and Robert Groden had seen them, and they did not question if it was Kennedy in the pictures. This was a slip of the tongue, because in the preceding pages the Committee was careful to list[4] very specific charges concerning the great disparity between the description of a large defect in the back of the President's head by the Dallas witnesses (*and* the President's widow, *and* the Secret Service men, *and* the people on the street—but the Committee did not mention *them!* It was easier for the committee to say that the Dallas doctors and nurses made a mistake, but not his widow and those close to him).

Keeton's three articles entitled "The Autopsy Photographs and X-rays of President Kennedy—A Question of Authenticity," beginning in the December 1977 issue of *The Continuing Inquiry,* a journal published by Penn Jones, Jr., were widely circulated among the assassination research community, and posed a serious challenge to the House Select Committee on Assassinations in the middle of their so-called investigation.

Keeton wrote: "After the long-awaited examination of the suppressed photographs and X-rays, two important facts emerge: 1) The location of some of the President's wounds as delineated in the original autopsy report and by the photographs and X-rays *cannot* be reconciled with other credible evidence, and 2) There are serious discrepancies between the original autopsy report and the photographs and X-rays concerning the location and characteristics of some of the President's wounds."

The Committee had to find a tame or controlled in-house critic to take over Keeton's charges and direct attention away from the many other problems with this evidence.

We note also that the Committee, with regard to numerous pieces of evidence, finds that the primary witnesses involved, including the autopsy surgeons, made a *mistake* with regard to the location of the head entry wound, for instance. They deferred to the photographs and X-rays as the best evidence. There were and are intrinsic proofs of forgery to which the Committee was quite blind, even though some of their own panel people tried to point out serious problems with the evidence, such as Dr. Angel noting the total lack of right frontal bone in the X-rays.

"To examine the autopsy photographs from the standpoint of identification of the victim we have considered two hypotheses:

1. That the subject shown in the photographs was not John F. Kennedy, but an unknown victim with a strong resemblance to the assassinated President.

2. That the victim in the photographs, in which the facial features are clearly visible, is indeed John F. Kennedy, but the body in which the face is not shown (particularly No. 32 through No. 37 which document the location of the critical wounds of the back and head) is that of another, unknown individual.[5]

There it is again: The question as to *who is it* that they photographed?

The Flap in the Back of the Head

A great controversy was started when *High Treason* questioned the authenticity of the autopsy photographs.

It had been implied that a flap of scalp was pulled up to cover a large exit wound and missing bone in the back of the skull. I may have been mistaken about its existence, and I did not fully understand this flap until I was able to locate additional witnesses who knew about it. The possible existence of a large flap in the back of the head seemed to conflict with the idea that scalp was missing in the back. I now understand that both were probably true.

Audrey Bell gave me a very explicit description of the flap, which was lifted for her by one of the doctors to show her the large defect. She is very sure that it was hinged at the top, and not at the bottom as in the photograph. She told me numerous times that "there was a lot of scalp missing in the back though."[6]

Autopsy personnel have also described this flap in extensive detail. James Metzler described it in exactly the same place and facing the same way as did Bell, to both myself and Mark Crouch, in the studios of WCHE, Crouch's radio station, in West Chester, Pennsylvania, on May 1, 1991. The description was repeated to me in the same detail by Jerrol Custer.[7] Dr. Robert McClelland also described this flap, but every one of these witnesses, and more, insists that it was hanging downward, hinged at the top to the left.

I believe it was hinged toward the left side of the head, almost blown off, and that the hand seen holding it in place over the back of the head in the photographs might be authentic, but that the photographs are greatly retouched all along the edge of the flap, which starts from behind the ear up high on the head and follows along the hairline to the back of the head, an inch or two inside the hairline.

This line, which Metzler described as looking like a can opener had opened it—when the wrappings were taken off at Bethesda—follows what Robert Groden said was a matte insertion line, showing where two pictures were composed as one. I think now that it is exactly what I told Groden it was in 1979 when Steve Parks of the *Baltimore Sun* and I first saw his leaked or stolen pictures: a very clever painting. The supposed "matte line" is out of focus because it is painted in to obscure the edge of the flap and make the head look intact in the back. The egg-shaped area of missing scalp described by every witness is also painted in. The actual process used was a matte overlay and not matte insertion, as Groden claimed.

In part, airbrushing is why the normal methods of detecting a forgery failed. The photographs had to be retouched, and they are certainly out of focus in the key area where the two parts of the scalp come together on the back of the head. The photo was also retouched to cover-up shredded and perforated scalp.

The vast weight of the evidence from all the witnesses who saw the body, including those at the autopsy, was that there was an area of missing scalp on part of the back of the head.

The picture is out of focus in that area and so there can be no edge. Some think that a hairpiece was used to cover the hole, but certainly not at any time on John Kennedy's head. Of course, the picture alleged by the government to be the back of John Kennedy may not be him. I think that in some of these pictures his face has been added to another corpse's head—in particular to the Right Superior Profile photograph in Groden's possession, which is not part of the Fox set.

Only the one area is out of focus to the camera. The rest of the picture, both the foreground and the background, is perfectly in focus, so we have a photographic impossibility.

Some time ago I showed copies of the autopsy photographs to a retired Maryland state police homicide investigator, Al Hranicka, and he immediately pointed out retouching on *several* of the photographs in addition to the picture of the back of the head. Specifically, he pointed to retouching along the hairline in the right temple area, and all along the hairline across the forehead in the Right Lateral Superior photograph. Of course, if there was a bullet entry hole showing in the right temple area, somebody would want to touch that up to hide it. But it is possible if not probable that the bullet from the front which we believe hit him struck farther back on his head and was a tangential shot that took off the back of his head. This is what most of the Dallas doctors, nurses, and Dealey Plaza witnesses believe.

In addition, the retired state police investigator said that the three large dark stripes hanging down from the apparent gaping wound on the top of the head (as the body lies on its back) were painted in. "This isn't real," he said about the stripes. He observed this in the black and white version of the color picture from the Groden set of pictures. In the color photographs, this area is very bloody red, and does not appear real. I am told that brain or other matter hanging down simply would not look like that.

Groden's Top-of-the-Head photograph in color, published in the tabloid *Globe*,[8] may be a hoax. The bright red is painted over whatever was there before. That red varied in intensity from print to print which Groden showed me over the years, and does not correspond to anything the witnesses saw, or to brain or scalp matter in real life.

I also feel that the stripes do not correspond to those in the black and white pictures, and are more exterior to the skull. In the black and white Top-of-the-Head pictures we see that two of the white stripes are clearly inside the head and show the brain and its convolutions.

We see so much more hair hanging down beneath and below those three white stripes, where there was supposed to be half of his head *and brain* missing. If we are being told that the area on the top of the head was really what was missing, then how come it is filled with brain right to the top of the head with just skull bone missing over it, at the apex of the head, when we know that a good quarter of the brain was blown out?

Baltimore city police forensic experts studied the photographs independently and felt that they were clearly retouched—airbrushed—in the same areas the Maryland state policeman pointed out, though they did not know about him or what he said. At the time, I did not know Mark Crouch, who was coming to the same conclusions.

Paul O'Connor then provided a set of photographs to the Baltimore policemen. He pointed out to the officers numerous examples of retouching and forgery in several pictures, all in addition to the forged picture of the back of the head. The fact that O'Connor himself had been a policeman and was present at the autopsy has motivated an intense investigation on their own time by some Baltimore police.

O'Connor repeatedly denounced the pictures depicting the throat wound: "The throat wound that I'm looking at now—it's garbage."

"What did it look like?"

"A more teardrop shape," he said, speaking of what remained of the bullet hole after Dr. Perry obliterated it to make his trach incision.

Since three different groups of policemen found retouching and forgery in the photographs, I think the matter is now beyond dispute. Our problem is that we are failing in our endeavors to gain access to the best copies available at the Archives. The Baltimore policemen wrote the Kennedy family lawyer—Burke Marshall—for permission to see these copies and were turned down on the basis that they were not experts. We had planned to get experts, but that did not matter to him. We recall that Marshall first granted permission to an unqualified urologist, Dr. John K. Lattimer.

We note that the Archives lately denies permission to see the rifle and other evidence. They will sell you a videotape of it though. Rick Waybright comments: "This is in violation of the law."[9]

No one has the right to keep this material secret any longer, and it appears at this juncture that Burke Marshall is part of the cover-up, whether intentionally or not. There were "rather heated negotiations" between Attorney General Ramsey Clark and Burke Marshall which resulted in the deed of gift of the autopsy materials to the government. But Robert Kennedy "was not sympathetic to the Government's need to acquire the autopsy material. Clark stated that he had only requested transfer of the autopsy photographs and X-rays and did not recall any discussions with Robert Kennedy about any other autopsy materials. Consequently the brain and the tissue segments were not an issue. . . ." (They presumably never left the possession of the Kennedy family.)[10] Burke Marshall told Clark, just after Robert Kennedy stepped down as Attorney General in 1965, that he did not want this material to come out.

Speaking of the alleged entry hole in the cowlick that shows in the photographs of the back of the head, Dr. Humes said: "Because I submit to you that, despite the fact that this upper point that has been the source of some discussion here this afternoon is excessively obvious in the color photograph, I almost defy you to find it in that magnification in the black and white."[11]

Watch what Humes is trying to tell us during this interview, along with Dr. Boswell, before a panel of doctors for the House Assassinations Committee. "The gentleman was in the dorsal recumbent position on an autopsy table, not the greatest photographic position in the world, and we had to hold his head up. One of us is lifting the head, flexing the neck, if you will, by holding the scalp, and to show the wound where it was in relation to the man's head."

DR. MICHAEL BADEN: In reviewing this material earlier today, you made an ink notation on the skull that we have here, localizing the entrance perforation to the right of the external occipital protuberance—in reviewing the skull and marking [sic] at this time and having reviewing [sic] all of the films and incorporating our discussion, is that still a valid representation? (This went against what the photographs and X-rays apparently show, as the Committee later noted.)

"Yes, I think so. . . . I think that's a reasonable representation. I think that we were making an attempt, and of course, we didn't have Polaroid in those days, like we might use now, to be sure that we had an image of what we wished, and it's interesting how technology changes things. We were attempting in that photograph to demonstrate that wound, and I feel that we have failed to demonstrate that wound."[12] *Failed to demonstrate that wound.* Humes makes it clear here that he is sticking to his original positioning of the entrance wound low down on the back of the head, and he says that the photographs and X-rays fail to show it where they saw it.

How come this did not alert anyone at that meeting to the fact that there was something seriously wrong with the photos and X-rays?

"The Panel continued to be concerned about the persistent disparity between its findings and those of the autopsy pathologists and the rigid tenacity with which the prosectors maintained that the entrance wound was at or near the external occipital protuberance."[13]

The next nail on the box demonstrating forgery or tampering with the autopsy photographs and X-rays is Dr. Humes's clear statements about having taken chest photographs, which are missing from the National Archives: "That's one photograph that we were distressed not to find when we first went through and catalogued these photographs [in 1966–67] because I distinctly recall going to great lengths to try and get the interior upper portion of the right thorax illuminated—you know the technical difficulties with that, getting the camera positioned and so forth, and what happened to that film, I don't know. There were a couple of films that apparently had been exposed to light or whatever and then not developed, but we never saw that photograph."[14] This is more evidence of Robert Bouck's "burn party."

How can photographs and X-rays disappear from the National Archives? Isn't there a *pattern* here of somebody tampering with this evidence?

In an intelligence operation, each person in each little office down a long corridor does not know what the person in the next office is doing. In this crime, we find that each piece of evidence, if viewed separately, may seem to prove the government theory, but not when viewed as a whole pattern.

The pattern in each of these murder cases where authentication of evidence is based on certain assumptions—evidence based on so-called scientific evidence that flew in the face of what the people who were there saw and remembered, and scientific evidence which clearly contradicted itself—is that the real facts were ignored or discounted. There is a *pattern*.

The pattern was one of the systematic extermination of liberal leaders in the U.S. Each murder was said not to be a conspiracy. Yet, we had a lot of deaths, and the deaths of a lot of witnesses. *Pattern* becomes a significant *fact* when it repeats itself enough. The totality of the patterns in these cases does not just strain credulity, but tells us that the case itself was all a lie in the first place. This is common sense, something those in charge of our destiny forget. They go to the experts, and rely on the federal police and intelligence agencies for wisdom in criminal matters.

The "Burn Party"

Mark Crouch tells us that on the night of December 6 or 7, 1963, just two weeks after President Kennedy was murdered, Robert Bouck went through his safe in the presence of James K. Fox, another Secret Service agent, and burned much of the photographic and X-ray evidence in the assassination of President Kennedy. If true, this was a great crime, but Bouck denies that it ever happened.

Crouch says that Fox told him that Bouck burned the materials because of fear that some of the evidence might conflict with what he thought *Life* magazine was about to publish the next day by way of frames from the Zapruder film. Well, somebody who ordered evidence destroyed had to be culpable, had to know that there was a conflict, that all the evidence did not say the same thing.

We can speculate that the safe in his office was used as a dead drop, that Acheson or someone higher than Bouck had access to it, and that they switched evidence right then. If evidence was destroyed for any reason, we can bet that it conflicted with the facts or other evidence. Bouck denies that anyone other than himself had the combination to his safe and that Edith Duncan (his secretary) was not privy to it.[15] There were plenty of highly trained safecrackers around Washington though.

They panicked and did not have too much time to decide what should survive. We do know that an awful lot is missing—the President's brain, the pathology slides, the interior chest photographs, and numerous other X-rays and photos—and the indications are that all that was missing long before it was ever turned over to Evelyn Lincoln (on April 26, 1965) and the Kennedy family in the National Archives, though it was never actually in their possession.

In fact, Robert Bouck told my chief investigator, Richard Waybright that "he felt that when he gave the materials to Mrs. Lincoln, he was actually giving them to the National Archives."[16]

In addition, it is not reasonable to me that any government official would release true copies of such materials even to the family.

In the fall of 1988, each of the personnel present at the autopsy at Bethesda described a large wound in the back of the head exactly where the Dallas doctors and nurses described it, each demonstrating with their hands but extending forward along the top of the head. This is the area where the FBI men at the autopsy wrote that there had been surgery, though perhaps mistaking the meaning of what the doctors said.

The men made it abundantly clear that there was no scalp on the part of the head we see covered with perfectly intact scalp, which covers the large defect extending into the occiput. They confirmed this to me when I filmed them, along with the Dallas doctors, April 6, 1991, and they drew on the head of a mannequin the area which the scalp did not cover when the head was put back together.

Floyd Riebe, a photographic technician who took the pictures of the body at Bethesda, said that the President had "a big gaping hole in the back of the head. It was like somebody put a piece of dynamite in a tin can and lit it off. There was nothing there." This is far more damage than could have been done by a military jacketed bullet, and could have only resulted from being shot by an explosive or frangible bullet, as appears when the head is struck in the Zapruder film. Riebe was shown the autopsy photographs, and strongly disagreed with them, saying, "The two pictures you showed me are not what I saw that night."

"What did it look like?"

(Demonstrating the back of the head.) "It had a big hole in it. This whole area was gone."

With regard to the pictures and X-rays, Riebe said, "It's being phonied someplace. It's make-believe."

Paul O'Connor, also at the autopsy, described an "open area all the way across into the rear of the brain." He demonstrated that the whole top of the head was gone clear to the back. The enlisted men who were at the autopsy, when asked about the small, neat bullet entry wound in the cowlick in the otherwise intact scalp on the rear of the head, said that they didn't know what that was or how it got there.

O'Connor was shown the autopsy photographs and he said, "No, that doesn't look like what I saw. . . . A lot worse wound extended way back here." And he demonstrated with his hand to the back of the head.

A set of autopsy photos reproduced in this book showed no part of the rear of the head missing. The only defect showing on the skull is a large hole on the top of the head extending far over to the left side, equally on the left and right sides, with a small flap of scalp and bone reflected back on the right, or open. There has never been any testimony or evidence that the large defect ever was on any part of the left side of the head.

The Zapruder film shows the flap of scalp and bone opening up on the right around the ear during the shooting, and the brain pressing outward. Evidently, the President's wife—as she held her dying husband's head in her lap—pressed this back into place, closing the wound, as it was not generally noticed in Dallas, except for a couple of doctors who noticed a fracture there, and a ridge of overlapping bone. The only thing that the witnesses in Dallas saw was the large hole in the back of the head with no scalp left. Nobody saw any large wound on the left, top, or front of the head. There was no large missing area across the top of the head at that time. The X-rays show a quite different wound *entirely* on the right front of the head and face with nothing on the left, or past the back half of the head.

The Central Independent TV four-part series made in England and shown around the world also had Dr. McClelland demonstrate the wounds. He drew a picture of a big hole in the back of the head. "It would be a jagged wound that involved the half of the right side of the back of the head. My initial impression was that it was probably an exit wound. So it was a very large wound. Twenty to twenty-five percent of the entire brain was missing. My most vivid impression of the entire agitated scene was that his head had been almost destroyed. His face was intact but very swollen. It was obvious he had a massive wound to his head. A fifth to a quarter of the right back part of the head had been blasted out along with most of the brain tissue in that area."

Dr. Paul Peters, then of Parkland Hospital, also was interviewed. He said, "We decided that the President was dead, and Dr. Clark, the chairman of the Department of Neurosurgery, had come in the meantime and he had walked up to the head of the patient and looked inside at the wound and shook his head. He had a large—about seven-centimeter—opening in the right occipital-parietal area. A considerable portion of the brain was missing there, and the occipital cortex—the back portion of the brain—was lying down near the opening of the wound. Blood was trickling out."

First, the Bethesda hospital personnel testimony strongly restated that there was a large hole in the back of the President's head. Dr. Charles Carrico said on television, "There was a large—quite a large defect about here [and he pointed to a large hole in the very back of the head] on his skull." Dr. Ronald Coy Jones said, "My impression was there was a wound in this area of the head [showing a large hole in the back of the head]. On viewing the alleged autopsy X-ray, he said, "Certainly I can tell you that the wound was not here [indicating the forehead from over the right eye back to the temple and to the top of the front part of the head where the wound shows on the X-ray]. There was no damage to the face that was visible." The alleged X-rays clearly show massive damage to the right front of the head extending into the temple, forehead, and face down to the eye, but no hole in the back of the head. The X-rays are incompatible with the photographs, which show no injury to the face.

Audrey Bell said, "There was a massive wound at the back of his head." Dr. Robert McClelland carefully pointed to a large hole in the back of the head and said, "It was in the right back part of the head—very large." All these witnesses were filmed independently, and each demonstrated the wound in exactly the same place. Dr. McClelland said, "A portion of the cerebellum fell out on the table as we were doing the tracheostomy." He was asked, "So the wound was very far back here?" (The interviewer points to the back of the head.) "Right," said Dr. McClelland.

"So the wound was in the back of the head?"

"Right." Six doctors in Dallas described seeing cerebellum on the table.

Then the television show began to point out the conflicts that have developed in the evidence. Dr. Michael Baden, who never saw the body, said on the same broadcast that the cerebellum was intact in the photographs of the wounds. Dr. McClelland addressed this problem directly: "That was one of my more vivid memories of the whole thing. It was particularly grim to see that portion of the brain ooze out of the wound as I stood there looking at it. That stays with you pretty much." Dr. Jenkins had described as late as 1977 the cerebellum protruding, but he changed his opinion after seeing the photographs, some made from the angle looking down at the top of the head. "It did look like cerebellum. It still looks like it, but it's obviously not—" he said, looking at the alleged photographs of the head wound. Fake photographs will cause witnesses to change their perceptions of what they saw.

Paul O'Connor, the autopsy technician from Bethesda, again strongly denounced the photographs on another show. "The whole side of his head was gone. I don't know where those things came from, but they are wrong. Totally wrong," he said of the autopsy photographs and X-rays.

The Photographs

There are two sets of autopsy photographs publicly known to exist outside of the National Archives—although this may be the first announcement of it. One of them—the "Fox" set—has been widely disseminated and in part was published in *High Treason*.

This gives rise to several questions, always keeping in mind Carl Bernstein's landmark article, "The CIA and the Media."[17] I'll answer the first question by stating that there were sets of the autopsy pictures spread all over Washington not long after the assassination. It is obvious that spreading forged pictures reinforced the official story of the assassination, that the President was shot only from behind. It is more than significant that the photograph of the right profile was not a part of this set. That picture fails to show the large exit wound described by Humes to the Warren Commission or seen in the Zapruder film. Such a picture would have been very difficult to forge, and I doubt that there was much time to make these forgeries. They were made as simply as possible: by retouching.

In addition, photographs of the X-rays were not disseminated. Although the skull X-rays showed a large blow-out in the appropriate area of the right front of the head, they would clearly conflict with the photographs of the President's undamaged face. I am sure they were made to be flashed at the appropriate people on the Warren Commission, if necessary.

Human nature being what it is, spreading around a few sets of these photographs at the time injects an element of terror and fascination into the body politic and into Washington itself. People don't question things like that. They view such macabre materials with the same horror and excited fascination as they watch the Amity Massacre Chainsaw Affair. It stirs more of the morbid curiosity in people than the dispassionate eye of the investigator looking for signs of forgery. Morbid curiosity is the perfect cover-up for truth. Key people in possession of or privy to such depictions of the dead President feel privileged, and don't ask questions. Their morbid curiosity is satisfied, as they are so overwhelmed with the horror and excitement of the priceless treasure they possess or have seen in others' hands. And they are also scared, which is the idea. The subliminal message is: Don't get the idea you are President the way Kennedy did, because this could happen to you.

Johnson, Carter, and Ford got the message. Nixon made the mistake of going to China and opening a détente there, so everything bad they had on him and the last of all the setups his warped personality amplified led to his downfall.

Robert Bouck, the former head of the Secret Service, denies having given permission to James K. Fox to make a set of the autopsy pictures for himself.[18] He did give the negatives to Fox, who was the man who took the film to the Navy labs to be developed,[19] and so he could have made a set for himself. Other sets could have been passed to other people. I sincerely doubt that Fox, a relatively simple man who ended life as a baker in a small town in Maryland, would have made copies and passed them out without being told to do so. I doubt that he was the source for the other sets privately distributed in Washington after the tragedy.

The color and black and white sets are not all identical, as there are different views, though some of the pictures appear to be identical colorized versions of the black and whites. A color picture of the face in right profile does not exist in the Fox set of eight pictures.

I am not alone in thinking that some are identical and yet not in their original format. Long after writing the above paragraph, I read something that I had missed before. Drs. Humes and Boswell were discussing the photographs with the panel of doctors at the National Archives in 1977.

DR. HUMES: These black and white photographs, both, were taken temporally that evening at a later hour than was this color photograph No. 26, in this case.

DR. BOSWELL: These two are essentially identical though.

DR. PETTY: Which two, would you just identify them for the—

DR. BOSWELL: No. 44 color and No. 17 black and white. These are almost identical, and I would assume that one was taken with one camera and then the other with another camera at the same time.

DR. HUMES: What? The color negative may have been developed, may have been printed black and white, Jay. Looks more like that to me.

DR. BOSWELL: Might have been. So they may be actually the same photograph.

DR. HUMES: I think they are.[20]

Seems rather strange, doesn't it? No wonder, as the House Committee commented, the photos are of such poor quality. They were taken on color film and then printed in black and white, and if my suspicion is correct, then retouched, tinted, and colorized anew from a black and white print, then rephotographed. A lot of detail gets lost that way.

Right Profile Photo

This picture was not one of those disseminated privately in Washington in 1963 and 1964. The reason might be that it appears to show a crease or shot that might have grazed along the right side of Kennedy's head starting near the temple until it entered the skull and took off the back of his head. And what may be the quite phony flap that we see opened out on the right side of the head just above and forward of the ear in the Back-of-the-Head photographs does not and could not exist in this photograph—of the right side of the head, the face in profile.

Here we come upon evidence of forgery in this particular picture. The color picture shows brilliant red stripes of brain or tissue coming down from the top of the head, somewhat on the outside of the hair. I was astonished when I first saw this, and mentioned it to Groden. His version of the scalp or brain hanging down on the top of the head promptly grew lighter.

This material is very bloodred, and shows prominently in the pictures, several inches long. In other views showing the top of the head as the body lies on the table there are three of these stripes, but in the black and white pictures, they are white or gray.

As Mark Crouch points out, we have a photographic impossibility. If the tissue matter is in reality white or gray, it will remain relatively the same color in a black and white picture. But if it is in reality red in color, and not white or gray, the tissue will go to black when printed in a black and white photograph. Red goes to black.

We printed this color picture in *High Treason,* but in black and white, since it did not exist among the Fox set, and it was the only photograph that shows the right side of the head. It is gravely important because it shows the right side of the head almost completely undamaged, contrary to Dr. Humes's testimony to the Warren Commission, which said the large defect was entirely in the right side of the head.[21] In fact, little if any real damage to the head is apparent at all in this photograph.

There are two rather strange structures on the right side, one of which is bat shaped and has a wing tip extended into the forehead a half inch and pointing at the right eyebrow. It might be scalp that has been cut and reflected downward. It could be several things. Knowing what the number of the photograph is and the sequence in which it was taken would help. If it was taken toward the end of the autopsy, that would be meaningful, but I doubt that it was taken at that time.

In addition, there is what Mark Crouch calls the "Devil's Ear," which is a shiny structure just above the ear and on the scalp. It is behind the area where there is an open flap on the Back-of-the-Head photographs, and does not correspond to the flaps. It does not show in other photographs.

The key thing about the photograph as we printed it in black and white is that the three long, wide stripes of tissue hanging down from the apex of the head are black, but they are *white*—in the photograph of the top of the head from the Fox set.

Cindy McNeill, a Houston attorney, has noted what Mark Crouch and I thought some years back, that the face looks waxen in this picture. She felt that perhaps a wax dummy was actually made to make the false pictures from. McNeill points out that photographs taken of President Kennedy the morning that he died showed a fairly large mole and perhaps a pimple of some kind near the right corner of his mouth. These are notably lacking in the above-mentioned autopsy photograph, which, as I have said elsewhere, does not altogether look like Kennedy. Perhaps that is why Robert Blakey leaked it to Robert Groden.

McNeill also notes that rigor mortis appears to be present, due to the manner in which one shoulder is off the table, though Paul O'Connor and Jim Jenkins say that a chock is under the shoulder. We know that the picture was taken at the beginning of the autopsy because there is no Y incision, but the body does seem quite stiff—too stiff for the beginnings of rigor mortis, as the autopsy report said. It began to be a problem as the hours went by. McNeill says that "the photos wherein the body is rolled over on its side for the posterior shots support the assumption the body is very rigid."[22]

McNeill writes that "the autopsy photographs of President Kennedy are actually photographs of a wax model. A cast was made of Kennedy's face and head [and perhaps his body] shortly after the completion of the autopsy. Subsequently the wax model was created complete with 'wounds' that would support the lone assassin theory."

Pencil marks left on the X-rays were made by Dr. John Ebersole some days after the autopsy when he was asked by the White House to provide measurements for a bust of Kennedy. Cindy McNeill speculates that those measurements were in fact made to provide a false head so that phony autopsy photographs could be made.

I don't think anyone would have to go to all that trouble, when all that was necessary was to airbrush the photos that were taken. In addition, the perfect wax face that we may be looking at in Groden's (and the National Archives') color pictures remains in serious conflict with the X-rays, which have the top right front of the face missing. What was the point?

It seems to me that we may in fact be looking at a wax face that was composited with some of the real face and body, but the purpose is to plant one more red herring in the evidence to confuse it greatly.

Either that, or during the "burn party" days after the autopsy, and some panic, too many pictures were destroyed, and they had to recreate them to fill out the inventory.

Back of the Head

There are apparently three different views of the back of the head (two in color), and an additional view which shows it, along with the President's back and the bullet hole there, several inches down from the shoulder.

When I took *High Treason* to the printer, I decided to include some of the autopsy pictures to illustrate forgery in them. That day Robert Groden met me, having with him his color photographs of the body. When I had first seen them in 1978, I had told him that I thought they were very clever paintings. Little did I know the trouble that observation would bring me in the following years. The pictures seemed to change each time I saw them. Different exposures, different views, and different information in them.

Now I had an opportunity to study them again for a half hour or so, but in poor conditions, sitting in a car in poor light. I noted something rather extraordinary on one of the pictures—that of the back of the head—which I had not previously noted. One of those pictures had a series of black crescents about a half inch long, a half inch apart, all along what Groden calls the "matte line." They are not in the latest version he showed us (Mark Crouch and Richard Waybright).

His pictures should have been published in toto to avoid suspicion and answer many questions about this case. Those in the Archives should have been published.

Unbeknownst to me, Groden went back to my printer the next day and switched all but one of his photographs for the Fox set of pictures. This caused me a great deal of trouble, for I did not know for almost two years that the pictures had been switched. I had repeatedly been set up, and this was the last straw.

Mark Crouch writes: "The publication of Groden's Right Superior Lateral photo in *High Treason* created much confusion in the research community. In 1990 I asked Groden if he could inventory the color photographs in his [Groden's] collection. Groden showed me five photographs which I designated G1–G5."

The problem with this inventory is that it does not correspond to my own 1979 inventory, when Groden first showed me the photos. Groden had a Stare-of-Death photograph, a photograph showing the massive defect in the head, and a right profile showing the large defect in the side of the head, all in color and now all missing, as well as a set of black and white prints.

Crouch goes on to write: "Groden also showed autopsy photos to David Lifton in 1979 and Lifton reported that he could read the imprint *Bethesda Naval Hospital* on the towel, but this imprint is not visible anywhere in the five photographs Groden showed me in 1990. The reason for these varied observations remains unclear. I informed Groden that I had contacted the FBI in regard to the question of legal consequences of possessing the photographs, and I felt that Groden was playing a shell game with the pictures out of fear of prosecution. The FBI had no interest in the 'leak' of the color photographs more than a decade earlier. Despite assurances from me, Groden continues to refuse the research community the opportunity to study these important forgeries. His reasons for these actions will have to await some explanation from him, since they seem totally illogical to those of us who know the evidence."[23]

The Flap

With regard to the alleged flap, I recall Robert Groden originally claiming that he saw a flap of scalp waving in the breeze in the Zapruder film after the fatal shot. Both Jim Metzler,[24] who was at the autopsy, and

Audrey Bell, the nursing supervisor at Parkland Memorial Hospital,[25] have described to me a large flap of scalp on the back of the head which covered up much of the huge defect. Groden now denies the existence of this flap.

Audrey Bell told me that she remembers coming into the emergency room and asking how the President was doing, and one of the doctors lifting up the flap of scalp in the back to show her the large hole in the back of the head. "All of the brain was missing there, in the back," she said.

They described a flap that was torn loose all along the hairline from behind the right ear down following the hairline to the back of the neck, about an inch or so into the hair from the hairline. The lacerated border of the scalp corresponds to what we thought was a matte line, where two photographs were put together to make a composite. I no longer believe this theory, but think it is just retouched. Metzler said the head looked like a can opener had gone around the edge of his head from behind the ear back and opened it up. So, if there was in fact a large but perforated flap of scalp with some missing areas there, the flap need only have been drawn back over the large hole and then the photos retouched to cover up the missing spots.

The most important information about this flap is that the scalp is intact where it is not supposed to be, according to one of the cover-up stories. It is intact 180 degrees around the other side of the head, toward the top, whereas the cover story has it cut loose where the surgeon's hand holds it up in the photograph, and intact all around the right edge of the head.

In addition, the scalp in the flap as Bell and all others have described it is badly torn with portions missing, something we don't see in the present photographs, where we are shown perfectly clean scalp and hair.

I am absolutely certain that all the Back-of-the-Head photographs are phony.

Back-of-the-Head Photo and the Focus Problem

Years ago I made the startling discovery that the photographs of the back of the head are out of focus in one specific area: all along what Groden calls the matte line. The picture is perfectly in focus in the background and foreground, and we have another photographic impossibility. One wonders if the lack of clarity the House Committee experts spoke of referred to that area which is out of focus, but they never specified.

Once again, I wonder why Groden, the photographic expert, never noticed this, or claims not to have done so.

Stare-of-Death Picture

There is a major problem with this picture in that the shadow of the head on the towel beneath the right ear should not be there, because the bright light of the camera's flash would have obliterated it.

In addition, the face looks like a mask and the right eye does not appear real. This picture may very well be a series of matte overlays assembled to make a composite. Tom Wilson, a computer image process specialist, says that the picture is made up from several different elements, and that the area inside the throat wound is the same as that of the eye and the shadow beneath the head.

Mark Crouch has pointed out a small black triangle in the hairline of the temple at the juncture with the forehead above the right eye in what is known as the "Stare-of-Death" picture. This triangle is reference black: blacker than anything else in the picture, and represents something to cover up. It can be nothing else, unless it is a red herring.

The reference-black triangle is apparently not in the color picture of the superior right profile that Groden possesses. Why not? Crouch says that the black area covers up either an incision, a bullet hole, or a tear. Groden says that it is a bruise, which he calls a subdural hematoma. The *Nova* show got Dr. Paul Peters to say this, basically. I said to him, "That's not a bruise. It's a *cut.*" It looks very precise, as if it were something that was done deliberately, but I can't preclude the possibility that it isn't a very nice, clean, accidental tear. Peters told me in a later interview that nothing like that was seen in Dallas.[26]

"There is no light at all passing through the negative," Mark Crouch says about the small black triangle. "It's not a bruise, it's a tear in the scalp. The key point is that it should be visible in the Fox 'Stare-of-Death' photo, and in fact, it is a) not visible, and b) the area where it should be is blacked out without a doubt."

"What could it be? Do you think it could be just an accidental tear? That's where the bullet was creasing along?"

"No! I believe it is evidence of a bullet—I've said it is an entrance wound. It doesn't have to be an entry wound. You said a key word right there: a 'crease.' It could have been a crease where the bullet sort of skirted and entered the skull."

Right Profile and the Bat Configuration

"Well, there is that straight line on the Right Profile picture. It's two or three inches long." This straight line starts at the base of a triangle pointing toward the right eyebrow and runs straight back on the head toward the top of the ear.

"It's the V that starts on the right part of the forehead above the eye and goes straight into the hairline toward the ear." We are speaking of a batlike shape on the right front part of the hair, with one wing tip (the "V") pointing toward the eye. The base, or trailing edge, of the wing is a straight line pointing at the right eye in one direction and toward the apex of the back of the head in the other direction. The whole batlike structure is also in the shape of the letter *W,* but spread wide apart.

I have grave difficulty with the Groden picture showing the face in superior right profile, the lens behind the head a bit, because the flap sticking out on the right side of the head does not correspond to anything in this picture, although there is a flaplike shape above the ear, very dark. It appears to be painted in to correspond with the flap sticking out on the side of the head in the Back-of-the-Head photographs.

In addition, Dr. Charles Crenshaw[27] and all the other Dallas witnesses insist that there was nothing like the flap we see sticking out of the right side of the head in the posterior photographs of the head.

"For whatever reason, that V incision that is evidenced in Groden's color photograph of the superior right profile is blacked out in the Fox pictures. The question that you ask then—is there something that is being hidden—what is being blacked out? Is there some evidence of a bullet hole or some other evidence of bullet trauma there that is being blacked out, that they later not worried about because an incision has been made through it?" Mark Crouch asks.

But the President's head was bowed somewhat when he was struck, and the straight line at the base of the bat-wing shape on the right side of his head points almost straight up and down, so it would not seem to be the track of a bullet along there. Joanne Braun speculated that it was an incision.[28]

Dr. Charles Crenshaw[29] and the other Dallas witnesses have convinced me that there was no such laceration on Kennedy's head anywhere in the front. Drs. Peters and Crenshaw believe that it is the type of cut made during an autopsy to reflect back the scalp. I note also what appear to be sutures along the edge of it.

The consensus among us is that the incision, like Perry's tracheostomy, obliterates an entry wound that struck Kennedy in the front of his head, near the right temple, at the hairline.

Yet, several of the autopsy witnesses say that it is a "laceration." Both Dr. Boswell[30] and Dr. Karnei,[31] who were at the autopsy, volunteered —without my bringing up the subject—that this straight line across the scalp is a "laceration." My question is, why would these doctors, who normally are so tight-lipped, want to be sure that I was so informed? They are aware that the phony pictures are out. Is there some knowledge among them that there had in fact been an entry wound in the right front or side of the head in the hairline which was easily obscured by an incision, if that is what it is?

How could such a long, straight edge running from front to back along the head and extending into the forehead a half inch and pointing at the right eye occur? I was told about the "laceration" as well, by the attendants at Gawler's Funeral Home. The bone was intact beneath it, but there was a simple tear in the scalp, according to those who were at the morgue. Others speculate that the underlying bone fractured at some point, breaking the skin and the scalp.

Which is the more credible? To my own mind, I feel that the final word must be that of the embalmers, who are trained and experienced. They learn a lot of forensics in the course of their work.

One last thought. The long line could be both: There might have been a crease and then the entry of a bullet. Then the crease or laceration was extended with a scalpel to reflect back the scalp. I have trouble with this because it seems to me that Kennedy's head, which was bowed at the moment it was hit, would have that crease pointing at the sky. This is evidence showing that the shot that hit him could not have come from the sixth floor, and instead came from down low, from the sewer in the curb just ahead, and that it took off the back of his head. It's just an indication. I continue to believe that the shot actually came from the manhole in front of the car on the edge of the overpass.

The fact that *all* the damage present in the X-rays is on the front of the head is greatly significant because we cannot otherwise explain the great effusion of internal head matter that came out of the right front of Kennedy's face which we see in the Zapruder film after the fatal head shot. Both the film and the X-rays are contradicted by a massive and conclusive amount of information showing that there was no such damage to the face or frontal bone.

In my opinion, some of Groden's color pictures are paintings. *There is no background in them,* and specifically the Superior Right Face in Profile picture, the Stare-of-Death picture which he once had, and the Back-of-the-Head pictures are largely paintings. Groden denies this, or that some are colorized and that some are identical to the black and whites.

Groden denies the possibility that his Zapruder print might be forged in some respect, yet he pointed out to us all the splices in it after others did so. Obviously, if the film has so many splices and frames actually missing, it is not beyond the realm of possibility it has been tampered with. I feel that there are some special effects in the film.

When I first saw Groden's pictures in 1978, one of them showed a large hole in the right side of the head through which one could look at the interior of the skull. This picture no longer is in his inventory. It was a view of the whole head in profile, and there was a large hole there. I cannot imagine what happened to it.

He also had a Stare-of-Death picture, which I described carefully in my notes. The right eye was quite clearly askew. This picture also has disappeared from his collection. The question is, what happened to them?

The Throat Wound

The throat wound is most clearly seen in the Stare-of-Death photograph. It is also seen in the Left Profile picture.

Paul O'Connor strongly believes that the throat wound is retouched, making the wound more jagged and perhaps larger than it was, and partly covering up the bullet wound that the incision in part obliterated. They saw a smooth incision at the autopsy. Retouching it makes it look like an exit wound.

The incision is not as large as some critics have made it out to be. I had previously been misled into thinking that it was quite a bit

The Groden color version of the Back-of-the-Head picture. Note the blood, so it is unlikely that this picture was taken at the end of the autopsy, as has been speculated. It would have had to be taken at the same time as the other black and whites, as the head is basically intact before the brain has been removed. But the scalp is too clean. Groden switched this picture from *High Treason* at the printer, substituting Mark Crouch's Fox black and white print. Why did he do this, when the ''matte line'' he talks about is far clearer in that picture, whereas in the black and white he substituted, the evidence of forgery is less clear? Mark Crouch has written that publication of Groden's photograph ''would have been far better at proving a case for matte insertion.''

Note also in the Back-of-the-Head pictures that the large egg-shaped or fist-size hole through the scalp that was described by all witnesses is not showing, proving that it has been painted over, airbrushed, and retouched to look like a normal head of hair if this is actually Kennedy's head.

These frames from the Zapruder film follow immediately after the head
shot that killed President Kennedy. The sequence that begins on the left
is taken from a video transfer. The vertical strip of frames on the far
right is taken directly from the film itself. Two reproduction
techniques are used because the video contains more information while
the film offers better definition. For example, the Blob is considerably
more obvious in the video than in the film frames. The Blob represents
a forgery since there is no known damage to the head in that area. The
Blob is most assuredly not a reflection of sunlight as some apologists for
the film have suggested.

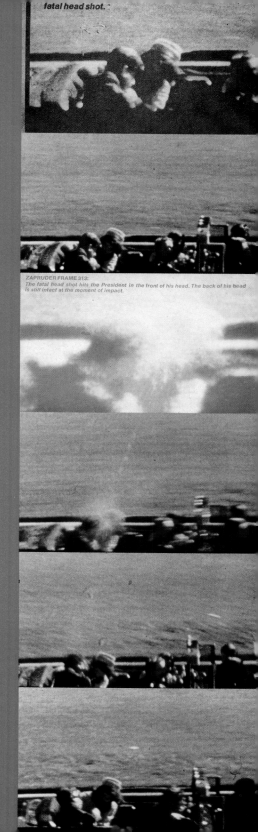

ZAPRUDER FRAME 313:
The fatal head shot hits the President in the front of his head. The back of his head is still intact at the moment of impact.

The Groden Top-of-the-Head photograph is identical in most respects to the corresponding Fox black and white photo, except that Groden claimed that the red in the photo had been enhanced. Note that certain things in fact are not the same. Some locks of hair and the size and shape of the red area are not identical. The photographer took both the color and the black and white photos with a stationary camera. Groden states that the *Globe*, a tabloid, enhanced the red in this picture. The *Globe* denies it.

larger than what Dr. Perry had done, and that therefore someone had cut it open farther in probing for a bullet. But after talking to all of those Dallas witnesses who remembered it and to whom I showed these photographs, I cannot believe that it was enlarged. Without exception, everyone said that what is seen in the picture is accurate. Dr. Perry strongly denied that he had ever questioned the picture or even been asked about it, since the whole purpose of the *Baltimore Sun* visit I organized was to question him about the Back-of-the-Head pictures.

The Bone Flap

Then there is the matter of the flap of bone and attached scalp opened out on the right side of the head just forward of and above the ear. This flap changes orientation with each movement of the camera for another angle and view. It does not stay firmly in the area where it starts. One might easily dismiss that with the observation that the scalp is sliding around on the head, but this might not permit the flap of bone to move as it does.

The flap is nowhere to be seen in the Stare-of-Death or Right Profile pictures, not even closed. The "Devil's Ear" is in the wrong place to be the flap. None of the Dallas witnesses[32] remembers it.

In light of the statements made to me by Jerrol Custer and Paul O'Connor[33] that the scalp did move loosely on the head and that there was little or no supporting bone beneath some intact scalp in the right temporal area where the flap is, I am inclined to think that it did in fact exist. But, as Custer said, the flap closed when the head was flat on the table, and it changed orientation in each picture as the head was moved around—because the scalp to which it was attached was not fastened on the head. Thus, it was hardly seen by anyone in Dallas. It is logical, though, that this is where a bullet entered, and Jim Jenkins describes a discussion at the autopsy of a gray area, where a bullet may have scraped the bone.

Jerrol Custer made it clear to me that the flap we see in the photograph was indeed there. "If you would have moved the head, that flap would have closed," he said. I asked, "Is that why it changed orientation each time the camera moved or the head moved?" "Yes, every time you moved that head."[34]

I doubt that gray would come from a brass military jacketed bullet, but it certainly could have come from some other type of bullet which more readily exploded on or in the head.

I believe that the large hole in the back of the head was connected to the area just above and in front of the right ear, where we see this flap when a piece of bone fell in between the two areas. This would be compatible with Dr. Humes's description before the Warren Commission that the hole extended all along the side of the head. The scalp was intact in between, or across the top of the head from ear to ear, and held the head together.

In Dallas they simply did not see the full extent of the wound. The head was shattered like an eggshell and could just barely hold much of its shape, held together by what scalp remained.

Robert Groden

Robert Groden, my former partner, published some of his color autopsy photographs in a seedy tabloid, the *Globe,* during Christmas week of 1991. Publication of these pictures in such a poor and undignified format threw most of us into great turmoil. I was horrified and greatly depressed. I had spent thirteen years trying to get Groden to show them to police forensic experts, and he refused. Some of the pictures may be hoaxes.

Although the first public showing of some of his clandestinely obtained materials in the *Globe* proves indisputably one of the forgeries I have been describing (the top of the head shows bright red stripes of an unreal material—paint) which conflicts with what happens when this is printed in black and white. That picture is clearly a fake, and the question is, who did it? The black and white pictures of the top of the head are real, according to all medical people who have seen them, although perhaps not Kennedy's head, and that material in the stripes is almost white. It cannot be red.

New Developments

At a conference in Dallas in the fall of 1991, Tom Wilson, a former executive at U.S. Steel, presented his findings with regard to his computer image processing of various visual evidence in the assassination of John F. Kennedy. Wilson made a number of claims that were astonishing, and if true, totally corroborated my findings as presented in this chapter with regard to forgery of the autopsy photographs.

Wilson discussed each point made in this chapter, plus some of his own, with regard to things that are wrong with these pictures, and in addition, the Zapruder film, which he believes to be substantially altered. Wilson uses what he says is a fairly simple technique employing a CCD array, (or scanner) of a quarter of a million sensors, converting the light reflected off the photograph into that many pixels, which are sorted on a Gray Scale, or 256 shadings of gray from black to white. To each pixel, he assigns an arbitrary color. He says he is able to note the depth of the paint used in airbrushing by forgers, and to a certain extent see what is beneath the paint, even in a later generation of a photograph.

Wilson, who has not published his findings, was instantly attacked by computer people who did not believe that he could do what he says he can do. For most of us, it is impossible to interpret the technical process involved, or to judge its validity or lack thereof. It will take time, therefore, to sort out both his process and the totality of his findings, to know if what he says, which corroborates my findings, are true.

Harold Weisberg wrote in *Postmortem:* "The pictures of the head must be truly miraculous if they show the entrance wound 'slightly higher than its actually measured site. . . .' "[35] Four inches higher.

The forgery of the autopsy photographs was the primary means whereby the overthrow of the elected President of the United States was covered up. That forgery is obvious and indisputable.

"This nation . . . was founded on the principle that all men are created equal, and that the rights of every man are diminished when the rights of one man are threatened. . . . It ought to be possible for every American to enjoy the privileges of being an American without regard to his race or color . . . to have the right to be treated as he would wish to be treated, as one would wish his children to be treated . . . this nation, for all its hopes and all its boasts, will not be fully free until all its citizens are free."

—John F. Kennedy

CHAPTER 16

THE AUTOPSY X-RAYS AND EVIDENCE OF FORGERY

If you draw a line from the tip of one ear across the top of your head to the other ear, that is roughly where the coronal suture is, which is a juncture of the frontal bone, or plate of the skull, composed of the forehead and the two major bones posterior to that on the left and right sides of the skull. Those are the parietal bones, separated by the sagittal suture. The sagittal suture runs front to back from the coronal suture to the occipital bone.

In 1977 a panel of doctors, anthropologists, and a dentist met privately at the National Archives with two of the autopsy doctors, James Humes, and Thornton Boswell. They had the alleged autopsy photographs and X-rays with them, and this discussion with regard to the skull X-rays Nos. 1, 3, and 6 followed.

"Well, I think the question that we all have is whether this is anterior to the coronal suture or posterior to it," Dr. Petty said. He was talking about whether the large hole in the President's head was forward of the right ear or behind it.

"Oh, there was damage that far forward?" Dr. Angel asked. He was an anthropologist from the Smithsonian Institution, now deceased. Angel was aware of the evidence that the back of the President's head was missing. He had before him photographs that showed no damage to the face or the back of the head, but he had conflicting X-rays showing the right front of the face missing.

"I believe so. I think the damage is quite apparent here in the lateral view of the skull by X-ray," Petty said.

"Yes, that's right," Angel said with a sort of bitter irony, as he could read the X-ray.

Dr. Baden then confirmed for us that the frontal bone was indeed missing: "And also on X-ray No. 1, the anterior-posterior view, right side."

"In that case, I'm puzzled by the missing bone here and the angles. . . ." Angel said. After a bit he said, "What's bothering me is what part of the flesh is that?"

"That's the cheek, the right cheek."

"If that's the right cheek, then it can't be—has to be more or less," Dr. Angel said.

"Yeah."

"It's really hard to be sure, square this with the X-ray which shows so much bone lost in this right frontal area."[1]

Humes makes it clear then that the X-rays were taken before any "manipulations were performed."[2] In a moment, Angel, still doing God's work, said, "So, in that case this exit wound is really in the frontal—it's in front of that notch there—it's in the frontal, see what I mean, it would have to be about here."[3]

And a bit later Dr. Petty says, "So that placing the outshoot wound in the right frontal bone toward the coronal suture is probably about where it was . . ."

HUMES: Uh-huh.

Edward F. Reed, a student X-ray tech present and assisting Jerrol Custer, was quoted as saying, "When I saw Kennedy and took the X-rays, he had a large gaping wound about the size of my fist in his right carotidal, temple, and frontal areas."[4] Jerry Custer remembers this wound, but it did not extend more than a very short way into the frontal bone.[5] This is where we now see a flap of scalp and bone sticking out of the side of the head in the photographs, by the right ear. Custer says that the large defect extended that far forward, but not into the forehead or eye region. He explains that the scalp held the head together and one could not then see all of the missing bone beneath it.[6]

In any event, one would think that this is where a bullet struck Kennedy.

The key point about the hole where the flap is by the right ear is that it does not correspond to the large amount of the frontal bone and right eye missing in the present X-ray. As seen in this chapter, there is clear evidence that that hole was greatly enlarged to appear to be an exit wound and to remove bone where an entering bullet scraped off part of itself.

Whether or not any of this happened at Bethesda is not clear, because the X-rays themselves are fake, and it was not necessarily Kennedy's head, but someone else's whom they killed for this purpose.

Reed goes on to say, "Even Commander Humes, who was doing the autopsy, didn't know exactly which way the fragments were going or where they were coming from. He couldn't find the bullets. I X-rayed his whole body and we only had fragments. He didn't have anything larger than four or five millimeters long."[7]

Humes and Boswell went passively along with placing the large exit wound in the front of the head, but they protested vigorously on other points that the X-rays and photographs showed, and they claimed that three weeks prior to the meeting, photos turned up which they were told about. "And we never had the privilege of examining the fragments, or photographs of this fragment that you now examined, until this afternoon, and I was unaware of its existence until about three weeks ago."[8] How convenient. In 1966 these same autopsy doctors spent some hours in the National Archives cataloging and marking each and every photograph and X-ray, and now all of a sudden, like the palm print on the alleged Oswald murder rifle, a new photograph shows up eleven years later and three weeks before this meeting!

Humes conveyed his disturbance about the fact that the interior chest photographs were missing.[9] And both he and Boswell were upset by the attempts to move the entry wound four inches from where they had placed it at the autopsy. I would be upset, too, if—as the other witnesses say—there was no such entry wound anywhere on the back of the head in the first place, and they had been made to produce an entry hole and place it near the hairline and the occipital protuberance, and then, to their dismay, find three years later that somebody else had moved it four inches.

A proof of the forgery, of the enormous lies that are being perpetrated, is the fact that there is a description of the large defect in the *back* of the head, the exit wound that everyone is trying to pretend is no longer there. Dr. Davis points it out to all: "We can see in X-ray film No. 2 extending in an upward direction from the region of the external occipital protuberance, with the upper portion of this in an area where there's a large defect in the posterior parietal bone."[10] The plain truth is, there could not have been an entry wound where they are trying to move it—into the cowlick of the head four inches above where it was observed at the autopsy—because there was no bone on that part of the back/top of the head.

The very next sentence Dr. Davis utters is even more revealing: "Now, there is radiopaque material, some of which appears to be even exterior . . ." Remember that the X-ray tech was made to tape pieces of bullet fragments to pieces of bone the next day and X-ray them. (See Chapter 10.) The Clark Panel found in 1968 that there was a large part of a bullet embedded on the outer table of the skull.

The student X-ray tech, Edward F. Reed, who helped Jerry Custer take the X-rays that day, was interviewed by a radiographer's magazine in 1988. It said, "Reed reports that his first action was to take AP and lateral skull films using a 2×4mm piece of scrap metal taped to the side of the skull for magnification purposes."[11]

To clarify one point, it is not possible that a student technician took X-rays of the President and then Custer and the other men verify that Custer took the pictures.

This piece of scrap metal may explain some of the problem the House Committee on Assassinations had in trying to explain things.

Jerrol Custer told Warren Patton in 1989 that he marked his X-rays. "What I did was put a marker on it [the radiographic plate]. I used my initials on it, just 'JC.' I put it right on top of the plate. A small metal marker." Patton asked him what the chances were that given the circumstances, this one time he didn't lay the marker on the plate. "Well, let's put it this way. I did it five days a week, eight hours a day. It became an automatic thing. And those initials are not on the X-rays that the Committee presented."[12]

Custer told me that "normally, I put my initials down on the plate, but one of the FBI guys said, 'No, we don't want identification on it whatsoever.' "

"That's strange!"

"That's what I thought. In fact, they wouldn't even let me put left and right markers on them."[13] In this business, everyone claims to have done what everyone else has done, and often forget who did what.

The Fakes

The X-rays alleged to be of Kennedy are either composites or false. The X-rays are what is called a "subtraction," which is a composite made from several different pictures. The day after the assassination, Custer was made to tape bullet fragments to bone fragments and make X-rays of them, but he did not have a whole skull X-ray.

It would appear that Custer himself made these up—or part of them —he says in the presence of Dr. John Ebersole and Dr. Loy T. Brown at the Bethesda National Naval Medical Center. (See Chapter 10.) Although Custer was told that they were for a "bust" of Kennedy, it would seem that these have to be the forgeries we now have.

Custer stated to me that he had what he thought was the skull cap— or roughly the bone in the back of the head underneath the cowlick, the next day, and taped a fairly large metal fragment to it near what would be the cowlick and made an X-ray. He believes that the film was then overlaid onto a skull X-ray to make it look like Kennedy's head.[14]

But the skull X-rays are something else as well. The head was reassembled at some point late at night, probably after midnight, when Dr. Ebersole says he took more X-rays.[15] It would not be logical to take more pictures that late at night unless they had in some way reconstructed the head. The search for bullets was over. We know from the autopsy report that three major pieces of bone came in late at night from Dallas, and Humes wrote that they "in aggregate roughly approximate the dimensions of the large defect described above."

It is of some considerable significance that the House Committee chose to keep secret whatever Dr. Ebersole, the acting chief of radiology at the autopsy, had to say in March 1978. His statements released to the press seemed to change 180 degrees after he went to Washington and presumably saw the X-rays again. Before Ebersole went there, President Kennedy had no back of the head, and when he went home the head was intact and the front of his head was blown out.

In addition, the House Committee got some skulls and had the autopsy doctors mark the wounds on them. The House wrote it up as follows: "The panel was concerned about the apparent disparity between the localization of the wound in the photographs and X-rays and in the autopsy report, and sought to clarify this discrepancy by interviewing the three pathologists, Drs. Humes, Boswell, and Finck, and the radiologist, Dr. Ebersole. Each was asked individually to localize the wound of entrance within any one of several of the above-referenced photographs after reviewing the photographs, X-rays, and autopsy report. In each instance, they identified the approximate location of the entrance wound on a human skull and within the photographs as being in a position perceived by the panel to be below that described in the autopsy report. . . . They also said it coincided with the rectangular white material interpreted by the panel as brain tissue present on top of the hair near the hairline. Each physician persisted in this localization, notwithstanding the apparent discrepancy between that localization and the wound characterized by the panel members as a typical entrance wound in the more superior 'cowlick' area *[about five inches above]*."[16]

This tends to indicate forgery of the X-rays more than reconstruction of the skull, since no one felt that there was any entrance wound in the cowlick area. If the skull had been reconstructed with the exact bones brought up from Dallas, as seems to have happened, then one of the bones might have had the entrance wound, except that the doctors placed it near the hairline, near the neck, where the bone was not missing. Then what was it that the "expert" panel of outside doctors were seeing as an entrance wound in the cowlick? The answer might be that the head was reconstructed in part with bones from somebody else's head, someone who was conveniently shot in the cowlick.

There was, of course, a body conveniently handy in the morgue that had available spare parts. He may very well have been selected for his close resemblance to John Kennedy as well.

Don't dismiss this, because nothing is too fantastic when governments are being overthrown and intelligence operations are involved.

If the above discrepancies between the autopsy doctors and their autopsy report and the X-rays don't indicate great crime, nothing will. It is a matter for the United States Senate at this point. And never mind that the doctors seemed to recant during their public testimony before the House Committee on television a few months later. That was just for show. They are still of the same opinion as they were in 1963.

It is my opinion that at least some of the skull X-rays are part of Kennedy's head, although composites could have been made up by shooting someone else in the head, beating on the skull to disrupt the wounds, and taping bullet fragments to skull fragments and connecting X-rays of those with the main film.

Other Forged X-Rays

Speaking of the posterior neck and shoulder, Dr. Humes testified that "we examined carefully the bony structures in this vicinity as well as the X-rays to see if there was any evidence of fracture or of deposition of metallic fragments in the depths of this wound, and we saw no such evidence, that is, no fractures of the bones of the shoulder girdle, or of the vertical column, and no metallic fragments were detectable by X-ray examination."[17]

We note that the X-rays that turned up before the Clark Panel several years later showed "several small metallic fragments present in this region."[18]

Since Humes was able to see quite clearly many small dustlike particles of metal in the head at the autopsy when they examined the X-rays being taken right then, we have a clear-cut case of a new, false X-ray being substituted for the neck to show a wound that had not been noted at the autopsy. It is unlikely that a military jacketed bullet would leave any dustlike particles at all if it did not strike bone in the neck, which this one apparently could not have done.

"We received skull fragments and bullet fragments in a small bag."

I do not believe that the doctors missed at the autopsy the metal that years later turned up on the X-rays. This is one more example of blatant forgery to invent another "Magic" Bullet wound higher on Kennedy's body than where he was actually struck.

Fragment Behind Eye

"The largest section of this missile as portrayed by X-ray appeared to be behind the right frontal sinus. The next largest fragment appeared to be at the rear of the skull at the juncture of the skull bone."[19] The Clark Panel found in 1968 that this later slug was "embedded in the *outer* table of the skull close to the lower edge of the hole . . . this fragment is round and measures 6.5mm. in diameter."[20]

How convenient that the bullet is round and can be measured at 6.5mm., the same diameter as Oswald's alleged bullets. The problem, though, is the fact that it is impossible for it to be on the *outer* table of the skull in the *back* (from where the bullet was coming) near an entry hole that did not exist in 1963.

There is an extensive discussion of the fragment behind the eye by Humes:[21] "A rather sizable fragment visible by X-ray just above the right eye . . . this one which was seen to be above and very slightly behind the right orbit."[22] The problem with this is, there is no bone there in the X-ray. Do they mean that the fragment was in the brain?

Dr. Ebersole is quoted as saying, "When the body arrived, and when it was removed from the casket, there was a very obvious horrible gaping wound at the back of the head. . . . Later on in the evening, between midnight and one A.M., a large portion of the skull was sent up from Dallas . . . that represented the back portion of the skull."[23]

When the President's head was filled with plaster for burial, we know that some of the skull bones were retained, but the full extent of what was kept was not clear.

In 1979 I showed the published copies of the skull X-rays to a radiologist. The first thing he noted was apparent surgery along the bottom of the right temple area. This would be the area where a shot from the front or the side probably struck JFK. Jim Jenkins reports that at the autopsy they noted gray metallic material on the edges of the bone in that area.

Mark Crouch has noted what appears to be surgery in a wide crescent just to the right of the midline of the forehead (just on the left side of the head over the eyebrow) with the very small marks left by bone nippers. This is why there is no right frontal sinus, because from that point on all the bone is missing. Jerry Custer, in examining this, also states that both areas of the skull X-ray show that surgery was performed.[24]

He also notes that in the lateral skull X-ray, the sella turcica is freefloating, and he says that this is impossible. The sella turcica is a sickleshaped structure seen in the middle of the temple-cheek area along a horizontal plane.

Perhaps this is what was meant by "surgery to the head area," in the FBI report of the autopsy. We don't know if this existed on the body before it came in. It seems unlikely.

All X-rays were taken in the morgue,[25] and the body never left it until it went to the White House.

Life magazine published a photograph of an apparently empty stretcher going into the morgue of the hospital at Bethesda, with the following caption: "Inside, a guard of honor waits while the body is prepared for burial."[26] David Lifton's *Best Evidence* included the same photograph, but with this comment: "When published in *Life*, the picture's caption stated that this stretcher was used to carry President Kennedy to the morgue. But persons I interviewed said the *Life* caption was incorrect—that this was the stretcher they were told was used to bring a stillborn baby to the morgue."

The authentication of the skull X-rays by the House Committee was a miserable failure.

The KRON-TV Show

In 1988 several witnesses at President Kennedy's autopsy came forward and spoke publicly to the central issue of the authenticity of the autopsy photographs and X-rays. What they said was startling.

Jerrol Custer, who took the X-rays at Bethesda, was shown copies of them and asked, "Is this the X-ray picture that you took and is this the wound that you saw on the President?"

"No. This area here was *gone*," he said, indicating the back of the head. "There was no scalp there. Not this area," he added emphatically, pointing out the very large missing area on the right in front of the ear in the alleged X-rays. "I don't believe this is the autopsy X-ray." He swept his hand from the front top of the head to the back of the neck. "This part of the head was gone." Custer very strongly disputed the photographs and X-rays, as did the other witnesses.

Jerrol Custer told me exactly what he told Sylvia Chase on KRON-TV in San Francisco.

I asked him if he had seen the Walter Cronkite show on the assassination. "That was very superficial."

"But was a flap of scalp there that could have been pulled up to cover the hole in the very back of the head?"

Custer replied, "There was a king-size hole in the back of the head, and that area was torn." From their observations at the autopsy at the time, Custer and the other enlisted Navy men all thought that the President had been shot from the front, and that the large hole in the back of the head was an exit. They themselves were quite stunned when they heard the results of the Warren Commission findings and what the autopsy report said—not entirely in line with each other either.

"Do you feel that the X-rays—you're absolutely sure in your own mind that they don't show what you saw that night?"

"Let's put it this way—in the lateral skull films it looks like part of the front of his face is gone. But if you look at the autopsy photographs, there's nothing gone there. His eye should have been completely gone on that film, which it never should."[27]

The Authenticator

The House Select Committee on Assassinations made a stab at authenticating the skull X-rays. It all boiled down to two teeth with more than one exhibit to compare it to, and a sinus cavity. Nobody inquired whether or not those parts of the skull the forensic dentists compared to dental X-rays supposed to be that of JFK were parts of composite X-rays made just for this purpose.

On July 18, 1991, I attempted to talk to Dr. Lowell Levine, the forensic dentist who worked on the famous Josef Mengele case, and who was used by the House Assassinations Committee. I say attempted, because for me it was a very tough interview. I never got close to the technical questions because Levine—who works for the New York state police—was too defensive, too much on the attack, too much in control, and not open to any real discussion. Dr. Levine's report on his authentication of the autopsy skull X-rays 1, 2, and 3 are in Volume 7 of the HSCA, page 53.[28]

He told me that he saw the original X-rays. I asked him, or tried to, "The original?"

"The whole original X-rays, there's absolutely nothing wrong with them."

"For the entire head, you mean?"

"Yeah. . . . They could not publish them intact. They were not allowed. They're owned by the family."

"Is that right?"

"The X-rays—there's absolutely nothing peculiar about 'em. We examined the original X-rays."

I tried to explain to Levine that the X-rays of the skull showed the whole right front of the face missing. I asked him why there was so much bone missing if they either cropped them or blacked them out somehow. "They had to be cropped," he explained, which, of course, had nothing to do with why the bone was missing. But cropping them was one more example of tainting the evidence preventing the public from adequately perceiving it. They didn't want the public to know what really happened.

The X-rays were faked to show a blow-out in that part of the head. Cropping them made my job that much more difficult.

"Is there a reason why?"

"Yeah . . . because they were not allowed by the owners of the X-rays to publish the entire picture . . . there's absolutely zippo . . . nothing wrong with the films."

Later: "I can tell you absolutely, positively, totally one hundred ten percent the X-rays were of Kennedy. . . . Okay . . . they totally comported with everything that, ah, with the findings of the panel." He sidestepped saying that they compared with the dental X-rays or whatever else he had.

He said that he did not think it peculiar that they found three envelopes of dental X-rays in the White House rather than in a dentist's office. "Prominent people want it that way," he said. "I have no problem with that. I don't remember a whole lot, but there was nothing unusual about 'em."

He told me that he was present when Humes and Boswell were interviewed by the panel of doctors for the House Committee. Not long after this interview with Levine, I talked to Dr. Earl Rose, who was there also, and who had been the Dallas medical examiner who tried to stop the body from being taking out of Texas.

I tried to reason with Levine: "Well then, you are aware that they [Humes and Boswell] were insisting that the entry wound in the back of the head was nowhere near where it was in that X-ray and the panel commented on the persistent disparity between its findings and those of the autopsy pathologists, who said that the entrance wound was at or near the occipital protuberance and it was found to be four inches higher than that on the X-rays. . . . Don't you think it was rather peculiar when the autopsy doctors were rather desperately trying to say—" He cut me off.

"But they were not *forensic* pathologists." There it is again. They made a mistake. They *did* make mistakes, but they could not be wrong about everything. They certainly would have seen and noted a bullet hole in the skull where it now is rather than four inches from there— especially since there was no bone in that part of the head. After all, they had a competent radiologist at the autopsy who was interpreting the films, and they had the head of the deceased in their hands. They would see and find the bullet hole, which they did, but not anywhere near where it now is.

Dr. Pierre Finck, who was at the autopsy and who collaborated on all the reports with Humes and Boswell (so we are told), was a forensic pathologist. He apparently came to the above meeting from his home in Geneva, Switzerland, and then shortly walked out, bored.

"Mr. Livingstone, look, let me, if I may, 'cause I'm not going to get in an argument with you. I'll give you my discernment, then I'm gonna go."

"Sure."

"It's not unusual. I can tell you you're wasting your time—or I think so. The medical evidence was very obvious. It was very simple and it's the type of stuff we look at all the time."

"Let me ask you in the frontal part of the skull X-ray that you saw . . . did you see that the bone was missing, or was it present?"

"I don't recall."

This was the beginning of a major memory problem with him. He couldn't recall from then on, and he didn't hang up.

"On the right side."

"I don't recall right now. I'd have to go back and look at the report. What I can tell you is that the X-rays totally comported with the findings of the pathology panel." Which said findings, of course, were almost totally dependent on his X-rays. Catch 22.

I mentioned that a radiologist told me that there appeared to be surgery to the edges of the frontal bone in the temple, and that bone was missing there, not to mention the rest of the right top front of the face. Mark Crouch noted the same thing in a different area—on the forehead, and he had been told by a doctor that it looked like nippers had been used there. These are the type of clippers that go through skull bone.

"There was absolutely no surgery to the skull."

We then got into another puzzle. This dealt with whether or not my radiologist friends had seen the original X-rays. His position was that if we didn't look at the original material, we couldn't know what we were talking about. "You have to look at the original material," he said.

"You know that we can't."

"Just file a Freedom of Information Act suit," he said.

I told him that "the presumption is that this material is a forgery."

"Mr. Livingstone—"

"Yeah?"

"I'm not going to get in an argument with you."

"I'm just trying to tell you the opposing viewpoint. . . ."

"Well, let me tell you, it's all interesting—but you're barking up the wrong tree."

"Ah, huh," I said.

"You know, feel free to do whatever you want, but—"

"Do you have a basis for saying that?"

"Sure, I looked at the original evidence and you haven't."

"Well, if that evidence . . ."

"I've got no other comment. The evidence that I looked at—the X-ray films—were absolutely, positively normal X-ray films that are taken every day and not tampered with."

"Did you see the photographs of the face—the President's face?"

"Yes."

"And did his face look normal to you?"

"You know, I don't recall, but all I can tell you—"

"But you'd remember if there was damage to his face?"

"I don't recall off the top of my head. We're talking about fourteen years ago, and I've probably seen thousands of cases."

"All right, let's put it this way, do you have any reason to believe his face was damaged?"

"I don't recall off the top of my head, you know, and I'd have to go back and—"

"Is there any medical testimony that his face was damaged?" I asked him.

"I do not recall, once again. As I said, you can do whatever you want, but do not quote me—you know, inaccurately."

"Yes, but what I am trying to find out is if what you saw is similar to what they printed showing that the top right front of the face is missing. That is the question here because, as you must know, there is no evidence whatsoever from anybody; in fact, to the contrary, everyone said his face was perfect, it was undamaged and in the photographs it is undamaged."

"You're telling me that the right front of his face was missing?"

"The skull that you verified as authentic has no right front of the face. The eye is missing, the right forehead, the right temple."

"Once again, the skull that I verified is authentic. You know by comparing it with the dental X-rays."

"What you verified was the jaw," I told him.

"What you need to do is to look at the original X-ray films. Okay? In other words, the original X-ray films are correct."

"No legitimate researchers in this case have been able to obtain this material."

Soon he was back at it: "If you haven't learned, you know, that you've got to look at the original evidence."

"It's not subject to the FOIA, you should know that. It's a contract with the Kennedy family and the National Archives and no FOIA suit applies."

These people get you running around in circles. He has already stated that there was an agreement with the Kennedy family that precluded showing the X-rays. He told us that he and the House Committee were not allowed to show the full skull X-rays. But he is going to beat me over the head with an impossibility, telling me that I would be able to get access if I file a Freedom of Information Act request.

The interview was within moments of its termination, and yet twice more he tried to send me to the original evidence. "I'm trying to help you by telling you that unless you see that—unless you see the original material . . ." And, "I've gotta go, but you take a look at the original evidence. . . ."

The authentication—that is the comparison of the autopsy skull X-rays with some dental and skull X-rays that were allegedly taken while Kennedy was alive—depends ultimately on perhaps two teeth and the right frontal sinus. Levine states that "it is my opinion that all films were taken on the same person, John F. Kennedy." He then goes on in the next paragraph to say that in X-ray No. 1 "the configuration of the frontal sinuses are quite distinctive. The right side is 'heart'-shaped, the left almost 'rhomboid.' "

The problem with this is, *there is no right frontal sinus* in autopsy X-ray No. 1. All of the bone where that sinus would normally be is missing.

This proves that either someone played a vast trick on Levine, or they think so little of us that they can simply make it all up, just as Lattimer describes adrenals in the X-rays—when one cannot see adrenals in an X-ray without dye—notwithstanding the fact that Dr. Karnei said Kennedy had no adrenals in the first place.

But there is still another problem with this. The antemortem sinus X-ray shows a definite "heart-shaped" right sinus cavity (it's not the frontal sinus but the maxillary sinus), Kathlee Fitzgerald writes. "Question: Did Levine mix up his medical terms [calling it "frontal sinus" instead of *maxillary sinus]?* Was his use of 'frontal' merely to indicate a sinus 'in the front' as opposed to 'the side'? After all, Levine is a dentist, not an M.D."[29]

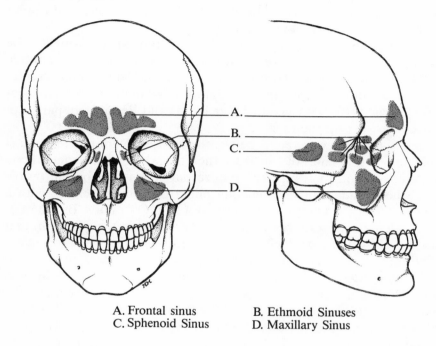

A. Frontal sinus   B. Ethmoid Sinuses
C. Sphenoid Sinus   D. Maxillary Sinus

Why did the House Committee publish poor and perhaps incomplete photographs of the X-rays at all? What do they prove other than to create a new storm of controversy by showing the top right front of the face missing? But nobody noticed this except me. There is something seriously wrong with the press and some other institutions in this country. A lot of us are trained either not to ask questions or ask the wrong ones. It also would seem that somebody on the Committee made sure that enough information did slip through the cracks to both stimulate and allow the real investigation to go forward.

Paul Hoch has suggested that part of the problem might lie in the publication by the House of enhanced versions of the X-rays. "As a layman, I wonder if the printing and/or enhancement processes applied to the X-rays, perhaps intended to show the fracture lines in better detail, might have involved turning up the contrast so much that thinner sections of bone appeared to vanish."[30] The problem with that is

that the A-P view has all the bone present on one side of the head—
and it is entirely missing on the other side in the front, an impossibility.
This sort of rumination and speculation (from an otherwise thoroughly
analytical person) is the kind that results in "jet effects" to explain the
backward movement of Kennedy's head when he was shot, and other
attacks on the physical laws of the universe.

I think our attention is being directed away from what we ought to be
noticing. Some of the congressmen on the Assassinations Committee
forced the publication of a portion of the medical data and representa-
tions of the autopsy X-rays and photographs, but once again we had co-
option by right-wing conservative Democrats and Republican party operatives to cover up the case.

If the X-rays that were published by the House Committee are in fact
Kennedy's X-rays and not forgeries, then the whole right frontal bone
was removed and then replaced before burial, but not by the morticians, who found it intact. Someone might have hit part of it with a
hammer, for all we know, as someone told Paul O'Connor. But there is
clear evidence that surgery was in fact performed in two places in that
bone, which would have facilitated its removal.

The three large pieces of bone were placed on the back of the head
—as Humes described their reconstruction—and a new X-ray was
made. During the time they had the back of the head together, the
frontal bone came out, and we have the X-ray showing all of that frontal bone missing, which would fool a lot of people into thinking that
there was an exit wound in the right front of the face, just where *Life*
magazine made you think it was when they published frames from the
Zapruder film a few days after the assassination.[31]

And they could even fool the Chief Justice of the United States, who
saw this material privately, into thinking that there was nothing wrong
with the back of the head.

There has been a great deal to cover up in the assassination of John F.
Kennedy, and it took a lot of people to do it, even those who were used
—either against their will or because they were easy. Some of the "critics" were turned around, and became a part of the cover-up, though
they may not have known it.

The main point is that the X-rays of the skull are fake, and the
evidence of that is intrinsic in the X-rays themselves.

> "There was nothing Robert Kennedy could do about
> . . . the cover-up that he knew Allen Dulles was
> perpetrating on the Warren Commission."
>
> —Harris Wofford, *Of Kennedys and Kings*

CHAPTER 17

THE ZAPRUDER FILM

The Zapruder film, an amateur home movie taken during the moments of the assassination by a Dallas dress manufacturer, has long been touted as the benchmark of the investigation. Every sort of claim has been made about it. Stamm and Thompson* first pointed out that it shows a head snap to the rear when the President is being struck by a bullet, and this, they say—according to the laws of physics—shows that the President was struck from somewhere in front of him rather than from behind.

The film gives us a time frame as well, as about 18.3 frames per second pass through the lens. From this we can calculate the time between some of the shots. The FBI had tested the bolt-action rifle attributed to Lee Harvey Oswald and knew that it required about two and a half seconds to eject a spent shell, reload, aim, and fire. The FBI experts thought that it could be done in the amount of time between apparent hits on the film, but just barely.

That analysis depended upon the real elapsed time between shots seen on the film, which was dependent on a subjective interpretation of whether John Connally was hit with a separate shot. If he was, as the film appears to show, then the single assassin theory is out the window. The film seems to show that Connally was hit sometime after Kennedy

---

* Probably the best and most extensive discussion of the Zapruder film and what it shows is to be found throughout Josiah Thompson's *Six Seconds in Dallas,* a book, though old, I still recommend (Berkley/Medallion; 1967). Other discussions are to be found in Harold Weisberg *Whitewash I* (1965), *Whitewash II* (1966), and *Photographic Whitewash* (1967). Copies may be ordered from Harold Weisberg, 7627 Old Receiver Road, Frederick, MD 21701.

was hit, as Connally has always maintained. If Kennedy and Connally were hit with two separate shots from behind, they came too close together to have been fired from the same rifle.

We don't need the film to prove John Connally was hit with a separate bullet. When Arlen Specter, the chief lawyer to the Warren Commission, asked Dr. Humes, "And could that missile [CE 399—the bullet that was found on the stretcher and alleged to have transited President Kennedy's back and come out of his throat] have made the wound on Governor Connally's right wrist?" he said, "I think that that is most unlikely. May I expand on those two answers?"

"Yes, please do," the future senator replied most graciously.

"Also going to Exhibit 392, the report from Parkland Hospital, the following sentence referring to the examination of the wound of the wrist is found; 'Small bits of metal were encountered at various levels throughout the wound, and these were, wherever they were identified and could be picked up, picked up and submitted to the pathology department for identification and examination.' The reason I believe it most unlikely that this missile could have inflicted either of these wounds is that this missile is basically intact; its jacket appears to me to be intact, and I do not understand how it could possibly have left fragments in either of these locations."[1]

Please do not compartmentalize the doctor's statement above, isolating it from the many other statements that will show that most of whatever he and the other doctors say cannot be disregarded—either because it conflicts with the theory that Specter and Ford invented, or that it conflicts with the autopsy photographs and X-rays which neither the Commission nor anyone else at the time really examined.

The theory is also out the window if the Warren Commission's other major assumption—that the first shot could not have been fired until the car was clear of the tree blocking the view from the alleged assassin's window—is wrong. The House Committee proved that the first shot occurred long before frame 210 of the Zapruder film. Although the House did not say it, the first shots could not have come from the window blocked by the tree.

The Warren Commission said it could be done—making three shots and two hits from the time the car came out from under the tree to the moment the President's head was hit six seconds later. But we all know it would have taken the best rifleman in the world with the best rifle to do the job, shooting down from a high window on a moving car as fast as he could reload, aim, and fire. It could not have happened, and any gunman in that particular window would have fired *toward* the car as it *approached* the window rather than as it drove away—unless the car was headed into an ambush and the gunman in the window had to wait until the car was inside the triangle, and the men in front of the car could fire directly at it.

Sequence

The evidence indicates that a gunman fired from low down and behind the President, striking him in the back at about Z frame 177.[2] Almost two seconds later, at about frame 208 or 210, the Warren Commission said another shot was fired from behind. Michael Kurtz, a history professor and assassination researcher, says that the bullet missed Kennedy and hit Connally because Kennedy moved suddenly, reacting to the shot that hit him in the back.

The House Assassinations Committee thought that Connally showed signs of reacting—of being hit at about frame 226. This is of course long after JFK was hit, and is consistent with Connally's insistence that he was hit with a different bullet.[3]

The problem with the latter is that Kennedy was struck in the neck sometime before Connally was hit and was either raising his arms in self-defense or clutching at the wound in his neck, which would be natural or involuntarily.

It is my belief that Kennedy was struck in the neck from the front. I have always believed that somebody had to get that bullet out before the autopsy began—unless it passed clean through the neck and out—but this remains pure speculation. There is simply no evidence of a bullet having exited the back of the neck. The autopsy doctors would have seen it, and by now told someone about it. Tom Wilson, a researcher, says that he can see with his computer image processing technique the exit wound from this bullet coming out of the back of John Kennedy's neck on a videotape of the Zapruder film. He also says that he can look right down the trajectory of that shot from front to back through the neck, and right into the skull through the large hole in the top of the head on the Zapruder film. He thinks Kennedy was shot twice in the head from the front.

At frame 312 of the film, President Kennedy is struck in the head. The fatal shot is also seen on the Nix and Muchmore films. The weight of the evidence indicates that this shot came from the manhole in front of the car, where the stockade fence joins the overpass. Others have thought that there was a simultaneous second shot that struck Kennedy in the head from behind. His body seems to move forward a bit just before a powerful shot hits him from the front, rocketing him backward. Kurtz says that the bullet that hit Kennedy from in front was a "dum-dum."[4]

Of course, both the House and the Warren Commission do not officially accept that JFK was struck from the front at any time, but the radiologist that the House consulted, Dr. David O. Davis, after close examination of the skull X-rays, said that Kennedy could have been struck from the Knoll if his head "was tilted to the left side, that is, with the right ear elevated and the left depressed."[5] His head is tilted exactly that way in the Zapruder film.

The House found that a bullet was in fact fired from the Grassy Knoll an instant after the head shot from behind. This is dependent upon how the Committee matched the police tape recordings of each shot to what they thought were corresponding frames of the film, and it is generally believed that the House was wrong in that placement. The House says the shot from the Knoll missed.

I agree that it missed. The House did not say there were just four shots on the tape, but indicated that there were "at least four shots," meaning that there were more. That was a shot from in front of the car, just a bit to the right, in the manhole facing the car, where the stockade fence joined the concrete railing of the overpass. We see many people gathered in exactly that spot in several photographs, just after the fusillade.

It was that shot that hit Kennedy in the head. If he had been hit from the Grassy Knoll or stockade fence, it would have taken off the left side of his head and thrown him violently sideways, and not backward as in the film. The left side of his head was not damaged at all.

All of this becomes a terrible game with words when one considers that an exploding bullet would make a large blow-out as it *enters* the head.

We do have what sounds like a double shot, a *bang-bang,* on the Dallas police tape that might correspond exactly to frames 312–313 or 327–328.[6] "It was right," Secret Service agent Clint Hill said, "but I cannot say for sure that it was rear, because when I mounted the car it was—it had a different sound, first of all, than the first sound that I heard. The second one had almost a double sound—as though you were standing against something metal and firing into it, and you hear both the sound of a gun going off and the sound of the cartridge hitting the metal place, which could have been caused by the hard surface of the head. But I am not sure that is what caused it."[7]

And when Arlen Specter questioned Secret Service agent Roy Kellerman, he asked, "Now, in your prior testimony you described a flurry of shells into the car. How many shots did you hear after the first noise which you described as sounding like a firecracker?"

"Mr. Specter, these shells came in all together."

"Are you able to say how many you heard?"

"I am going to say two, and it was like a double bang—bang, bang."[8]

Some descriptions were that a "fusillade" was fired. Of course, there is ammunition that makes little sound, and that which makes a lot of noise. I believe there were decoy gunmen at the ambush, and those with quiet ammunition who were being covered by the others, who could get away more easily.

Penn Jones, Jr., a former Texas newspaper owner and assassination researcher, having had much combat experience at Anzio and other battles, believes that it was an exploding bullet. So do some of the veterans who saw the wounds at the autopsy. There is certainly evidence for an exploding bullet in terms of the sort of shrapnel that was found in the car and in the skull. It did not appear to be or perhaps could not have been the military jacketed bullet that was supposed to have been used, which is designed to pass on through bone without coming apart.

But Kurtz, whose academic work on the case is little known, then makes an interesting proposal. He says that there is an indication that "the gunman on the sixth-floor southeast corner window of the Depository also focused on the President's head. Now, at Zapruder frame 327, he fired the final shot in the carefully planned crossfire. Discharged less than a second after the Knoll shot hit the President, this shot entered the rear of the skull near the top of the head, and it exploded out of the huge hole in the front caused by the shot from the Knoll."[9]

Of course, there was no hole in the front at all.

Authenticity

I question the authenticity of the Zapruder film. Let us examine for a moment how Time, Inc., got the film. Abraham Zapruder's lawyer was Sam Passman, to whom he was related, a partner in Passman, Jones in

Dallas. Zapruder took the film to Passman—the man who actually arranged the sale to *Life* magazine for $150,000 (Zapruder told the Warren Commission he was paid $25,000, which was true, but omitted to mention the remaining five payments for the same amount of money, which were yet to come). Nobody ever criticised him for doing things the good old American way.

Passman's partner, Shannon Jones, just happened to have done a lot of work for the CIA in Texas, and had been in the OSS in World War II. Jones leased hangars for the CIA in Brownsville and in the Guatemalan operation, and painted and armed planes. Jones was also the lawyer for Joe Civello, the top Mafia chieftain in Dallas who was arrested at the famous Appalachian conference of Syndicate leaders, and who reported to Carlos Marcello in New Orleans. Zapruder's son was a long time FBI agent.[10]

While we are talking about this, it is worth pointing out how many times we find the Mob working "hand in glove," as Congressman Henry Gonzalez told me in 1976, with government agencies. David Ferrie, a famous figure in the Clay Shaw investigation in New Orleans, flew planes and performed many other tasks for Carlos Marcello, and was a contract agent of the CIA at the same time.

Let's use common sense when we analyze the facts and the evidence, and not fall into the pits dug for us by official bodies. If the film shows a huge wound to the right side of the face, as it does, then *all* the witnesses who saw the dying or dead President and *all* the autopsy photographs are *wrong*. Common sense tells us that they *all* can't be wrong.

Common sense, therefore, tells us that the film is wrong. That it is a fake. But almost nobody ever dared question it, and the persons most closely connected to it deny this possibility. We are used to accepting the word of the experts—even if self-proclaimed—without question.

Professor Paul Hoch of the University of California at Berkeley obtained with the aid of a Freedom of Information Act suit some papers indicating that NPIC, the National Photographic Interpretation Center, a CIA department, made a study of the Zapruder film. The Secret Service brought the film to them. The question is, when? The papers are not dated. Why not?

The question arises as to whether it was possible to get the film to Washington and returned to Dallas by the next day. There would be no problem with that if supersonic jets were used. Abraham Zapruder and *Life*, presumably, would have to be deluded, and a false paper trail laid.

There are receipts among the papers indicating that three prints and perhaps an original film were processed and printed by NPIC, which would almost certainly—if the indication of an original is correct— mean that they had the film the night of the assassination, and the business of developing and copying the film in Dallas is hoaxed up.

Professor Philip Melanson suggests in his article "Hidden Exposure: Cover-up and Intrigue in the CIA's Secret Possession of the Zapruder Film"[11] that the film could have been tampered with. He says that the technology existed in 1963 to resize images, remove frames, and create special effects.

The Blob

I have long wondered about a large apparent effusion of brain matter or flesh that spills from the right side of the face and temple region just after the President receives a shot to the head.

We do not see this so much in the Groden "optically enhanced" version of the film, but we do see it in a rather extraordinary fashion in the much clearer Thompson version, which was made for the House Assassinations Committee. The material spewing forth from the head appears to stick out several inches and be about a half foot wide. It is spread all across the face. One would assume that it is an exploded face or brain, and it cannot all be an optical illusion from reflections of sunlight off Jackie's hat and from the small flap of bone that evidently opens up at that point, as Groden has led us to believe. In fact, close study of the succeeding frames in which we see this blob—until the head disappears from view to the left, in Jackie's lap—indicates that the blob covers exactly that part of the face shown to be missing in the autopsy skull X-rays.

We see a small flap of bone with scalp attached on the right side of the head in some of the autopsy photographs but not in others. Trouble with the flap is, it changes orientation in relation to the rest of the head as the camera moves around the head. And it does not exist at all in the autopsy photograph of the right side of the head. There is a bat-wing-shaped structure on the head in the general area, but much too large to be the flap, and in the wrong place.

Groden claims that Mrs. Kennedy closed up the alleged flap on the way to the hospital, where it was not seen. But the autopsy staff say the

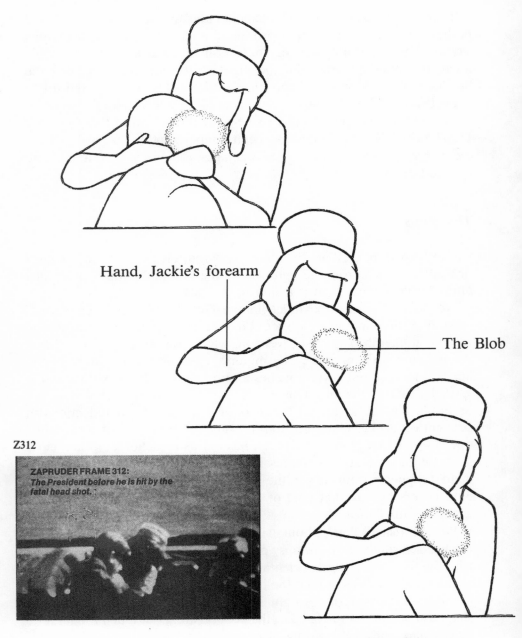

Hand, Jackie's forearm

The Blob

Z312

ZAPRUDER FRAME 312:
The President before he is hit by the fatal head shot.

A frame from the Zapruder film after the fatal head shot. Note the large blob on the right front of the face, which corresponds to the missing area of bone in the X-rays. Yet there was no damage to the face reported by any witness, nor is any damage visible in any photograph of the face.

flap we see in the picture is not in the right place either, or did not exist at all.

No entry wound was noted in Dallas in the right temple or face area, and, in fact, no defect in the bone or skull was seen there by any witness. "You saw the President's face, though, at a later time as you have described?" Arlen Specter asked Roy Kellerman, the Secret Service agent who was sitting in the right front seat of the President's limousine when he was killed.

"Yes. . . . While he lay on the stretcher in that emergency room, his collar and everything is up and I saw nothing in his face to indicate an injury, whether the shot had come through or not. He was clear."[12] There are many other statements that there was no damage at all to any part of the President's face, and none to the contrary.

Since the doctors and nurses all carefully noted a very small wound in the throat, at the most five millimeters across, and perhaps only two or three millimeters, it would not seem rational that the head wound we see in the film existed: Someone in Dallas would have noted such a wound, which seems gigantic in the Zapruder film.

Corresponding to the gigantic wound in the right front of the face and forehead-temple area is a total loss of bone in the X-ray alleged to be of President Kennedy's head. We know that this would be impossible without the face being blown away, if it represents a shot from behind. If the bone had fallen in during transport to Bethesda, it would show somewhere in the X-rays. It does not. If it had fallen in, the face would have fallen in with the body on its back, and there is no sign of the bone anywhere in the skull. The face shows no sign of being unsupported by bone, and in fact looks perfectly undamaged. No doctor I have spoken to said that a face would remain normal if the underlying bone was gone.

The missing bone in the skull X-rays has to represent a blow-out of the face, which did not in fact happen.

The photographs of the head show that parietal bone on both sides of the top of the head as far as the coronal suture is missing. We would have seen the blob coming out of there if the film was on the up and up, and not on the face, as we now see it in the film. Dr. John Lattimer says that the blob is a "flap," but this is about as inaccurate an observation as his seeing the adrenals in the X-rays.

It is my opinion, therefore, that the Zapruder film has some animated special effects: The large effusion we see sticking out from the head is painted in for those few frames before the head falls into Jackie's lap.

The purpose of this special effect is to encourage the idea in Earl Warren's head that the President was shot from behind. The brain did not show any loss of material from the frontal cerebral lobes, and in fact could not, according to the supplemental autopsy report, have lost any material at all, having the weight of a normal brain. The alternative is that President Kennedy had an abnormally large brain, which some of us would prefer to believe. In addition, they found a large fragment in the brain just behind the forehead above the right eye.

We see the strange blob for more than twenty-five frames, far too long for it to be any sort of defect in the film. In addition, for optical reasons, it cannot be an artifact, because it is quite clear and distinctive for those twenty-five frames. What is not clear and distinctive is the President's head, which seems to disintegrate and disappear by the time it is drawn into Jackie's lap. In one frame there is no face or head at all to the right of the line extending upward from the President's ear, and I see Jackie clearly to the right of and beyond the ears, where the rest of the head should be.

One might get the idea from this that Kennedy's head was indeed blown off and nothing but a "stump." But that raises too many questions. Far too many witnesses have insisted that there was no damage at all to the President's face, and there certainly is none in the autopsy photographs.

As Dr. Paul Peters told me in 1979, "His face and the front of his head was perfect."

It is not reasonable that Mrs. Kennedy somehow stuffed back into the head what appears to be the whole right front part of the brain. The flap as seen in the photographs is far too small for such a huge blob to exit from, and it is in the wrong place. There were no known fracture lines in the skull area that would have allowed so much tissue to exit and stick out from the head.

The X-ray shows the front of the face and forehead missing, so the plotters quite clearly fabricated evidence that would cover up a shot from the front to the head. They kept secret the pictures of the face and did not expect them to become public. They kept them, though, to confuse the evidence—telling the story both ways, and to leave some evidence for the smart money to know what really happened. Keeping it was insurance for the plotters protecting their back.

* * *

In addition, I notice a sort of jerk in the film at the moment of the head shot, which would indicate a possible frame missing. Shortly before this, six frames have been removed from the film in two places. The first splice is at Z 157. Kennedy appears to be reacting to something. Next, a few frames later, we see a tree trunk split and the crucial frames around Z 210 and Z 212 seem to be missing.

Additional tampering with what this film says was evidenced by the fact that the crucial frames at the instant the President was hit in the head were reversed by both the Warren Commission in their publication of the film frame by frame and by the *Life* magazine presentation. Those frames in their proper sequence show the President's head rocketed backward by the force of a rifle shot from the front.

Had that backward movement not been on the film, I don't think we would have ever heard about the jet effect, a supposed physical reaction to a force that would cause an object to move in the direction from which the force came. This violates Newton's Second Law of Physics, as I understand it.

Every force has an equal and opposite reaction.

It seems to me that after all the talk from the critics of a shooter hitting President Kennedy in the head from the Grassy Knoll, ninety percent of the theory for which is based on the fact that Kennedy is driven almost straight back into the seat, it is not reasonable that the shot came from the Grassy Knoll nearly perpendicular to the car, as Groden and many others claim. Kennedy would have been thrown sideways with the shot, into Jackie, by their reasoning. For this reason, reporter Earl Golz and I believe that the shot came from the manhole in front of the car.

Critics and researchers can use their ouija boards and photographic enhancements until Doomsday trying to find the shooter on the Grassy Knoll, but I doubt if it will ever be proved.

In a quiet but intellectually blistering exchange at Professor Jerry Rose's June 1991 State University conference at Fredonia, New York, the soft-spoken Ken Degazio of Fort Erie, Ontario, a high school physics teacher, engaged my friend, the self-made expert and JFK assassination case gadfly on trajectories and jet effects, Robert Cutler. Cutler, along with Dr. John Lattimer (another jet-effect nut), who largely believes the Warren Report, attempted to restate the jet-effect theory: that the head would go in the direction *from* which the bullet came. Cutler invoked Newton's Third Law of Motion in his paper, which states that when two objects interact, such as a bullet with a head, they exert equal but opposite (in direction) forces on each other.

Degazio wrote me that "the collision of a bullet from the rear with Kennedy's head would result in the bullet exerting a forward force on Kennedy's head (action force) resulting in the forward acceleration of Kennedy's head (by Newton's Second Law). On return, Kennedy's skull exerts the same but *opposite* (i.e. rearward) force on the bullet (reaction force), resulting in the bullet being decelerated (and possibly smashed by the impact force exerted on it by Kennedy's skull). . . . As you can see, Newton's laws reflect common sense notions: that a bullet from the rear impacting on Kennedy's skull would impel his head forward (Newton's Second Law) and that on this impact a *force is exerted on Kennedy's skull* (accelerating and smashing it) *as well as* a *force exerted on the bullet* (slowing it down and possibly smashing it, Newton's Third Law).

Cutler said that he believes that Kennedy was shot from the rear and that his head moves forward between frames 312 and 313 of the Zapruder film, something others have noted. But then there is what he calls a "reaction" and it moves backward—a movement quite obvious to everyone. "It is this third point which I was objecting to: The reaction is *not* the rearward motion of Kennedy's head, but rather the reaction force exerted *on* the bullet *by* Kennedy's skull. If this is what Cutler was getting at, he was wrong as to the meaning of the Third Law." Newton's Third Law of Motion is inviolate. "It has survived the twentieth century revolutions in physics (relativity and quantum mechanics) and more than three centuries of experiments and observations; it is the foundation for the law of conservation of momentum, also inviolate. But Cutler, whether deliberately or unintentionally, by implication was grossly distorting Newton's Third Law, using it to—apparently— explain the subsequent rearward motion of Kennedy's head after Z 313. There is no time delay to the Third Law, but, more important, the Third Law is in fact no more and no less than a statement about the effect the skull has on the bullet impacting on it, and vice versa."[13] Getting hit *twice* in the head in the same instant from opposite directions can explain a lot of things, too.

NPIC

Paul Hoch, a longtime researcher and author, also the publisher of an important assassination newsletter called *Echoes of Conspiracy,* in 1976 obtained certain documents regarding the Zapruder film with a Freedom of Information Act request. One of the group of documents released to him (No. 450) indicated that at some point the CIA had access to the film at their National Photographic Interpretation Center. Unfortunately, there is no date, so this information can possibly mean nothing, but the fact that there is no date in itself tells us a lot.

One of the documents apparently refers to the original film and indicates that four prints were made from it. One of these is a "test print."

Professor Philip Melanson writes that "in any criminal case, the integrity of evidence depends upon its *chain of possession:* who had it when, how and for what purposes before it came into the possession of official investigators to be analyzed by them. . . . [The documents] provide considerable support for allegations of a CIA cover-up and for allegations regarding possible CIA manipulation of evidence. There is now good reason to question the evidentiary integrity of the Z film. Moreover, it is clear that before the FBI had obtained the film, CIA experts had already analyzed it and had found data which strongly suggested a conspiracy."[14]

Officially, on the day of the assassination Abraham Zapruder took the film to a photo studio in Dallas and had an original and three copies made. He sold the original and one copy to *Life* the next day, and gave the other two copies to the Secret Service on the day of the assassination. They gave one to the FBI the following day.

The Secret Service during that period, as Professor Melanson points out, had some dependence on the CIA for technical services, and lacked sophisticated photo interpretation facilities of its own. Document 450 indicates that the Secret Service turned over a copy of the film to the CIA's NPIC, but did not say when they did it. It is not only not clear when they asked the NPIC to analyze it, but whether or not this is the way it happened—that the Secret Service had it first and gave a copy to NPIC.

The question is, also, whether or not the original and three copies processed and printed by the NPIC were the three that Zapruder ordered or were new and in addition to those he had made. In other words, was the original film really developed in Dallas, or immediately flown to Washington and developed at the NPIC, where it could be analyzed on the spot?

Of course, if the evidence was faked in JFK's murder, it would appear that here was a good opportunity to do it the night of the assassination. The conspirators, obviously operating at a high level of government, had to take a look at the film in order to know what information it revealed about the true nature of the murder. Or, it could simply represent a need to investigate.

But Melanson reports that a notation in the nine pages of item 450 says that it took two hours to process and dry the film, one hour to make a print test, one hour to make three prints, and one and one half hours to process and dry prints, "referred to work being done with the original film, not a copy. My discussions with a half dozen photo laboratories confirm this point—processing refers to developing an original. If the NPIC had been working with a copy, the first step would have been to print, then process. The NPIC notation "print test" refers to a short piece of film printed from the original and used to check the exposure —to see if the negative is too light or too dark—before printing copies from the original. Thus there is a strong indication that the NPIC had the original.[15]

In 1982 attorney Bernard Fensterwald received more documents relating to the Zapruder film and the NPIC through a lawsuit under the Freedom of Information Act. These documents had been withheld from Paul Hoch in his earlier requests which resulted in the nine pages he received in 1976. They concerned "the CIA's response to a Rockefeller Commission query about the NPIC analysis."[16] Among other things, the newer documents revealed that they brought a copy of the film to John McCone, the CIA's director, "late in 1963."

We have to ask how come *they don't give us an exact date for this.* The NPIC conducted their analysis, "late that same night." The document further states that Secret Service agents were there and took the film with them that night.

This sounds suspiciously like the night of the assassination.

Melanson asks what happened to the other three copies of the film made by the NPIC. We can only imagine that those were the three ordered to have been made by Zapruder, who, presumably, did not know that all of this was going on, that his film may even have been out of Dallas.

*   *   *

Among documents sent over to the National Archives from the Secret Service in 1979 was a letter from Secret Service agent Forrest Sorrels of the Dallas office explaining to Director James Rowley how they came to have copies of the film. He said that after the film was developed, he was given two copies and airmailed one copy to the chief in Washington.[17]

As Melanson suggests, the film was probably flown that night to Washington, and we would assume that the Secret Service would be so interested to see what it showed that they would have taken it over to the NPIC that night and analyzed it. And wouldn't they want to see the original rather than a less clear copy?

Melanson concludes his article with these remarks: "If, as appears to be the case, it was the original of the Z film that was secretly diverted to the CIA laboratory on November 22, 1963, then the means and the opportunity for sophisticated alteration did, in fact, exist—alteration that even the most expert analysis would have difficulty in detecting. By the 1960s, cinematography labs had the technical capacity to insert or delete individual frames of a film, to resize images, to create special effects. But it would take an extraordinary sophistication to do so in a manner that would defy detection—the kind of sophistication that one would expect of CIA photo experts.

"Between Zapruder and the Secret Service, they had possession of all three of the Dallas-made copies for nearly twenty-four hours. With the original at the NPIC and with three copies made there, it is possible that if the film was doctored, the three NPIC copies of the doctored film were substituted for the three Dallas-made copies." Or that all the copies went to the NPIC "and the switch was made there. . . .

"It is possible that the film of the century is more intimately related to the crime of the century than we ever knew—not because it *recorded* the crime of the century, as we have assumed, but because it was itself an instrument of conspiracy."

Does forgery invalidate the entire film? It would seem so, but not necessarily. Most or all of the evidence in this case appears to be tainted, but there are ways of weighing evidence so as to determine what part of it may still stand. If part of a piece of evidence is sufficiently corroborated, it may have value.

I'm not always sure what we need the Zapruder film for, nor am I sure what it proves. It may in fact prove nothing. Dr. Charles Wilber said to me that he thought "the film was overused and over-relied upon."[18]

The CIA evidently needed the film for training,[19] unless "training" is a euphemism for something else. We would hope that when they train their assassins, or otherwise subject them to desensitization, that that isn't what "training" means, as in *A Clockwork Orange*.

The main thing that the Zapruder film shows is that the President was rocketed backward, evidently from a powerful shot from the front. But that was attacked on the grounds that there was a jet effect which drew him backward in the direction of a shot that came from behind. I personally think the idea is ridiculous, but I can't prove that it isn't so.

The "jet-effect" fantasy has fooled a lot of people in this case, but not most of us.

Mark Crouch writes: "A bullet striking the President's head would begin to transfer its energy into the skull and brain at the second of impact. Much of this energy would be spent as the bullet pierces the skull and tears through the brain. In order for the 'jet effect' to work, the energy of the mass which is forced from the front of the head would have to be greater than the energy applied by the impact at the back of the head.

"Jet effect works in jet engines because energy is indeed added to the equation in the form of heat created by the burning of great amounts of fuel. The poor President's head was not an engine which could add energy and thusly force the body backward.

"In the home movie made by Dr. Lattimer, which is occasionally shown on assassination specials, where a human skull is filled with plaster of Paris, placed on a ladder, and then a rifle shot is fired from the rear, the skull somersaults backward. The effect being witnessed here has nothing to do with jets. The effect is caused by the fact that any stationary object at rest, when struck at its base, will generally spin backward in the direction from which it was struck, like a billiard ball.

"I have yet to see, nor do I know exists, any film where the skull is attached to a mass equivalent to a human body, then fired upon and seen to recoil backward. My response to any argument that tried to trump up a pseudo-scientific theory as to why the body snaps backward is 'From what source did all this energy come which could cancel out the forward thrust and then force the body backward so violently?' Unlike many theories in this case, energy cannot be drawn from thin air."[20]

Dr. Lattimer, who is primarily responsible for the crazy idea of the "jet effect" to explain the backward movement of the President's head (the car almost stopped before this, and had not started to move out), and who is also a principal apologist for the Warren Report, is the one who reported that he saw the adrenals in the autopsy X-rays, adrenals that had completely atrophied and that cannot be seen in an X-ray without dye if they exist.

And so it goes. Some billed the Zapruder film as perhaps the most important film in history. I think it's just one more cheap trick, one more lie about the truth, one more perversion and distortion of the evidence having the ultimate effect of desensitizing us and dehumanizing us to the murder of John Kennedy.

> "A man does not show his greatness by being at one extremity, but rather by touching both at once."

> —Albert Camus, *Resistance, Rebellion and Death*

CHAPTER 18

AN INTERVIEW WITH ONE OF THE BETHESDA DOCTORS

Dr. Joseph Theodore Brierre, a pathologist, knew Dr. Humes and Dr. Boswell "real well."

"In fact, Jim Humes was put in charge of the case and he was told to actually do the whole case, put the tissues through the technicon [a machine that processes tissue], do the microscopic, and do the final summary before he was ever allowed to go home. It took him three days. He had to stay at the hospital and do it, and then he asked me to proofread the autopsy report. You noticed that the adrenals are not there? My first reaction to Jim was: 'Where is the description of the adrenal glands?' "

"He told me, 'I was told not to report that.' "

"Did he do the pathology on the adrenals?"

"I guess he did. That's the way you do all autopsies. But he was told not to report it, and he said to me, 'And don't ask me anything about it!' I gathered that one of the admirals told him to delete the description of the adrenal glands."

"If he had Pott's disease, you can see why Burkley or someone would have wanted it covered it up."

"Yes."

"I understand that it was a relatively easy thing to pick up in those days?"

"Oh, *of course!* And, my only assumption from that—although I've never said anything about it, since I was just the low man on the totem pole up there—was that he *did* have Pott's disease. As a matter of fact, I had noticed pictures of Kennedy over the last three years, and he seemed to be getting very cushinoid, and I assumed he was receiving exogenous steroids. From Cushing's disease—hyperplasia of the adrenals. If he had his adrenals knocked out and was taking exogenous steroids, that would give you a cushinoid appearance just like it does athletes. I reasoned that that was what was going on."

"You distinguish that from Addison's disease?"

"Addison's is the opposite of Cushing's. Addison's is adrenal hypoplasia, or atrophy, and Cushing's is adrenal hyperplasia, or excessive adrenal activity. One would become cushinoid if one was receiving exogenous steroids, given steroid shots to replace his adrenals. One could only assume that this guy had no adrenals. So I assumed that he had Pott's disease.

"I don't know if anyone will ever find out the truth. Maybe Dr. Humes will talk about it now, but he wouldn't talk to me about it then."

"Did anyone else agree with you? Did you discuss it with anyone else then?"

"Oh, a lot of us discussed it, you know, behind his back, and thought that was a logical conclusion. Cushing's disease is an excess of steroids, not adrenaline."

"When I was up close to him I noticed that he was sometimes rather yellow or brown, and I assumed that that was from the malaria," I said.

"There was a picture of him very shortly before his death, around August, when he was on a beach in California. He looked more suntanned—and he was getting more bronze in color," the doctor said.

"He was very bronze," I said.

"He was very bronze, and he had really bulked up his musculature. He just really looked like a guy that was taking steroids. When he became President, he brought this woman—Janet Travell—who was treating him with injections in the back of procaine, I guess, or xylocaine, Supposedly he thought she was the most wonderful thing on earth, because she was relieving his back pain.

"Kennedy was supposed to be a smart man, but he really availed himself of some crappy medical care. Of course, Admiral Burkley was nothing but an alcoholic. The bastard didn't know how to spell medicine."

"He had misdiagnosed it. If he had failed to pick it up, then they would want to cover it up!"

"Yeah, sure! And that is exactly what I thought all along. I think it's a well-known fact that Kennedy had had tuberculosis. So, naturally, the tuberculosis could have spread to the spine and to the adrenal glands. I'll tell you, this is a cover-up beyond belief," he said.

* * *

"Humes had his hands tied behind his back. Humes was going to retire the next year, and he was already doing pathology at Suburban Medical Hospital over in Bethesda, and he got so much bad publicity from this that he actually had to leave the state when he went into private practice, and he went up to Detroit. He was a terrific pathologist, and he became head of the entire Catholic pathology system in the whole state of Michigan."

"They hounded him so much, he just left and went up to Michigan."

"A very significant number of X-rays and photographs of the body were taken and never developed. They are supposed to be examined in seventy-five years, at the anniversary of the death. They took one picture and one X-ray and developed them to make sure the exposures were correct, and then they took the rest and sequestered them somewhere."

"Were you in the autopsy room?"

"No, I was the Officer of the Day. I had no access to the room itself. It was cordoned off."

"Have you talked to Dr. Humes?" Dr. Brierre asked me.

"Years ago when he was in Detroit, for about an hour, but I can't say I got anything from him. He was very gracious, but he was obviously muzzled," I said.

Dr. Brierre laughed. "Boy, *had he been*, I'll tell you that! I just think that is a pathetic situation. Burkley shut him up. They weren't forensic pathologists in the first place, and there was a lot of criticism that a forensic pathologist didn't handle the case. Nevertheless they had some good and fairly expert people there. Pierre Finck was a ballistics expert, and in those days there were only ten or twelve forensic pathologists in the United States. It's only more recently become a specialty. You could say that he dealt in forensics, because that was his special field of interest."

"Was Humes silenced with regard to—"

"Absolutely clammed up completely."

"He couldn't discuss the case."

"No. No. He asked me to proofread the protocol, and then when I asked him the question about the adrenals, he clammed up and that was the end of the discussion. And he never said another word. From then on—and he was in charge of the residency at Bethesda—from then he actually never came to work anymore. He was downtown all the time at the Warren Report hearings."

"He sat in on them?"

"Oh, yeah, he was there all of the time."

"Because they asked him too?"

"I don't know. He might have been there to protect himself."

"Do you think that about the adrenals, it was Burkley that told him not to talk about it?"

"I really think it was Burkley that told him to shut up. All he told him to do was delete it from the report, and delete any evidence that he might have about it."

"Do you think it was because Burkley was trying to protect himself?"

"Yeah. That's what I think. I think Burkley, he didn't know how to do anything. He didn't know anything about medicine. He missed the diagnosis and everything else. I don't think Kennedy would have lasted a second term if he had been elected."

"Because he was under Burkley's care?"

"Yeah. He probably would have died. I think Kennedy was a very sick person, besides his philanderings and everything. . . ."

"But wouldn't that flow from the steroids?"

"Yeah, oh, definitely. They'll really boost your energy level."

"I mean the libido?"

"Yeah."

"I don't know that much about medicines, but wouldn't the steroids boost your sexual energy?"

"Oh, definitely!"

"It seems to me a little bit unfair to judge character on that basis, because doctors really didn't know much about the effects of steroids at that time."

"No, they sure didn't. Oh, God, it was being given out by the ton. And that doctor in New York was giving him amphetamines."

"Dr. Feelgood? Dr. Jacobson?"

"Yeah, that's him."

"Do you think there is any other cover-up going on in the assassination or the autopsy, and that Humes and Boswell were victims of it?"

"No, I think they did a straightforward autopsy. The protocol was exactly like I would have done an autopsy, only the description of the adrenals is left out. Otherwise it is a kind of a straightforward type of protocol. But it wasn't a strictly forensic protocol as most forensic pathologists would have done it. Jim Humes did some funny things. We had a work sheet that we used in the morgue at Bethesda, and Jim marked all of his notes on that piece of paper, and then he got in hot water because he told people that he had burned that after he had transposed his description onto formal paper. So what? I don't see what difference it would make because that piece of paper was just like a little memo to him.

"His hands were tied from the start. He was told that afternoon, 'Don't leave Bethesda. You are going to do the autopsy.' "

"Did you ever hear anyone describe the face being missing or damaged?"

"Actually, none of them would talk to me about it. But I would assume from the copies of the X-rays I saw in Lattimer's diagrams that the face was missing."

"How firm are you on the Pott's disease diagnosis?"

"Oh, I believe that's what he had."

"He could have developed it anytime during his life. Sometime during childhood a person will develop what we call a Ghon complex, which is a tuberculoma in the lung. The antibody system will overcome it and it will be suppressed, and then at some time later in life, like when you are given steroids, this thing will be activated and spread throughout the body. One of the things it will do is cause Pott's disease."

"And that is in the spine?"

"Yes, in the spine in the immediate vicinity of the adrenal glands, which lay right against the spine right there. It almost inevitably gets involved."

"Does atrophy or calcification of the adrenals follow Pott's disease?"

"It's a part of Pott's disease."

"Do you think that the Pott's disease proceeded his adrenal insufficiency?"

"Well, it has to develop for you to become insufficient."

"You say he would have died in his second term. Would that be from the steroids?"

"I wouldn't say directly from the steroids, but from all the other things that were going wrong with him."[1]

"Anyone who opposes us, we'll destroy. As a matter of fact, anyone who doesn't support us we'll destroy."

—Egil Krogh

CHAPTER 19

OTHER DEATHS

This chapter could be called "Strange Deaths 2," except that it is a general discussion of some other major political killings in the United States which followed the assassination of President Kennedy. My book *High Treason* briefly outlined the death of numerous witnesses in that case.

Here we are talking about the murders of Martin Luther King, Jr., and Robert Kennedy, the attempted murders of George Wallace, Presidents Gerald Ford and Ronald Reagan, and the assassination of Allard Lowenstein. Others might mention the fact that some sixteen famous popular singers died within a short space of time, all of whom came out against the Vietnam War. The death of John Lennon sometime later might fit our discussion here in terms of its possible political meaning. These entertainers spoke to many millions of young people, and their opposition to official policy may have marked all of them for death. Not to speak of the apparent extermination of the whole high command of the FBI, and the death of J. Edgar Hoover.

In reading the FBI's file on their investigation of the assassination of President Kennedy, I discovered that they performed in a pretty honest and straightforward fashion. Elements of the FBI continued to hold on to the belief that John Connally was struck with bullets different from those that struck Kennedy, which meant a second gun, but were unable to adequately investigate the murder due to the tremendous political power of those who led the conspiracy.

Critics have argued that J. Edgar Hoover was involved in some manner in overthrowing John Kennedy, but it seems to me that though Hoover made his mistakes and though his actions may be construed to have protected and nurtured organized crime in this country, and though he was a close friend of President Lyndon Johnson (who many think was himself involved in or privy to Kennedy's assassination), Kennedy's successor, and who was probably blackmailed as Hoover seemed to do to every president and a lot of those in other political office, I think Hoover ran the federal police agency in the best interests of the United States as he saw them. I cannot believe that Hoover was involved in JFK's murder. I do feel that Hoover's death, as the *Harvard Crimson* long ago reported, may have been other than natural, and I feel that it was because he and the men directly under him who died at the same time perhaps constituted a grave threat to the conspirators who were moving to control the whole operation and direction of the United States government.

We also note that Jim Hougan, author of *Spooks* and *Secret Agenda,* speaks of the deaths of numerous lawyers in the Washington, D.C., area during that period up to and including the time of Watergate, which was the beginning of the end of the Nixon presidency.[1]

In addition, as in the assassination of John F. Kennedy, witnesses appear to have been murdered in many of the cases that follow, including the whole Watergate nightmare that befell this nation in our time of troubles.

And finally, perhaps *finis* was written to the nightmare of Watergate with the deaths of Martha Mitchell, the cantankerous and dipsomaniac wife of the attorney general under President Nixon—who was doing her best to alert the country about a crooked administration—and the wife of E. Howard Hunt, the chief of the Watergate burglars. Not only did Dorothy Hunt die on United Airlines Flight 553 on December 8, 1972, other passengers who lost their lives included Michelle Clark, the CBS reporter who was traveling with Mrs. Hunt; Congressman George Collins of Chicago; and several lawyers tied to the oil companies enmeshed in some of Nixon's threatening scandals.

Mrs. Hunt, the alleged bag lady, was paying off the Watergate burglars and their families. She and her husband, former CIA agent Howard Hunt, were said to possess boxes of documents implicating Nixon in crimes that would "impeach him eight times over." The crash of her plane and the death of Martha Mitchell—who also knew too much about the Watergate affair, the embezzler Charles Vesco, Nixon's brother and nephew, who were involved with Vesco, and the Mob connection to the Nixon administration—remain suspicious to this day.

* * *

Some people questioned the official findings in many of the crimes we have been investigating, such as the assassinations of John and Robert Kennedy and Martin Luther King, Jr. The critics of the critics might say that there will always be those who will not accept the official story on anything. It is, of course, the prerogative of citizens in a democracy to question. There must be a loyal opposition on every issue, even in a criminal case. Every accused person is entitled to legal representation to be sure that everything is on the up and up and that they get fair treatment.

I think any act of political violence in this nation must always be closely examined, and the fact that a few people at first, and later many, begin researching such an occurrence is an act of patriotism for most of them. Some, of course, are also looking to make money out of it, but that is the American way. Commercialism alone will not invalidate their research. And, of course, there are many for whom such research and detective work is intriguing, interesting, and absorbing, and for them we are all very grateful.

Robert Kennedy, June 5, 1968

The assassination of Robert F. Kennedy seemed to be an open and shut case. Few people questioned the apparent obviousness of the accusation that Sirhan Sirhan, a disgruntled and unhappy Palestinian immigrant, shot Robert Kennedy on June 5, 1968, at the Ambassador Hotel in Los Angeles. Sirhan was captured at the scene, a gun in his hand, firing.

From the first day some people did not accept the official version of RFK's assassination on the night that he won the California primary and proved that he would likely become president. Researchers went looking for the "girl in the polka-dot dress." Sandy Serrano, an RFK campaign worker, had said that a girl in a white polka-dot dress had screamed "we shot him!" just after the assassination.[2]

Allard Lowenstein, a New York lawyer and strong supporter and friend of the Kennedy family, especially did not believe it, and researched the case himself. About the time Lowenstein developed hard evidence proving that there was a second gunman in Robert's death, he was murdered in his office. More about his murder later in this chapter. We recommend Lowenstein's article in the *Saturday Review,* February

19, 1977: "The Murder of Robert Kennedy, Suppressed Evidence of More Than One Assassin?"

Sirhan's pistol, a .22-caliber Iver-Johnson, held eight bullets, all of which were fired (according to the police), assuming the gun was fully loaded, which we do.

Six persons were wounded or killed. Five of the victims were standing behind Kennedy and each received one bullet (and survived), and Robert Kennedy was struck three times, according to the autopsy report. Two of those bullets struck him in the armpit from behind, and one entered the back of his head. This is a total of eight bullets. Still another bullet went through the shoulder pad of his jacket, and thus we have nine bullets.[3]

There are more bullets.

There was a wild melee and the five other victims were shot during it, but *also,* bullets quite clearly struck two door frames behind Kennedy, and the ceiling panels. The number of these bullet strikes taken together with the eight wounds in the victims add up to more than the number of bullets in Sirhan's gun, assuming it was fully loaded. In fact, they add up to thirteen shots. Sirhan did not have time to reload the pistol.

Three bullets were found in wooden door frames, and one bullet hit a door hinge.[4] This assumes that one of these bullets either passed through the body of one of the victims or was the one that went through Kennedy's shoulder pad. Otherwise, we have fourteen shots.

None of the other five victims had gunpowder on their skin or clothes. Only RFK had such burns or powder. Three of the bullets that hit Kennedy or his jacket had upward trajectories. "The most sophisticated forensic techniques were unable to prove that the fatal bullet was fired from Sirhan's gun," wrote Dr. Thomas Noguchi. Noguchi, the coroner who conducted the autopsy, went on to write: "I have never said Sirhan killed Robert Kennedy." In fact, he makes clear in his book that Sirhan *could not have killed Kennedy.*

"All four bullets that hit Robert F. Kennedy in the pantry of the Ambassador Hotel traveled from down to up, from right to left, from back to front, and were fired at contact range, between one and five inches from the senator," as Jack Kimbrough, a writer and investigator, wrote the district attorney of Los Angeles. Kennedy received no frontal wounds.

Soot shows up when a gun is held inches from the victim, and Kennedy's hair was full of it. Kennedy was shot from very close, the muzzle almost touching his head. This is undisputed.

The bullet that struck his skull broke into many pieces in the brain and could not be linked to any gun.

Eyewitnesses who stood directly next to the "second gun" have described to our investigators how that pistol blazed away at Kennedy. Booker Griffin, a Kennedy campaign worker, said that a third man had a gun out. Witnesses have said that police officers, or men in police uniforms, came onto the scene and took them away from the area, then moved them out of the city and gave them new jobs and lives. Some were given the impression that they were in a witness protection program and it was for their own benefit, but in fact the so-called LAPD police officers were conspirators involved in the plot.

One might ask why they simply didn't kill these eyewitnesses, but too many deaths too soon would arouse much more suspicion, so time was needed for things to cool off. Later on people would be shot or stabbed or die mysteriously.

The door frame hit by a bullet was the one through which Kennedy had just passed as he came down from the stage of the ballroom of the Ambassador Hotel.

The police later claimed that one of the bullets that had gone through a ceiling tile hit the floor above and ricocheted downward, making yet another hole in another tile, and struck Elizabeth Evans Young in the head. This is how they explained away two of the apparent additional shots.

"Unfortunately for this theory, Mrs. Young had lost a shoe and was, in fact, stooping over to retrieve it when she was hit in the forehead by a bullet that was traveling upward. Furthermore, not all of the bullet was removed from Mrs. Young's head, but the part that was removed weighed almost thirty-one grains—a considerable achievement for a bullet that had weighed only thirty-nine grains before penetrating two ceiling tiles each about three fourths of an inch thick, and bouncing off concrete as well as presumably going through either Senator Kennedy's chest or his shoulder pad," Allard Lowenstein wrote.

As for the third bullet hole in the tiles, it was "lost in the ceiling interspace."

Photographs were taken by the LAPD of policemen pointing to what they stated was a bullet embedded in a door frame, and later policemen clearly indicated to former D.A. Vincent Bugliosi (famous for prosecuting the Charles Manson case) that they had in fact removed that bullet. But it disappeared from the evidence and the police went to a lot of trouble to deny that they had ever said there was a bullet there.

"Los Angeles law-enforcement agencies had a funny reaction to Sergeant Wright's shifting recollections. . . . The LAPD discouraged one of these men from signing a statement about what he saw, and the district attorney of Los Angeles County and the attorney general of California battled successfully to prevent the subpoenaing of these men to testify under oath about what they knew."[5] Why, we may ask, if the local authorities had nothing to hide?

"Official photographs from the court proceedings showed, moreover, three separate door frames in which holes had been circled by LAPD investigators. Some of the door frames had been booked into evidence —which, unless the LAPD had taken to collecting door frames as a hobby, suggests that there was something about those particular frames that made them worthy of preservation. If it were subsequently determined that there were no bullet holes and that there had been no bullets in the frames, some records ought to exist supporting the conclusion. I asked to see these records or to have the door frames examined by experts; then it was discovered that the frames, together with the relevant ceiling tiles, had been "routinely" destroyed by the LAPD. Nor was I able to obtain any record of these tests.

"Another peculiar fact has also emerged: two bullets that experts say bore traces of wood were booked into evidence even though, according to the LAPD, the two bullets were 'found on the front seat of Sirhan's car.'

"No one in authority seems to be puzzled by the two bullets on the front seat of Sirhan's car. Did Sirhan have a secret penchant for shooting into wooden fences and then hacking the bullets out and carrying them around on the front seat of his car? Did Sirhan find two .22-caliber bullets that happened to have wood on them lying in the street?

"In view of what is now known, is it unreasonable to wonder if more than eight bullets might have been recovered from the scene of the shooting, since more than eight bullets were actually booked into evidence?"

We can see why Lowenstein died of a gunshot wound. It is not so difficult to find a madman, put a gun in his hand, and direct him at a target. Madmen will do anything at times. They can even be hypnoprogrammed. That was what the CIA program MK/ULTRA was all about. We are speaking of Sirhan, David Hinckley, Dennis Sweeney, and the rest of the accused. Kind of like the Nazis putting some mental patients in Polish uniforms and mowing them down at a German border post in 1939 as a pretext for attacking Poland and starting World War II.

"Moreover, in Los Angeles, even the evidence on which the official conclusions are based has been kept secret. The Warren Commission, whatever its failings, at least made available much of the material collected during its investigation. But the ten volumes of material collected during the investigation of the RFK case have been withheld from everyone—and this despite repeated promises by virtually every official involved to do precisely the opposite," Lowenstein said.

The ceiling panels and door frame were then taken down and destroyed by the LAPD within a year of the assassination. Jack Kimbrough is a chief researcher in this case, and has struggled for a long time to get it properly reinvestigated. Dr. William Harper of Pasadena is also a critic of the official version and has made important discoveries. The late Lillian Castellano, assassination conspiracy investigator, was able to get a court order forcing the LAPD to give up their photographs showing the bullets in the door frames.

In April 1988 the AP and the *San Francisco Examiner* reported that more than 2400 photos taken during the shooting or the investigation that followed were destroyed. "There was no explanation in the 50,000 pages of documents as to why the pictures were burned or why such items as ceiling tiles and doorjambs from the scene of Kennedy's death were destroyed in the months following the assassination." John Burns, the state's chief archivist, said that the 2400 photographs were destroyed two and a half months after the assassination. "This is a very unusual murder file [but] I'm not absolutely satisfied that any questions are answered." He said that the biggest surprise was the amount of evidence destroyed, and that he could not explain it. Let's again state this in the toughest possible language. When you have certain strange things happen to evidence or to witnesses in a case, suspicion has to be raised. In *every one* of these cases, evidence appears to be faked, planted, or it disappears. Of course they are all linked.

We have the same pattern as in the assassination of John F. Kennedy.

We must also discuss the deaths and other mysterious happenings in the RFK case.

Cathy Sue Fulmer, twenty-three, questioned by police as the possible girl in the polka-dot dress, overdosed on drugs and died in a motel in Los Angeles on April 17, 1969.

David Scheim, assassination investigator, mathematician, and National Institutes of Health analyst, told William C. McGaw and Thomas G. Whittle in their *Freedom* article that the following had problems: Theodore Charach, investigating this case, was threatened by a man with a knife and told to turn over his evidence. Betty Dryer, Charach's assistant was knifed. Wald Emerson, financially backing research into the assassination, was repeatedly threatened by anonymous callers.

Dr. William Harper, mentioned above as a chief crime scientist investigating this case, was shot at and his car struck with a high-powered-rifle bullet as he was driving—not long before he was going to testify.

One of the main problems in the RFK assassination case is that the coroner, Thomas Noguchi, found that the bullet that killed Robert Kennedy was fired from two to three inches behind his head. There was soot all over that area of the skull, with a circular tattoo pattern of unburned powder grains on his right ear. Noguchi conducted his own test on pigs' ears with a similar handgun to determine the exact distance needed to create an identical pattern, and he found that the gun was no more than three inches from Kennedy's head.

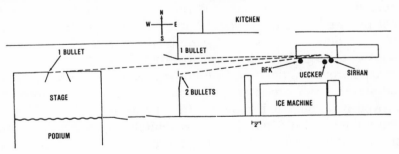

The photographs taken during the shooting clearly show that Sirhan Sirhan was about eight feet *in front* of Robert Kennedy, who was facing him, and could not possibly have shot Kennedy in the back of the head.

Karl Uecker, the hotel's maître d', was at all times directly between Kennedy and Sirhan, who faced Kennedy as he came into the pantry. Uecker personally grabbed Sirhan and wrestled the gun away from him. He has repeatedly stated that Sirhan was never closer than a few feet and faced Kennedy at the time the shooting began. Sirhan could not possibly have shot *any* of the bullets that hit Kennedy. The shot that killed him, striking Kennedy behind the ear, could not have come from Sirhan's gun.

In addition, none of the fatal bullets was ever linked to Sirhan's gun, and no tests were ever conducted on that gun.

There can be no doubt from the hard evidence in this case that there was a second gun. Who wielded it? And who redirected Kennedy from the stage into the pantry at the last moment, changing his route of exit from the ballroom? Who led him to his doom?

A security guard, one Thane Eugene Cesar, walking with Kennedy carried a similar .22-caliber Iver-Johnson pistol. That gun was never turned over to the police and never test-fired to compare the ballistics of its slugs with those that struck Kennedy. Cesar did have the gun out of his holster, according to witnesses. Cesar then disappeared from the face of the earth, and has never been found.

Allard Lowenstein wrote that "the harder I've tried to get answers, the more resistant the Los Angeles authorities have been. There seems to be an official cover-up in progress, one of truly impressive proportions. Evidence has been destroyed, facts have been misstated or flatly denied, and incorrect testimony has been given."

An example of the distortion of eyewitness testimony by the authorities follows: "Karl Uecker [as Lowenstein wrote] is the witness most frequently cited by the district attorney to support the claim that Sirhan's gun was at Kennedy's head. But Uecker has never said that Sirhan's gun was at Kennedy's head, not to the grand jury, nor at the trial, nor in a subsequent interview with *Stern* magazine, nor to me personally.

"To the contrary, Uecker says that Sirhan's gun could not possibly have fired the bullets that hit Senator Kennedy, according to the autopsy report, because Sirhan's gun was in front of Uecker's own nose. Furthermore, he insists that he knocked Sirhan onto a steam table after only two bullets had been fired. If this is true, there is no way that Kennedy could have been hit at close range by four bullets from Sirhan's gun. . . . Nobody saw Sirhan get past the steam table, yet if he did not pass the steam table, his gun couldn't have been fired next to Kennedy's head—even if he had made a titanic unnoticed lunge past Uecker."

Later on Lowenstein says: "A few witnesses did see another gun in the pantry—and they saw it in the hand of a man who was walking directly behind Senator Kennedy. This man, a part-time security guard, subsequently acknowledged not only that he had a gun on him but also that he had removed it from its holster after the shooting started.

"The trial of Sirhan never dealt with the ballistics issues or with such questions as the distance of the weapon from the victim or, for that matter, with any of the other evidentiary problems we are discussing: *The trial dealt exclusively with the issue of Sirhan's mental competence.*"

Several tape recordings were made during the shooting, and they recorded the shots. In particular, one recording was made by Andrew West of the Mutual radio network as he stood within a few feet of Robert Kennedy. In 1982 Dr. Michael Hecker, an acoustics scientist at the Stanford Research Institute, conducted tests on the tapes in the presence of assassination investigator Kevin Cody, who reported that Dr. Hecker declared that there were "no fewer than ten gunshots" on the tape (the revolver only held eight bullets).

The tape recorder had not been turned on when the first shots were fired, and Paul Shrade had already been hit. This would mean that there were at least four more shots fired before the recorder registered ten shots. This would mean that fourteen shots were fired.

Cody writes that following this test, six more tapes became available from CBS, ABC, NBC, and others, and that all the tests confirmed the above findings. In addition, tests of all the tapes made during the shooting indicated even more shots.[6]

Robert Kennedy had come out strongly against the Vietnam War, a war he and his murdered brother had started to take the United States out of, a war we could not win, did not plan to win, and ultimately did not win, gaining nothing but vast debts unpaid to this day, and a greatly torn social fabric stained with the human tragedy of those who fought and died, or who came back damaged and neglected.

We recommend that the reader interested in the RFK slaying read *The Assassination of Robert F. Kennedy: A Searching Look at the Conspiracy and Coverup, 1968–1978* by John G. Christian and William Turner.[7] The publisher unaccountably withdrew this book from stores. It remains, however, the best overall work dealing with the assassination of Robert Kennedy. In addition many articles on Robert Kennedy's assassination were published by Duncan Harp.[8]

Martin Luther King, Jr., April 4, 1968

As a result of the efforts primarily of Coretta Scott King, the widow of the Reverend Dr. Martin Luther King, Jr., a bill was passed in 1976 in the House of Representatives that resulted in new investigations of the assassinations of her husband and President John F. Kennedy. "I don't have the facts, but at this stage I say it appears there was a conspiracy in the death of my husband," Mrs. King said in November 1975. Nearly three years later the House Committee found that there "probably was" a conspiracy in both cases. King died on April 4, 1968, at the Lorraine Motel in Memphis, Tennessee. Trouble is, the House did not have the courage to get to the bottom of either murders, or any others on our list.

"The way he was documented and followed around by Hoover and the CIA when he was abroad, it would have to have been attached to the forces of our government that felt he was a threat to the system as it existed." Mrs. King referred to the CIA and FBI chief J. Edgar Hoover.

"The FBI has acknowledged that it undertook a harassment campaign to discredit King but concluded that James Earl Ray acted alone in King's assassination."[9]

"We were operating an intensive vendetta against Dr. King in an effort to destroy him," said an Atlanta FBI agent to the House Select Committee on Assassinations. And Hoover did his best to slander King, telling Jack Anderson that James Earl Ray was hired to kill King by a man whom they said was cuckolded by him.[10]

It is absolutely clear to me, after reviewing all the known evidence in the case, that renegades in the FBI and perhaps the local police set up King's murder. It is clear simply from the manner in which any new evidence in the case has been treated. Or, rather, covered up. It is clear that J. Edgar Hoover was greatly afraid of King and the possibility that he would become a messiah, and if King ever turned away from nonviolence, he might—in Hoover's demented paranoia—lead a violent revolt. That is what I believe the rationale was for killing this man.

As the Canadian police have repeatedly said, James Earl Ray, the convicted assassin, simply could not get in and out of Canada without help, plus assume the identities and obtain the passports and papers of three Canadian citizens who looked like him, and in one case had the same scars.

In addition, in violation of the extradition treaty, the U.S. government quite clearly presented false documents to the government of Great Britain when it sought to extradite Ray.

Ray was brought back to the United States, where he was put in a cell with bright lights shining on him at all times, two guards within five feet of him, television cameras recording his every move and breath.

We have a constitutional clause stating that no cruel or unusual punishment will be meted out in this country. But it apparently doesn't apply to political prisoners. Ray was broken down, and when he was about to come to trial, he pleaded guilty in fear of being electrocuted for a crime he shortly thereafter insisted he did not commit. Clearly, he was coerced into his confession.

Other witnesses say that Charles O. Stephens, the only witness to say that he saw Ray running from the rooming house after the shot, was too drunk to see anything, let alone stand up. Nobody saw anyone fire from the rooming house either. Not only that, it would have been all but impossible to fire a rifle from the bathtub, as the state claimed.

Ray says that he did not know what the conspirators planned to do. He thought he was involved in just smuggling, but saw later how he had been set up and drawn in. Ray wrote Senator James Eastland in 1969: "I personally did not shoot Dr. King . . . but I believe I may be partly responsible for his death." Ray claimed that a man named Raoul told him to buy the rifle that was later found near the scene of the crime, telling him it was to be shown to a gun runner. Raoul was a mysterious character he met with in Canada and elsewhere, and who he believed was behind the plot. Ray felt that "much of the evidence" was in Los Angeles and New Orleans. He was sent to those places by Raoul, and altogether had been given some $12,000 over a period of months.

Crawdaddy published a sketch made by police from eyewitness descriptions of the man seen running from the scene of the crime. Alongside it is a picture of one of the three tramps marched back from the railroad yards behind the Grassy Knoll in Dallas on November 22, 1963, just after President Kennedy was shot. The picture is of the man we call "Frenchy," known by that name because of the European cut of his clothes. He would appear to be identical to the man seen at the murder of King five years later.

We would suppose that this is the same "Jack Armstrong," a pseudonym given to a man reporter Wayne Chastain suspects was one of the real killers. Researcher Richard E. Sprague wrote in *People and the Pursuit of Truth*[11] that Gary Patrick Hemming, a CIA contract employee, said that "Frenchy" was another mercenary working from a yacht owned by anti-Castro sympathizer Larry LaBorde. . . . "Frenchy" was really a French-Canadian. He was said to be close to Loran Hall, William Seymour, and Lawrence Howard (all of whom figured prominently in the JFK case) but that they probably did not know his real name.

Sprague writes that the similarity of the man in the 1968 sketch to the photograph of "Frenchy" is so "striking . . . but also it was so strong as to make one conclude the sketch was made from the tramp photograph itself.

"It is important to recall that the sketch of the King 'killer' was broadcast and published long before the names Eric Starvo Galt, Ramon George Sneyd (both real people in Canada, but whose identities were used by Ray), or James Earl Ray were known. It was released, in fact, only a short time after the assassination."

Researcher Jeff Paley took a copy of the sketch and the photograph of "Frenchy" to the Memphis police, who told him to go to the FBI, since they had taken over full control of the case. "The officer immediately pushed the pictures across the desk, and although Paley protested that he was ignoring important new evidence, the agent refused to deal with the questions and discontinued the conversation. Paley gave up further efforts and returned to New York." The professionals don't want to hear from us, I think. We, the people.

Ray says it was Raoul who came out of the rooming house just after the shooting and dropped a bundle on the sidewalk. He jumped into the backseat of the white Mustang and Ray drove off. After a few blocks the man got out, and Ray never saw him again.

The sketch that witnesses drew of the small man who ran from the boardinghouse in no way resembles Ray.

Author William Bradford Huie had told Richard Sprague and Trent Gough that he had located three barmaids in Atlanta and Montreal that had seen Ray and Raoul together. Huie said that they identified Raoul from the sketch, and Ray from police pictures. Sprague tells us that after he showed the sketch of the man in Memphis and the November 22, 1963, Dealey Plaza picture of "Frenchy" to Huie, "from this time forward [William Bradford] Huie and [Percy] Foreman dropped all statements regarding a plot to kill Dr. King, and, even more interesting, in the existence of Raoul. When Huie published his third article [in *Look*] he treated Raoul as a figment of Ray's imagination, failing to mention that he had told researchers he found witnesses who had seen Ray and Raoul together."

Sprague writes that Huie said that Ray was just a liar.

Only after Ray got a new hearing and took Jim Lesar as his lawyer did he make a positive identification of "Frenchy" as Raoul. For reasons best known only to attorney Bernard Fensterwald, indicates Sprague, none of the evidence identifying Raoul as "Frenchy" or the backing of the murder plot by four wealthy industrialists was brought out at Ray's new hearing.

Ray has since not talked about his identification of "Frenchy" as Raoul either.

Richard E. Sprague (not to be confused with the first chief counsel of the House Select Committee on Assassinations, Richard A. Sprague) writes that "first, if the executive agencies sensed that Ray's brother, Jerry, was involved in the case, it seems rather certain they would have publicized the point because (a) the role of the younger Ray would have provided a plausible "conspiracy theory" to the plot-minded already aware of the great discrepancies in the case against James Earl Ray and (b) this sort of plot would easily fulfill the schematic already mapped out by the FBI, i.e., that James Earl Ray was motivated by racist and pathological impulses to murder Dr. King." Sprague also doubts that Jerry Ray had professional credentials for smuggling, and soldier-of-fortune type employment.

Wayne Chastain believes that one Jack Youngblood, also a mercenary and military intelligence spy, was involved in the murder along with Raoul and an unwitting Ray.

Harold Weisberg, through his attorney, Jim Lesar, brought a Freedom of Information Act suit in order to free the files and evidence the government claimed that it had against James Earl Ray. It is to be noted that evidence in criminal cases is supposed to be a matter of public record. When Weisberg, who knew that there was a cover-up in the case, finally got a look at that evidence, he saw why it was being kept secret: Not a single fingerprint of Ray's was found in his rooming house, in the bathroom where he was supposed to have fired the fatal shot, nor on his furniture, his car, or anywhere else where they claim he was.

"They've sworn falsely, they've misrepresented, they've deceived the courts," Weisberg said. They fooled the British government. That is what the U.S. thinks of extradition treaties.

Even the autopsy report, which Weisberg got through his suit, conflicts with what the state had said about the bullet and the wounds.

In 1977 a woman said her husband, a retired police officer, was offered a half million dollars to assassinate King.[12] The man had written Representative M. G. Snyder of Kentucky, and told him that several agents of the FBI and several police officers, including a chief of detectives, a captain, a lieutenant, and a sergeant, all in one police department were involved in the murder.[13] This would appear to be the Louisville, Kentucky, police, in the context of the AP article in the *New York Times* of March 24, 1977.

A key article that led to the establishment of the House Assassinations Committee at the same time in 1976 was written by Wayne Chastain of the Pacific News Service and published in the *San Francisco Examiner & Chronicle,* October 10, 1976: "Did lawmen set up King?" Chastain was a reporter in Memphis where King was shot, and he was one of the first people on the scene. He wrote: "Martin Luther King, Jr., may have been the victim of 'security stripping'—a technique used by intelligence agencies to expose a victim to assassination by removing his protection.

"This theory persuaded the U.S. House of Representatives to create a special twelve-member committee to investigate both the 1968 King murder and the 1963 assassination of John Kennedy. The black caucus in the House, acting on new information in the King case, was responsible for breaking a stalemate and pushing the investigation through, according to several committee appointees."

Newsday reporter Les Payne found in scores of interviews that Ed Redditt, a black Memphis police detective in charge of protecting King, was removed from his post across the street from the motel where King was shot just two hours before the slaying. Redditt's contingency plan to seal off the area in the event of trouble was "never implemented" and the assassin got away.

The director of the police department, Frank Holloman, a retired FBI agent of twenty-five years, had removed Redditt, saying that he was the target of a murder plot. This was clear intimidation. Redditt never heard another thing about the plot after that day. Redditt said that Holloman told him of the plot in the presence of a man he identified as being from the Secret Service. He also said that representatives of the FBI, military intelligence, the National Guard, and other agencies were there. Redditt's assistant said that he, too, left his post before the slaying.

Someone in the King entourage relieved four members of an informal bodyguard just before the murder as well. And "the only two black firemen assigned to the fire station across from King's hotel, Redditt's command post, were also 'stripped away,' " Chastain wrote. One of the firemen, Floyd Newsum, was told that the transfer order came from the police department.

Holloman, writes author Mark Lane, "served J. Edgar Hoover in a more personal manner" for eight years. "Holloman was the FBI inspector in charge of Hoover's personal office in Washington. Holloman told me that he had met with Hoover every day during that eight-year period."[14]

Ray's former attorney, Arthur Hanes (whom Ray had fired two days before his trial was to begin), said at a hearing that he was positive that the rifle found near the scene of the crime was not used to kill Dr. King. Hanes was the former right-wing mayor of Birmingham, Alabama.

In spite of that fact, he said that the British government should not have extradited Ray because the assassination of Dr. King was a political killing. He had also worked for both the FBI and the CIA. He told a hearing that the slug that was taken from King's body "was as perfect as a slug fired for test purposes." If it had been fired from Ray's rifle, experts could have established this.

Also, Tennessee law states that if a judge dies during a trial or part of the appeal process, a new trial must be ordered. Judge W. Preston Battle died at his desk three weeks after the trial, an appeal from Ray in his hands.

"Arthur Murtagh, a former FBI agent in Atlanta [King's hometown] has said agents in the Atlanta office 'literally jumped for joy' when they learned King had been assassinated. He said the FBI intelligence squad in Atlanta was assigned to 'somehow or other get King to bring him down, break him, or destroy him.' " This same FBI intelligence squad was then assigned to investigate the murder. Murtagh said that his superiors washed out leads suggesting a right-wing conspiracy.

This FBI man then went on to say that "had a more thorough investigation been conducted by the FBI, I believe links would have been established between the King assassination and the Kennedy murders —both those of JFK and RFK."

Murtagh said that the FBI "intentionally and deliberately" avoided looking at conspiracy leads in both cases.

Former agents said that the FBI would set off fire alarms where King was going to speak, planted false stories in the newspapers in hope that colleges would stop giving honorary degrees to him, interfered in his personal and private life by making anonymous calls to his friends, even to his wife. They sent his wife a tape recording of her husband at a party in which she was not present, intending to get King in trouble at home.

Ed Redditt further states that King was clearly lured to Memphis by deliberate provocation of the problems there. Violence was instigated in order to get King on the scene so that he could be shot. The Reverend Jesse Jackson said, "Dr. King would never have returned to Memphis if the violence had not happened."

"After the violence, apparently intended by the militant group to discredit him, King vowed to return to prove that he could still lead a peaceful demonstration," Chastain wrote.

A Memphis policeman had infiltrated the Invaders, the black militant group that disrupted the march of the sanitation workers. He was "one of the most provocative members," very active in planning confrontations, and he was one of the four men supposed to be informally guarding King.

The man shortly left the Memphis police department and may have gone to Washington. Redditt ran into him sometime later in Memphis. The man claimed to be with the CIA and begged Redditt not to blow his cover.

A man who claimed that he was an advance man and a security worker for King went to the Lorraine Motel and changed the reservation for King from a ground floor suite to a room overlooking the pool on the second floor, with a balcony. If King went out on that balcony, he was a much better target. When King's entourage arrived, they were mystified by the room switch and did not know who had made the change.

Wayne Chastain, writing for the Memphis *Press-Scimitar,* uncovered a man who he feels was a part of the gun team. He calls him "Jack Armstrong," though Chastain knows his real name. "Armstrong" was identified as being in the restaurant below Ray's room an hour before the killing. Chastain believes the man then visited several people in Memphis some days after the shooting, all of whom called the police. He claimed to one of them, Russell X. Thompson, a lawyer, that his roommate had shot King, and not from the rooming house, but from the bushes in front of the motel. Several eyewitnesses later said that that was where the gunman fired from, and no one but the government claimed that the gunman had fired from the rooming house across the way.

"Armstrong" also said that Robert Kennedy would be shot if he won the California primary, which is what happened two months later.

James Earl Ray recognized a photograph of the man whom he said he had seen twice the day of the killing, and thought that he was a gun runner for Raoul. As Alan MacRobert wrote, "His real life reads like something out of an international spy novel. A Southern-born gun runner and soldier of fortune, he made his living fighting in, or against, most of the Latin American revolutions from 1954 to the early sixties, after fighting as a guerrilla behind North Korean lines."

The assassination of the Reverend Martin Luther King caused a great explosion of race riots in many cities in the United States upon his death. Violence was the very thing King did not want to see happen. This saintly black man had fought nonviolently to bring about change in the heinous racism and segregation that rotted the United States, making a lie of its pretence as the defender of freedom.

Many people died in those riots, and a vast amount of property was destroyed in the fires that consumed the ghettos of some cities, not set by whites, but set by black provocateurs. Innocent people were pushed forward to face the clubs of police, and one of the darkest episodes in American history took place.

In fact, America itself seemed to explode from that moment forward as increasing unrest over educational values, curriculums, and racial policies gripped the college campuses. It can be argued that the Vietnam War was undertaken in a much stronger way then in order to deflect attention from the trouble at home. Soon the campuses erupted in protest against that war, which nobody seemed seriously to want to win or end. All these problems gave the Nixon administration ammunition for creating its own police operations, and clamping down as best it could. The Pentagon had some fifty thousand informers on college campuses, and the FBI's COINTEL (counterintelligence) program threatened the very heart of America's Bill of Rights and liberty. The nightmare that was Watergate can be said to date from the murder of Martin Luther King, Jr., and so much of this flowed from the assassination of President John F. Kennedy—when the pace of orderly change possible within the framework of a peaceful country facing its problems and iniquities was overturned by the bullets of Dallas.

James Earl Ray was accused and convicted of the murder in a kangaroo court, later claiming that the assassination was a conspiracy of which he was an unwitting part. "I was down the street about three blocks from where King was shot, checking a leak in a tire, when it happened," Ray said. "My fingerprints were on the gun—but I had handled it—I had given it to Raoul." He had first heard of King's death while driving his white Mustang toward Mississippi. Ray panicked when he heard on the car radio that he was wanted for the crime and began a flight that ended with the London arrest.

Ray was not an educated man, and he was totally inept as a robber. He had little experience in the outside world, having spent much of his life in jail. He had no history whatsoever of violence, and in reviewing the evidence claimed against him, it simply is not credible that he could have done any one of the many things attributed to him without a lot of help. Not just ordinary help, either, but it would have taken the boiler room of a major intelligence agency, or their moonlighters and graduates, to produce the false identities and travel arrangements Ray had.

The important thing to remember concerning James Earl Ray is that he had other identities: Paul Bridgeman, Ramon George Sneyd, Eric Starvo Galt, to name a few, and he could not have obtained Canadian passports, driver's licenses, and other identification, passed in and out of the United States after escaping from prison, gone to Europe after the murder of King, and been in both Lisbon and London at the same time, as the police claimed: He could not have done all of this without help.

Let's get into how other writers and the media help cover up these crimes. As Harold Weisberg, the father of assassination research in twentieth-century America, said, William Bradford Huie in his book tried to explain the Galt identity this way: "He chose Eric S. Galt, and since there is a real Eric S. Galt in Toronto, the assumption has been that Ray saw his name in print. But he [Ray] says no. Between Windsor and Toronto he passed the city of Galt, and he says he chose Galt when he saw it on an exit marker. He says he chose Eric only in the process of seeking something different from the more common names."

Weisberg writes in *Frame-up*:[15] "There is a lemming in this writing. Ray took the name Eric *Starvo* Galt. Huie says Eric *S.* Galt. Thus, he avoids the need to explain the odd middle name, which cannot fit this scheme. Aside from the astounding resemblance of Ray to the real Eric Galt and two other Canadians, Paul Bridgeman and Ramon George Sneyd, whose identities he had assumed, complete with identical scars, it is asking too much to believe Ray could have made up so unusual a name and, with the right middle initial, caught a live one he also resembles."[16]

We know that there was an FBI vendetta to disrupt King, and his accused assassin claimed in 1988 that he was framed to cover up an FBI plot to kill King.[17] It is known that Hoover hated King because King's calls for economic and social justice threatened the status quo.

In an application for a pardon hearing, Ray, in an AP interview, named four men who he believes were involved in the conspiracy: Randolph Erwin Rosenson, Carlos Miguel Hernandez, "Raoul," and David Graiver, whom Ray says he saw with "Raoul" in Nuevo Laredo, Mexico, in October 1967. The House Select Committee on Assassinations interviewed Rosenson in June 1977. Ray said that all of these people were involved in illegal narcotics smuggling, into which he had been drawn by Raoul.[18]

Ray said that he didn't think he would ever get a parole. "I think the only way I'll get out of here is through a jury. If they wouldn't grant me a trial, I don't see how they'll grant me a parole." One would think that Ray was railroaded so that he pleaded guilty, in fear of his life, and never had a chance to speak or defend himself. He claimed that the FBI had threatened to jail his father and brother if he didn't sign a confession.

Ray said that the government refuses his requests to review the evidence alleged against him, has never conducted ballistics tests on the alleged murder weapon, and has suppressed witnesses and investigations that could have cleared him. "Since they won't, they must be hiding something," Ray said of the FBI.

Ray was identified from fingerprints on a rifle tossed in the doorway of a building near the side of the assassination. It hardly seems likely that an assassin would leave evidence dooming him at the scene so deliberately.

Aides to King believe that Ray did not shoot King, and that the FBI was in fact plotting the civil rights leader's death.

J. Edgar Hoover, May 1, 1972

Hoover was a bigot who conducted a vendetta against King. Jack Anderson wrote on December 17, 1975, that "the FBI vendetta against Dr. King didn't end with his murder. The old FBI bulldog, J. Edgar Hoover, who had tried to blacken King's name while he was alive, also tried to tarnish his death."

Hoover had made an "incredible attempt to panic King into committing suicide, it seems to me, which abrogates any right he may have to confidentiality. Yet I was reluctant to believe ill of Hoover. But in late 1970 I happened to be on an airplane with the late Hale Boggs, then House Democratic leader. He told me how members of Congress were being intimidated, if not blackmailed, by Hoover. He said that the FBI would come upon a skeleton—a woman, a vice, a shady business associate—and then get word to him that an accusation against him had reached the FBI and they wanted to alert him so he could be on his guard. From then on, the congressman was likely to be a captive of Hoover's."[19]

Perhaps the facts to mention first in discussing the death of J. Edgar Hoover is that in the same month an attempt was made to kill George Wallace, who held the balance of power in the coming presidential election, and the Watergate burglaries were occurring. The first burglary of Democratic Party National Headquarters occurred at the Watergate on May 27, 1972, and the second Watergate burglary occurred on June 17, 1972, during which time the burglars were discovered and arrested.

President Nixon had called in J. Edgar Hoover the preceding December and asked him to resign. Hoover refused. He had the power not only to stand up to presidents, but to defy them, and Hoover, a complex man who had his own rules and priorities, openly resisted numerous moves made by Nixon. John Mitchell, Nixon's law partner in New York whom Nixon had appointed attorney general, had asked the FBI to wiretap various newsmen and even people in Nixon's own administration. Hoover at first flatly refused, but agreed to some of it only under strict agreements with written orders traceable to the White House showing that they had ordered these acts, which, of course, were illegal.

In the summer of 1971 Hoover was engaged in very tough fighting with the White House to try to protect the integrity of his FBI, and in addition he resisted strongly the attempt by the White House to create its own police operation. Nixon was clearly going to do things as president that not only were unconstitutional, but far beyond what any president of this country would think of doing. Some presidents were not without blemish in trying to protect themselves and attack their enemies, but none remotely proposed to do or tried to do the things that Nixon did.

Hoover had vetoed a White House intelligence force in 1971. Break-ins of his apartment were sworn to by Felipe DeDiego under the direction of former FBI man G. Gordon Liddy. DeDiego was a past associate of E. Howard Hunt, former CIA man and leader of the Watergate gang working for CREEP (Committee to Reelect the President).

Attorney General John Mitchell had ordered the FBI to wiretap various newsmen and national security council people. Hoover finally caved in, but demanded to keep the original transcripts in his office safe so that they could not be altered. Mitchell then told Robert Mardian (his close friend) to have the transcripts removed from Hoover's safe and taken to John Ehrlichman's safe in the White House. The man who was made to do this was a high-ranking FBI executive, William Sullivan, who shortly thereafter died in a strange hunting accident, during a period when many of his colleagues at the FBI also suddenly died.

As Jim Hougan wrote in *Spooks,* there surely was a "spook" war going on in Washington.

It would have to be assumed that from that moment on, Hoover was a marked man. The Nixon administration had previously established its intent to "destroy" those who got in its way. The Committee to Reelect the President (Nixon) then set up its own intelligence operations with former FBI and CIA employees and renegades who became the political police and brownshirts of the Nixon neo-Nazi faction.

Hoover's cause of death was listed as hyperactive cardiovascular disease, and yet no autopsy was performed. The *Harvard Crimson* reported on December 12, 1973, in an article by Mark Frazier, that a source, alleged to be a past associate of E. Howard Hunt, said that two burglaries of Hoover's home were performed, and during the second, a thyon-phosphate-type poison was put on Hoover's toilet articles, which caused an immediate heart seizure.[20]

A source said that the break-ins at Hoover's home were to retrieve documents that the White House thought would be used to blackmail President Nixon. Again, we repeat that Hoover originally believed that separate bullets had struck Governor Connally and President Kennedy, and that the Lee Harvey Oswald who allegedly defected to the Soviet Union was an impostor.

The man who replaced Hoover, L. Patrick Gray, covered up events both in the Watergate burglary and in the shooting of George Wallace. Those cover-ups significantly aided the reelection of Richard Nixon.

If Hoover's death was from natural causes, it sure came at a convenient time for the Nixon White House.

Attempted Assassination of George C. Wallace, May 15, 1972

Governor George Wallace of Alabama was shot down during a political appearance at a shopping mall in Maryland. His alleged assassin was again a disgruntled lone nut.

First we need to look at the political realities relevant at the time. The front runner in the Democratic Party primaries was Senator George McGovern, a former bomber pilot from the Pacific campaign, and an avowed liberal. McGovern was a good, kind, and decent man, very tough in his way, as so many veterans of the World War II were, but also a bit weak in the face of the awesome power that the Republican Party was beginning to use or condone to destroy their enemies.

Governor Wallace ran in the primaries as a Democrat, and although McGovern had gathered considerably more delegates to the Democratic National Convention, Wallace had actually had more people vote for him. Wallace was a southern conservative Democrat associated with the bad old days of racism and segregation. But in his state, unknown to the vast majority of militant northern liberals, Wallace was considered very liberal, decent, and backed by large numbers of blacks. He just came across all wrong to many northerners. When I met him, I was impressed by his intelligence and tenacity, and did not overly fear him, knowing he had to walk a difficult line between the virulent racism of northern Alabama and more decent instincts.

But McGovern was the better candidate, though it might be argued that the Democratic Party had already been co-opted by its opponents among the Republicans and radical rightists who nominated the weakest possible man—weakest in terms of his ultimate voter appeal. If McGovern won the nomination, he could be counted on to lose, *unless* it was a three-way election: between three parties.

That was in fact going to happen, because Wallace planned (and in fact did) to run as the candidate for the American Independent Party, in which case the vote and the electoral college would be split three ways. The only possible outcome in that case would be the triumph of George McGovern for president, since Wallace would draw votes from the Republican Party. Nixon was in deep trouble over the Vietnam War at that time, and what finally won for him was a huge lie from Henry Kissinger saying "peace is at hand" and the shooting of Wallace.

But in the earlier months of the year, it was clear to the strategists of the White House that Wallace was a greater threat than McGovern. Wallace had won surprising victories in Michigan and in Maryland, a state that in the same election voted for the very liberal Senator Joseph Tydings, a close friend of the Kennedy family, a state that had given a vast majority to the young Senator Kennedy in his run for the presidency a dozen years before. Wallace couldn't have been all bad.[21]

The gunman, Arthur Bremer, had at a stroke taken out the biggest single threat to Nixon's reelection: George Wallace. And Wallace himself does not believe that Bremer was acting on his own. But Bremer had already been fitted into the "lone nut" frame before he even had the gun.

Within hours the Nixon White House ordered its burglars, employed by the president's campaign organization, to invade the assassin's apartment and see what they could find. Interestingly enough, the FBI, who had already been there, did not secure the property, and all manner of journalists, tourists, and others ransacked the place.[22]

There was always a suspicion that Bremer had that look, the aura of a programmed assassin. Something did not ring true about him or his diary, which seemed to have been written by the same person who wrote Lee Harvey Oswald's diary, and that of Sirhan Sirhan.

He, like James Earl Ray, traveled around with someone who might be construed to be his controller, a man who was shortly found dead in Canada. Then two other contacts died quickly.

Wallace was shot with a five-shot .38-caliber revolver, found at his feet. They claimed it had been fired five times. Three other people were shot, and the four victims suffered eleven different wounds. Officially no one else, including police present, fired their weapons. Doctors at the hospital said that Wallace was hit four times and maybe five times, which means that each of the bullets that hit him had to go through him and hit someone else.

One bullet went through the right upper arm (1). (See diagram for numbers that locate the wounds.) Another bullet went through the right forearm (2).

Two more bullets hit Wallace in the chest. One struck him on the right side (3) and the other in the right-hand region of the chest (4). "It was considered possible, although not certain, that these wounds were

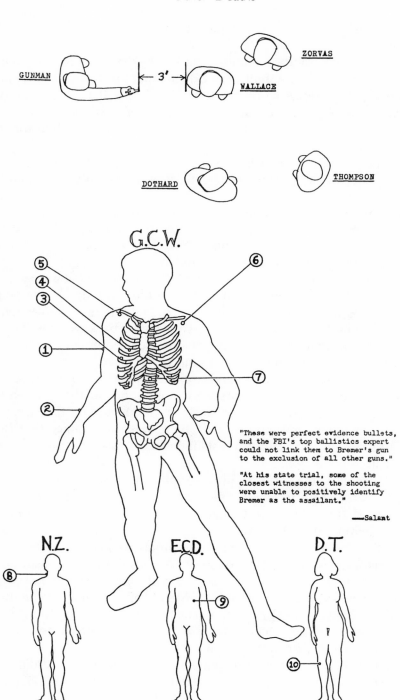

GUNMAN

WALLACE

ZORVAS

DOTHARD

THOMPSON

G.C.W.

"These were perfect evidence bullets, and the FBI's top ballistics expert could not link them to Bremer's gun to the exclusion of all other guns."

"At his state trial, some of the closest witnesses to the shooting were unable to positively identify Bremer as the assailant."

—Salant

N.Z.

E.C.D.

D.T.

caused by the same bullets that passed through the Governor's right arm."[23]

The description of the wounds gets murky from there on. Salant continues: "One of the bullets hit ligaments of the intestine and brushed the large intestine on the left side. One bullet penetrated the Governor's stomach. It was not certain which of these bullets was the one that lodged in the patient's back (7), which paralysed him for the rest of his life.

One bullet made a superficial wound of the right shoulder (5) and another bullet made a glancing superficial wound of the left shoulder blade (6).

Bullet number seven lodged against the first lumbar vertebra, just below the ribs. Dr. Schanno speculated that the bullets that caused the wounds in the governor's arm might also have entered his abdomen and chest, but he was not certain on this point."

The wounds in the right shoulder and left shoulder blade were superficial and evidently the bullets causing them did not lodge in the body.

Two bullets were removed from Wallace. He sustained four wounds of entrance and two of exit, plus the two glancing back wounds. This is at least eight wounds. Three other persons received bullets, for a total of eleven wounds. One bullet was found in the pavement.

None of the bullets was matched to the revolver found at the scene. Bremer's finger- and palm-prints were not found on the gun, which seems very strange. No evidence was presented proving that Bremer had fired the alleged weapon. In fact, there was no evidence that Bremer had fired any gun. Paraffin tests indicated to the contrary, that he had not fired a weapon.

Yet the remarkable series of photographs taken by CBS cameraman Laurens Pierce seem to clearly show Bremer repeatedly firing his gun at Wallace.[24] It would seem, though, as in some of the other cases we are investigating, that someone else was there firing at Wallace as well.

Even the Wallaces believe that a conspiracy backed up Arthur Bremer in his attempt to kill the governor. A conspirator or conspirators would most likely be those persons who had "the most to gain" from eliminating a presidential candidate, Mrs. Wallace said.[25] "But then when I saw the [Thomas] Eagleton catastrophe and some other things that happened, I think McGovern in a sense was done in, too," Mrs. Wallace told the *Christian Science Monitor.*

All sorts of dirty tricks were played on Democratic candidates in those years. Muskie found himself uncontrollably crying in Maine after apparently being sprayed with an irritating substance and made a fool of himself in a way which undoubtedly cost him a victory. Thomas Eagleton had a big thing made of his former emotional problems and had to quit as vice presidential candidate, sabotaging the McGovern candidacy.

Other Related Deaths and Disappearances

The man who died in July 1972 in Canada—Dennis Salvatore Cossini—seemed to be a double agent who was identified with Cuban intelligence, as had Frank Sturgis, a CIA operative working for Fidel Castro and later arrested as one of the Watergate burglars working for President Nixon.

Cossini was supposed to have met with Bremer in Ottawa when Nixon was staying there.

Cossini was found to have died from an overdose of heroine. The trouble is, there is no evidence that he had ever used it. His friends felt that Cossini had been killed with an injection of the junk. When he died, Cossini had a syringe, a pistol, several false draft cards, and a false Wisconsin driver's license.

Then, interestingly enough, all the records of Cossini's death in Canada disappeared. John J. McCleary, a friend whom Cossini had called not long before he died, drowned in the fall of 1972. McCleary's phone number was in Cossini's address book, and McCleary's father drowned at almost the same time, but far away.

Another close friend, Edward Contor, died within a short time of Cossini's death.

Herbert Spenner was shot to death about then. He was a beer-drinking buddy of Arthur Bremer, and headed the German-American bund in Milwaukee, which Bremer frequented.

Earl Nunnery, who said he was a witness to a conversation between Bremer and someone else, has disappeared. Another friend of Bremer's, Michael McHale, has disappeared. Bremer's friend Michael Cullen was deported to Ireland. He was supposed to be a hypnotist and "a master of behavior modification and psychological programming."[26]

Watergate-Related Deaths

James Glover and James Webster, February 1972

James Glover and James Webster were two political aides of Congressman William Mills, and were killed in a car wreck. The *Washington Post* reported on May 23, 1973, that an illegal $25,000 contribution from President Nixon's reelection campaign committee was given to Webster.

Hale Boggs, July 1972

Hale Boggs was a prominent congressman from Louisiana who confided his doubts about the findings of no conspiracy by the Warren Commission, of which he was one of the seven members. He disappeared in an airplane over Alaska one month after President Nixon's men were arrested burglarizing the Watergate. The *Los Angeles Star* reported on November 22, 1973, that "Boggs had startling revelations on Watergate and the assassination of President Kennedy."

Dorothy Hunt, December 8, 1972

Dorothy Hunt, the wife of E. Howard Hunt, had also worked for the CIA, and was an experienced agent. But by the time of her death she had about had it and announced that this would be her last trip as the "bag lady" to pay everybody off. She took off on United Airlines Flight 553 for Chicago on December 8, 1972, with a large amount of money, reputed to exceed $100,000 in cash.

The day after the crash, White House assistant Egil Krogh was made undersecretary of transportation and supervised the NTSB and FAA, which investigated the crash. A few days after that, Nixon's assistant, Alexander Butterfield, was made the head of the FAA, and a few weeks after that Nixon's appointment secretary, Dwight Chapin, was sent to Chicago to work for United Airlines.

The plane crashed in the streets of the city, and it was blamed on equipment malfunction. (See Chapter 20.)

James Krueger and Ralph Blodgett

James Krueger and Ralph Blodgett were killed in the same plane with Dorothy Hunt. They were attorneys for Northern Natural Gas. These men may have been linked to Attorney General John Mitchell and knew about stock given by the El Paso Natural Gas Company to Mitchell after his Justice Department vacated an antitrust suit against El Paso.

Blodgett told his friends before he got on the plane that he would not be alive before the day was out.

(See Chapter 20 for a more extensive treatment of this crash.)

Richard Lavoie, December 27, 1972

Richard Lavoie died of a heart attack. He was guarding Dita Beard, an employee of ITT, at a time when a vast scandal swirled around that company's payoff to Nixon's campaign chest. ITT was trying to stave off antitrust suits threatened by John Mitchell's Justice Department. When the story broke, Dita was moved from Washington to Denver, where she had a heart attack—which she survived. Howard Hunt went to see her in a disguise.[27]

President Lyndon Baines Johnson, January 20, 1973

The coincidence of President Johnson's death during a spate of Watergate-related deaths may mean nothing, but Johnson knew where the bodies were buried, and just a few weeks before he died was quoted in the *San Francisco Chronicle* as saying, "We've been running a damn Murder, Incorporated, in the Caribbean." Johnson had been making statements to reporters and friends that he believed that the CIA was involved in President Kennedy's death, and since he died, his mistress, Madeline Brown, has stated that Johnson had told her that Kennedy was going to be killed, that it would be in Dallas, and when it was going to happen.

William Mills, May 24, 1973

William Mills, a Maryland congressman, was found shot to death the day after it was revealed that he had received $25,000 from Nixon's reelection committee. He had an alleged suicide note pinned to his body.[28]

George Bell, June 30, 1973

Charles Colson, special counsel to the White House, said that George Bell, his assistant, was responsible for the "enemies list." This was a list of two hundred politicians and celebrities that Nixon considered a political threat to himself and his reputation.[29] The cause of Bell's death was not specified.

Lou Russell, July 31, 1973

Lou Russell was an old friend of Nixon's who worked for James McCord. He knew a lot, especially about call girls used in Washington for political blackmail. He supposedly died of natural causes, but again at a key time in history. See Jim Hougan's *Secret Agenda*,[30] for an extensive discussion of Lou Russell and Watergate.

Jack Cleveland, November 1973

Jack Cleveland was to be questioned about a possible payoff to the CIA industrialist billionaire Howard Hughes. Cleveland was the partner of President Nixon's brother Donald.[31] The president's family were implicated in various deals, and his nephew lived abroad with the world-class swindler Robert L. Vesco during his run from justice in the United States.

Beverly Kaye, December 1973

Beverly Kaye worked for the Secret Service in the White House and her job was, among other things, to store the tape recordings which the Secret Service made of President Nixon. She was the secretary of agent John Bull and she must have known what was on the famous "eighteen-minute gap" that Nixon's secretary, Rose Mary Woods, erased from one of the tapes. She had been telling her friends what she thought about the culpability of Nixon and his aides from what she had heard on the tapes. The eighteen-minute gap contained information about other assassinations. Kaye died in the White House of a "massive stroke" at the age of forty-two.[32]

Murry Chotiner, January 30, 1974

Murry Chotiner, an attorney for almost two hundred gangland gamblers and racketeers in Los Angeles, and long-time close associate and political fixer of Richard Nixon, died when his car was hit by a government truck. The *Los Angeles Times* claimed that Chotiner had probably received the clandestine tape recordings made by the wiretappers who had burglarized the Democratic Party headquarters in the Watergate building.[33]

José Jãoquin Sangenis Perdimo, 1974

José Perdimo, another Cuban with the code name of "Felix," with the CIA at the Bay of Pigs. He had worked with Howard Hunt and Bernard Barker.

Lee Pennington, Jr., October 1974

Two years before his death, Lee Pennington, Jr., was the CIA agent dispatched by the Agency to enter James McCord's home shortly after he was arrested in the Watergate break-in and find and destroy documents linking McCord to the CIA. Richard Helms, DCIA at the time, kept this fact a secret, but after Helms was replaced by William Colby, he told Senator Howard Baker about it.[34]

He died of an apparent heart attack.

Rolando Masferrer, October 5, 1975

Rolando Masferrer, a Cuban, was killed by a car bomb. He had worked with Howard Hunt, Frank Sturgis, and Bernard Barker, and had been employed by the CIA. He knew about assassination attempts against foreign leaders.[35]

Martha Mitchell, Memorial Day, June 1976

Only a day or two after the arrest of the burglars in the Watergate affair, which was gradually to become a nightmare that absorbed the nation until President Nixon resigned, Martha Mitchell was pushed around by security guards working for her husband, the attorney general. Her hand was slashed and her shoulder was damaged. She was forcibly injected with a drug that made her hysterical. But from that time on, she never stopped fighting, for it might be said that she brought down the president as much as anyone did.

Martha Mitchell was at first laughed at when she made her late-night drunken calls to reporters, trying desperately to tell them what was really going on. On September 10, 1973, *Newsweek* published an article called "How Much Does Martha Know?" and in it quoted Martha Mitchell as saying Nixon "planned the whole goddamned thing," referring to the Watergate break-in.

Martha called UPI reporter Helen Thomas and told her that "Nixon was a direct party to the Watergate cover-up," she said about the Watergate break-in. And another time she said "Nixon is involved with the Mafia. The Mafia was involved in his reelection campaign."

Good enough reason to be bumped off. She was kidnapped and carted off to a hospital, and after some months separated from her husband and tried to make a new life. She died a few years later at the Sloan Kettering Cancer Center in New York City of hemorrhage, with myelonoma and pneumonia. If somebody didn't help her get cancer, the strains she had lived with undoubtedly helped her along.[36]

Allard Lowenstein, March 13, 1980

I believe that the murder of Allard Lowenstein, a New York lawyer and Kennedy family friend, was engineered to frighten Ted Kennedy at a time when he had just won six of the eight crucial industrial states in the primary, and demonstrated that in spite of Chappaquiddick and all the character assassination concomitant with that tragic event would be elected president. A win of seven of the largest industrial states yields sufficient electoral votes to obtain the presidency. Illinois was not legitimately lost by Edward Kennedy due to the fact that John Anderson changed parties, ran as an independent, and split the vote three ways. The only state Kennedy legitimately lost was Ohio, traditionally written in stone as a rock-ribbed Republican state during the reign of the Tafts there.

Lowenstein wrote that "it took Watergate and the discoveries that I was seventh on Nixon's enemies list and that even Government agencies had taken an improper interest in my affairs to persuade me to look into the assassinations: If obscure people had been singled out for illegal attention, why was it unthinkable that some of our important leaders might also be singled out for illegal attention by someone?"[37]

In this regard, it might be mentioned that Herbert Mitgang wrote a most important article in *The New Yorker* some years ago, called "The Policing of America's Writers,"[38] and it can be mentioned that in the murders of Robert and John Kennedy and that of Martin Luther King, Jr., police are implicated as participants. In spite of all the progress America has made in combatting racism, it is still a serious problem. The fact is that racism is deeply rooted in some of America's police, and that any liberal who speaks for better treatment of minorities is a target and on somebody's list.

FBI Deaths

In addition to the death of J. Edgar Hoover, a spate of expirations took place in 1977. All were deeply involved in the investigation of President Kennedy's murder. And, it is important to note, all these deaths took place when the House Assassinations Committee had been set up to investigate the murder of Dr. Martin Luther King, Jr., and that of

President John F. Kennedy. Numerous witnesses started dying very quickly, too, as fast as the House investigators found them—some on the same day, as did George DeMohrenschildt, Oswald's close friend, and Mafia kingpins Sam Giancana, Charles Nicoletti, and Johnny Roselli. All might have been presumed to shed some light on the investigation, including and especially the FBI men. Once again we are faced with the question: "Is it coincidence, or conspiracy?" to paraphrase the title of Bernard Fensterwald's excellent book.

First of all, we are not in a position to determine if the deaths of the FBI men were murders. In the case of the murder of a great public figure such as President Kennedy and some of the others mentioned above, a certain amount of evidence is released, or surfaces, to satisfy, scare, or confuse the rest of us. But when obscure bureaucrats die, even those high up in some agency, very little investigation or evidence—if any—might be available. All we have are patterns.

William Sullivan

In the case of the high command of the FBI, six agents died in six months, and one of them, William Sullivan, died by gunshot, though it was put down as a "hunting accident." Sullivan was head of the Bureau's counterespionage section in 1963. According to journalist Jim Marrs, the counterespionage section included assassinations among its duties.[39] We are reminded of the FBI's assault on Martin Luther King, Jr., and admitted murders by G. Gordon Liddy when he worked for the FBI.

Less than two weeks after John Kennedy died, Sullivan sent a memo saying that there was no evidence that Lee Harvey Oswald was put up to the killing in any way by a foreign country, including Castro's Cuba.[40] The possible importance of this lies in the fact that a great deal of effort was going into a project to make Oswald look like a Cuban or Russian agent, and this continued for many years until the fallback position of Oswald as Mob agent became de riguer. But in the days immediately after the assassination, numerous false stories were planted linking Oswald to foreign powers or agents. The fact that a high-ranking official of the FBI—Sullivan—and undoubtedly others were not duped by this disinformation campaign of renegade CIA agents certainly put them in a bad light with the conspirators, and when Congress threatened to have a real investigation of the crimes thirteen years later, Sullivan and the others in the FBI who died might have paid for their integrity in this matter.

A few random deaths among FBI members at the time of the new congressional investigation, deaths of persons who were connected to the investigation of the assassination, certainly would—like the deaths of numerous Dallas witnesses—scare others into silence or perjury.

Hoover had been against the idea of the Warren Commission all along and had told that to Sullivan and two other aides, according to the Senate Intelligence Committee in 1976. The committee's report quoted Hoover as saying: "The thing I am most concerned about . . . is having something issued so we can convince the public that Oswald is the real assassin." What did he mean by "real"? If Oswald didn't do it, then who did Hoover think did it?

Sullivan became unhappy with Hoover, and in 1971 this dissatisfaction came to a head, according to Jim Marrs in the Fort Worth *Star-Telegram* of November 10, 1977, when Sullivan came to work to find Hoover had locked him out of his office. Sullivan had told the Intelligence committee not so long before he died that Hoover had leaked the secret FBI report on JFK's death to "blunt the drive for an independent investigation of the assassination."

Sullivan's name repeatedly came up on the White House tapes made by President Nixon and his men discussing their displeasure with the information Sullivan provided about political surveillance ordered by Johnson and Kennedy.

Sullivan told the Intelligence committee, headed by Senator Frank Church: "Never once did I hear anybody, including myself, raise the question, 'Is this course of action which we have agreed upon lawful, is it legal, is it ethical or moral?' We never gave any thought to this line of reasoning because we were just naturally pragmatic."

He told the *Los Angeles Times* in 1973 that "J. Edgar Hoover was a 'master blackmailer.' He suggested that the director had lost control of himself and was verging on senility before his death. A year later Mr. Sullivan submitted a paper to a meeting of the Roscoe Pound–American Trial Lawyers Foundation in which he said that the FBI, as then organized, posed a threat to the civil liberties of the country.

"The weaknesses of the FBI have always been the leadership in Washington, of which I was a part for fifteen years," he wrote. "I accept my share of the blame for its serious shortcomings."[41]

Sullivan had also stated that radical groups such as the Weathermen were far more of a threat to the United States than domestic Communists. This got him into deep trouble with Hoover, who depended on hyping up the Communist menace to obtain large funding for his budget. We also know that Hoover tried to pretend that organized crime did not exist in the United States, another one of those contradictions in terms.

Sullivan, who headed up the JFK assassination investigation for the FBI, mistaken for a deer, was shot and killed by the son of a New Hampshire state policeman on July 16, 1978.[42]

Regis Kennedy died shortly after he was interviewed by the House Assassinations Committee in 1978. Kennedy had a most interesting involvement in the investigation of the assassination of President Kennedy, being the FBI agent who interviewed David Ferrie in jail shortly after he was arrested November 24, 1963, and alibied him.[43] He protected Carlos Marcello, saying that he was just a "tomato salesman." Gary Shaw showed a large number of "mug" shots to Beverly Oliver, and she identified Kennedy from them as being the FBI agent who took her movie camera and film away from her the day after the assassination.

Louis Nichols was seventy-one when he died in June 1977 of a heart attack. He was the number three man under Hoover.[44]

Alan H. Belmont was seventy and a former assistant to Hoover and testified to the Warren Commission. He died after "a long illness" in August 1977.[45]

James C. Cadigan was sixty when he died after a fall in his home, according to the *Washington Post*. He was a document expert who testified to the Warren Commission.[46]

Donald W. Kaylor died of a heart attack at age fifty. He was a chemist in the fingerprint section of the FBI.[47]

J. M. English, who also died of a heart attack, was an agent involved in the investigation of Kennedy's death.[48]

Clyde Tolson, Hoover's companion and a top official at the FBI, died in 1975 when the issues of numerous political murders and foreign assassinations were in the news every day and major investigations were being conducted by the Senate Intelligence Committee. Cause of death unknown.

More Attempted Assassinations

Gerald Ford

The first question is, how come Lynette "Squeaky" Fromme wasn't being watched? Fromme was the girl who took a shot at President Gerald Ford in Sacramento on September 5, 1975, during his short presidency. She was also a key member of the Charles Manson ghoul family, and along with Sandra Goode were about the last remaining hard-core members who had not regretted their association with Manson. Manson had been captured after his followers had murdered and mutilated the pregnant actress and lover of director Roman Polanski, Sharon Tate, and several others. Some say the group committed as many as thirty-five killings.[49]

Squeaky Fromme had gone to the offices of the *Sacramento Bee* not long before Ford's visit and asked them to print a letter from Manson saying that if Gerald Ford continued to violate the law, there would be a massacre. The newspaper gave it to the police, who shared it with the Secret Service.[50]

Nothing happened. The Secret Service did not interview Fromme. When Ford came to town, she put on a flaming red robe and came up to within two feet of Ford and shot at him. Where was the Secret Service then? An agent grabbed the gun from her, but anyone would have tried to do that. How come she got so close?

To quote Vincent Bugliosi, the former district attorney who put Manson away: "The Sara Jane Moore incident spotlighted the Secret Service's utter incompetence even more than the Fromme case. A week after Squeaky's attempted assassination, the president goes to San Francisco, where Sara Jane Moore had already called inspector Jack O'Keefe of the San Francisco police department to say that she was inclined to test the presidential security system when Ford appeared at Stanford on Sunday. The police placed her under arrest, seized her gun —a .44-caliber automatic—and then told the Secret Service about her. The Secret Service checked on Sara Jane Moore and concluded she wasn't going to do anything because she'd been an informant for the

FBI." The San Francisco police said they would keep her in jail until Ford left, but the Secret Service said to let her go.

The next day she shot at Ford.

Ronald Reagan

One more lone gunman—John Hinckley—emptied his gun from close range at President Ronald Reagan two months after he took office. If we add up all the bullets that seem to have been shot from the gun, all the wounds suffered by five people, we get more bullets than were in his gun.[51]

John Hinckley had spent the previous night in a hotel across from Secret Service headquarters which was crawling with agents. Hinckley's brother knew George Bush's son quite well and was going to have dinner with him the next night, the night after Hinckley shot President Reagan.[52] There are a lot of questions about this event that have never been asked.

The newspapers made it clear that Hinckley had three different guns, including a .45. If he had planned to kill Reagan, he would have used that gun, and not a .22.[53] Evidently, somebody wanted only to scare Reagan, who would not have been struck, but a bullet ricocheted off his car and hit him.

Reagan had begun a retreat from the tough policies announced in his campaign, but he became very hard-line on his foreign policy after that, and systematically began ruining the American economy, which serves certain interests quite well, but not that of the nation or the world in general.

The real bottom line of American political history for the past century and a quarter or more is that the elected government both on the national and local level is a charade. Powerful men unafraid to use violence to intimidate or kill any elected official and terrorize the rest run this country. They have insured that the Secret Service itself cannot do its job, and each president who comes into power has certain experiences, violent and nonviolent, that right away tell him where the real power is. He has to go along with the program.

Each official of any significance has a loaded gun at his head, and is the victim of his own guards. In Byzantium, the sultan's guards became his keepers.

Our government is the second oldest significant one on the face of the earth, after Great Britain. Nothing is as it appears. The idea with which we are raised, that the government is true to its citizens, began to erode strongly with the Warren Report, the Gulf of Tonkin incident, and Watergate. This progressive loss of trust continues to the present, and little of what we are told can be believed. There are layers and layers of meaning behind each act or public statement. "Watch what we do, not what we say," the Nixon gang alerted us.

CHAPTER 20

NIXON AND WATERGATE

I feel that the real reason Nixon was pursued over the Watergate break-
ins was that there were a series of murders connected with Richard
Nixon's presidency.

Not only was the liberal-centrist leadership that represented the majority of Americans crippled, but numerous others—witnesses, journalists,
lawyers, bureaucrats, and ordinary people were liquidated. Some of
these deaths were discussed in Chapter 19. Watergate itself saw a number of deaths, including an entire planeload of people in a crash onto
the streets of Chicago under very strange circumstances.

The natural liberal impulse of most enlightened and educated people
—of fair play for our fellow man—was all but extinguished after years
of slander and smear aimed at associating the majority liberal-centrist
population of the United States with the left and with communism.
Nothing could have been farther from the truth, but the center core of
this nation was up against propaganda specialists trained in smear techniques and murder aimed at foreign targets by our intelligence agencies
in a period when they were out of control and shot full of renegades,
often in the pocket of private industrialists with their own radical, simplistic, uninformed, and dangerous agendas.

The philosophy of putting the state above the individual was of
course anathema to America's majority liberals, but we also—as a nation—have a tradition of public service and charity. President Ken-

nedy's inaugural dictum that we should dedicate ourselves to public service was in keeping with this philosophy, but there was another, selfish, and radical imperative in the shadows that would surface in the "me" generation providing a mask for corporate consolidation of our lives beneath massive power which usurped the authority of the state. In other words, free enterprise and rugged individualism is as much a con game as is the Statue of Liberty for so many oppressed people in the U.S. The totems of our country, free enterprise and individualism, are a mask for what has become bank and corporate control of our lives. The corporations are the new state. There is increasingly less chance for anyone to attempt or achieve what we always called the American Dream.

Richard Nixon's presidency laid the groundwork for turning back the clock, for overthrowing the very liberalism that asked us to be constructively charitable to the downtrodden in our country, and for paving the way for a now-entrenched corporate society.

The liberal movement in the United States never really recovered from the assault that began with Nixon's ascendancy, and has been on the defensive ever since. At the time, the number of Republicans had declined to a small percent of those registered to vote, and yet Ronald Reagan was elected. Why?

The Democratic Party had been co-opted by its enemies, and only the weakest candidates could be put forth. This was, quite simply, due to intelligence agency techniques long tested abroad against other political parties and then applied here. After all, for the doubter, Nixon's campaign was run by these same intelligence agency operatives who had been employed by the Committee to Reelect the President.

American party politics had become a charade by then, a charade without meaning. The budgets for the political and social programs enacted by the liberals were raided and padded by secret agencies who concealed their own vast fiscal requirements in Health, Education, and Welfare, the U.S. Forest Service, the Environmental Protection Agency, and so forth. There are agencies the public doesn't even know about.

Ronald Reagan ruined the nation's economy. He was elected with a lie: to balance the budget. Reagan, a puppet of banking and financial interests more interested in promoting defense industry failures than weapons that worked, took America to the edge of financial ruin. The

United States, thanks to Ronald Reagan, became and remains the world's leading debtor nation. To a certain extent we have become an economic colony of the western world.

But the main point of this chapter is to show the groundwork that was laid for such economic destruction of America's industrial base. That has its source in Nixon's presidency and John Kennedy's murder, when the liberal majority leadership was decimated. The Democratic Party, by far the majority party, could no longer lead. It was subverted and its leadership manipulated, controlled, and finally so weakened that the party was ravaged by internal dissent, and the presidential candidates it put forward were the weakest available.

The one job left for America at the end of the century was world cop. We all know what the average person thinks of cops. They aren't highly respected, and they don't always feel so good about themselves and their work because of it. They see things in black and white, and they don't always see their own faults.

Watergate and Nixon not only began to turn back the clock and attack the liberalism that had fought racism, ignorance, and economic oppression so effectively, but eventually began to defeat it. Americans are now being reduced to a service-oriented economy founded on the minimum wage. Many young people have no hope of owning their own homes, their own businesses, or their own farms, and that was traditionally the foundation of a strong nation.

Flight 553

On Friday, December 8, 1972, a United Airlines plane took off from Washington National Airport for Chicago. It was a few months since E. Howard Hunt, the former CIA agent, broke into the campaign headquarters of the Democratic Party at the Watergate.

The plane carried an interesting bunch of people. Not everyone died when Flight 553 crashed on the streets of Chicago, but the principals in the cast did die. Among them were Howard Hunt's wife, Dorothy, Congressman George Collins, who was linked to the oil companies connected to Nixon's scandal, Michelle Clark, a CBS correspondent, and several attorneys.

A bitter pattern of events underlies this period of American history. There were repeated political assassinations; the death of numerous witnesses in each case; stolen, planted, or forged evidence; deliberate official cover-up, as well as distortion by the media.

E. Howard Hunt had been indicted some months before for the Watergate burglary, and was not allowed to travel, so he sent his wife, also a former CIA operative, to pay off the Cubans who were involved in the Watergate plot. We might recall that certain Cubans involved in the Bay of Pigs operation were implicated in the assassination of President Kennedy, and Howard Hunt knew nearly all the Cubans active in this country who had been involved in it.

It is clear that much of the scandal over the Watergate break-in that forced Nixon to resign revolved around political assassination. John Ehrlichman, H.R. Haldeman, and others indicated this in their writings, which seem greatly censored (sometimes self-censored), even today.

Roy H. Sheppard, a federal employee, had received Hunt's papers and stored them just after Hunt's arrest. Then shortly before Dorothy took off for Chicago, UPI reported that Sheppard had burned the papers. Jack Anderson reported that that was not the truth, and that the papers had been returned to Hunt in August 1972.

It is believed that Dorothy Hunt carried with her on that trip some of the most damaging documents, and that is why the plane was brought down. Ask anyone who lived in Chicago then.

There were sixty-one people and six crew members on the plane, a Boeing 737. And, surely, the plane was *sabotaged*. This is the evidence.

One of the other significant people on that plane was Harold Metcalf, an agent with Nixon's newly created drug task force, DALE (Drug Abuse Law Enforcement). He carried a gun, which he told the captain about. Metcalf sat in the very rear of the plane.

Congressman George Collins was also on the plane. He had been questioned by CBS correspondent Michelle Clark soon after the Watergate arrests that summer, to see what he might be able to tell her about the break-in.

And there were two lawyers for Omaha's Northern Natural Gas Company, Ralph Blodgett and James W. Krueger. Connected with them were Wilbur Erickson, president of the Federal Land Bank of Omaha, and Lon Bayer, attorney for the Kansas-Nebraska Natural Gas Company.

Officials of the Omaha gas company had been indicted three months before, charged with bribing local officials to put through a gas line in Illinois and Indiana. The company fought back with papers that apparently blackmailed Attorney General John Mitchell, a very close friend of the president. These "Mitchell papers" "purported to reveal illegal acts of conspiracy between former Attorney General John Mitchell and the Justice Department with Northern's fiercest competitor, the El Paso Natural Gas Company (which employed Mitchell's law firm), along the lines of the ITT scandal,"[1] which so severely damaged the Nixon presidency—along with Watergate.

Charges against El Paso were dropped. At the same time, "Mitchell, through a law partner as nominee, received stock interest in El Paso." El Paso then contributed heavily to Nixon's campaign for reelection. "The favorable decision to drop antitrust charges was worth an estimated $300 million to El Paso."[2]

Northern's lawyers had been "warned that they would never live to reach Chicago."[3]

Dorothy Hunt wasn't traveling alone on that plane either. With her was Michelle Clark of CBS.

"Michelle Clark had learned from her inside sources that the Hunts might be getting ready to 'blow the White House out of the water,' and that before Howard Hunt was hung out to twist slowly in the breeze he would 'bring down every tree in the forest.' "[4]

James McCord, Hunt's co-conspirator, testified that by the time of Dorothy Hunt's trip, things had reached a crisis, and that "Mrs. Hunt was unhappy with her job going all over the country to bribe defendants and witnesses in the bugging case. She wanted out."[5] Hunt was uneasy and wanted confirmation that he would get executive clemency and sufficient money to cushion any punishment that would befall him, according to Barboura Freed.

It was cloudy over Chicago when Flight 553 made its approach. The air controllers never warned the plane that it was coming in too rapidly, according to the available evidence. The plane was flying thirty knots too fast, which may or may not have been a factor. The approach controller "forgot" to give the plane a "cleared approach" as well.

Freed writes: "In the absence of clearance, any experienced pilot would normally hold at some fix and maintain his last assigned altitude" until told it was safe to come down. Instead, the plane stayed on its course for a landing at Midway. The pilot, Captain Wendell L. Whitehouse, was a very experienced captain, with eighteen thousand flying hours. Something had gone wrong.

Flight 553 was then passed from the controllers at O'Hare to those at Midway, about nine miles from the airport. Official reports placed the hand-off at 5.3 nautical miles out, but unpublished official documentation placed the hand-off at 8.9 miles from the airport. "O'Hare approach control had made a premature hand-off, and from the evidence they did so without giving Midway any information on 553's excessive speed or other in-flight factors."

Investigators found that Midway gave two contradictory orders within seconds: They told 553 to keep coming in for a landing, and at the same time they told O'Hare they were sending her around a second time.

Midway had little modern equipment such as that at O'Hare, and the runway that 553 was to come in on was suddenly changed to one without any glidescope or precision radar at all, at the opposite end of the field. Flight 553 had no way of knowing its height and angle. There was a "localizer"—a signal the plane received that gave its flight path to the pilots in relation to the runway, but just as the plane was headed down, "the localizer either stopped working or was somehow lost to the aircraft."

No one knows why the plane was redirected to another runway as it was coming in. There were no winds that could affect a landing, and no reason that anyone can think of to explain this.

Captain Whitehouse radioed: "Is Kedzie Localizer off . . . off the air, is that it?"

Both this radio request and another are not in the official reports. Buried in the fine print of the NTSB (National Transportation Safety Board) report was the fact that the Kedzie Outer Marker was turned off, which would have told the plane exactly where it was through the clouds more than three miles from the runway.

According to Midway, they waved off 553 for fear it would hit a small plane that was trying to land. They said they did this 3.3 nautical miles out. Later they said they did it just before 553 disappeared from their radar screens.

The plane came out beneath the clouds 1.7 miles from the runway, but far wide of it. A stewardess screamed, "Get down in a crouch!"

"The nose of the Boeing 737 'pitched up'; the engines wound laboriously; 'spooling up,' the aircraft 'stalled,' suspended in midair, shuddering in its death throes. Then Flight 553 plummeted to earth 1.5 nautical miles on the southeast course to Midway, in a working-class neighborhood of one-story bungalows," writes Freed. The plane crashed at 2:29 P.M., and from that moment on, the FBI was in charge of the crash site for the first time in history. Not the FAA (Federal Aviation Agency) or the NTSB.

There was no distress call from the plane before the crash. Nothing. A ham operator claimed to have overheard the pilot accusing the control tower of gross error and sabotage before the plane went down.

The crashing plane cut through phone and electrical lines, blacking out the entire area, which was—some might say—conveniently cut off from the outside world. But the plane came in on its belly in the middle of the city, and everyone did not die. Some passengers survived to tell the story.

There was an "almost immediate materialization of 'police,' using the easiest and most practical synonym for plainclothes official-looking strangers."[6] This matter was thoroughly researched in Chicago by Citizens' Committee to Clean up the Courts (CCCC) investigator Sherman Skolnick and others. Something very strange began to happen when that plane came down.

"Witnesses living in the crash zone told of 'FBI types' parked on side streets in unmarked cars, and of others arriving at the time of the crash. These 'officials' were in the crash area before the fire department, which received a '3-11' call within one minute of the crash—even though all telephone lines in the area were down."

We all know what sophisticated military hardware can do. Smart bombs can come in the garage door, hang a right, and enter the side window of the car door. We undoubtedly can cause an airliner to nose up, stall out, and come down where we have men waiting to locate the documents they want at the crash scene.

Local investigators, led by the CCCC—famous in the Chicago area— who at one time brought down the governor of the state, charged that immediately after the crash, over 200 FBI and DIA (Defense Intelligence Agency) men came in and took over the area. None showed credentials when asked by local police or anyone else. The head of the NTSB, John Reed, testified that he had complained to the FBI because FBI agents had taken over their job in the crash and were interviewing witnesses before the NTSB could, and had listened to the tower tapes before anyone else, and then *confiscated* the tapes! We know from the John F. Kennedy murder that as soon as federal agents intervened, witnesses refused to talk to others, and evidence was thereafter compartmentalized and buried.

Chairman Reed indicated to the FBI that in view of the death of Dorothy Hunt, the above constituted suspicious behavior, and "has raised innumerable questions in the minds of those with legitimate interests in ascertaining the cause of this accident."

At first the FBI said that only a dozen agents had been involved, but later they said that fifty were on the crash scene. William Ruckelshaus, the former acting director of the FBI, admitted that they had done all of the above. Ruckelshaus told the *Washington Post* on June 14, 1973, that in cases of possible sabotage the FBI had primary jurisdiction.

The FBI at the time of the crash was directed by L. Patrick Gray, an otherwise unblemished man who had gotten into some trouble helping to cover up the Watergate crimes. It would clearly appear that the FBI had prior information that Flight 553 was going to be sabotaged. No one has been able to find out if that is true.

There are never fifty FBI agents available at one time without prior arrangement. The FBI office was forty minutes away from the crash site. Local authorities and police "who were initially no more than half a minute away found the FBI already at the crash." They reported that the FBI did not want their help and sent them away from the center of the crash site.

It is then reported that the FBI interfered with rescue teams. "They kept a medical team away from the plane, even though a member of the team swore that he had heard someone in the crash screaming. The FBI had the least-injured persons evacuated from the crash area first, contrary to established practice of speeding the most injured to possible life-saving medical treatment. FBI agents, not medics, separated the dead from the living and stripped the dead of all belongings and identification."[7] These boys must have trained in Iraq.

We are reminded of the men with phony Secret Service credentials on the Grassy Knoll on November 22, 1963, when John Kennedy was murdered.

"The FBI cordon was complete, but one man managed to penetrate it—an executive aide to Congressman George Collins, one of the passengers. The aide happened to have some old military ID on him. Once on the inside, he claims that he saw a man in coveralls climbing out of the split fuselage of the Boeing 737. The aide recognized the man as an operative of the CIA. Other witnesses claimed to have seen operatives of the Defense Intelligence Agency."

Interestingly (and tragically), the Operation Gemstone charts which E. Howard Hunt and G. Gordon Liddy had designed "diagrammed the illegal manipulation of flight communications and electronic signals."

As Barboura Freed wrote, did Dorothy Hunt think of those Gemstone charts as that plane went down, or "did she think of the other Watergate women victims and what had happened to them: Martha Mitchell, drugged, kicked, and held captive beyond even the control of her powerful husband, and Dita Beard, kidnapped and drugged by Liddy and interrogated for hours on end by Howard Hunt. Poor Dita Beard, who had suffered a 'heart attack' on another United Airlines flight between Dulles and Denver."[8] Dorothy Hunt was now very dead. The federal drug agent sitting in the back of the plane, Harold Metcalf, survived.

Charles Colson, President Nixon's counsel told *Time* magazine: "I think they killed Dorothy Hunt."[9] Colson, perhaps the most vicious of them (if that was possible) changed after that and got religion.

Ten thousand dollars was found in Dorothy's purse, according to the officials quoted in the press. Hunt claimed that she was taking it to her cousin to invest. Other reports make it well past $100,000. Her husband collected a quarter of a million dollars' insurance on his wife.

The day after the crash the former head of Nixon's "plumber's" unit —Egil Krogh, Jr.—which employed Howard Hunt, was made undersecretary of transportation. "This put Krogh in a position to supervise the National Transportation Safety Board and the Federal Aviation Agency —the quasi-independent agencies authorized to investigate airline crashes." Of course this did not make the news.

Krogh later went to jail for burglarizing the offices of Daniel Ellsberg's psychiatrist. This was part of Nixon's "dirty tricks," for which he was forced to resign. When the Watergate scandal forced Krogh to resign, "witnesses before the Senate Commerce Committee would testify that Krogh played a leading role in at least one attempt to intimidate members of the National Transportation Safety Board during the time they were investigating the Midway crash."[10]

"Egil Krogh was only the first of the Watergate personalities to move into a post from which he could oversee the investigation. The second was Alexander Butterfield, 'ex' CIA, secretary to the Cabinet, the White House aide in charge of secretly taping presidential conversations and telephone calls, and the one who revealed the existence of those secret tapes to the Senate Watergate Committee. On December 19, 1972, President Nixon named Butterfield head of the Federal Aviation Agency."[11]

Then Dwight Chapin, Nixon's appointments secretary and dirty tricks supervisor, was made an executive in the Chicago office of United Airlines in January 1973. Shortly thereafter, in February, "according to consumer advocates there, he warned the media to steer clear of any question of foul play in the crash or any hint of a cover-up by the NTSB, FAA, Boeing Aircraft, Pratt-Whitney, or United Airlines. If the newsmen failed to obey, Chapin threatened to use Nixon's communications czar Clay Whitehead to break up the networks. United had already prohibited its own employees from talking and had refused immediately after the crash to release information or even to disclose the home addresses of its crew members."

Herbert W. Kalmbach, Nixon's personal lawyer and Gemstone bagman, had worked for United Airlines. He was also the lawyer for Marriott, which catered the food and drinks for the plane. Marriott's exec VP was the president's brother, Donald.

The NTSB blamed the captain and his two copilots. It went down as "pilot error." But before that the NTSB thought that the plane had stalled. It wasn't clear how this could happen in level flight in that situation though. Captain Whitehouse was known as one of the best pilots there was, and he was also an experienced stunt pilot.

Nothing much could be learned from the tapes. It took four days to clean the oil from the flight recorder. "Had the tape been broadly edited and left purposely incomplete?" Barboura Freed asks. Any information that would have given a clue as to the cause of the crash was missing from the tapes.

The *Chicago Tribune* reported that the tail flight recorder had stopped recording fourteen minutes before the crash. How could this happen? And how could it have been found by sanitation workers, whose commissioner had given it to the NTSB? "It was hardly possible that the well-made, highly insulated, tightly secured instruments—built to survive far worse crashes—had been loose, just lying in the street to be swept up by custodians. Had the commissioner gotten them from someone else, possibly the FBI?" Freed asks.

A week after the crash an FAA employee telephoned Sherman Skolnick, investigator for the CCCC, paralyzed and confined to a wheelchair. "I'm calling you from Midway Airport. Flight 553 was sabotaged. I'm risking my life to tell you . . . you better get your group working on this—people were murdered." Skolnick then received 1300 pages from the official crash file of the NTSB on the flight. In order to account for the documentation, he publicly said that he had stolen them, which everyone knew was impossible because of his handicap.

Perhaps the key to this puzzle is a document that said that the pilot's body had contained a high count of cyanide, four times more than he could have breathed from burning cabin plastic before dying, which is the way most victims of air crashes expire. In addition, five other passengers also had breathed too much cyanide before dying. Skolnick charged that CBS had demanded Michelle Clark's body for immediate cremation for this reason. He claimed that the pilot was not at the controls when the plane went down. Why?

The NTSB got its own expert, Dr. Paul W. Smith of Oklahoma City, who claimed that the Cook County coroner had made a mistake in his calculation of the cyanide found in the bodies. He said that the cyanide count in the blood of the pilot was only 3.9 micrograms per milliliter. "But Dr. Smith admitted that this *was the highest blood-cyanide reading he had ever recorded in a crash victim.*"[12]

Investigators working for Skolnick's group, Alex J. Bottos and Joseph Zale, were also coordinating with the Justice Department's Organized Crime Strike Force. Two days after the crash they were startled to see things taken from the plane in the possession of the Sarelli mob: $40,000 more of Dorothy Hunt's money and the infamous "Mitchell Papers" taken from Krueger's suitcase.

Bottos "claimed also to have seen $2 million in American Express money orders, traveler's checks, and postal money orders drawn on the National City Bank of New York. Also, invaluable written evidence of executive 'high crimes' abstracted from E. Howard Hunt's eight cartons of 'White House Horrors,' that included *pre*-Watergate complicity in assassinations in both North and South America and plans for future Gemstone operations. Bottos was not allowed to testify to any of this at the crash-cause hearing."[13]

"Was it Hunt and Carlstead who had given the Sarelli mob a post-crash contract to get the 'Hunt Papers' and valuables?" asks Freed. It was rumored that the papers were fenced for $5 million. Who bought? Nixon and El Paso Natural Gas?

What did happen was that Bottos was arrested and sent to what Jack Anderson calls the federal political prison in Springfield, Missouri, on April 9, 1973. He was released forty days later after intense inquiries by his former employer, the Indiana Crime Commission. The ICC then called a press conference and accused the Organized Crime Strike Force of fraud for silencing its own witness.

Before this had happened, Bottos had confronted Harold Metcalf, the federal agent who survived the crash, in a safe house in Indiana. "Did you know the plane was sabotaged?" He didn't get an answer, and Metcalf fled after indicating the plane was not supposed to have been sabotaged but implying something went wrong. He ran away before he said anything more.

The final NTSB Blue Book Report did not clarify anything. It was not clear as to whether the plane had been waved off and was making a second approach, for instance. And, as Barboura Freed writes: "Even if 553's speed had been sufficiently slow over a period of time long enough to trigger the onset of the stickshaker stall warning, the pilots could not fail to respond. The signals are so startling that only the unconscious could miss them. . . . NTSB could not prove that enough time had elapsed for 553's entry into a stall regime in level flight.

"Quite possibly, 553 had suffered aircraft malfunction or sabotage while still up in the cloud cover, and then rapidly descended, disoriented, and imbalanced. What ground witnesses and passengers described as a 'climb and stall' at 1.7 nautical miles out might have been only the end result of trouble—the doomed twin engine aircraft making a brief rally for control and balance before continuing its fall to the ground.

"Equally possibly, 553 could have suffered mechanical malfunction or sabotage after emerging below the clouds. But if all were well and its brief climb characteristic of an ascent from an untroubled final approach, why did its nose tip up so steeply? Why did its engines wind 'laboriously'? Why did the missed approach maneuver not succeed? And why was 553 fourteen blocks far wide to the right of runway 31-L when 'wave-off instructions for a missed approach from 31-L call for a left turn to 180° and a climb to two thousand feet?"[14]

Thomas Togas, a witness on the ground, had first said that "I heard a boom, looked into the sky, and saw the plane with one engine apparently ablaze. It was about two hundred feet high at the time and had not yet hit any buildings or trees. I recognized it as a 737. I used to fuel those planes at Midway." The newspapers got back to Togas a few days later and distorted what he had said so that it didn't sound like something had happened to the plane *before* it went down.

Freed suggest that a pressure detonator was used to bring the plane down. What we have here, as she says, is a cover-up and we can't have a cover-up without a crime.

On June 24, 1974, the *Washington Post* quoted Charles Colson as saying that Richard Nixon was a prisoner of the CIA, in the White House, something that John Ehrlichman (Nixon's number two assistant after

Vice President Lyndon Johnson, Attorney General Robert Kennedy, and President John F. Kennedy

South Vietnam President Ngo Dinh Diem, center, talks with General
Maxwell D. Taylor, and U.S. Ambassador Frederick Nolting at his
Saigon palace September 11, 1962.
AP / WIDE WORLD PHOTOS

Undersecretary of State George Ball, right, and Secretary of Defense
Robert McNamara brief reporters at the Pentagon.
AP / WIDE WORLD PHOTOS

Dean Rusk, Secretary of State during the Kennedy and Johnson administrations.
AP / WIDE WORLD PHOTOS

President-elect Kennedy with his soon-to-be Secretary of Defense Robert McNamara, the youthful president of the Ford Motor Company, December 13, 1960.
UPI / BETTMANN

**Senator John F. Kennedy after his spinal operation in December
1954 leaves the New York hospital accompanied by his wife for a
flight to Palm Beach, Florida, and several months of recuperation.**
AP / WIDE WORLD PHOTOS

Watergate burglar E. Howard Hunt embraces Cuban exile Manuel Artime, a leader of the ill-fated Bay of Pigs invasion.

G. Gordon Liddy showing off a German Luger.

**Martin Luther King, Jr., addresses thousands of participants in the
"March on Washington" who had gathered in front of the Lincoln
Memorial on August 28, 1963.**
AP / WIDE WORLD PHOTOS

Martin Luther King, Jr., on the same balcony of the Memphis motel where he was shot by an assassin. This photograph was taken Wednesday, April 3, the day before the shooting. Standing next to King, tieless, is Jesse Jackson. At right is the Reverend Ralph Abernathy.
AP / WIDE WORLD PHOTOS

James Earl Ray following his capture after he and five other inmates escaped from prison in June 1977.
AP / WIDE WORLD PHOTOS

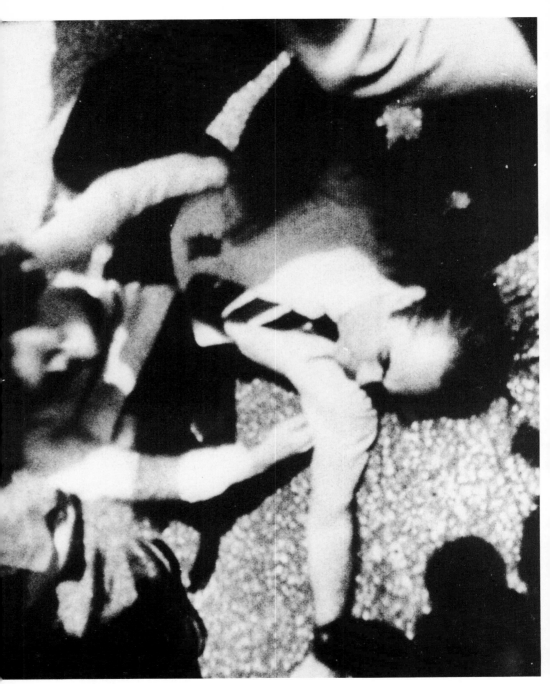

**Alabama Governor George Wallace lies on the ground after being
shot at a political rally in Laurel, Maryland, on May 15, 1972. Mrs.
Wallace is kneeling over her husband. The dark spot on Wallace's
shirt is a blood stain.**

Arthur Bremer is taken into custody by police officers moments after shooting Alabama Governor George Wallace in Laurel, Maryland.
AP / WIDE WORLD PHOTOS

New Orleans District Attorney Jim Garrison at a 1968 press conference.
AP / WIDE WORLD PHOTOS

Director Oliver Stone on the set of the movie *JFK* in Dallas during the filming in April 1991.
AP / WIDE WORLD PHOTOS

The Dallas Conference. This was the first time witnesses who were at the autopsy of President Kennedy at Bethesda Naval Hospital were brought together with witnesses from Parkland. Left to right: Floyd Riebe, Paul O'Connor, James Curtis Jenkins, Harrison E. Livingstone, Aubrey Rike, Dr. Robert McClelland, Nurse Audrey Bell, and Dr. Phillip Williams.
PHOTO COURTESY OF AL FISHER, FISHER PRODUCTION GROUP

H. R. Haldeman) outlined in his novel, *The Company*. Colson told *Time* that "I think they killed Dorothy Hunt."

Colson pursued a life of charitable and religious activities and work with a prison ministries organization after his close brush with power in the Nixon White House. At the time his repentance and newfound faith was not entirely believable and was viewed as one means of getting out of a much stiffer sentence for perhaps more crimes than he was publicly known to have committed. It might be suggested from his activities that he not only suffered from a great deal of guilt and a conscience (something rather rare in that gang), but also had a very close shave himself with the ultimate.

It was CIA director Richard Helms that pushed Robert Mullen to hire Howard Hunt. Nixon was upset about this. Helms was the liaison between the Warren Commission and the CIA, and if anyone was in a position to cover up the real nature of John Kennedy's assassination, and, for exile Cuban complicity, the CIA's assassination plots against Castro, it was Helms, according to the House Select Committee on Assassinations.[15]

Forty-five people died in the crash of Flight 553.

"However close we sometimes seem to that dark and final abyss, let no man of peace and freedom despair. For he does not stand alone. If we all can persevere, if we can in every land and office look beyond our own shores and ambitions, then surely the age will dawn in which the strong are just and the weak secure and the peace preserved. . . . Never have the nations of the world had so much to lose or so much to gain. Together we shall save our planet or together we shall perish in its flames. Save it we can, and save it we must, and then shall we earn the eternal thanks of mankind and, as peacemakers, the eternal blessing of God."

—John F. Kennedy to the United Nations

CHAPTER 21

THE PRESIDENTIAL PARTY

Evelyn Lincoln

I first talked with President Kennedy's former secretary, Evelyn Lincoln, on April 21, 1991. I had been reluctant, or perhaps afraid, to speak with her before, as I often was when trying to talk to persons who had been close to the dead president they loved. It is not pleasant to think that you might upset some of these folks, who all carry a deep suffering.

But some are glad to talk, and Evelyn Lincoln was very friendly to me. She has strong views about the assassination and who was involved.

"You were on *Air Force 1* coming back from Dallas with the coffin?"

"That's right."

"Did you see Jacqueline Kennedy get into that ambulance at Andrews Air Force Base with Robert Kennedy and with the coffin?"

"No, I didn't. I was too taken up with my own grief. I wasn't noticing anyone."

"You were on the lift coming down from the plane with the coffin?"

"I was the one that was supposed to get off *Air Force 1* with Jackie at that time. But just before we were to get off, Bobby Kennedy came storming through the plane, and he took over and I was right behind him."

"Yes."

"As far as knowing—they got off ahead of me. But as far as looking where they went, I can't give you any idea on that. I was right behind Jacqueline and Bobby. But I remember they went one way and I went another."

"Did Jacqueline ever talk to you after that about those events that day?"

"You mean at the hospital?"

"Yes."

"No. It was a Catholic wake, more or less, up on the seventeenth floor of the hospital at Bethesda, when we were talking about our association with the President. About our happy memories about him. There was no discussion about anything."

"At some later date, weeks later, did you ever talk to her about what happened that day?"

"No. The only thing—I remember coming into Parkland Hospital, and Dr. Burkley telling me that he had gone, and Jackie was sitting outside of the place where he was being kept—they were doing the autopsy or whatever they were doing, and I went up to her and tried to console her. Then I went into the small room outside . . . and that is the only thing that I remember."

"Did it ever occur to you that there was some larger plot, some conspiracy?"

"The grief is so overpowering. You don't think about anything. You just think about how sad it is, because for the last six months of his presidency he was in the best health, and he really looked like a president. And it was just unbelievable that they could do that to him."

"Well, see, many of us will never get over that. And we are all working on this case, and researching it."

"That's great."

"Yes."

"I'm sorry. I'd like to help you with thoughts about who did it or anything like that, but we were just grief stricken, that's all!"

"I understand that you had possession, at least figuratively, of the autopsy materials—the photographs and X-rays."

"I never looked at any of that. Nothing. I kept it, and then Bobby moved it into another room. It was all sealed up. I never saw any of it."

"It stayed in your office for a while?"

"For a very short while."

"In what kind of a box?"

"It was in a sort of a trunk, and it was locked up. I had no access to it."

"But do you remember when it was moved? How long afterward?"

"Oh, no. I have no idea. I don't really have anything to add to what you already know. You've got to work on your own on that."

"You never had any feeling in the White House that something strange was going on with any of the military officers?"

"No, no. I have my theories about who did it, but that is just my idea. I have all kinds of theories on that."

"Could you give me one of them?"

"It was a conspiracy. There was no doubt about that."

"Where do you think it came from?"

"Well, you know . . . there were a lot of hating people around. There were a lot of evil people about."

"Especially in Texas?"

"Well, that, yes. That's basically where it started. But . . . J. Edgar Hoover was involved in it."

"Did you ever talk with Hoover? Did you get bad feelings from him, that he hated Kennedy?"

"Oh, well, you knew that because Bobby was the attorney general, and he was J. Edgar Hoover's boss!"

"You feel that Hoover in some way might have been involved?"

"Oh, sure. Oh, sure."

"And how about some military people there?"

"The CIA and the Mafia."

"Yes."

"And the underworld, because Bobby was investigating the Mafia and all that, you know."

"Yes."

"You can tie them all in."

"They were all in it together."

"I always thought Garrison knew more about it than any of the rest of them, so I am very happy that they are making that film." (The Oliver Stone film, *JFK*.)

Marty Underwood

Marty Underwood was an advance man first for President Kennedy—
placed there by Mayor Richard Daley of Chicago—and then for President Lyndon Johnson. He was with Kennedy on the Texas trip, and flew
back with the body to Washington, and was asked to stay on by LBJ,
which he did. He is retired and lives in Baltimore.[1]

He was one of the few included in the presidential party who spoke
out at any length about the assassination and his theories or feelings
about it. He actually did some investigating of the murder for Johnson,
and talked about it on *Evening Magazine,* a national television show.
His conclusion, after talking to a leading CIA operative in Mexico City,
was that the Mob was somehow involved.

I mentioned to him that we believe the autopsy photographs were
faked. "Oh, I'm sure they were forged. You know, the Warren Commission was a set-up. Johnson had to set that thing up. We had to whitewash it. Christ, with the mental state of the country—if they had
thought for a minute that Castro or anybody was behind it, they would
have gotten after them. That Warren Commission, they didn't have the
staff—

"Johnson knew all about it and who did it. He understood it was a
domestic conspiracy. In addition, his mistress says that LBJ told her
about what was going to happen, and that he had foreknowledge."

"Did she bring in H. L. Hunt?"

"No."

"Her name is Madeline Brown.

"Yeah, I know. I met her.

"You know that she insists that Johnson told her before it happened
that it was going to happen?"

"Well, I always doubted that."

"Of course we pulled Kennedy out that day, you know. Out of the
hospital before they could do an autopsy. It was strictly against the law,
but . . ."

"Yeah."

"We had to actually force that sheriff off into the corner."

"Somebody pulled a gun on Dr. Rose, right?"

"*Well,* I think the Secret Service showed their guns! But it was pandemonium, and they weren't going to let them have the body."

"Did you get a look at the head wounds?"

"No. I didn't. I could have, but I didn't."

"Do you know if they took any photographs or X-rays that day?"

"I don't think they did. I don't really believe they did, but I don't know. I have to be very honest with you, I don't know."

"Do you remember any descriptions of those wounds yourself?"

"No. See, that's what I told you, I was very far out. I was one of the chief advance men, but my job was completely away from that, so . . . Kenny O'Donnell would have been a great source for you."

"I was going to write Dave Powers a letter today, but he is hard to talk to."

"He's hard to talk to, and you've got to remember these were brothers. You have to remember that the Kennedy family—you didn't get inside that family, I don't care how good you were or who you were. Kenny was the closest. They talk about Bobby or anyone else, but Kenny was in the operating room a long time, you know.

"Of course Kenny got drinking. Hell, I used to wet-nurse him. He couldn't hold anything on his stomach for six months afterward. They all blamed themselves, you know. There were a couple of suicides in the thing, with the Secret Service and everything. It's just a goddamned shame with Kennedy and so on."

"Do you remember who committed suicide?"

"I don't remember. I think there were a couple . . ."

"Clint Hill—"

"He was the one who ran down on the back of the car, and actually Jackie pulled him in.

"I don't think that Dave Powers was in the operating room. Kenny and Jackie were in there. She wouldn't leave. Of course you'll never get to her, I am sure."

"Were you on the plane with the coffin?"

"Yeah."

"Do you remember the ambulance trip to the airport from Parkland?"

"No. I'll tell you why I don't. Kenny O'Donnell came out to me and said, 'Marty, we don't know whether this is a plot—maybe they're after Johnson, maybe they're not. We don't know. Get the vice president, and get them back to the plane.' And that is what we did."

"What I need to know is—did that ambulance make a stop at the funeral home? Did it stop anywhere on the way to the airport?"

"Well, I was on the plane. We got in the plane and pulled all the curtains down, and that was a half hour before the ambulance even got there."

"So you went straight from the hospital to the—"

"To the plane with Johnson, yeah. . . . Because they didn't know if this was a plot or what."

"But you were basically in Kennedy's detail, right?"

"I was Kennedy's guy. Then I turned over and became head of Johnson's detail."

"Were you at all times in the rear of the plane, or were you up forward in the plane in the staff cabin?"

"I was probably four seats from the rear, in the regular part of the plane."

"In the forward part where Johnson's party was?"

"Yeah."

"Did you go in the back part of the plane at any time?"

"No. Jackie was back there, and the only time she left was when Johnson asked her. I thought it was very gracious of her to come up for the swearing in."

"From your statements on *Evening Magazine,* you know that this was a pretty high-level plot."[2]

"Well, I thought it was," Marty said. "You know, I think I was the first one who ever came out and said so, on a program like *Evening Magazine*! I think I am the only one that ever blew the whistle on the thing, because I got so goddamned mad through the years at all this hokey-pokey stuff and nobody gettin' the truth. And they did a lousy job! They did a stinkin' lousy job!"

"They had the scoop of the century—"

"You said on *Evening Magazine* that everyone was sworn to secrecy."

"Well, that was Kenny O'Donnell."

"And you had heard that JFK would be assassinated in Dallas? You said that on the show—"

"John Connally went to him, and—"

"Connally tried to warn him?"

"Oh, Connally tried to warn him. As I told you, I was in Houston the night before. For three or four days in Houston that's all we heard. In fact, I called the White House on the thing. . . . In Dallas we were getting ready to start the motorcade and Connally, Kenny O'Donnell, and Dave Powers and everybody talked to Kennedy and said, look, let's put the bubble top up. And he said, 'No, this is Jackie's first trip and the people love her, and I'm going to keep it down.' It was his idea all the way."

"You said J. Edgar Hoover was in it up to his neck."

"*Oh!* He was! He hid the Oswald file on us. Christ, if we had had the Oswald file, Oswald would have been—I'm sure you know how that operated. He would have been contacted a day or two ahead and he would have been either put under house arrest or gotten out of town. The Book Depository, for Christ sake, would have been swept from one end of the town to the other."[3]

Marty said that he was already on the ground when the lift with the President's casket and widow came down from the plane's door at Andrews. He went directly into the office and did not see Jackie get in the ambulance. "Kenny O'Donnell gave me two quick phone calls to make, and I took off.[4]

"I made two calls and headed for the White House.

"All I know is Bobby came in and wouldn't shake hands with Johnson and just brushed right by him."

"Were you in the after cabin when he came on the plane?"

"Yeah."

"He went down on the lift at Andrews, right?"

"Yeah. Bobby and Larry O'Brien and Kenny O'Donnell."

"Dave Powers won't touch anything with a ten-foot pole. He just clammed up completely."

"Do you think it's because he knows something?"

"I wouldn't be surprised. I know Tip O'Neill. Kenny O'Donnell went up in front of that committee on the Hill and said that he'd heard only one shot, and he told Tip O'Neill, well, no, he didn't . . . he'd heard two or three. And he said why don't you tell him the truth. Kenny and Dave were twins, you know. They were always together.

"He was a hell of a nice guy. He stayed on with Johnson, you know. I got to know him real well. I took him and Kenny and Larry O'Brien out to the airport the night before in Houston, and got them on the plane. They didn't want to go. I took the President."

"You worked for Johnson?"

"I worked for him. I became his chief advance man, until he went out of office."

"You must have heard some of the rumors about a conspiracy going around?"

"Oh, let me tell you something, they were around. But I did an awful lot of checking. Probably the best friend I had was Wyn Scott, who was head of the CIA for Central America. If Lyndon Johnson was mixed up in it in any way, I think I would drop over tomorrow, because I checked to see if it was true. There is a lot of Lyndon Johnson–bashing around. I just don't believe it. I did a lot of checking on that for him. Every once in a while one of the damn papers will come out and run one of those damn articles. He'd get all upset and I didn't blame him. I'm just as sure as my name is Marty Underwood that Johnson didn't have a damn thing to do with it."

"I don't think so either. I think he was a genuine humanitarian."

"Absolutely."

"He might not have liked the Kennedys personally, but . . ."

"Well, let me tell you this quickly. He and Jack Kennedy got along great. Bobby was the source of terrible friction! Oh, *terrible!* Bobby just hated his guts and he hated Bobby's guts."

"Bobby rubbed people the wrong way, that was for sure," I said.

"You know, in California, when they finally decided the vice-presidential candidate was going to be Johnson, . . . Bobby didn't know it until he heard it on the radio. He came back and just raised *hell!* They picked Johnson, and Kennedy would have never been elected without Johnson. *Never!*"

"There were so many things that fell through in Dallas. Any advance man who had any sense at all would never have taken him down that route."

"Well, the route was changed just before . . ." I said.

"Yeah, I know. You don't take a guy down a route like that."

"Was there any Secret Service man that you were suspicious of?"

"No, there really wasn't. You know, there were a lot of rumors—that Clint fell off, or that his gun went off, or two or three others—I don't believe that really!"

"Yes."

"You know that Texas trip was the first political trip Jackie ever took with the President? He insisted on going when Marty Underwood and everyone else was calling the White House for a week saying, Christ, there's too many rumors going, don't come, you know. But that was the main reason he went, and then he wouldn't let 'em put the top up, you know. They had a hell of a fight there for about five minutes that day, before they started the motorcade. I don't mean a fight, but, ah—"

"A hot discussion."

"But Jackie wanted it up and Kenny O'Donnell wanted it up, and Connally wanted it up. He wanted the people to see Jackie, so, he was just—heh, there's a Lord up there and he calls the shots in the end.

"Well, if they hadn't gotten him there, they would have gotten him down at the ranch or somewhere down the line that day. No doubt about it. They wanted him and they got him.

"When my son Marty was about twelve, President Johnson had him down on the ranch a few times. He really loved him. Like a kid will do, one time he said, 'Well, Mr. President, how about the assassination?' and Johnson said to Marty, 'Well, Slim, your dad and I will never live to see it, but the truth will come out someday.'

"He told me one night, and I don't want to keep laboring on things you are not even interested in, but why I was so close to Johnson—I wasn't married at the time, I was divorced, and I used to take Marvin Watson [a presidential assistant] when he wanted to go home or something, and Johnson never went upstairs until twelve o'clock. He'd sit in that office—Everett Dirkson or someone would come down and they'd have a bloat of freedom, as they used to call it, out of the bottle.

"He told me one night, 'You know, I've got two cancers. One is Vietnam, and the other is the fact that they still bring up the fact that I had something to do with the assassination.' It bothered him until he died. A sad thing."

Malcolm Kilduff

On April 17, 1991, I spoke to Malcolm Kilduff, a very interesting man who was with Kennedy when he died. He filled in for Pierre Salinger as press secretary on the fatal trip, and had the unhappy job of telling the assembled reporters that the President had died and what had happened at the hospital. He later got into the newspaper business, and edited and published newspapers in Kentucky.

He had worked for the State Department in Washington in public affairs and traveled a lot with Secretary of State Dean Rusk before working for Kennedy.

*　*　*

He described the motorcade vehicles. "The press pool car had Merriman Smith, Jack Bell, myself, Bob Clark of ABC, and Bob Bascomb of the *Dallas Morning News,* plus the driver, who was an employee of Southwest Bell Telephone. I'm sure you read of the fight between Merriman Smith and Jack Bell over the use of the telephone. Merriman Smith was using the phone and Jack Bell from the backseat tried to grab it from him, and he hit me in the head! Funny."

"At the press conference at Parkland you pointed your finger at the right temple area. And you said he 'died of a gunshot wound to right here.' And you put your finger on your right temple."

"I was wrong at that time, because it wasn't until I went downstairs right after that and the doctors told me. But when I saw him downstairs, it was clearly in the left side of his head."

"Was missing?"

"Yeah."

"And that was the piece, it was alleged, that was found in the street."

"That was supposed to be occipital bone," I said.

"Yeah."

"When you say left side of the head, you mean forward of the left ear?"

"Yeah."

"Would it include the eye area?"

"I would say no. You see, when you look at the Zapruder film, it shows him grabbing his throat first, pitching forward, his hands grabbing his throat, right? Okay, now, that bullet, to my mind and for all the evidence presented so far, shows that that bullet went into the back of his head and came out just above his tie, because of the marks on his tie and on his shirt."

"Those marks were scissor marks, when they cut off his tie. . . ." I said.

"I'm talking about blood, and also that oblong-shaped hole that was in the front of his neck. Now, in the Warren Commission Report there is that drawing—it is not a photograph—it is a drawing of his head."

"Do you think that drawing in the Warren Commission Report showing the bullet coming into the back of the neck and coming out of the throat, you think that is accurate?"

"Yes. Because first of all, I'm sitting in the right front seat, three cars back. So I immediately turn around and I look up. What am I looking at? I am looking at the window of the School Book Depository. Why am I looking at that? Because to me that is where the shots are coming from.

"I'm not thinking of any yo-yo on the Dealey Plaza knoll, the Grassy Knoll, or any of that bullshit. I'm looking where I hear a noise coming from. Now, that is the only defense to my position. If the shots weren't coming from there, why did I bother to look there?"

"Yes, but that does not preclude the possibility of shots coming from elsewhere also."

"In my opinion, all three shots came from my right ear, sitting in the right front seat of that car. And they did not come from the Grassy Knoll across the way, and they did not come from the overpass, which has been another suggestion, and they did not come through the windshield of the car and strike him in the neck. There was some sort of a nick in that windshield. But it was not a hole."

"Do you accept the Warren Commission findings?"

"With one exception. I do not accept the so-called 'Magic' Bullet Theory that the first shot went through Kennedy into Connally, out of Connally and landed on the floor in perfect condition. No, I can't buy that one. And I can't buy that one for two reasons. Number one, the bullet has passed through so much mass, it had to have been tumbling. To have then entered Connally, it would have—if Connally had stayed in his position of looking forward, then that bullet, under the optimum set of circumstances, would have entered his back and come out his left chest.

"But instead it did not," Kilduff said. "Again, the Zapruder film shows Connally starting to turn to his left. There is a clean entry bullet wound in Connally's *right* back coming out in his *right* chest, which by his turning around, to about a forty-five-degree angle to see what was going on in the backseat, he felt the second shot enter—always felt that he did—felt the second shot hit him and came through just beneath his breast.

"And I have been swimming with Connally in the pool at the White House, and I saw a clean scar in his back, and also it did not tumble much as it exited his right chest. If he had remained seated forward after that, it would have gone into his heart. But if you turn him left a bit, then it comes in beneath his shoulder blade, and it comes out his right breast, because by that time he was turning to see what was happening.

"I've talked to Connally about it several times, and his feeling on that and mine are precisely the same. I mean, that doesn't make it necessarily so."

"Where would you say that shot came from?"

"My thought process—you may think I am absolutely crazy that I can remember my thought process—but my thought process was that we were a week away from Thanksgiving. And that we were in Texas, and fireworks. And I said it must be a firecracker. This is between the first and second shot, and that takes several seconds to go through that, about four, five, five and a half seconds. There was a much longer period of time—a matter of one, two, three seconds between the first and the second shot—than there was between the second and the third.

"It was a very short period of time between the second and the third shot."

"The neck wound came from in front—"

"I don't buy that."

"All of the medical witnesses state that there was no damage whatsoever to the face."

"I don't understand how they could possibly say that when the left part of his forehead looked like—when I got over to the car—looked like two pounds of ground beef."

"The left part of the forehead?"

"The left part of his forehead."

"And there was no damage to the eye at all?"

"Oh, you couldn't even tell, there was so much blood and gore. They found that piece of the skull, over by the curb, either later that afternoon or the following morning, with hair on it."

"Well, the person who found it was a medical student who took it to doctors and they stated that it was occipital bone. It was flown to Bethesda Hospital. It is known as the Harper fragment."

"That came from the left temple?"

"No. Occipital means right in the back of the head. You know where that little bump is on the back of your head?"

"Yes."

"There was no bone missing in the forehead, according to all the reports."

"Also," Kilduff said, "if you take those frames from Zapruder, there is something definitely entering his head *ahead* of his head. It looks like an explosion. Now, you know that when *Life* magazine finally got ahold of the Zapruder film, they printed two versions: There was the first rush copy, and they took that off the stands (I have a copy of this original one), and then the second version came out, and those frames had been substituted, which I always thought was rather peculiar. I suppose it was for the sake of taste, because it was this plume coming out of his head. Of course, since that time, it has been printed many times. But that clearly is going forward and it's not coming out of the back."

"Yes," I said. "You can see that happening in the film, and it's very difficult to interpret. There are some theories that the film itself has been tampered with. We know that things happened to it when it was at *Life*. Some of the frames are missing, and there were splices, and that sort of thing. But whether or not there was some forgery in those frames—312, 313, and so on, are not clear.

"Two chairmen [Jones and McClelland] of two surgery departments of two major universities insist to this day that the throat wound was an entry wound from the front. . . . And they also insist, quite a lot of them, that the President had been shot in the head from the front and the large blow-out in the head corresponds to—" I said.

"The blow-out was in the left front. The Zapruder film shows that. Frames 313, 314, 315."

"As you know, the face was not damaged at all. No witness saw any damage to the head past the midline of the skull, forward of the right ear."

"Forward of the *right* ear? No! Forward of the left ear, they did. I did. The bullet came in on the right side and exited the left side. What splatter there was."

"Well, all the medical testimony from both hospitals was that the back of the head was missing. The back of the head up to the top of the head. In other words, from the hairline up to the cowlick area and almost to the top of the head. That was gone.

"The back of the head?" Kilduff was incredulous.

"The whole back of the head."

He told me that Senator Ralph Yarborough was hysterical at Parkland and they thought they would have to restrain him. Says he would not make a very good witness.

I said, "People heard different things in the motorcade according to where they were or where they were standing. But people on the Knoll knew that there was a gunman right behind them. Some of them were soldiers who hit the dirt right there."

"That's right, they did. I saw one man put his child down."

"I talked to him the other day, by the way."

"I was kind of looking at him before I turned around and looked up in the window of the School Book Depository. And I go back to what I said earlier, that if there was nothing going on up in that window, why did I bother to turn around and look up there? I don't think it was an echo."

I told Kilduff that the killer would have shot at the car as it came toward the window rather than when it was going away from it. But he says, "No, he wouldn't have. He had the windshield in the way. [This is false because the window looked down into the car, well above the windshield.] I would have waited until it turned left, because I would have—of course, you have to get into the theory also that he wasn't really after Kennedy, too, that he was actually after Connally because of his bad discharge from the Marine Corps, and Connally had been Secretary of the Navy—"

"But he could always shoot at Connally!"

"Yeah, but this would have been more dramatic, but that I don't want to get into it because it is obfuscating what you and I are talking about now. My own deep-seated belief is that he was actually after Connally. I've been saying that for years. And I've talked to John Connally about it. And John feels the same way. He had reason to shoot Connally, and he didn't have a motive to shoot Kennedy."

"Tell me something, how come Oswald didn't have gunpowder burns on his face?"

"Who knows? Beats hell out of me!"

"How come there were no fingerprints on those weapons?"

"Maybe he was wearing gloves, I don't know. He could have gotten rid of gloves, the time he allegedly shot Officer J. D. Tippit." The shooting of Tippit, the officer who was killed shortly after the assassination, was pinned on Lee Harvey Oswald, and that shaky accusation created the syllogism that if Oswald killed Tippit, he must have killed Kennedy, for which there was even less evidence.

"How about—"

"You can 'how about' from now until Christmas. All I can attest to is what my reaction was at the moment it happened, where I looked, and what I thought. And that is the only thing that I can state. So far as speculation is concerned, it's a dangerous thing to speculate on when you don't have the facts. And I don't think any one person has all the facts. If any one person had all the facts, we wouldn't be almost thirty years later trying to unravel the fucking thing!"

"That's it."

"We are still talking about Julius Caesar and Brutus, and the doctor in the Booth and Lincoln case. I mean, this thing is going to be argued about when you and I are long gone."

"Mrs. Kennedy sat by that casket in that aft section where the seats had been removed, which was after the bedroom section. And where the swearing in took place was just forward of the bedroom section. And then Kenny O'Donnell, Dave Powers, and Mrs. Kennedy stayed back with the casket in the after section where four seats had been removed, and then they took the casket out of the plane and onto a fork lift out that service door.

"I was right there in the aft section when they took it down. I was not on the fork lift. Bobby was on that."

Kilduff went with LBJ to the White House and stayed on until 1965. He was close friends with Kenneth O'Donnell when O'Donnell ran for governor of Massachusetts.

Kilduff heard only three shots and then indulges in some explanations. "If there is anything I have been sure of in my life, it's three shots, and if there is anything else I am sure of, it's that they came from the School Book Depository where I was looking. I could see that window where the shots were coming from up there. But that is where the sound was coming from. In the Zapruder film, also, where are the Secret Service agents looking? They are all turning around, looking over their right shoulders and in that window. Every single one of them. Not just one, not two." [This is untrue. They are each looking in a different direction. The President has been hit, as we clearly see in the Altgens photograph, clutching his throat, and the Secret Service men are doing nothing at all, looking every which way, evidently confused by the echoes and their hangovers from the night before.]

"That House Committee, that's the biggest joke in the world! They started out—they had some bird on there—it was [Robert] Blakey. Blakey called me over one day and he asked me, 'What we'd like from you is what evidence you can give us that would help us substantiate or help us prove a conspiracy theory.'

"I said, 'Wait a minute! What the hell kind of a House investigation are you conducting when you've already made up your mind what you are trying to prove?'

"He said, 'Oh, I didn't mean to say that!' and I said, 'Oh, the hell you didn't!' I said, 'Unfortunately, I don't think there was a conspiracy. All I can tell you is what I saw and what I heard. What you do with that is up to you.' I never heard another goddamned word from him. And that was in late seventy-six or seventy-seven."

"So, you don't think there was any plot?"

"No. I think everyone wants to find more of a reason for having lost a president than just the simple act of a maniac. Of a man who was avenging his less-than-honorable discharge from the Marine Corps, and that he was after Connally. And I totally realize the question that comes up, well, why doesn't he pick a better place and a better time? Well, he wanted to do what was the most dramatic. Well, that was a bad rifle. And there are many witnesses to this, that he had that rifle bench-tested well and that that rifle fell to the left and down, which would account for that first shot. So he was aiming at Connally, and of course the motorcade sped up there a little bit, as there were very few people there in Dealey Plaza. And going down that little incline there, no matter how little it sped up, that bullet aimed at Connally would have naturally gone into Kennedy, who was sitting right behind Connally. You can see how it would have happened if you can accept the theory that the shots were coming from the sixth floor of the School Book Depository. That to me is what simplifies it. Not that I am looking for simplicity. I am merely trying to make sense out of something that so many have tried to complicate."

> "My soul is scorched. . . . If we are God's creation,
> we're part of it and all the sources are inside of us.
> So I just totally believe in consciousness, and the
> soul's existence, and you have to live accordingly."
>
> —Marina Oswald Porter

CHAPTER 22

MARINA OSWALD PORTER

Out of the blue one day, Marina Oswald called me.[1] I had not spoken with her before, and it was a big surprise. Marina, the widow of the accused assassin of President Kennedy, had not been in America long when the nightmare descended upon her life.

She was very pleasant and friendly. In the past I had obtained her address from close friends who researched the assassination of the President, and who had befriended her and spoken with her. I had then sent her a copy of *High Treason,* and she told me that she had read those parts of it first which pertained to her.

Marina has led a quiet life since the assassination, being a housewife, and raising two intelligent daughters. She was fortunate in finding a husband, a prosperous businessman, who takes good care of her and protects her. Meanwhile, she reads what she can on the assassination and gradually fills in some of the blanks in her understanding of what happened during those terrible days in 1963, when her husband was accused of killing both President Kennedy and a police officer.

Marina spoke with a Russian accent, of course, but her handling of English was good, and she had mastered many idiomatic expressions.

But I was little prepared for how truly tragic this lady is.

She said, "I'm suspicious of everything and everybody." I told her that that was a smart way to be.

"Oh, no, not smart. It's because I've been burned so many times that I'm thrown in cold water. So only because I have been approached by other people as well and I wonder who's in cahoots."

She was sorting her way through the maze of critics, researchers, government agents, and apologists dealing with the assassination of President Kennedy. Can you imagine coming to this country from a faraway land, barely able to speak the language, all but alone, and being caught up in the maelstrom of fear, politics, terror, intrigue, and horror connected with that assassination, with two small children, and having her husband first arrested and accused of the murder of the President, and then shot dead in a police station?

"I wonder who's together, and who's with nothing to do, in between. So I read your letter and you asked me . . . do you mind if I call instead of write to you because it's difficult for me? My English is not perfect."

"It's okay."

"I have to stick to the dictionary."

"It's fine."

"It takes me forever."

She wanted to know if there was anyone who agreed with us that the films of the body had been tampered with. "In the medical profession, because if he's one against ten, that's very suspicious to the public." She was in the labyrinth, in the maze of intrigue and politics that had covered up the case for twenty-eight years, and she knew if someone had an idea and stood alone, no one would believe it.

I told her that few people knew of my belief that the photographs and X-rays had been forged, but that my book was coming out. "We don't say that the body was necessarily altered."

"See, that's the reason nobody pays any attention and that's the reason for confusion among the public, because everybody scream, 'I'm sorry, my theory is right.' You know? 'And I'm on the right path.' Because I think that's the reason the public is confused."

"Yes, I understand."

"I'm thinking they heard so many fairy tales and the official truth that have been spoken but they just simply—oh, well, another book and somebody playing with that theory. I can talk until I'm blue in the face, which I did. You write the books to no benefit at all, to simply entertain. You say they are breaking the case open. How legally can that possibly be done because everything right now is hearsay. Am I right? Please convince me differently."

I tried to explain why I thought this time there was some hope that what we were trying to say about the case would have an effect, but I don't think I convinced her of much.

"I appreciate every effort that you're making, but how can I help—because I am so powerless?"

I said that I noticed that when she was on the Jack Anderson show it seemed that every time she started to say something he often cut her off. She said, "Because the time was so limited. You know how television works. You have two or four seconds to reply, and you're a little bit nervous. So you are approached with the questions that you know what they want you to answer, but you have your own idea as to how to express yourself in a limited time. And I'm tired of going on television when I'm just like a button—it doesn't solve anything."

She said, "I only know what the researchers supplied to me. And I have a reputation: 'Well, she says whatever was convenient to her.'" Marina then took issue with a quote in my book to the effect that she had been tutored by Isaac Don Levine before the Warren Commission. "What upsets me is you said my testimony is inconsistent and I have been blamed for you know what. I have heard that so many times from the press, I do not know what you mean by that. Because I testified for the Warren Commission and I signed it. I do not know. I read some of the little parts sometimes and I'm very embarrassed because I so sound like a second-grade dropout, and my Russian I have to admit was pretty good at the time, and I take pride in it. So I did not sound like a little donkey. Apparently it was very important to portray me in a certain way. I was completely honest, but the Secret Service or whoever interrogated me from day one. And they would play a part between two of them like the Secret Service were good guys and the FBI were not. I guess it's still that way."

"You were scared, weren't you?"

"Definitely, I was. I had to protect myself and not to tell more—than the written law required. I didn't want to harm him, let's put it that way. A wife has to protect her husband. Even in death."

She kept returning to my statement that she had been inconsistent in her testimony and asked me where I got that. I explained that the Warren Commission has said that about her, as well as many others studying her testimony. Of course there might have been translation problems, but no one has gone over this carefully. "If you have any questions—do you know what I mean—just ask me directly." She was very direct and very prepared.

"I'll tell you what: I was so tired [just after the assassination] that I just wanted to get out and I didn't care what I answered. Just let me go!"

"Wasn't it true that to a certain extent they coached you—they told you what to say?"

"No, that's not true at all."

"Not at all?" I said.

"I had an interpreter and a government lawyer. How it was translated, I do not know."

"All right."

"Well, that's the truth. Okay another thing is—I did take those pictures of Lee."

Marina was speaking of the famous "Backyard" pictures of Lee Harvey Oswald holding a rifle, wearing a pistol on his hip, and holding up copies of the *Militant* and the *Daily Worker,* two more antagonistic newspapers it is hard to imagine.

"I took them one Sunday. Yes. I swear on my children I'm telling the truth. I do not remember how many. Because I didn't want it; I didn't like it; but two [pictures] I definitely took."

She said that Lee had asked her to take them, and that she thought she took only two or three, no more.

Later on she said, "I'm not liar by nature. It's very difficult for me. I'd rather not [lie]."

Marina said (and told Larry Howard of the JFK Assassination Information Center in Dallas) that she took the "Backyard" pictures, but they were not the same ones as those in evidence. She said that she had her back to the staircase, which we see in the background of the present photographs, off to the left side. Therefore they could not be the Warren Commission exhibits because the staircase would not be visible. Marina's belief is that she took some photographs of Oswald in the backyard of the house where we see him in the official pictures, but "nobody ever asked me where I was standing."[2]

"These aren't the pictures I took." She told Howard that it was early in the morning, about ten o'clock. The sun was out. Howard said, "She was backed up to the staircase. What I'm thinking is that the pictures she took—maybe the quality wasn't very good, so they had to redo them. Whoever faked them got the idea to fake them from the ones she took. Who knows, maybe Oswald faked them.

"She remembered the rifle and the pistol, but not the clothes that he had on in the pictures. She said that Oswald went around to the mailbox and got the copies of the newspapers and posed with them."

Once again, the type of criticism Harold Weisberg has expressed privately to me and to others is pertinent: Why would anyone fake some evidence that is clearly betraying itself as fake? Not so clearly, perhaps. My only answer is that the conspirators weren't that smart, weren't that careful—in fact did not have to be—and did not have much time to do better.

I told her that other researchers and some police authorities felt the pictures were faked, with Oswald's face being pasted on. I told her that Oswald himself had said, before he was shot to death in police head-quarters, that the pictures were faked. She said that "man who is drowning—maybe he was searching for self-preservation—and denied this at the time, is that possible too?"

She said that she agreed with the conclusions of the Warren Commission. "I agreed with them wholeheartedly not because they forced me or threatened me. I respect them. They are honorable people who reach for the truth and their conclusion was so. I agreed because with all the evidence that I have and they presented to me, that was the only conclusion that I could draw."

They had to prove it to her, too, the wife of the accused assassin.

"But now do you think that Lee shot President Kennedy?"

"I said that when I made that statement *long ago*. I believe in that." (Emphasis hers)

"But what do you believe now?"

"I don't believe that now."

"And why don't you believe it now?"

"Because a lot of evidence exists that pointed in a different direction."

"Do you think he knew some of the people he was spying on and that he thought he was working for the government?"

"I discovered things about Lee after his death. I did not know that much at all before. If you assume that he was working for the government, only then certain things will make sense."

She asked me if I thought Oswald was innocent. "Yes, of course."

"Can you prove that in a court of law?"

I made the case to her for Oswald's innocence.

She said, "I don't mind to go on the stand if I have enough evidence to back me up. But I don't want to make a donkey out of myself again."

I proposed to her that she come to a press conference I planned, and speak out.

"I appreciate it, but I'll let the professionals do what they are going to do. I'm just a simple person living a simple life definitely in the hard way, who can't afford the luxury of flying there and going there."

I digressed to say that I hoped that things were going well for her in her private life.

"It's scary."

"Scary?" I asked.

"My soul is completely—" She hesitated.

"Pardon me?"

"I said, my spirit and the soul are completely destroyed. It's hard. You know what I mean?"

I felt for her very deeply. Those who have been through it cry for others who express the same pain.

But the soul cannot be destroyed.

She quickly changed the subject to say that the General Edwin Walker incident was true, that Oswald was supposed to have told her he took a shot at Walker. "I wasn't there. I wasn't a witness—I didn't see that Lee did it. If you didn't see him do it, you cannot say that he actually did it. I wasn't there around the Walker place, but that's what he told me. When he came, you know, late. That's the truth. I did not make this up." But she said that she had no idea why he told her this or why he did it, if he in fact did it.

The House Assassinations Committee wrote that "according to Marina Oswald, he [Oswald] probably used the rifle in an attempt in April to kill Edwin A. Walker, a retired army general who had been relieved from his post in West Germany [by President Kennedy] for distributing right-wing literature to his troops.[3] . . . Marina Oswald, because of her testimony, played a central but troubling role in the investigation of the Warren Commission. A great deal of what the Commission sought to show about Oswald rested on her testimony, yet she gave incomplete and inconsistent statements at various times to the Secret Service, FBI, and the Commission. Marina's role in the committee's investigation was less central. . . ."[4]

I asked her about his character, if he was very complicated, if he was two people. . . ."Are you talking about schizophrenia?"

"In other words, it's possible that he could have done the Walker shooting or had the 'backyard' pictures taken as part of his job as an intelligence agent of some kind?" I asked her.

"I prefer to think the last paragraph of what you said."

"That he did these things because he was directed to do them?"

"I think so."

Later she said, "I did not want the government to know that those pictures of Walker's house and Lee existed. I never took a picture in my life, except this time. Because I didn't know anything about photography. So I thought that if I destroyed the pictures, that was going to be it. I never thought about negatives."

About Oswald she said, "I wasn't married to an angel. I could be married to a thief, but he didn't rob that bank at that time."

I suggested that Oswald had been set up—asked to tell his wife that he had taken a shot at Walker's house (even if he had not done so), asked to make the "backyard" pictures so that later on he could be depicted as violent.

"He wasn't stupid, but maybe he can't outsmart somebody who is smarter than you are. Not every man can admit that you have all the cards. That somebody had the edge."

The edge?!

"I do not know who he met or what was. My only speculations come from the searchers [researchers], and my little calculations. It's a personal thing, to assume that he was working for the government. I think connections with George DeMohrenschildt—his strong ties with him means something."

We spoke of the death of DeMohrenschildt, the fabled Russian count and Texas oilman long connected to intelligence operations who befriended and respected Oswald. The day the House Committee on Assassinations found him on the same day that Edward J. Epstein found him, he was dead. Epstein, the author of *Inquest* which questioned the conclusions of the Warren Commission, believes that Oswald was a Soviet agent and that that fact had to be covered up.

What a story DeMohrenschildt told! The unpublished manuscript he was writing at the time of his death in 1977 and printed by the House Committee throws a bit more light on the subject. It tells us how deeply Lee Harvey Oswald truly liked President Kennedy.

"Another thing was that lots of Lees had been running around which wasn't Lee! Lots of people impersonate Lee."

"I've heard that." I asked her about one of the incidents, and she said that she had never been to the gun shop the Warren Commission said she and Lee had gone to.

"So in your mind you didn't feel that he was capable of shooting at the President?"

"For twenty-five years I tried to find out the reason. I digged into everything, including my conscience. I tried to find the reason why would he do such a thing, and I could not. So after I made my speculations maybe because of communism or this and that. Because it didn't make any logical explanation to me why John Kennedy, because he adored that man. That I would never ever believe."

"You say he adored John Kennedy?"

"Oh, yes."

I then made out a case for Oswald's innocence again, and she said, "So, everything, like in the court of law, the prosecutor would say everything that you say is irrelevant. . . . Testimony can be broken, you know."

After some discussion she said, "But it's no threats to you, you know. You have a good name and everything. My life and my children's life are at stake too. I read some books, I saw some movies. I'm a little bit equipped with the knowledge."

She wanted to know if the police could tell if a gun had been fired. "For example, if it's the evidence, I stay with the gun, with the body laying in front of me. And I say, well, I didn't shot anything. Can they take this gun away from me and examine it or test that it has been fired or not?"

"Yes, if the gun had been fired that day, it is a very simple matter to test to know if it had not been fired, they would know that right away."

"Was that test done?"

"There's nothing in the evidence about it. In other words, it was negative. The gun had not been fired."

Marina asked me: "Was it assumed by the researchers negative because of the paraffin test, or on the examination of the gun?"

"Well, both. It's true because he did not have any burns on his face, and he would have had to have burns on his face if he had fired a rifle. Secondly, there was never any evidence entered to show the rifles had been fired. They couldn't put that in because they had not been fired."

"Okay, but this evidence exists?"

"The paraffin test, yes. That exists, but there was never any rifle test, or at least there is no record of it, and never any evidence to show that the gun had been fired."

She kept asking if the evidence existed anywhere. I didn't have a good answer. "Well, I doubt that it exists. I think they destroyed that."

"But you remember that rifle—the Mannlicher-Carcano?"

"They asked me that. My answers were very contradictory even in the Warren Commission testimony, but I don't want to talk about it. I know what it looks like at the time. I never examined it or touch it. I don't know anything about it. Because I don't like to touch it."

We indulged in small talk awhile, as I had no more questions. It was like the day years before when I called up Jacqueline Kennedy's office and Jackie picked up the phone, and I didn't have the courage to start asking her the questions I wanted answered so badly.

"I talk to you and so many people, but no matter which one, you're going to get different information."

"I know that your soul has suffered greatly for twenty-seven years. I know people who have suffered greatly," I said.

"I am so scorched. My dream was . . . it was my dream to become American citizen."

"Did you get citizenship?"

"I don't want to."

"You don't want to?"

"I belong to the earth, and that's it. I'm that disappointed."

"Well, hopefully things are changing."

"Is it really?"

"Well, yes, it has. It's come a long way. It's not healed, it's not perfect."

"You have such apathy in the country right now."

"Well, that's true. It's like they're blindfolded."

"In a way I was blindfolded for very many years. But when you know the truth, it's a crime not to do something about it."

"That's what we are trying to do."

"But your hands are tied up, you know, we aren't very adequate," she said.

She said that she heard a Russian artist on television make the comment that the people usually deserve the type of government they have. "And you know, that kind of makes sense to me."

I said, "Governments are really like kings, you know—"

"They *think* they are, see, but big powerful people are nothing. And we all just specks on the earth. I feel about myself as a person that I'm nothing, and my soul rebels against that."

I said, "But what this country really is all about is that it does have the capacity to look at itself and criticize itself."

"But they don't do anything about it."

"No, but it often learns, grows, and changes as a result. You may not realize this because you weren't born here, and you're not that familiar with its history, but America has gone through vast changes over the last two hundred years."

"What pains me the most is such beautiful people—the majority of them—in this country, and they're so betrayed," she said.

"I agree with that."

"But just by few."

There was more philosophy discussed in this interview, and even though the evidence was important for historical purposes, perhaps the philosophy between an American and a Russian was even more important.

Marina said, "We are American, we have a freedom, but they never question—we have freedom to talk, you have freedom to print, to say anything, but when you try to do *something,* that's different story. If you don't have the pull, if you don't have the money, you're a loser. Rich people can get away with murder, but you could not even prove, if you do not have the means, that you're innocent."

She may not be a citizen, but she felt that she was an *American.* That was something, when you think about it, after what she has been through. She felt accepted by the people around her. Of course, in Texas, Lee Harvey Oswald was a hero to some bastards.

Then she apologized for being in such a "foul mood."

"I hope you are not taking a lot of tranquilizers or something," I said.

"Oh, I never do, I never did."

"I was afraid that somebody had you doped up."

"Oh, no, no. In fact, I took only two Valiums in my life and I'm allergic to them."

"Can I say something to you? Try to take heart. Try to find some faith and hope now that you haven't had, maybe, for a long time, but try to go out and look at what a beautiful day it is, you know. . . ."

"Only that keeps me alive, the nature. I'm not a religious person. I'm not in organized religion."

"But you have a soul, Marina."

"But I do not believe in a mighty—a universal God. I don't care which religion you are or not at all."

She said, "If we are God's creation, we're part of it and all the sources are inside of us. So I just totally believe in consciousness, and the soul's existence, and you have to live accordingly."

Then again she spoke of life and the case. "I'm just simply disappointed. Every time, even the good book of yours—something good will come along—it's just extra burden, extra hurt, because you know that nothing—that you are helpless. That's the thing. . . . Every time I believe in somebody or something, I say to them, thanks a lot. Nobody supports you. So that's why I think it's hard to win. If all of you researchers united, you will be much more powerful voice or force to deal with than individuals. I hope you're not offended by my suggestion."

She said: "We don't need another book. We need evidence and we need action. I don't mean to prosecute somebody. I'm not that evil or that vicious. Simply admit the truth and go from there. So I hope I didn't ruin your weekend?!"

No, she made my weekend.

"When he shall die, Take him and cut him out in little stars. And he will make the face of heaven so fine That all the world will be in love with night, And pay no worship to the garish sun."

—Shakespeare, *Romeo and Juliet*

CHAPTER 23

THE ROSCOE WHITE AFFAIR

I was the only person privileged to hear all of Ron Laytner's exclusive interview in August 1990 with Geneva White conducted for London's *The Mail on Sunday*.[1] She is the widow of the Roscoe White, the man she and her son, Ricky, state was the gunman on the Grassy Knoll.

Geneva White worked for Jack Ruby during a brief spell just prior to the assassination.

Geneva was in the advanced stages of lung cancer at the time of the interview, and died a few months later. It was said that she was inarticulate, crazy, and that too much of her other talk about UFOs and such would discredit her, so she was kept under wraps.

I was highly skeptical after private detective Joe West had announced a few months before[2] that the gunman on the Grassy Knoll was Johnny Roselli. A *Baltimore Evening Sun* reporter called me the night before the press conference[3] was set up in Dallas to introduce Ricky White, to read me the notice on the AP wire that had just come in. To his surprise, I read him the main points of my fax from the JFK Information Center, which had alerted me. The Center participated in the announcement, as they normally help a lot of people without passing judgment.

Gary Shaw told me: "We didn't say this was the truth or the solution to the assassination. But that the American people ought to be aware of the story and it deserves close scrutiny. We made no claims. We believe this young man has a story to be told."[4]

I talked with Ricky White on the phone, and although all who met him felt that he was completely honest, I did not think that there was

463

any *hard* evidence there. At this point Ricky is primarily a witness to the story that there once was a diary, which he found and which he says was in his father's handwriting, and to finding some alleged CIA cables that dealt with apparent assassination directives—a happenstance I consider extremely unlikely—and other materials. The diary describes Roscoe White's shots at JFK from the Grassy Knoll and shooting Officer Tippet while trying to take Oswald to Redbird Airport. Geneva White solidly corroborates all this.

In 1975 or so there was a robbery at the White home and a number of things were taken, among which was a new and different "backyard" photograph of Lee Harvey Oswald. The robbers were caught in Arizona and the FBI discovered this photo, which they turned over to the Senate Intelligence Committee, which was conducting a superficial investigation of President Kennedy's assassination. From there it went to the House Assassinations Committee and is mentioned in 6 HSCA 141, paragraph 362.

With the stupidity and blindness for which their staff is now famous, the HSCA never bothered to investigate how the Whites acquired the picture, or what else they might know. And the Whites knew a lot.

I listened with great care to Geneva and Laytner, and I found her and her story credible in almost every respect. She was the *real* witness, the witness who overheard Jack Ruby and her husband planning the murder of President Kennedy.

Harold Weisberg jumped all over this story shortly after during an appearance on *Inside Edition,* pointing out the mention of Redbird Airport as the destination for White and Oswald as having its source in Richard H. Popkin's *The Second Oswald.* This does not in itself expose White's story as a hoax.

Weisberg also pointed out that Ricky White stated that the diary gave the code name of one of the assassins as "Saul," and this is a more telling revelation, since "Saul" is also to be found in the book *Appointment in Dallas* by Hugh McDonald. McDonald explains that he made up the name "Saul" as a means of protecting the identity of his informant. This is a problem because the White diary, if authentic, predated McDonald's book.[5]

Nevertheless, I think that Harold jumped on this story too fast, and it also shows how one of us in the critical community is often used to discredit others.

This leaves us with otherwise credible testimony from Geneva and her son, now corroborated by several other witnesses, we are told. Unfortunately, I have not seen the corroboration myself, so cannot pass judgment on it.

We have to question why a mother and her son would reveal this information about a deceased husband and father. This would have to be an awfully good family of actors, if not true. It is unfortunate that Ricky is being financed by a company that is asking a half million for the exclusive rights to his story. Nothing discredits us faster than somebody putting a price tag on evidence we come up with.

The JFK Information Center had a lot of problems with a detective named Joe West, who retained the alleged CIA cables and would not turn them over to the rightful owners (the Whites), to the Center, or to Attorney General Jim Mattox of Texas, who announced on August 8, 1990,[6] that he was going to look into new assassination evidence as a result of presentations to him by researcher Gary Shaw and the late Washington lawyer and leading assassination researcher Bernard Fensterwald. Mattox stated that after all, *his* mother had told him that Ruby frequented the restaurant where she waitressed, and that "she saw Mr. Ruby and Oswald eating dinner there together."

Neither the "investigation" nor Mattox lasted long. Soon he was out of office.

Joe West was responsible for the May 1990 story that it was Roselli on the Grassy Knoll. Some close to the situation think that someone long ago may have forged the diary and planted it. But would it have been worth it to the conspirators to go to such trouble and detail?

We still have the testimony of Geneva saying she overheard the assassination being planned by Ruby and her husband, but there are just too many coincidences: That she worked for Ruby, that her husband was in the Marines with Oswald, went to Japan on the same ship, both were from Texas, and they both—according to family members—appear in a photograph of a squad of marines in the Philippines.

The cables implied orders to White to kill Kennedy, but the JFK Center could not produce the originals at the press conference, which highly embarrassed everyone, due to Joe West's expropriation of them the day before. Also, there was nothing to prevent the FBI from taking them, as they took the diary, so copies—both Xerox copies and retyped copies—were produced. The originals were in fact damaged by age. Shaw says, "The FBI destroyed Oswald's note to FBI agent James Hosty. Gordon Shanklin [his boss] ordered Hosty to destroy the note and then denied that he had done so, but Hosty and three other FBI personnel testified that they had seen the note and that it was ordered destroyed."

The Dallas contingent of assassination researchers still harbor resentment toward the FBI and other agencies with regard to their behavior in the assassination investigation and other acts in the 1960s. I see no reason to maintain this vendetta today, since J. Edgar Hoover is dead and the FBI has become a much more professional organization over the years.

A strong dispute arose over the authenticity of the cables. John Stockwell, a former CIA officer living in Dallas, said that yes, the Agency would put something like that in writing. Admiral Bobby Inman ridiculed the idea.[7]

I was incredulous that the ideas expressed in the cables could be put in writing, but my sources tell me that any hit man on government business would not move an inch until he had such an order in writing locked up in a vault somewhere. He needed the protection to document that he had acted on orders.

A preacher also flits in and out of this story. The Reverend Jack Shaw was with Roscoe White as he lay dying after a mysterious fire—a fire his son says was no accident but intended to kill White. Shaw says that White confessed his murders (more than one) to him. Shaw also says he has tapes of Geneva White revealing what she knew. At one point Shaw mentioned to newsmen that he worked for the CIA. I went to the home of the Reverend Shaw and his wife, along with my chief investigator, Richard Waybright, and I was impressed with his honesty and knowledge of the case. "I am convinced that Roscoe White did shoot President Kennedy," he told us. "I believe that Roscoe was telling the truth, and had no reason to lie."[8]

Shaw said that he was trying to corroborate Geneva White's story that she had been given shock treatments which were intended to obliterate the memory of the conversations her husband had with Jack Ruby.

Shaw said that "Rock" White had an affair with a woman who worked at the office of Jaggars-Chiles-Stovall, which was being used by the conspirators as their operation headquarters for the assassination. The proprietors did not know they were being used in this fashion.

Jaggars-Chiles-Stovall did top-secret map work for the military. Lee Harvey Oswald worked there for a while after his retrieval from the Soviet Union as an alleged defector, which seems strange, because that work required a security classification and proven loyalty to the United States. Unless they knew he was all right.

Geneva had previously been quoted in *The Odessa American* as saying, "There is no doubt in my mind that my husband did shoot Kennedy."[9]

Geneva says she carried a terrible load of guilt when she learned her husband was a hit man. She first had some idea of his real employment when she overheard Roscoe plotting the assassination with Ruby. But what got her to eavesdrop at the door to Ruby's office was overhearing the name Sue, a woman Roscoe was having an affair with.

She questioned her husband later on, but learned little.

Meanwhile, Ruby caught her listening to them and seized her by the arm. "What shall we do with her now?" he said, very angry. "Now we have to kill her." Her husband, Roscoe, talked Ruby out of that and they agreed to give her electroshock treatments.

How they got the idea to use electroshock for this purpose remains a mystery to me, but apparently it did in fact erase her memory. Ricky discovered the diary years later, and after sitting on it for some time told his mother what was in it. She then told him what she could remember about Roscoe and the assassination. In the intervening years Geneva was a sorry case, half destroyed by the "treatments." Now, dying, she conducted her interview with Laytner while being fed oxygen and chain-smoking at the same time. The former "rail girl" for Ruby who earned $200 a night was very gracious to her journalist guests during this interview.

She talked about working for Ruby, and we have a photo of her showing off her legs to Ruby in his office. She was a B girl at the Carousel Club, and said that Jack was always very nice to her. She said she was paid for "recommending drinks to customers and dancing with them." Since her son was present, she couldn't explain her employment in any other language. After all, her husband was just starting out as a policeman. His son says that the CIA placed him with the Dallas police department undercover.

Ron Laytner, of *The Mail on Sunday,* is of the opinion that because Roscoe was a cop, Ruby reimbursed him for the hit on the President by paying his wife $200 a night. She was, of course, astounded by making so much money, and presumably shared it with her husband. Trouble is, a B girl in such a club can easily make $200 a night on her own.

She said that shortly after the assassination and Oswald's arrest, Roscoe hustled them out of town for three days.

I have little faith in what the attorney general of Texas might do. It's all BS as far as I'm concerned. The man is a political animal, and he may not be in office too long, so he is going to do what is politic. This case just isn't going to get any action from those people. And it wasn't long before this so-called "investigation" of the White case was ended.

If this was on the up and up, Mattox would have sent his man or gone himself instantly to the witness and taken evidence. But that would be like Earl Warren and Gerald Ford going to the gangster Jack Ruby and sitting with him for much of a day and refusing to take Ruby out of Dallas, where he felt he could speak more freely. This whole thing is already in a class with that, because Ricky White has been trying to get this story out for years. One good way is to force disclosure by putting a price tag on part of it, in this case, *his* story. The press conference at the JFK Center seems to have worked.

Geneva described going to the rifle range near their house with her husband and Oswald, and said that Oswald was a real bad shot. That we already know. She said he was innocent and didn't shoot Kennedy.

The Whites lived catercorner to the Tippits after the assassination. Geneva White says that they knew the Tippits well, and that after Tippit was killed his family was taken care of by those in the conspiracy.

The story is that when Roscoe White asked Tippit to drive Oswald to Redbird Airport, Tippit balked, suspecting that they were involved in the assassination he had just heard about, and White had to shoot him right then. Oswald ran away. There is a report that an extra police shirt was found in the backseat of Tippit's car, and we surmise that this belonged to Roscoe, who changed his clothes there. It is also thought that Tippit's car was the one that stopped at Oswald's house and beeped, and then picked him up just down the street.

Geneva describes a later trip to New Orleans without her husband. There, Charles Nicoletti, the mobster, approached her and threatened to torture and kill her children if she ever talked. Nicoletti was one of those who died about the time the Senate Intelligence Committee and the House Assassinations Committee wanted to talk to him, along with John Roselli and Sam Giancana, also dead. "They were the apple of my eye," Geneva White said, crying, as she described the threat to the reporters from London. She was in terror when the names of Johnny Roselli and Sam Giancana came up, who she says were involved with Nicoletti.

The Geneva White story indicates a much greater role for the Mob.

She said, "We at first thought the assassination was more Mob," but she later realized "it was more CIA."

We get a picture of policemen who straddled the line, who rubbed shoulders with or who were in the confidence of the local underworld and Jack Ruby, and/or who through military service were connected to intelligence operations and radical rightist operations run in the area by General Edwin Walker, who hated JFK for his politics and for firing him.

During the entire interview with Geneva, she was level-headed and credible and got the confidence of the reporters from London. She seemed totally rational and *The Mail on Sunday* reporters completely believed her, finding no part of her story questionable other than the "Saul" matter.

On September 21, 1990, a new controversy arose when a headline screeched across America: "Diary Claiming Policeman Killed Kennedy Called Hoax." This particular story by Reuters mixed up a document Geneva found in her garage, which was a bunch of notes she had made in the margins of a hymn book, with the diary. More accurate stories published in the *Dallas Morning News* the same day made clear that this was not the diary spoken of by Ricky and Geneva and written by Roscoe White. Nevertheless, the public was highly confused by the distortions of the wire services. Part of that distortion is the result of private detective Joe West trying to convince the press that the diary was Roscoe's. Ricky White issued a statement saying that there was no connection at all, and John Stockwell also called the diary a fake.

Unfortunately, nothing may come of this angle, since the principals are all dead. It'll have to come from some other guilty party who was involved in it with them and can prove it.

"It was warfare in the shadows, ambush and murder and torture, leaving behind a trail of burned villages, shattered families and weeping women."

—Arthur M. Schlesinger, Jr.,
A Thousand Days

CHAPTER 24

PRESIDENT KENNEDY AND THE ISSUE OF HIS INTENT TO WITHDRAW FROM VIETNAM

Vietnam was the most nearly unsolvable problem faced by modern presidents.* There had been unremitting fighting in Indochina after World War II. The 1954 Geneva Conference had outlined a settlement that included popular elections, but nobody, including the United States, ever intended to honor that agreement.

John Kennedy first got into trouble over Vietnam in 1951, when, as a young congressman, he had gone there to see for himself what the situation was.

Kennedy was given the usual briefing at the embassy in Saigon, and he "asked sharply why the Vietnamese should be expected to fight to keep their country part of France," Arthur Schlesinger writes.[1] This caused a problem right away, upsetting the American diplomat in charge, and later the French commanding general complained to the American minister.

"In Indochina," Kennedy said on his return to Washington, "we have allied ourselves to the desperate effort of a French regime to hang on to the remnants of empire. . . . To check the southern drive of communism makes sense but not only through reliance on the force of arms. The task is rather to build strong native non-Communist senti-

---

* The best overall discussion of Kennedy's intentions is to be found in Arthur M. Schlesinger, Jr., *Robert Kennedy and His Times* (Boston: Houghton-Mifflin, 1978); and *Vietnam Legacy* New York: (Ballantine Books, 1985).

ment within these areas and rely on that as a spearhead of defense rather than upon the legions of General de Lattre. To do this apart from and in defiance of innately nationalistic aims spells foredoomed failure."[2] On *Meet the Press* he said, "Without the support of the native population, there is no hope of success in any of the countries of Southeast Asia."[3]

There had been many voices promoting the idea that the United States should intervene and help the French, and there were many voices to say that we should take over from them when France was defeated in Vietnam in 1954. Young Senator John Kennedy made a speech from the floor of the Senate in 1954. He said: "Unilateral action by our own country . . . without participation by the armed forces of the other nations of Asia, without the support of the great masses of the people [of Vietnam] . . . and, I might add, with hordes of Chinese Communist troops poised just across the border in anticipation of our unilateral entry into their kind of battleground—such intervention, Mr. President, would be virtually impossible in the type of military situation which prevails in Indochina . . . an enemy which is everywhere and at the same time nowhere, 'an enemy of the people' which has the sympathy and covert support of the people."

What Kennedy said in 1954 was still true in 1963.

Theodore Sorensen writes: "That year [1954] he had watched the French with a courageous, well-equipped army numbering hundreds of thousands suffer a humiliating defeat and more than ninety thousand casualties. Now the choice was his. If the United States took over the conduct of the war on the ground, he asked, would that not make it easier for the Communists to say we were the neo-colonialist successors of the French? Would we be better able to win support of the villagers and farmers—so essential to guerrilla warfare—than Vietnamese troops of the same color and culture?"[4]

The Geneva Accords had planned for both North and South Vietnam to be neutral, but the Soviets and China determined that North Vietnam was to remain in the socialist camp.

Sorensen[5] tells us that China's intention was to drive the western nations out of Asia. But too many roots had been put down, and the West saw the struggle as part of the Cold War, the Domino Theory, and more especially within the Balance-of-Power construct. In addition, it is difficult for a nation whose old men recall that America's involvement as a combatant in the greatest and most destructive war the world has ever known was precipitated over this very spot of land halfway around the world—difficult for that nation to simply sign off on that piece of land. Pearl Harbor—the Japanese attack on the United States—was a direct result of our oil embargo against Japan for its conquest of Vietnam and Indochina.

Under President Eisenhower, some American advisors had been sent to South Vietnam following intense CIA activity there under Lieutenant Colonel Lucien Conein and General Edward Lansdale. The reason was to support an insurgency by North Vietnam, which our government felt violated the plan for neutrality between the two states. North Vietnam's attitude was that they had thrown the French out, and it was not for the purpose of creating two countries.

Dominoes

Americans felt that a victory by North Vietnam would be a victory for China, if not the Soviet Union, two great powers who were at each other's throat at the time, vying for control of the eastern half of the world if not the world. Both sent weapons and material to North Vietnam.

The Domino Theory was based on the experience of the events both leading up to World War II, when one country after another fell to Germany and Japan, and the experience after that great war, when one country after another in Eastern Europe was subverted and overthrown by Communists and became locked in a deadly and destructive embrace with the Soviet Union.

The Cold War thus ensued, as the few nations on the western rim of the vast Eurasian continent struggled to survive and rebuild after the terrible devastation of World War II, and all of the West felt sorely pressed to stand against the almost irresistible tide of communism.

Tragically, Vietnam became a part of that struggle.

Kennedy knew upon assuming the presidency that he was enmeshed in the deeper mysteries of statecraft. He took leading Republicans into the foreign policy and national security side of his administration for the sake of political peace, and perhaps this was a big mistake, because these men at every turn counseled war. They wanted to invade Cuba with our armed forces to back up the CIA-led Cubans at the Bay of Pigs invasion.

*   *   *

South Vietnam had very special problems. A million Catholics had fled North Vietnam and moved into South Vietnam, a country whose Buddhist people were deeply tied to their own land. Someplace had to be found for the refugees. The Mandarins were universally disliked by the native population. The Ngo brothers, themselves Catholic and from North Vietnam, took over South Vietnam, forcibly resettling this vast throng on land in the agricultural South Vietnam.

The great disruptions caused by the migration of over a million people into South Vietnam caused the insurgency. The South Vietnamese attacked the new people, but this is not how we learned of it. It was filtered through the news to become a Communist-led insurgency. Then a North Vietnam–led insurgency. Our CIA operatives in the area then made all that happen.

The problem in South Vietnam was small when we got into it, and it would have eventually solved itself, but the more we plunged in there, the bigger the problem became. The more money we spent, and the more men we sent, the more we were committed—the more we lost, and the bigger the enemy got. As Dean Rusk wrote in his memoirs, he and our government had underestimated the will of North Vietnam, and their capacity to fight.

The decision had been made in 1954 by the United States to draw the line against Communist expansion at South Vietnam. "This far and no farther" was our attitude. We could have picked a better place to draw the line, one perhaps with desert terrain and not jungle, not a place with many millions of intelligent and industrious people so alien and hostile to us.

The government we supported in South Vietnam bitterly antagonized and provoked its own people, to the point where Buddhist leaders were immolating themselves in public places to the horror of the world. We had trained the Vietnamese to fight as though they were in Europe, not in a jungle and countryside such as existed in Vietnam, and we therefore created that much more of a problem when the Communists vastly escalated their effort in South Vietnam in response to what was happening there.

Escalation

Sorensen tell us that John Kennedy's "essential contribution was both to raise our commitment and to keep it limited. He neither permitted the war's escalation into a general war nor bargained away Vietnam's security at the conference table, despite being pressed along both lines by those impatient to win or withdraw. His strategy essentially was to avoid escalation, retreat or a choice limited to those two, while seeking to buy time."[6]

In October 1961 Kennedy sent General Taylor and his deputy National Security Advisor, Walt Rostow, to Vietnam on a fact-finding mission. The Vice President, Lyndon Johnson, had proposed that the United States make a major commitment, but Kennedy was wary. He did not send the Secretary of State, Dean Rusk, and perhaps this was an error, because from the moment of the Taylor-Rostow trip, a more military solution for a long time dominated the advice he was getting.

Chester Bowles had proposed creating a neutral belt of nations in Southeast Asia, and Kennedy was caught between a rock and a hard place, not wanting to see South Vietnam fall to the Communists, and at the same time finding that he had to take a stand somewhere against the world to the heavy pressure the Communist countries were making at the beginning of his presidency. "It was an imaginative proposal, but it seemed either too early or too late. Its opponents contended that it would be taken as a deliberate abandonment of regimes which depended on us and a monumental United States retreat—all in exchange for empty promises from Moscow and Peking. Instead, there seemed a strong case for trying the Johnson approach and making an increased effort to stabilize the situation in South Vietnam."[7]

Contrary to the notion that Kennedy left the Vice President out of things—quite clearly from this example—Lyndon Johnson was listened to and not left out. What this meant was that Secretary of State Rusk had abrogated a diplomatic approach to the tender ministrations of the Defense Department. Schlesinger says it was a "conscious decision. . . . Rusk doubtless decided to do this because the military aspects seemed to him the most urgent. Kennedy doubtless acquiesced because he had more confidence in McNamara and Taylor than in State. The effect, however, was to color future thinking about Vietnam in both

Saigon and Washington with the unavowed assumption that Vietnam was primarily a military rather than a political problem."[8]

Taylor and Rostow told Kennedy that Vietnam was viable enough to offer major backing. Taylor pushed right then for ten thousand men to go in a combat capacity, but Kennedy limited the effort to advice and flying helicopters.

Rostow and Taylor expressed faith in Ngo Dinh Diem, but felt that changes had to be made in the way he did things. They were at least alert to that. They also felt the program of assistance they recommended could work only if the infiltration from the north stopped, which it did not. "If it continued, then they could see no end to the war."[9] They talked about the possibility that we would have to strike back across the border.

"He did not like, however, the proposal of a direct American military commitment. . . ." Schlesinger writes. The President was attracted by the idea of strengthening the Diem government with advisors and that was it. This was his reaction to the Taylor-Rostow proposals overall:

"They want a force of American troops. They say it's necessary in order to restore confidence and maintain morale. But it will be just like Berlin. The troops will march in; the bands will play; the crowds will cheer; and in four days everyone will have forgotten. Then we will be told we have to send in more troops. It's like taking a drink. The effect wears off, and you have to take another."[10]

Basically, Taylor indicated that the problems were simply military, and he ignored the real import of the underlying political, social, and economic causes that would doom any attempt that made it the "white man's war." As Arthur Schlesinger writes, Kennedy believed that in that case we would be thrown out just as the French had been a decade earlier.

But, "reflecting on the situation and reposing particular confidence in McNamara and Taylor, Kennedy prepared to go ahead. Moreover, given the truculence of Moscow, the Berlin crisis and the resumption of nuclear testing, the President unquestionably felt that an American retreat in Asia might upset the whole world balance. In December [1962] he ordered the American build-up to begin."[11]

Robert McNamara said on his first visit to Vietnam in 1962: "Every quantitative measurement we have shows we're winning this war." That is how we got into body counts a few years later. Statistics lie, and those counts led us halfway to our doom.

The fact is that Taylor and the others led Kennedy to believe that the war was as good as won in Vietnam, and his State of the Union address at the beginning of 1963 indicated that. "The spearpoint of aggression has been blunted in South Vietnam."[12] In fact, this is as good a reason as any to believe that Kennedy had every justification to start planning to withdraw. In my view, he had been tricked.

Kennedy kept the commitment set by Eisenhower and our government long before, but he did not let it get out of hand as it would have had he listened to almost any one of his advisors. The reason is that Kennedy had a long view of history and how war comes about. He knew very well just what would happen to us if we went any further. He understood the situation there better than anyone else in the nation.

The world understood that when there was a major public commitment like the one we had to Vietnam since 1954, to fail to honor that commitment would be to put into question our integrity, our reliability, and our resolve.

Kennedy's plan was to keep the commitment at a level that we could stand for as long as he thought we could stand it, and then when it could be stood no more, he made the decision to quit. That killed him.

As long as Kennedy was alive, the CIA, which he had begun to reshape, was in charge of the war in Vietnam. That brought its own problems, but it emphasized an entirely different type of military commitment, tactic, and strategy. The military did not begin to take over the warfare there until Kennedy was dead, in 1964, when units of Marines landed. Even then they never controlled the general strategy.

In 1961 and 1962 Kennedy bought the counterinsurgency concept put forward by Maxwell Taylor. At least it wasn't big-time war. What Kennedy did was make a show of strength so that he did not look weak. Counterinsurgency was a good cover. He beefed up our advisors there and told the military to prepare to send combat troops if needed. He talked a good game, but he did not intend ever to go further. That, too, helped seal his fate, because it was misleading and comes across to more simplistic souls as double-talk, as moral failure. As betrayal.

"Kennedy recognized far more clearly than most of his advisors that military action alone could not save Vietnam," Sorensen says.[13]

Sorensen writes that after the coup that overthrew and killed the Ngo brothers, so soon before Kennedy himself died, "no early end to the Vietnam war was in sight. The President, while eager to make clear that our aim was to get out of Vietnam, had always been doubtful about the optimistic reports constantly filed by the military on the progress of the war. In his Senate floor speech of 1954 he had criticized French and American generals for similar 'predictions of confidence which have lulled the American people.'

"The Communists, Kennedy knew, would have no difficulty recruiting enough guerrillas to prolong the fighting for many years. The struggle could well be, he thought, this nation's severest test of endurance and patience. At times he compared it to the long struggles against Communist guerrillas in Greece, Malaya and the Philippines. Yet at least he had a major counterguerrilla effort under way, with a comparatively small commitment of American manpower. He was simply going to weather it out, a nasty, untidy mess to which there was no other acceptable solution."[14]

Buying Time

Kennedy sought to buy time "to make the policies and programs of both the American and Vietnamese governments more appealing to the villagers—time to build an antiguerrilla capability sufficient to convince the Communists that they could not seize the country militarily—and time to put the Vietnamese themselves in a position to achieve the settlement only they could achieve by bringing terrorism under control."[15]

The idea was to get back to the Geneva agreement. We know that Kennedy negotiated one deal after another that worked out fine but which antagonized radical rightists who thought he was soft, who thought we did no wrong and any compromise was cowardly.

Shortly after Kennedy took office, he had a study prepared on Laos, and the military recommended sending *combat* troops. From that moment on, from May 1961, Kennedy was in trouble because the military and their many supporters were for war and they were for it from the beginning.

In 1961 the CIA, State Department, Defense Department, White House, and U.S. Information Agency were asked to prepare a recommendation on Vietnam. The report called for the commitment of *combat* troops.

NSAM 273

On January 31, 1991, a Top Secret draft of National Security Action Memorandum 273 was released at the John F. Kennedy Library in Boston. It was dated November 21, 1963, the day before President Kennedy died, when Kennedy was in Texas. Frank Mather, a researcher in Boston, promptly discovered the memorandum and turned it over to me. The NSAM had McGeorge Bundy's name on it. Bundy verified to me that it was a "first cut."[16] Others who did not talk to Bundy about it have said that it was a forgery, and many people familiar with 273 believe that it was an order that reversed Kennedy's decision to withdraw from Vietnam and represented foreknowledge or even participation in the coup by Bundy. I think that is preposterous.

It is doubtful that President Kennedy could have seen or known about or sanctioned this document, since he was in Texas. But in fact the memorandum may have had little or no effect when it was signed days after the assassination. NSAM 273 was somewhat changed when Johnson signed it.* Only the most tortured argument might demonstrate that it then reversed Kennedy's publicly repeated policy of withdrawing United States troops from Vietnam. NSAM 273 may be insignificant in the history of the escalation. It has become a suspicious document to scholars trying to trace the reversal of American policy, which led us into a wider war. They point at 273 as a reversal of the President's orders.

George Lardner wrote in *The Washington Post,* "That is nonsense. In a memo LBJ signed after that Sunday meeting, he explicitly stated that the 1,000 troop withdrawal would be carried out. And it was. There was no abrupt change in Vietnam policy after JFK's death."[17] The 1,000 men were withdrawn, but this was offset in the following weeks. In addition, to escalate the war at the moment President Kennedy was buried would look rather obvious. Lardner does believe, however, that Kennedy did not plan to withdraw, and that the withdrawal was a device . . . "A way of putting pressure on the Vietnamese to take up more of the burden."[18] This is, of course (along with his source), absurd, as the evidence presented in this chapter shows.

Almost four months later[19] NSAM 288 began the process of heavy

---

* See Appendix for copies of both the draft and the signed NSAM 273.

American involvement in Vietnam. The emotional and social wounds of that war still run deep. But it is 288 that truly began to heavily involve the United States in Vietnam in a major war, not 273.

Dave Powers and Kenny O'Donnell wrote in *Johnny, We Hardly Knew Ye:* "The President's order to reduce the American military personnel in Vietnam by one thousand before the end of 1963 was still in effect the day he went to Texas. A few days after his death, during the morning, the order was quietly rescinded." Were they referring to NSAM 273?

I am indebted to Professor Peter Dale Scott for his incisive and penetrating analysis of NSAM 273 and its effects, long before the full document was released.[20] Scott assembled a good picture of the Top Secret paper from bits and pieces that were quoted in the Pentagon Papers.

It is possible, though, that many have put too much emphasis on the word "win" in the draft of NSAM 273. This word can be interpreted to mean many things and raises semantic problems. Kennedy could talk about somebody winning but not mean that *we* have to do the fighting for them, which he made clear in a statement just before he died.

Under President Eisenhower the CIA was allowed to engage in certain covert operations which Ike felt were inappropriate for the military to handle. But the size and intent of these operations were kept from Eisenhower. When Kennedy was elected, he inherited all of this. The CIA was conducting "vast operations in Indochina and Tibet, and its U-2 spy plane flights over the Soviet Union had seriously compromised this policy because the operations could not be kept secret. . . ."[21]

Kennedy Attempts to Change the System

President Kennedy learned his lesson at the Bay of Pigs. After an informal investigation in the White House, he fired the high command of the CIA, including the director. It was clear that Kennedy had been deceived, and that there had been an attempt to entrap the United States and its military into a larger adventure.

"The policy announced by Kennedy in his monumental NSAMs 55, 56 and 57 was based upon a direct turnabout of the assignment of responsibility for covert operations from the CIA to the military. This policy, primarily the work of General Maxwell Taylor, placed the responsibility for Cold War planning and paramilitary operations, i.e., clandestine activities, on the shoulders of the Joint Chiefs of Staff."[22]

But the military did not want this. "These men all believed that warfare and the utilization of military forces were a formal affair and that the military were not to be used in any other country, large or small, in violation of that state's sovereignty," Fletcher Prouty writes.[23] Prouty worked closely with the Chiefs of the General Staff, and was their liaison with the CIA for years.

Prouty briefed the generals on NSAM 55, which Kennedy had signed himself. He writes: "It did not take long to see that these military men, all chiefs of their services, were not Cold Warriors, and did not intend to be."[24] Kennedy had written: "I regard the Joint Chiefs of Staff as my principal military advisor responsible both for initiating advice to me and for responding to requests for advice. I expect their advice to come to me direct and unfiltered."[25]

Prouty says you could hear a pin drop. "They had never been included in the special policy channel—which Allen Dulles had perfected over the past decade. . . . They did not want to get involved. But their services did get involved inevitably whenever CIA operators approached the individual services for support. . . . Despite this logistical support, they rarely, if ever, participated in the overall operational planning with the CIA—even for such enormous 'secret activities as the Bay of Pigs invasion of Cuba.' "[26]

Prouty tells us that there was little discussion after the briefing. NSAM 56 required an inventory of the paramilitary assets in the armed forces, and a longtime CIA operative, General Edward G. Lansdale, was assigned that task. Prouty believes that Lansdale, along with General Lucien Conein, is in the photographs taken at Dealey Plaza.

The third NSAM, 57, "was a strange document." Prouty says that "the primary thrust was contained in an enclosure that proposed the establishment of the Strategic Resources Group for initial consideration of all paramilitary operations and for approval, as necessary, by the President."[27] Kennedy thereby set up his own committee to examine all overt military operations in advance.

Reversing Kennedy

But there was a covering letter attached to it. This letter contained a recommendation that "the Special Group [5412 Committee] will perform the functions assigned in the recommendation to the Strategic Resources Group."[28]

Prouty says for such an important paper, its language was a surprise. "The message of the directive is carried in the enclosure, yet it is negated by the sentence cited above that assigns the responsibility for 'paramilitary operations' back to the system used by the National Security Council and the CIA since 1954. The confused language that does this is a 'recommendation' about a 'recommendation.' "[29]

The enclosure contained in 57 was written by General Maxwell Taylor, but the cover letter reversing the Taylor procedure was "written and signed by McGeorge Bundy."[30]

McGeorge Bundy called General Charles Cabell, the deputy director of the CIA, the morning of the Bay of Pigs invasion and canceled the air strikes against Cuban planes. Kennedy approved those same air strikes the day before.[31]

"By concluding that the Special Group [5412 Committee] would 'perform the function' of the new Strategic Resources Group, NSAM 57 left the former Cold War Operations system in place with one stroke of the McGeorge Bundy pen. This circumscribed the role of the Strategic Resources Group.[32]

"The JCS recognized this loophole immediately and slipped through it. They did not want the job of clandestine Cold Operations. With its toe firmly in the door as a result of the loophole in NSAM 57, the CIA began an argument that effectively neutralized NSAM 57 and the other directives."[33]

The rest of the NSAM made it clear that the military was to handle large paramilitary operations, but this sparked off a territorial battle, as the CIA then tried to claim as large an operation as possible. "What eventually came about in Vietnam, when the first U.S. military troops under direct military command landed at Da Nang in March 1965, was a direct result of the policy outlined in NSAM 57. The warfare in Indochina that had begun in 1945 under the OSS had become too big for the CIA. With the landing of the U.S. Marine battalions, under the command of a Marine general, the nature of the warfare that had been carried out under the aegis of the CIA changed. It took twenty years for the clandestine work of the CIA to achieve that level—and it was not accomplished during JFK's lifetime."[34]

Later Prouty tells us—along the lines of my own thinking—"As presidential administrations come and go, the bureaucracy lingers on to perfect its ways and this is nowhere more sinister than in the domain of the CIA and its allies throughout the government. It has learned to hide behind its best cover—i.e., that it is an intelligence agency."[35]

Was Kennedy Withdrawing?

Bundy prepared the draft of a National Security Memorandum (273) which Kennedy could not have seen or approved, and it may actually have countermanded another order of the Administration which had been made public policy. But I don't see the evidence for it, and, admittedly, the issue is not as clear as Peter Dale Scott and Frank Mather would like to make it.

At the beginning of October 1963, after Secretary of Defense Robert McNamara and General Maxwell Taylor had returned from an inspection in Vietnam, it was announced by the Administration: "U.S. Troops Seen out of Viet by '65."[36] It was also made publicly clear that one thousand or more troops would leave by the end of 1963.

A few weeks later and two days before Kennedy died, it was again stated in a public announcement that more than one thousand troops would be withdrawn from Vietnam before the end of the year, only five weeks away.

Days after Kennedy died, there was an emergency meeting of the National Security Council. The new president, Johnson, under the impression that Kennedy had approved NSAM 273, signed it into law. From that moment forward, the covert escalation of the war against North Vietnam, known to half the world but kept from the American people, began to inextricably carry America into Vietnam and the great tragedy and national upheaval that followed.

Professor Scott told me that "the draft of NSAM 273 brought significant changes in policy, because there is the question of commitment, and there is the question of starting the 34A office planning against North Vietnam, which led to the Tonkin Gulf incident."

Scott says that for the first time, NSAM 273 announced (secretly) that the "central objective" was to help South Vietnam "to win." Previously, the idea was simply to help them.

NSAM 273 contained "a quiet cancellation of the November 20th plans to withdraw troops, disguised by a public reaffirmation of a previously announced 'objective' with respect to withdrawal."

"It contained an order to 'all senior officers of the government' to avoid any criticism of U.S. Vietnam policy."

And it contained a directive to the State Department "to develop a 'case' which would demonstrate Hanoi's control of the Vietcong."[37]

There is a general feeling among many who have studied the Pentagon Papers that "with respect to events in November 1963, the bias and deception of the original Pentagon documents are considerably reinforced in the Pentagon studies commissioned by Robert McNamara. Nowhere is this deception more apparent than in the careful editing and censorship of the Report of the Honolulu Conference on November 20, 1963 [two days before JFK died], and of National Security Action Memorandum 273, which was approved four days later. Study after study is carefully edited so as to create a false illusion of continuity between the last two days of President Kennedy's presidency and the first two days of President Johnson's . . . incompatible pictures of continuous 'optimism' and 'deterioration' are supported generally by selective censorship, and occasionally by downright misrepresentation.

". . . National Security Action Memorandum 273, approved 26 November 1963. The immediate cause for NSAM 273 was the assassination of President Kennedy four days earlier; newly installed President Johnson needed to reaffirm or modify the policy lines pursued by his predecessor. President Johnson quickly chose to reaffirm the Kennedy policies. . . . Military operations should be initiated, under close political control, up to within fifty kilometers inside of Laos. *U.S. assistance programs should be maintained at levels at least equal to those under the Diem government so that the new GVN (Government of Viet Nam) would not be tempted to regard the U.S. as seeking to disengage.*

"The same document also revalidated the planned phased withdrawal of U.S. forces announced publicly in broad terms by President Kennedy shortly before his death: 'The *objective* of the United States with respect to withdrawal of U.S. military personnel remains as stated in the White House statement of October 2, 1963.'

"No new programs were proposed or endorsed, no increases in the level or nature of U.S. assistance suggested or foreseen. . . . The emphasis was on persuading the new government in Saigon to do well those things which the fallen government was considered to have done poorly. . . . *NSAM 273 had,* as described above, *limited cross-border operations to an area 50 kilometers within Laos.*"[38]

Scott tells us that, "if the author of this study is not a deliberate and foolish liar, then some superior had denied him access to the second and more important page of NSAM 273, which 'authorized planning for specific covert operations, graduated in intensity, against the DRV,' i.e., North Vietnam. [See Appendix.] . . . The second page of NSAM 273 was a vital document in closing off Kennedy's plans for a phased withdrawal of U.S. forces."

The covert operations contemplated in 273 "set the stage for a new kind of war [which led to the Tonkin Gulf incidents] but also through the military's accompanying observations as early as December 1963, that 'only air attacks' against North Vietnam would achieve these operations' 'stated objectives.' "

The "stated objectives" proposed in CINCPAC's OPLAN 34–63 of September 9, 1963, were rejected by Kennedy in October 1963 and first authorized by the first paragraph of NSAM 273.

"The Pentagon studies, supposedly disinterested reports to the Secretary of Defense, systematically mislead with respect to NSAM 273, which McNamara himself had helped to draft." Did these guys know what they were doing, or is this bureaucratic drift? When conflicting signals are given, when one person is or thinks he is the boss—and everybody else tries to get a different result by maneuvering the President, and nobody is playing it straight, then there is not just a fundamental flaw in the government, but often serious trouble.

There is a theory that the Pentagon Papers were released because by 1968 the CIA was having serious reservations about the continuing course of the Vietnam War and wanted to get out. Release of the papers, it was thought, would help expose the lies that led us into it in the first place. But the war was to go on for four more years.

Plan to Withdraw

On October 20, 1963, the White House gave an estimate attributed to McNamara and Taylor that one thousand men or more could be out by the end of the year. It was not a promise, just an estimate. On October 5 Kennedy had decided to implement the plan to withdraw, and this was authorized by NSAM 263 on October 11. But this was not made public until the Honolulu conference of November 20. An accelerated withdrawal plan was made public then, but the Pentagon Papers do not mention this.

The dispute during Kennedy's presidency was between trying to win the conflict in Vietnam and simply assisting the South Vietnamese in their struggle. "In this conflict the seemingly innocuous word 'objective' had come, in the Aesopian double-talk of bureaucratic politics, to be the test of a commitment. As early as May 1961, when President Kennedy was backing off from a major commitment in Laos, he had willingly agreed with the Pentagon that 'the U.S. objective and concept of operations' was 'to prevent Communist domination of South Vietnam.' "[39] In November 1961, however, Taylor, McNamara, and Rusk attempted to strengthen this language by recommending that "we now take the decisions to commit ourselves to the objective of preventing the fall of South Vietnam to communism."[40]

"Despite this advice, Kennedy, after much thought, accepted all of the recommendations for introducing U.S. units, *except* for the 'commitment to the objective' which was the first recommendation of all. NSAM 111 of November 22, 1961, which became the basic document for Kennedy's Vietnam policy, was issued without this first recommendation."

What we had then was a struggle between hard-line cold warriors that wanted a "commitment" that flowed from the "objective" to defeat the Communists. In my opinion, the hard-line foreign policy establishment men closest to Kennedy perceived him as soft and ambiguous on the issue, and they saw Vietnam as an opportunity to serve up a defeat to Communists in general. These men ultimately had their wish and committed the United States to a long and hard war, which we catastrophically lost. Kennedy, advised by General Douglas MacArthur and others, had the foresight not to so engage this country's resources and lives. "This commitment, as presented by Taylor in November 1961, would have been open ended, 'to deal with any escalation the Communists might choose to impose.' "[41]

Both General MacArthur and General de Gaulle told Kennedy that the domino theory in the modern nuclear age is ridiculous. O'Donnell described these meetings in *Johnny, We Hardly Knew Ye,* and says that Kennedy came out of the meeting with MacArthur "stunned. That a man like MacArthur should give him such unmilitary advice impressed him enormously." MacArthur was a five-star general—and a very great man, as any history will show—and told Kennedy that our domestic problems were more important than Vietnam.

Reversal

Two years later Taylor and McNamara were still at it and "tried once again: by proposing to link the withdrawal announcement about the one thousand men to a clearly defined and public policy 'objective' of defeating communism. Once again Kennedy, by subtle changes of language, declined to go along. His refusal is the more interesting when we see that the word and the sense he rejected in October 1963 [which would have made the military 'objective' the *overriding* one] are explicitly sanctioned by Johnson's first policy document, NSAM 273."[42]

The document was approved at the first business meeting the new president had after Kennedy died. I wish to let Scott try to explain his point of view that 273 rather than NSAM 288, which came along months later, reversed Kennedy's program. After all, Dave Powers, Kenny O'Donnell, and others thought the same thing. "The importance of this meeting, like the document it approved, is indicated by its deviousness. One can only conclude that NSAM 273's [paragraph 2] public reaffirmation of an October 2 withdrawal 'objective,' coupled with 273's [paragraph 6] secret annulment of an October 5 withdrawal plan, was deliberately deceitful. The result of the misrepresentations in the Pentagon studies and Mr. Gelb's summaries is, in other words, to perpetuate a deception dating back to NSAM 273 itself."[43] On the same page, Scott writes that "the secret effect of NSAM 273's sixth paragraph [which unlike the second was not leaked to the press] was to *annul* the NSAM 263 withdrawal decision announced four days earlier at Honolulu, and also the Accelerated withdrawal program: 'both military and economic programs, it was emphasized, should be maintained at levels as high as those in the time of the Diem regime.' "

In my opinion, the operative sentence in paragraph 6 of NSAM 273, which says, "Programs of military and economic assistance should be maintained at such levels that their magnitude and effectiveness in the eyes of the Vietnamese Government do not fall below the levels sustained by the United States in the time of the Diem Government" does not *in se* prove either a retraction of Kennedy's orders to take a thousand men out at that time, and the rest out by 1965, nor does it prove a reversal of his overall intent to totally withdraw.

One can get into severe semantic disputes over this. The fact is that NSAM 273 and the word "win" can apply *only* to the government of

South Vietnam and not to U.S. troops, which had not been involved in combat up to then. It could certainly have been used by someone to cancel the withdrawal plan, but does not in itself cancel that plan. There is simply no documentation for holding the line or escalation until NSAM 288, March 17, 1964.

As soon as Kennedy was dead, the words "overriding objective and commitment" began to appear, and "at least two separate [Pentagon] studies understand the 'objective' to constitute a 'commitment:' NSAM 273 reaffirms the U.S. commitment to defeat the VC in South Vietnam.[44] This particular clue to the importance of NSAM 273 in generating a policy commitment is all the more interesting, in that the government edition of the Pentagon Papers has suppressed the page on which it appears." (We now have it, years later, and it is in the Appendix.)

General Maxwell Taylor, whom Kennedy had trusted, was now in the driver's seat. On January 22, 1964, he wrote a memorandum saying NSAM 273 "makes clear the resolve of the President to *ensure victory* [emphasis mine] over the externally directed and supported Communist insurgency in South Vietnam. The Joint Chiefs of Staff are convinced that in keeping with NSAM 273, the United States must make plain to the enemy our determination to see the Vietnam campaign through to a favorable conclusion. To do this, we must prepare for whatever level of activity may be required and, being prepared, must then proceed to take actions as necessary to achieve our purposes surely and promptly."

From the moment John Kennedy was shot to death, Lyndon Baines Johnson was a captive of an increasingly escalating war effort that Kennedy had kept the lid on for three full years.

McNamara told a congressional committee that "the survival of an independent government in South Vietnam is so important . . . that I can conceive of no alternative other than to take all necessary measures within our capability to prevent a Communist victory."[45]

The military was getting ready to conduct aerial bombing against North Vietnam, and "the basic policy is set that we are going to stay in Vietnam in a support function as long as needed to win the war."[46] Scott says, "The new President's decisions to expand the war by bombing and to send U.S. troops would come many months later. But he had already satisfied the 'military' faction's demand for an unambiguous commitment, and ordered their 'political' opponents to silence."

The military had pushed since 1961 for the deployment of whatever forces—including combat troops—in Vietnam to insure victory. It would appear that they never examined the historical imperatives or the military realities, and they were opposed by those who supported the idea of "counterinsurgency." Kennedy was looking for a political solution.

While all this was going on, the military was intervening in Laos with jet overflights from Thailand, among other things. "These same over-flights, according to Roger Hilsman, had been prohibited by Kennedy." These were in violation of the Geneva agreements. Thailand was very angry with the U.S. at that time in 1962 as well, and boycotted the South East Asia Treaty Organization (SEATO).

A little further back in time, when the Vietnamese had defeated France and had thrown them out after the battle of Bien Dien Phu, it was agreed at Geneva that there would be elections in Vietnam. The United States, wishing to usurp the region France had so grudgingly given up, prevented those elections, and let Vietnam be divided into two countries, North and South. This was the origin of the serious trouble there. The western-oriented government we supported, run by the Catholic Ngo brothers, turned out to be a ruthless authoritarian dictatorship causing more unrest than the Communist regime in the north.

As Bernard Fall tried to tell us, there were two Vietnams far back in time, with stone walls like the Great Wall of China dividing them, and the two peoples were somewhat different, though with the same common origin. We had intervened in a dispute as old as time.

Withdrawal

Of course, those close to Kennedy, such as Kenneth O'Donnell and Dave Powers, have said that Kennedy was determined to get us totally out of Vietnam, but we don't really know if Kennedy was aware of all that was going on there, the covert actions that would insure that we could not get out.

The evidence is clear enough to me that he was determined to get out. Kennedy had to attempt to withdraw, knowing that he had strong opposition within the government and the power structure.

Assistant Secretary of State Roger Hilsman said that "we instituted a lot of planning in the State Department about how to withdraw, but we never dared send one of those pieces of paper to the Pentagon." Michael Maclear writes that Hilsman said that Kennedy trusted Defense

Secretary McNamara, but not the military—"We thought that somebody on his staff might well undercut and destroy. So this whole documentary evidence of the other option—the option of withdrawal—is
still not on public record."[47]

But it is, and Arthur Schlesinger wrote me[48] that JFK had a withdrawal plan, which is described in Chapter 31 of *Robert Kennedy and
His Times,* "a plan that Kennedy requested from the Pentagon in July
1962 and that was approved in May 1963 [and canceled by LBJ in
March 1964]." The plan is to be found in the Pentagon Papers.[49]

The fact is that Rusk, McNamara, Taylor, and Johnson believed very
strongly that we had to win that war and defeat the Communists, and so
Kennedy was up against the most powerful men in his own government
without really knowing how duplicitous they could be.

Intent

On October 2 Kennedy had announced through his press secretary at a
press conference that one thousand military training personnel could
be withdrawn by the end of the year because the training of the Vietnamese had progressed well enough.[50] In his press conference of October 31, Kennedy talked about some of the troops coming out. There
was no doubt in anyone's mind that we were withdrawing.

The key point is that there were no troops in combat in Vietnam at
any time during Kennedy's presidency. He had merely provided men
who could train the South Vietnamese. Revisionist historians have tried
to say that Kennedy got us into Vietnam, but nothing could be further
from the truth.

At another press conference on November 14 he said that the exact
number of men to be withdrawn that year would be decided at the
Honolulu conference scheduled for November 20, two days before he
was to die. Kennedy demanded a "full-scale review" of U.S. policy in
Southeast Asia when Diem was killed.

On the twentieth at this major meeting were Lodge, Bundy, Taylor,
McNamara, Rusk, McCone, and fifty other major officials. Everybody
but Robert Kennedy and LBJ. Kennedy himself was on the way to
Texas. Only RFK was left in Washington. From Honolulu, some of the
top people were to fly on to Japan, and they were airborne heading for
the Orient when the news came that Kennedy was dead. McGeorge

Bundy had returned to Washington November 21, and wrote NSAM 273 while JFK was already in Texas and out of touch.

Pentagon Paper IV.B.4 tells us that at that November 20 conference in Honolulu it was secretly agreed that the accelerated plan for withdrawal from Vietnam agreed to in October would be maintained. The conference issued a press release that "reaffirmed the United States plan to bring home about 1,000 men of its 16,500 troops from South Vietnam by January 1."[51]

Death of the Ngo Dinhs

When the Ngo brothers were killed, Kennedy realized he had to begin terminating our involvement. It would seem that he also felt that Vietnam was in the good hands of General "Big" Minh, who replaced the Ngos in the coup. Kennedy would give the general some support, but would withdraw our military advisors. Some might feel that the coup overthrew an obstacle to ending the war: a repressive regime that provoked the situation. JFK may have felt that with the Ngos out of the way, things would go better without us, and his previous decision to get out was now written in stone. He also probably thought that the situation became more hopeless with the junta that took over. Before, his moves toward withdrawal also had a symbolic quotient: He was trying to push the Ngos into better treatment of their population.

Professor Peter Dale Scott closes his landmark article "The Kennedy Assassination and the Vietnam War" by saying: "NSAM 273, it seems clear, was an important document in the history of the 1964 escalations as well as in the reversal of President Kennedy's late and ill-fated program of 'Vietnamization' by 1965. The systematic censorship and distortion of NSAM 273 in 1963 and again in 1971 by the Pentagon study and later by the *New York Times* raises serious questions about the bona fides of the Pentagon study. . . . It also suggests that the Kennedy assassination was itself an important, perhaps a crucial, event in the history of the Indochina war. . . ."

Any intent on the part of others to escalate the war had to have been without Kennedy's knowledge. Johnson signed NSAM 273 without hesitation, and from that moment on he began to escalate American involvement in the peninsula, though it more properly dates from NSAM 288, four months later. Whatever failings Kennedy had, he would not have changed so quickly such a long-thought-through policy change—a change contemplated for three years—and then made it so public. That policy was based on the recommendations of his own Chairman of the Joint Chiefs, and his Secretary of Defense, although he may have put the words in their mouths.

The remaining question is, did the change in South Vietnam's government three weeks before Kennedy died, after the October 2 announcements of intent to withdraw, change the equation in Kennedy's mind? Did it cause him to reverse his policy?

William Bundy, the brother of the author of NSAM 273, wrote me[52] to say that his unpublished manuscript goes into the subject of JFK's intent at the time of his death. "Then came the Buddhist crisis and the turmoil over Diem, and by fall we were much less sanguine, as I believe was JFK. At that time, in early September, he made a very strong statement about *not* pulling out and holding fast *[Public Papers of the Presidents]* and about the stakes involved: domino theory, etc. By early November, as the Honolulu conference with Lodge affirmed clearly, the field reports were disturbed to alarming. For a recent source, see Prados, *Keepers of the Keys,* p. 200. So far as I know, although JFK did on October 2 order the withdrawal of the first 1000 advisors (in the plan I helped draw up in the spring, leaving a much larger number still to go), there is no evidence that I know of, that between then and his death he ever reaffirmed the idea of withdrawal by 1965. Certainly his senior advisors had come to feel it was at best a long-shot hope, and they unanimously concurred in November and December in LBJ's program of continuing to support SVN (again Prados is illuminating and basically correct)."

Is this whole issue a case of inertia?

William Bundy, in his same long letter to me, alludes to Schlesinger's opinion that "he would have decided to withdraw when the going got steadily more muddy: others, at least equally close, like my brother, doubt it while believing he would have done things differently than LBJ. I myself, in my MS, said I simply could not tell, and that it seemed to me unwise and even unworthy to speculate about it. But of one thing I am reasonably sure: as of his death, he had not made up his own mind."

Even though I don't agree with this, I think we have to judge the matter on what Kennedy very carefully made public in the few weeks before he died. In the past Kennedy carefully alerted the country to whatever change of course we were about to undertake.

Pierre Salinger knew Kennedy as well as anyone did. On May 21, 1991, he wrote me from London to say that in his private discussions with the President, the President made it clear that he had come to believe that no military solution was possible and that the Vietnam situation needed a negotiated diplomatic solution.

Salinger, the senior editor of ABC News for Europe, said that "the biggest impact on Kennedy's decision not to involve himself in a ground war in Vietnam came from General MacArthur." As far as I am concerned, this is the definitive answer to the question.

William Bundy concludes his letter to me by saying, "What I most emphatically do not believe is that LBJ thought he was changing any firm policy of Kennedy's." In other words, Bundy says that Kennedy was not withdrawing, and LBJ confirmed that through action, or that— as some have commented—NSAM 273 does not in fact indicate any escalation or reversal of the plans to take the thousand men out. NSAM says nothing, and therefore Bundy is correct in saying that it did not change any firm policy of Kennedy's.

Of course, too many bureaucratic documents are written so that they can be read two different ways, and history can become rather difficult to sort out on that basis.

"All in all, I come out where Prados does, that the idea of withdrawal, never firmly nailed down as policy, was a good idea overtaken by events and the flow of the situation in SVN."

Bundy adds something important here. "It is surely significant that NSAM 273 was in draft before JFK died, and that its draftsman [his brother] supposed he was reflecting JFK's view."

On October 2, 1963, the Taylor-McNamara report was presented by the President's press secretary as being the program for the U.S. At that press conference it was announced that we would be pulling our men out of Vietnam, and the Taylor-McNamara report of that same day recommended all men (advisors) to be out by 1965.

It is worth it to digress for a moment and note the origins of that report. McNamara and Taylor went to Vietnam all right. "While touring Vietnam, the President, Bobby Kennedy, and General Krulak were setting down the outline of their report aided by frequent contact with McNamara in Saigon via 'back-channel' communications of the highest secrecy—that would contain precisely the major items desired by the President in the manner in which he wanted them. This report was written and produced in the Pentagon by Krulak and members of his SACSA staff.

"Krulak is a brilliant man and an excellent writer. He set up a unit in his office and the author was one of its members, to write this report. We had cots set up and teams of secretaries working around the clock. The report was filled with maps and illustrations throughout. It was put together and bound in leather with gold-leaf lettering for President Kennedy. As soon as it was completed, it was flown to Hawaii to McNamara and Taylor so that they might study it during their eight hour flight to Washington and present it to the President as they stepped out of the helicopter onto the White House lawn.

"Let no one be misled. That McNamara-Taylor report to Kennedy of October 2, 1963, was, in fact, Kennedy's own production. It contained what he believed and what he planned to do."[53]

This was to be the policy of the United States, as announced by the President's press secretary. NSAM 263 was signed a few days later, formalizing the Taylor-McNamara report as being the course of action we were to follow. Fletcher Prouty helped write that report, which was written for McNamara and Taylor.

In other words, Kennedy had decided, had determined to follow the policy that Generals de Gaulle and MacArthur had recommended, drawing from their infinitely long experience in the region, so painfully learned in World War II.

To this day we have powerful men from that administration, Ball and Rusk, the assistant secretary and secretary of state, claiming that Kennedy was taking us into Vietnam. But McGeorge Bundy's NSAM 273, drawn up the day before Kennedy died, although speaking of an intent to *win* in South Vietnam, a term I feel Kennedy would have ultimately taken out of the paper, reaffirmed that which we see in NSAM 263, which referred to the McNamara-Taylor Report of October 2, outlining a program for withdrawal.[54] In other words, the NSAM that McGeorge Bundy wrote has enormous contradictions in it—a commitment to win (paragraph 1), a commitment to withdraw (paragraph 2), and not to withdraw (paragraph 6). Kennedy would not double-talk his own administration in this manner. Not like this, in a secret communication? Whom would he have been trying to fool?

The evidence seems clear that 273 is not Kennedy's paper but Johnson's. It just happened to have been written the day before Kennedy died when he was away. Kennedy was getting out. NSAM 273 commits the U.S. to war against North Vietnam in paragraph 7, something far beyond anything Kennedy would have agreed to: "7. Planning should include different levels of possible increased activity, and in each instance there should be estimates of such factors as: A. Resulting damage to North Vietnam; B. Plausibility of denial; C. Possible North Vietnamese retaliation; D. Other international reaction."

Rusk writes that in hundreds of conversations with Kennedy, he never heard him hint that he wanted to withdraw. Where was Rusk on October 2 during Pierre Salinger's press conference at the White House announcing the schedule for withdrawal?

A note of clarity comes with learning more about Dean Rusk's Far East background. He was a staff officer for General "Vinegar Joe" Stilwell in the Burma-India-China theater during World War II, and he was later assistant Secretary of State for Far Eastern Affairs. He was President of the Rockefeller Foundation when Kennedy chose him to be Secretary of State. Once again we have the "Far East" establishment wedded to the wealthy American pro-war Establishment.

It is true that Rusk advised Kennedy of the consequences of military involvement. "I didn't necessarily oppose sending combat troops," he admits. "I just wanted Kennedy to realize that this was truly a fateful decision with enormous consequences."

A cable Rusk sent to Kennedy turned up among the Pentagon Papers, saying that "it is difficult to see how a handful of American troops could have decisive influence. While attaching greatest possible importance to the security of Southeast Asia, I would be reluctant to see the United States make major additional commitments of American prestige to a losing horse."

But he stayed with President Johnson when Kennedy died, and helped form his Vietnam policy, recommended in a memo the bombing of North Vietnam in 1965, and the landing of the first U.S. combat troops in South Vietnam. "I was wrong," he wrote much later. After Hanoi took a terrible beating during their 1968 Tet offensive, and at the same time inflicting heavy damage, he "thought Hanoi might come to the conference table and call the whole thing off. I was wrong." The war dragged on and on for years.

We are sifting through the ashes of a dead administration in the hope of learning more, in the hope of taking the human experience a notch higher, in the hope that the mistakes of the past will help us avoid similar mistakes in the future. The major lesson of the Vietnam War was one of miscalculation. Very big mistakes were made, and so many relate to misperceptions about the enemy. There was something very wrong with our intelligence estimates, just as there was with the fabri-

cated body counts that played so large a role in the war. The CIA ran
that war, and the CIA and everybody else was wrong about just everything.

Except Kennedy. He was as right as anyone could be regarding that
war. He tried to stay put, and then ease out of it.

William Bundy wrote me on April 27, 1991, that "there was no Kennedy decision to 'withdraw from Vietnam,' only a decision to start reducing the American advisory presence by 1000 men, which I believe
was contingent on progress being made. Since the unanimous advisors'
judgment by the time of his death was that it was *not* being made, it is
entirely speculative to try to guess what he would have done in the
essentially new situation late that November."

This is an example of a high official playing one more semantic game
and ignoring facts. We have it from Kennedy's intimates that he intended to pull out. The decision to pull out men and in fact pull out all
men was recommended by the Chairman of the Joint Chiefs and the
Secretary of Defense only a few weeks before, and it was not contingent
on anything. The decision was based on the assessment that not even a
change in government would change the swamplike nature of affairs in
South Vietnam.

The President's press secretary had announced on October 2 that
"the military program in South Vietnam has made progress and is
sound in principle."

Although the same press conference announced that we would continue to help SVN suppress the insurgency, Salinger also said, "Secretary McNamara and General Taylor reported their judgment that the
major part of the U.S. military task can be completed by the end of
1965. . . ." And that one thousand men were to be withdrawn by the
end of 1963.

One more caveat remains to the revisionists: They would claim that
Kennedy's announcements of a plan to withdraw were intended as only
a threat, and a notice of our displeasure to those in Vietnam, and
unless things changed, we would in fact withdraw.

This theory overlooks the fact that our government was really withdrawing, and men were coming back when John Kennedy died. No
government plays the kind of game that might be implied here. No
government would start to bring men back if it didn't mean to keep its
word, and things just do not work like the few who might state the
above theory.

A final word from McGeorge Bundy on the mysterious NSAM 273

first draft dated November 21, 1963. Some tried hard to convince me that it was a forgery, and others tried very hard to believe (and spread the word all over the country) that it meant that Bundy, or whoever forged it, had foreknowledge of President Kennedy's impending murder, and wanted the document ready for Johnson to sign immediately, under stress, just after Kennedy lay dead. Bundy wrote me a final letter on the subject, and his letter destroys the forgery scenario as well as the idea that the paper had much if any real significance. He also lays to rest with this one letter a few more misconceptions generated by other academic minds:

"I did indeed go to the meeting in Honolulu. Since that is so, I think it is probably true that I did the 'first cut' at an NSAM. My guess is that it was nothing more than an attempt at a paper that would reflect both JFK's general policy and the particular results of the Honolulu discussion. I certainly do not myself think, looking back at it, that the phrase about helping the South Vietnamese to 'win their contest' should be read as a change of policy. . . . I really do not think there is anything very complicated about the draft memorandum. I think that those other suggestions attempt to read much too much into a relatively simple paper."[55]

O'Donnell and Powers wrote that in the spring of 1963, at a personal meeting with the President, Senator Mike Mansfield strongly criticised our policy in Vietnam to the President and others. Kennedy was angry with Mansfield for being so totally opposed to everything we were doing there, but Kennedy also said that he was even more angry with himself for agreeing with Mansfield. O'Donnell heard Kennedy agree with Mansfield on the need for a complete military withdrawal. But Kennedy made it clear that such a total withdrawal would have to wait until 1965, when he was reelected.

When Mansfield left the room, Kennedy told O'Donnell: "In 1965. I'll be damned everywhere as a Communist appeaser. But I don't care. If I tried to pull out completely now, we would have another Joe McCarthy Red scare on our hands, but I can do it after I'm reelected. So we had better make damned sure that I *am* reelected." Later he told O'Donnell that when he took us totally out of Vietnam it would make him "one of the most unpopular presidents in history."

Later on O'Donnell asked JFK how we could get out of Vietnam. "Easy. Put a government in there that will ask us to leave." This is basically what happened. The government of "Big" Minh—a government we allowed to happen by withdrawing support for the Ngos and the announcement of our withdrawal from Vietnam—did not want us there, but they, too, were shortly replaced by those who did.

Senator Mike Mansfield confirmed Kennedy's plan to withdraw from Vietnam to the *Washington Post* on August 3, 1970. "He had definitely and unequivocally made that decision." Mansfield confirmed his quotes in O'Donnell and Powers's book. "President Kennedy didn't waste words. He was pretty sparse with his language. But it was not unusual for him to shift position. There is no doubt that he had shifted definitely and unequivocally on Vietnam, but he never had the chance to put the plan [the 1965 withdrawal] into effect."

It seems to me that this is the definitive statement on the conflict we are trying to resolve. Mansfield was probably the closest outsider, and a very powerful man in the Senate.

On August 4, 1970, O'Donnell told the *Washington Post* that he didn't think that Secretary of State Rusk had been told of Kennedy's plans. We know from Rusk's later book that he thought Kennedy was going to stay in Vietnam, which might indicate that he was a figurehead Secretary of State.

Clearly, if Kennedy did not tell him, it is an indication that he was afraid of certain powerful people in the administration, and Rusk was a creation of the most powerful interests in the country. We know from the previously quoted statements by Rusk that he was for the war.

He said that McNamara was aware of the plan for withdrawal, which, of course, is quite true. But McNamara later led us into massive escalations of the war.

O'Donnell said that the idea of withdrawal had never been presented in clear terms to the National Security Council. But we know that everyone on the Council had many talks with Kennedy and that all but perhaps Rusk knew of the plan. Much of the above was published in a *Life* article by Kenneth O'Donnell, August 7, 1970, excerpted from his book.

Tom Wicker, on August 4, 1970, noted in the *New York Times* that "others who believe themselves knowledgeable about Mr. Kennedy differ" with O'Donnell. "It often has been pointed out that Mr. Johnson ordered military intervention in 1965 while surrounded by virtually the same advisors who would have counseled Mr. Kennedy, had he lived. Moreover, it was Mr. Kennedy, not Mr. Johnson, who ordered the first substantial 'escalation' in late 1961. The editors of *Facts on File* comment in *The Kennedys and Vietnam* that according to Wicker, "Kennedy's last major statements on the war 'are conflicting.'"

In the same article, Wicker makes it clear, though, that Kennedy had already proven himself after suffering "in the Bay of Pigs episode both a defeat and a disillusioning exposure to military solutions; he had tested himself against the redoubtable Khrushchev; in the 1962 missile crisis he made plain to the world his personal strength and determination. . . . It suggests that he would not have been under quite the same human and political pressures as those that undoubtedly acted on Mr. Johnson in 1965 and on Richard M. Nixon in April 1970." This was when he sent troops into Cambodia.

This is the "balls theory of history." Johnson and Nixon never quite knew if they had them. The traditional manner for a politician to prove that he has balls is to go to war and have other men die for him. Stand tough.

On November 14, just after the coup in Vietnam overthrew the Ngo brothers, Kennedy held a press conference. He told the newsmen about the planned meeting on November 20 in Honolulu, and that it was an attempt to assess the situation: "What American policy should be, and what our aid policy should be, how we can intensify the struggle, how we can bring Americans out of there." His goal was "to bring Americans home, permit the South Vietnamese to maintain themselves as a free and independent country, and permit democratic forces within the country to operate—which they can, of course, much more freely when the assault from the inside, and which is manipulated from the north, is ended." This was his last public comment on the problem before he died.[56]

David Ormsby-Gore said that "the great feeling I had from him then was that he would not have gone into any mass involvement of troops."[57]

Representative Frank Thompson said that Kennedy told him that he was committed to send in 20,000 troops, but then planned to phase out the operation, Ralph Martin writes. "He could not have been more firm or specific."[58]

Under Secretary of State George Ball reported at one time something else. "I have great doubt that he would have done anything different than Johnson did. It was a kind of creeping thing. It was hard, at any point, to say, 'This is enough and no further.' And he probably would have said, as Johnson did, 'I'm not going to be the first president to lose a war.'"

"I told him then that, if we went down the course, we'd have three hundred thousand men in Vietnam in five years' time and we'd never see them again."

"George, I always thought you were one of the smartest guys in town," Kennedy said, "but you're crazy as hell, it isn't going to happen."[59]

Robert McNamara, the secretary of defense, said, "We were all in the Cabinet room a month before he died. We were discussing his authorized withdrawal of a thousand troops from Vietnam by December. There was a lot of pro and con at the meeting, but the final decision was Kennedy's. His reason there was that our role in Vietnam should be limited to training and assisting Vietnam to carry on their war, but it was their country and their responsibility and their war. All we could do, and should do, he said, was to provide the hardware and a certain degree of training. That means the helicopter pilots too."[60]

Kennedy said to Larry Newman, as reported by Ralph Martin, "The first thing I do when I'm reelected, I'm going to get the Americans out of Vietnam. Exactly how I am going to do it, right now, I don't know, but that is my number one priority—get out of Southeast Asia. I should have listened to MacArthur. I should have listened to de Gaulle. We are not going to have men ground up in this fashion this far away from home. I'm going to get those guys out because we're not going to find ourselves in a war it's impossible to win."[61]

Mary McGrory said that "he would not stand for long the sight of pine coffins coming back from a futile battle." He had not taken the hawk course in the Cuban Crisis, bombing the missiles. He had not taken the hawk course on Laos, sending in troops, Martin tell us.[62] Not with the Berlin Wall or the Bay of Pigs.

Sorensen says the war as it later became would not have happened. He would never have sent combat divisions into South Vietnam, or bombed North Vietnam. Sorensen was the closest to Kennedy.

Kennedy said on September 2, 1963: "I don't think that unless a greater effort is made by the Government [of South Vietnam] to win popular support that the war can be won out there. In the final analysis it is their war. They are the ones who have to win it or lose it. We can help them, we can give them equipment, we can send our men out there as advisors, but they have to win it, the people of Vietnam against the Communists. We are prepared to continue to assist them, but I don't think that the war can be won unless the people support the effort and, in my opinion, in the last two months, the government has gotten out of touch with the people."[63]

At Kennedy's last press conference he talked about the plan to withdraw. "Well, as you know, when Secretary McNamara and General Taylor came back, they announced that we would expect to withdraw a thousand men from South Vietnam before the end of the year, and there has been some reference to that by General Harkins. If we are able to do that, that would be our schedule." This was Kennedy's public position. In private he expressed the feeling that he was damned if he withdrew and damned if he did not withdraw, and that he might lose the election if he moved too quickly. He felt safe only in a token withdrawal, and then a complete withdrawal after the election in 1964.

Robert Healy wrote in the *Boston Globe* of December 16, 1988, that "the point is that Kennedy was moving toward the same pattern for settlement as he had followed in Laos, where negotiations had brought about a neutral government and the withdrawal of troops."

As previously stated, it was reaffirmed at the Honolulu meeting only two days before Kennedy died that the withdrawal plans would continue. "Rusk and McNamara had said in a formal statement at the end of the Honolulu meeting that three hundred U.S. troops would leave South Vietnam December 3 and that one thousand more would depart before 1964. This would leave about 15,500 American troops in the country."[64]

Johnson held a meeting Sunday morning, November 24, at the White House and "pledged that his administration would continue to pursue the U.S. policies on South Vietnam that had been established by the late President Kennedy. The White House made this disclosure after Mr. Johnson met with U.S. Ambassador Henry Cabot Lodge, who reported on a one-day strategy meeting on Vietnam that he had attended with other U.S. officials in Honolulu November 20th. . . . Johnson reportedly had emphasized at the White House meeting that: (a) the U.S.'s principal policy in Vietnam remained continued assistance to the new government to help it win the war against the Vietcong; (b) the U.S. stood by its October 2 decision to withdraw some U.S. troops from Vietnam. . . ."[65] We were to help South Vietnam "win" the war. Not buy time, but *win*. The language in Bundy's "first cut" began to be reinterpreted to ultimately mean that helping them "win" meant putting in our combat troops.

On January 22, 1964, General Taylor wrote to the secretary of defense: "The Joint Chiefs of Staff consider that the United States must:

i) commit additional U.S. forces, as necessary, in support of the combat action within South Vietnam, and (j) commit U.S. forces as necessary in direct actions against North Vietnam."

Here we have quite clear and loud advocacy of war by the men whom Kennedy had controlled. Now they were out of control.

Kennedy clearly did not think it looked good. He wrote McNamara on September 21, 1963, and said: "The events in South Vietnam since May 1963 have now raised serious questions both about the present prospects for success against the Viet Cong and still more about the future effectiveness of this effort. . . ."

William J. Rust writes: "Although Kennedy's government was hopeful, the President had come to doubt Vietnam's manageability. He had learned painfully from Diem's assassination that the U.S. could influence events there but not necessarily control them."[66]

Two days before Kennedy died, Michael Forrestal reported that Kennedy had asked about South Vietnam's viability. "It was the first time that he ever got really philosophical and reflective about Vietnam with me.

"But the question still lingers. What would President John F. Kennedy have done about Vietnam had he lived? . . . My guess is that he would not have crossed the covert action-advisory threshold, would not have bombed North Vietnam, and would not have committed U.S. ground troops to South Vietnam. Undoubtedly, Kennedy would have put off the really hard choices in Vietnam until after the 1964 election. Like Lyndon B. Johnson, he would have campaigned as a man of restraint and moderation—a sharp and reassuring contrast to the triggerhappy image of his opponent, Senator Barry Goldwater," Rust writes.

"At this point Kennedy might well have chosen the negotiations route, realizing full well that it would eventually mean Communist domination of Vietnam, Laos, and Cambodia and a divisive search for scapegoats at home. Such bitter consequences, however, could have appeared preferable to becoming a co-belligerent in a war where virtually every U.S. military and political initiative had failed. Indeed, Kennedy's own failures in Vietnam might have created an unshakable skepticism about the efficacy of bombing the north and of sending ground troops into the south."[67]

Rust tells us that the assassination of the Ngo brothers had an intense effect, deeply shocking him. General Maxwell Taylor was with Kennedy when he got the news of the murders. "Kennedy leaped to his feet and rushed from the room with such a look of shock and dismay on his face which I had never seen before."[68]

"It shook him personally . . . bothered him as a moral and religious matter," said Forrestal. "It shook his confidence, I think, in the kind of advice he was getting about South Vietnam."[69]

Of course Taylor and many other American officials were not so shocked. "The execution of a coup is not like organizing a tea party. Its a very dangerous business," Taylor said. "Revolutions are rough. People get hurt," Roger Hilsman told Marguerite Higgins.[70]

With the Ngo family out of the way, President Kennedy felt that he had the option to bring the war to a close on his own terms.

Kenneth O'Donnell and Dave Powers wrote: "The President's order to reduce the American military personnel in Vietnam by one thousand before the end of 1963 was still in effect the day he went to Texas. A few days after his death, during the morning, the order was quietly rescinded." These men were as close to John Kennedy as his wife was.

And Malcolm Kilduff, who was with him when he died, had this to say: "There is no question that he was taking us out of Vietnam. I was in his office just before we went to Dallas and he said that Vietnam was not worth another American life. There is no question about that. There is no question about it. I know that firsthand."[71]

They would know the truth of what was in his mind.

"I have positively solved the assassination of
President John F. Kennedy."

—Jim Garrison, February 24, 1967

CHAPTER 25

THE GARRISON AFFAIR

Lee Harvey Oswald was born and grew up in New Orleans. He still had family there in 1962, when he returned from the Soviet Union. He lived for a time in Fort Worth and Dallas, then returned to New Orleans in 1963, where he remained until not long before he allegedly killed President Kennedy.[1] As a high school student Oswald was in a Civil Air Patrol group in New Orleans whose leader was one David Ferrie,[2] a person who forever figured prominently in possible conspiracy scenarios of the assassination. Ferrie was asked to step down just before Oswald joined that particular CAP group, but Ferrie remained close to it and was in contact with Oswald.

Oswald, upon arrest in Dallas an hour after the assassination, was taken to jail, where he remained unrepresented by a lawyer until the moment of his death. He had tried unsuccessfully to obtain a lawyer. It was claimed that Dean Andrews, an attorney in New Orleans, received a call from a "Clem Bertrand" who asked him to go to Dallas and represent Oswald.[3]

In the period leading up to the assassination, Ferrie, an enigmatic and mysterious figure, was closely connected to Carlos Marcello of New Orleans,[4] the Mafia chieftain for all of the South excluding Florida.[5] Attorney General Robert Kennedy, the fiercest enemy the Mafia and the Teamsters ever had in the United States, had previously deported Marcello from the United States without due process.[6] Ferrie allegedly flew Marcello back,[7] and they were in court at the moment Kennedy was assassinated, winning an acquittal that day on immigration and other charges.[8] It was later alleged that the district attorney of New Orleans, Jim Garrison, and some of his staff had connections to Marcello and the Teamsters, or in some way was protecting organized crime.[9]

Ferrie was deeply involved with the CIA's operations against Cuba, flew planes for them, trained and armed guerrillas,[10] was a priest in a heretical Catholic church, and indulged in other aberrant behavior often involving young boys and men. Ferrie also worked for a former FBI agent, Guy Banister.[11] He had been a pilot for Eastern Airlines until he was fired after being arrested on a morals charge.[12] I met Ferrie and remember him as an intense and sinister, cynical, disgusting, disheveled individual who was excited at the prospect of preying upon the vulnerable, the helpless, and the innocent.

Banister had his office at 544 Camp Street, which was the same small building where Lee Harvey Oswald claimed to locate his Fair Play for Cuba Committee operations in late 1963, though some pamphlets Oswald handed out,[13] had the address 4907 Magazine Street stamped on them and others had the 544 Camp Street address.[14] In June 1963 Oswald handed out his leaflets on the dock where the U.S. Navy aircraft carrier *Wasp* was berthed.

One can only conclude from the available evidence that Oswald operated out of Banister's office. Banister had been in the Office of Naval Intelligence during World War II, and he had been the chief of the FBI's Chicago office. He was primarily engaged in counterintelligence operations in the New Orleans area, and that meant that he spied on and kept massive files on leftists and pointed provocateurs at them, of whom Oswald was obviously one. At the same time, arms and ammunition passed through his office, destined for the exiled Cubans who continually prepared attacks on Cuba and hoped for an invasion.

On the day of the assassination of President Kennedy, for unaccountable reasons Ferrie drove in one of the worst rainstorms on record to Houston, Texas, with two other men, Alvin Beauboeuf and Melvin Coffey, and then to Galveston and waited two hours in a skating rink to receive a phone call. Meanwhile, Jack Martin, an investigator who also worked for Banister, became deeply disturbed after a fight and pistol whipping from Banister and went to the police in New Orleans. He told them that David Ferrie was probably involved in the assassination, that Ferrie knew Oswald well and had taught him to shoot with a telescopic sight.

Martin, though a drinker, was credible enough to the police that when Ferrie returned on November 24, he was arrested along with his roommate (Layton Martens) and questioned. Regis Kennedy, an FBI agent, came in to question Ferrie after the police and the Secret Service were done with him.

Kennedy then got Ferrie off, and although the matter was mentioned by the Warren Commission,[15] it was essentially dropped. It is worthwhile to note that Regis Kennedy had a laissez faire attitude toward Carlos Marcello, whom Ferrie also worked for. The FBI man was often at meetings in 1961 of anti-Castro Cubans.[16]

Gary Shaw tells me that Regis Kennedy has been identified by Beverly Oliver as the FBI agent who took her movie camera and film away from her the day after the assassination.[17] She had filmed the motorcade as the President was shot, but the film has disappeared from the evidence. She knew Jack Ruby well. It may be unreasonable to believe that Regis Kennedy did in fact go to Dallas for a day and then return in time to interview Ferrie.

Three years passed, during which the Warren Commission performed its show investigation and issued the cover-up theory known as its Report. Then one day in November 1966, Senator Russell B. Long of Louisiana was riding tourist class on an airplane with Jim Garrison, who had always been troubled by the arrest and release of David Ferrie. Long expressed his severe doubts about the findings of the commission,[18] just as the prominent congressman from Louisiana, Hale Boggs, a member of the commission, did. Long also had ties to the Teamsters, and led an effort to get Jimmy Hoffa, the president of the Teamsters union, out of the jail Robert Kennedy had finally succeeded putting him in.[19] Hoffa and the Teamsters were at that time and for many years synonymous with the Mafia.

Garrison said he was troubled by indications that the plot to kill the President had been hatched in New Orleans, and he suspected that some of those involved were still there. Garrison, normally highly visible, went into seclusion and studied the published evidence, reading the volumes produced by the Warren Commission and whatever else was available. He studied the case against Oswald and concluded that Oswald not only didn't kill Kennedy, but that there were several gunmen —one was in the sewer alongside the car; two were in front. He felt sure that there was a plot by the CIA Cuban group partly based in New Orleans, led by someone named Clem Bertrand, that killed the President.

How Clem Bertrand became Clay Shaw has never been documented. Jim Garrison writes in his book *On the Trail of the Assassins* a sort of personal history of those times, that his investigators were gradually able to obtain statements from people in the French Quarter of New Orleans that Clay Shaw, a prominent businessman with a secret homosexual life, used the name Clay Bertrand when he was prowling the famous gay bars of the district.[20] "Clem" became "Clay."

For what followed, Scott Van Wynesberghe writes in *The Third Decade* that a "malevolent force," which involved the Teamsters, hung over it all.[21] Van Wynesberghe details the Teamsters' connections with some of those on Garrison's staff, and even one of the judges involved in the case.

Garrison put some of the people in his district attorney's office to work on the Kennedy assassination, and had spent about $8000 when reporter Jack Dempsey of the New Orleans *States-Item* got wind of how he was spending the taxpayers' money and mentioned it in his column. This got John Wilds of the city desk interested and he put Rosemary James on the story with Dempsey, to act as "good cop." The hardnosed Dempsey was the bad cop, and he hated Garrison about as much as Perry Russo hated John Kennedy because of the Bay of Pigs. Russo was to become the chief (and probably phony) witness in this setup.

A lot of people had assumed that the Warren Report had closed the case and for that reason wanted to let sleeping dogs lie. As Senator Long was later to say, Garrison had a perfect right to do what he was doing—conduct a criminal investigation into the assassination. In fact, when it later came to a hearing, a three-judge panel summarily threw out the Warren Report, refusing to admit it into evidence.

But Garrison, in over his head, was already in another kind of trouble. Plenty of people did not want the case investigated, and there was a ravenous media primed to ridicule Garrison and make his investigation public before it was complete.

"But there's something else that Oliver Stone left out of his movie, something that disturbed a lot of reporters in New Orleans in those days," Jack Payton wrote about the time Stone's movie *JFK* came out. "It's the fact that whatever you thought of Garrison or his screwball theory, somebody put together a carefully orchestrated campaign to discredit him right from the beginning. Most of the reporters in New Orleans knew that shortly after Garrison went public with his accusations, the Justice Department sent down a special task force from Washington to keep tabs on what he was up to. The offices of the U.S. Attorney and the local FBI got huge increases in staff. That was about the same time that strange rumors started floating around. Reporters, myself included, started getting strange telephone calls from people who wouldn't identify themselves. . . . You would try to check these things out and always end up getting nowhere. Even so, some of it would show up in the media, attributed to unnamed sources. One I remember in particular was from a man who said Garrison was a noted pederast and had a record of molesting young boys at the New Orleans Athletic Club. Others suggested marital infidelities, financial improprieties, or ties to the local Mafia clan."[22]

The kindest way of discussing the sad history that followed is to say that the glare of the public spotlight unbalanced Garrison and those who worked for him so that mistakes were made and their hand was forced. One of his staff, for instance, told Ferrie in advance what was going on.

In those days it was often the practice to surprise a defendant with unexpected witnesses or evidence in a criminal proceeding in spite of the rule in this country that defendants have a full right of discovery and disclosure. They have the right to face their accusers and prepare a defense. From the beginning of the Garrison affair, these failures and conflicts in prosecutorial methods was at the root of the nightmare and sensationalism that followed. One might bring into this discussion the matter of ethics, since the same questions arose over the actions of Oliver Stone and his producers of *JFK*.

What was the effect of the whole business? Years later the chief counsel of the Assassinations Committee, G. Robert Blakey, stated that (though it was not an official finding either explicit or implied) Carlos Marcello was involved in the assassination of President Kennedy. David Ferrie worked for Marcello. If there were Mafia ties to the government of New Orleans and Louisiana, as many have always believed, then the trial sacrificed some scapegoats and deflected attention away from Marcello and the Teamsters.

It was later well demonstrated that Shaw was on more than intimate terms with the CIA,[23] but so what? Garrison does not present any hard evidence in *On the Trail of the Assassins* or other writings that Shaw was involved in the plot to kill Kennedy. He convicts him only for allegedly talking about killing the President, something thousands of people probably did. Even the evidence Garrison claims (talk) is not illegal unless it is in the form of an overt threat. Garrison writes: "Had the jurors been aware of Shaw's Agency connection, the verdict might possibly have been different."[24] This is very lame reliance on guilt by association. Garrison goes on to write: "Even as it was, every juror Lane questioned agreed that the prosecution had established that President

Kennedy had been killed as the result of a conspiracy. To me, this was important. The jurors had acquitted Shaw as an individual, but they had *not* accepted the federal government's great lie about the assassination."[25]

Reporter Jack Payton wrote: "Few of us came away with much confidence in the government's official version of the truth, the Warren Commission Report. . . . Many of us got to interview Garrison, and I did several times, and each time I came away bewildered. Here was a man who was intelligent, a lot better read than most of the reporters covering him. But he was a lousy public speaker, often ponderous and sometimes almost inarticulate—certainly nothing like Kevin Costner in the movie. He seemed perfectly sane and totally aware of the powerful forces gathering to oppose him. Yet here also was Garrison, a previously obscure district attorney, making monstrous accusations he didn't have a chance in hell of proving. He was completely out of his depth, and we all knew it. Whether his conspiracy theory had merit became almost irrelevant after a while. There was simply no way he could prove it with the tools at his disposal as district attorney of Orleans Parish in Louisiana."[26]

Garrison's explanation for the failure of his case is to blame the assault of forces—including the major media—from the Attorney General of the United States (Ramsey Clark) to the Chief Justice of the Supreme Court (Earl Warren). He likened this to Hemingway's *Old Man and the Sea* having his great fish picked apart by sharks before he could get it home. "Looking back, I can see that this is pretty much the way it turned out when we finally got Clay Shaw to trial in Criminal District court. . . . Our office had been infiltrated by the federal government, and Bill Boxley had stolen many of our files. As if that were not enough, a week or two before the trial began, Lou Ivon learned that the young Englishman from Oxford who was in charge of our archives had given copies of many of our files to the defense. Almost as important, some of our key witnesses—e.g., David Ferrie, Gordon Novel, Sandra Moffett—had died or been scared off or moved from New Orleans with no chance of my extraditing them."[27] It is highly doubtful that anyone in this group, and the others he later discusses, either knew anything, would talk, or were credible.

That doesn't mean that Garrison wasn't on the right track all along. It means only that he really had no hard evidence and all the rest of the smoke-and-mirror show is just that: a show. Gary Rowell describes an interview of Garrison by one of the gadflies of this research where

Garrison claims that the House Assassinations Committee had a "f—king confession from one of the guys participating in the meetings. As an accessory. On tape. Hours. Dates, places, trips to Dallas in preparation . . . It's corroborated by a thousand things that I've sent up."[28] We would sure like to know about that tape.

A prosecution witness, Charles Spiesel, who might have been planted on Garrison, used to fingerprint his daughter every day when she came home from school for fear that someone had substituted her.[29] But Garrison found this out only during the trial when his witness was cross-examined. It did not do his case much good with one more kooky witness being exposed a bit too late. Somebody didn't do their homework.[30]

Like so much of what is said and done in the research community, the example of Garrison provides a few hard facts and a lot more loose talk, mistakes, excess, lies, and wrong statements. He is almost a model for slick and not so slick operators who get into the "conspiracy business" looking for exposure, success, and a buck.

Walter Sheridan of NBC went to New Orleans with a crew to investigate the investigation. Sheridan formerly worked for Robert Kennedy, and knew that the Kennedys had conducted a secret investigation of the assassination and that it pointed in the direction of Hoffa, Marcello, some Texas oilmen, and a few involved with the CIA in the New Orleans and Dallas area. Garrison later accused Sheridan of trying to bribe his star witness, Perry Raymond Russo, and placed criminal charges against him. It was this sort of heavy-handed tactic against members of the media, not to speak of someone very close to the Kennedy family, that made great trouble for Garrison. Sheridan told Robert Kennedy that Garrison was a fraud.

The New Orleans *States-Item* had begun a parallel investigation of their own, led by star reporters Rosemary James and Jack Wardlaw. They soon became aware that *Life* magazine had a team in New Orleans, and the local reporters and their paper were not willing to be scooped by out-of-towners. The *States-Item* published the story on February 17, 1967, and all hell broke loose. Overnight Garrison's investigation became a circus, the Scopes trial, and the Lindbergh case all rolled up into one. Hundreds of reporters and photographers descended upon the Big Easy from all over the world, and like amoebas crawling across the scum of the pond absorbed everything they could find.[31] It was great for business on Bourbon Street, which Big Jim had gone to some trouble to clean up, but it was not what the Jolly Green Giant's (as Jim Garrison was also known) flair for publicity had contemplated. Garrison had a lot of local support, and a group of businessmen calling themselves Truth and Consequences put up the cash for Garrison's further inquiries. Nobody believed the Warren Report.

Garrison did not have a case against anyone, even though he could prove a conspiracy in the assassination based on the work of other researchers. That was a far cry from having a defendant who could be convicted in court of law. Conspiracy in most jurisdictions requires an overt act.* But there is nothing like having a defendant for conducting a fishing expedition.

And Garrison needed a defendant.

On the seventeenth of February, when the story broke in the local paper, Garrison had no defendant, though he had been contemplating arresting David Ferrie as a conspirator in the assassination. Going on the offensive, David Ferrie went down to the *States-Item* and talked to reporters, telling them that he was picked by Garrison as the getaway pilot in the assassination. Five days later Ferrie was dead. The coroner at first said that his examination showed that Ferrie had died before midnight of the twenty-first. But George Lardner, the reporter who handles national security matters for the *Washington Post,* said that Ferrie was still alive when he left his apartment at four in the morning after a four-hour interview starting at midnight.[32]

Lardner writes: "I was probably the last man to see Ferrie alive. Is Stone [Oliver] suggesting that I interviewed a dead man? In fact, the coroner originally said Ferrie died around midnight, then redid that aspect of the autopsy after I told him he was wrong. This man died a natural death."[33] Although I respect Lardner, I find this rather odd, and especially find his medical opinion strange. It has to be one of the

---

* Conspiracy requires the persons involved to *agree* that they *will* perform the act, which is either unlawful, such as murder or fraud, or that they will obtain a lawful goal through illegal means. Talking about killing someone is just that: talk. They have to agree that they will do it. Trying to prove such a crime or that a person agreed to help with it can be all but impossible due to the hearsay rule. Law enforcement authorities who agree to use illegal means, such as an illegal search, intimidated or bribed witnesses, and perjured testimony are in a criminal conspiracy—reason enough for the press to malign the perpetrators.

Louisiana law required that "one or more of such parties does an act in furtherance of the object of the agreement or combination."

few times in history, if not the only time, when a scientist changes his findings on the basis of a reporter telling him that the man was not dead when he said he was.

There was a suicide note, of course, and the finding was that Ferrie died of a berry aneurysm, which is the rupture of a blood vessel. A hard blow on the neck could do it, but they failed to spot any tissue damage that indicated murder.[34] "We waited too long," Garrison told me.

Interestingly enough, another figure in the case—Eladio Del Valle—whom Garrison's men had located three days before, and to whom they promised to protect was found hacked to death in Florida about the same hour. In fact, quite a lot of strong-arm types died about the time they talked to the big show investigations in these cases. All is just coincidental, of course.

Two days after these deaths Garrison felt the chasm opening beneath his feet. He had to do something. He began making statements to the throng of newspaper people that had flooded back into New Orleans. Starting to dig a hole for himself, Garrison announced that he had "positively solved the assassination of President John F. Kennedy," and would arrest everybody involved.[35]

He went on, digging deeper. "The only way they [the Kennedy plot suspects] are going to get away from us is to kill themselves."[36] Did he want them to die?

As Rosemary James and Jack Wardlaw wrote: "And then came the real jawbreaker for quizzical newsmen chewing up the D.A.'s every word: 'The key to the whole case is through the looking glass. Black is white; white is black. I don't want to be cryptic, but that's the way it is.'" Nobody understood this too well except the gay community, which used the term "through the looking glass" to mean the gay world. That's where Ferrie was from, and where Big Jim had evidently been rooting around.[37]

"I have no reason to believe that Lee Harvey Oswald killed anybody on November 22, 1963," Garrison said, making sure that the political and media establishment that had fallen into line behind the Warren Commission was forced into opposition, since they were committed to the official story. One thing Garrison was good at was antagonizing his potentially greatest enemies. Soon he was threatening and even arresting reporters and witnesses. This greatly antagonized journalists.

Before the story broke to the press, Garrison had another chief witness, David L. Lewis, who did some private investigation work. He was with Guy Banister's secretary, Delphine Roberts, one day when Cuban exile Carlos Quiroga came in with a Leon Oswald. A few days later he saw Quiroga, Oswald, and David Ferrie in the office together. When Jim Garrison's investigation came along three years later, Lewis decided that Leon Oswald might have been Lee Harvey Oswald.[38]

So far, he had only guilt by association.

Harold Weisberg tells me that Earling Carothers Garrison (he named himself Jim) was in the process of issuing arrest warrants for Robert Perrin, husband of Nancy Perrin who figured in the Warren Commission investigation, as a conspirator when he pointed out that Perrin had died of arsenic poisoning the year before John Kennedy was assassinated.

But Perrin might not have been dead at all, as Garrison investigator Bill Boxley (real name is William Wood) thought.[39]

Garrison's handling of the press was working against him. His close friend, David Chandler, a reporter and now correspondent for *Life,* said that he was "outraged by his irresponsible behavior."[40]

Garrison needed to arrest *somebody* and have a defendant. He had information from a witness that Lee Harvey Oswald, David Ferrie, and Clay Shaw had been seen together.

That is *all* that he had. Even if it were true, and the alleged conversations about killing Kennedy were accurate, it did not *prove* a conspiracy. It was guilt by association. Circumstantial evidence cannot prove a conspiracy charge. There was no overt act in the evidence. Garrison had to show the operation of a conspiracy.

Clay Shaw

On the day that Ferrie died, February 22, 1967, a twenty-six-year-old insurance salesman—Perry Raymond Russo—of unstable mental background, long treated by psychiatrists, wrote a letter to Garrison saying he knew Ferrie. Two days later Russo gave an interview on WDSU-TV in which he said: "I never heard of Oswald until the television [sic] of the assassination."[41] The next day Garrison sent Andrew Sciambra to interview Russo, and showed him a photograph of Clay Shaw. Russo said he had seen him at a speech given by President Kennedy, and at David Ferrie's gas station, which Ferrie had bought after Kennedy died.[42]

But then Russo said that Lee Harvey Oswald had been a past roommate of David Ferrie, which contradicted what he had said on television the day before. They had to draw a beard on the picture of Oswald for him to say that it looked familiar. Oswald has never been known to have worn a beard. Even then, Russo did not know the name of the roommate of Ferrie, though "the name Leon rings a bell."[43]

Jack Payton, a young reporter, lived next door to Perry Russo and thought he was weird. "Russo, like the rest of Garrison's suspects or witnesses, was a misfit, not the kind of person you would depend on to prove a conspiracy as far-reaching as Garrison's. When he finally got called to the stand, Russo admitted under cross-examination that he remembered his crucial testimony only after being hypnotized."[44]

The coroner of New Orleans, Nicholas Chetta, who performed the autopsies on a number of the star characters in this drama, including David Ferrie and Robert Perrin, administered "truth serum" (sodium pentothal). Does it not seem strange that the coroner of Orleans Parish would be performing this chore? Later Russo was hypnotized and left with posthypnotic suggestions, a session at which Dr. Chetta was also present. Chetta died of a heart attack the following year. His sometime assistant and close associate, Dr. Mary Sherman, also died under questionable circumstances, and his brother-in-law and sometime assistant Dr. Henry Delaune was murdered on January 26, 1969.[45]

Actually Russo claimed only that he heard Ferrie "joking" in the summer of 1963 about how easy it would be to kill Kennedy or any president.[46] I need to point out that nobody in this country can be prosecuted for "joking" about killing someone. That is not and cannot constitute the crime of conspiracy, though the Secret Service or police might have an interest in those who are reported to banter about such things.

Russo also said that he had seen Lee Harvey Oswald in New Orleans at a time when the Warren Commission had proven (or so they thought) that Oswald was in Mexico.[47]

During the truth serum session, Russo was asked if Clem Bertrand had ever appeared at Ferrie's apartment. *Life* editor Richard Billings, who years later wrote the Report of the House Assassinations Committee, was present when Russo placed a tall, white-haired gentleman named Bertrand in Ferrie's apartment. Russo said that he never heard the name Bertrand before. Clem Bertrand had become Clay Shaw in Garrison's mind by then.

Then it was arranged for Russo to have a clandestine look at Clay Shaw on March 1, 1967, and after an identification by Russo, Shaw was arrested on the spot. He was charged with conspiracy to murder Presi-

dent Kennedy. Van Wynesberghe points out that the booking procedure itself was a violation of Shaw's rights. The arrest forms were later
ruled inadmissible. It was later claimed that Shaw gave the booking
officer the alias Clay Bertrand, but this is in dispute, and Shaw's defense attorneys claimed that the name was added to the arrest forms
later.[48]

From that moment on it was a debacle. Clay Shaw had friends in high
places, and the director of the CIA, Richard Helms, expressed considerable concern about his prosecution,[49] as did numerous others in government. Garrison was considered a renegade and was read out of the
association of former FBI agents. Shaw, the former director of the
International Trade Mart, had undoubtedly been involved in intelligence operations in World War II and certainly had performed those
functions in his capacity as a world-traveling businessman, as did many
patriotic Americans in those days. The Mob was considered as patriotic
as the next guy in the battle against the worldwide Communist conspiracy, and was used to stifle leftist influence in the unions, at that time a
major political force. Partnership with the government helped entrench
the Mob in our affairs, as would any deal with the devil.

For a populist harboring ambitions for a seat in the United States
Senate, or to be governor, one needed the votes of the common man in
Louisiana, and Garrison started out on a path that normally would have
won him a lot of votes, having a tremendous issue (the assassination of
John Kennedy) and a sounding board that would get him in the news
everyday. But it all turned to shit and blew up in his face. It was one of
the biggest political blunders of modern times.

When Robert Kennedy prosecuted the Mob and put in jail union
leaders like Hoffa, he was messing with the fundamental political organization of the nation, a partnership of the intelligence agencies, the
military, the Mafia (who did the dirty work) and the establishment.
Garrison, possibly seeking political gain, inserted himself into this, in a
quixotic quest that he had to have known could not succeed because he
had no case against Shaw. If he didn't know that, this literate and
intelligent man was ultimately stupid. The whole thing was a charade.
Marcello was protected at the moment he beat the deportation rap,
Hoffa was sprung from jail, and there was an *appearance* that *someone*
in an official capacity, no matter how local, was trying to reinvestigate
Kennedy's death at a time when many citizens were making known that
they believed there was a conspiracy. Maybe the whole thing was a put-
up job from the start, and Shaw was expendable in spite of his wartime

medals and decorations. The doubting public had to be pacified while savaging their hopes. The big-name up-front critics of the Warren Report, provocateurs for the most part, co-opted the investigation and seized it from the many inspired amateurs who might have broken the case.

Countries need diversions and entertainments, especially when there are domestic and international problems. In America in the late 1960s attention needed to be directed away from such failures as the program to prosecute the Mob, the civil rights marches, and the major start-up of the war in Vietnam. Circuses. That Garrison gave us. All the critics at first had their hopes up, and then they were set against one another.

Two years after Shaw was arrested he was acquitted by a jury after only one ballot and less than an hour of deliberation. Russo was thoroughly discredited as a witness, and there was no other witness except one, Vernon B. Bundy, a heroin addict who was utterly unbelievable. Was this a plot against Garrison run by CIA operatives? No. There was no case to start with. Shaw lost his house and spent $200,000 defending himself. He died under strange circumstances, to put it politely, like so many others. His neighbors say they saw the body go into his house on a stretcher before he was taken out.[50]

Aftermath

Garrison went down the garden path. He spent a vast amount of time, as many of us researchers do, proving (or attempting to do so) a conspiracy in the case, but his investigation did not link a conspiracy to the men he was arresting, indicting, and trying. He may have proved a conspiracy, but at the expense of a lot of people's lives. Scott Van Wynesberghe points out three solid achievements: The Zapruder film was repeatedly shown in the courtroom, which spoke volumes for what really happened on November 22, 1963; the Clinton, Louisiana, witnesses presented solid testimony that they had seen Oswald and Ferrie together, with perhaps Clay Shaw or someone who looked like him (Guy Banister looked like him); the Clinton witnesses were examined by the House Assassinations Committee and their testimony was confirmed;[51] and Shaw's own testimony placed him in proximity to two of Ferrie's roommates, whom he knew: Layton Martens and James Lewallen.[52] Garrison also obtained the testimony of Kennedy autopsy sur-

geon Dr. Pierre Finck as well as other testimony that further established evidence of a conspiracy *in se.*

But that is about it. None of Garrison's investigation linked anyone
to any conspiracy. All Garrison had was hearsay, which in most instances is not admissible.

Of course the death of David Ferrie didn't help, but it is doubtful
that Ferrie would have—even if he were involved—described a plot.

Like some of the other big names in the critical community, perhaps
Garrison lacked scruples. He attempted to capitalize on a few facts and
get as much mileage out of them as he could with little regard to the
consequences. I find that this is a human character trait he has in
common with a lot of people. Too many enter the fray with a big ego
and think they can bluff or bull their way through for whatever is to be
gained. I don't see that the media has many scruples with regard to this
case either, considering their failure to properly investigate it. Those in
government had no scruples, covering up the case. Like Diogenes, I
look for an honest man. The entrance of an errant knight from Hollywood into the lists, like so many young swains of high motivation and
great passion but lacking in brains and experience, will not break the
case apart.

As brilliant and intelligent a man as Garrison was, he was in over his
head. He couldn't control the actions of all of his staff either. And he
himself was made unstable by the events as they began to unfold. He
inspired great passion, just as the film made about him and the assassination of President Kennedy by Oliver Stone has inspired great passion
and debate. The same thing was happening all over again twenty-four
years later, with the same people involved, including Jim Garrison playing his greatest adversary, Chief Justice Earl Warren.

Garrison carried on his life, running for election, losing, winning,
ending up a respected appeals court judge. He was durable and a survi-
vor in spite of declining health. He lived to see a movie made about him
and his investigation.

There is another issue underlying all this, and that is the sometimes
fatal flaw in our judicial system. We have a fundamental tenet that
citizens are innocent until proven guilty. It doesn't always work that
way. The flaw is that far too often people are indicted on flimsy evidence, on circumstantial evidence, on perjured or bought testimony,
testimony obtained with promises of leniency in other charges. People
are indicted when there is reasonable doubt that they did it. If there
was an honest examination of the evidence by prosecutors beforehand

and they had a reasonable doubt, then they should not arrest or indict because there can be no conviction if there's a reasonable doubt. That is the law of the land.

But they do it, and this major flaw (which allows so many to get off in court) is there because too often a case can be rigged if the defendant is unable to obtain a proper defense. The political problem of the prosecutor is solved by convicting somebody—anybody—for a crime. After all, there have to be arrests and convictions to keep the social lid on. It's like a body count. An arrest and accusation of even an innocent person will often satisfy the wolves.

The standard of reasonable doubt which every jury must apply to a criminal defendant should be applied before anyone is indicted. But it isn't, and Jim Garrison failed to do that. He just bulled ahead. Weisberg wrote me: "I know what did and did not happen at the Shaw trial, and before they started impaneling the jury, I learned with some shock what their alleged case was, and I predicted they would lose and deserved to."[53]

Garrison made the ultimate error. He antagonized the press. Oliver Stone repeated it and compounded it, so we are destined to live the whole business all over again. I have no doubt they did it deliberately. That's show biz! After all, Garrison sold his book to Stone, who made a movie called *JFK* that isn't about JFK at all.

CHAPTER 26

THE OLIVER STONE MOVIE *JFK*

"What this entire, relentlessly didactic and polemical movie does is make one wonder about Oliver Stone. To some observers, there is nothing to wonder about. In their view, Stone's entire cinematic oeuvre—*Platoon, Wall Street, Born on the Fourth of July,* and the rest—has been marked by dishonest renderings of history, simplistic moral constructs, and a kind of puerile fatuousness about the 1960s," the *Chicago Tribune* pontificated. "The danger is that Stone's film and the pseudo-history it so effectively portrays will become the popularly accepted version. After all, what can scholarship avail against Kevin Costner, Sissy Spacek, Donald Sutherland, et al on the big screen with Dolby Stereo?"[1] Having added its weight to the enormous crescendo that swept the nation about the film, the *Tribune* then said that "it's time that the documents and all the physical evidence from the Kennedy assassination—pictures, films, tissue samples, and the rest—be made public and available for examination. . . . If our history since November 22, 1963, demonstrates anything, it is the cleansing effect of public exposure and the corrosive effect—as in *JFK*—of secrecy."

Now begins the tale of one of the greatest brouhahas in American political, intellectual, and filmmaking history.

Harold Weisberg is the grandfather of assassination research and has now become respected by the same media that used to ridicule him. It is to him that much of the media turns when they have questions about the latest fad or theory put forth by buffs, writers, and others attempting to mine the rich vein of confusion and misinformation surrounding the case. For it is Weisberg, right or wrong, who sits in judgment upon all those charlatans and frauds, upon the earnest but misguided, or those who may have made a truly new discovery.

521

Weisberg worked with Jim Garrison at first until he was fed up and turned against him. Garrison had written the foreword to Weisberg's book *Oswald in New Orleans,* and otherwise thought highly of Weisberg's work, which was the first published detailed analytical criticism of the evidence in the assassination of the President. Weisberg wrote Oliver Stone.[2] "I told Stone about Garrison sometime before he started shooting film. I warned Stone in advance," Weisberg wrote me a week before the scheduled release of the forty-million-dollar film, when the hype from Hollywood was reaching a pitch.[3] The movie by then had made the cover of *Life* and *Newsweek,* and every newspaper and magazine had written about it.

The day I received this letter from Weisberg, there he was on the *CBS Evening News* with Dan Rather,* who saw the assassination that terrible day in Dallas almost three decades before. Rather started off the program with this: "One of Hollywood's best-paid filmmakers mixes fact, fiction, and theory in a new film about the killing of John F. Kennedy. What happens when Hollywood mixes facts, half-baked theories, and sheer fiction into a big-budget film and then tries to sell it as truth and history?"

Mark Phillips, the CBS reporter, continued: "On a Hollywood sound stage, Oliver Stone, two-time Oscar winner, is adjusting history, creating his version of how and why John F. Kennedy was killed. It's a version that differs dramatically from the Warren Commission account of one deranged gunman acting alone." Phillips explains that Stone says the murder was over Vietnam.

Mark Phillips goes on, videotaping in Weisberg's basement, where Weisberg has scores of file cabinets filled with thousands of FBI documents released to him over the years. "Weisberg says: 'Jim Garrison's investigation was a fraud. And Oliver Stone hasn't produced history as he says, but he created another fiction.'" George Lardner, Jr., had a few weeks before written in the *Washington Post:* "Garrison's investigation was a fraud."[4] Lardner, though, acknowledges "that a probable conspiracy [in the assassination] took place."[5]

What do people mean by history? The battle is on for *who* is going to

---

* During a TV broadcast, Dan Rather had reversed the direction of Kennedy's head snap when he was struck with the fatal bullet, saying the head went forward rather than rocketing backward, as it does, when he narrated the Zapruder film decades before. The television viewer was not allowed to actually see the film; Rather told us what he wanted us to think was on it.

define just what that history is. The Warren Report is not writ in stone, not yet "history"—it's still only an opinion or a theory—and history is written by the winners. Nobody has won just yet.

Rather's real purpose seems to be to turn the public away from any criticism of the Warren theory. He used Weisberg, twisting and distorting some of his key points. I agree with Weisberg that Stone does not have the right to change the history of what happened in those years, just as Stone's original script had Jim Garrison waving an autopsy picture of President Kennedy at the jury and saying, "This is the finally released and official autopsy photo." The pictures have never been released. It is this sort of false representation that got Stone into trouble with most of the research community, or at least with those of us whom he either couldn't buy or did not try to deal with. He thereby alienated the very people who might have kept his movie straight, and instead rounded up the usual suspects, the disinformation specialists in the research community, the has-beens.

Was the movie intended to be a vindication of Garrison somehow? Vindicating what? Why make a movie centered on Garrison's personal life? As a vehicle to discuss the conspiracy that murdered Kennedy? As a metaphor, as Stone said—a composite? But if the film doesn't talk about what Garrison's investigation did to a lot of people's lives, in most cases—if not all—those completely innocent of anything having to do with the investigation, what good is it? If it does not talk about Kennedy's life and work, what good is it? Does it describe what Kennedy went through that morning to get out of bed and get into his back brace? The pain he lived with? Instead, they hired a nobody to play Kennedy, and a terrible actor to play Garrison.

Does this movie have any connection with the realities we have touched upon? Stone deifies and tries to vindicate Garrison by overlooking the man's serious flaws and what was wrong with what he did. When asked about this, Stone says that he did not have time in a three-hour movie to get into questions of character. Pardon me, but isn't that what movie-making is about, aside from storytelling? Character? A true artist can demonstrate character on the silver screen in a trice.

Dan Rather had one final word at the end of his television news broadcast: "And now the public is going to live with the pain and the uncertainty of that dark day in Dallas once more. For much of Stone's audience, this powerful movie by a skilled artist is the only version they'll know. Call it art or call it history, it's bound to make an impression." Stone had the last word, saying, "It's only a movie. They can go in and you can either believe it or not."

There are many problems with all of this.

The Problem

The issue has been raised as to whether or not Oliver Stone had the right to make his film without public discussion beforehand, then to release that film and subject it to normal criticism. Most people in the media don't think so, and neither do I.

Stone chose to make various and conflicting public statements beforehand, such as in his *Dallas Morning News* interview,[6] and an interview in New Orleans.[7] In Dallas he said that "I am making a movie first and foremost. I'm not doing a school lesson here, and I don't have a documentarian's responsibilities. I have a dramatist's responsibilities to an audience." Wrong. This is what got him into deep trouble with Harold Weisberg, Jon Margolis of the *Chicago Tribune*,[8] and George Lardner of the *Washington Post*,[9] who insists that Garrison is a fraud to being with. Who or what that history (of the assassination) is has not been made clear, and that is what we have been arguing about all these years. The real issue is that neither Stone nor anyone else has the right to make composite characters out of Perry Raymond Russo, as he does in the film, "metaphors" out of Jim Garrison, and so on. He has to tell the truth. We make the rules, not him.

"I've taken the license of using Garrison as a metaphor for all the credible researchers," Stone said. "He's an all-encompassing figure."[10] This statement is guaranteed to make enemies of those who do not want to be lumped together with Garrison, and thus discredited. In a sense, Garrison certainly is a metaphor, since we have all have had some of the problems he had when the sky fell in on him as a result of his own excesses, but only a few other big-name critics of the Warren Report actually engaged in hoaxes, and to put all together as one composite figure certainly does distort the reality of who and what Garrison and the others really were, each different in their own way, and each just as dangerous.

To renounce a "documentarian's responsibility" is to renounce his integrity, his citizenship, his caring. Perhaps Stone felt trapped, having publicly committed himself to Garrison and Garrison's story, then realizing that there was something wrong with it. It was the Hollywood mind at work, dealing in images rather than in facts and honesty. And changing course in midstream.

Margolis jumped into the fray with his *Tribune* article headed JFK MOVIE AND BOOK ATTEMPT TO REWRITE HISTORY. "Whether or not it is a gift, artistic talent conveys a responsibility. Those who can sway emotions ought to know what they are talking about, lest emotions be swayed toward foolishness," Margolis writes, and what he has to say—in part—deserves reprinting here. "Unhappily, there is no law of nature that ordains that talent will be accompanied by knowledge, much less by wisdom, and the ill-informed poet, painter, musician, or novelist is a commonplace in our time. Most do little harm because art, even popular entertainment, has far less impact than either its practitioners or its critics like to think. People are smarter than artists or critics, and know better than to confuse novels, movies, or plays with reality. . . . Still, some insults to intelligence and decency warrant objection. Such an insult now looms. It is *JFK* . . . based largely on a book called *On the Trail of the Assassins* by Jim Garrison."

Margolis and other critics who wrote about the movie jump on one primary point: "Garrison writes that the less than conclusive testimony of one waitress 'constituted the totality of the witness testimony identifying Lee Oswald' as the man who killed a Dallas patrolman after shooting the President. There were in fact six witnesses who either saw the patrolman get shot or saw the armed gunman running from the scene. All six identified Oswald." Not that that testimony ever held water.

Should I be climbing all over Stone when he is getting across key points in my research such as the fact that the autopsy photos show the head intact when all the medical evidence demonstrated that this was not true, and that there were more than four shots fired?[11] Yes, because Stone has an obligation not to trade on other people's research (he does not properly credit them) and to not discredit the case for conspiracy as a whole by deifying Garrison.

Stone says: "I feel I've behaved responsibly. I've done all my homework. I have tried to include all the credible evidence. . . . But we're not doing a documentary. Most of all, I felt a tremendous need to make as many people as possible aware of what really happened that day. For me as a filmmaker, that means doing it cinematically."[12] I assume that this last statement means fictionalizing. The fact is, the film mentions almost *no* evidence showing conspiracy, and instead presents only theory (in the person of Donald Sutherland and his monologue) as *evidence* of conspiracy.

The movie, about Jim Garrison, is in fact propaganda. The mixing of a political agenda with art is the most dangerous business there is, even if we agree with what it says because of the power over people's minds.

We are concerned about the means versus the end here, something the big-name writers in the "critical community" often ignore. The facts in the film should be totally accurate. We don't need any Hollywood embellishments with metaphors and alternative myth-making.

"My feeling is that Jim Garrison was an extremely courageous individual who took extremely long odds and pointed a strong finger at government cover-up. That took guts in the 1960s, when the FBI and CIA were sacred cows. And don't forget he had 23 years of military service, was three times elected district attorney of New Orleans, and is now an appellate judge. He's hardly a buffoon. Garrison was the first to see that the JFK assassination wasn't just a matter of trajectories and bullet fragments in Dealey Plaza. He called into question the larger issues, especially the government's willingness to lie to the public—and this was before Watergate," Stone said.[13] True, but it nevertheless ignores the many other issues that have been raised.

One of those issues is that Garrison's case rested on Perry Russo's identification of Clay Shaw and his claim that he saw Shaw with Oswald. Why was he left out of the movie? Russo's statements would appear preposterous, as they did to the court in 1969, because they were obtained under hypnosis. Stone instead creates a composite character of Russo and other witnesses, indicating that he knows very well that this evidence is fake and he is afraid to present the Russo story for what it was. In other words, Stone is trying to make the trial and the case look a lot better than it was by avoiding historical truth and fictionalizing.

The New Orleans *Times-Picayune*[14] said that Garrison knew his case amounted to nothing, but he cynically pursued it to get publicity. "In short, the accusation is that Oliver Stone doesn't know what he is talking about in his film."[15]

The *New York Times* goes on to quote Stone: "I didn't want to make a movie of the Garrison book only. He is the protagonist, but the book ends essentially in 1969, and I wanted to push the movie into the new ground that was uncovered after 1969 and pre-1969—the autopsies, the bullets, the work of other researchers. So I've taken dramatic license. It is not a true story per se. It is not the Jim Garrison story. It is a film called *JFK*. It explores all the possible scenarios of why Kennedy was killed, who killed him, and why. What actually happens in the movie is that you see different scenarios, different possible conclusions." The film *never* does this at all.

Then Stone gets into what he thinks his movie is about, which bears scant relationship to his script. He claims that it is like the 1951 Japanese epic *Rashomon* in which the same event is seen from several points of view rather than a "straightforward, unequivocal defense of any particular theory." (This is another completely false statement about his own film. He has one idea *only* to sell.)

Of course, without consulting those who are on the cutting edge of this research, how can he know what he is talking about?

"Oliver Stone Fights Back" came the word in Elaine Dutka's article in the *Los Angeles Times*.[16] Aubrey Rike, the ambulance driver who helped put Kennedy in his casket, complained to me about the amount of blood Stone was slinging around the emergency room at Parkland Hospital. I told Dutka about it, and she led off her article with Rike's criticism. Stone told Dutka: "This isn't history, this is movie-making. I'm not setting out to make a documentary."

Dutka wrote: "At issue is not only the artist's responsibility when dealing with a subject in the public domain, but whether these critics— in the press and elsewhere—are curtailing creative freedom by prejudging a work-in-progress."

Stone replied to the pre-judgments by likening them to what happens in an authoritarian state. He said: "It's interesting that the *Washington Post* is applauding the Soviet media for its new openness, its willingness to expose Stalin's mass murders, while impugning my project before the American people can assess it. It's hypocritical, a double standard, ironic at best."[17]

Stone asks a cogent question in this article of his own in the *Washington Post*—when he was allowed equal time after Lardner's attack on the movie he had not yet made: "Why is Lardner so worried about our movie? Why is he so concerned that the investigation not be reopened? Lardner admits to a conspiracy, so why is he so afraid people might see it? If I am the buffoon he and Outlook's demonizing cartoon make me out to be, no one will really believe my film. I can't but feel there is another agenda here. Does the *Washington Post* object to our right to make a movie our way, or does it just object to our disagreeing with its views that the Warren Commission was right?"

*   *   *

We have raised the question as to whose history is being rewritten in the movie. Everyone from Weisberg to Lardner has complained about Stone's tampering with this history. The fact is that the so-called six-witness testimony that Oswald shot Tippit never held water, and is as thin as Garrison's charges against Shaw. The plain fact is that Oswald's handgun had not been fired and no one has ever offered evidence that it had been.

Margolis, who calls Garrison bizarre (twice)—Lardner calls him "zany"—points out that in the first Stone script he has Lyndon Johnson behind the plot to kill President Kennedy. Needless to say, this is prima facie crazy. Some evidence has been put forward by Johnson's former mistress and a lawyer, Craig Zirbel, in a book called *The Texas Connection,* but it is unreasonable to supposse that Johnson planned Kennedy's murder or ordered it. "To remember Lyndon Johnson is not to love him. But the suggestion that Johnson would stoop to murder, stupidly plotting with men he knew enough to distrust, is even less credible than was Johnson at his worst."[18]

Margolis concludes by saying: "Simple-mindedness has always been Stone's weakness. . . . None of his other movies posed the danger that millions of young people, ignorant of recent history and influenced by Stone's technique, may henceforth believe that a president of the United States got the job by having his predecessor bumped off. There is a point at which intellectual myopia becomes morally repugnant. Stone's new movie proves that he has passed that point." The problem with Margolis and others of a like mind is that they make clear that they reject conspiracy theories and claim that Stone is therefore rewriting history, or what they *think* is history, according to the Warren Report. In fact, the history of the assassination was rewritten by Congress when they found in 1979 that there *was* a conspiracy in the crime. The large majority of the public believes this. They don't need to be protected by journalists on that score.

Stone told the *Los Angeles Times* that we have a "Fascist security state running around this country."[19] This is the kind of excessive statement that both Garrison and Stone are known for, which defames the nation and which is simply not true. Stone wonders why the media is dumping on him. It doesn't occur to him that his own big mouth, like Garrison's, is getting him into this trouble. More especially, it doesn't occur to them that when they make public statements like this, *everyone* has a right to scrutinize them, as they have become very public and what they are doing legitimately concerns everyone. We have a perfect right to criticize the critics. This is a democracy, and it is *our* history. A film is as open to scrutiny as were the deliberations of the Warren Commission. There are fundamental issues of ethics and journalistic responsibility involved.

At times in its past, our government has overstepped its authority and impinged on our freedoms, but it never became a Fascist state and could not. Yes, a certain amount of surveillance exists or existed in the past that went beyond what was required, but Stone's statement is the statement of an extremist and is a valid reason why the press, even the liberal press, would call him to task—the man has so much power to influence opinion here and over the world. Certainly we have a right to investigate when the man appears at times as nuts as the people he wants to expose.

Stone repeatedly told reporters that his film offers several possible conspiracy scenarios. "I hope my responsibility is apparent in the work, but the work cannot be prejudged," he told Jay Carr.[20]

Controversy sells books and movies. Time-Warner, the company making the movie and reviewing it in their magazine, *Time,* gets to sell it on HBO and Cinemax, which they own. Stone has always hyped up his movies beforehand, explaining what he is going to do as though it were the Holy Grail and he were a New Wave French director in 1956.

Oliver Stone may have thought that he was engaging in the normal hype for a film prior to its release, but in so doing he initiated the very public discussion he now feels is unfair.

"What we're doing is we're sort of acting like detectives," Stone said.[21] "It's entertaining, it's a thriller," Stone told Forrest Sawyer.[22] "I tried to put all the researchers into Garrison's case." No way did we get in there. This was strictly Garrison's theory of the conspiracy, plus some outdated medical evidence exposed by Weisberg and a handful of others. Therefore, the movie did not go any further than what was known in 1967 about the medical evidence.

Stone admitted to Forrest Sawyer that the meeting with Mr. "X" (Fletcher Prouty) did not happen as it does in the movie.

Harold Weisberg described Stone as a "great monster." Stone, in making a film that relies partly on this man's research, must take notice. He is not completely free to do what he wants. Weisberg said that Garrison's investigation "was not in any sense investigation. He was making it up as he went along."[23] William Gurvich, chief aide to Garrison, had quit him abruptly in June 1967 because he believed the investigation had no basis, and went to work for Clay Shaw's defense team.[24] He told Forrest Sawyer on ABC-TV's *Nightline* that "I know that there was no evidence."[25]

"If they can make up a myth, why can't Oliver?" Jack Lemmon said on the way into the premier in Hollywood. What we were treated to in the hoopla that followed were the utterances of the Hollywood mind hard at work on a tough intellectual problem that went right by them.

There is a doctrine of responsible journalism. Not only do alleged facts have to be corroborated, but journalists abide by certain unspoken rules of conduct and ethics. This is even more true where crimes are concerned, as in the murder of President Kennedy. When Stone enters the field of journalism, as he has, he must play by the rules. He is not completely free. If he engages in unethical behavior, he must account for it.

At this point probably every major assassination researcher is against both Stone and his film. Why? He started out praising these people and tried to buy some of them. He has seriously disrupted our work at a key moment. He has wrecked relationships and is making a cartoon of the most serious affair in American political history. The very idea of having famous but weak or silly stars in his film makes a joke of the great tragedy we have suffered and are still suffering. To make it worse, he has Robin Hood playing the key role, dancing with wolves.*

The *Washington Post* and George Lardner, Jr., were trying to tell Stone and Hollywood something of great importance. Other signals should have been picked up when Lardner's by-line read "George Lardner covers national security issues for the *Washington Post.*" Alarm lights went on when the same article made it clear that Harold Weisberg had joined forces with the *Post* and given them Stone's script. In fact, every communication Stone made to the *Post* was sent to Harold Weisberg by the *Post* for response.

Harold Weisberg in fact motivated the entire onslaught of the *Washington Post* against the Stone film when he wrote Lardner, and told me that "writing about the Stone movie was not Lardner's idea, not the *Post*'s. I interested them. I gave Lardner the script and access to any of my Garrison records he wanted. He read every word of his story to me before he submitted it, and there is no inaccuracy or unfairness in it.

---

* Kevin Costner directed and acted in a film called *Dances with Wolves,* and played Robin Hood in another film about the same time. Some writers said that Stone was dancing with facts.

Based on what I gave him and what he could have used, it is under-stated."[26]

Stone's lawyers claimed in a threatening letter to numerous people who opposed his script after it was pirated and published, even sold in college film classes, that it was a trade secret. Granted each industry has customs that can govern in a lawsuit and be interpreted as law, Stone has intervened in our business where the rule is one of total disclosure.

Stone signed numerous key witnesses to exclusive contracts right in the middle of our research, killing it, and our own documentary.

As *Time* magazine noted in highly critical articles, Stone interfered in all other documentaries being prepared in this case. "According to Hollywood sources, the director has worked hard to block a movie based on Don DeLillo's 1988 book *Libra,* a fictionalized account of the assassination. 'Stone has a right to make his film, but he doesn't have a right to try and stop everyone else from making their films,' said Dale Pollack, president of A&M films, which has been trying to make the DeLillo movie."[27]

The *Time* article points out that various scenes in the secret first script, were removed from the film later on, such as a scene depicting David Ferrie being murdered by fantastic (and invented) characters named Bull and Indian whom we later see in the Texas School Book Depository, and the scene depicting the autopsy pictures being held up to the jury. Of course, such crazy and historically inaccurate scenes would not have been removed had the script not been stolen and spread around so excluded critics and experts could point out to Stone (though communication was very difficult) how silly some of it was.

The problem that I and others in the research community have is that we were unable to get any real input into the final product because of the iron secrecy Stone succeeded in imposing. We were all working for the same goal: to have an accurate and correct movie, but Stone did not seek first-class advice.

Then there is Mr. "X" in the film, who is Fletcher Prouty, whose writings were extensively used in the movie. Stone hired Prouty as a consultant, and relied upon him for an exposition of the conspiracy. Prouty is a friend of mine whom I respect for his writing and what he has to say. He has often been the victim of unfair charges, but he sometimes makes mistakes. Stone went to some trouble to make a prop from an old newspaper belonging to Prouty, the *Christchurch Star,* which was published some hours after the AP wire came through containing the news that Kennedy had been shot. Prouty sold Stone on the idea that the newspaper could not have had the information when they had it without it being planted by an intelligence agency.

I called the *Christchurch Star,* which is sixteen hours ahead of Dallas central standard time, in New Zealand and learned the precise hour the wire came through and when the paper went to press that afternoon (November 23, 1963, which was actually the afternoon of November 22). My examination of the information it published about Oswald was nothing that was not in the AP wires within two hours of Oswald's arrest, and it was nothing at all that would not be known to any journalist covering the case, from the preexisting files on Oswald's arrest in New Orleans and the newspaper accounts of his defection to the former Soviet Union, to the police reports.

"I had trouble knowing what was fact and what was not fact," Forrest Sawyer said, referring to the movie. "Stone takes dramatic license by mixing in facts or what he represents as facts with fictionalization. You have Garrison delivering a very powerful speech to the jury that never happened, which were Oliver Stone's words, in large part."[28]

At the moment the film was released, *Life* weighed in with what was probably the best, though shallow, article of an incredible year, called "Why We Still Care: A New Movie About the Assassination Reopens an Old Controversy." The title was emblazoned on its cover with a black and white photograph of Jack Kennedy sailing his boat. *Life* is owned by Time-Warner as well. Though it failed to mention some of the leading researchers, the *Life* article certainly managed to provide exposure for very many of those who have devoted their lives to bringing out the truth in the case.[29] The magazine did not have much of an ax to grind, being more of a picture magazine than one of ideas or news, and did not dig too deeply beneath the surface. It was better than the other articles, not for those reasons, but because it gave more of an overview, with less bias.

Speaking of the CIA, Stone told Mark Seal: "They bring down governments. This is their job. Why isn't it conceivable that an outlaw organization such as the CIA that does this abroad would do it domestically?"[30] Some of this statement, of course, is true. But there is an excess of language here, and that is the problem. He defames the CIA by calling it an outlaw. The CIA has done a lot of good, but as an institution, with all its flaws, it did not and could not have killed JFK, as many think.

"They don't kill you anymore," Stone told a reporter, "they poison your food. You get sick. You don't die. You get sick, and you get incapacitated for a year or two . . . and you get strychnine laced in your system. Or else they simply discredit you in the media, which is probably a lot more sophisticated way of doing it, like they did Garrison, you see. They just made fun of him. They ridicule you as a beast. As a monster. As a buffoon. And they do a good job of it. And the movie has to overcome."[31] A moment later Stone said that "they're into satellite taps now. You don't have to go into the phone system." He had his phone swept for bugs and found nothing. This demonstrates how deep the director's paranoia had gone, and it is a shame—right or wrong as he may be.

Perhaps the answer lies in this observation: "Stone always looks haggard. . . . His entire being exudes exhaustion—the result of his year-long war with a hostile press, combative assassination buffs, and zealous defenders of the Warren Commission, all of whom have attempted to portray Oliver Stone as the biggest assassination buffoon since Jim Garrison. 'There's a thousand and one vultures out there,' groans Stone, 'crouched on the rocks, saying, "Ah, here comes Stone." They want to come down and just peck out my eyes and rip my guts out. I'm such a target in a way, because I've attacked big things. And now I've got not only the usual Hollywood vultures on my tail, I've got a lot of the paid-off journalist hacks that are working on the East Coast with their recipied political theories, who resent the outsider, the rebel with a different theory.' "[32] The man doth protest too much.

Part of the underlying social or philosophical conflict in this mess stems from the differing mind sets of the East and West coasts. As Rosemary James of New Orleans, one of the first reporters close up to the Garrison affair in 1967, said about the land of the laid-back lotus eaters: "Now comes a gullible from La-La Land with a $60-million budget who wants to regurgitate all of that garbage . . ."[33] James said in the same letter that "I know for a fact that Garrison deliberately proceeded with a fraudulent case against Shaw," and that Garrison selected a scapegoat for political purposes, then set about destroying one of the most creative business and cultural leaders New Orleans ever produced. Stone responded to this letter by saying that "the truth is that the prosecution was sabotaged by the federal government from day one."

The bottom line of Duane Byrge's review of *JFK* in the *Hollywood Reporter* is that "while Oliver Stone has certainly stirred up the waters, with good conscience and, in JFK's own parlance, 'with vigah,' most people are likely to regard *JFK* as BS."[34]

Stone had a double standard. He publicly promoted his notion of morality and pontificated upon virtue and truth. Privately, like so many others in Hollywood, he and his producers ran all over the little people to get what he wanted.

When Garrison, Mark Lane, and Stone made blanket charges that the CIA or the FBI killed Kennedy, they were basically way over the line. First of all, no responsible researcher in this case ever said anything like that. Granted, *whatever* we say is often *distorted* to sound like we've said more than we actually said. If we say a few out-of-control renegades did it, they say we said the *Agency* did it!

Stone did not need to recreate the phony and gory hospital scenes and the murder itself. He could have used the existing footage, but he has made a charade of it by re-creating it. He has a nobody playing John Kennedy and that in itself is objectionable. The point is that our country has a fast-rising level of violence in part because of films and TV shows whose producers revel in such violence, who make life cheap and guns alluring. This film is not at all about John Kennedy as a human being. What can we feel for him when he is shot? What can young people who know little about John Kennedy feel when they see him murdered?

If Stone knew in his own mind what it is he really intended to do, an "entertainment" or a "docudrama," perhaps there would not be so much trouble. If he had not tried to be so secretive, perhaps he would not have so many people against him. But if he intended to make a docudrama about John Kennedy's murder, he had to be *absolutely accurate* about every last detail. That murder concerns this nation to its core. We cannot have assassination as a political instrument in this country, and we cannot have anyone making light of it or making a cartoon of it.

With all his flaws, Jim Garrison deserved better than *JFK*. Garrison was born in Denison, Iowa, and spent his youth in Iowa and Chicago. He always talked like a northerner before Kevin Costner played him with a hoked-up southern accent, which Garrison had never acquired. The *Washington Post* had this to say about Costner's performance: "Stone's dramatic efforts are dulled by Costner. As Garrison, he's a dead, vacant performer. Perhaps the milquetoast casting is ironically appropriate: the real story's about Kennedy. Someone with a personality would only get in the way."[35] More like a timid dweebe, to use Costner's highschoolese. Garrison deserved a great impersonator.

Stone says that the murder of John Kennedy was a seminal event for him and for the country. "It changed the course of history. It was a crushing blow to our country and to millions of people around the world. It put an abrupt end to a period of innocence and great idealism. . . . The movie is not, as Lardner suggested, the 'Jim Garrison story.' It does use the Garrison investigation as the vehicle to explore the various credible assassination theories, and incorporates everything that has been discovered in the twenty years since Garrison's efforts. It does not purport to 'solve' this murder mystery. What I hope this film will do is remind people how much our nation and our world lost when President Kennedy died, and to ask anew what might have happened and why. In the words of Thomas Jefferson, 'Eternal vigilance is the price of Liberty.' " Stone then points out how the *Washington Post* has steadfastly stuck to the Warren Report, in spite of all reason.

Fine words, these. But Stone really doesn't do what he says he will do. The film does not remind us of what we lost when Kennedy died because Kennedy is never alive in the film. Those of us who remember don't need Stone. The film cheapens our memory. Those of us who thought there was a conspiracy have always asked what happened and why. *JFK* tries to tell young people what to think without giving them anything with which to back up their ideas. As for a piece of vigilance, it is more like vigilante justice.

The Reviews

The movie was premiered in Hollywood on December 18, 1991, in Dallas the next day, and in New Orleans and the rest of the nation on the twentieth. Days before the premier, *Newsweek* and *Time* hit the stands with their appraisals,[36] and in the case of *Newsweek* the cover of the magazine proclaimed "The Twisted Truth of *JFK:* Why Oliver Stone's New Movie Can't Be Trusted." Three frames from the movie, parallel to the corresponding frames of the Zapruder film, show Jackie on the trunk of the limousine retrieving part of her husband's head.

In one of several articles in the *Newsweek* story, David Ansen ends with grudging praise: "What [Mr.] 'X' tells us may be more than many people can or want to swallow. No one should take *JFK* at face value: It's a compellingly argued case, but not to be confused with proof. But my hat is off to the filmmaker—and Warner Bros.—for the reckless chutzpah of the attempt. Make no mistake: this is one very incendiary Hollywood entertainment. Two cheers for Mr. Stone, a troublemaker for our times."

The most violent attack on the film came from George F. Will of the *Washington Post.* He called it a cartoon history, and wrote: "In his three-hour lie, Stone falsifies so much, he may be an intellectual sociopath, indifferent to truth. Or perhaps he is just another propagandist frozen in the 1960s like a fly in amber, combining moral arrogance with historical ignorance. He is a specimen of the 1960s arrested development, the result of the self-absorption encouraged by all the rubbish written about his generation being so unprecedentedly moral, idealistic, caring, etc. He is one of those 'activists' who have been so busy trying to make history, they have not learned any. . . . Intellectually, Stone is on all fours with his mirror images, the Birchers, who, like Stone, thought Earl Warren was a traitor. Stone and they are part of a long fringe tradition, the paranoid style in American politics, a style ravenous for conspiracy theories."[37]

Will goes on with one more slam: "Why is actor Kevin Costner lending himself to this libel of America? Is he invincibly ignorant or just banally venal? Nothing else can explain his willingness to portray as a hero Jim Garrison, who, as New Orleans district attorney, staged an assassination 'investigation' that involved recklessness, cruelty, abuse of power, publicity-mongering, and dishonesty, all on a scale that strongly suggested lunacy leavened by cynicism. . . . *JFK* is an act of execrable history and contemptible citizenship by a man of technical skill, scant education, and negligible conscience."

Vincent Canby's *New York Times* review entitled "When Everything Amounts to Nothing" said that the movie clarified nothing and that the conspiracy "remains far more vague than the movie pretends. . . . *JFK,* for all its sweeping innuendos and splintery music-video editing, winds up breathlessly running in place. The movie will continue to infuriate people who possibly know as much about the assassination as Mr. Stone does, but it also short-changes the audience and at the end plays like a bait-and-switch scam. . . . It builds to a climatic courtroom drama, the details of which it largely avoids, to allow Kevin Costner, the film's four-square star, to deliver a sermon about America's future with an emotionalism that is completely unearned."[38]

Canby says that the film did succeed in presenting the case for the idea that there actually was a conspiracy, but "beyond that, the movie cannot go with any assurance. . . . The only payoff is the sight of Mr. Costner with tears in his eyes. . . . The film's insurmountable problem is the vast amount of material it fails to make coherent sense of. . . . Mr. Stone is Fibber McGee opening the door to an overstuffed closet. He is buried under all the facts, contradictory testimony, hearsay, and conjecture that he would pack into the movie.

"By the time *JFK* reaches the Clay Shaw trial, most uninformed members of the audience will be exhausted and bored. The movie, which is simultaneously arrogant and timorous, has been unable to separate the important material from the merely colorful. After a certain point, audience interest tunes out. It's a jumble.

". . . The movie remains an undifferentiated mix of real and staged material. Mr. Stone's hyperbolic style of filmmaking is familiar: lots of short, often hysterical scenes tumbling one after another, backed by a sound track that is layered, strudellike, with noises, dialogue, music, more noises, more dialogue. It works better in *Born on the Fourth of July* and *The Doors* than it does here, in a movie that means to be a sober reflection on history suppressed."

Canby ends by saying: "When Walter Matthau turns up for a brief, not especially rewarding turn as Senator Russell B. Long, *JFK* looks less as if it had been cast in the accepted way than subscribed to, like a worthy cause. The cause may well be worthy; the film fails it."

Desson Howe writes in the *Washington Post* that "despite its three hours, *JFK* is absorbing to watch. It's not journalism. It's not history. It is not legal evidence. Much of it is ludicrous. It's a piece of art or entertainment. Stone, who has acknowledged his fusing of the known and the invented, has exercised his full prerogative to use poetic license. He should feel more than mere craftsman's satisfaction at the result."[39] Howe writes that the first order of business in this film is *entertainment.* "As such, Stone creates a riveting marriage of fact and fiction, hypothesis and empirical proof in the edge-of-the-seat spirit of a conspiracy thriller."[40]

Howe also tells us what the message is: "Kennedy angered right-wing elements by trying to pull out of Vietnam and by not liberating Cuba during the Bay of Pigs incident. Messing with the war machine was his fatal flaw. This wasn't just a conspiracy. It was a junta."

Stephen Hunter wrote that "the movie is ultimately incoherent—Stone never makes sense out of the New Orleans angle to the conspiracy—and seems to veer in strange directions to accommodate all sects of assassination dialectic. Assassination scholars will be somewhat dumbfounded at the cavalier method by which the movie credits all 'discoveries' to Garrison and his team, though much of the information was developed later by others."[41]

Hunter, writing in the *Baltimore Sun,* goes on to say: "Yet still and all, *JFK* is entertaining, if only because the cast of characters in the New Orleans underground is so bizarre . . . though Stone comes danger- ously close to homophobia in his insistence of camping up the sexual orientation of some of the characters." (Gay and lesbian groups were deeply offended. He edited out scenes that would offend the city of Dallas, his host for much of the filming.)

Hunter continues: "The movie is curiously at its worst when it needs to be at its best—and it's also at its most reprehensible. It offers up as heroic and admirable Garrison's decision to prosecute Shaw, though even on the evidence the film itself offers, he had no case at all. The case, of course, was dismissed in an hour. When a prosecutor ruins a man in order to get himself his own day in court, and a film director canonizes him for it, that seems to me the biggest proof of an American coup d'état and evidence that indeed, the Fascists have taken over."

Some Facts

Unfortunately, *Time*'s extensive coverage of the film falsified many statements.[42] For instance, we find this comment: "The bullet that hit Kennedy's head was found in the limousine, and tests indicated that it came from Oswald's rifle. Moreover, frame 313 of the Zapruder film clearly shows brain matter spraying forward." Nothing is too clear in Z 313, and no bullet was found in the limousine, only fragments. There is no way that a fragment can be linked to a rifle.

Time gropes on: "Neutron activation tests indicate that the fragments in Connally's wrist did come from the bullet in question." This is a completely false statement. The tests were not conclusive, and there was more metal in his wrist than is missing from the "Magic" Bullet.

In a more serious example of double speak, another trick is being played on the unsuspecting when *Time* says: "The Evidence: Over the years some witnesses have come forward to say they saw the alleged conspirators together at parties and at a rally in rural Louisiana. This was Garrison's key contention in his 1969 trial of Shaw, but the jury rejected it. [We have here the mixing of two different groups of witnesses. The Clinton, Louisiana, witnesses, for instance, have been acknowledged by the House Assassinations Committee to be correct in having seen the men together.] Even many conspiracy theorists doubt the credibility of the witnesses." Which witnesses? We accept the credibility of the townspeople of Clinton that they saw Lee Harvey Oswald and David Ferrie together with either Clay Shaw or Guy Banister. What is not to be believed was the testimony of Perry Russo, but *Time* has done its dirty work by linking researchers with skepticism of *all* witnesses.

Time tells us that Stone is saying: "Open your eyes wide, like a child's. Look around. See what fits. And Costner's summation is right out of an old Frank Capra movie in its declaration of principle in the face of murderous odds. Lost causes, as Capra's Mr. Smith said, are the only causes worth fighting for."

Time's reviewers gave grudging respect and praise to the film. They had to in order for their parent company, Time-Warner, to get their money back. *Time* ends its review with this: "To Stone's old enemies, *JFK* may be another volatile brew of megalomania and macho sentiment. To his new critics, the film may seem deliriously irresponsible, madly muttering like a street raver. But to readers of myriad espionage novels and political science fictions in which the CIA or some other gentlemen's cabal is always the villain, the movie's thesis will be familiar high-level malevolence. *JFK* is Ludlum or le Carré, but for real. Or —crucial distinction—for reel. Memorize this mantra, conspiracy buffs and guardians of the public respectability: *JFK* is only a movie. And, on its own pugnacious terms—the only terms Oliver Stone would ever accept—a terrific one."

The View from on High

The film is a kaleidoscope of cascading, fast-changing images with everything jam packed so tight that nothing of substance has any meaning. You get one message: *There was a conspiracy.* It is a kind of Hard Rock impressionism—a product of our culture and era, and it demeans and degrades the message. But it is fair to report that other longtime researchers in the case such as Gary Shaw liked it, and felt that the film accomplished what we have not been able to do in twenty years of trying to revive interest in the Kennedy assassination. There was a run on libraries for books on the case, and many editions sold well in stores.

My partner, Mark Crouch, had a private interview with Oliver Stone in which Stone explained his motives. He wanted "to counter the Warren Commission myth with our own myth—to create an alter myth to give the kids of the new generation." He put it this way to *Time:* "I'm giving you a detailed outlaw history, or countermyth. A myth represents the true inner spiritual meaning of an event."[43]

I find this language deeply disturbing, that Stone would call a conspiracy a myth. I suppose in a very distorted fashion whatever is presented in story form could be called a myth, true or not, but for us it is the truth, not a myth. (I am not speaking, of course, about anything having to do with the Shaw trial, but the outlines of the conspiracy itself, on a high level. How else could the autopsy evidence be faked?)

Sadly, the major networks and magazines repeated many of the falsifications of the evidence in the case.

For instance, several points were brought out on ABC's *Nightline* and other shows: That "atomic" testing proved that the "bullet" found in the car, or the "bullet" found in Connally's leg came from Oswald's rifle, 2) that the bullet fell out of Connally's leg and was found on his stretcher, 3) that there was scientific proof that the jet effect worked on human heads, which would go backward if hit from behind, 4) that *Nova* and certain tests proved that the trajectory of the "Magic" Bullet could have struck both men at the same time.

One bullet might have struck both men at the same time by some miracle considering how they were seated, but it certainly would not come out of Connally in almost pristine condition after striking his bones. The media ignored all the tests that prove that the official story could not have happened.

With regard to the Parkland bullet, the crew that found it made it clear that it was on the stretcher of a small boy and could not have been on Connally's—meaning it was planted there. In addition, the autopsy surgeon, Dr. Humes, testified that the bullet had to have come out of John Kennedy's back, and therefore could not have been the same bullet that struck Connally. Humes also made it clear to the Warren Commission that he knew that fragments had been found in Connally that prima facie demonstrated that they could not have come from the pristine, nearly undamaged "Magic" Bullet.

The so-called jet effect has been dealt with at length in Chapter 17. None of the so-called experiments conducted was with living human heads, nor were they attached to bodies. Films of executions show that a human head moves rapidly backward when struck with a bullet from the front. In addition, the statements made by Forrest Sawyer on ABC-TV about the jet effect assumes an exit hole in the front, as he said that matter was expelled from such an exit hole. He assumes the front exit hole because that is where it appears in the Zapruder film. This is a far cry from the neuromuscular reaction we hear about more often causing the backward head snap. It's also a far cry from a large exit hole in the back, which would have caused, according to this distorted reasoning, the head to go backward. There wasn't any exit hole in the front that would have caused such a reaction.

Former President Gerald Ford defended his findings on the Warren Commission, albeit after carefully couching his language to make it clear that they *"did not find* [author's emphasis] evidence of conspiracy." Ford has always left the door open with that language, knowing that three of the other seven men on the commission never agreed with what the most conservative members of the commission wanted. Ford said, "that Stone nor anyone had produced another identical gunman, nor another gun, nor any new bullets. The Garrison approach is pure fiction. There was a neuromuscular reaction that made his head go backward when he was hit in the neck."[44]

This shows how crazy, uncaring, inattentive, and incompetent Ford is. The so-called back-of-the-neck shot he speaks of was not the fatal head shot.

As for the so-called atomic testing, I dealt with this in *High Treason* when I discussed the neutron activation analysis tests.[45] Suffice it to say that the tests were never released by the Warren Commission because they did *not* prove that the fragments that were found were from the same lot of lead as that of the "Magic" Bullet found at Parkland. The fragments could only be shown to be similar. Millions of bullets might have been made from the same lot of lead, so it would be impossible to prove that they came from a particular weapon. The bullet found at Parkland was clearly a piece of frame-up evidence planted there so that it would connect to the alleged Oswald rifle when found. But the bullet did not actually go through a body or hit bone, or it would not look so perfect.

This is the gist of the counterattack launched on this film by the journalists, parroting the official line put out by David Belin, Arlen Specter, and Gerald Ford, the resident defenders of the Warren Report.

The End

It is worth ending this chapter with what Robert Spiegelman, a professor of mass communications and sociology, had to say. He was an advisor on the film, and says there is a lot more at stake than the fate of this film. "This outcry is a continuation of the assault on the 'L word,' the liberal values and tradition which Camelot and Kennedy—and these days Oliver Stone—symbolize. And it constitutes a very dangerous precedent. Films critical of the official version of history aren't abundant as it is. If Stone's work can be targeted, imagine the chilling effect it can have on others without his clout and financial backing."[46] Important and predictable words these, emanating from an L.A. junior college, except that they carry all the myopic vision of an academic who misses the point of the conflict. Stone certainly chilled the other films that were being made. Of course, it takes a lot of power, money, and ferocious drive and determination to make a big film, and people will even kill to protect their interests, and certainly sweep aside anyone who gets in their way or asks questions.

Some in this research say that whatever is necessary to keep the case alive, even if hoked up, they will do. I draw the line at falsification of anything, and I have spent years investigating the claims of other researchers whom I find have perpetrated a fraud. We make enough mistakes as it is. I hope that the Stone film will rekindle interest in the case, and possibly open it up again.

Stone could have cut all of the Garrison part in the movie and shown us the boardrooms of America—Brown & Root that built Cam Ranh Bay in Vietnam, and Bell Helicopters—shown us what really happened after that murder, the mad borrowing of the Treasury to raise money for the war, the bodies coming back from Vietnam, the release of Carlos Marcello from charges the day Kennedy died, the Mob having a field day making money in rackets, the accelerated conglomeration of companies that has ruined much of the social and economic structure of this nation. Man, there was one hell of a movie there, even with a fictional character to hold it together, but he blew it. He took for his hero someone all the media of the United States were down on and tried to canonize him, tried to use him for his vehicle. That's like going to a junkyard, digging up a scrapped car from the bottom of the pile, and trying to fly with it.

The film has a line in it when the prosecution of Clay Shaw is in trouble and the police officer who booked Clay Shaw is not going to testify that Clay Shaw told him his alias was Clay Bertrand. "That's our case!" Garrison says in a panic. Stone admits here that Garrison had nothing but that to go against Shaw, not enough to indict someone in conspiracy to murder the President. Even Dean Andrews admitted that he made up the name and persona of Clem Bertrand.[47]

The whole point of John Kennedy's assassination and that of other leaders in the sixties was to get rid of those knights on white horses. No more leaders of great honesty or charisma will be allowed to enter the political arena because it is against the wishes of those who actually govern and who have found a way, with gun in hand, to get around the idea of honest elections and true democracy. No more strong leaders, only weaklings who are front men for a committee that governs us behind the scenes. The power behind this does not want anyone whom the public can look to for real leadership, and in a way Stone's film serves this purpose. But he wrote *finis* to the case in 1969 as though nothing did in fact happen after that. He did not help us get out our new evidence, which he knew about. After many promises about what he was going to do with the new developments in the case, what we got was a presentation of conspiracy theory according to "Mr. X" as evidence. Theory is not evidence.

Scott Van Wynsberghe, a prominent Canadian assassination researcher, wrote me and said this: "I wonder if *JFK* the movie is beginning to divert too much energy away from JFK the assassination. It's now an issue on its own—which, sadly, is what became of the Garrison affair, and we know what damage that did to JFK research."[48]

Sure enough, there was a powerful reaction to the film, and everybody and his brother came forward to step into the limelight and mislead the public. New York City was absorbed for a week by the statements of a Mob lawyer, Frank Ragano, who claimed that "Hoffa Had JFK Killed" and that Jimmy Hoffa, former head of the Teamsters union who disappeared, had Ragano tell Carlos Marcello and Santos Trafficante (both major Mob bosses) to kill Kennedy.[49] Ragano, facing imprisonment on tax charges, must have figured to curry favor with the government and came out with his wholly unsubstantiated and misleading interpretation of the conspiracy that killed Kennedy. Not that I am trying to protect the Mob. They certainly were marginally involved.

All sorts of people came out of the woodwork to get into the act: G. Robert Blakey, former chief counsel of the House Assassinations Committee said that Ragano's story "is the most plausible, most coherent [assassination] theory."[50] The article goes on to say that the report of the Committee "concluded that Trafficante, Marcello, and Hoffa all had the motive, means, and opportunity" to kill Kennedy. We have heard this distortion and falsification of the findings of his own Committee over and over by Blakey since 1979, and it is tiresome. *JFK* the film has provided him one more opportunity to mislead the public.

That statement is being taken out of context by everyone who seeks to deflect attention from the fact that there was an entirely different conspiracy, and point at the Mob as the culprit. We are not being told what the conclusions were about possible Mob involvement. The Committee had this to say: "It may be strongly doubted, therefore, that Hoffa would have risked anything so dangerous as a plot against the President. . . ." It further states that he "was not a confirmed murderer" and was known to counsel against violent death as a solution to anything.[51]

After a massive investigation of organized crime, the committee, while noting that Marcello and Trafficante had the means, motive, and opportunity to assassinate the President, in fact discounted the possibility and stated clearly that "it is unlikely that Marcello was in fact involved in the assassination of the President,"[52] noting that Marcello was successful because he was very prudent and not reckless. "He would be unlikely to undertake so dangerous a course of action as a Presidential assassination."[53] With regard to Marcello, the Committee concluded that "Trafficante's cautious character is inconsistent with his taking the risk of being involved in an assassination plot against the President. . . . It is unlikely that Trafficante plotted to kill the President."[54]

No, the Mob did not have the means, motive, and opportunity to forge the autopsy evidence of the President.

In the fourth week of its release, ABC's *Primetime* launched another powerful attack on *JFK* with much sophistry.[55] Gerald Ford made an appearance. Ford said, as many others did, including Louis Stokes, the former chairman of the House Committee on Assassinations, and Senator Edward Kennedy, that all the secret records should be released. The former president claimed to know what was in them and that he had nothing to fear and that the records would add nothing whatsoever to our knowledge of the case.

*   *   *

People will go on believing there was a conspiracy, as the majority has done through most of these years, but they are being told by the media and by many prominent people that nothing will be done. There is no action that the public can be stirred to by this movie. There will be no street demonstrations or marches.

If the movie had been made honestly and not taken up the story of Jim Garrison, it might have caused the case to be reopened. But it seems to me that this film had the real intent of co-opting the major new evidence of forgery.

We have stupid and uncaring leaders. Our government is weak, led by puppets of a bankrupt and corrupt business and financial establishment. We cannot expect them to truly look at the evidence in this terrible murder, or to be honest. For the plain truth is that for the same reason that Oliver Stone lacked the integrity to make an honest movie, this country's leaders lack the integrity to conduct an honest investigation.

The King truly is dead.

"There is another great traveler in the world, and this is the travel of a world revolution in a world of turmoil. . . . We should not fear the twentieth century, for this world-wide revolution which we see all around us is part of the original American revolution. When the Indonesians revolted after the end of World War II, they scrawled on the walls, 'Give me liberty or give me death' and 'All men are created equal.' Not Russian slogans, but American slogans. When they had a meeting for independence in Northern Rhodesia, they quoted Jackson, they quoted Franklin Roosevelt. They don't quote any American statesman today. . . ."

—John F. Kennedy

CHAPTER 27

A PROPOSAL

Three different men claim to have taken the autopsy X-rays. Each appears to be within a different time frame. We have two different times offered for the start of the autopsy, and some autopsy personnel insist that they saw Mrs. Kennedy arrive after they were working on the body. We have different caskets being described, and two bodies present in the morgue. Some of the crew insist on having seen a body bag. No bullets were found in the body, only some fragments. There are severe conflicts on nearly every piece of evidence in this case, which shows conspiracy when taken together with other facts.

The evidence is clear that there was a major domestic conspiracy in the murder of President Kennedy, and not just in the cover-up. We base this on the forgery of the autopsy photographs and the retouching of the X-rays and the manner in which the autopsy report was fudged and later misinterpreted. Observations of medical personnel in Dallas—almost thirty years later—indicate that two of the shots came from the front. There is every reason to believe that there were three gunmen, and not fewer. The photos and witnesses prove two bullet holes in the back and "neck." The films show a shot from the front. We know that John Connally was in fact hit by a different bullet from the one that struck Kennedy. We know that we are dealing with a planted bullet that allegedly hit both men, because there is and was more metal in John Connally than was missing from that "Magic" Bullet. The recordings made during the assassination have strong indications of more than three or even four shots.

Somebody had the wherewithal to reassemble the skull and make a fake X-ray showing an intact back of the head, which covered up for a shot from the front, *if it was in fact Kennedy's skull.* But my investigation so far indicates that the frontal bone was never out of the right top face and forehead. I don't know how they did it, but I cannot believe that the X-rays represent a total reconstruction and altering of the head. The X-rays have to be, therefore, forged composites, or "subtractions," much as I don't want to offend Dr. Levine, who says they are authentic.

We have X-rays that clearly show an imperfectly rebuilt skull with no large defect in the back, the skull cap having been put back on. This is what tricked Earl Warren. Dr. John Ebersole said, "Later on in the evening, between midnight and one A.M., a large portion of the skull was sent up from Dallas . . . that represented the back portion of the skull."[1]

Actually, three large fragments of bone were brought up from Dallas. The autopsy report says, "Received as separate specimens from Dallas, Texas, are three fragments of skull bone which in aggregate roughly approximate the dimensions of the large defect described above. At one angle of the largest of these fragments is a portion of the perimeter of a roughly circular wound presumably of exit which exhibits beveling of the outer aspect of the bone and is estimated to measure approximately 2.5 to 3.0 cm. in diameter. Roentgenograms of this fragment reveal minute particles of metal in the bone at this margin." This statement is important because Humes can be speaking only of the skull cap —the rear apex of the head that was torn off and seen lying in the car— and he told the Warren Commission that *the bullet could have exited only from behind.*[2] He didn't want to say that *two* bullets hit Kennedy, one from the front and one from behind.

Clint Hill described the fact that the back of the President's head had been lying in the backseat of the car.[3] "Both Dr. Humes and Dr. Burkley informed the committee that these fragments were placed back in the skull of the President"[4] and no doubt X-rayed, giving us the apparent composite we now have, a skull that looks like an assembled puzzle. If these three bones were the Harper fragment, or piece of occipital bone, the skull cap itself, and another large piece of parietal bone, then they would have been able to fill up the missing area in the back of the head for the purposes of making the false X-ray, and thus masking the large exit wound. The X-ray seems to show the skull cap—the top rear or apex of the skull merely sitting on the head, as though it were reassembled, with the fracture lines very imperfectly joined, as we see in the X-ray.

I have presented clear evidence provided by radiologists that the frontal bone was cut both through the forehead toward the top of the head, following roughly the midline between the eyes, and in a large sweeping semicircle in the right temple-cheek area. That large piece of frontal bone seems to have been removed. The sella turcica is left unattached. But the autopsy staff I spoke with deny that the frontal bone was cut or removed.

O'Connor, Jenkins, Boswell, Karnei, Humes, and others insist that the right forehead was intact. Nobody says it wasn't. But there isn't any right forehead in the X-rays.

It is worth repeating the following story, since it may fit with something that someone remembers: A "Dr. "Morgan" or "Miller" in the Baltimore–D.C. area called Paul O'Connor late one night and said that someone—we'll call him X—took a ball-peen hammer to the head either at Walter Reed or Bethesda. O'Connor thinks he said it was Bethesda—"to disrupt the wound and the physical characteristics of the wound." Paul thought that X had something to do with it. X transferred out after the autopsy.[5]

He said that "I was told by this so-called Dr. Michael Miller that the body was altered at Walter Reed or at Bethesda and he thinks it was Bethesda and put back in the coffin and taken around the corner and down back of the hospital to the morgue."[6] Dr. Charles Crenshaw of Parkland says he also thinks it was tampered with at Bethesda.[7]

Once again we must keep in mind the large amount of missing frontal bone, which was described by the Clark Panel,[8] and noted by Dr. Angel when the House doctors interviewed Humes and Boswell.[9] O'Connor clearly described to me all the bone missing from the flap sticking out just in front of the right ear which we see in the photographs of the back of the head—all the way back to the occiput.[10] This is about the same as the large defect Humes described to the Warren Commission.[11] It seems somewhat larger to us than what the public thought, but Paul O'Connor says that we cannot see all of it because the scalp was intact over the top of the head and held the head together between the ears. The main part of the large defect was visible in the back of the head only upon lifting up the flap.

Humes is a bit confusing because in the above Warren Commission testimony he speaks of the scalp being intact past a certain ill-defined point, once again making us wonder if someone else's body was there.

We know that they kept some bones that were not buried with the body, and the Harper fragment was not brought to Washington until the next day.[12]

We have to account for whatever happened between the time the body arrived and the start of the autopsy, and nobody has ever done that. It is not logical that everyone just sat around and waited, and it did not take that long to take some pictures. Waited for what? For Dr. Pierre Finck to show up?* That is too much like a show. So many things don't add up about this autopsy—that it is clear that some of the witnesses are lying about something major and/or the record has been fogged by a sophisticated shell game and plot.

Theory

If the body was tampered with, and *if* bullets were removed, let's start with this scenario. The body comes in and is removed from the casket in the morgue and put on the table. The sheets are removed. Jerry Custer says that he and Reed were then asked to leave and wait until called. Dr. Ebersole is brought in to take some X-rays before anything is started, and everyone has to be cleared to avoid the radiation. Sibert and O'Neill, the two FBI men, are busy checking credentials and making a list outside. O'Connor is sent on an errand. Jenkins is in the chemical room. No one is in the gallery and everyone has been cleared from the autopsy room. We are still off the record because the autopsy has not begun, as Mark Crouch tells me. He says that this is the way courts and governments operate.

Dr. Ebersole stated in a deposition to the House Committee that prior to commencing the autopsy he took several X-rays of the skull,

---

* Interestingly, Dr. Finck was also at the autopsy of Robert F. Kennedy five years later, before he moved to Geneva, Switzerland.

chest, and trunk of the body, and that he used portable X-ray equipment.[13] He said that he hand-carried the X-rays to the fourth floor to develop them. Then he took them downstairs again. Of course, the room was cleared during X-rays, and it is conceivable that it stayed clear and operations were performed before everyone was allowed to come back in.

But, we have someone else who says that he is sure all the pictures *were developed right there in the autopsy room.* Who? Francis X. O'Neill, the FBI man who was there. He told me that "to the best of my knowledge, the X-rays were developed right in the room. Developed on the spot. We were right there. They did not have to leave the room."[14] There was no lab there. Unless, of course, somebody brought down the necessary chemicals and tanks and set it up during the possible pre-exam for the possible operations to remove the bullets before the autopsy began. A lot of time could be saved by developing some of the films there instead of going upstairs. They could have been developed in the chemical room, which was part of the morgue.

Later on, when Custer and Reed were taking what they thought were the first X-rays, they had to go upstairs each time to develop them. The real first (and crucial) X-rays that were needed to find bullets had to be done right away, and Ebersole took them, though he may not have known what for. If O'Neill is right when he told me that the X-rays were developed right there, something the crew deny happened (at least some of them were out of the room), the lab or adjoining area was set up to develop the X-rays then, saving quite a bit of time.

Normally, a radiologist would never take X-rays himself, especially in the military, as Ebersole tells us he did. The staff deny that the doctor operated the machine at any time. I believe that he must have, since the record is clear that photos and X-rays were taken before the Y incision, and we know that the X-ray technologists were not in the room at any time before that.

There is something very suspicious about the above. It is my opinion that within a few minutes, as soon as they had some X-rays and had located what they were looking for, the throat and brain were quickly operated upon and the bullets removed—while everyone was still out of the room.

Either a tangential shot, or a bullet striking Kennedy on the right side of or frontal part of the head, took off the back of the head. It might not have left much lead behind, if any. But we have indications from the film that Kennedy was also struck from behind, as the Warren

Commission said, and that bullet, as some told the Warren Commission, could not have come from the sixth floor window, let alone high up. The bullet, or part of it, lodged behind the right eye, and they had to get it out of there because it contained ballistic evidence that it came from a gun other than the one attributed to Oswald, and from a different box of bullets. Dr. Humes discusses the fragment behind the right eye at length during his testimony before the Warren Commission, as previously quoted. The question is, did they take the right forehead out to remove the fragment, then take a skull X-ray, then replace the frontal bone so that it was undetectable to the morticians? Certainly not that "the X-ray and photo evidence which has superseded the written autopsy report, and dominated the record, was not fabricated days, weeks, or years after November 22, 1963, as part of a 'cover-up,' but was created on the night of November 22, 1963, *before* [emphasis added] the official autopsy got under way, and probably in conjunction with the plan to alter the President's body."[15] This predicates that the skull was already altered *before* the X-rays were taken, which was not true. No one describes the right forehead missing. In addition, the false X-ray we now have could not have been taken before the autopsy began.

Some very quick photographs were taken immediately, and that might account for their poor quality, commented upon by the House Committee. Some of these photographs show no Y incision having been made. We know of no photographs that survived the "burn party" which show the Y incision or the interior torso, though such photographs were taken.

Audrey Bell, who saw the flap on the rear of the head lifted so that she could see the extent of the large defect, says that anyone knowing what they were doing could have compressed the brain and slipped out what remained of it.[16] The brain dehydrates and grows smaller as time passes and leakage occurs. By the same token, it could have gone back into the head along with the cerebellum. In addition, another possibility exists in view of the statements made by Governor Connally's wife. She said that all the way to Parkland Hospital in the fatal limousine, Jacqueline Kennedy kept saying, "They've killed my husband and I have his brains in my hand. . . ."[17]

It is not clear if this means his entire brain or if it refers only to the part that was blown out or fell out after the shot. It tends to indicate that it refers to the whole brain, which I don't really believe, in which case somebody put it back in the head. Since the doctors described the cerebellum as having come out of the head, and this was not true at the autopsy, we have a further indication that the brain was replaced, and that the brain stem had been partly severed by the shot. In order to put the brain back into the head properly, Dr. Clark (perhaps) had to cut the brain stem. This could be the clean transection of the brain stem which Jenkins noted, and can explain Clark's reluctance to talk about the case, which he has never done—but I don't believe this scenario since there is no evidence whatsoever to support it. Some call a deductive conclusion evidence, but it's not, and is not a fact. This is all within the realm of speculation and theorization.

Dr. Peters—whom Jackie stood beside—told me that Jackie had only bits of brain in her hands—not the whole brain or even a large part of it.

The X-rays may have shown a slug inside the chest. How else would the lungs be bruised and the other internal damage which was reported both at the autopsy and in Dallas have occurred? The Dallas doctors put chest drainage tubes in, or started to, because something seemed punctured inside Kennedy's chest. But the fluid they thought was in the chest may have simply been what came down from the throat and trachea wound, and was not the result of any penetration of the chest by a missile. It is possible that the bullet that struck him in the throat hit the vertebra and was reflected down into the chest. It did not go up, we conclude, because there was no damage to the floor of the skull. As the FBI men suspected at the autopsy, a bullet made of ice hit him in the throat with a paralytic agent and melted.

It would seem that one of the two apparent bullet holes in his back did enter the chest and stop, but the probing that the autopsy personnel described makes it clear that there was only superficial penetration. That was only one of the two apparent holes in the back. The upper "hole" on the shoulder may be painted on the photograph, as was the "entry" hole in the cowlick, or be just a clot.

Tampering

After the first X-rays were taken by Ebersole, a quick operation was performed by the conspirators to remove the bullets in the brain and throat. This would take only a few moments. O'Connor told me that in fact everyone did not leave the room during the taking of the X-rays. The conspirators would have been those who stayed or returned to the morgue, during which time it could be assumed that X-rays were still being taken, but actually after the X-rays were exposed and rapidly developed, a quick operation was performed.

After this quick operation to remove the evidence, everyone except Custer and Reed came back into the room. The Y incision was made, and then Custer and Reed are brought back in to take what they think are the first, but are actually additional X-rays. During this set of X-rays, everyone is again removed from the room to avoid radiation. Custer and Reed are then sent off to develop the X-rays, and those in the hallway see Mrs. Kennedy, actually more than an hour after she had to have arrived.

Meanwhile everyone is waiting in the halls for the autopsy to begin, and for Dr. Finck to arrive. Everyone is called back in, and the X-ray techs and the photographers go to work again.

The Y incision was made right away to mask an operation to get the bullet out of the chest. Who did this?

Jerry Custer says that he held the skull cap in his hand the next day and taped a bullet to it and X-rayed it. Is that possible? Is the buried skull at Arlington only made of plaster and rubber in the back?

If this conspiracy reached into Bethesda Naval Hospital, when the body came in at seven P.M. those privy to the plot would have to have been already in place.

As for the forged X-rays and photographs, this must have been done very soon after the autopsy. I believe that the photographs—in particular the photograph of the back of the head—was merely retouched. I cannot explain how this was done so that it successfully fooled those experts who studied them for that purpose for the House of Representatives, but the evidence is too overwhelming in favor of this retouching.

The X-rays seem to me to be composites made from a reconstruction of the back of Kennedy's skull and part of an X-ray from someone else's head which has had the right top front of the skull behind the face cut away and removed. Jerry Custer called them "subtractions." It is possible that that bone was removed after midnight without everyone being present. After all, a lot of hours had passed and some might have taken a break somewhere. Ebersole says he took X-rays about one A.M. Then the frontal bone was replaced. The plotters then had an X-ray that was actually from Kennedy's head and which showed that the only bone missing was from a shot from behind which blew out part of his face. Of course such damage did not happen. Evidently, the X-ray was never shown to anyone for three years after the autopsy, as it must have occurred to the plotters that it greatly conflicted with all the other evidence, which showed no damage to the face. I feel that I have established a chain of witnesses in my interviews which precludes any such tampering and reconstruction before the body was ready for the coffin. The X-rays are simply fake.

It seems probable that some sort of decoy arrangement was made, in spite of many denials. The Bethesda Naval Hospital did not have a high fence around it, and thousands of people had gathered. Reporters and photographers had infiltrated the hospital. The logical thing to do was to fly the body in, as the men have said. The Air Force officer's casket, its hearse and helicopter, if any, became a decoy, or simply fooled people. The men did not actually *know* any of this for sure, and most of them did not know who was in what casket, but the stories we hear are typical of the kind of scuttlebutt the Navy is famous for—good enough reason to make them sign an order compelling them to keep their mouths shut.

If the body had been stolen, somewhere along the line it would have had to be removed from its casket and put into a body bag and taken in some other casket by helicopter to Bethesda. I do not believe that the body was or could have been operated on in any other place. The two-casket theory and body bag have been examined elsewhere. That doesn't mean that the body wasn't in fact stolen, but I think there would be supporting evidence for it by now. If there had been a decoy system set up, there would be no reason to deny it now, unless the body really was stolen—which for the reasons outlined elsewhere appear to be impossible. The decoy setup also appears to be impossible because it depends on the body having been removed from its casket, and we have no hard evidence of that, only deductions based upon the supposed body bag and the two caskets. I cannot believe that the body could be removed without the Kennedy entourage knowing it, and word getting out.

Unfortunately, there is more of a stone wall around the Kennedy entourage than any other aspect of this case, making it impossible to investigate various elements.

Several of the men recall another body being at the morgue. Jim Jenkins has described often enough that the body of an officer first was in a shipping casket, and then in an expensive viewing casket, which we know was sent in. The men therefore not only saw President Kennedy's casket, but a shipping casket and then the third one, or the viewing casket for the officer. Jerry Custer told me that the Air Force major came in a shipping casket.[18] It is quite possible that when the body was taken out of the shipping casket in the cold room and that casket was removed, the body was wheeled into the morgue just as Jenkins recalls, though thinking it was Kennedy. "Shipping" is undoubtedly nothing less (in this case) than a simple casket, not a military shipping coffin per se.

Then, realizing that they were not going to perform an autopsy and that Bethesda was merely the transshipment point, he was wheeled back into the cold room and put into the expensive rosewood casket. Since almost nobody was present, there is little testimony on any of this, and it is hard to draw a conclusion.

It is clear to me that the acute nervousness, reticence, and confusing and greatly conflicting testimony of the doctors, and the many great discrepancies in the medical evidence show that the doctors have to know something that they cannot tell under any circumstances, although none of them may have knowledge of the conspiracy itself. The doctors know that something momentous and untoward was behind that tragically flawed autopsy and its fake photographs and X-rays. They know it because they questioned the photographs and X-rays themselves, however covered over this might have been by the House of Representatives.

William Bruce Pitzer

Lieutenant Commander William Bruce Pitzer was found dead of a gunshot wound on the right side of the head *at Bethesda Naval Hospital* on October 29, 1966.[19] Dennis David was the source for an article that expressed his opinion that Pitzer, a close friend, would not have committed suicide, and states that Pitzer was left-handed.[20] Pitzer, according to David, had filmed the autopsy.[21]

Plus, numerous other reasons were presented to me by Pitzer's family as to why he could not have killed himself, and why they believe his death had something to do with John Kennedy's assassination and the pictures he took at the autopsy.

Pitzer died on the day the Kennedy family transferred the autopsy materials—which they had not seen—to the National Archives.[22] On that same day, the trunk containing the autopsy materials was opened for inspection at the Archives and it was found that *all* the material listed under item No. 9 was missing: paraffin blocks of tissue sections, 35 slides presumably of tissue sections, another group of 84 slides, a stainless steel container which we can assume held the brain, and boxes containing 58 slides of blood smears taken at various times in Kennedy's life.[23]

Three days later, on November 1, 1966, three of the autopsy doctors, and the photographer, John Stringer, examined the photographs and X-rays and began to make some amazing discoveries.[24] Coincidence is not proof of foul play, but as countless people have previously noted, there are far too many coincidences in this case.

I have now seen, after years of effort (thanks to Joyce Pitzer's and Washington lawyer Jim Lesar's help) the autopsy report of Bruce Pitzer (See Chapter 7 in *High Treason*). Nobody in his family believes the Navy claim that he died a suicide. After all (according to Dennis David), Pitzer was in the gallery filming the entire autopsy with a movie camera, and David, a chief petty officer at the time—who had helped bring in the casket—helped Pitzer edit the film. David was a bridge partner and close friend of Pitzer's for many years and used to baby-sit for his children. They all believe he was murdered.

What the film might have been used for we do not know. Nor do we know if it was made for personal reasons. Dennis David wrote the following to researcher Joanne Braun: "As to Bill Pitzer's involvement, I never asked him, 'Were you there?' or 'Did you do the filming?' I have always assumed he did, but cannot verify that he was in the autopsy room that evening. I do know that he had the film in his possession at one time. When he and I looked at a portion of the film, we remarked only on the extent of injury, apparent point of entry, etc. Bill also had some 35mm slides which, again I assumed, were excerpts from the film. I would say the films which *I viewed* with Bill were prior to the commencement of the postmortem, as there was no evidence of a Y incision on the torso, nor was the scalp incised and peeled forward on the face as would be done during a postmortem."[25]

In another letter to Joanne Braun, David wrote that "the film slides I viewed with Bill Pitzer showed much the same as the pictures which you enclosed. First, I had seen and helped treat gunshot wounds and from training and experience had some idea of their effect on human flesh. Even high-powered rifle or pistol (375, M-1, M-16, etc.) entry holes are substantially smaller than their exit. It is inconceivable that anyone even vaguely acquainted with gunshot wounds would conclude that the massive wound in the *rear* of JFK's skull could have occurred from a rear-entry projectile, unless it was from grenade or mortar shrapnel, which tears and rends flesh and bone rather than pierces it. What appeared to be an entry was near the point of the arrow you drew on the right lateral picture. Also, the extension of the original tracheotomy incision to attempt to obliterate what appears to be an entry wound reinforces our impression of a frontal attack. The tracheotomy appeared to be approximately twice the length necessary."[26] David also wrote that Dr. Boswell told him a few days later that the casket that he helped unload from the black hearse in fact contained Kennedy's body.

Pitzer's autopsy report contains no mention whatsoever of gunpowder burns. If the man had shot himself, there would be a specific pattern of burns on his head and even his clothes. There is nothing indicating that he was shot from a distance. This should have been properly investigated by local authorities, but it was not.

The following is from Pitzer's autopsy report: "The body when first seen was clothed in civilian attire consisting of a blue knit shirt with undershirt, gray trousers, black loafer-type shoes, and blue socks. The head and face are partially covered by clotted blood. Bloodstains are present over the anterior portions of the shirt, undershirt, and both hands. Small bloodstains are also splattered over the trousers. After removal of the clothing the body is seen to be that of a well-developed well-nourished Caucasian male appearing to be of the stated age of 49. The head is slightly asymmetrical due to a large hematoma on the left side. The head is covered by a balding gray hair. Penetrating wounds are present in the right temporal and left parietal areas. The wound in the right temporal area is oval and measures 0.6 × 0.8 cm. in greatest dimension. An area of charring of the skin surrounds the wound. The wound with the charred area measures 1.5 cm. × 1.3 cm. No additional wounds are noted on the right side of the head and no powder burns of the skin surrounding the area are noted. This wound is judged to be the entrance wound and is located 3 cm. anterior to a perpendicular from the point where the upper anterior helix of the right ear attaches to the head. The wound is also 3 cm. above this point and is located in a diagonal measuring 4 cm. anterior and upward. It is located 6 cm. posterior and is slightly elevated from the lateral canthus of the right eye. . . .

"Sections from the margin of the entrance wound would reveal marked basophilic degeneration and hyalinization of the underlying collagen. Scattered throughout these tissues are prominent collections of a dark brown to black granular material presumably representing nitrates. The neighboring portions of the skin reveal moderate basophilic degeneration of the collagen, but no lesions of the epidermis or deposits of a foreign material are present."

I am told of a Dr. Raymond who was also found shot to death at Bethesda, and who had been at the autopsy. His widow, who worked in a bank, described many details of the autopsy to an acquaintance. Unfortunately, I am unable to find any record of a Dr. Raymond who is deceased and who might have been in the military or at Bethesda Naval Hospital, or who might have known something about the assassination.

Crimes committed at Bethesda Naval Hospital are within the jurisdiction of the State of Maryland. The attorney general and his assistants have repeatedly denied that they have jurisdiction, and indicate that local authorities in the county do. At first the state wrote me that there was no local jurisdiction because Bethesda is a federal base. The law is that if it is an "open" base, as this one is, the local authorities can and must come in whenever a crime is committed. The state then tried to tell me that the statute of limitations had passed. There is none in a murder case, and I believe there is none for accessories after the fact in murder.

The State of Maryland has as much right and duty to investigate these cases as the State of Texas has to investigate the murder of President Kennedy, since the federal government may never have had jurisdiction in that case. Perhaps on the basis of crimes being committed in conjunction with a conspiracy by military or civilian federal personnel, federal jurisdiction would obtain, but if the federal government will not act, it is incumbent upon the states so to do.

The evidence in this case more properly calls for an investigation in the United States Senate. I've been saying that for a long time, and it will never happen. Nobody there has that kind of courage.

Kennedy

One of the purposes of this book is to point out that our democratic system has been circumvented by what we have called *the secret team* of military officers, intelligence officers, government officials, and those outside of government closely allied with them.* The history of Kennedy's three years in office seems to demonstrate the basic conflict between him as the President, and the unelected factotums who were in a position to wrest it away.

The essence of Kennedy's presidency, other than the large historical facts of it, was one of struggle with these men who sought to maneuver and control him, and who ultimately overthrew him. They had all but physically paralyzed Kennedy. He spent much of his time in a special chair, slept on boards, took heavy medications, wore a back brace, and walked with a cane or crutches when not in public. And he was a young man. And this man was never known to complain.

We have to keep this country honest because it has more power than any country in the world, the power to utterly crush any opponent. Criticism of its activities may help us keep our country on an even keel. Constant awareness of its sins, crimes, and omissions is a way of preserving our Constitution and faith in our system of government. Revealing such crimes as John Kennedy's murder is part of that process. Americans have always felt that the First Amendment allows them to criticise their government. And this country has always had as one of its saving graces the ability to criticise itself and admit its mistakes.

Historical criticism serves that purpose. I'm just following tradition.

We can draw certain definitive historical conclusions at this point while most of the witnesses are still alive. Unless one of the participants in the conspiracy talks, or in our lifetime leaves some sort of documentation, we shall never know much more than what I have to say in this book.

---

* I recommend Bill Moyers' *The Secret Government: The Constitution in Crisis* by Bill Moyers, CBS correspondent and former top aide to President Lyndon Johnson, as a good opening primer on the subject. See the bibliography for information.

> "I think continually of those who were truly great.
> . . . The names of those who in their lives fought for
> life, Who wore at their hearts the fire's center. Born
> of the sun they traveled a short while towards the
> sun, And left the vivid air signed with their honour."
>
> —Stephen Spender

CHAPTER 28

WHAT REALLY HAPPENED

There are those among us who sit in judgment on the rest of us about our morals. These people have all the answers. They think they know what is right and wrong. And, in my opinion, this played a role in John Kennedy's death.

The Warren Commission

The Warren Commission's handling of President Kennedy's autopsy report is not credible. Questions remain about its findings, and there is a question as to whether or not Senator Arlen Specter and former President Gerald Ford—a president essentially appointed by Richard Nixon and never elected, and who then covered up for Nixon by pardoning him before he could be indicted—had made themselves accessories after the fact in covering up the murder of President Kennedy. Men working for Nixon are suspected of having participated in numerous political murders in the United States, including that of President Kennedy. I have maintained that their introduction of deadly violence into our political process was the real reason for Watergate. The burglary and cover-up could not possibly have been the only reason for President Nixon's forced resignation.

Specter and Ford invented an implausible theory (the "Magic" Bullet Theory) to place the blame on a dead scapegoat who could not defend himself. In addition, Specter extensively bullied witnesses and distorted the evidence in 1963, just as we have seen him do in 1991 to Anita Hill. Both Ford and Specter ultimately advanced their careers, having put the possibility of conspiracy in Kennedy's death behind them.

The conspiracy that killed President Kennedy was at least to some extent hatched and operated out of Dallas/Fort Worth. The plotters controlled the police and the city government there. Numerous of their relatives and connections were in the military and in the CIA and the DIA in Washington. Some of those, like General Charles Cabell of Dallas, had been fired by Kennedy. The Chief of the Western Hemisphere Division, David Atlee Phillips, and numerous others from the CIA were from Dallas or Fort Worth.

After the echoes of the shots quieted, officials saw what had happened and shifted their allegiance if they weren't a party to it beforehand. Some of Kennedy's people stayed with Johnson and benefited. Some of those stayed through a sense of duty, but others were opportunists, or stayed because they had no loyalty to the principles and policies of a dead president.

The Presidency

Before I go on, let me quote something from Harris Wofford's *Of Kennedys and Kings.* He wrote that Chester Bowles and others were uneasy. Wofford is talking about the period that led up to the massive involvement of the U.S. in Vietnam after JFK died. "American armed forces had not been sent into action in Cuba, Indochina, the Dominican Republic, or on the autobahn, but all of these affairs were cliff-hangers. He [Bowles] was concerned about the narrow perspectives of the 'military mind,' and the undue influence military leaders had on primarily political questions." After eight years of General Eisenhower as president, that was understandable.

"But that did not fully explain the tendency of the Democratic administration to reach for military answers to political problems. Bowles thought 'militarized liberals' were in part a reaction to years of being charged with softness on communism. However, a larger reason for the narrow escapes, he began to fear, was the new administration's—and Kennedy's—lack of a 'genuine sense of conviction about what is right and wrong.' " The Cold War seriously distorted our national life for a long time, then.

Bowles wrote in his journal: "Anyone in public life who has strong convictions about the rights and wrongs of public morality, both domestic and international, has a very great advantage in times of strain, since his instincts on what to do are clear and immediate. Lacking such a framework of moral conviction or sense of what is right and what is wrong, he is forced to lean almost entirely on his mental processes; he adds up the pluses and minuses of any question and comes up with a conclusion. Under normal conditions, when he is not tired or frustrated, this pragmatic approach should successfully bring him out on the right side of a question.

"What worries me are the conclusions that such an individual may reach when he is tired, angry, frustrated or emotionally affected. The Cuban fiasco demonstrates how far astray a man as brilliant and well intentioned as President Kennedy can go who lacks a basic moral reference point."[1]

Kennedy liked Bowles, and called him in for a talk when it looked like Bowles might be eased out. Bowles had outlined where our foreign policy ought to go, and by then it appeared that Rusk was not the man for the job. His "whole approach was the antithesis of how the Secretary operated," Wofford tells us.[2] Bowles discovered that he was becoming the scapegoat for the weaknesses of the State Department.

After months of public bickering and continuous calls for Bowles to be ejected from the administration, including the rancor of the President's brother, who considered Bowles a "gutless bastard," Kennedy made Bowles a roving ambassador, gave him special responsibilities, and got him out of the line of fire from the old guard in the State Department. Kennedy was listening, and tried to accommodate all parties. It wasn't easy being president. Kennedy could take criticism and learn from it.

Installing a general as president in the 1950s reinstituted the wartime psychological discipline and controls over the population which the power controllers of the United States wanted. They saw the benefit of such a highly disciplined, organized militaristic state as it existed in America during World War II.

Beware of the military-industrial establishment, Eisenhower warned us as his parting shot as president, turning it over to young John Kennedy.

The men of iron mountain did not expect John Kennedy to be elected. They expected Nixon, who was bought and paid for, to be elected. In addition, the way things were set up, both parties were being co-opted by the power controllers, and they assumed that whoever was elected, they could control him and his administration. John Kennedy did not work out that way because ultimately he could not be controlled. Since then, his memory and the history of his government had to be slandered with misinformation so that people would not care what had happened to him. If you could somehow claim or imply that he or his brother killed Marilyn Monroe (there is not a shred of credible evidence that she was murdered), then his assassination was justified. Or if you could falsely state that "he got us into Vietnam," then it didn't matter. The attitude was that he was out of control and had to be gotten out of the way.

The Evidence

This is what I believe and what I believe the evidence clearly shows.

There was beyond any doubt a conspiracy to murder President Kennedy. We know this from the forgery of the autopsy evidence, which was used to cover it up, and the planting of considerable evidence implicating Oswald, some of it before he was arrested. Considerable evidence disappeared shortly after the murder, and considerable evidence was faked. There were more shots than could have come from one gunman firing with that shoddy rifle within that time frame. There were at least three gunmen firing. Anyone trying to shoot Kennedy from the alleged sniper's window would have done it as the car *approached* the Texas School Book Depository, not when it was going away—when it was an impossible feat of marksmanship. Also, we know it was a conspiracy when J. Edgar Hoover himself lied and said there was a tree blocking the view from that window as the car approached it. There are no six-story-high trees in all of Texas.

A critic might say that the crime was covered up in order to prevent a war or international problems, or disorder in the United States. This was not the case. The murder was covered up by those who benefited from it or wanted JFK dead. They used fools and dupes, those whom they frightened into complicity and perhaps willing accomplices on the Warren Commission and in the police agencies and other official bodies who played some role in looking into the murder.

The fact is that nobody wanted the truth to come out because everybody suspected what it was and it was just too hard to handle.

We know that it was a conspiracy not solely because of the police recordings made during the shooting that revealed at least four shots and maybe more, and which—until presented more perfectly—proves little, but because the medical evidence shows that the President was hit from the front. There was more lead removed from John Connally than could have come from the "Magic" Bullet found at Parkland (CE 399) —which means that two different bullets hit the two men and could not have been fired from the same rifle within the time it took to load, aim, and fire.

A fragment found on the outside back of Kennedy's skull X-ray could have come only from the front.

We know that there was a conspiracy because the evidence shows that Oswald was set up as the patsy long before the murder took place, and in fact his whole identity as we learned of it in the Warren Report was fabricated to create a lone-nut gunman, even though there is plenty of evidence showing he did not fire any shots that tragic day, nor was he at all what he was made out to be by Gerald Ford[3] and the rest.

It seems to me that Gerald Ford, a Republican congressman on the Warren Commission, demonstrates both through his co-invention of the "Magic" Bullet Theory and the publication of his book—using classified information which he was not permitted to publish—a vested interest in convicting Lee Harvey Oswald, postmortem, of the murder of President Kennedy. He seems to have been rewarded with the appointment as vice president by the very man who may have been protected by the Warren Commission, Richard Nixon, whom Ford then replaced as an unelected president.

Ford then promptly pardoned Nixon before Nixon could even be indicted, a precedent unheard of in American history or jurisprudence. I find this whole affair most suspicious.

There is a key concept here which we went into in Chapter 24. In a murder case we have to ask about motive, and who benefited. A great debate has raged about whether or not Kennedy was taking us out of Vietnam. That is the question here—so what evidence do we have, ultimately, to resolve it one way or another?

From the moment of Kennedy's death it was ordained that we were going to go to war in Vietnam. The history of the period shows that numerous individuals around Kennedy at the time of his death helped lead us into that war, which was ultimately disastrous for the United States—as it had been for France before us. If a country does not practice austerity and pay off its wars, future generations have to pay for them. War debt can bring down a nation. It rots a country, festering like an open wound. This began the process that led us from being the richest country in the world to the world's leading debtor nation.

General Edward Lansdale and Lucien Conein wore military uniforms but were CIA. The military was their cover. The Far East and, in particular, Southeast Asia was their beat. There was long a rumor in the Washington area that the Far Eastern section of the CIA killed President Kennedy, along with propaganda specialists and Bay of Pigs operatives from the Western Hemisphere division. They were also connected to Richard Nixon. In the end Nixon was just another of their victims. There are many people entrenched in the upper levels of the bureaucracies and the military who are in a position to push the president around. It is exceedingly difficult for anyone to control them, and this secret team, a conglomeration of persons in those areas of government, have the power to create and direct foreign policy on their own, carry it out, and, if necessary, ruin or exterminate any opposition.

Various factions of this bunch are in the pockets of the most powerful and wealthiest of the Establishment, known as the "club," but, at times, there are competing interests and conflicting policies and goals. Lesser mortals, such as some of the Texas oilmen and their allies in the military and the intelligence agencies, may have their own agenda, and take matters into their own hands.

Certainly, the mayor of Dallas in 1963, whose brother, a general, had been fired by Kennedy as Deputy Director of the CIA, was in a key position in the terrible events of that year when a Texan became president.

Lansdale and Lucien Conein were prominent in the Far Eastern Section, along with Desmond Fitzgerald. There was a matrix of men in whose lives the Far East was either a primary interest or played a big part; Dean Rusk was with Stilwell in the China, Burma, India theater; Dave Powers fought there; McGeorge Bundy was with Army intelligence during the war. That war, World War II, shaped a lot of these men. Kennedy himself suffered from that war to the day he died.

Bundy's brother, William, the longtime CIA man, was married to the daughter of former Secretary of State Dean Acheson, and both were strong members of the Eastern establishment that had for decades controlled American foreign policy. One needed to play ball with their decisions and direction, and Kennedy was going off on his own direction. He had started to go against many powerful men.

It was Professor William Yandell Elliot of Harvard who had talked Kennedy into taking Rusk for secretary of state instead of McGeorge Bundy, and this caused some trouble. William Bundy and Acheson wanted McGeorge Bundy for secretary of state. He had for allies the Alsop brothers, who were powerful political columnists whom Kennedy feared. They became the enemies of liberalism in our foreign affairs, and they particularly disliked Chester Bowles.

The Ivy League establishment is incestuous. One way to cement ties between many of the ruling families is to intermarry. That bond of intimacy helps to hold everything together. Jackie and John Kennedy were no exceptions. Jackie had a reputation as a swinger. Before she met John Kennedy she lived in Paris and dated a young Air Force attaché there named Godfrey McHugh.

Godfrey McHugh was from a wealthy family and had close ties with some of the rich Texas oilmen. In fact, the night before Kennedy's assassination, General McHugh was at the home of two brothers, Robert N. and E. J. McCurdy, both oilmen in Fort Worth. They both intensely disliked Kennedy, as did every other oilman in Texas.[4]

These men would sit in judgment on Kennedy's morals. *Time* wrote that by the time he had become president, Kennedy had slept with 1600 women. There are a lot of people like this. I am not here to argue the morality of this, the fairness to his wife or otherwise. Women threw themselves at Kennedy, and his wife had lost a couple of children, which can kill sexual desire in a woman. Eventually, life and sexuality must go on. Kennedy needed affection and warmth.

The argument is made by militants that if someone needs sex to reaffirm that they are alive, then there is something wrong with them. This is a crazy idea, and there is something truly wrong with the fool who says this. The act of procreation is the life force itself, and when someone lives with death every day, with suffering, with pain, and when someone like Kennedy had repeatedly been given the last rites, then he had to have reassurance that he was alive. Intimacy with another provides that reassurance, and reason has nothing to do with it.

In the old days the newspapers viciously attacked presidents who had a little something on the side. Thomas Jefferson suffered the slings and arrows of the press due to his longtime love affair with his slave and mistress, Sally Nemmings. Sometime after that the press learned to keep its nose out of private presidential business.

President Cleveland had an illegitimate child, and, of course, General Eisenhower had a long romance with his driver in World War II.

President Harding also had a long affair.

President Roosevelt had always deeply loved Lucy Mercer and kept her close to him during his presidency. In fact, she was with him when he died at Warm Springs, Georgia, and his death was not made known until she could leave the area.

These men were mortal, and is a man a man if these things do not happen at one time or another? Or is a woman a woman if it doesn't happen? I don't mean to say that those who are entirely faithful to their partners are any less a man or a woman. I am just saying that we are all human and have either our faults or different ways of doing things. We have learned to become a lot more tolerant since John Kennedy. If he showed us the way with his private and personal crusade, he did us the biggest favor anyone has ever done. Our society needed drastic transformation. At long last we are an almost open and tolerant society.

Godfrey McHugh

And it seemed that some of Jackie's exes, such as Godfrey McHugh, her old friend from the Paris days, were gotten jobs at the White House. McHugh just happened to be with JFK when he was shot, and on *Air Force 1,* where the body was, flying back to Washington. McHugh just happened to be connected to the Dallas oilmen, and connected to General Charles Cabell, whom Kennedy had fired after the Bay of Pigs.

Godfrey McHugh was listed in *Who's Who in the CIA,* a book confirmed in the Pentagon Papers as being accurate. Other sources say that a U.S. military attaché at an embassy abroad is almost guaranteed to be CIA connected or employed.

Fort Worth, just a few scant miles from Dallas, was McHugh's home of record, although he was born in Belgium and educated in Paris. He seems to have something in common with Dr. Pierre Finck, who was the Belgium-born Army doctor at President Kennedy's autopsy.

McHugh was in the air attaché business, and had no real background in military science. An attaché at an embassy was a liaison, and this served the White House's purposes just fine. It is true that high-ranking officers wondered at the President's choice of McHugh for his aide, since he was in no way an expert on military matters. But they were pleased because they knew and liked McHugh and it was easier for them to have access to the President through him—an experienced diplomatically oriented liaison.

But they also wondered how he got that job, and perhaps John Kennedy never knew of his wife's romantic link to McHugh in their Paris days. She evidently had put in a word for him in order to keep him around. It is natural that she would want some old friends around, as Kennedy kept his Boston Irish cronies in house to keep his feet on the ground and his head screwed on straight.

If the body was stolen from *Air Force* 1 in Dallas, the time it was done was during LBJ's swearing in, when only General McHugh was on guard, and not before.

Penn Jones, Jr., who retired from the military a brigadier general, a veteran of Anzio and other tough battles, has this to say: "Since the assassination was planned and executed by the military of the United States, we feel now that General McHugh was a high-ranking traitor for the military inside the Kennedy camp. We hope we are wrong, and we hope McHugh will defend himself, but the evidence so far indicates treachery." McHugh is now dead.

Four or five of the key Secret Service agents in the President's guard at Dallas did not live too many years after the assassination. There seem to be certain classes of witnesses who died, but none of the medical personnel, for instance, who certainly got the message that others (who mattered less) were being killed.

The problem arises when there is a possibility that the government might be compromised by the President's bedroom liaisons. One of Kennedy's more or less regular women turned out to be involved with two famous Mafiosi.

Kennedy's détente with the Soviet Union was a fact by 1963, and the militant cold warrior sect didn't like it one bit, because they would lose all their marbles.

All this terror—nuclear weapons, the Cold War—was staged to keep the rest of us in line until going on with it any longer would bankrupt the nation. We are declaring a victory and quitting. The Cold War was an unspoken conspiracy between the U.S. and the U.S.S.R. It kept Germany divided for as long as possible, and that was the important thing.

But Kennedy was in a lot of pain, and, as Marilyn Monroe said, "I relieved his back pain." He needed it, and he deserved it.

And if it was discovered at the autopsy that Kennedy had TB of the spine and the adrenals, it meant that his military doctors had not diagnosed it, or had misdiagnosed it. Perhaps deliberately. He wasn't being treated for TB, he was being sabotaged.

What we do know is that the adrenals never made it into the autopsy report, which is extraordinary. There must be some reason for this, for even if they were missing this would have been noted, and I don't believe there would be any reason for the family to want to hide the fact if the autopsy report showed he had Addison's disease. So what? It would evoke more sympathy.

You can bet in this case that something is being withheld, hidden until the year 2039 because it doesn't support the government's case. It is just too damaging to the official story. You can also bet that it isn't in the National Archives any longer. The Archives have become a show window exhibiting fakes. The real evidence is behind the scenes, somewhere else, or was gotten out long ago.

Kenny O'Donnell, a bombardier on B-17s in the European theater, was the liaison with the FBI and the Secret Service. He, too, is dead now. "[Dr. Earl Rose, the Dallas County Medical Examiner], told me Kennedy was just another murder case," O'Donnell confided in his sister.[5] Strange, but Earl Rose said the same thing to me the day before I heard it from Justine O'Donnell, Kenny's sister. "It was just another murder case to me," Rose said. I didn't really think he cared too much either, except to say that he would have done a much better job than his colleagues performed at Bethesda. He was more professional.

Fletcher Prouty insists that Lansdale and Conein were present in Dealey Plaza the day Kennedy was killed, and that Lansdale's back appears in the background of some of the "tramp" photographs (pictures of men taken into custody from the railroad yards and box cars behind Dealey Plaza shortly after JFK was killed). These men were all let go. Their arrest reports were finally found by Larry Howard among the Dallas police records released in early 1992. Their names are Harold Doyle, John Forrester Gedney, and Gus W. Abrams. (See Appendix.)

I have trouble with Prouty's identification of Lansdale in these pictures. "I would know that back anywhere," he told me. His stronger reason for saying it is Lansdale in the photographs is that he knew Lansdale was there. Lansdale told him that he was going, Prouty says.

Tampering with the Body

I think that it is possible, but not probable, that the body was operated on before it ever got to Bethesda. The obvious or easiest place to do it would be on the airplane. The statements of some witnesses indicate that somebody may have gotten to the body before the autopsy and tampered with it. Somebody got the slugs out.

But tampering is only slightly possible, and there is no hard evidence to support this theory. And it wasn't necessary when forgery would cover-up the facts.

Nevertheless, it does seem reasonable that somebody did in fact get at the body and remove a bullet or bullets. There was no bullet found in the neck, and no evidence that the floor of the skull was penetrated by a bullet coming in the neck and exiting through the back of the head. The films and photographs make clear that the President was shot in the throat some seconds *before* his head blew apart, so the head shot could not have come through his neck from the front.

But, clearly, an *exploding bullet* struck the head. No part of it could be traced to any gun. Before the fatal head shot, fired by a crack sniper at what amounted to almost close range, it is likely that paralysing ice bullets hit the throat and perhaps the back, and so, were not found. No trace of metal was found in these wounds. The bullets that hit Connally were shots intended for Kennedy. Connally had to have been hit *twice*.

Either the bullet that struck Kennedy's neck was removed in Dallas, or it exited at the back of the neck and the exit wound simply was never noticed at the autopsy, or deleted from the public record part of the autopsy.

It seems to me to be true that the bullet that struck Kennedy in the back did not penetrate more than an inch or two and then fell out of his back.

The head wound was clearly made by a bullet intended to do great damage. The sharpshooter making this shot was to follow the first hits which were intended to freeze JFK in place and make a better target out of him.

I'm certain that the conspirators had a medical ally at Parkland, just as Jack Ruby was seen there by Seth Kanter immediately after the crime. Ruby probably planted the "Magic" Bullet.

There are repeated mentions of a "post" or partial autopsy at Parkland, by Bill Greer (The Ashville *Citizen-Times,* November 6, 1983), by Evelyn Lincoln in a casual mention to me and by Ken Raley. These could all be slips of the tongue or memory merge.

Only Jacqueline Kennedy and the two missing nurses can finally answer the question as to *if* the body was unattended for a short time in the ER at Parkland.

I accept the opinion of every Dallas witness that the wound in the throat was an entry wound. Dr. Perry indicated to me that the wound as shown in the photograph is accurate, but distended due to the flexion of the neck.[6] The trach incision was large enough for someone to either dig in the throat with their fingers or for the insertion of forceps to remove a bullet, as Dr. Crenshaw suggested to me. The trach wound did not have to be enlarged.

A bullet might have fallen out of the neck, of course, but I doubt that. There was claimed to be damage to one of the cervical vertebrae, and that would not have been caused by a bullet that entered below the neck in the back, struck the bone, and came out the throat. The government seriously distorted the evidence in order to make it sound like the bullet that hit Kennedy from behind hit him in the back of the neck, which it did not.

I also find it very hard to believe that a bullet struck JFK in the back and fell out. That is what is claimed explains one of the two bullet holes in the back, which is well established as having not penetrated the chest. But a spent bullet would fall out, yes.

As for the brain, there is no solid statement from even James Curtis Jenkins that the brain stem had been previously cut. He only thinks that it was, if I understand him correctly. The whole speculation of prior removal of the brain may be one more red herring among many. But if the first X-ray of the skull showed a large slug in the brain that might contain sufficient forensic information to indicate other weapons or bullets than the official story allowed, then the brain may very well have been operated on.

In my opinion, there was sufficient opportunity at Bethesda to do so clandestinely.

Finally, the severe conflicts in some of the facts indicate a sinister event. I find it impossible to believe that all the conflicts are simply coincidences or accidents. That is, when two different groups of credible witnesses are half an hour apart on both the arrival time of the body and the start of the autopsy, when the groups of witnesses at both hospitals saw at the one location a cerebellum completely out of the head and at the other a cerebellum in the head with no apparent damage, when the top of the head is entirely missing in one hospital and not at the other, when the X-rays cannot possibly depict the wounds as anyone remembers them and seriously conflict with the photographs of the face, when the photographs are clearly retouched, then one has evidence of a major tampering with the evidence.

In fact, part of me finds it very hard to believe that they had Kennedy's body at Bethesda.

Reason tends to indicate that somebody removed bullets from the body, and that is why there is a discrepancy in the time the body was received. But the stories we have heard for the past years about body alteration and tampering did not deal with the actual evidentiary issues as I have outlined them, and misled us with numerous red herrings.

The Plot

The real government of the United States does not work the way we are taught in school. That is all a front. The real government of the United States is elsewhere, other than in Washington, and the real power brokers have so much power that mere politicians are just flunkies. We now have a weak government, like Japan. If someone slips through the cracks and gets elected without sanction by the power brokers, that person will be taken under control one way or another, or neutralized or eliminated.

Nobody, *but nobody,* gets to be president without being a puppet of the powerful business interests that own America. Anybody who thinks —once in office—that they are free to do what they want or free to make decisions that run counter to the needs and will of the most powerful people is marked.

Kennedy was a marked man from not long after the start of his administration. It was clear from the Bay of Pigs debacle that he could not be controlled. It was clear from that time that he was going to be resistant to whatever was being done in Southeast Asia and its ultimate effect on the United States. For these reasons he was tested by the real power group in America, from which he sprang.

Kennedy's government was a coalition government. He did not have a mandate to govern with a free hand because he was not elected by a majority of those who voted. He had beaten Richard Nixon, a member of the "club," by only one hundred thousand votes, and Nixon had been picked to win by the power brokers. Each had less than half of the votes cast.

But our elections are rigged from the start. *All* of those who have any chance of winning the presidency have long been picked by the power elite, as had Kennedy. Our history is replete with instances where mediocre men achieve the presidency and become statesmen, but some became mere puppets. Kennedy began to rub the wrong people the wrong way, as he became his own man and a statesman.

The oil companies ruled America at that time, and they believed that there was oil off Vietnam. The Texas oil people had great power and they wanted more. They had their own people in the CIA and in the military, people high up in the pipeline and very loyal to their Texas partners.

Kennedy had threatened to remove the oil depletion allowance, which gave the oil people a great advantage over the rest of us, allowing vast fortunes to be built up by the likes of John D. Rockefeller and H. L. Hunt.

The 112th Military Intelligence unit in Dallas was ordered to stand down from alert just prior to the murder. Why? Later on they were unable to determine just who told them to do that. But it took this military unit out of action insofar as they might have provided protection for the murdered President.

Edward Lansdale was from the Far East Section in the CIA, his military uniform a cover. He had a long involvement with Indochina and a personal stake in preventing its fall to the Communists.

Kennedy knew that whatever men he had in South Vietnam were there as a shield for all of Southeast Asia, that the real countries to protect were Malaysia and Indonesia, nations with resources of oil and other strategic materials. Japan had attacked us at Pearl Harbor in order to get at the oil in Indonesia when we cut off Japan's oil—a response to Japan's invasion of Indochina, i.e., Vietnam.

Oil ultimately is the life blood of the modern world, and countries and people will kill over it. Make war over it.

There are some comments worth making about William Bundy's letter of April 27, 1991. Bundy, a democrat and liberal, had worked for the Agency for ten years, and he says that he did not agree with invading Cuba. "I did not feel we should invade Cuba, at any time." Critics would say (and have done so) that if Bundy felt that way, he would have or should have spoken to somebody about it. He "had enough clout to speak with General Erskine or even with McNamara and to tell them that. He might have stopped it. I never heard of any of the men in those positions disagree with the invasion plan; so Erskine and McNamara supported it with tons of money, equipment, ships and all the rest." Bundy's brother worked in the White House.

William Bundy wrote to me that he has "no personal recollection" of NSAM 273. He was in a key position with respect to such papers as 273. His brother had written it and sent it over to him.

Then note how he waffles the real question. He says: "273 . . . had little or no effect."

Certainly a vast amount of money was made on the morning of the assassination with selling short on the New York Stock Exchange. Somebody had advance notice.[7]

Questions are raised about the existence of a cabal to kill President Kennedy and to provide LBJ with an alternative program without delay.

We had a group of high officials remaining in the government after Kennedy died who then led us into a full-scale war in Vietnam, presaged with the NSAM 288 of March 17, 1964. Some of these men, who were clearly opposed to President Kennedy's plan to withdraw, became the de facto handmaidens of the conspiracy that killed him. It is not unreasonable to suppose that some of them had foreknowledge of the murder, and that some even participated in the plot.

It seems to me that this is the ultimate proof of the conspiracy. Unless one posits that Robert McNamara, General Maxwell Taylor, and the others were such tools that they simply went along with whichever way the wind blew, it must be assumed that for them all to unite behind a policy after Kennedy died—which he clearly opposed—and carry it through at vast cost to this nation and others, they sanctioned the murder. None of them either protested the killing or investigated the simple facts that would have shown that there was a conspiracy and that the conspiracy had to have employed government men in order to work. In addition, it is too simple-minded to suppose that they all just put their trust in the Warren Commission, when any fool in government would have known full well that there was no real investigation going on, and that the Warren Commission itself was politically compromised.

After all, most of those both on the Warren Commission and in the Administration were from the high-level banking and financial interests that controlled the nation and its policy. Certain specific short-term interests gained from the war. The evidence is blatantly clear that the murder came from within that Establishment.

When we see that the real power people in our country didn't believe in our own form of government, it can be better understood why they supported so many ruthless authoritarian regimes like South Korea and Chile. At the same time, those regimes, like our own, sometimes give the illusion of democracy.

You see, somebody has a gun at the head of the elected government in this country, and has had since 1963, and a lot of these people do not believe in our form of government. They use, manipulate, and control it.

The other side of the coin is that the secret foreign policy establishment (or the "club") operating through the "secret team," believes in government by committees of experts. They are absolutely opposed to the idea of elections, and feel that elections open the door to demagoguery, if not waste and inefficiency. If they had their way, there would be no public debate of issues, and nobody would be elected to promote a particular side of an issue. The whole notion of elections and democracy and a pluralistic society is anathema to these anachronistic plutocrats.

But they dare not raise their heads with such ideas in public for fear of being run out of the country, or worse, so they have found a way of putting a gun to the head of whoever is elected and making sure that they get their way.

Kennedy was a great threat. He understood very well Thomas Jefferson's suggestion that we have to overthrow the government every generation, because even in those halcyon days it was clear that when people become entrenched in the bureaucracy and can't be fired, we are all in trouble.

Such a flaw in national organization brought down the Communist states in the early nineties. People could not be fired, and they could not be motivated, so the nations rotted and failed.

The conspirators just could not plan for the overall cancer as it would inflict an old, settled government such as ours. Our Constitution, culture, creativity, and now our economy, and, to a certain extent, our society has got a smothering blanket over it.

*   *   *

There was a lot of hate in 1963. And there are those who stand in judgment of us, and those who felt left out.

The *Washington Post*'s Ben Bradlee was very close to John Kennedy. Kennedy thought he was a friend. They shared a lot. But Bradlee saw a Kennedy "who barely resembled the almost sacred figure described by the Camelot school. He was exceedingly vain, incredibly foul-mouthed, petty, penurious, insensitive, spiteful, eager for salacious gossip, and extremely manipulative. He slipped secret government documents to journalists in return for favors, got drunk, favored abortion, and denigrated liberals."[8]

We all have different sides to our character and none of the above can negate greatness. All great people are flawed and have critics.

James Jesus Angleton, the CIA's counterintelligence boss, had some more bad things to say. "JFK at least experimented with marijuana, cocaine, hashish, and acid in the White House." But prove this. Corroborate it. After all, Coca-Cola originally contained cocaine. There was a time when half the housewives in America were addicts, and nobody knew what it was doing to us.

It was felt—according to Reeves and others—that the President was under the influence of "Dr. Feelgood," Max Jacobson, who had him on amphetamines during his time in the Oval Office. It was otherwise rumored that a mix of vitamins was given to JFK that also contained amphetamines, which were prescribed to millions of people in those days for appetite control.

The historian Herbert Parmet felt that Kennedy's judgment was questionable with regard to many of the landmark policies and actions of his administration. Of course, this might reflect, as it did for his other critics, a political judgment. Then we have the low blow of linking the possible existence of Addison's disease, which is nothing more than an adrenal insufficiency, to his decisions and judgment. The innuendo was that because he had this medical problem he was unsuited to be president, liable to be impaired during crisis, and that his judgment was affected, for which there is no medical evidence or history.

Parmet saw evidence of panic, macho recklessness, and lack of moral principle.[9] "JFK's approach to civil rights . . . was basically political and pragmatic. . . . The President's relations with Congress . . . faltered in part because of his preoccupations with personal enjoyment." Now we are getting down to it. Sweeping generalizations by third-rate academics and gossip columnists pointing out what we already knew: All heroes' feet are made of clay.

Liz Smith says: "And the conclusions drawn in this book [Thomas C. Reeves's *A Question of Character*] about JFK's adultery are simply remarkable. One wonders that he didn't end up in a jar at Harvard, as the old joke goes. The Secret Service had to take special precautions to conceal his lechery, conducting him in and out of New York's Carlyle Hotel in New York with flashlights through tunnels. He had Judith Campbell [Exner] to the White House twenty times, invited her on *Air Force 1*, and begged her to attend White House functions."

Tell me, could a man with an almost broken back perform all the bedroom feats this man has attributed to him?

One hears other salacious and scandalous stories intending to show that JFK was immoral. But then, so was Thomas Jefferson, William McKinley, Franklin Roosevelt, and Warren Harding. In fact, probably most presidents except Richard Nixon and Jimmy Carter had a mistress. After all, these were older people for whom marriage withered, and the spice of life is what keeps us going. The total judgment of a person's moral structure should not be based on whether or not he has affairs. We all have faults and vices. It seems to me that Kennedy's vices were far preferable to other common and more serious political corruption in the White House.

Yes, because if the partying Secret Service was keeping lookout while Jack Kennedy was dallying in order to reaffirm life and that he was a man, in order to go back to his office and fend off yet another attempt to embroil the world in war, then maybe there was someone in his personal guard who did in fact betray him, who did in fact see only the too-human side of him and who did not see the great things he did. And that person or persons betrayed him. They set him up, sat in a bar until four A.M. the night before he was killed, and left him unprotected the next day, not reacting for ten or more seconds during the shooting until he was sure to die from his wounds.

Maybe somebody in his guard helped cover things up before the autopsy began, helping get at the body and removing what bullets there were.

The driver of the fatal limousine certainly did nothing for ten seconds, his foot on the brake, looking around, checking it all out until the President was good and dead.

Who Benefited?

The mayor of Dallas, who was in the fatal motorcade that day, Earle Cabell, was sent to the House of Representatives the following year. He was the one who was able to arrange a rather exorbitant payment to Vernon Oneal, the funeral director in Dallas who provided the casket that was used to transport the President to Washington. Oneal got his casket back, too.

Assistant chief of police Charles Batchelor, in charge of security precautions for both President Kennedy's motorcade and Oswald's transfer, who lost both Kennedy and Oswald, was rewarded by being made chief of police of Dallas.

Cabell's brother, the de facto Director of the CIA, whom Kennedy had fired, went to work for Howard Hughes, the multibillionaire, in a very lucrative job.

Another Texan, Lyndon Baines Johnson, became president.

The Republicans benefited when the assassination signaled mass defections from the Democratic Party. The whole South showed its true colors and defected. John Connally and Arlen Specter became Republicans, along with countless other conservative southern democrats, ultimately decimating the Democrats, isolating its liberals and associating them with leftists.

Defense industry benefited as NSAM 288—authorized by Johnson—signaled once and for all that we were going to war in Vietnam, and the huge Texas oil companies, construction firms, and defense industries made a fortune in that terrible war over the next ten years. They were all backers of Johnson and had wanted him to be president, and not Kennedy.

The deregulators and those who wanted to strip the federal government of what power it had to effect social change benefited. The banks and their backers, at first, made a vast fortune, until it all came full circle and their own stupidity caught up with them.

But in the end I don't think anybody gained. We all are the worse for the loss of John Kennedy. As I have said before, there will never be anyone like him again.

On August 17, 1991, just two days after speaking with Joe Hagen, president of Gawler's Funeral Home, which prepared John Kennedy's body for his coffin, I interviewed his assistant, Tom Robinson. On that terrible night of the autopsy of November 22, 1963, Tom had the heart-breaking task of putting the President back together in case his widow or the family would want to open the coffin and look at him one last time.

Tom washed and combed the hair and knew there was no slug there. It has been said before, but it is vital because we have two or three honest men making the same report. This is what Robinson told me:

"A lot of the scalp in the back was gone. We used a piece of rubber there, in the back."

"Did you cover the missing area of scalp with a hairpiece?"

"No. We didn't have to. No one could see the hole on the pillow," Robinson told me.

"No, no hairpiece was used. We didn't have to, because the part of the back of the head where scalp was missing was placed on the pillow, and no one could see it. There was a hole in the pillow to take care of leakage, and that covered up the missing area.

"The body had been cleaned up before we got it. The face was perfect and undamaged except for a small laceration about a half inch into the forehead, which I covered up."

I asked him if any of the frontal bone or bone behind any part of the face, forehead, or front top of the head underlying the scalp was damaged.

"It may have been fractured [and I couldn't see that], but it was perfectly intact. I don't think any of it had been removed or replaced before we got it. The face was perfect. It would have fallen in without the frontal bone."

"There was one very small hole in the temple area, in the hairline. I used wax in it, and that is all that I had to do. I just put a little wax in it."

"What side was it on?"

"I can't remember for sure, but I think it was on the right side." In another interview he told me that the skull was penetrated in two or three more places by shrapnel, which he filled with wax. These places were near the eyes.[10]

There was only one significant hole of any kind in the head beside small puncture wounds, and that was the large defect. He said that it was in the very back of the head and could not be seen with the head on the pillow. The scalp back there was badly mangled and "some of it was missing."

Enough was missing that it could not be pulled over the missing bone, but that they did not do anything about it because that space was unseen, on the pillow. Otherwise, beyond washing and combing the hair, the head needed no work, and no hairpiece was used. All that he told me was identical to what I had been told by Paul O'Connor, Jim Jenkins, Floyd Riebe, Dr. Karnei, and Commander Boswell.

His face was perfect and did not require work of any kind, and the frontal bone underlying it was intact, but slightly fractured.

"There was not enough scalp to pull together over that large wound in the back. The big hole was only in the back. We filled the skull with plaster and put back the bones, but we did not have all of the bones and could not completely cover over the hole in the back.

"I do not remember any bone being missing on the top of the head."

"Tom Robinson said there was no bone missing in the face."

"I told you that," Joe Hagen said when he got back to me. "I couldn't remember any bone missing in the face or from the frontal bone. That was pretty well intact to the best of my memory. Tommy Robinson was right there, hands on, during the whole thing and put his head back together, so he would be the guy who would know better than anyone else other than the pathologists themselves. He was there."

The men have all insisted to me that the evidence they saw at the autopsy showed clearly that Kennedy had been shot on the side of his head above and to the right of his ear, and that it took off the back of his head. None of them recalls either of the entry holes claimed to be in the back of the head in the autopsy report, or shown in the alleged autopsy photographs four inches away from where the report placed it.

Dr. Humes may have tried his best to let us know that something was greatly wrong when he told the Warren Commission that the bullet to the head "could not have but exited from behind." He said that in the same breath that he used to say that there was a bullet entry hole on the margin of a piece of bone that he thought fitted in the large defect in the back of the head.[11]

After Lincoln's and Roosevelt's, Kennedy's death was the most terrible loss this country has ever suffered. We are still traumatised by it, and there is a great vacuum in our affairs because of it.

And I don't think many of us will ever get over the assassination. I don't think this *nation* will get over it or be the same for a long time, if ever. It has left a black cloud in our national life and history that will forever be with us and cost us, and some of us will forever be trying to solve the mystery of John Kennedy's death.

God bless him.

Appendix

The Autopsy Photographs

Mark Crouch and I shared the autopsy prints with Steve Mills, a photo analyst in Hermiston, Oregon, who also talked to John Stringer. Mills wrote the following:

I spoke with John Stringer, the autopsy photographer, on January 19 and 20, 1992, and he clarified some matters. He said that he used two light sources, each on a stand on both sides of the camera. The 4×5 view camera was on a tripod, and identical photographs were taken both in color and black and white panchromatic film by changing film holders. He did not think that one of his light stands was at any time on the opposite side of the table from his camera. He repeated that there was no damage at all to Kennedy's face. He said that he had asked Floyd Riebe, the enlisted photographer, to take some pictures of the scene—the room and the people in it. Riebe took about five when a Secret Service man seized his camera and exposed the film. Riebe took no further pictures.

Stringer felt that there was something wrong with the photographs that he has seen, and that it first of all related to the color photographs having been printed in black and white, and that both color and black and white were several generations down the line.

F1 and F2 (Fox 1 and 2, Stare-of-Death photos.) F1 has the words U.S. NAVAL HOSPITAL on the corner of the towel under the head, but the words are washed out of F2, and shadows and tile are also visible in F1 and not F2 (a lighter exposure was a first attempt and F2 was to correct the problem.) The room area is visible in F1, and F2 has been "burned in" in printing to mask that. F2 was also burned in to bring out the name on the towel. This is evidenced as well by the blue stripe being darker to the left of JFK's head in F2 than it is to the right. This technique is known as burning and dodging. The path of light from the enlarger to the printing paper is manipulated by small shapes on wire handles, thus allowing an area to receive sufficient exposure. Surrounding areas can be "burned in" while that area is being "dodged." That is how Robert Groden's color version of F4 has lost its background.

The most striking difference between F1 and F2 is the shadow of the right shoulder. F2 was probably taken after placing the block under that shoulder, and F1 before. The other shadows do not show enough change to credit this to

583

a shift in flash position. In fact, it appears that the camera is mounted on a tripod or stand. The nose shadow has not changed.

F4 (Left Profile). Here the left ear supports your assertions about the smudges of blood on his right ear.

I feel this photo shows his head is high enough (three to four inches) above the towel to account for the stripe visible both above and below the right ear in the various poses. This does not preclude staging, however.

The splice line appears to be where the phone line goes. What is that dark line to the left? It has no reflection.

Notice the first tile in the top row just left of the splice. Its upper right corner should have the brightest reflection of all the corners within the axis of the flash, yet it's the dullest.

Does the phone being here place him on the "proper" table?

F5 (showing the President's back, and back of the head). Clearly, the back wound in its proper Humes location. Here, as in F3, the back of the head is in focus when it should not be. The crown is on a plane roughly equal to the doctor's wrist and shouldn't be so sharp. The back of his head shows no detail in my copy.

F6 and F7 (top of the Head). Here's where it gets interesting. The record says the photos (black and white) were taken with panchromatic film. Pan records red and blue as nearly equal shades of black. Yet the blue stripe is light gray in every available view. You can make pan sec blue as gray with a blue filter, but this darkens the red. A red filter will lighten the red, but it darkens the blue.

Orthochromatic film, unfiltered, records blue very lightly and red very darkly. This makes perfect sense in F1 through F5. Yet, here's a supposedly bloodied scalp in F6 and F7 recorded as light gray. This can be done with a red filter on ortho film, but the blood drops on the towel show me this is not the case. The scalp can't be gray and three bloody spots still be dark if a filter was used.

It is common to use ortho film in forensic photography to show differences and details in red and blue areas. But this is no proof.

The record declares one type of film, and the photos declare either another or fraud. They also show Groden's color shots to be fraud. Let me explain.

1) Let's say it was pan b/w. F6 and F7 would have to be shot with a blue filter to lighten the stripe. That would darken the supposedly bloody scalp. You can't have it both ways, i.e., light red *and* light blue, so there's no red filter either. This would not work.

So, if it's truly pan film, then the scalp is not bloody skin but brain matter.

2) Let's say it's ortho film. The blue stripe will always be light and the red will always be dark. No filter is required if the scalp is really brain tissue, but a red one is still needed to lighten blood. But here the bloody spots prove this is not the case once again. So do the bloody marks on his shoulder.

So, here's the result: They probably used ortho film and no filtering of any kind. *That is brain* and *not scalp.* We can see that *no combination of film and filtration can give you b/w photos that will jibe with Groden's colors. They have to be fake.* Of course, you already thought so, but there's a good reason to go on feeling that way.

There's more: in both F6 and F7 there's a clear laceration of the scalp. This is the work of a scalpel. Humes must have been referring to this when he declared surgery (to the top of the head). This and the V notch.

You can't call the area scalp when it's been mangled in such a way.

I can't make out any detail in the V-notch area in the two prints I have.

F8 (The Large Defect). Here's where the real story is. My view of this photo is best in the vertical with the ruler to the right and the scalp peeling left. The Committee called this anterior-superior. It's actually posterior-superior to posterior only. This one may be red filtered.

Near the center and slightly lower and to the right you will find in the focused area the back of the sinuses and a lacerated right eye. Around these the skull is notched and mostly gone.

I'm convinced that this photo matches the X-ray. Here at the bottom now is a deep notch that would correspond to the in shoot Humes describes.

Out of focus along the back of the skull is what the Committee saw as a semicircular notch that was medicolegal evidence of exit. How true! This places it where all the witnesses saw the exit wound.

It's no overstatement to say that the whole story is in this one photo.

The problems I see with my assertion are that viewed this way, the head appears to be detached. (Author's note: Radiologists I consulted said that the skull in the X-ray is not attached to a body.) At least in my print. The detail at the bottom is dark and confusing. Clearest to me is how this photo would match the X-ray, viewed as I suggest.

There are bones missing, or set aside to give us a clearer view, that would support his right ear. This is quite far into the autopsy, I would say.

Stringer took all the autopsy photographs, both b/w and color. He used a view camera (the type with bellows and the cloth hood) specifically, a Linhoff 4×5. This camera was on a tripod, hence the similarity of poses. He had an assistant bring him film from the lab to the autopsy room. Stringer turned all the film holders over to the Secret Service. He expressed concern about the discrepancy in accounting for numbers of plates and holders, as you see in the Clark Panel data. Stringer said, "I know what I gave them." He thinks they are counting empty holders. No elaboration on that point by him.

Stringer said it was Riebe's roll of 120 film that was deliberately ruined. Riebe took no other photos.

The films used were Kodak Ektachrome slide film and a panchromatic black and white film. No filters were used. Lighting was a single strobe flash. (This varies from the two light sources Stringer described to the author.) Stringer expressed how difficult the job was with all the people in the room. As to the photos in the Archives, he saw them and signed off in 1966. He has not seen that set since. The photos we are seeing (the Fox set) he feels are "copies of copies of copies," and are based on color originals.

He said he was present throughout the autopsy, and was "there until the undertaker came."

His conversation was generally pleasant and forthcoming, but he volunteered nothing more than his feeling of being disturbed that the autopsy photos have been made public. I asked pointedly if he thought these were more or less accurate versions of what he photographed that night. I was hoping for a response that might hint at fraud, or help at least by pointing in some direction. That's when he told me that they were "copies of copies of copies." He thought the reason for the lighter area on top of the head was due to loss in copying, and specifically, he feels these black and whites are from color originals.

That brings me back to our dilemma about why that navy blue stripe is light (Author's note: In one of the pictures it is two entirely different shades on either side of the head.) and the red areas are very black. Color negatives (he shot color slides, but color negs are only one more step; you simply copy the slides) can be used in making black and white prints. There is a specific black and white paper for this called Kodak Panalure. It is used commonly by wedding photographers to give the couple b/w prints from their color photos. The reason for Panalure is that it will see the colors of a color negative correctly and render grays that compare to the true scene.

If you print b/w from color negatives using standard b/w paper, you will have generally good results, but the blues will be lighter and the reds will be darker. Sounds familiar, doesn't it? Stringer may be saying more than the obvious, but he did say they were copying color originals. What I thought was the result of ortho b/w film was something else (if he is right).

Let's see if I can write a scenario showing how we got from Stringer's originals to what you and I have seen. You begin with color slides and b/w negatives. To view color slides is simple. But for the Warren Commission or anyone else to see them, you have to leave the original and go to either reversal prints (made directly from the slides; this paper goes positive, requiring no negative) or color negatives, then color prints.

With these color prints you can do all the manipulation (artwork, mattes, overlays, etc.) you want to. You simply rephotograph the doctored prints on color negative film and make new prints. Or rephotograph on slide and b/w 4×5 film to substitute with the originals. Or you can do both.

What we most likely have is a set of black and white copies that at one point were printed using color negatives, and are not from the original black and white negatives in any way.

We're still left with a problem, since there exists a set of color prints, some of which are essentially identical to the black and whites. The solution is to follow the rules for red and blue and how they are responded to by various combinations of film and paper. What is most obvious is that one or both are fraudulent. There's no possible way that they can both be from their respective originals.

I compared the two top-of-the-head shots as you asked. One was published by Groden in the *Globe* and the other was one of the black and white prints taken from the same angle. The differences are many. There are missing locks of hair in the color print. The "flap" over the right temple is too red in the color and too large if the black and white shot is red. A comparison of equal prints would reveal much more. (Groden refuses to allow this.)

I think you need to get more out of Stringer while there's time. Get him to say if these photos represent what he photographed that night, or does he think they've been retouched.

There are so many ways to manipulate color and shades of gray in photographs that saying "this is how it was done" can be dangerous. What helps in this case is that we know what some of the original colors were and can track their likely path knowing what the original film was. The biggest aid is the fact that the dominant colors were red and blue, the two hardest to manipulate simultaneously without revealing your method.

The result of my best efforts to analyze these photos is that they are all suspect. None of them are from the originals. The color shots that Groden has were not the source of the Fox set either. His colors may be hand done, but I'd have to see better copies even to guess.

We've been fed crap just to keep us amused and confused. There are bits to be gleaned from these photos, but little more. Except to say they aren't what they're supposed to be.

On the question of painting or drawing in, I feel that the major area that you find surrounded by half moons (Groden's unpublished color picture) is all photograph. There is much artwork involved in inserting a new scene into an existing photograph. The addition would have been laid over the area they wanted to hide, possibly some retouching being done to obscure the edge between new and old. Most of the retouching would be done at the new generation. Then you make one more copy and all future prints from that negative. These are the ones you have seen.

I agree that you can see the marks of retouching in your copy. I can even see some near the lower portion of the insertion in my copy of *High Treason*. Most of the artwork was probably done with an airbrush.

As to digitally altering the image, this could not have been done in the mid-sixties. Even now the process is easily detectable.

I don't see any possibility of faking the bullet hole without making a composite first. There may be a genuine bullet hole in whomever the scalp belongs to, but it does more closely resemble artwork (as Dr. Humes suggested when he viewed these photos).

I have an opinion about the source of the scalp image that may give you pause. First, it is not of the area of scalp it is intended to portray. Not Kennedy's or anyone else's. Take a look at it with the rest of the picture blocked from view. To me, it appears to be a top view of a head facing the camera. In other words, it is backward. Second, the area that looks like the cowlick is "in space" compared to where it would be were the scene genuine. The skin past it toward the upper left continues on a relatively flat plane, again inconsistent with reality.

The notion put forward in *High Treason* about successive copies of this photo bringing out the edge of the insertion is only somewhat valid. It is the result of the varied contrast between Kennedy's real hair and hair that appears wet.

The out of focus area along what Groden called the matte insertion belongs to both halves of the composite. Each was focused on a particular area. On Kennedy, the focus was farther in than the nearer point, which was whatever was left of the back of his head. If the cowlick was there, it was very fuzzy. The new part was focused at the nearest point and gradually goes out of focus to the farther points. These two out of focus areas are both genuine parts of each half but are carefully blended together. This area did not need to fool the stereo-viewing of the House Committee—since nothing out of the ordinary will reveal itself in stereo-viewing a flat original. Now, if the photo you had access to were in any way retouched, this could be revealed by the stereo method. That is, if blending or spotting or airbrushing had been done on the very print you work from. But copy it once, and all that is hidden from stereo-viewing. For them to say no evidence of retouching was found is both the truth and a lie. There is no evidence *on* the prints, but there is plenty *in* them.

Something else of interest to me about this photo is the ruler. It should cast a shadow over the left shoulder, given the apparent source of flash. The shadow it casts on the back of JFK's head seems contrived, its angle is too parallel with the ruler. The ruler's brilliant reflection indicates precisely where the flash is. There is a rule in reflectivity called the family of angles. To get that strong a reflection, the ruler becomes like the bank of a pool table. If the camera and flash are known, the validity of the photo can be more precisely known. However, that type of study would be beyond my scope. A good subject for computer enhancement.

N E W S   C O N F E R E N C E   #1265

AT THE WHITE HOUSE

WITH PIERRE SALINGER

OCTOBER 2, 1963

6:52 PM   EDST

WEDNESDAY

MR. SALINGER: This is a White House statement, and it is of some length.

Secretary McNamara and General Taylor reported to the President this morning and to the National Security Council this afternoon. Their report included a number of classified findings and recommendations which will be the subject of further review and action. Their basic presentation was endorsed by all members of the Security Council and the following statement of United States policy was approved by the President on the basis of recommendations received from them and from Ambassador Lodge.

1. The security of South Viet Nam is a major interest of the United States as other free nations. We will adhere to our policy of working with the people and Government of South Viet Nam to deny this country to Communism and to suppress the externally stimulated and supported insurgency of the Viet Cong as promptly as possible. Effective performance in this undertaking is the central objective of our policy in South Viet Nam.

2. The military program in South Viet Nam has made progress and is sound in principle, though improvements are being energetically sought.

3. Major U. S. assistance in support of this military effort is needed only until the insurgency has been suppressed or until the national security forces of the Government of South Viet Nam are capable of suppressing it.

Secretary McNamara and General Taylor reported their judgement that the major part of the U. S. military task can be completed by the end of 1965, although there may be a continuing requirement for a limited number of U. S. training personnel. They reported that by the end of this year, the U. S. program for training Vietnamese should have progressed to the point where 1,000 U. S. military personnel assigned to South Viet Nam can be withdrawn.

4. The political situation in South Viet Nam remains deeply serious. The United States has made clear its continuing opposition to any repressive actions in South Viet Nam. While such actions have not yet significantly affected the military effort, they could do so in the future.

MORE

Page 2 - #1265

5. It remains the policy of the United States,
in South Viet Nam as in other parts of the world, to
support the efforts of the people of that country to
defeat aggression and to build a peaceful and free
society.

Q. Pierre, did the Secretary bring a message
from Ambassador Lodge?

MR. SALINGER: No, but the President has been
in the closest touch with Ambassador Lodge and, of course,
Secretary McNamara and General Taylor had very extensive
consultation when they were there.

Q. How many troops do we have in South Viet Nam?

MR. SALINGER: I couldn't tell you that.

Q. Could you give us an unclassified figure,
Mr. Sylvester?

MR. SYLVESTER: No.

Q. Does this mean the military effort will
end in 1965?

MR. SALINGER: I will let the statement stand
by itself and this will be for all departments of Government.

Q. The statement says this should be completed
by 1965.

MR. SALINGER: I think the statement is extremely
clear.

Q. Can you tell us how long we have been in
South Viet Nam with military personnel, approximately?

MR. SYLVESTER: I would have to get the exact
figure for you.

Q. Can you get the number of troops?

MR. SYLVESTER: No, sir.

Q. How long did the NSC meeting last?

MR. SALINGER: The NSC meeting lasted about 50
minutes.

Q. Can you say who was there?

MR. SALINGER: NSC members and others.

Q. How many other than 1,000 will they be
pulling out of there?

MR. SALINGER: I couldn't say.

Q. Can you give us an estimate?

MORE

Page 3 - #1265

MR. SALINGER: <u>OFF THE RECORD</u>:

* * * * * * * *

I might say that we are just not about to answer that.

* * * * * * * *

Q. You say success. Does that refer to any
one period of time?

MR. SALINGER: No, I think the statement speaks
for itself.

Q. Does that mean the Vietnamese military
program or the combined program or what?

MR. SALINGER: It means the overall military
program.

Q. Can you tell us who was in the meeting?

MR. SALINGER: Members of the Security Council
and others.

Q. Who were the others?

MR. SALINGER: It was a wide representation from
many departments of the Government.

Q. Could we find out? If we are going to less
than 1965, how long we are going to be in there roughly
might help.

MR. SALINGER: We will get that.

Q. Would you say between 20 and 30 were at
the meeting?

MR. SALINGER: Yes.

THE PRESS: Thank you.

E N D

White House Report

U.S. TROOPS SEEN OUT OF VIET BY '65

PACIFIC
STARS AND STRIPES

AN AUTHORIZED PUBLICATION OF THE ARMED FORCES IN THE FAR EAST

FIVE-STAR EDITION

10¢ DAILY
15¢ WITH SUPPLEMENTS

Vol. 19, No. 276   Friday, Oct. 4, 1963

Koufax, L.A. Top N.Y. 5-2

Compiled From AP and UPI

NEW YORK—Lefthander Sandy Koufax set a World Series strikeout record Wednesday as he pitched the Los Angeles Dodgers to a 5-2 victory over the New York Yankees in the first game of the fall classic.

Catcher John Roseboro powered the Dodgers to the win with a three-run homer into the right field stands off New York starter Whitey Ford capping a four-run outburst in the second inning. Bill Skowron, a former Yankee, drove in the other runs with two singles.

Koufax, 25-5 during the regular season, struck out 15 Yankees, one more than Carl Erskie of the Brooklyn Dodgers did against the Yankees, 10 years ago to the day.

Roseboro set another Series record with a total of 18 putouts on strikeouts and fouls to smash the mark held by Mickey Cochrane of the Detroit Tigers and Roy Campanella of the old Brooklyn Dodgers.

The Yanks, who managed to get only 6 hits off Koufax, scored all their runs in the eighth inning on a homer by Tom Tresh. The crowd of 69,000 at Yankee Stadium also saw the team strikeout mark set. The total of 25 strikeouts for the two teams bettered the old mark of 22 established by the St. Louis Cardinals and the St. Louis Browns in 1944.

SANDY KOUFAX

President Kennedy gets a firsthand report on the situation in the Republic of Vietnam from General Maxwell D. Taylor (left), chairman of the Joint Chiefs of Staff, and Defense Secretary Robert McNamara. (AP Photo)

WASHINGTON (UPI) — The White House said Wednesday night after hearing a report from a two-man inspection team that the U.S. military effort in the Republic of Vietnam should be completed by the end of 1965.

The White House said the situation in the Southeast Asian country was "deeply serious."

The statement came after President Kennedy met for nearly an hour with the full Security Council to hear a detailed report on the Vietnamese situation from Defense Secretary Robert S. McNamara and General Maxwell D. Taylor, chairman of the Joint Chiefs of Staff.

McNamara and Taylor returned to the U.S. early in the day after an on-site survey.

Highlights of the White House statement:

1—The U.S. government will continue to support the people and government of south Vietnam in their battle against the aggression of the communist Viet Cong.

2—McNamara and Taylor conceded that improvements could be made in the current military program but they thought progress had been made recently.

(Continued on Back Page, Col. 2)

JFK Signs Military Pay Bill

WASHINGTON (AP) — President Kennedy signed Wednesday, with "great pleasure," a bill granting an average 14.4 per cent pay increase to most of the 2.7 million men and women in the U.S. armed forces.

In a cabinet room ceremony, Kennedy used more than a dozen fountain pens to sign the measure, which will cost the government $1.3 billion a year. It is the biggest military pay boost in history.

Kennedy said that, while he is impressed with new and powerful weapons, he is mindful (Continued on Back Page, Col. 1)

1931 GANG KILLINGS
Valachi Fingers Genovese

WASHINGTON (AP)—Joseph Valachi Wednesday linked Vito Genovese—the man he says now runs a U.S. criminal syndicate from a prison cell—to the 1931 violent deaths of two gangland bosses.

Tracing the history of the syndicate known as La Cosa Nostra,

Valachi did not name Genovese as the actual killer, but told the Senate investigations subcommittee:

1) The shooting of Guiseppi Massaria, alias Joe the Boss, in a Coney Island (N.Y.) restaurant in April 1931 was set up by "Charles Lucky, Vito Genovese

and Ciro Terranova."

2) Salvatore Maranzano, gunned down the following September, had been in a meeting that day with Genovese and Charles Lucky.

Massaria and Maranzano at the time were leaders of rival (Continued on Back Page, Col. 2)

Weather

Tokyo Area Forecast
Friday: Cloudy; High 68, Low 58
Saturday: Partly Cloudy; High 74, Low 56
Wednesday's Temperature: High 73, Low 67
(USAF Weather Central, Fuchu AB)

TOP SECRET

THE SECRETARY OF DEFENSE
WASHINGTON

2 October 1963

Comm. Print Bk 12
NVM   11/29/71

MEMORANDUM FOR THE PRESIDENT

Subject: Report of McNamara-Taylor Mission to South Vietnam

Your memorandum of 21 September 1963 directed that General Taylor and Secretary McNamara proceed to South Vietnam to appraise the military and para-military effort to defeat the Viet Cong and to consider, in consultation with Ambassador Lodge, related political and social questions. You further directed that, if the prognosis in our judgment was not hopeful, we should present our views of what action must be taken by the South Vietnam Government and what steps our Government should take to lead the Vietnamese to that action.

Accompanied by representatives of the State Department, CIA, and your Staff, we have conducted an intensive program of visits to key operational areas, supplemented by discussions with U.S. officials in all major U.S. Agencies as well as officials of the GVN and third countries.

We have also discussed our findings in detail with Ambassador Lodge, and with General Harkins and Admiral Felt.

The following report is concurred in by the Staff Members of the mission as individuals, subject to the exceptions noted.

I. CONCLUSIONS AND RECOMMENDATIONS

A. Conclusions.

1. The military campaign has made great progress and continues to progress.
2. There are serious political tensions in Saigon (and perhaps elsewhere in South Vietnam) where the Diem-Nhu government is becoming increasingly unpopular.
3. There is no solid evidence of the possibility of a successful coup, although assassination of Diem or Nhu is always a possibility.
4. Although some, and perhaps an increasing number, of GVN military officers are becoming hostile to the government, they are more hostile to the Viet Cong than to the government and at least for the near future they will continue to perform their military duties.
5. Further repressive actions by Diem and Nhu could change the present favorable military trends. On the other hand, a return to more moderate methods of control and administration, unlikely though it may be, would substantially mitigate the political crisis.

SECRET

TOP SECRET

6. It is not clear that pressures exerted by the U.S. will move Diem and Nhu toward moderation. Indeed, pressures may increase their obduracy. But unless such pressures are exerted, they are almost certain to continue past patterns of behavior.

B. Recommendations.

We recommend that:

1. General Harkins review with Diem the military changes necessary to complete the military campaign in the Northern and Central areas (I, II, and III Corps) by the end of 1964, and in the Delta (IV Corps) by the end of 1965. This review would consider the need for such changes as:

    a. A further shift of military emphasis and strength to the Delta (IV Corps).

    b. An increase in the military tempo in all corps areas, so that all combat troops are in the field an average of 20 days out of 30 and static missions are ended.

    c. Emphasis on "clear and hold operations" instead of terrain sweeps which have little permanent value.

    d. The expansion of personnel in combat units to full authorized strength.

    e. The training and arming of hamlet militia at an accelerated rate, especially in the Delta.

    f. A consolidation of the strategic hamlet program, especially in the Delta, and action to insure that future strategic hamlets are not built until they can be protected, and until civic action programs can be introduced.

2. A program be established to train Vietnamese so that essential functions now performed by U.S. military personnel can be carried out by Vietnamese by the end of 1965. It should be possible to withdraw the bulk of U.S. personnel by that time.

3. In accordance with the program to train progressively Vietnamese to take over military functions, the Defense Department should announce in the very near future presently prepared plans to withdraw 1000 U.S. military personnel by the end of 1963. This action should be explained in low key as an initial step in a long-term program to replace U.S. personnel with trained Vietnamese without impairment of the war effort.

4. The following actions be taken to impress upon Diem our disapproval of his political program.

    a. Continue to withhold commitment of funds in the commodity import program, but avoid a formal announcement. The potential significance of the withholding of commitments for the 1964 military budget should be brought home to the top military officers in working level contacts between USOM and MACV and the Joint General Staff; up to now we have stated $95 million may be used by the Vietnamese as a planning level for the commodity import program for 1964. Henceforth we could make clear that this is uncertain both because of lack of final appropriation action by the Congress and because of executive policy.

TOP SECRET

2

THE WHITE HOUSE
WASHINGTON

October 11, 1963

Mr. Smith:

Secretary McNamara has

approved the attached draft

NSAM.

Michael V. Forrestal

~~TOP SECRET~~   *8* October 1963   DRAFT   *1A*
EYES ONLY

NATIONAL SECURITY ACTION MEMORANDUM NO. _____

TO: Secretary of State
         Secretary of Defense
         Chairman of the Joint Chiefs of Staff

SUBJECT: South Viet Nam

At a meeting ~~in the Cabinet Room~~ on October 5, 1963, the President *single*
considered the recommendations contained in the report of Secretary
McNamara and General Taylor on their mission to South Viet Nam.

The President approved the military recommendations contained in
Section I B (1 - 3) of the report, but directed that no formal announcement be made of the implementation of plans to withdraw 1,000 U.S.
military personnel by the end of 1963.

After ~~extensive~~ discussion of the remaining recommendations of
the report, the President approved an instruction to Ambassador
Lodge which is set forth in State's *Department telegram no.* 534 to Saigon, ~~a copy of which~~
~~is attached.~~

Copies furnished: Director McCone
                  Administrator Bell

~~TOP SECRET~~
EYES ONLY

THE WHITE HOUSE

WASHINGTON

~~TOP SECRET~~- EYES ONLY   October 11, 1963

NATIONAL SECURITY ACTION MEMORANDUM NO. 263

TO: Secretary of State
       Secretary of Defense
       Chairman of the Joint Chiefs of Staff

SUBJECT: South Vietnam

At a meeting on October 5, 1963, the President considered the
recommendations contained in the report of Secretary McNamara
and General Taylor on their mission to South Vietnam.

The President approved the military recommendations contained
in Section I B (1-3) of the report, but directed that no formal
announcement be made of the implementation of plans to withdraw 1,000 U.S. miltitary personnel by the end of 1963.

After discussion of the remaining recommendations of the report,
the President approved an instruction to Ambassador Lodge which
is set forth in State Department telegram No. 534 to Saigon.

McGeorge Bundy

Copy furnished:
   Director of Central Intelligence
   Administrator, Agency for International Development

                    cc:
                       Mr. Bundy
                       Mr. Forrestal
                       Mr. Johnson
       ~~TOP SECRET — EYES ONLY~~ NSC Files

DECLASSIFIED
E. O. 11652, SEC. 3(E), 5(D), 5(E) AND 11
Committee Print of Pentagon Papers
BY MSS   NARS, DATE 7/15/77

THE WHITE HOUSE

WASHINGTON

~~TOP SECRET~~ - EYES ONLY   October 11, 1963

NATIONAL SECURITY ACTION MEMORANDUM NO. 263

TO: Secretary of State
        Secretary of Defense
        Chairman of the Joint Chiefs of Staff

SUBJECT: South Vietnam

At a meeting on October 5, 1963, the President considered the
recommendations contained in the report of Secretary McNamara
and General Taylor on their mission to South Vietnam.

The President approved the military recommendations contained
in Section I B (1-3) of the report, but directed that no formal
announcement be made of the implementation of plans to withdraw 1,000 U.S. miltitary personnel by the end of 1963.

After discussion of the remaining recommendations of the report,
the President approved an instruction to Ambassador Lodge which
is set forth in State Department telegram No. 534 to Saigon.

                                McGeorge Bundy

Copy furnished: cc:
    Director of Central Intelligence
    Administrator, Agency for International Development

~~TOP SECRET~~ - EYES ONLY

TOP SECRET - EYES ONLY   October 11, 1963

NATIONAL SECURITY ACTION MEMORANDUM NO. 263

TO: Secretary of State
     Secretary of Defense
     Chairman of the Joint Chiefs of Staff

SUBJECT: South Vietnam

At a meeting on October 5, 1963, the President considered the recommendations contained in the report of Secretary McNamara and General Taylor on their mission to South Vietnam.

The President approved the military recommendations contained in Section I B (1-3) of the report, but directed that no formal announcement be made of the implementation of plans to withdraw 1,000 U.S. military personnel by the end of 1963.

After discussion of the remaining recommendations of the report, the President approved an instruction to Ambassador Lodge which is set forth in State Department telegram No. 534 to Saigon.

           McGeorge Bundy

Copy furnished:
 Director of Central Intelligence
 Administrator, Agency for International Development

DECLASSIFIED
E.O. 11652, SEC. 3(E), 5(D), 5(E) AND 11
Committee Print of Pentagon Papers
BY MZE NARS, DATE 7/15/77

TOP SECRET - EYES ONLY

November 21, 1963

MEMORANDUM FOR

    THE HONORABLE WILLIAM BUNDY

Attached is a first cut at a document which
the President might look over with Cabot on Sunday and might then put out in appropriate ways
to the Government.   You will probably want
to compare it with your own notes and check
with Bob McNamara to see what additions and
subtractions would be desirable.

    McGeorge Bundy

~~TOP SECRET~~ ATTACHMENT

11/21/63
DRAFT

~~TOP SECRET~~

NATIONAL SECURITY ACTION MEMORANDUM NO. _____

The President has reviewed the discussions of South Vietnam which occurred
in Honolulu, and has discussed the matter further with Ambassador Lodge.
He directs that the following guidance be issued to all concerned:

    1. It remains the central object of the United States in South Vietnam
to assist the people and Government of that country to win their contest
against the externally directed and supported Communist conspiracy. The
test of all decisions and U. S. actions in this area should be the effectiveness
of their contribution to this purpose.

    2. The objectives of the United States with respect to the withdrawal
of U. S. military personnel remain as stated in the White House statement
of October 2, 1963.

    3. It is a major interest of the United States Government that the
present provisional government of South Vietnam should be assisted in
consolidating itself and in holding and developing increased public support.
All U. S. officers should conduct themselves with this objective in view.

    4. It is of the highest importance that the United States Government
avoid either the appearance or the reality of public recrimination from one
part of it against another, and the President expects that all senior officers
of the Government will take energetic steps to insure that they and their

~~TOP SECRET~~

TOP SECRET　　　　　　　　　　　　　- 2 -

subordinates go out of their way to maintain and to defend the unity of the
United States Government both here and in the field.

More specifically, the President approves the following lines of
action developed in the discussions of the Honolulu meeting of November 20.
The office or offices of the Government to which central responsibility is
assigned is indicated in each case.

5. We should concentrate our own efforts, and insofar as possible
we should persuade the Government of South Vietnam to concentrate its
efforts, on the critical situation in the Mekong Delta. This concentration
should include not only military but political, economic, social, educational
and informational effort. We should seek to turn the tide not only of battle
but of belief, and we should seek to increase not only our control of land but
the productivity of this area wherever the proceeds can be held for the
advantage of anti-Communist forces.

(Action: The whole country team under the direct supervision of the
Ambassador.)

6. Programs of military and economic assistance should be
maintained at such levels that their magnitude and effectiveness in the eyes
of the Vietnamese Government do not fall below the levels sustained by the
United States in the time of the Diem Government. This does not exclude
arrangements for economy on the MAP account with respect to accounting
for ammunition and any other readjustments which are possible as between

TOP SECRET

- 3 -

MAP and other U. S. defense resources.   Special attention should be given
to the expansion of the import distribution and effective use of fertilizer
for the Delta.

(Action: AID and DOD as appropriate.)

7. With respect to action against North Vietnam, there should
be a detailed plan for the development of additional Government of Vietnam
resources, especially for sea-going activity, and such planning should
indicate the time and investment necessary to achieve a wholly new level
of effectiveness in this field of action.

(Action: DOD and CIA)

8. With respect to Laos, a plan should be developed for military
operations up to a line up to 50 kilometers inside Laos, together with
political plans for minimizing the international hazards of such an enterprise.   Since it is agreed that operational responsibility for such undertakings
should pass from CAS to MACV, this plan should provide an alternative
method of political liaison for such operations, since their timing and
character can have an intimate relation to the fluctuating situation in Laos.

(Action: State, DOD and CIA.)

9. It was agreed in Honolulu that the situation in Cambodia is of the
first importance for South Vietnam, and it is therefore urgent that we should
lose no opportunity to exercise a favorable influence upon that country. In
particular, measures should be undertaken to satisfy ourselves completely

TOP SECRET   - 4 -

that recent charges from Cambodia are groundless, and we should put

ourselves in a position to offer to the Cambodians a full opportunity to

satisfy themselves on this same point.

(Action: State)

10. In connection with paragraphs 7 and 8 above, it is desired

that we should develop as strong and persuasive a case as possible to

demonstrate to the world the degree to which the Viet Cong is controlled,

sustained and supplied from Hanoi, through Laos and other channels. In

short, we need a more contemporary version of the Jorden Report, as

powerful and complete as possible.

(Action: Department of State with other agencies as necessary.)

                                        McGeorge Bundy

TOP SECRET

FILE COPY

~~SECRET~~   March 17, 1964

NATIONAL SECURITY ACTION MEMORANDUM NO. 288

TO: The Secretary of State
             The Secretary of Defense
             The Secretary of the Treasury
             The Attorney General
             The Chairman, Joint Chiefs of Staff
             The Director of Central Intelligence
             The Director, United States Information Agency
             The Director, Bureau of the Budget
             The Administrator, Agency for International
                Development

SUBJECT: Implementation of South Vietnam Programs

1. The report of Secretary McNamara dated March 16, 1964 was considered and approved by the President in a meeting of the National Security Council on March 17. All agencies concerned are directed to proceed energetically with the execution of the recommendations of that report.

2. The President, in consultation with the Secretary of State and the Secretary of Defense, has designated the Assistant Secretary of State for Far Eastern Affairs to coordinate the execution of the recommendations in the report.

McGeorge Bundy

DECLASSIFIED
E.O. 12356, Sec. 3.4
NLJ NSC # 76 E00514
By _____, NARA, Date 12-4-87

cc:
    Mr. Bundy
    Mr. Forrestal
    Mr. Johnson
    NSC Files

~~SECRET~~

COPY LBJ LIBRARY

~~TOP SECRET~~   November 26, 1963

NATIONAL SECURITY ACTION MEMORANDUM NO. 273

TO: The Secretary of State
            The Secretary of Defense
            The Director of Central Intelligence
            The Administrator, AID
            The Director, USIA

The President has reviewed the discussions of South Vietnam which
occurred in Honolulu, and has discussed the matter further with
Ambassador Lodge. He directs that the following guidance be issued
to all concerned:

    1. It remains the central object of the United States in South
Vietnam to assist the people and Government of that country to win
their contest against the externally directed and supported Communist
conspiracy. The test of all U. S. decisions and actions in this area
should be the effectiveness of their contribution to this purpose.

    2. The objectives of the United States with respect to the withdrawal
of U. S. military personnel remain as stated in the White House statement of October 2, 1963.

    3. It is a major interest of the United States Government that the
present provisional government of South Vietnam should be assisted
in consolidating itself and in holding and developing increased public
support. All U. S. officers should conduct themselves with this
objective in view.

    4. The President expects that all senior officers of the Government
will move energetically to insure the full unity of support for established
U. S. policy in South Vietnam. Both in Washington and in the field, it
is essential that the Government be unified. It is of particular importance
that express or implied criticism of officers of other branches be
scrupulously avoided in all contacts with the Vietnamese Government
and with the press. More specifically, the President approves the
following lines of action developed in the discussions of the Honolulu
meeting of November 20. The offices of the Government to which
central responsibility is assigned are indicated in each case.

                              ~~TOP SECRET~~   (page 1 of 3 pages)

5. We should concentrate our own efforts, and insofar as possible we should persuade the Government of South Vietnam to concentrate its efforts, on the critical situation in the Mekong Delta. This concentration should include not only military but political, economic, social, educational and informational effort. We should seek to turn the tide not only of battle but of belief, and we should seek to increase not only the control of hamlets but the productivity of this area, especially where the proceeds can be held for the advantage of anti-Communist forces.

(Action: The whole country team under the direct supervision of the Ambassador.)

6. Programs of military and economic assistance should be maintained at such levels that their magnitude and effectiveness in the eyes of the Vietnamese Government do not fall below the levels sustained by the United States in the time of the Diem Government. This does not exclude arrangements for economy on the MAP account with respect to accounting for ammunition, or any other readjustments which are possible as between MAP and other U. S. defense resources. Special attention should be given to the expansion of the import, distribution, and effective use of fertilizer for the Delta.

(Action: AID and DOD as appropriate.)

7. Planning should include different levels of possible increased activity, and in each instance there should be estimates of such factors as:

     A. Resulting damage to North Vietnam;

     B. The plausibility of denial;

     C. Possible North Vietnamese retaliation;

     D. Other international reaction.

Plans should be submitted promptly for approval by higher authority. (Action: State, DOD, and CIA.)

8. With respect to Laos, a plan should be developed and submitted for approval by higher authority for military operations up to a line up to 50 kilometers inside Laos, together with political plans for minimizing the international hazards of such an enterprise. Since it is agreed that operational responsibility for such undertakings should

TOP SECRET   -3-   November 26, 1963

pass from CAS to MACV, this plan should include a redefined
method of political guidance for such operations, since their timing
and character can have an intimate relation to the fluctuating
situation in Laos.

(Action: State, DOD, and CIA.)

9. It was agreed in Honolulu that the situation in Cambodia is
of the first importance for South Vietnam, and it is therefore urgent
that we should lose no opportunity to exercise a favorable influence
upon that country. In particular a plan should be developed using
all available evidence and methods of persuasion for showing the
Cambodians that the recent charges against us are groundless.

(Action: State.)

10. In connection with paragraphs 7 and 8 above, it is desired
that we should develop as strong and persuasive a case as possible
to demonstrate to the world the degree to which the Viet Cong is
controlled, sustained and supplied from Hanoi, through Laos and
other channels. In short, we need a more contemporary version
of the Jorden Report, as powerful and complete as possible.

(Action: Department of State with other agencies as necessary.)

/s/

McGeorge Bundy

TOP SECRET   (page 3 of 3 pages)

Appendix   *609*

POLICE DEPARTMENT
CITY OF DALLAS
CPS-JS-356

ARREST REPORT
ON
INVESTIGATIVE PRISONER

RT. THUMB PRINT

FIRST NAME	MIDDLE NAME	LAST NAME	DATE	TIME
GUS	W.	ABRAMS	Nov 22,63	4:30

RACE: WHITE ☑ COLORED ☐   SEX: MALE ☑ FEMALE ☐   AGE 53   DATE OF BIRTH 29.0   NONE   HOME ADDRESS

ADDRESS WHERE ARREST MADE: ELM & HOUSTON   TYPE PREMISES (IF BUSINESS, GIVE TRADE NAME ALSO): RAILROAD YARDS

CHARGE: Pour & In Robbery   BUSINESS WHERE ARREST MADE HAS: BEER LICENSE ☐ LIQUOR LICENSE ☐ STATE LIC. NO.

HOW ARREST MADE: ON VIEW ☐ CALL ☐ WARRANT ☐   LOCATION OF OFFENSE (IF OTHER THAN PLACE OF ARREST)

COMPLAINANT (NAME—RACE—SEX—AGE)   HOME ADDRESS—PHONE NO.   BUSINESS ADDRESS—PHONE NO.

WITNESS   HOME ADDRESS—PHONE NO.   BUSINESS ADDRESS—PHONE NO.

WITNESS   HOME ADDRESS—PHONE NO.   BUSINESS ADDRESS—PHONE NO.

PROPERTY PLACED IN POUND (MAKE, MODEL, LICENSE NO. OF AUTO)   PROPERTY PLACED IN PROPERTY ROOM

NAMES OF OTHERS ARRESTED AT SAME TIME IN CONNECTION WITH THE SAME OR SIMILAR OFFENSE:
HAROLD DOYLE W/M/33   John F. GEDNEY W/M/38

NAME OF AND/OR INFORMATION CONCERNING OTHER SUSPECTS NOT APPREHENDED

OTHER DETAILS OF THE ARREST

These men were taken off a train box car in the rail yards right after President Kennedy was shot. These men are passing through town. They have no jobs or any means of making a living.

CHECK ALL ITEMS WHICH APPLY:
DRUNK ☐ DRINKING ☐ CURSED ☐ RESISTED ☐ FOUGHT ☐   INJURED BEFORE ARREST ☐   INJURED DURING OR AFTER ARREST ☐   OFFICER(S) INJURED ☐   SPECIAL REPORT ☐

ARRESTING OFFICER: W.T. Chambers   I.D. NO. 1057   ARRESTING OFFICER   I.D. NO.

OTHER OFFICER   I.D. NO.   OTHER OFFICER   I.D. NO.

INVESTIGATION ASSIGNED TO   CHARGE FILED   FILED BY   DATE   DATE - TIME TO CO. JAIL

RELEASED BY Beck 11-26-63 9¾   H.C. BOND BY   DATE-TIME   COURT   DATE   TIME

DISTRIBUTION: (REMOVE CARBON—CHECK ORIGINAL FOR RECORDS BU.—CHECK COPY FOR EACH BUREAU CONCERNED)
RECORDS BUREAU ☐   SPEC. SER. BUREAU ☐   HOMICIDE ROBBERY ☐   AUTO THEFT ☐   BURGLARY THEFT ☐   FORGERY ☐   JUVENILE ☐   TRAFFIC ☐

USE REVERSE SIDE IF MORE SPACE NEEDED

PHOTOREPRODUCTION FROM
DALLAS MUNICIPAL ARCHIVES AND RECORDS CENTER
CITY OF DALLAS, TEXAS

POLICE DEPARTMENT
CITY OF DALLAS
CPS-JB-586

ARREST REPORT

ON

INVESTIGATIVE PRISONER

RT. THUMB PRINT

FIRST NAME	MIDDLE NAME	LAST NAME	DATE	TIME
HAROLD	—	Doyle	Nov 22 63	4 am

RACE WHITE ☑ COLORED ☐ SEX MALE ☑ FEMALE ☐ AGE 32 DATE OF BIRTH 12-8-30 HOME ADDRESS Rod Jacket, West Virginia

ADDRESS WHERE ARREST MADE Elm & Houston TYPE PREMISES (IF BUSINESS, GIVE TRADE NAME ALSO) Rail Road Yards

CHARGE Inv. Co. Vag. & Robbery.

BUSINESS WHERE ARREST MADE HAS: BEER LICENSE ☐ LIQUOR LICENSE ☐ STATE LIC. NO.

HOW ARREST MADE ON VIEW ☑ CALL ☐ WARRANT ☐ LOCATION OF OFFENSE (IF OTHER THAN PLACE OF ARREST)

COMPLAINANT (NAME—RACE—SEX—AGE) HOME ADDRESS—PHONE NO. BUSINESS ADDRESS—PHONE NO.

WITNESS HOME ADDRESS—PHONE NO. BUSINESS ADDRESS—PHONE NO.

WITNESS HOME ADDRESS—PHONE NO. BUSINESS ADDRESS—PHONE NO.

PROPERTY PLACED IN POUND (MAKE, MODEL, LICENSE NO. OF AUTO) PROPERTY PLACED IN PROPERTY ROOM

NAMES OF OTHERS ARRESTED AT SAME TIME IN CONNECTION WITH THE SAME OR SIMILAR OFFENSE
Gus W. Abrams W/M/53   John Forrostor Gedney W/M/38

NAME OF AND/OR INFORMATION CONCERNING OTHER SUSPECTS NOT APPREHENDED

OTHER DETAILS OF THE ARREST

These men were seen getting on a box
car on a train right after President Kennedy
was shot. These men are all passing
through. They have no jobs etc.

CHECK ALL ITEMS WHICH APPLY:
DRUNK ☐ DRINKING ☐ CURSED ☐ RESISTED ☐ FOUGHT ☐   INJURED BEFORE ARREST ☐   INJURED DURING OR AFTER ARREST ☐   OFFICER(S) INJURED ☐   SPECIAL REPORT ☐

ARRESTING OFFICER W. E. Chambers I.D. NO. 1087   ARRESTING OFFICER   I.D. NO.

OTHER OFFICER   I.D. NO.   OTHER OFFICER   I.D. NO.

INVESTIGATION ASSIGNED TO   CHARGE FILED   FILED BY   DATE   DATE - TIME TO GO. JAIL

RELEASED BY Buck DATE - TIME 11-4-63 9:35   H.C. BOND BY   DATE - TIME   COURT   DATE   TIME

DISTRIBUTION: (REMOVE CARBON—CHECK ORIGINAL FOR RECORDS BU.—CHECK COPY FOR EACH BUREAU CONCERNED)
RECORDS BUREAU ☐   SPEC. SER. BUREAU ☐   HOMICIDE ROBBERY ☐   AUTO THEFT ☐   BURGLARY THEFT ☐   FORGERY ☐   JUVENILE ☐   TRAFFIC ☐   ☐

USE REVERSE SIDE IF MORE SPACE NEEDED

POLICE DEPARTMENT
CITY OF DALLAS
CPS-JB-556

ARREST REPORT
ON
INVESTIGATIVE PRISONER

RT. THUMB PRINT

FIRST NAME	MIDDLE NAME	LAST NAME	DATE	TIME
John	FORRESTER	Hedney	Nov 29, 63	4⁰⁰

WHITE ☑ COLORED ☐ MALE ☑ FEMALE ☐ AGE 38 DATE OF BIRTH 3/3/25 HOME ADDRESS none

ADDRESS WHERE ARREST MADE: ELM & HOUSTON   TYPE PREMISES: TJP RAILROAD YARDS

CHARGE: Inv. of VAG, ROBBERY

HOW ARREST MADE: ON VIEW ☑ CALL ☐ WARRANT ☐

NAMES OF OTHERS ARRESTED AT SAME TIME: HAROLD DOYLE W/M/32 — GUS W. ABRAMS W/M/53

OTHER DETAILS OF THE ARREST

These men were taken off a box car in the railroad yards right after Pres. Kennedy was shot. They are passing through town. They have no means of support

ARRESTING OFFICER W. S. CHAMBERS I.D. NO. 1081

RELEASED BY Bell 11-16-63 9⁰⁰ AM

PHOTOREPRODUCTION FROM
DALLAS MUNICIPAL ARCHIVES AND RECORDS CENTER
CITY OF DALLAS, TEXAS

APPENDIX "E"

                                    10 Moulton Street
                                    Cambridge, MA 02238
                                    Telephone (617)491-1850
                                    Telex No. 92-1470

BOLT BERANEK AND NEWMAN INC.

18 February 1983

G. Robert Blakey
Professor of Law
Notre Dame Law School
Notre Dame, Indiana 46556

Dear Bob,

    This letter conveys our suggestions for further studies of the acoustical
evidence that we examined for the House Select Committee on Assassinations.

    We have read the report that Norman Ramsey's committee wrote for the Na-
tional Academy of Sciences (NAS). That report can be divided into two parts.
One part analyzes some data that pertain to the Barber hypothesis, while the
order part contains opinions about our report. Only within the former part
do we find important and original information.

    Barber discovered a very weak spoken phrase on the DPD Dictabelt recor-
ding that is heard at about the time of the sound impulses we concluded were
probably caused by the fourth shot. The NAS Committee has shown to our satisfaction that this phrase has the same origin as the same phrase heard also
on the Audograph recording. The Audograph recording was originally made from
the Channel 2 radio. The common phrase is heard on Channel 2 about a minute
after the assassination would appear, from context, to have taken place. Therefore, it would seem, and the NAS Committee concludes, that the sounds that
we connected which gunfire were made about a minute after the assassination
shots were fired.

    Upon reading the NAS report, we did a brief analysis of the Audograph dub
that was made by the NAS Committee and loaned to us by them. We found some
enigmatic features of this recording that occur at about the time that individuals react to the assassination. Therefore, we have doubt about the time
syncronization of events on that recording, and so we doubt that the Barber

hypothesis is proven. The NAS Committee did not examine the several items of evidence that corroborated our original findings, so that we still agree with the House Select Committee on Assassinations conclusion that our findings were corroborated.

It appears to us that further analysis is needed to decide whether the Barber hypothesis is correct. If it can be proven that our indications of shots do not coincide with the assassination, then that would invalidate our findings. But if this cannot be proven, then it still seems necessary to further the acoustical analysis to increase confidence in the conclusions to be derived from the acoustical evidence. In the following paragraphs we present our ideas on how these further studies should be done.

A. STUDY ORIGINALITY AND INTEGRITY OF RECORDED ACOUSTICAL EVIDENCE

1. Phase demodulate the power hum on both recordings.

The phase of the 60 Hz power mains to which both recorders (Dictabelt and Audograph) were connected would contain modulations (perturbations) caused by various electrical equipment on the grid. We recommend both channels to be analyzed for phase modulation using a velocity tracking phase lock loop (PLL) which uses an analog phase detector and a servo response optimized to estimate 60 Hz phase deviations within about a 100 Hz modulation bandwidth. The PLL should be preceded by a very sharp bandpass filter, centered at the power frequency (nominally 60 Hz).

2. Compare phase modulation on the two channels as a function of time.

The Channel 2 recording is discontinuous in time, owing to the voice-actuated recording switch. The task is to match the phase modulations on the two channels, so as to determine where each part of the Channel 2 recording fits on the Channel 1 recording - if anywhere.

3. Study the gain discontinuity and power-hum harmonic-strength discontinuities seen on the Channel 2 recording at about 12:30 (nominal time of the assassination).

Look for phase discontinuities in hum here. Look for other indications of a splice or overlay.

4. Look for indications of double recording on both channels, by examining the number of hum signals that have been recorded.

This can be done by very narrow filtering or by looking for beats in the hum waveforms.

The results of these four studies should determine whether both recor-

dings are single recordings or whether they have been superposed. The correct time alignments between Channel 1 and the various segments of the Channel 2 recording should be established also. If the common phase was recorded originally and sumultaneously on both channels, and if both recordings
are faithful copies of the originals, then the Barber hypothesis is true.
And if true, the recorded sounds that we decided were probably gunfire would
not be gunfire. But, if not provable as true, then the truth must be found
as the most likely choice between the Barber hypothesis, our interpretation
of the acoustical evidence, or any other interpretation that may enjoy corroboration of any kind.

The studies listed under "A" can probably show whether the Barber hypothesis is proven or not. If not proven we recommend studies "B".

B. ENHANCED ECHO PATTERN MATCHING

Owing to time and funding limitations, our original study devoted only
about three days to the process of matching the acoustical reconstruction
echo patterns with the sound patterns we had found on the DPD recording.
This study "B" would be undertaken to add some additional features to the
matching process and to perform the matches in a systematic way on a computer. We suggest the use of crosscorrelation, where both waveforms (echo patterns and DPD recording) would be pre-processed as follows: Each 10 ms time
window would be characterized by the amplitude and phase of the largest peak
occuring within the window. Amplitude would be quantized into two or three
values, separated by about 10 dB. The best quantization would need to be
studied in light of the expected uncertainty in the directivity pattern of
the motorcycle-mounted microphone.

The matching process would amount to the continuous crosscorrelation of
each of the echo patterns (about 500) with 60 sec of the DPD recording (6000
crosscorrelation values per echo pattern). The results of this effort would
provide the data necessary to recompute the probabilities that four shots are
uniquely revealed by the DPD recording. In other words, if the Barber hypothesis cannot be proved, the results of this study would increase the confidence with which the acoustical evidence can be said to reveal gunshot times
and origins. If the results show that gunshot sounds are probably not on the
DPD tape, then our original conclusions would be rejected. If the results
show that gunshots probably are on the tape, then we suggest the following
studies "C" to further increase confidence in the result, and in particular,
the conclusions about the third shot.

C. ADDITIONAL WORK OF THE WEISS AND ASCHKENASY (WA) TYPE

Owing to time and funding limitations, Weiss and Aschkenasy applied their
analytical extension of our pattern matching procedure to the third shot only. We suggest that their procedure be applied to the other three shots as
well. The WA procedure will need to be extended to include the third (verti-

cal) dimension for the TSBD-originated shots, because the source-reflector-receiver is not in a horizontal plane. There is little doubt about the origin and approximate timing of these other shots and so if their procedure works for them too, then their procedure will be validated independently of the controversial third shot.

We found that WA had placed the onset of the third shot echo pattern at about 300 ms earlier than had our pattern matching procedure. The NAS Committee decided that this inconsistency was an error, and therefore supported their view that either or both of the tests were wrong. We pointed out to the NAS Committee that both the relevant signals on the DPD tape and the echo pattern contain two similar bursts of echoes that are separated by about 300 ms, and that we had simply matched on the second. The second burst is an echo of the first burst after its sound is reflected from the face of the DCRB, which is nearly perpendicular to a line connecting the Knoll with the microphone and about 150 ft from the microphone. We suggest that the WA procedure be repeated with explicit attention paid to this reflecting feature.

If the results of "C" show that the other three shots do not allow an accurate position of the motorcycle microphone to be found, or if the positions that are found are inconsistent with our knowledge of the motorcycle trajectory, then the truth of the third shot from the Knoll would be in question. If the results do produce an acceptable motorcycle trajectory, then the truth of the third shot from the Knoll would be greatly enhanced. In this latter event, we suggest studies "D" that are designed to improve the credibility of the acoustical evidence by answering questions that have arisen about the compatibility of our interpretation of the acoustical evidence with non-acoustical evidence.

D. COMPATIBILITY OF ACOUSTICAL WITH NON-ACOUSTICAL EVIDENCE.

1. Comparison of shot instants with "jiggle" analyses.

There are at least three separate analyses of the jiggle of the Zapruder camera, presumably in reaction to the gun shots. These three analyses have yielded different results, so our first suggestion is to compare them. A quantitative analysis of camera/operator motion induced by both muzzle blast and shock wave is needed first to enable those jiggle features to be identified that are most likely to have been caused by gunfire directly - as opposed to features caused by psychomotor action.

Once a best estimate is made from the jiggle data about the timing of each event that could be a shot, then these times would be compared to the times found by studies "C". These comparisons must include tape speed corrections as well as time-of-flight corrections.

2. Estimate motorcycle speed

We believe that a harmonic analysis of the amplitude modulation on the motorcycle noise can determine the motorcycle speed as a function of time on the DPD recording (with ambiguities due to gear position). We suggest that this analysis be done, to show the speed trajectory during times around 12:30. This trajectory would establish whether the motorcycle was moving along in the motorcade or not. We note that if the NAS Committee were correct, then the now-apparent slowing of the motorcycle did not occur until about one minute after the assassination. If this analysis confirms the now-apparent slowing of the motorcycle, then the NAS idea that the motorcycle radio passed a Channel 2 receiver to hear the "hold everything" would be voided.

3. Measure doppler shift on siren sounds

A few minutes after the assassination, the sounds of sirens are heard on the Channel 1 recording. There appears to be a doppler shift as the sounds first intensify and then fade away. We suggest that the instantaneous frequency as a function of time be estimated and plotted. From this can be estimated the closest point of approach and relative speeds of the motorcycle and the siren vehicle. These estimates will enable one to chose among the various explanations of the origins of the siren sounds.

4. Photographic examination of McLain's trajectory

It is important to compare our best photographic estimates of McLain's trajectory with our best acoustical estimates - those from "C". We understand that further work has been done here, but not having seen it we don't know if an adequate analysis has been done.

You have also asked us to estimate the cost of doing the studies that we have suggested. We offer the following figures as a guide. It is assumed that those who do the work have the necessary equipment and skills in hand.

A.1	1 mm (scientist) and 1 mm (technician)
A.2	1/2 mm (scientist)
A.3	1 mm (scientist and 1/2 mm (technician)
A.4	1/2 mm (scientist and 1/2 mm (technician)
B	5 mm (programmer) and 4 mm (scientist)
C	2 mm (scientist) and 6 mm (technician)
D.1	2 mm (scientist) and 2 mm (technician)
D.2	1 mm (scientist) and 3 mm (technician)
D.3	1 mm (scientist) and 2 mm (technician)
D.4	1/2 mm (scientist and 2 mm (technician).

As a rough estimate, the cost of a programmer or a technician would be about $50/hour, and the cost of a scientist would be about $70/hour.

The NAS Committee report contained a list of 13 studies that they suggested could shed additional light on the subject. We are in general agreement with their suggestions. All of their suggestions are incorporated in some way in our suggestions, except for their Nos. 2, 6, and 10.

We hope this list of topics for further study will be useful to you. Although we do not wish to perform any of these studies ourselves, we will discuss our ideas with whichever investigators you decide upon.

                                        Very truly yours,

                                        James E. Barger
                                        Chief Scientist

JEB:bd

Notes

ABBREVIATIONS USED FOR CITATIONS:

WR: Warren Commission Report (*New York Times* edition used unless otherwise stated.)

3 H 67: volume 3, p. 67, hearings of the Warren Commission Report

CD: commission document

CE: commission exhibit

3 HSCA 422: volume 3, p. 422, Appendix to the Report of the House Select Committee on Assassinations

Report: HSCA Report.

Chapter 1

1. Arthur M. Schlesinger, Jr., *A Thousand Days: John F. Kennedy in the White House* (Boston: Houghton Mifflin, 1965) p. 739.
2. Howard L. Rosenberg, *Atomic Soldiers, American Victims of Nuclear Experiments* (Boston: Beacon Press, 1980); Thomas H. Saffer and Orville E. Kelly, *Countdown Zero: GI Victims of U.S. Atomic Testing* (New York: G. P. Putnam's Sons, 1982).
3. Theodore C. Sorensen, *Kennedy* (New York: Harper & Row, 1965) p. 384.
4. Sorensen, p. 384.
5. Schlesinger, p. 724.
6. Schlesinger, pp. 724–5.
7. Schlesinger, p. 726.
8. William J. Rust, *Kennedy in Vietnam* (New York: Da Caps, 1987) pp. 122–3.
9. The August 24 cable, Rust, p. 124.
10. Rust, p. 125.
11. Rust p. 128.
12. Rust p. 128.
13. August 31, 1963.
14. p. 129.
15. Rust p. 129.
16. *New York Times,* August 4, 1970.
17. *Washington Post,* August 4, 1970.
18. Kenneth P. O'Donnell and David F. Powers, *Johnny, We Hardly Knew Ye* (Boston: Little, Brown, 1972), p.
19. *Washington Post,* August 3, 1970.
20. *New York Times* News Service.
21. Schlesinger, p. 978.
22. Sorensen, p. 758.

Chapter 2

1. Gail Cameron, *Rose* (New York: Berkley, 1972, p. 107); Rose Kennedy, *Times to Remember,* Garden City, N.Y.: Doubleday, 1974, p. 175.
2. Joan Meyers, ed., *John Fitzgerald Kennedy: As We Remember Him* (New York: Atheneum, 1965) p. vi.
3. Rose Kennedy, p. 20; Doris Kearns Goodwin *The Fitzgeralds and The Kennedys* (New York: Simon & Schuster, 1987), p. 314.
4. Rose Kennedy, p. 202.

5. Rose Kennedy, p. 203.
6. Rose Kennedy, pp. 282, 216.
7. *New York Times, The Kennedy Years* (New York: Viking Press, 1966), p. 31; Evelyn Lincoln, *My 12 Years With John F. Kennedy* (New York: Bantam, 1966), p. 46; Goodwin, p. 175; Cameron, p. 145.
8. Joan and Clay Blair, Jr., *The Search For JFK* (New York: Berkley Publishing, 1976), p. 17.
9. Rose Kennedy, *Times,* p. 215.
10. Blairs, p. 46.
11. Cameron, p. 107.
12. Cameron, p. 107.
13. Rose Kennedy, p. 174; Collier and David Horowitz, *The Kennedys: An American Drama* (New York: 1984), p. 17; Summit Books, *New York Times,* p. 17; Cameron, p. 149.
14. Collier and Horowitz pp. 61, 66.
15. Rose Kennedy, p. 201.
16. Blairs, p. 34.
17. Collier and Horowitz, p. 66.
18. Collier and Horowitz, pp. 80–1; *New York Times;* Blairs, p. 94.
19. Collier and Horowitz, p. 175.
20. Blairs, p. 181.
21. Blairs, p. 182.
22. Blairs, p. 241; see also Robert J. Donovan, *PT 109: John F. Kennedy in World War II* (New York: McGraw-Hill, 1961).
23. Blairs, p. 333.
24. *New York Times,* p. 21.
25. Blairs, p. 348.
26. *Journal of the American Medical Association,* July 10, 1967, p. 129.
27. Interviews with Dr. Joseph Theodore Brierre, August 7, 1991; Dr. Doyle Rogers, May 29, 1991.
28. Interview with Dr. Janet Travell, September 4, 1991.
29. Janet Travell, M.D., *Office Hours Day and Night* (New York and Cleveland: World Publishing Company, 1968), pp. 3, 5, 7.
30. Michael Baden, *Unnatural Death* (New York: Random House, 1989), p. 14.
31. 7 HSCA 243.
32. 7 HSCA 243.
33. Interview with Dr. James Nicholas, August 27, 1991.
34. LBJ Library.
35. Interview, August 27, 1991.
36. Goodwin, p. 734.
37. Blairs, pp. 588–89.
38. Blairs, p. 592.
39. Collier and Horowitz, p. 202.
40. Blairs, p. 593.
41. Collier and Horowitz, p. 202.
42. Arthur M. Schlesinger, Jr., *Robert Kennedy and His Times* (Boston: Houghton Mifflin, 1978), p. 55; Collier and Horowitz, p. 158.
43. Blairs, p. 596.
44. Blairs, p. 596.
45. Blairs, p. 596.
46. Blairs, p. 593.
47. Blairs, p. 593.
48. Blairs, p. 595.
49. George W. Thorn, *The Diagnosis and Treatment of Adrenal Insufficiency.*
50. Powers and O'Donnell, pp. 112, 116.
51. Blairs, p. 597.
52. Ibid; Rose Kennedy, p. 145; Powers and O'Donnell, p. 113; *New York Times,* p. 31; Lincoln, p. 45; Goodwin, p. 775.
53. Blairs, p. 599.

54. Rose Kennedy, p. 145.
55. Blairs, p. 571.
56. Interview, August 27, 1991.
57. Journal of the American Medical Association, "Induced Hypoadrenalism, Orthopedic Surgery" 1954–5.
58. Blairs, p. 602.
59. Blairs, p. 602.
60. Blairs, p. 603; *New York Times,* July 5, 1960.
61. *New York Times,* November 11, 1960.
62. Blairs, p. 102.

Chapter 3
1. Anthony Summers, *Conspiracy* (New York: McGraw-Hill, 1980), pp. 295–6; Other key Schweiker quotes—*U.S. News & World Report,* September 15, 1975; AP of September 8, 9, 1975; *Newsday,* November 21, 1975; *San Francisco Chronicle,* November 22, 1975, May 14, 1976 (AP), June 24, 28, 1976 (AP); *San Francisco Examiner,* May 14, 1976; *Oakland Tribune,* May 19, 1976, and by Tad Szulc, May 28, 1976 (UPI), *The Investigation of the Assassination of President John F. Kennedy: Performance of the Intelligence Agencies,* Senate Intelligence Committee Report, Book V, April 23, 1976.
2. Roy Kellerman, 2 H 76, 78, 79, 84, 90, 92, 104.
3. 2 H 85.
4. 2 WCH 376.
5. HSCA report, p. 483.
6. Special Agents Francis X. O'Neill, Jr., and James W. Sibert, FBI report of November 26, 1963.
7. O'Neill and Sibert report.
8. AP, November 24, 1966; *Baltimore Sun,* November 15, 1966.
9. 7 HSCA 114-114, 246-7, 251-2, 25-6, 260-1.
10. 1 HSCA 323-333.
11. 7 HSCA 218, 221, 222; Clark Panel Report, *Maryland State Medical Journal,* March, 1977, p. 69.
12. *National Examiner,* February 6, 1990.
13. *Ramparts,* 1968, p. 56.
14. 1988.
15. John L. Davis, *Mafia Kingfish* (New York: McGraw-Hill, 1989); David E. Scheim, *Contract on America* (New York: Shapolsky Publishers, Inc., 1988); G. Robert Blakey and Richard N. Billings, *The Plot to Kill the President: Organized Crime Assassinated JFK—The Definitive Story* (New York: Times Books, 1981).
16. The *Baltimore Sunday Sun Magazine,* May 1 and 8, 1977.
17. 6 WCH 121.
18. Interview of July 7, 1991.
19. Interview of August 17, 1991.
20. William Manchester, *The Death of a President* (New York: Harper & Row, 1967), p. 294.
21. Letter to the author, August 20, 1991. Mr. Long is not alone in this suspicion.
22. Dallas conference with the author, April 6, 1991.
23. Interview of May 20, 1991.
24. Manchester, pp. 297–305; interview with the author, July 27, 1991.
25. Interviews with Ken Raley, August 16, 1991, and September 30, 1991.
26. See *High Treason.*
27. Interview of September 30, 1991.
28. Interview of August 17, 1991.
29. Interview of October 28, 1991.
30. Penn Jones, Jr., *Forgive My Grief, Vol. I* p. 174 (author may be contacted at Rte. 3, Box 356, Waxahachie, TX 75165); *The Continuing Inquiry,* February 1977, p. 16; *The Third Decade,* November 1987, p. 6.
31. AP, April 25, 1964.
32. 7 HSCA 189.
33. 7 HSCA 189.

34. Interview of July 27, 1991.
35. *The Third Decade,* March 1990. Jerry Rose, "The Body Switch: A Parkland Scenario,"
36. Price exhibits, 21 WCH 162; 259-60. See also 2 H 126 and 142 for the exit of Mrs. Kennedy and the coffin.
37. Author's interview with Audrey Bell, March 26, 1991.
38. *The Third Decade.* Harrison E. Livingstone, "Concerning David Lifton and 'Best Evidence,' "
39. February 27, 1965.
40. Interview of August 28, 1991.
41. Affidavit of December 29, 1990.
42. Letter to the author, July 1, 1991.
43. Interviews of May 27, 1991, and September 28, 1991, with Mark Crouch at WCHE, June 1, 1991.
44. Interview of September 28, 1991.
45. Malcolm Couch and David Belin, 6 H 159.
46. AP reports *(Chicago Daily News)* of November 22, 1963.
47. Interview of Donald Rebentisch, May 27, 1991 and news accounts, *Ft. Worth Star Telegram,* January 24, 1981, and the *Miami Herald,* January 25, 1981.
48. 7 HSCA 15.
49. KRON-TV, Sylvia Chase, "The Men Who Killed Kennedy," 1988, and television taping by the author and Albert Fisher in Dallas, April 1991.
50. Interviews of the author, and television taping by the author and Albert Fisher in April 1991, presented in this book in the chapter on the Parkland testimony.
51. Interview of August 27, 1991.
52. Earl Warren, *The Memoirs of Chief Justice Earl Warren* (New York: Doubleday, 1977), p. 371.
53. 2 H 353.
54. 2 H 354.
55. Interview with Art Smith, *The Continuing Inquiry,* July 1978, and Gil Delaney of the *Lancaster Intelligencer-Journal,* March 9, 1978—two days before Ebersole went to be deposed before the House committee.
56. August 17, 1991; August 15, 1991.

Chapter 4

1. 21 WCH 241-2; 6 H for testimony.
2. Interview of July 21, 1981; also *Boston Globe* interview by Ben Bradlee, Jr., arranged by the author, May 2, 1981.
3. 21 WCH 239-40.
4. 21 WCH 203; Diana Bowron testified to the Warren Commission, 6 H 134-9.
5. Interview of April 5, 1991.
6. Interview of October 10, 1991.
7. 7 HSCA 274.
8. Interview of April 5, 1991.
9. Letter to the author, December 11, 1981.
10. Interview of July, 1979.
11. Interview of April 3, 1991.
12. Interview of October 10, 1991.
13. 6 H 10.
14. Interview of October 10, 1991.
15. Interview with Henry Gonzalez, November 23, 1976.
16. Chapter 2.
17. Interviews of July 12, 1980 and September 21, 1991.
18. CD 1245.
19. CD 1245.
20. Price exhibit No. 2, 21 WCH p. 153.
21. Price exhibit No. 7, 21 WCH p. 162.
22. Interview of 12, 1991.
23. April 6, 1991, Dallas filming.
24. 21 WCH 237.

25. 21 WCH 153.
26. 21 WCH 242.
27. CD 1245.
28. 23 WCH 884—CE 1974.
29. 2 WCH 97.
30. Interview of October 10, 1991.
31. Many interviews and letters with the author.
32. Interview of October 10, 1991.
33. Interview of August 10, 1979.
34. 3 H 366-90, 6 H 7-18.
35. Interview of October 10, 1991.
36. Letter of December 21, 1981.
37. Interview of October 27, 1991.
38. 2 WCH 143, William Greer.
39. 2 WCH 98
40. WR 59; 2 WCH 98 and from transcripts of AF 1.

Chapter 5

1. 7 HSCA 15.
2. Mary Barelli Gallagher *My Life With Jacqueline Kennedy* (New York: Paperback Library, 1970), p. 116.
3. Kenneth O'Donnell, *The Witnesses,* p. 80; 7 H 455.
4. Interview of September 23, 1991.
5. Manchester, p. 390.
6. Manchester, p. 390.
7. Jim Bishop, *The Day Kennedy Was Shot* (New York: Funk & Wagnalls, 1968), p. 337.
8. Bishop, p. 338.
9. Manchester, p. 398.
10. Roy Kellerman, 2 H 102; WR 59.
11. Kenneth O'Donnell, 2 H 455; WR 59.
12. 2 H 102-3.
13. 7 HSCA 8.
14. 2 H 349.
15. 7 HSCA 11; ibid.
16. Interview of September 23, 1991.
17. Many interviews with the author, and public appearances, and Edward F. Reed, interview with Warren Patton, *RT Image,* November 21, 1988.
18. Interview of September 23, 1991.
19. Interview of September 23, 1991; also to Warren Patton.
20. KRON, November 1988, statements to the author at various times.
21. 1 HSCA 239-244; 7 HSCA 109-113.
22. 7 HSCA 221; 223; 249. The reader should study closely 7 HSCA pp. 217–230 with regard to both the fragments on or in the head, and the missing bone and fractures in the X-rays.
23. James Jenkins to the author, October 8, 1990.
24. Interview of September 21, 1991.
25. Interview of September 23, 1991.
26. Interview of September 21, 1991.
27. Manchester, p. 294.
28. Interview by the author and Mark Crouch with James Metzler, June 1, 1991.
29. Interview of October 8, 1990.
30. Interview of October 8, 1990.
31. Interview of March 25, 1991.
32. Interview of May 24, 1991.
33. Interview of May 24, 1991.
34. Interview of June 16, 1991.
35. 7 HSCA 15.
36. Interview of May 29, 1991.

37. Interview of October 14, 1990.
38. Interview of October 8, 1990.
39. UPI in the *Miami Herald,* January 25, 1981; AP, *Fort Worth Star Telegram,* January 24, 1981.
40. *Miami Herald,* January 25, 1981; *Fort Worth Star Telegram,* January 24, 1981.
41. Interview of May 27, 1991.
42. Manchester, p. 397.
43. Interviews with Joseph Hagen, Tom Robinson, and John Van Haeson of Gawler's Funeral Home, Paul O'Connor, and James Jenkins.
44. Interviews with Joseph Hagen, August 15 and 28, 1991; Tom Robinson, August 17 and October 6, 1991.
45. Interview of December 28, 1988; "Inside Edition," June, 1989; Interview of July, 1979 and February 12, 1991.
46. Interview with James Curtis Jenkins of July 14, 1991.
47. Interview of August 27, 1991.
48. Interview with Francis X. O'Neill, May 20, 1991.
49. 7 HSCA 8.
50. Author's interviews of June 8, 9, and 11, 1991.

Chapter 6

1. 2 H 349.
2. 2 H 455.
3. Wilber, p. 131.
4. 2 H 363.
5. 21 H 152.
6. 7 HSCA 273-4, interview of January 11, 1978.
7. Letter to the author, July 25, 1991.
8. CE 291.
9. Note of October 10, 1991.
10. Interview of July 14, 1991.
11. Letter to the author, July 25, 1991.
12. Letter to the author, October 12, 1991.
13. Interview of March 25, 1991.
14. Dr. Philip Williams, April 6, 1991.
15. Interview of September 5, 1991.
16. Interview of October 7, 1991.
17. Interview of September 23, 1991.
18. Art Smith, *The Continuing Inquiry,* July 1978.
19. *RT Image,* Nov 21, 1988.
20. *Lancaster Intelligencer-Journal,* March 9, 1978.
21. *Lancaster Intelligencer-Journal,* March 9, 1978.
22. 2 WCH 351.
23. 2 WCH 352.
24. 2 WCH 353.
25. 2 WCH 256.
26. Interview of September 23, 1991.
27. Interview of September 23, 1991.
28. Interview of September 23, 1991.
29. Interview of September 23, 1991.
30. Interview of September 23, 1991.
31. Smith.
32. 7 HSCA 246, 251, 254, 256.
33. 1 HSCA 326-330.
34. 2 WCH 360.
35. 7 HSCA p. 119.
36. Interview of September 23, 1991.
37. 2 WCH 361.
38. Interview of October 27, 1991.

39. Jones, Dulaney, McClelland, Peters, Bell, Interview of April 2–6, 1991.
40. *Philadelphia Inquirer,* March 10, 1978.
41. Trial of Clay Shaw, Jim Garrison, *Heritage of Stone* (New York: Putnam, 1970), Josiah Thompson, *Six Seconds in Dallas* (New York: Berkley, 1976), p. ix; Gary Shaw and Larry Harris, *Cover-up,* p. 195–7; Dr. Charles Wilber, *Medicolegal Investigation of the President John F. Kennedy Murder,* Springfield, Ill.: Charles Thomas & Sons, p. 256.
42. 2 H 93.
43. 2 H 143.
44. Interview of May 20, 1991.
45. FBI Report of November 26, 1963, File No. 89-30-31.
46. 2 WCH 361.
47. 2 WCH 376.
48. Wilber pp. 129–30.
49. Wilber, 130.
50. WR, p. 59.
51. Wilber, p. 130.
52. 7 HSCA 15.
53. Interview of September 23, 1991.
54. Interview of September 23, 1991.
55. Interview with Warren Patton, December 2, 1988.
56. 7 HSCA 11.
57. 7 HSCA 11 (58).
58. 2 H 78-9.
59. 2 WCH 80-1.
60. 2 WCH 94.
61. 2 WCH 124.
62. 2 WCH 138.
63. 2 WCH 139.
64. 2 WCH 140.
65. 2 WCH 141.
66. 2 WCH 141.
67. 2 WCH 141.
68. Testimony 5 H 178-81 (edited version). Mrs. Kennedy said more, and the rest of the quote above can be found in Harold Weisberg, *Postmortem* (self-published, 1975), p. 380, and Shaw and Harris, p. 23.
69. 2 WCH 143.
70. *Maryland State Medical Journal,* March 1977.
71. 2 WCH 94; and Greer, 2 WCH 128.
72. Interview of September 23, 1991.
73. Smith, July 1978.
74. Affidavits of Dr. Donald Siple and others.

Chapter 7
1. 7 HSCA 243-4.
2. 2 H 361-2, 367, 371, 373; 7 HSCA 257; 1 HSCA 331.
3. Interview of August 27, 1991.

Chapter 8
1. Report of Richard Waybright to the author, November 16, 1990.
2. 7 HSCA 243-265.
3. 7 HSCA p. 115.
4. 7 HSCA p. 61.
5. 7 HSCA p. 249.
6. 7 HSCA 249.
7. Interview of October 7, 1991.
8. Interview of August 27, 1991.

9. Interview of October 6, 1991.
10. Interview of October 7, 1991.

Chapter 9

1. Art Smith, July 1978.
2. 2 WCH 361.
3. 7 HSCA 249.
4. Smith, July 1978, p. 3.
5. Interview of October 14, 1990.

Chapter 10

1. Interview of October 29, 1990.
2. Interview of November 22, 1991.
3. 7 HSCA 15-16.
4. Interview of September 23, 1991.
5. Interview of November 22, 1991.
6. Interview of October 29, 1990.
7. Interview of November 22, 1991.
8. Interview of August 29, 1991.
9. Smith, July 1978.
10. March 10, 1978.
11. March 10, 1978 interview with Jack Severson of the *Philadelphia Inquirer.*
12. *Maryland State Medical Journal,* March 1977, p. 77.
13. Interview of September 23, 1991.
14. Interview of October 8, 1990.
15. Interview of October 8, 1990.
16. Interview with the author, April 28, 1991.
17. Interview of January 4, 1988.
18. Interview of January 4, 1988.
19. Interview of January 4, 1988.
20. Interview of March 20, 1991.
21. Interview of March 25, 1991.
22. Interview of March 25, 1991.
23. Interview of March 26, 1991.
24. Interview of March 26, 1991.
25. Interview of November 22, 1991.
26. Interview of September 23, 1991.
27. 2 H 349; 1 HSCA 324.
28. 7 HSCA 11:61, 2 H 363; Sibert & O'Neill pp 3–4.

Chapter 11

1. Interview of October 8, 1990.
2. Interview of March 25, 1991.
3. Interview of March 25, 1991.
4. Interview of October 8, 1990.
5. Interview of March 25, 1991.
6. Interview of May 24, 1991.
7. Interview of May 24, 1991.
8. Interview of June 16, 1991.
9. Interview of May 24, 1991.
10. Interview of May 24, 1991.
11. Interview of June 6, 1991.
12. Interview of June 16, 1991.
13. Interview of October 7, 1991.
14. Interview of August 27, 1991.
15. Interview of May 24, 1991.
16. Interview of May 24, 1991.

17. Interview of April 28, 1991.
18. Interview of April 28, 1991.
19. Interview of April 30, 1991.
20. Interview of July 14, 1991.
21. Interview of May 29, 1991.
22. 2 H 354.
23. Interview of October 19, 1991.

Chapter 12

1. Author's personal interview along with Kathlee Fitzgerald of August 15, 1991; interview of August 28, 1991; Manchester, p. 433.
2. 7 HSCA 261.
3. Interview of May 18, 1990.
4. Interview of April 20, 1990.
5. Interview of April 20, 1990.
6. Interview of April 20, 1990.
7. Interview of April 20, 1990.
8. 7 HSCA 254, *see also* 251.
9. Interview of April 20, 1990.
10. Interview of June 11, 1990.
11. Interview of June 11, 1990.
12. Interview of May 18, 1990.
13. Interview of May 18, 1991.
14. Interview of May 26, 1991.
15. Interview of May 26, 1991.
16. Interview of May 26, 1991.
17. Interviews of May 27, June 1, and September 28, 1991.
18. Interview of June 8, 1991.
19. Interview of May 9, 1990.
20. Interview of May 9, 1990.
21. Interview of May 9, 1990.
22. Interview of May 9, 1990.
23. Interview of May 9, 1990.
24. Interview of April 28, 1991.
25. Interview of June 9, 1991.

Chapter 13

1. Interviews with the author of April 29, 1990, and May 11, 1990.

Chapter 14

1. April 6, 1991.
2. Interview with Tom Robinson, October 6, 1991.
3. *Best Evidence Research Video.*
4. Interview of May 6, 1990.
5. 21 WCH 153.
6. 21 WCH 162.
7. Author's interview of September 1, 1991.
8. *Robbins' Pathologic Basis of Disease.*
9. Interview with Dr. Ronald Buggage, the Johns Hopkins University Hospital, November 19, 1991.
10. Jurgen Ludwig, *Current Methods of Autopsy Practice,* New York: W. B. Saunders, 1979, p. 666.
11. W. F. Sunderman, *Normal Values in Clinical Medicine*
12. 7 HSCA 130.
13. Interview with Dr. Humes, December 10, 1980.
14. November 25, 1966; "JFK Autopsy Doctor Admits Sketch Error," AP of November 24, 1966.

Chapter 15

1. 7 HSCA 70.
2. 7 HSCA 46.
3. 7 HSCA 46.
4. 7 HSCA pp. 37–8.
5. 7 HSCA 47.
6. Interviews of September 22 and October 10, 1991.
7. Interview of September 27, 1991.
8. *Globe,* December 31, 1991.
9. Interview of October 11, 1991.
10. 7 HSCA 28.
11. 7 HSCA 261.
12. 7 HSCA 261.
13. 7 HSCA 115.
14. 7 HSCA 253.
15. Interview with Richard Waybright, and report, November 16, 1990.
16. Report of Richard Waybright to the author, November 16, 1991.
17. *Rolling Stone,* October 20, 1977.
18. Interview with Richard Waybright, report to the author of November 16, 1990.
19. 7 HSCA 23–4.
20. 7 HSCA 245.
21. 2 WCH 351, 352.
22. Letter to the author, November 5, 1991.
23. Letter to the author, December 9, 1991.
24. Interviews of May 27, 1991 and June 1, 1991.
25. Interview of September 22, 1991.
26. Interview of October 10, 1991.
27. Interview of September 21, 1991.
28. Joanne Braun, "New Evidence of Body Tampering," *The Third Decade,* March 1991.
29. Interview of September 21, 1991.
30. Interview of September 1, 1991.
31. Interview of August 27, 1991.
32. Harrison E. Livingstone, *High Treason* (Baltimore, Md.: The Conservatory Press, 1989), Chapter 2, *Boston Globe* Interviews, 1981, arranged by the author.
33. Interviews of September 23, 1991.
34. Interview of September 23, 1991.
35. Weisberg, p. 577.

Chapter 16

1. 7 HSCA 249.
2. 7 HSCA 249.
3. 7 HSCA 250.
4. "Radiographer Remembers JFK," *RT Image,* November 21, 1988.
5. Interview of September 23, 1991.
6. Interview of September 23, 1991.
7. Interview of September 23, 1991.
8. 7 HSCA 248.
9. 7 HSCA 253.
10. 7 HSCA 254.
11. *RT Image,* p. 6.
12. Interview with Warren Patton, June 20, 1989.
13. Author's interview of September 23, 1991.
14. Interview of September 23, 1991.
15. Smith, July 1978.
16. 7 HSCA 114.
17. 2 H 361.
18. Clark panel report, p. 13.

19. Sibert and O'Neill, FBI report.
20. *Maryland State Medical Journal,* March 1977.
21. 2 H 353.
22. 2 H 353.
23. Gil Delaney, interview with Dr. John Ebersole, *Lancaster Intelligencer-Journal,* March 9, 1978.
24. Interview of September 23, 1991.
25. Delaney.
26. *Life,* November 29, 1963; also in *Life's* memorial edition.
27. Interview of January 4, 1988.
28. See also public testimony, September 7, 1978, 1 HSCA, p. 149.
29. Letter of September 20, 1991.
30. Paul Hoch, *Echoes of Conspiracy,* November 24, 1989.
31. *Life,* November 29, 1963, p. 24.

Chapter 17

1. 2 WCH 374-5.
2. Michael Kurtz, *Crime of the Century* (Chattanooga, Tenn.: University of Tennessee Press, 1982), p. 222.
3. 7 HSCA 54-6.
4. Kurtz, p. 222.
5. 7 HSCA 226-7.
6. Kurtz, p. 226; HSCA Report 81.
7. 2 WCH 144, testimony of Clinton Hill.
8. 2 WCH 76.
9. Kurtz, p. 222.
10. Interview with James Niell, August 10, 1976.
11. *The Third Decade,* November 22, 1984.
12. 2 WCH p. 82.
13. Letter to the author, September 16, 1991.
14. Philip Melanson, "Hidden Exposure: Cover-Up and Intrigue in the CIA's Secret Possession of the Zapruder film," *The Third Decade,* November 1984.
15. Melanson, p. 15.
16. Melanson, p. 17.
17. Melanson, p. 19.
18. Interview of September 4, 1991.
19. Melanson, p. 17; CIA Memos of October 28 and April 23, 1975, Docs. 1472-492-BJ and 1627-1085.
20. Mark Crouch, FAX to the author of September 1, 1991.

Chapter 18

1. Interview of August 7, 1991.

Chapter 19

1. Jim Hougan, *Spooks* (New York: William Morrow, 1978); *Secret Agenda* (New York: Random House, 1984).
2. For a description of the girl, see William W. Turner and John G. Christian, *The Assassination of Robert F. Kennedy* (New York: Random House, 1978), pp. 69–70.
3. Thomas Noguchi, M.D., *Coroner* (New York: Pocket Books, 1984) pp. 101–110.
4. William C. McGaw and Thomas G. Whittle, *Freedom,* January, 1986, p. 6.
5. Allard Lowenstein, *Oui,* May 1976, pp. 45–46, 116–119.
6. *Cover-ups,* March 1985, p. 6.
7. New York: Random House, 1978.
8. Duncan Harp, "The Tangled Web, an Inquiry into the Assassination of Senator Robert F. Kennedy," copyright 1977.
9. AP, November 28, 1975, Nairobi, Kenya.
10. *San Francisco Chronicle,* December 17, 1975.
11. *The Continuing Inquiry,* July 1977.

12. *The New York Times,* March 20, 1977.
13. AP, March 20, 1977.
14. Mark Lane, *Washington Newsworks,* August 26–September 1, 1976; also in *The Continuing Inquiry,* September 1976.
15. *New York: Outerbridge & Dienstfrey, 1971.* This is a brilliant book and we recommend it highly. It may be ordered directly from the author, Harold Weisberg, 7627 Old Receiver Road, Frederick, MD 21701. Enclose $12.50 for the book, postage, and handling.
16. Weisberg, p. 53.
17. AP, November 23, 1988.
18. *The Nashville Tennessean,* November 2, 1980.
19. *San Francisco Chronicle,* December 17, 1975.
20. See also Mark Frazier, "Ervin Committee, FBI Investigate Hoover Death," *Harvard Crimson,* December 12, 1973.
21. Theodore White, *Making of the President 1972* (New York: Atheneum, 1973).
22. *New York Post,* June 21, 1973.
23. Frank Salant, *The Continuing Inquiry,* October 1976.
24. *Life,* The Year in Pictures edition, 1968.
25. UP, November 26, 1975.
26. Sybil Leek and Bert R. Sugar, *The Assassination Chain* (New York: Corwin Books, 1976).
27. J. Anthony Lukas, *Nightmare* (New York: Bantam Books, 1977), pp. 249–50.
28. Lukas, *Nightmare,* p. 196.
29. Lukas, *Nightmare,* pp. 17–18.
30. New York: Random House, 1984.
31. Lukas, *Nightmare,* pp. 90–92, 497–98; John Dean, *Blind Ambition* (New York: Pocket Books, 1977), p. 61.
32. Malcolm Abrams, "Thirty Watergate Witnesses Have Met Violent Deaths" in *Midnight,* September 12, 1976, p. 20.
33. Dean, *Blind Ambition,* pp. 12–13, 23–24.
34. Lukas, *Nightmare,* pp. 285, 336.
35. George M. Evica, *And We Are All Mortal* (self-published, 1978), p. 322.
36. Bernard Fensterwald, *Martha, the Mouth, Coincidence or Conspiracy?* pp. 131–2, 503.
37. Lowenstein, *Oui,* p. 46.
38. October 5, 1987.
39. Jim Marrs, "Ex-Agent Sixth to Die in Six-Month Span" in *Fort Worth Star-Telegram,* November 10, 1977.
40. Mark North, *Act of Treason* (New York: Carroll & Graf Publishers, Inc., 1991), p. 461.
41. *Washington Post,* November 10, 1977.
42. *The Continuing Inquiry,* February 1980.
43. Ferrie alibi: *Report of the House Select Committee on Assassinations,* pp. 105 and 114 note 5; On Marcello, 9 HSCA 70; and on threat, 9 HSCA 81. See also Summers, p. 506; Rosemary James and Jack Wardlaw, *Plot or Politics, The Garrison Case & Its Cast,* p. 152.
44. *Fort Worth Star-Telegram,* November 10, 1977.
45. *The Continuing Inquiry,* February 1980.
46. *The Continuing Inquiry,* February 1980.
47. *Fort Worth Star-Telegram,* November 10, 1977.
48. *Fort Worth Star-Telegram,* November 10, 1977.
49. *Time,* September 15, 1975.
50. Keith Powers, "The Woman in Red—An Earlier Threat" in the *San Francisco Chronicle,* September 6, 1975.
51. Jack White, "Here We Go Again" in *The Continuing Inquiry,* April 1, 1981.
52. Earl Golz, "The Assassination Attempt" in *The Dallas Morning News,* April 1, 1981.
53. Gary Mack, "Network Tapes Reveal a Second Reagan Gunman" in *The Continuing Inquiry,* August 1981.

Chapter 20

1. Barboura Morris Freed, "Flight 553: The Watergate Murder?" in *Big Brother and the Holding Company* (Palo Alto, Ca.: Ramparts Press, 1974), p. 131.

2. Freed, p. 132.
3. Freed, p. 132.
4. Freed, p. 130.
5. Freed, p. 129.
6. Freed, p. 136.
7. Freed, p. 139.
8. Freed, p. 140.
9. Freed, p. 150.
10. Freed, pp. 142–143.
11. Freed, p. 143.
12. Freed, p. 150.
13. Freed, p. 154.
14. HSCA Report, p. 128.

Chapter 21

1. Interview of February 12, 1991.
2. *Evening Magazine,* syndicated television show, November 21, 1988.
3. Interview of February 12, 1991.
4. Interview of April 7, 1991.

Chapter 22

1. Interview of May 12, 1991.
2. Report, House Select Committee on Assassinations, p. 54., and 6 HSCA. Jack White produced a home video called *Fake* demonstrating the forgery of the "backyard" photographs. His address is 301 W. Vickery Blvd, Ft. Worth, TX 76104.
3. Report, House Select Committee on Assassinations, p. 52.
4. Report, House Select Committee on Assassinations, p. 55 note 11. See also Peter Dale Scott, *Crime and Cover-Up,* pp. 35–38.

Chapter 23

1. Tapes and interview with Ron Laytner, August 10, 1990.
2. Interview of May 11, 1990.
3. Interview of August 6, 1990.
4. Interview of November 6, 1991.
5. Hugh McDonald, *Appointment in Dallas* (New York: The Hugh McDonald Publishing Corp., 1975).
6. *Dallas Morning News.*
7. AP wire story, August 6, 1990.
8. Interview of October 26, 1991.
9. No date, but quoted in the *Dallas Morning News,* August 8, 1990.

Chapter 24

1. Schlesinger, *A Thousand Days,* p. 321.
2. Schlesinger, *A Thousand Days,* p. 321.
3. Schlesinger, *A Thousand Days,* p. 321.
4. Schlesinger, *A Thousand Days,* p. 654.
5. Schlesinger, *A Thousand Days,* p. 649.
6. Schlesinger, *A Thousand Days,* pp. 651–2.
7. Schlesinger, *A Thousand Days,* p. 545.
8. Schlesinger, *A Thousand Days,* p. 545.
9. Schlesinger, *A Thousand Days,* p. 546.
10. Schlesinger, *A Thousand Days,* p. 547.
11. Schlesinger, *A Thousand Days,* p. 548.
12. Schlesinger, *A Thousand Days,* p. 550.
13. Schlesinger, *A Thousand Days,* p. 655.
14. Schlesinger, *A Thousand Days,* pp. 660–61.
15. Schlesinger, *A Thousand Days,* p. 652.

16. Letter of September 11, 1991.
17. *Washington Post,* May 13, 1991.
18. *Washington Post,* May 13, 1991.
19. On March 17, 1964.
20. Peter Dale Scott, Paul Hoch, and Russell Stetler, eds., *The Assassinations, Dallas and Beyond: A Guide to Cover-ups and Investigations* (Vintage New York: 1976).
21. Fletcher Prouty, "The Erosion of National Sovereignty," *Freedom,* October 1986.
22. Prouty,
23. Prouty,
24. Prouty, p. 19.
25. Prouty, p. 19.
26. Prouty, p. 19.
27. Prouty, p. 19.
28. Prouty, p. 19.
29. Prouty, p. 19.
30. Prouty, p. 19.
31. *Operation Zapata* (Frederick, Md. University Publications of America, 1984), p. 20.
32. Prouty
33. Prouty, p. 19.
34. Prouty, p. 21.
35. Prouty, p. 36.
36. *Stars and Stripes* headline, October 4, 1963.
37. Scott et al., p. 413.
38. U.S. government edition, *Pentagon Papers,* IV.B3, pp. 37–38; Senator Gravel edition, II:457–59; emphasis added.
39. NSAM 52 of May 11, 1961, in *Pentagon Papers* (New York: Bantam, New York Times), p. 126.
40. Rusk-McNamara memorandum of November 11, 1961, in *Pentagon Papers,*
41. *Pentagon Papers,* p. 148.
42. Scott et al., p. 414.
43. Scott et al., p. 411.
44. U.S. gov't edition, *Pentagon Papers,* IVB.5. p. xxxiv; Gravel edition, II:223; U.S. government ed., IV.B.3, p. 37; Gravel edition, II:457.
45. U.S. Congress, House Committee on Appropriations, *Department of Defense Appropriations for 1965, Hearings,* 88th Cong., 2nd session (Washington, D.C.: GPO, 1964), Part IV, p. 12; pp. 103–104, 117–118.
46. U.S. Congress, Committee on Foreign Affairs, *Winning the Cold War: the U.S./Ideological Offensive, Hearings,* 88th Congress, second session (February 20, 1964). Statement by Robert Manning, Assistant Secretary of State for Public Affairs, p. 811.
47. Peter Arnett and Michael Maclear, *The Ten Thousand Day War, Vietnam: 1945–1975* (New York: St. Martin's Press, 1981), p. 81.
48. Letter of May 23, 1991.
49. *Pentagon Papers,* Gravel edition II:75–81.
50. John F. Kennedy, *Public Papers of the Presidents,* 1963 (Washington, D.C.: Government Printing Office, 1964), pp. 759–760. Gravel ed., II:188.
51. *New York Times,* November 21, 1963.
52. Letter of May 10, 1991.
53. *Freedom,* January 1987, pp. 34–36.
54. Paragraph 2 of NSAM 273.
55. Letter of September 11, 1991.
56. *Facts on File,* p. 418 and *Public Papers of the Presidents,* November 14, 1963, p. 459.
57. Ralph Martin, *A Hero for Our Time—An Intimate Study of the Kennedy Years* p. 464.
58. Martin, p. 464.
59. Martin, p. 464.
60. Martin, p. 465.
61. Martin, p. 465.
62. Martin, p. 464.

63. P. 366 HT; *Facts on File,* 1963, CBS Evening News interview with Walter Cronkite, September 2, 1963.
64. *Facts on File,* pp. 45, 418.
65. *Facts on File,* November 21–November 27, 1963, p. 418.
66. Rust, p. 179.
67. Rust, pp. 179–182.
68. Rust, p. 175; Taylor, *Memoirs.*
69. Rust, p. 175.
70. Rust, p. 175.
71. Interview of April, 17, 1991.

Chapter 25

1. Harold Weisberg, *Oswald in New Orleans: The Case for Conspiracy with the CIA,* (New York; Canyon Books, 1967). Forward by Jim Garrison.
2. 9 HSCA 110. The House Committee conducted an extensive investigation to determine if Oswald and Ferrie knew each other when Oswald was in high school, and they were able to find out more than was known in 1963, saying, "The records themselves lent substantial credence to the possibility that Oswald and Ferrie had been involved in the same CAP unit during the same period of time." See 9 HSCA 103–15, which presents numerous witnesses who knew both and otherwise had to know each other. The House did not make this too public.
3. Bertrand: 5 H 614; 11 H 330–37, 339; Andrews testimony: 11 H 325–39.
4. Proof that Marcello and Ferrie knew each other well: 9 HSCA 107 and *Report,* HSCA 143. See also pp. 143–45, 147; 4 HSCA 485; 10 HSCA 105, 111–22, 132, 203; Scott Van Wynesberghe, "Dead Suspects Part III," *The Third Decade,* March 1987; Ferrie and Marcello: *The Continuing Inquiry,* January 1979; Summers, *Conspiracy;* James and Wardlaw, *Pest or Politics*—extensive discussion about Ferrie throughout; Bernard Fensterwald, *Coincidence or Conspiracy* (New York: Zebra Books, 1977) pp. 295–305, and see Index.
5. Fensterwald, 306–16, and see Index; Role in organized crime: 9 HSCA 18, 61–69, 93, 102, 420, 422.
6. Deportation: 9 HSCA 58, 61–64, 69–76, 84.
7. Report, HSCA 143, note 26.
8. Report, HSCA 144.
9. Van Wynesberghe, *The Third Decade,* May 1988, p. 11; Summers, p. 498 mentions the meeting between Garrison and John Roselli a month after Ferrie died.
10. James and Wardlaw, p. 45; Report, HSCA 142–45, 147, 170, 180; 4 HSCA 483–85; 5 HSCA 464; 9 HSCA iv, 103–15; 10 HSCA 105–22, 127, 131–32; 12 HSCA 392.
11. Summers, p. 328.
12. Summers, p. 329.
13. James and Wardlaw, p. 9.
14. Summers, p. 315.
15. 7 H 14, 29–31.
16. James and Wardlaw, p. 152.
17. Interview with Gary Shaw, December 13, 1991; also in his book *Cover-ups.*
18. James and Wardlaw, pp. 47, 154–55.
19. James Kirkwood, *American Grotesque,* p. 154; Walter Sheridan, *The Fall and Rise of Jimmy Hoffa,* p. 426.
20. Jim Garrison, *On the Trail of the Assassins* (New York: Sheridan Square Press, 1988), pp. 86–87.
21. Scott Van Wynesberghe, *The Third Decade,* "Dead Suspects, Part VI, Clay Lavergne Shaw," May 1988. This article is recommended to researchers as an extended discussion of the Shaw prosecution, the people involved, and Garrison.
22. Jack R. Payton, St. Petersburg *Times,* Chicago *Tribune,* December 26, 1991, etc.
23. Victor Marchetti, *True* magazine, April 1975; *Hunt v. Weberman,* S.D. Fla. 1979; *Hunt v. Liberty Lobby,* S.D. Fla., No. 80-1121-Civ.-JWK, deposition of Richard McGarrah Helms, June 1, 1984, p. 37.
24. Garrison, *Trail,* p. 251.

25. Garrison, *Trail,* p. 251.
26. Jack R. Payton, St. Petersburg *Times,* December 26, 1991.
27. Garrison, *Trail,* p. 228.
28. Gary Rowell, *The Continuing Inquiry,* November 1981, and *The Third Decade,* January 1991.
29. Garrison, *Trail,* pp. 236–37.
30. State of Louisiana v. Clay Shaw.
31. I am indebted to Mark Crouch for this imagery, though he was referring to certain prominent researchers.
32. James and Wardlaw, p. 40.
33. Lardner, *Washington Post,* June 2, 1991.
34. James and Wardlaw, p. 41.
35. James and Wardlaw, p. 46.
36. James and Wardlaw, p. 47.
37. James and Wardlaw, p. 47.
38. James and Wardlaw, p. 47.
39. Jones, *Forgive My Grief III,* p. 38, 41, 43, 45.
40. James and Wardlaw, p. 49.
41. Interview on WDSU-TV, February 24, 1967; *Orleans,* Weisberg, *Oswald,* p. 237; James Phelan, *Scandals, Scamps, and Scoundrels,* p. 152; Kirkwood, p. 144; *Counterplot,* Epstein, p. 48.
42. Weisberg, *Oswald,* p. 237; Phelan, p. 152; *American,* Kirkwood, p. 144; Epstein, p. 48. James and Wardlaw, see also Van Wynesberghe, *The Third Decade,* May 1988, p. 4.
43. Phelan, pp. 152–53; Kirkwood, pp. 144–45, 205; G. Robert Blakey and Richard N. Billings, *The Plot to Kill the President* (New York: Times Books, 1981), p. 50; Van Wynesberghe, *The Third Decade,* May 1988, p. 5.
44. Jack R. Payton, St. Petersburg *Times,* December 26, 1991.
45. Groden and Livingstone, Chapter 7.
46. Weisberg, *Oswald,* p. 237; Phelan, p. 152; Kirkwood, p. 144; Epstein, p. 48; Van Wynesberghe, *The Third Decade,* May 1988, p. 4.
47. James and Wardlaw, p. 81.
48. Van Wynesberghe, *The Third Decade,* May 1988, p. 5; Kirkwood, pp. 353–59.
49. Garrison, *Trail,* p. 234; *True,* April 1975, Victor Marchetti. p. 324, *On the Trail of the Assassins,* note 234.
50. Bird, "Clay Shaw Is Dead at 60"; Phelan, p. 174; Bernard Fensterwald, p. 454.
51. Clinton witnesses; *Report,* HSCA, 142–43, 145; 4 HSCA 482, 484; 10 HSCA 4, 114, 132, 203; Fensterwald, pp. 298–99.
52. Van Wynesberghe, *The Third Decade,* May 1988, pp. 12–13. Sources for the first, second, and third statements are as follows: Mark Lane, *Rush to Judgment* (New York: Dell, 1975), p. xxvii; Fensterwald, pp. 298–99, Clinton witnesses: *Report,* HSCA, 142–43, 145; 4 HSCA 482, 484; 10 HSCA 4, 114, 132, 203; Kirkwood, pp. 314–15, 370–72, 407.
53. Letter to the author, December 12, 1991.

Chapter 26
1. Editorial, *Chicago Tribune,* December 26, 1991.
2. Letter of Harold Weisberg to Oliver Stone on February 8, 1991.
3. Letter to the author, December 12, 1991.
4. *Washington Post,* May 19, 1991, D1.
5. *Washington Post,* June 2, 1991, p. D3, last paragraph.
6. *Dallas Morning News,* April 14, 1991.
7. *Times-Picayune,* June 9, 1991.
8. *Chicago Tribune,* May 13, 1991.
9. *Washington Post,* May 19, 1991.
10. *Hollywood Reporter,* August 15, 1991.
11. *Hollywood Reporter,* August 15, 1991.
12. Jay Carr, film critic at the *Boston Globe,* writing in *Hollywood Reporter,* August 15, 1991.
13. Carr, August 15, 1991.
14. *Times-Picayune,* June 9, 1991.
15. *New York Times* quoting *Times-Picayune,* June 12, 1991.

16. *Los Angeles Times,* June 24, 1991.
17. *Washington Post,* June 2, 1991.
18. *Chicago Tribune,* May 13, 1991.
19. *Chicago Tribune,* May 13, 1991.
20. *Hollywood Reporter,* August 15, 1991.
21. *Nightline,* December 20, 1991.
22. *Nightline,* December 20, 1991.
23. *Nightline,* December 20, 1991.
24. Rosemary James & Jack Wardlaw, Pelican Press, 1967 p. 149.
25. *Nightline,* December 20, 1991.
26. Letter to the author, December 19, 1991.
27. *Time,* Hays Gorey and Martha Smilgis, June 10, 1991.
28. *Nightline,* December 20, 1991.
29. *Life,* December 1991.
30. *Texas Monthly,* December 1991, p. 166.
31. *Texas Monthly,* p. 166.
32. *Texas Monthly,* p. 164.
33. *Hollywood Reporter,* December 16, 1991; and letter of Rosemary James to the *Times Picayune.*
34. *Hollywood Reporter,* December 16, 1991.
35. *Washington Post,* December 20, 1991.
36. Both *Newsweek* and *Time* articles are dated December 23, 1991.
37. George F. Will in *Pittsburgh Post-Gazette,* December 27, 1991; *Washington Post.*
38. *New York Times,* December 20, 1991.
39. Desson Howe in *Baltimore Sun,* December 20, 1991.
40. *Washington Post,* December 20, 1991.
41. *Baltimore Sun,* December 20, 1991.
42. *Time,* December 23, 1991.
43. *Time,* December 23, 1991.
44. *Nightline,* December 20, 1991.
45. Livingstone, pp. 60, 62, 64–65, 200–201, 331.
46. Elaine Dutka in *Los Angeles Times,* June 24, 1991.
47. *Times-Picayune* December 15, 1991.
48. Scott Van Wynesberghe, letter to the author, December 31, 1991.
49. *New York Post,* January 14–15, 1992, p. 00.
50. *New York Post,* January 15, 1992, p. 7.
51. Report, HSCA 178. *See also* 174–79 with regard to a known discussion Hoffa had about an assassination attempt.
52. Report, HSCA 172.
53. Report, HSCA 172.
54. Report, HSCA 175.
55. *Prime Time,* January 16, 1992.

Chapter 27

1. Delaney, *Lancaster Intelligencer-Journal,* March 10, 1978.
2. 2 H 360.
3. 2 H 141.
4. 7 HSCA 13.
5. Interview of May 26, 1991.
6. Interview of May 26, 1991.
7. Interview of September 21, 1991.
8. *Maryland State Medical Journal,* March 1977, p. 74.
9. 7 HSCA 249.
10. Interview of September 23, 1991.
11. 2 H 351-2.
12. 2 H 140.
13. 7 HSCA 11.
14. Interview of May 20, 1991.

15. David S. Lifton, *Best Evidence* (New York: Carroll & Graf, 1988), p. 668.
16. Interview of September 22, 1991.
17. Nancy Dickerson, *Among Those Present* (New York: Random House, 1976), p. 93.
18. Interview of October 8, 1990.
19. Penn Jones, Jr., *Forgive My Grief, III,* p. 95, 196; Harrison E. Livingstone, *The Third Decade,* January 1988.
20. Art Peterson, "A JFK Death," *The News-Sun,* Waukegan, Ill., May 1, 1975. This article refers to Dennis David as a source without naming him as the "Lake County informant," and discusses the death of William Bruce Pitzer.
21. Interviews of April 22, 1990, May 12, 1990, April 25, 1991, and June 4, 1991.
22. 7 HSCA 28.
23. 7 HSCA 27.
24. Their inventory is contained in Weisberg, p. 565.
25. Letter of September 11, 1991.
26. Letter of October 31, 1991.

Chapter 28
1. Harris Wofford, *Of Kennedys and Kings* (New York: Farrar, Straus & Giroux, 1980), p. 367.
2. Wofford, p. 367.
3. Gerald R. Ford and John R. Stiles *Portrait of the Assassin* (New York: Simon and Schuster, 1965),
4. Manchester, p. 88. See also Jones, *Forgive My Grief IV,* pp. 29–30.
5. Interview with Justine O'Donnell, July 28, 1991.
6. Interview of June 14, 1991.
7. Lincoln Lawrence, *Were We Controlled?* New Hyde Park, N.Y.: University Books, 1967.
8. Thomas C. Reeves, *A Question of Character: A Life of John F. Kennedy* (New York: Free Press, 1991), p. 6.
9. Liz Smith, syndicated column, May 23, 1991.
10. Interview of October 6, 1991.
11. 2 H 360.

Bibliography

Journals:

The Continuing Inquiry. Journal of assassination research, no longer published.

Cover-Ups. Journal of assassination research, no longer published.

Echoes of Conspiracy, 1525 Acton St., Berkeley, CA 94702. Journal of assassination research, published sporadically at present.

The Third Decade. This journal of research on the John F. Kennedy assassination is published by Jerry Rose at the State University College, Fredonia, New York, 14063. $15 for one year, $26 for two years, $36 for three years. This is currently the best journal published in the field.

Reports:

Report to the President by the Commission on CIA Activities Within the United States. New York: Manor Books, 1976.

Senate Intelligence Committee Report on Foreign Assassinations. *Alleged Assassination Plots Involving Foreign Leaders.*

U.S. House of Representatives Select Committee on Assassinations. *Investigation of the Assassination of President John F. Kennedy.* Washington, D.C.: Government Printing Office, 1976–78.

U.S. Senate. *Final Report of the Select Committee to Study Governmental Operations with Respect to Intelligence Activities.* 1976.

Books:

Ashman, Charles. *The CIA–Mafia Link.* New York: Manor Books, 1975.

Bishop, Jim. *The Day Kennedy Was Shot.* New York: Funk & Wagnalls, 1968; Bantam Books, 1969.

Blair, Joan and Clay. *The Search for JFK.* New York: Berkley Publishing, 1976.

Blumenthal, Sid, with Harvey Yazigian. *Government by Gunplay: Assassination Conspiracy Theories from Dallas to Today.* New York: Signet, 1976.

Bowart, William. *Operation Mind Control: Our Secret Government's War Against Its Own People.* New York: Dell, 1978.

Buchanan, Patrick. *Who Killed Kennedy.* New York: Putnam, 1964; MacFadden, 1965.

Canfield, Michael, with Alan J. Weberman. *Coup d'Etat in America: The CIA and the Assassination of John F. Kennedy.* New York: Third World Press, 1975.

Cameron, Gail. *Rose.* New York: Berkley Publishing, 1972.

Collier, Peter and David Horowitz. *The Kennedys: An American Drama.* New York: Summit Books, 1984.

Christic Institute. *Inside the Shadow Government.* Washington, D.C.: The Christic Institute, 1988.

Curry, Jesse. *JFK Assassination File.* Dallas, Texas, American Poster & Printing Co., Inc., 1969

Dean, John. *Blind Ambition.* New York: Pocket Books, 1977.

Evica, George Michael. *And We Are All Mortal.* 1978. Available from the University of Hartford, 200 Bloomfield Avenue, West Hartford, CT 06117.

Fall, Bernard B. *The Two Vietnams: A Political and Military Analysis.* New York: Praeger, 1964.

Fensterwald, Bernard. *Assassination of JFK by Coincidence or Conspiracy?* New York: Zebra Books, 1977.

Flammonde, Paris. *The Kennedy Conspiracy: An Uncommissioned Report on the Jim Garrison Investigation.* New York: Meredith, 1969.

Ford, Gerald R., with John R. Stiles. *Portrait of the Assassin.* New York: Simon & Schuster, 1965.

Fox, Sylvan. *The Unanswered Questions About President Kennedy's Assassination.* New York: Award Books, 1975.

Galloway, John. *The Kennedys and Vietnam.* New York: Facts on File, Inc., 1971.

Garrison, Jim. *Heritage of Stone.* New York: Putnam, 1970; Berkley Publishing, 1972.

————. *On the Trail of the Assassins.* New York: Sheridan Square Press, 1988.

Goodwin, Doris Kearns. *The Fitzgeralds and The Kennedys.* New York: Simon & Schuster, 1987.

Hepburn, James (pseudonym, author unknown, but thought by French Intelligence and American sources to be William W. Turner). *Farewell America.* Vaduz, Liechtenstein: Frontiers Publishing Company, 1963. This is a fictitious publishing company, but book is available from Al Navis, Handy Books, Toronto.

Hinckle, Warren and William Turner. *The Fish Is Red.* New York: Harper & Row, 1981.

Hougan, Jim. *Secret Agenda.* New York: Random House, 1984; Ballantine, 1985.

————. *Spooks.* New York: William Morrow, 1978.

Joesten, Joachim. *Oswald: Assassin or Fall Guy?* Marzani & Munsell, 1964.

Jones, Penn, Jr. *Forgive My Grief.* Rt 3, Box 356, Waxahachie, TX. 75165.

Kantor, Seth. *Who Was Jack Ruby?* New York: Everest, 1978.

Kennedy, Rose. *Times to Remember.* Garden City, N.Y.: Doubleday, 1974.

Lincoln, Evelyn. *My 12 Years with John F. Kennedy.* New York: David McKay, 1965; Bantam Books, 1966.

Lukas, J. Anthony. *Nightmare.* New York: Bantam Books, 1977.

Manchester, William. *The Death of a President.* New York: Harper & Row, 1967; Popular Library, 1968.

Marchetti, Victor and John D. Marks. *The CIA and the Cult of Intelligence.* New York: Knopf, 1974.

Marks, John. *The Search for the Manchurian Candidate.* New York: Times Books, 1979.

Martin, Ralph G. *A Hero for Our Time—An Intimate Study of the Kennedy Years.* New York: Macmillan, 1982; Fawcett Crest, 1983.

Meagher, Sylvia. *Accessories After the Fact: The Warren Commission, the Authorities, and the Report.* New York: Bobbs-Merrill, 1967; Vintage, 1976.

Melanson, Philip H. *Spy Saga: Lee Harvey Oswald and U.S. Intelligence.* New York: Praeger, 1990. Praeger was a famous (and documented) CIA front, so their publication of this book is of interest in itself.

Milan, Michael. *The Squad: The U.S. Government's Secret Alliance with Organized Crime.* New York: Shapolsky Books, 1989.

Miller, Tom. *The Assassination Please Almanac.* Chicago: Henry Regnery Co., 1977.

Moyers, Bill. *The Secret Government: The Constitution in Crisis.* P.O. Box 27, Cabin John, Md.: Seven Locks Press, 1988, 20818; (301) 320-2130; $9.95 plus postage and handling.

New York Times. The Kennedy Years. New York: Viking Press, 1966.

North, Mark. *Act of Treason: The Role of J. Edgar Hoover in the Assassination of President Kennedy.* New York: Carroll & Graf, 1991.

Noyes, Peter. *Legacy of Doubt.* New York: Pinnacle Books, 1973.

O'Donnell, Kenneth P., and David F. Powers. *Johnny, We Hardly Knew Ye.* Boston: Little, Brown, 1972.

Oglesby, Carl. *The Yankee and Cowboy War.* Mission, Kansas: Sheed, Andrews and McNeel, 1976.

Oswald, Robert, with Myrick and Barbara Land. *Lee: A Portrait of Lee Harvey Oswald.* New York: Coward-McCann, 1967.

O'Toole, George. *The Assassination Tapes: An Electronic Probe into the Murder of John F. Kennedy and the Dallas Cover-up.* New York: Penthouse Press, 1975.

Popkin, Richard H. *The Second Oswald.* New York: Avon Books, 1966.

Prouty, L. Fletcher. *The Secret Team: The CIA and Its Allies in Control of the United States and the World.* New York: Prentice Hall, 1973.

Roffman, Howard. *Presumed Guilty.* Madison, N.J.: Fairleigh Dickinson University Press, 1975.

Rust, William, J., and the editors of *U.S. News & World Report. Kennedy in Vietnam.* Scribners 1985; Da Capo, 1987.

Salinger, Pierre. *With Kennedy.* Garden City, N.Y: Doubleday, 1966.

Sauvage, Leo. *The Oswald Affair: An Examination of the Contradictions of the Warren Report.* Cleveland: World Publishing Co., 1966.

Scheflin, Alan W. and Edward Upton, Jr. *The Mind Manipulators.* New York: Paddington Press Ltd., 1978.

Scott, Peter Dale. *Crime and Cover-up: the CIA, the Mafia, and the Dallas-Watergate Connection.* Berkeley, California: Westworks, 1977.

Scott, Peter Dale, Paul Hoch, and Russell Stetler. *The Assassinations, Dallas and Beyond: A Guide to Cover-ups and Investigations.* New York: Vintage Books, 1976.

Schlesinger, Arthur M., Jr. *A Thousand Days: John F. Kennedy in the White House.* Boston: Houghton-Mifflin, 1965.

———. *Robert Kennedy and His Times.* Boston: Houghton-Mifflin, 1978; Ballantine, 1985.

Sculz, Tad. *Compulsive Spy: The Strange Career of E. Howard Hunt.* New York: Viking, 1974.

Searls, Hank. *The Lost Prince: Young Joe, the Forgotten Kennedy.* New York & Cleveland: World Publishing Co., 1969.

Shaw, J. Gary. *Cover-up: The Governmental Conspiracy to Conceal the Facts About the Public Execution of John Kennedy.* 1976; write Cover-

Up, P.O. Box 722, 105 Poindexter, Cleburne, Texas 76031. Recommended reading.

Shaw, J. Gary, Dr. Charles A. Crenshaw, and Jens Hansen. *Conspiracy of Silence: Three Days at Parkland.* New York: Penguin, 1992.

Sorensen, Theodore C., *Kennedy.* New York: Harper & Row, 1965.

———. *The Kennedy Legacy.* New York: New American Library, 1970.

Subject Index to the Warren Report and Hearings and Exhibits. New York: Scarecrow Press, 1966; Ann Arbor: Michigan University microfilms, 1971.

Summers, Anthony. *Conspiracy.* New York: McGraw-Hill, 1980; Paragon House, 1989.

Thompson, Josiah. *Six Seconds in Dallas: A Microstudy of the Kennedy Assassination.* New York: Bernard Geis Associates, 1967; Berkley Publishing, 1976.

Thornley, Kerry. *Oswald.* Chicago: New Classics House, 1965.

Turner, William W. and Christian, John G. *The Assassination of Robert Kennedy—A Searching Look at the Conspiracy and Cover-up, 1968–1978.* New York: Random House, 1978.

Weisberg, Harold. *Whitewash.* Vols. I-IV write Weisberg at 7627 Old Receiver Rd., Frederick, MD., 21701. *Whitewash,* Vols I & II New York: Dell, 1967.

———. *Oswald in New Orleans: The Case for Conspiracy with the CIA.* New York: Canyon Books, 1967.

———. *Postmortem.* Self-published, 1975. 7627 Old Receiver Rd., Frederick, MD., 21701.

Weissman, Steve. *Big Brother and the Holding Company. The World Behind Watergate.* Palo Alto, California: Ramparts Press, 1974.

White, Theodore. *Making of the President 1972.* New York: Atheneum, 1973.

Wilber, Charles. *Medicolegal Investigation of the President John F. Kennedy Murder.* Charles Thomas & Sons. Springfield, Ill.: 1978.

Wise, David, and Thomas B. Ross. *The Invisible Government: The CIA and U.S. Intelligence.* New York: Random House, 1964; Vintage, 1974.

―――. *The Espionage Establishment.* New York: Random House, 1967; Bantam, 1968.

Wofford, Harris. *Of Kennedys and Kings.* New York: Farrar, Straus, & Giroux, 1980.

There are many others books on the subjects of assassination and intelligence, and about Kennedy, but those above are the most important. The appendix to the report of the House Select Committee on Assassinations is crucial to study the case, but only 20 sets were printed for libraries and the public.

Additional Sources

Readers are urged to visit and support the JFK Assassination Information Center at West End Market Place, 603 Munger Street, Suite 310, Dallas TX 75202, (214) 871-2770. Larry Howard has put up a monumental struggle to open and keep open the doors of this effort, which presents in visual terms our point of view. There is a movie, and books can be obtained. The Center makes a major effort to find and report to the public any new information in the case.

The Assassination Archives and Research Center (AARC) was founded in 1984 by Bernard Fensterwald, Jr., and Jim Lesar, two Washington attorneys who had long had an interest in political assassinations. Fensterwald once served as speech writer and campaigner for his Harvard classmate, John Kennedy. He was also the lawyer who represented Watergate burglar James McCord when McCord cracked the cover-up through his famous letter to Judge John Sirica. He and Lesar both represented James Earl Ray, the alleged assassin of Dr. Martin Luther King, Jr., in his attempts to get a trial. Lesar has handled most of the Freedom of Information Act litigation for requesters seeking records on the assassinations of President Kennedy, Senator Robert F. Kennedy, and Martin Luther King, Jr. The AARC is a unique and valuable repository of information on political assassinations and related matters, such as intelligence activities and organized crime. It is also a contact center for authors, researchers, and members of the media, and many of them have donated their own manuscripts and research materials to the AARC. Fensterwald provided virtually all the financial support for the AARC until his death in April 1991. As a result, the AARC's very existence is now threatened and it is urgently in need of financial support. Contributions are tax deductible and may be sent to: The AARC, 918 F St., N.W., Washington, D.C. 20004. The AARC's new president is Jim Lesar. Annual membership is $25.00, but large contributions are needed.

For new and used or hard-to-get books on the Kennedy assassination and related matters, the following stores are recommended: The Last Hurrah Bookshop, 937 Memorial Avenue, Williamsport, PA, 17701, (717) 327-9338; M & A Book Dealer, P.O. Box 2422, Waco, TX 76703; The President's Box Bookshelf, P.O. Box 1255, Washington, D.C. 20013, (703) 998-7390; Cloak and Dagger Books, 9 Eastman Avenue, Bedford, NH 03102, (603) 668-1629; and for new copies of *Farewell America,* call Al Navis at (416) 781-4139—Handy Books, 1762 Avenue Road, Toronto, ONT, M5M 3Y9, Canada.

Index

2.95